Principles of Environmental Economics and Sustainability

Recent years have witnessed considerable consolidation between the disciplines of environmental and ecological economics at research level, but until now textbooks in the area have done little to reflect this. Ahmed Hussen's book is to date the only one to reconcile the two standpoints.

The central focus of the book will continue to be on this systematic integration of both mainstream and ecological approaches to environmental economics, and an acknowledgement that enduring solutions to major contemporary environmental challenges can be obtained through studies based on a well-conceived and balanced interdisciplinary approach. However, this third edition also contains much that is new. Chiefly, brand new chapters appear covering the following topics:

- The economics of climate change
- The economics of biodiversity and ecosystem services
- 'Green' accounting and alternative economic and social indicators of sustainability
- The business case for environmental sustainability
- An Appendix that provides a brief historical account of the development of ecological economics

The result is a comprehensive introduction to the main facets of environmental and ecological economics—a text that boldly refuses to put up barriers between disciplines and takes a holistic approach to vital issues.

This student-friendly textbook contains a variety of study tools including learning points, boxed features, case studies, revision questions and discussion questions, and an Appendix that provides students with a review of basic economic principles relevant to the study of the environment and its management. Written in a clear and accessible style, this book will prove an excellent choice for introducing both students and academics to the world of environmental economics.

Ahmed Hussen is Professor of Economics at Kalamazoo College, Michigan, USA.

Principles of Environmental Economics and Sustainability

An integrated economic and ecological approach

Third edition

Ahmed Hussen

Routledge
Taylor & Francis Group

LONDON AND NEW YORK

First edition published by Routledge 2000
Second edition published by Routledge 2004
2 Park Square, Milton Park, Abingdon, Oxon OX14 4RN
Third edition published 2013

Simultaneously published in the USA and Canada
by Routledge
711 Third Avenue, New York, NY 10017

Routledge is an imprint of the Taylor & Francis Group, an informa business

© 2000, 2004, 2013 Ahmed Hussen

The right of Ahmed Hussen to be identified as author of this work has been asserted by him in accordance with the Copyright, Designs and Patent Act 1988.

All rights reserved. No part of this book may be reprinted or reproduced or utilised in any form or by any electronic, mechanical, or other means, now known or hereafter invented, including photocopying and recording, or in any information storage or retrieval system, without permission in writing from the publishers.

Trademark notice: Product or corporate names may be trademarks or registered trademarks, and are used only for identification and explanation without intent to infringe.

British Library Cataloguing in Publication Data
A catalogue record for this book is available from the British Library

Library of Congress Cataloging in Publication Data
Hussen, Ahmed M.
    Principles of environmental economics and sustainability : an integrated economic and ecological approach / by Ahmed Hussen. — 3rd ed.
        p. cm.
    Includes bibliographical references and index.
    1. Environmental economics. 2. Ecology. 3. Environmental policy. I. Title.
    HC79.E5H875 2012
    333.7—dc23   2012011802

ISBN: 978-0-415-67690-8 (hbk)
ISBN: 978-0-415-67691-5 (pbk)
ISBN: 978-0-203-09624-6 (ebk)

Typeset in Perpetua and Bell Gothic
by Keystroke, Station Road, Codsall, Wolverhampton.

Printed and bound by CPI Group (UK) Ltd, Croydon, CR0 4YY

Contents

Illustrations

FIGURES

TABLES

EXHIBITS

CASE STUDIES

Preface

The third edition of this textbook is motivated by the same objective as the two editions before it. It is written to present the economic and ecological principles essential for a clear understanding of complex contemporary environmental issues and policy considerations. However, the third edition introduces several additional features, including *four* new chapters. These new chapters cover the following topics: the economics of climate change; biodiversity conservation; alternative monetary and physical indicators of sustainability; and the business cases for sustainability. The title of the book is modified and adds the term 'sustainability' as part of the main heading. This is done to reflect the expanded and comprehensive coverage of environmental sustainability in this edition.

In addition, there is no chapter from the previous edition that has not been modified and updated, and the modifications made to six of the chapters (Chapters 2, 3, 6, 7, 11 and 12) have been extensive.

ORGANIZATION

The book consists of *sixteen* chapters, which are grouped into *five* parts. What follows is a brief description of each part:

Part I Environmental economics: perspectives

This part consists of the first three chapters. These chapters introduce students to fundamental economic, ecological and institutional concepts and theories that are essential for a course in environmental economics with an interdisciplinary perspective. Chapters 1 and 2 explore the economic and ecological perspectives on the relationship between the human economy and the natural environment. In Chapter 3, the economic, technological and ecological determinants of the waste absorptive capacity of the environment are explored. In addition, this chapter explains the basic economic and institutional factors essential in unraveling the root causes for market failure and its possible remedies. The three chapters in Part I attempt to cover all the *core* concepts and theories that will be repeatedly used throughout the rest of the book.

Part II The economics of pollution control and environmental valuation

This part consists of *five* chapters (Chapters 4 to 8). These chapters cover the basic topics included in a standard environmental economics course, including: the costs of environmental pollution-control technologies; the determinants of environmental-damage costs; the design of and choice of policy instruments; the macroeconomic effects of environmental regulation; the economic valuation of environmental amenities and disamenities; and the economics of environmental project appraisal and valuation (i.e., cost–benefit analysis and other alternative methods of project evaluation).

The analysis in this part of the book is done from a predominantly neoclassical perspective using both comparative static equilibrium analysis and the framework of welfare economics. However, even in this seemingly traditional part of the book, concerted efforts are made to critically evaluate the major findings of each chapter from an ecological perspective.

Part III The new scarcity

This part consists of *two* chapters (Chapters 9 and 10). These are *new* chapters and cover two pressing contemporary global environmental issues. Chapter 9 offers an extensive and comprehensive discussion of both the science and economics of climate change. Chapter 10 presents theoretical arguments for biodiversity conservation. The main objectives of this chapter are to understand: (1) the factors contributing to the loss in biodiversity; and (2) the link between losses in biodiversity and the supply of ecosystem services.

Part IV Sustainable development and the limits to growth

This part is composed of five chapters (Chapters 11 to 15). The unifying theme of these five chapters is *sustainability*, that is, major concerns arising from the unintended social, environmental and economic consequences of rapid population growth, economic growth and consumption of natural resources. It is a long-term view of resource adequacy (or wellbeing) and generally implies conflict between present and future generations.

Chapter 11 provides extensive discussion on the Malthusian 'variations' of the arguments on limits to economic growth. The causes for the impending limits are primarily discussed on the basis of population growth and resource scarcity.

Chapter 12 presents the view that neoclassical economists have taken, primarily to show why there are no limits to economic growth. This optimism is principally based on the viability of continued technological advances.

Chapter 13 presents the theoretical foundation for the economics of sustainability. This chapter establishes *three* specific sustainability rules with varying implications on intertemporal resource use and/or conservation.

In Chapter 14 the concept of environmentally adjusted national income accounting is explored. In addition, this chapter includes extensive discussion of *four* sustainability indexes that can be used as a measure of sustainability or unsustainability at an aggregate level.

Chapter 15 examines how the private sector can be a constructive partner in achieving sustainable development goals. The focus of this chapter is to show real-world cases in which private firms, inspired by visions of eco-efficiency and/or eco-effectiveness, are beginning to substantially reduce the material and energy wastes in their production activities.

Part V Environmental sustainability in developing countries

This part is composed of a single chapter, Chapter 16, which analyzes the population, resources and environmental problems of the developing nations. The main focuses are on poverty and environmental degradation. The solution to the rapid and continued environmental degradation that is evident in poor nations requires not only economics and ecological understanding of the problem(s) under consideration, it also requires an understanding of the social, cultural and political circumstances of the most relevant stakeholders—the people living in developing countries. This book makes a concerted effort to discuss the significance of several social, cultural and political factors that are identified as being crucial to the ongoing search to find lasting solutions to the environmental woes in developing countries.

UNIQUE FEATURES OF THE BOOK

Unlike other textbooks in this area, this book is written with the belief that *a course in environmental economics cannot be treated as just another applied course in economics*. It must include both economic and ecological perspectives and, in so doing, must seek a broader context within which environmental and natural resource issues can be understood and evaluated. In this regard, the book does not approach environmental and natural resource problems from only, or even predominantly, a standard economic perspective. To emphasize this point, the new edition has a subtitle that reads 'An Integrated Economic and Ecological Approach'.

The book contains a chapter, Chapter 2, that is exclusively devoted to providing students with basic concepts and principles of ecology. This chapter has been revised extensively and it has a sharp focus on *three* important principles of ecology and their broad implications for the functioning of the human economy and the biosphere. These three principles are: ecological interdependencies; the laws of thermodynamics of matter–energy; and ecological succession. This chapter also contains discussion of the broader implications of the growing dominance of a single species, humans, on natural ecosystems.

What are the justifications for a chapter that deals exclusively with ecology in a textbook that is written for students who may not be in science fields? The simple and straightforward answer to this question is that it provides students with a scientific foundation for understanding key themes covered in other chapters, such as: (1) the waste assimilative (absorptive) capacity of the natural environment (Chapter 3); (2) the biophysical determinants of the pollution-damage function (Chapters 4 and 7); (3) the causes and impacts of climate change (Chapter 9); (4) the contributions of ecosystem services to the economy and the causes of biodiversity loss (Chapters 7 and 10); (5) the nature of the biophysical limits to economic growth (Chapters 11, 13 and 14); (6) the limits to energy savings through technological advances (Chapters 11, 12, 13 and 14); (7) the design of products and production processes that are eco-friendly and the evaluation of product and material lifecycles (Chapter 15); (8) the biophysical (i.e., in terms of flow of matter–energy) interactions between the biosphere and the human economy (Chapters 11 and 14); and (9) the design of physical indicators of sustainability and the physical symptoms of unsustainable systems (Chapters 14 and 16). Furthermore, there is no chapter in this textbook that does not in some way include concepts covered in Chapter 2.

However, incorporating a single chapter on ecology *per se* would not be sufficient justification for the claim that this book differentiates itself from its competitors by taking 'an integrated economic and ecological approach' to the study of environmental economics. Thus, in addition to providing a stand-alone chapter on ecology, this text incorporates concepts, theories, methodologies and perspectives that are uniquely attributable to ecological economics—a relatively new subfield in economics.

Ecological economics was founded with the belief that pressing environmental problems require interdisciplinary approaches that focus on the links between economic, social and ecological systems. This book seriously engages the ecological economic position that views the human economy as a subsystem of the biosphere (i.e., the earth's life support system), implying that biophysical reality has implications for the functioning of human economy that are much more far-reaching than has been acknowledged by the proponents of mainstream economic thought. Appendix B presents a brief historical sketch of the development of ecological economics. This appendix should be read after reading Chapter 2.

Another important feature of this book, which may seem somewhat at odds with the position expressed above is this: no compromise is made in the use of relevant mainstream economic theories and methodologies.

The text is written with an assumption that students have completed a one-semester course in microeconomics. Furthermore, Appendix A at the end of the text provides explanations of fundamental economic concepts that are specifically relevant to environmental economics. In Appendix A, economic concepts such as basic demand and supply analysis, willingness to pay, consumers' and producers' surplus, Pareto optimality, and alternative economic measures of scarcity are thoroughly and systematically explained. The material in this Appendix is referenced throughout the text (especially in Chapter 1 and Chapters 3 to 8). Appendix A could also serve as a good review for economics students and a very valuable foundation for students specializing in fields other than economics.

Finally, this book is primarily a theoretical exposé of environmental and resource economics. The emphasis is on the systematic development of theoretical principles and conceptual frameworks essential for a clear understanding and analysis of environmental and resource issues. To catch the imagination and attention of students, as well as to reinforce their understanding of basic theoretical principles, case studies and 'exhibits' are incorporated into most of the chapters. These are taken from brief magazine articles, newspaper clippings, articles and summaries of empirical studies from professional journals, and publications from government and private research institutions.

Let me end this part of the book with these important remarks. This textbook is not written to defend or promote a particular brand of economic perspective on the environment. While it should be left for others to judge whether a balanced approach has been used in analyzing and discussing pressing environmental issues from different perspectives, at the very least readers will notice the concerted efforts that have been made to expose the mainstream views of environmental economics, as well as the arguments of its most ardent critics. This is not intended to make the mainstream economics perspectives on the environment less useful, but rather to make them more tenable and complete.

OTHER NOTABLE FEATURES

The book is well-researched, as is evident by the long list of references at the end of most of the chapters, and it includes carefully thought out review and discussion questions at the end of chapter.

Each chapter of this book is written to stand on its own. This is done so that users of the book can freely move from chapter to chapter without significant loss of continuity. However, this comes at a cost, i.e., some degree of repetitiveness.

Acknowledgements

The experience of being the sole author of a textbook on a subject matter which requires an interdisciplinary focus has indeed been daunting. Undoubtedly, the completion of this project would not have been possible without the help and encouragement of many professional associates, students and family members. In this sense, I cannot truly claim to be the sole author of this text.

I would like to extend my thanks to several individuals who read and edited a section or a full chapter(s) at some stage of my effort to write this book. Most notable among these people are: Paul Olexia, Rajaran Krishnan, Chuck Stull, Tim Moffit, Jacquelyn Gardner, Fumie Hussen, Sophia Hussen, Cynthia Leet and Genevieve Leet.

I would also like to thank my students Molly Waytes K'12 for her significant contributions to Exhibit 10.3, and Samantha Weaver K'09 for reading and providing me with valuable comments on Chapter 9.

As was the case in the previous two editions, the new edition uses numerous quoted remarks, exhibits and case studies. These items are not included for mere appearance or style; they significantly contribute to the effectiveness of the book in conveying certain important ideas. Obviously, my debt to those whose work I have quoted and summarized is immeasurable. However, I have the sole responsibility for the interpretation placed on these works.

I would like to express my sincere gratitude for the valuable comments I received from four anonymous reviewers during two separate stages of the review process for the third edition. I am especially indebted to the two reviewers who read the entire manuscript and provided me with specific and detailed comments and suggestions. Not only did the book benefit from these comments and suggestions, but it was also personally gratifying to realize that there are people within my own profession who both appreciate my work and take it seriously.

It would have been impossible to start and complete this project without the encouraging words and substantive support that I have received from my editor, Robert Langham. As always, it has been a real pleasure to work with Rob and his two editorial assistants, Louisa Earls and Natalie Tomlinson. I would also like to thank Dan Harding for his meticulous and masterful work in copy-editing the book, and for the personal interest he has exhibited regarding its content. My sincere gratitude goes also to Stewart Pether, the production editor, not only for effectively shepherding the production stage of the book but also for involving me in every step of the production process'.

Finally, I would like to dedicate this edition to Fumie, my wife. I am forever indebted to her unconditional commitment to my personal wellbeing and professional growth.

Acronyms

As a general rule, my preference is to use acronyms only when they are absolutely needed. Below are the acronyms that are used on more than a few occasions.

ARP	acid-rain program
BAU	'business as usual' approach
CBA	cost-benefit analysis
CBD	Convention on Biological Diversity
CD	sustainable development
CDM	Clean Development Mechanism
CEA	cost-effectiveness analysis
CFCs	chlorofluorocarbons
CNC	critical natural capital
CSR	corporate social responsibility
CVM	contingent valuation method
DfE	design for the environment
DICE	Dynamic Integrated Model of Climate and the Economy
EANIA	environmentally adjusted national income accounting
EDP	environmentally adjusted net domestic product
EFP	ecological footprint
EIA	environmental impact assessment
EKC	environmental Kuznets curve
EPA	Environmental Protection Agency
EPE	environmental protection expenditures
ESS	ecosystem services
FCCC	Framework Convention on Climate Change
GDP	gross domestic product
GHGs	Greenhouse gases
GS	genuine net savings
GW	Global warming
IAS	Invasive alien species
IMF	International Monetary Fund
IPCC	Intergovernmental Panel on Climate Change
ISEW	index of sustainable economic welfare

LCA	life cycle assessment
LCD	life cycle design
MCC	Marginal control cost
MD	Millennium Development Goals
MDC	Marginal damage cost
MSB	Marginal social benefit
MSC	Marginal social cost
NGOs	non-governmental organizations
NIE	New Institutional Economics
NNP	net national product
NPV	net present value
OECD	Organization for Economic Co-operation and Development
OPEC	Organization of Petroleum Exporting Countries
ppm	parts per million
RFF	Resources for the Future
SEEA	System of integrated Environmental and Economic Accounting
SMS	safe minimum standard
SNA	system of national accounts
SP	stated preference
SSE	steady-state economy
TDT	theory of demographic transition
TEC	transferable emission credit
TPI	turning-point income
UNDP	United Nations Development Programme
UNEP	United Nations Environmental Programme
UNSD	United Nations Statistical Division
WB	World Bank
WBCSD	The World Business Council for Sustainable Development
WCED	World Commission on Environment and Development
WMO	World Metrological Organization
WTA	willingness to accept
WTP	willingness to pay

Introduction: What is environmental economics all about?

THE ECONOMIC NOTION OF NATURAL AND ENVIRONMENTAL RESOURCES

The concept of natural resources

The study of natural resources involves theories and concepts that are continually evolving with the passage of time and with our improved understanding of the natural environment. For example, the pre-classical or Physiocratic school (1756–78) and classical economists (1776–1890) typically used *land* as a generic term to describe natural resources or the natural environment (air, water and landmass), in general. To these economists, land represented one of the three major categories of basic resources essential to the production of goods and services—the other two being labor and capital.

This three-way classification of basic resources or factors of production persists, although our understanding of natural resources and their roles in the economic process has changed markedly. Advances in the natural and physical sciences have increased our knowledge of the laws that govern the natural world. Furthermore, as the human economy continues to expand, its impacts on the natural world have become sizable and potentially detrimental. Consequently, our conception of natural resources tends to be influenced by our current understanding of the human economy and its interrelationship with the natural world.

Broadly defined, natural resources include all the 'original' elements that comprise the earth's life-support systems: air, water, the earth's crust and radiation from the sun. Some representative examples of natural resources are arable land, wilderness areas, mineral fuels and nonfuel minerals, watersheds, and the ability of the natural environment to degrade waste and absorb ultraviolet light from the sun. Exhibit A explains the conventional classification of natural resources in terms of two major categories: renewable and nonrenewable natural resources. It is important to understand the difference between these two concepts right from the outset since, as will be observed throughout this book, they convey important implications regarding environmental and resource management.

EXHIBIT A   RENEWABLE VERSUS NONRENEWABLE RESOURCES

Natural resources are generally grouped into two major categories: renewable and nonrenewable natural resources. *Renewable resources* are those resources that are capable of regenerating themselves within a relatively short period, provided the environment in which they are nurtured is not unduly disturbed. Examples include plants, fish, forests, soil, solar radiation, wind, tides and so on. These renewable resources can be further classified into two distinct groups: biological resources and flow resources.

Biological resources consist of the various species of plants and animals. They have one distinctive feature that is important for consideration here. While these resources are capable of self-regeneration, they can be irreparably damaged if they are exploited beyond a certain critical threshold. Hence, their use should be limited to a certain critical zone. As will be explained later, natural biological processes govern both the regenerative capacities of these resources and the critical zone. Examples of this type of resource are fisheries, forests, livestock and all forms of plants.

Flow resources include solar radiation, wind, tides and water streams. Continuous renewal of these resources is largely dictated by atmospheric and hydraulic circulation, along with the flow of solar radiation. Although these resources can be harnessed for specific use (such as energy from solar radiation or waterfalls), the rate at which the flows of these potential resources are regulated is largely governed by nature. *This does not, however, mean that humans are totally incapable of either augmenting or decreasing the amount of flow of these resources.* A good illustration of this would be the effect that greenhouse gas emissions (in particular carbon dioxide emissions) have on global warming.

Nonrenewable resources are resources that either exist in fixed supply or are renewable only on a geological timescale, whose regenerative capacity can be assumed to be zero for all practical purposes. Examples of these resources include metallic minerals such as iron, aluminum, copper and uranium; and nonmetallic minerals such as fossil fuels, clay, sand, salt and phosphates.

Normally, nonrenewable resources are classified into two broad categories. The first group includes those resources that are recyclable, such as metallic minerals. The second group consists of non-recyclable resources, such as fossil fuels.

Environmental versus resource economics

In economics, the study of natural resources is subdivided into two major subfields: environmental economics and resource economics. These two subfields differ in focus. Environmental economics seeks to assess the *damages* inflicted on the natural environment (air, water, and landmass) when it is used for the disposal of waste (a byproduct of all forms of economic activities). The damages may manifest themselves in various forms, such as present or future losses to humans in the form of damaged health, lower productivity, degradation and/or depletion of resources, and reduced enjoyment of nature (i.e., loss in environmental amenities). Given this, in environmental economics the focus of inquiry is on finding the most efficient way(s) to reduce environmental damages. It should be pointed out from the outset that this subject matter, environmental economics, is the primary focus of this textbook.

On the other hand, in resource economics the focus is on determining the rate of the extraction of nonrenewable resources and the harvest of renewable resources over time. The key issue is to identify the time path of the rate of withdrawals of renewable and nonrenewable resources from the natural environment with an objective to maximize the total economic value of the resources under consideration. The overarching economic concerns are premature exhaustion of nonrenewable resources and the undue degradations of renewable resources.

It should be clear from the above discussion that environmental and natural-resource economics differ in one important way. In environmental economics the focus is on assessing present and future damages arising from the *disposal* of the byproducts of economics activities into the environment. On the other hand, in natural-resource economics the emphasis is on the rate of resource (renewable and nonrenewable) *withdrawal* from the environment. That is, *environmental economics deals with what is put into the environment and resource economics with what is being removed from the environment.*

Clearly, these two subject matters cannot be unrelated, given that what is disposed (as waste) into the environment is likely to affect the quality or quantity of what can be withdrawn from the environment and vice versa. For example, determining the 'optimal' rotation of timber harvest from a particular forest reserve may be regarded as a subject that belongs to resource economics. However, if a sustained use of this forest reserve is an important consideration, such activity (timber harvest) cannot be done without considering its environmental impacts, such as a possible loss of biological diversity (i.e., the diversity of the species and genes, and the ecological process that supports life in this particular forest reserve). Another example is the recent global awareness that a societal choice such as using a particular energy resource (such as fossil fuels, nuclear, biofuels, solar, wind, etc.) cannot be effectively determined without careful consideration of its impact on the environment (such as global warming).

ENVIRONMENTAL ECONOMICS: SCOPE AND NATURE

As a subdiscipline of economics, environmental economics started in the 1960s—the early years of the so-called environmental movement. It was not until 1974 that the field became officially institutionalized with the establishment of the dedicated *Journal of Environmental Economics and Management* (Ropke 2004). However, despite its brief history, over the past three decades it has become one of the fastest-growing fields of study in economics. The growing popularity of this field parallels the increasing awareness of the interconnectedness between the economy and the environment—more specifically, the increasing recognition of the significant roles that nature plays in the economic process as well as in the formation of economic value.

As discussed earlier, environmental economics deals with the assessment of environmental damages arising from human uses of the air, water and landmass for waste disposal arising from all sorts of human economic activities. Human activities that cause environmental degradation may have three broadly recognized origins.

First, the human economy extracts or harvests basic resources (such as crops, coal, iron ore, and so on) to be used as *raw materials* in the production of goods and services. In this regard, environmental economics focuses on the extent and nature of the damages caused to the natural environment due to human activities stemming from the harvest and/or extraction of raw materials from nature. Examples are: the deformation of landscape and the loss of vegetation caused by mining activities, soil erosion and soil fertility losses resulting from intensive farming practices, the loss of biodiversity from deforestation, and so on.

Second, environmental economics focuses on the adverse effects of pollution on the natural environment (including humans) directly emanating from the production and consumptions of goods and services. Some representative examples include: municipal solid waste and untreated sewage effluent, emissions of sulfur and carbon dioxide from coal-burning power plants, effluent streams discharged from pulp and paper mills, agricultural runoffs carrying fertilizers, and the release of toxic wastes into the atmosphere from chemical plants.

Third, even a 'passive' use of the natural environment for recreational and educational purposes, such as 'ecotourism', could inflict considerable damage on nature. Hence, allowing access to nature for human recreational and educational use alone can create considerable disturbance to some sensitive natural environments.

The above discussions suggest that environmental damages have multiple sources. More specifically, the damages could originate from the extraction and harvest of raw materials, the production of goods and services, and even the passive use of the natural environment for recreational and educational purposes. The important message is that, contrary to what appears to be the conventional wisdom, environmental economics does not deal only with the damaging effects of pollution (waste) arising from factories in the production process of goods and services. In other words, the health of the natural environment cannot be ascertained or fully understood without careful examination of what the human economy *takes* (extraction and harvesting of resources), what it *makes* (goods and services), and what it *wastes* (effluents, emissions and byproducts), as the three are intimately inter-related (Hawken 1993).

Another way to look at the environment is in terms of the services it provides to the economy. These services can be delineated into three components: resources for production, assimilative capacity to absorb pollution, and enjoyment of nature (amenity value). Thus, the opportunity cost of damages inflicted to the environment is the loss of some combinations of these three services.

With this rather broad definition of the scope and nature of the tradeoffs between increased human economic activities and damage to the environment in mind, the list below addresses some of the major topics covered in environmental economics, which are all issues addressed in this book:

- An ecological understanding of the structure and functioning of natural environment (ecosystem);
- The nature of the tradeoffs between environmental degradation and economic goods and services;
- The economics and institutional factors responsible for environmental degradation;
- The ineffectiveness of the market, if left alone, in the 'optimal' allocation of environmental resources;
- Assessing the monetary value of environmental damages—damage cost;
- The extent to which technology can be used to ameliorate environmental degradation—pollution-control cost;
- Public-policy instruments that can be used to slow, halt and reverse the deterioration of environmental resources;
- The macroeconomic effects of environmental regulations;
- The conceptual, methodological and practical issues associated with evaluating the benefits and costs of environmental projects, such as a project to clean up toxic waste dump;
- Environmental concerns that are characterized by considerable economic, technological and ecological uncertainties, such as global warming and biological diversity loss;
- Ethical and moral imperatives for environmental resource conservation—concern for the welfare of future generations;

- Alternative indicators of sustainability and the necessity and viability of sustainable economic development;
- The needs and challenges associated with meeting the requirements of internationally binding environmental treaties;
- The business case for sustainability; and
- The interrelationships among population, poverty and environmental degradation in the developing countries of the world.

This list by no means exhausts the issues that can be addressed in environmental economics. However, these topics illustrate some of the fundamental ways in which environmental economics is different from other sub-disciplines in economics.

First, the ultimate limits to environmental resource availability are imposed by nature. This is because the origin, interactions and reproductive capacity of environmental resources are largely governed by nature. Thus, no serious study of environmental economics can be done without a good understanding of some basic ecological principles— a subject matter that is addressed in Chapter 2.

Second, most of these resources have no readily available markets: for example, clean air, ozone and the genetic pool of a species.

Third, no serious environmental economic study can be entirely descriptive. Normative issues such as intergenerational fairness and distribution of resources between the poor and rich nations are very important.

Fourth, most major environmental problems (such as acid rain, global warming, deforestation and the associated loss of biodiversity) transcend national boundaries, and thus require regional and/or international cooperation for their resolution.

Fifth, uncertainties are unavoidable considerations in any serious study of environmental and natural resource issues. These uncertainties may take several forms, such as prices, irreversible environmental damage, or unexpected and sudden species extinction. Such is the nature of the subject matter that we are about to begin exploring in this book.

REFERENCES AND FURTHER READING

Hawken, P. (1993) *The Ecology of Commerce*, New York: Harper Collins.

Howe, C. W. (1979) *Natural Resource Economics*, New York: John Wiley.

Ropke, I. (2004) 'The Early History of Modern Ecological Economics', *Ecological Economics* 50: 293–314.

Part I

Environmental economics: Foundational concepts, theories and perspectives

The word *paradigm* . . . is more commonly used today to mean a model, theory, perception, assumption, or frame of reference. In the more general sense, it's the way we 'see' the world –not in terms of our usual sense of sight, but in terms of perceiving, understanding, [and] interpreting.

(Covey, S. R. 1989: 23)

The three chapters that constitute Part I have one thing in common. They all cover the concepts, theories and perspectives that are the foundation for the subject matter addressed by environmental economics. The first two chapters examine the economics and ecological perspectives of environmental resources and their implications for the economic and the natural world.

Chapter 1 examines what could be considered the mainstream economists' 'pre-analytic' vision of the economy and its relationship with the natural world. What can be observed from the discussion in this chapter is the treatment of the natural environment as one of the many 'fungible' assets that can be used to satisfy human needs. In this regard, the emphasis is on the general problems of resource scarcity. This being the case, the roles of consumers' preferences, efficiency, markets and technology are stressed.

Chapter 2 is intended to provide the reader with the assumptions and theories vital to the understanding of the ecological perspectives of natural resources and the environment—elements crucial to the sustenance of the human economy. More specifically, in this chapter economics students are asked to venture beyond the realm of their discipline to study some basic concepts and principles of ecology. The inquiry on this subject matter is quite focused and limited in scope. The primary intent is to familiarize students with carefully selected ecological concepts and principles so that they will have, at the end, a clear understanding of an ecologist's perspective of the natural world and its relationship with the human economy. In the final analysis, the major lesson of this chapter is the recognition of biophysical limits that are considered to be relevant to the sustainable use of environmental resources.

The last chapter of Part I, Chapter 3, covers two subjects fundamental to environmental economics. First, the basic ecological and technological factors that influence the relationship between economic activity (i.e., production of goods and services) and waste absorptive capacity of the environment are examined. This effort provides an important initial glance at the ecological and technical determinants of the environmental damage function.

The second subject covered in Chapter 3 focuses on the institutional factors that, at the fundamental level, make the allocation and management of environmental resources uniquely problematic. More specifically, attempts are made to delve into the factors that help to explain why a system of resource allocation that is based on, and guided by, individual self-interest (hence, private markets) fails to account for the 'external' costs of environmental damages: market failure. It also addresses the difficult choice of institutional arrangements (including government intervention) that are inherent in any effort to correct market failure.

Chapter 1

The natural environment and the human economy: The neoclassical economic perspective

LEARNING OBJECTIVES

After reading this chapter you will be familiar with the following:

- The peculiar nature of the standard economics conception of environmental resources as factors of production.
- How, under certain ideal conditions, market price(s) may serve as an indicator of 'absolute' and 'relative' resource scarcity.
- The extent to which factor substitution and technological change may be used to ameliorate resource scarcity, including environmental resources.
- A schematic view of a market-oriented economy and how it relates to the 'natural' environment in accordance with the neoclassical worldview.
- The axiomatic assumptions and, at the fundamental level, the analytical principles that are cornerstones of the standard economic conception of the natural environment and its interactions with the human economy.

This is a vital chapter for the understanding of the ideological foundations of the school of economic thought that is dominant today, with respect to the efficacy of the market system to generate reliable indicators of resource scarcity, the bounds of resource substitutability, and the extent to which the human economy is viewed as dependent on the natural environment (i.e., the concern for general resource scarcity).

1.1 INTRODUCTION

It is safe to say that mainstream economists have a peculiar conception of the natural environment (i.e., all living and non-living things occurring naturally on earth), including how it should be utilized and managed. The primary aim of this chapter is to expose the *axiomatic* assumptions and, at the fundamental level, the analytical principles that are the cornerstones of the standard economic conception of the natural environment and its interactions with the human economy. This is a crucial issue to address early on because it helps to clearly identify the ideological basis of neoclassical economics, the dominant approach to economic analyses since the 1870s, as it is applied to the management of the natural environment.

How do neoclassical economists perceive the role that the 'natural' environment plays in the human economy? For our purpose here, the natural environment could be defined as the physical, chemical and biological surroundings that humans and other living species depend on as a life support. As shown in Figure 1.1, in specific terms the economy is assumed to depend on the natural environment for three distinctive purposes: (1) raw materials production—which includes the extraction of nonrenewable resources (such as iron ore, fossil fuels, etc.) and the harvest of renewable resources (such as timber, fodder, genetic resources, dyes, etc.); (2) the disposal and storage of wastes; and (3) the provision of ecosystem services and amenities (such as pollination, habitat and refuge, water supply and regulation, nutrient cycling, climate regulation, aesthetic enjoyments, and so on).

Thus, broadly viewed, the economy is assumed to be completely dependent on the natural environment for raw materials, the disposal and assimilation of waste materials, and for the provision of ecosystem services that are essential for supporting and sustaining life. Even when they are accused (as they often are) of taking the services from nature for granted, neoclassical economists are fully aware of the critical significance of ecosystem services to life on earth including humans.

If economists appear to have overlooked or even ignored the contributions of ecosystem services, it is primarily because they have yet to come up with adequate ways of imputing the value of the contributions of ecosystem services to the human economy at the margin (more on this in Chapter 7).

This much remains indisputable, however. Since the earth is 'finite' there exists a *theoretical* upper limit for resource extraction and harvest, and the disposal of waste into the natural environment. Furthermore, nature's ability to provide ecosystem services is also adversely affected in direct proportion to the amount of resource extraction and harvesting and the disposal or discharge of waste into the natural environment. Thus, as with any other branch of economics, fundamental to the study of environmental economics is the problem of *scarcity*: the tradeoff between economic *goods* and *services* and the preservation of the quality of the natural environment. What this suggests is that increased production of goods and services will ultimately have the effect of diminishing the health and/or the productive capacity of the natural environment.

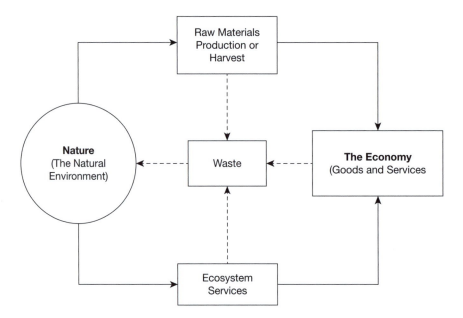

Figure 1.1 *A schematic look at how the human economy for its production of goods and services depends on the natural environment for raw material production, provision of ecosystem services and disposal of waste.*

To understand the full implications of these trade-offs it will be instructive to have a clear picture of some *fundamental* (and in some sense axiomatic) assumptions that the standard economics approach uses with respect to the natural environment, and how they are related to or influenced by the activities taking place within the human economy:

■ Environmental resources are 'essential' factors of production. A certain minimum amount of these resources is needed to produce goods and services.

■ Environmental resources are of economic concern to the extent that they are *scarce*, and resource scarcity including the environment can be measured (indicated) by market *price*.

■ The scarcity of environmental resources can be augmented either through factor substitutions and/or technological advances.

■ Nothing is lost in treating the human economy as separate from natural ecosystems—the physical, chemical and biological surroundings that humans and other living species depend on as a life support. That is, the natural ecosystem is treated as being outside the human economy and exogenously determined. Note that to indicate this, in Figure 1.1, the human economy and the natural environment are drawn as two distinctly separate entities. The full extent of the implications of this worldview will be discussed in the next chapter.

From the above discussions it should be evident that, at the fundamental level, the following three issues are central to the standard economics worldview with respect to the 'association' of the natural environment and the economic process: (1) the extent to which market prices adequately signal resource scarcity, including the environment; (2) the extent to which factor substitution and technological advances can be used to augment natural resource scarcity; and (3) the extent to which the human economy can be viewed as an 'open system' for both its material and energy use.

As shown in Figure 1.1, in an open system that is typified by a linear process in which materials and

energy enter one part of the system (in this case the Human Economy) and then leave either as products or byproducts/wastes. An open system of this nature can be sustained indefinitely only by a continuous flow of free energy-matter from an external source, in this case nature (more on this later). The rest of this chapter will address these three issues one step at a time.

1.2 THE MARKET AS A PROVIDER OF INFORMATION ON RESOURCE SCARCITY

> The relevant measure of scarcity is the cost or price of a resource, not any physical measure of its calculated reserves.
> (Simon 1984: 580)

From the perspective of neoclassical economics, the market system is considered to be the preferred institution for allocating scarce resources. Under certain assumed conditions the market system, guided by the free expressions of individual consumer and producer choices, would lead to the maximization of the wellbeing of society as a whole—the so-called invisible hand theorem (see Section A.3 of Appendix A for a formal analysis of this theorem using basic demand and supply analysis). The market system accomplishes this wonderful feat using price as a means of gauging resource scarcity. In this section, an attempt will be made to explain, at a very basic level, how market price indicates resource scarcity.

Under normal conditions, no payment is made to inhale oxygen from the atmosphere. On the other hand, although less essential than oxygen for our survival, no one would expect to get membership to a local golf club at no charge (i.e., zero prices). Why is this so? The answer to this question is rather straightforward and can be explained using Figures 1.2 and 1.3.

In Figure 1.2, the prevailing market equilibrium (or market clearing) price, P_e, is *positive*. Hence, a unit of this service, membership at a golf club, can be obtained only if one is willing and able to pay the prevailing market price. In other words, this service can be obtained only at a cost. On the other hand, in Figure 1.3 supply exceeds demand everywhere.

Figure 1.2

Demand and supply and market clearing (equilibrium) price, P_e, for a local golf club membership. The service of a local golf club is scarce because at zero price quantity demanded far exceeds quantity supplied—creating a shortage.

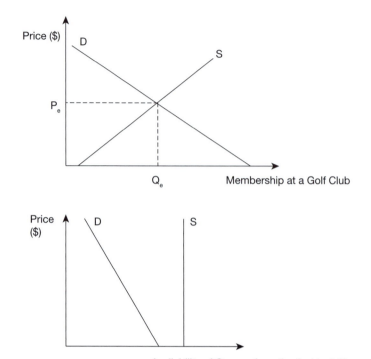

Figure 1.3

Demand and supply of oxygen. Oxygen is treated as a free good, because at zero price quantity supply exceeds quantity demanded—a surplus.

Under this condition, the price for this resource will be *zero*, hence, a *free good*. This case clearly explains why our normal use of oxygen from the atmosphere is obtained at zero price. Thus, economists formally define a scarce resource as any resource that commands a positive price. In this regard, market price is an indicator of absolute scarcity.

Therefore, for economists the market is invaluable to the extent that it provides information about the scarcity values of a potentially endless number of resources at a given moment in time. Based on this market information, it is possible to make further insights about resource scarcity. For example, relative (as opposed to absolute) scarcity could be effectively constructed using a ratio of two market-clearing prices.

Suppose there are two resources, gold and crude oil. Let X and Y represent gold and crude oil, respectively. Then P_x/P_y (the ratio of the market prices of gold to crude oil) would be a measure of relative scarcity. To be more specific, suppose, the price for gold is $1000 per ounce and the price for crude oil is

$80 per barrel. In this instance, the relative price would have a numerical value of 12.5. In what sense does this number measure relative scarcity?

Obviously, this number suggests that gold is relatively scarcer (or more costly) than crude oil. Furthermore, under ideal market conditions, the above numerical value would suggest that the value or the cost of the resources (labor, capital and raw materials, etc.) used to extract and bring an ounce of gold to the market is 12.5 times more than the barrel of crude oil. Hence, this provides the justification for why the market price of an ounce of gold should be 12.5 times that of a barrel of crude oil. Note that this kind of analysis can be done for any pair of natural resources as well as goods and services.

Information of this nature can be extremely valuable in making societal decisions on resource allocation at the margin. For example, as will be evident from the discussion in the next section, relative price plays an important role in the determination of factor-substitution possibilities, such as natural capital (e.g., forestland for carbon sequestration) versus human-made capital (e.g., the technology needed for geologic carbon sequestration). Carbon sequestration refers to the capture or storage of carbon dioxide as a means of mitigating the contribution of fossil-fuel emissions to global warming (more on this in Chapter 9).

Unfortunately, market-generated information on resource scarcity has its own limitations. For instance, in our earlier example the market price for a barrel of crude oil was given as $80. Does this price actually include the damage (cost) of carbon dioxide to the atmosphere when crude oil is refined, transported and used to run motor vehicles or other related activities? The implication here is that there could be situations in which the market price fails to fully account for all the costs of either extracting or using resources. The extent to which this claim may be valid, particularly as applied to environmental resources, will be explored in Chapter 3. In fact, it will not be an exaggeration to say that 'getting the prices right' is one of the fundamental subject matters addressed in environmental economics.

However, 'correcting' for possible market price distortion constitutes only a part of the challenge, given that most ecosystem services (such as waste assimilation and detoxifications, soil formation and maintenance, seed dispersal and nutrient cycling, maintenance of biodiversity, and so on) are not traded through normal market mechanisms. Thus, to assess the consequences of different courses of action, it is not enough to know that ecosystem services are valuable, it is also important to know how valuable they are, and how that value is affected by different sets of decision variables. This subject is dealt with in Chapter 7 using the term 'environmental valuation' —the various methods of imputing money values on environmental goods and services.

The second fundamental principle that influences and shapes the mainstream economic approach to environmental and natural resource management is technology, and the role it plays in the amelioration of natural-resource scarcity. A brief but formal discussion of the general characteristics of scarcity augmenting (resource-saving) technological advances is the subject matter of the next section.

1.3 FACTOR SUBSTITUTION, TECHNOLOGICAL ADVANCES AND RESOURCE SCARCITY

> The existence of a finite stock of resource that is necessary for production does not imply that the economy must eventually stagnate and decline. If there is continual resource augmenting technological progress (and factor substitution), it is possible that a reasonable standard of living can be guaranteed for all time.
>
> (Dasgupta and Heal 1979: 197)

At a fundamental level, factor substitution suggests that basic resources are used in combinations. Furthermore, resources are generally considered to be *fungible*. That is, one kind of resource (such as machinery) can be freely replaced by another (such as a labor) in the production process. Or, one type of energy resource (such as petroleum) can be replaced by another form of energy (such as natural gas). For example, in Case Study 1.1 below, it is shown that water purification for the city of New York can be attained by investing either in the preservation of a 'natural' capital (a forest watershed) or in building a filtration plant (a 'manufactured' capital). In other words, human-made capital can be replaced by natural capital and vice versa.

To explain the essence of factor substitution and its implications formally, let us suppose that the average annual water needs (in gallons) for New York City over the next decade is known and, as shown in (see page 15) Figure 1.4, it is represented by a negatively sloped curve labeled as Q_0. Note that this constant output of water, Q_0, can be produced by using various combinations of two inputs: natural capital (a forest watershed) and human-made capital (filtration plant). As shown in the horizontal and vertical axes of Figure 1.4, let the variables N and M represent the natural and human-made capitals, respectively.

Hence, from Figure 1.4, it is quite evident that an infinite combination of natural and human-made capitals can be used to provide the city of New York with its required level of annual water-purification, Q_0. For example, two pairs of these infinite combinations are (N_0, M_0) and (N_1, M_1). One readily

CASE STUDY 1.1 ECONOMIC RETURNS FROM THE BIOSPHERE

Garciela Chichilnisky and Geoffrey Heal

The environment's services are, without a doubt, valuable. The air we breathe, the water we drink and the food we eat are all available only because of services provided by the environment. How can we transform these values into income while conserving resources?

We have to 'securitize' (sell shares in the return from) 'natural capital' and environmental goods and services, and enroll market forces in their conservation. This means assigning to corporations—possibly by public–private corporate partnerships—the obligation to manage and conserve natural capital in exchange for the right to the benefits from selling the services provided.

In 1996, New York City invested between $1 billion and $1.5 billion in natural capital, in the expectation of producing cost savings of $6 billion–$8 billion over ten years, giving an internal rate of return of 90–170 percent in a payback period of four to seven years. This return is an order of magnitude higher than is usually available, particularly on relative risk-free investments. How did this come about?

New York's water comes from a watershed in the Catskill Mountains. Until recently, water purification processes by root systems and soil microorganisms, together with filtration and sedimentation during its flow through the soil, were sufficient to cleanse the water to the standards required by the US Environmental Protection Agency (EPA). But sewage, fertilizer and pesticides in the soil reduced the efficacy of this process to the point where New York's water no longer met EPA

standards. The city was faced with the choice of restoring the integrity of the Catskill ecosystems or of building a filtration plant at a capital cost of $6 billion–$8 billion, plus running costs of the order of $300 million annually. In other words, New York had to invest in natural capital or in physical capital. Which was more attractive?

Investing in natural capital in this case meant buying land in and around the watershed so that its use could be restricted, and subsidizing the construction of better sewage treatment plants. The total cost of restoring the watershed is expected to be $1 billion–$1.5 billion . . .

To address its water problem New York City has floated an 'environmental bond issue,' and will use the proceeds to restore the functioning of the watershed ecosystems responsible for water purification. The cost of the bond issue will be met by the savings produced: avoidance of a capital investment of $6 billion–$8 billion, plus the $300 million annual running costs of the plant. The money that would otherwise have paid for these costs will pay the interest on the bonds. New York City could have 'securitized' these savings by opening a 'watershed saving account' into which it paid a fraction of the costs avoided by not having to build and run a filtration plant. This account would then pay investors for the use of their capital.

Source: *Nature*, 391, February 12, 1998, pp. 629–630. Reprinted by permission.

observes from this that the city of New York can reduce its reliance in the use of its forest watershed for water filtration (such as a move from N_0 to N_1) by increasing the capacity of its water filtration plants (such as a move from M_0 to M_1) and still produce the same level of water output, Q_0.

In other words, it is possible to substitute natural capital with human-made capital and produce the desired level of water output, Q_0, and vice versa. The

broader implication of this observation is that the city of New York has a choice regarding what combinations of these two inputs to use to attain its desired level of water output, Q_0. Of course, the final choice depends, as discussed in the previous section, on the *relative* price (or relative scarcity) of these two resources.

However, a closer look at the slope of the constant output curve in Figure 1.4 indicates that each incremental reduction in natural capital, N, would

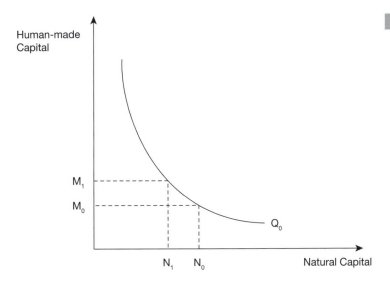

Figure 1.4

Substitution possibilities between natural and human-made capital. The output level Q_0 can be produced using the input combinations of either (N_0, M_0) or (N_1, M_1), or several other combinations of N and M along the constant output curve, labeled as Q_0.

require a progressively increasing amount of human-made capital in order to produce the desired amount of output, Q_0. In other words, the *opportunity cost* in terms of other inputs sacrificed (in this case, human-made capital) increases at an *increasing rate as natural capital becomes scarce*.

The two most important lessons to be drawn from the above discussion are the following:

1. Environmental resources can always be substituted by other factors of production, but it would be at an *increasing opportunity cost*. That is, the successive reduction in environmental resources (such as a forest watershed) requires an incrementally larger increase in other factors (such as human-made capital) in order to maintain the production of a constant level of output. It is in this sense, therefore, that the scarcity (availability) of environmental resources would become a concern.

2. However, even if it may occur at an increasingly higher cost, the existence of factor substitution suggests that the scarcity of any resource (including the environment) can be augmented through substitutions of other factors of production.

In the above discussion of substitution possibilities, production technology was assumed to remain con-

stant. In other words, factor substitution possibilities were discussed assuming no change in the current techniques (or state of the art) of production. However, in a dynamic economy, technological advances that entail a fundamental change in production techniques is normal. If this is the case, it would be instructive to provide a brief outline of the broader implications of changes in production technology to the issue of natural resource adequacy (scarcity).

In production analysis, technological advancement is defined as the ability to produce a given amount of output by using less of *all* inputs (but not necessarily by the same proportion). For example, in Case Study 1.1 the same amount of water can be produced by using *less* of both natural and human-made capitals. Figure 1.5 is used to illustrate this point.

Figure 1.5 is similar to Figure 1.4 in all respects except that the curve representing the constant water output, Q_0, is allowed to *shift* downwards to indicate that the same level of output can be produced using less of both inputs (N and M). For example, before the assumed technological advance it took the N_0 and M_0 amount of the two inputs to produce the annual water needs for the city of New York. However, as shown in Figure 1.5, with technological progress the same amount of water can be produced using less of both inputs, N_1 and M_1. Thus, it is in this specific way

Figure 1.5

Resource conservation through technological advances. The same amount of output, Q_0, can be produced by using less of both inputs; that is, (N_1, M_1) instead of (N_0, M_0).

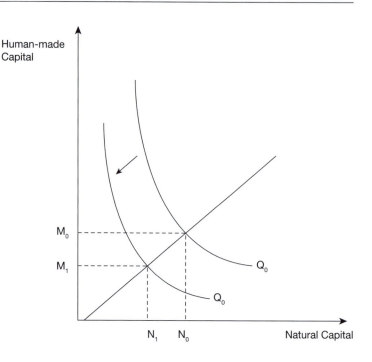

that technological advance implies the possibility of producing a given level of output with less of both inputs, thereby conserving resources including the environment.

To summarize the discussion in this section, the scarcity (availability) of natural resources cannot be adequately addressed without careful consideration of technological factors such as factor-substitution possibilities and technical advances in production (Solow 1991). This will be particularly evident when the focuses of the discussion are: (1) pollution-control technology in Chapter 4; and (2) the perennial debate on 'biophysical' limits to economic growth and the emerging sustainable development paradigm in Chapters 11, 12 and 13.

The third and the final issue that needs to be considered in this chapter is how, at the fundamental level, the proponents of the neoclassical school of economics perceive the interrelationships (inter-connectedness) between the human economy and the natural world. To what extent and in what specific ways is the human economy dependent on the natural environment? Is there evidence of inconsistencies in how the human economy is designed to function within the laws of nature? If so, would it matter?

These are the kinds of issues addressed in the next section.

1.4 THE HUMAN ECONOMY AND THE NATURAL WORLD: THE NEOCLASSICAL WORLDVIEW

> A curious event in the history of economic thought is that, years after the mechanistic dogma has lost its supremacy in physics and its grip on the philosophical world, the founders of the neoclassical school set out to erect an economic science after the pattern of mechanics—in the words of Jevons, as 'the mechanics of utility and self-interest.' . . .
> A glaring proof is the standard textbook representation of the economic process by a circular diagram, a pendulum movement between production and consumption within a completely closed system.
> (Georgescu-Roegen 1993: 75)

In this last section of the chapter, a very broad view of the human economy is presented with the following three objectives in mind: (1) to provide a schematic view of the basic institutional components of a market-oriented economy; (2) to show how the flow of materials (inputs and outputs) are circulated within a 'self-contained' human economic process; and (3) to discover the implied relationships (if any) between the human economy and the natural world.

As a working definition, an *economy* can be understood as a complex institutional mechanism designed to facilitate the production, consumption and exchange of goods and services, given resource scarcity and technology, the preferences of households, and the legal system for resource ownership rights (Randall 1987). All economies are alike in the sense that they are devised to help facilitate the production, consumption and exchange of goods and services, and they are constrained by resource scarcity and technology. On the other hand, economies differ in the degree of empowerment given to households and firms in their ability to make economic choices, and

the legal view of property ownership rights. For example, in a capitalist and market-oriented economy, freedom of choice and private ownership of property are strongly held institutional principles. In contrast, in a centrally planned economy, the production and distribution of goods are dictated by bureaucratic choices, with resource ownership retained by the state.

This section will use a circular flow diagram (an approach familiar to those who have taken a course in introductory economics) to present a schematic view of the basic institutional components of a market economy. The circular flow diagram in Figure 1.6 is designed to show that the operation of a market-oriented economy is composed of the following *four elements*:

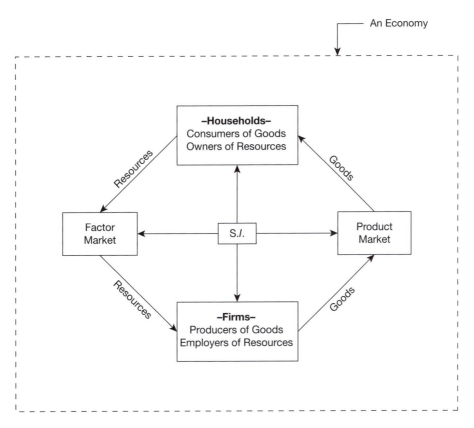

Figure 1.6 *Circular flow diagram of the economic process. An economy is composed of a flow of commodities (in the form of basic resources, goods and services); social institutions, primarily markets and legal tenders; and people (broadly identified as households and firms).*

1. *Economic Entities* (households and firms): House-holds are the final users of goods and services and the owners of resources. In a market economy, given resource scarcity, the primary goal is to find effective ways to address the material needs of consumers (households). At least in principle, *consumers' wellbeing (the maximization of consumers' utility) is the primary goal of a market-oriented economy*. While households are final users of goods and services, firms enter the economic process as transformers of basic resources (labor, capital and natural resources) into goods and services, and this is done in response to consumers' preferences (demand).

2. *Commodities*: Flow of resources both as factors of production and final goods and services. In broad terms, these resources are recognized as being directly or indirectly capable of satisfying human wants and are scarce, being found in limited quantities and/or qualities.

3. *Markets*: An institutional arena in which exchanges (buying and selling) of final goods and services and factors of production (labor, capital and natural resources) take place. Traditionally, economists group markets into two broad categories, namely, product and factor markets. The *product market* is where the exchange of *final* goods and services occurs. In this market, demand and supply provide information about households and firms, respectively. The *factor market* refers exclusively to the buying and selling of basic resources, such as labor, capital and natural resources. In this sub-market, demand imparts market information about firms and supply provides information about households as resource owners. That is, households are the suppliers of labor, capital and natural resources, while firms are the buyers, who, in turn, use these items to produce final goods and services for the product market. Clearly then, the role played by households and firms in the factor market is the reverse of their role in the product market.

   In both the product and factor markets, information about resource scarcity is transmitted through *prices*. As discussed earlier, these prices are formed through the interactions of market demand and supply, and under certain conditions, can be used as reliable indicators of both present and future resource scarcities (for more on this see Sections A.2 & A.4 of Appendix A).

4. *Non-Market Public and Private Institutions*: A market does not function in a vacuum; that is, for a market to operate efficiently, *ownership rights* need to be clearly defined and enforced. This requires the establishment of public agencies designed to articulate and enforce the rules and regulations by which ownership rights are attained, relinquished (transferred) and enforced (more on this in Chapter 3). In addition, *competition* in the marketplace is fostered through public intervention in some instances. Governments also create and regulate the supply of money.

   The public and quasi-public entities (social institutions) that legislate the rules for assigning resource-ownership rights, create and regulate money supply, and regulate the degree of competition in the marketplace are represented by the *box* at the center of Figure 1.6. It can be observed that what flows from this box to households, firms and markets are not physical goods but information services (in the form of rules and regulations). In general, the main function of these flows of information is to ensure that economic agents (households and firms) are playing by socially predetermined rules of the game. In this regard, ideally, social institutions are perceived as playing a similar role to that of a conductor of an orchestra or a traffic director at a busy intersection.

   Viewed in this way, social institutions have important economic functions. However, they should not be assumed to be either *perfect* or *costless* (North 1995). When they are not functioning well, the information communicated through them could distort market signals (prices) and in so doing, significantly affect the allocation of scarce resources. This will become evident in Chapter 3, which specifically deals with environmental resources.

Several lessons can be drawn from the above depictions of the human economy:

1. The human economy is composed of *three* entities: people, social institutions, and flow of commodities (as factors of production and final goods and services).

2. Since the value of resources is assumed to emanate exclusively from their usefulness to humans, the economic notion of resources is strictly *anthropocentric*. What this implies is that basic resources (such as the various services provided by the natural environment) have no *intrinsic* value. Something is of intrinsic value if it has value in its own right, or for its own sake (Attfield 1998; DeGregori 1987).

    For example, in Case Study 1.1, the worthiness of a watershed service (water purification process by root systems and soil microorganisms) is identified solely by its *commercial* value. The fact that the watershed under consideration may have other, non-economic, value is not considered. These other services include flood control, air purification, generation of fertile soil, and production of a range of goods from timber to mushrooms, as well as sites for recreation, inspiration, education, and scientific inquiry.

3. In the production sector, what is being continually created is *value*. Trees are cut and used to make chairs only if the *monetary* value of the chairs exceeds the *monetary* value of the woods used to make the chairs. Similarly, in the consumption sector, what is continually being created is an influx of *utility* from the final use (consumption) of goods and services. Therefore, in the human economic system, matter and energy from the natural environment (i.e., factors of production) are continuously transformed to create an immaterial (psychic) flow of value and utility. As will be evident in the next chapter, this observation is quite inconsistent with a purely ecological worldview of the transformation of matters and energy and the ultimate implications of this natural process to all living and non-living entities in nature.

4. In the above simple model, no explicit consideration is given to the extent to which the material flow (commodities) in the human economy is dependent on the natural ecosystem. The fact that the economic process continually depends on the natural world for both the generation of raw material 'inputs' and absorption of waste 'outputs' (see Figure 1.1, p. 10) is simply taken for granted. As Georgescu-Roegen put it, 'The patent fact that between the economic process and the material environment there exists a continuous mutual influence which is history making carries no weight with the standard economist' (1993: 75).

    More specifically, the natural environment (i.e., all living and non-living things occurring naturally on earth) is simply viewed as a 'gift of nature' ready to be exploited by humans and in strict accordance to the laws of demand and supply. Or, as O'Neill and Kahn (2000: 333) put it, the environment is viewed as 'the constant and stable background for economic activity'.

A basic understanding of ecological principles is needed in order to fully understand and appreciate the above criticisms of Georgescu-Roegen, and O'Neill and Kahn and Chapter 2 is devoted to this end. Most importantly, Chapter 2 is an essential reading if one wishes to fully understand the necessities and implications of the emerging sustainable development paradigm.

1.5 CHAPTER SUMMARY

The primary objective of this chapter has been to present the neoclassical or standard economic worldview of the natural environment and its roles in the economic system at the fundamental level. This involved presenting the key axiomatic assumptions and theoretical explanations that have been considered critical in the construction of the basic foundation for standard environmental and resource economics. With this in mind, the following are the key issues addressed in this chapter:

- The natural environment is viewed as having three distinctive functions. It is the source of basic raw materials to the human economy. It functions as a repository and eventually a decomposer of the waste materials emanating from the production and consumption sectors of the human economy. Finally, the natural environment provides humans with valuable amenities and ecosystem services.

- Environmental resources are considered to be of economic concern only to the extent that they are considered *scarce*—demand exceeds supply at zero prices.

- The *economic value* of scarce environmental resources is ultimately determined by consumers' preferences. Furthermore, consumers' preferences are best expressed by a market economy, and as such the market system is the preferred institution for allocating scarce resources, including the natural environment (more on this in Chapter 3).

- Given that economic value is determined solely by human preferences, the neoclassical worldview of environmental resources is strictly *anthropocentric*; that is, environmental resources have no *intrinsic* value, as such.

- Environmental (natural) resources are 'essential' factors of production. An economy cannot produce goods and services without the use of a certain minimum amount of natural resources. However, to the extent that resources are *fungible*, that is, one kind of resource (such as natural capital) can be freely replaced or substituted by another (such as human-made capital) in the production process, natural resources need not be seen as the sole or even primary factor in determining an economy's production capacity.

- Scarcity of resources (including environmental/natural resources) is continually augmented through technological advances.

- According to the neoclassical worldview, the human economy, as depicted in Figure 1.6, is composed of people, flow of commodities (or the flow of matter–energy at the fundamental level), and human institutions. The primary focus of the human economic system is not so much on the conversion of matter–energy that are found in nature to goods and services (i.e., the production process), but rather the generation of *utility* —an immaterial flux of satisfaction to humans. In this worldview, it appears that the link between the flow of matter–energy in the economic system and the natural environment is very much overlooked, if not completely ignored. The next chapter deals with the implications of this important oversight or omission to both the human economy and natural ecological systems.

REVIEW AND DISCUSSION QUESTIONS

1. Carefully review the following economic concepts and make sure you have a clear understanding of them: Neoclassical economics, absolute scarcity, relative scarcity, natural capital, human-made capital, factors substitution, technical advance, an economy, households, a firm, product and factor markets, utility, environmental amenities, and intrinsic value.

2. Identify the following:
    (a) The three distinctive contributions of the natural environment to the human economy.
    (b) The three roles of social institutions in a market economy.
3. Read the following statements. In response, state 'True', 'False' or 'Uncertain' and explain why:
    (a) Environmental resources should be of economic concern only if they are scarce.
    (b) Factor substitution possibilities render the problem of natural-resource scarcity (such as water) as manageable.
    (c) Relative price is important because it serves as a quick way to read opportunity cost.
4. Refer to Figure 1.4, where factor substitution possibility between human-made capital (M) and natural capital (N) was discussed using the New York water-filtration project as a case study. Try to make a similar analysis assuming that Q_0 represents the total amount of carbon dioxide (CO_2) emissions that needs to be controlled, and M and N represent CO_2 emission control by technological means, and carbon sequestration through the preservation of forest ecosystem, respectively. In your analysis make sure you discuss the following issues: factor substitution possibilities, the limit to factor substitution possibilities, and the effect of technological advances on factor substitution.
5. To view the human economy in isolation from the natural environment is not only misguided but also dangerous. Comment.

REFERENCES AND FURTHER READING

Attfield, R. (1998) 'Existence Value and Intrinsic Value', *Ecological Economics* 24.

Covey, S. R. (1989) *The 7 Habits of Highly Effective People: Powerful Lessons in Personal Change*, New York: Simon& Schuster Inc.

Dasgupta, P. S. and Heal, G. M. (1979) *Economic Theory and Exhaustible Resource*, Cambridge: Cambridge University Press.

DeGregori, T. R. (1987) 'Resources are Not; They Become: An Institutional Theory', *Journal of Economic Issues*, 221, 2: 1241–63.

Georgescu-Roegen, N. (1993) 'The Entropy Law and the Economic Problem', in H. E. Daly and K. N. Townsend (eds.) *Valuing the Earth: Economics, Ecology, Ethics*, Cambridge, MA: MIT Press.

North, D. C. (1995) 'The New Institutional Economics and Third World Development', in Herris, J. et al. (eds.) *The New Institutional Economics and Third World Development*, London: Routledge.

O' Neill, V. R. and Kahn, J. (2000) 'Homo Economus as a Keystone Species', *BioScience*, 50, 4: 333–7.

Randall, A. (1987) *Resource Economics: An Economic Approach to Natural Resource and Environmental Policy*, 2nd edn., New York: John Wiley and Sons.

Simon, J. L. and Kahn, H. (1984) *The Resourceful Earth: A Response to Global 2000*, Oxford: Basil Blackwell

Solow, R. M. (1991) 'Sustainability: An Economist Perspective', in R. Dorfman and N. Dorfman (eds.) *Economics of the Environment: Selected Readings*, 3rd edn., New York: W.W. Norton.

The natural environment and the human economy: The ecological perspective

No serious student of environmental economics can afford to ignore the subject matter of 'ecology,' the widely embracing science which looks at the interrelationship between living species and their habitats.

(Pearce 1978: 31)

LEARNING OBJECTIVES

After reading this chapter you will be familiar with the following:

- The notion of 'general' resource scarcity—that the human economy is bounded by a non-growing and finite ecological sphere. As such, nature acts as both a source of and a limiting factor to the basic material requirements of the human economy.
- What 'ecosystem' means and, at a rudimentary level, an understanding of the basic constituents of the 'structures' and 'functions' of a natural ecosystem.
- Ecological principles that are critical to understanding the basic prerequisites for 'sustainable' human co-existence with nature. These include:
  (a) Ecological interdependencies;
  (b) The laws of transformation of matter–energy; and
  (c) Ecological succession as it relates to the notions of biodiversity and ecological resilience.
- The causes and ecological implications of the growing dominance of humans over nature.

This chapter is worthy of a great deal of attention simply because it contains the basic scientific concepts and principles that are essential for understanding several of the environmental and resource concerns that are prevalent today, such as: the limits to energy conversion technology; the determinants of environmental damage cost function; the value of biodiversity; the causes and consequence of climate change; and the ways of achieving environmental sustainability. In this respect, the concepts covered in

Chapter 2 truly serve as foundations for most of the chapters in this book.

2.1 INTRODUCTION

Consistent with the discussion in Chapter 1, in broad terms, environmental resources include the living and non-living endowment of the earth and, for that matter, the entirety of the *biosphere* (the layer of air, land and water that supports life). The primary objectives of this chapter are twofold: (1) to establish a clear understanding of the *basic principles* governing the nature, structure and function of ecosystems (i.e., the subsystems of the biosphere); and (2) to demonstrate the functional *linkages* (relationships) between the biosphere (the global sum of all ecosystems) and the human economy. Below is a summary of these basic ecological principles and linkages. This summary provides an introductory overview of the key ecological tenets discussed throughout this chapter.

■ Environmental resources of the biosphere are *finite*. Hence, environmental resources are scarce in *absolute* terms.

■ In nature, everything is related to everything else. Moreover, survival of the biosphere requires recognition of the *mutual interdependencies* among all the elements that constitute the biosphere.

■ At a functional level and from a *purely physical* viewpoint, the biosphere is characterized by a *continuous transformation of matter and energy*. Furthermore, the transformation of matter and energy is governed by immutable *natural laws*.

■ *Material cycling* is essential for the revitalization and sustainability of all the subsystems of the biosphere, including the human economy. In well-functioning ecological systems, only solar energy would come from outside, while all byproducts (wastes) would be constantly reused and recycled within.

■ *Nothing remains constant* in nature. Furthermore, changes in 'ecosystems' do not appear to occur in a *linear* and predictable manner. However, measured at a *geological timescale*, the natural tendency of an ecological community (species of plants, animals and microorganisms living together) tends to progress from simple and unstable relationships (pioneer stage) to a stable, resilient, diverse and complex community.

■ The human economy is a *subsystem* of the biosphere and it would be dangerously misleading to view natural resources as just factors of production lying outside the confines of the larger system as implied in the discussion of the last section of Chapter 1.

■ Furthermore, from a purely physical viewpoint, the human economy consists largely of the transformation of matter and energy from one form to another. *Matter can be recycled but energy cannot*.

■ The natural disposition of the technological human has tended towards the *simplification* of the natural systems eventually leading toward less stable, resilient and diverse ecological communities.

The above list of ecological principles and pronouncements represents the foundation for the bio-centric (ecological) perspective on the relationship between the biosphere and the human economy. This perspective is bio-centric in the sense that it does not explicitly recognize the main output of the economic system—non-material flow of *utility* or 'enjoyment of life' that are discussed in the last section of Chapter 1. It describes nature and the interactions that occur in nature between living and non-living matter in *purely physical* (energy and matter) terms. These are clearly evident from the following specific observations relating to Figure 2.1:

1. The clearly demarcated circle (symbolizing the earth and its finiteness) represents the biosphere.

2. By placing it inside the circle, the human economy is perceived as a subsystem of the biosphere. The box inside the circle indicates that the growth of the economic subsystem is 'bounded' by a finite ecological sphere.

3. The figure suggests that the human economy is dependent on the biosphere for its continuous withdrawal (extraction and harvest) of material *inputs* and for repository of *waste* (outputs)— degraded matter and energy that are the eventual byproducts of the economic process.

4. The biosphere (hence, the human economy) requires the presence of a continuous flow of external energy—the sun.

5. While both the human economy and the biosphere are regarded as 'open systems' with regard to energy (i.e., both systems require an external source of energy—the sun), the biosphere taken in its entirety is regarded as a 'closed system'

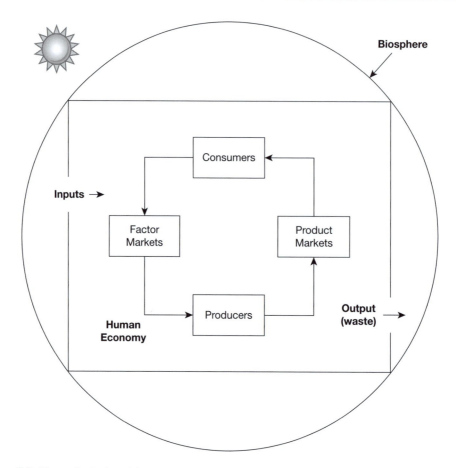

Figure 2.1 *The ecological worldview conceptualizes the human economy as being: (1) bounded within the confines of the biosphere; and (2) entirely dependent on the biosphere for inputs (i.e., basic resources) and outputs (i.e., disposal/storage of wastes), and energy from the sun.*

with respect to matter. It is important to note that this is in stark contrast to the way the human economy is depicted in Figure 1.6—the circular flow diagram presented in the last section of Chapter 1. Figure 1.6, representing the neoclassical worldview, actually treats the human economy as an 'open system' with regard to *both* energy and matter. That is, the human economy is continually dependent on both the *inputs* of energy and matter from external sources and the *output* to external repositories.

The upshot is clear: A worldview as represented by Figure 2.1 illustrates the principle that the human economy is completely and unambiguously depen-

dent on natural ecological systems for its material needs. Furthermore, the human economy (as a subsystem) cannot outgrow the biosphere. The implication of this is that the growth of the economic subsystem is 'bounded' by a non-growing and finite ecological sphere.

A comprehensive and systematic understanding of the extent to which nature acts as both a *source* and a *limiting factor* to the basic material requirements of the human economy demands a good understanding of the following *four ecological principles* (laws). A brief outline of these four principles and their broader implications is provided below. This will be followed with a detailed discussion of each of these principles in the remaining four sections of this chapter, Sections 2.2 to 2.5.

Ecology is a branch of science that systematically studies the relationships between living organisms and the physical and chemical environment in which they live. Hence, the *first principle* to consider is the presence of ecological *interdependencies* between living (including humans) and non-living matter, and the implications of interdependency on the relationships between the human economy and the natural world. This is discussed thoroughly in Section 2.2. The important lesson to be learned from the discussion in this section is that the human economy cannot be viewed in isolation from the natural ecosystem or biosphere. Instead, the economy is a subsystem of the environment, both as a source of raw material inputs and as a 'sink' for waste output.

The *second ecological principle* emerges from the mere recognition that what is evident in the biosphere is a *continuous transformation* of matter and energy. Furthermore, this transformation appears to be governed by some immutable laws. Thus, Section 2.3 provides a thorough discussion of the laws of transformations of matter–energy and their broad implications to the functioning of human economy and the biosphere. The important lesson to be learned from the discussion in this section is the recognition of biophysically determined limiting factors to the growth of both ecological and economic systems.

The *third principle* deals with a notion known as *ecological succession*: how natural ecosystems, if left alone, evolve through gradual (evolutionary) processes from 'simple' to more complex and interrelated systems, characterized by a movement towards stability, diversity and resilience. As will be evident in the discussion in Section 2.4, this particular area of ecological study (i.e., the process involving the transitioning of natural ecosystems from immature to mature stages) contains the seeds for many of the controversies in ecology. Nonetheless, one important lesson to be drawn from the discussion in Section 2.4 is the significance of biodiversity to the health and sustainability of natural ecological systems (including humans).

The *fourth principle* deals with the risk factors involved when a single species (in this case, humans) asserts dominance at the expense (or even demise) of many other species. Here, the ecological law under consideration means that, as Benyus (1997: 5) aptly put it, 'a species cannot occupy a niche that appropriates all resources—there has to be some sharing'. Thus, Section 2.5 describes the circumstances by which humans came to dominate nature. Furthermore, it explains the specific ways that human technology has led to the simplification (through biodiversity loss) of natural ecological systems and the possible implications of this trend to the survival of the biosphere.

The important lesson to be learned from the discussion in Section 2.5 is the warning to humans that, as a biological species, our long-term survival is ultimately threatened by developing niches that enable us to over-exploit the earth's stored-up supply of resources with the single-minded goal of achieving continued economic progress. In this respect, principle four is the corollary of principle one because it re-emphasises the fact that species depend upon each other and upon shared resources.

Why read a chapter on ecology?

For those of you who are outside the science field, this chapter may cover materials that you are encountering for the first time. For this reason, serious attempts have been made to write the chapter in ways that are palatable even to students who are unfamiliar with ecology. However, this is not to suggest that it will be an easy reading. It will require time commitments that are normally associated with learning new ideas and their implications to the world, and life in general. However, the rewards of reading the rest of this chapter carefully will be undoubtedly quite considerable to anyone who aspires to have a clear understanding of the scientific foundation of:

- The waste assimilative (absorptive) capacity of the natural environment (Chapter 3);
- The pollution-damage function (Chapter 4);
- Environmental valuation (Chapter 7);
- Climate change (Chapter 9);
- Biodiversity loss and risks associated with (Chapter 10);

- Energy-saving potentials and limitations through technological advances (Chapters 11, 13 and 14). These chapters deal with the general topics of limits to economic growth, sustainable development, and indicators of sustainability; and
- Designing products and production processes that from inception account for material reduction, reuse and recycling (Chapter 15).

2.2 ECOLOGICAL INTERDEPENDENCY AND ITS IMPLICATIONS

> Nature is by definition cyclical; there is virtually no waste in the natural world that does not provide food for other living systems. If there were waste, we wouldn't have survived four billion years of evolution, because linear systems use up and exhaust resources.
>
> (Hawken 1993: 38)

What is an ecosystem?

The logical starting-point for the study of ecological interdependencies is the *ecosystem*. An ecosystem includes living organisms in a specified physical environment. Most importantly, it refers to the multitude of interactions between the organisms, and the non-biological factors in the physical environment that limit their growth and reproduction, such as air, water, minerals and temperature. Viewed this way, an ecosystem practically means the 'house of life' (Miller 2010). The definition of boundaries and the spatial scale of an ecosystem can vary. An ecosystem can be as small as a pond or as big as the entire earth (see Figure 2.2 for a picture of a forest ecosystem). One can, therefore, refer to the ecosystem of a pond or the ecosystem of the entire earth. What is important in each case is the definition of boundaries across which inputs and outputs of energy and matter can be measured (Boulding 1993).

Ecosystem structure and function

Generally, an ecosystem is composed of *four* components: the atmosphere (air), the hydrosphere

(water), the lithosphere (earth) and the biotic (life). The first three comprise the *abiotic* or non-living components of the ecosystem, whereas the biosphere is its *biotic* (living) component. It is important to recognize that the living and non-living components of an ecosystem interact with each other. The dynamic interaction of these components is critical to the survival and functioning of the ecosystem, just as breathing and eating are essential to the survival of animals. Furthermore, these components are capable of coexisting so that the ecosystem itself is alive (Miller and Spoolman 2010; Schneider 1990). For example, soil is a living system that develops as a result of interactions between plant, animal and microbial communities (living components) and

Figure 2.2 *A picture representing a forest ecosystem. What makes this image of a forest one of an ecosystem is not one single being such as the trees. It is rather the interactions of the trees (the seemingly dominant feature of the ecosystem) with the air, water, rocks and the various living organisms that use the forest shade as their habitats and source of sustenance.*

parent rock material (abiotic components). Abiotic factors such as temperature and moisture influence the process of soil development.

In the ecosystem, the *abiotic* components serve several functions. First, the *abiotic* components are used as a habitat (space), and an immediate source of water and air for organisms. Second, they act as a reservoir for the six most important elements for life: carbon (C), hydrogen (H), oxygen (O), nitrogen (N), sulfur (S) and phosphorus (P). These elements constitute 95 percent of all living organisms. Furthermore, the earth contains only a *fixed* amount of these elements. Thus, the continual functioning of the ecosystem requires that these elements be *recycled* since they are critical to the overall welfare of the ecosystem.

The *biotic* (living) component of the ecosystem consists of three distinct groups of organisms: the producers, consumers and decomposers. The *producers* are those organisms capable of *photosynthesis*: the production of organic material solely from solar energy, CO_2 and water. This organic material serves as a source of both energy and mineral nutrients, which are required by all living organisms. Examples include terrestrial plants (such as trees and crops) and aquatic plants (such as phytoplankton).

The *consumers* are organisms whose survival depends on the organic materials synthesized by the producers. The consumers represent organisms of all sizes ranging from large predator animals (such as elephants and whales) to small parasites (such as mosquitoes and even bacteria). The consumers' dependence on the producers may take different forms. Some consumers (herbivores, such as rabbits) are directly dependent on primary producers for energy. Others (carnivores, such as lions) are indirectly dependent on primary producers.

The last group of living organisms is the *decomposers*. These include microorganisms, such as fungi, yeast, bacteria, etc., as well as a diversity of worms, insects and many other small animals that rely on dead organisms for their survival. They survive and obtain energy by decomposing materials released by plants and consumers to simpler compounds, such as CO_2, H_2O, phosphate (PO_4) and so on. This, as will be shown shortly, is what keeps material cycling within the ecosystem.

The discussion has so far dealt with what is known as the *structural organization* (i.e., how the components and the relationships of biotic and abiotic elements of an ecosystem are organized and defined) of the ecosystem. The next step is to examine not only how the basic components of an ecosystem are organized, but also how they become integrated through transformation of matter and energy. However, for any movements or transformations of energy and matter to occur—in other words, for the ecosystem to perform its intended function—an external source of *energy* is needed. For our planet, the primary source of this energy is solar radiation: the energy from the *sun*. Solar energy, then, fuels the flow of energy and matter in an ecosystem. The fundamental question is: Where does *life* start and end in this system that, from a *purely physical* viewpoint, is manifested by a continuous transformation of matter and energy?

The biotic component of the ecosystem relies on the ability of producers (terrestrial and aquatic plants) to directly convert solar energy to chemical or stored energy in the form of organic matter. This transformation of one form of energy to another is accomplished through the process of *photosynthesis*. Essentially, it involves the synthesis of organic matter from simpler inorganic compounds—such as carbon dioxide CO_2, H_2O, amonium nitrate NH_4, phosphate PO_4, etc.—obtained from soil, water, or atmosphere) fueled by solar radiation. From this, it should be evident that the abiotic components of the ecosystem are linked to the photosynthetic process—the production of an energy base to support life. Also through photosynthesis, the flow of materials becomes linked to the flow of energy, which will be explored further in Section 2.3.

It is important to recognize that the producers are indispensable to the biotic component of the ecosystem. Without these organisms it would be impossible to create the organic matter (plant tissues) essential for the growth and reproduction of other organisms (consumers and decomposers, which as will be shown shortly play an important role in material cycling).

While the nature of the dependency between the producers and other forms of organisms may appear to be linear at this fundamental level (the flow of the material is from producers to consumers and decomposers), the functioning of the ecosystem as a whole is characterized by mutual interdependencies among many species at each level—a food web (Miller and Spoolman 2010).

As shown in Figure 2.3, the consumers depend on producers for energy, various nutrients and oxygen. Oxygen is the byproduct of photosynthesis. The producers, in turn, depend on consumers and decomposers for CO_2 and on decomposers and abiotic processes for mineral nutrients such as nitrogen and phosphorus. All members of the biota, through respiration, release CO_2. Finally, by consuming the dead plants and animals, the decomposers convert organic compounds into inorganic compounds, which plants can use. Thus, in the natural environment, survival and 'proper' ecosystem functioning dictate mutual interactions (interdependence) among organisms and between them and the abiotic environment (Miller and Spoolman 2010).

Based on the discussion so far, at a fundamental level and from a *purely physical* viewpoint, a functioning (living) natural ecosystem is characterized by a constant transformation of matter and energy. Furthermore, an ecosystem will continue to function (remain alive) to the extent that it is not buried by the weight of its own internally generated waste. This can be avoided only through continuous *material cycling*, which is the next topic of discussion. In fact,

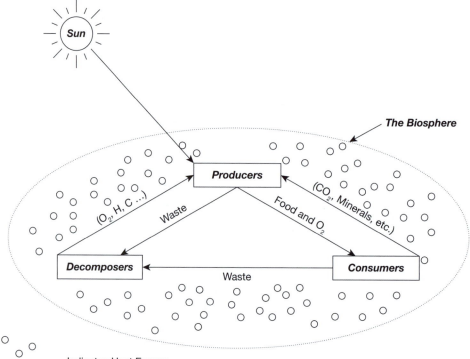

Figure 2.3 *The basic lifecycle process. The biotic component of an ecosystem is composed of three major groups of organisms: the producers, consumers and decomposers. As indicated by the direction of the arrows, functionally these three groups of organisms are mutually interdependent. The ability of the producers to convert solar energy to chemical or stored energy is what starts the biological cycles, and the sustainability of these cycles, among others, depends on the presence of a continuous flow of energy from an external source (sun).*

as indicated above, the waste from one component of the community becomes a resource for other components—waste is food.

Material cycling

As is evident from an earlier discussion (see also Figure 2.3), the natural recycling process starts with the formation of plant tissues through the processes of photosynthesis and biosynthesis. At this stage, oxygen is released into the environment. Virtually all of the molecular oxygen, O_2, in the atmosphere and in the oceans has originated from photosynthesis. In many ecosystems the second major stage of recycling occurs when animals, in their effort to metabolize the stored energy from plant tissues, release CO_2 and organic wastes. Microorganisms, however, perform the major recycling (decomposition). That is, the microorganisms ultimately break down dead organic matter into its simpler (inorganic) components. This recycling is particularly important because the amount of mineral elements found in the ecosystem (especially nitrogen and phosphate) is finite, and can limit the growth and reproduction of organisms.

However, decomposition may not always be complete. The oxidation process involved in decomposition largely depends on the availability of oxygen, moisture content and the temperature of the ecosystem under consideration. For example, oxidation takes place at a much faster rate in a tropical forest than at the bottom of a lake or in a desert. Thus, in nature material recycling is not 100 percent efficient, and some amounts of organic matter may remain only partially decomposed. This incompletely decomposed organic matter, accumulated and aged over a period of time, forms peat, coal and petroleum—that is, fossil fuels. This is the basis of the energy that is so crucial to the modern human economy. It is also a large reserve of carbon that gets released rapidly when fossil fuels are burned and contributes to global warming by releasing CO_2 into the atmosphere at an unprecedented rate.

The recycling of materials is not limited to the biological and material cycles in an ecosystem. The well-known atmospheric cycles (such as those of carbon, nitrogen and sulfur) contribute to the circulation of these elements within the various components of the ecosystem. Furthermore, it is through atmospheric cycles that the concentration of these elements in a given environmental medium is maintained or regulated. For example, the atmosphere is composed of approximately 20 percent oxygen, 79 percent nitrogen, 0.9 percent argon (which is not significant biologically) and 0.03 percent CO_2 (an amount that has been increasing over the past 200 years).

It is very important to note that, within an ecosystem, the atmospheric cycles cannot be viewed in isolation from geological and biological cycles. For example, there is a large reserve of nitrogen in the atmosphere, and only a small number of microorganisms are responsible for converting atmospheric nitrogen to a form that plants can use through a process called *nitrogen fixation*, whereas there is no large reserve of nitrogen in rocks. Thus, nitrogen fixation is the critical process of converting unavailable gaseous nitrogen from the atmosphere to available (inorganic) nitrogen for plants. Furthermore, physical and chemical processes associated with volcanic activities and the combustion of fossil fuels also can increase the availability of useful nitrogen to ecosystems.

In addition to the atmospheric cycles, hydrogen cycles and geological processes also contribute to the constant recycling of materials in the ecosystem. For example, it is through erosion and water movement that nitrates, sulfates and phosphates in the soil, rock and sediment can be freed and returned to the roots of plants. This process is particularly important for the recycling of phosphate, as there is a large reserve of phosphorus in rocks and virtually none in the atmosphere. Thus, the process of converting available (inorganic) phosphorus in rock to available phosphate for plants is primarily a physical and chemical process (erosion).

Therefore, on the basis of the above discussions, the cycling and recycling process of the ecosystem is all-encompassing and demands the interaction of every facet of the ecosystem. In fact, the decomposition and recirculation of materials in the ecosystem are referred to as *biogeochemical* cycles: for example, the nitrogen cycle, phosphorous cycle, carbon cycle, and so on (Miller and Spoolman 2010; Pearce 1978). Given this, it is not difficult to imagine how human activities that disrupt these cycles can have significant negative impacts on ecosystem processes.

Lessons learned

In summary, Section 2.2 has covered the following:

■ In a natural ecosystem, living and non-living matter have *reciprocal* relationships. Survival and 'proper' ecosystem functioning dictate mutual interactions (interdependence) among organisms, and between them and the abiotic environment.

■ At a fundamental level and from a *purely physical* viewpoint, a functioning natural ecosystem is characterized by a constant transformation of matter and energy. This constant transformation maintains the existence of biological organisms.

■ Material recycling is essential for the growth and revitalization of all the components of the ecosphere (Miller and Spoolman 2010). In every natural ecosystem, what is a byproduct (waste) for one organism is a resource for another, essentially creating closed-loop material recycling. Consequently there is no such thing in nature as waste: in effect, *waste is food*. Furthermore, in nature materials are continuously circulated through the biosphere by a combination of atmospheric, geological, biological and hydrological cycles. These cycles are essential for maintaining the long-term equilibrium of the elements in the atmosphere, hydrosphere and lithosphere. Furthermore, since the biosphere (the sum of all the ecosystems on earth) is a closed material system, it is also through closed-loop material cycling that material needs are sustained to perpetuity.

■ If the health, and ultimately the survival, of the biosphere require recognition of the mutual interdependencies among all the elements that constitute it, strictly from an ecological view-

point the human economy cannot be viewed in isolation from the natural ecosystem or biosphere as depicted by the circular diagram, Figure 1.1. Instead, *the economy is a subsystem of the natural environment* on which it depends, both as a source of raw material inputs and as a 'sink' for waste (output) as shown in Figure 2.1. As will be further explored in Chapters 11 through 13, this vision of the human economy as a subsystem of the biosphere has very profound implications for the question of what should be the size (scale) of the human economy relative to the natural ecosystem. What is being implied here is that a properly scaled human economy or technology should allow a diversity of other creatures to thrive.

Let us now turn to the vital role that energy plays in the continual functioning and revitalization of a natural ecosystem and biosphere as a whole. The fundamental issue that will be addressed in the next section is the question of why the sustaining of natural ecosystems (including the human economy) requires the continuous flow of energy from external sources. The answer to this puzzle, as will be shown shortly, has a great deal to do with a natural law that governs the transformation of energy.

2.3 THE LAWS OF TRANSFORMATIONS OF MATTER–ENERGY AND THEIR IMPLICATIONS

> Economists are fond of saying that we cannot get something for nothing. The entropy law teaches us that the rule of biological life and, in man's case, of its economic continuation is far harsher. In entropy terms, the cost of any biological or economic enterprise is always greater than the product. In entropy terms, any such activity necessarily results in a *deficit*.
>
> (Georgescu-Roegen 1993: 80)

Introduction

The previous section briefly examined the crucial role that energy plays in the functioning of the natural ecosystem. That is, the availability of the chemical energy (in the form of organic molecules) that supports all forms of living organisms and the maintenance of the circulation of matter within the ecosystem requires a continuous flow of energy from an external source or sources. For our planet, this external source of energy has been primarily the sun's radiation.

Why is it that natural ecosystems need to have a continuous flow of energy from an external source? An adequate response to this question demands a discussion of the laws governing the transformation of matter and energy. As working definitions, *matter* may be identified as anything that occupies a space and has mass, and *energy* may be viewed as an entity that lacks mass but contains the capacity for moving and/or transforming an object(s): in other words, energy is the capacity to do work.

A living ecosystem is characterized by a continuous transformation of matter and energy. Several laws of physics govern the flow and transformation of matter and energy. Of these, two laws of thermodynamics are especially relevant to our understanding of the functioning of the natural ecosystem. These are discussed below as they specifically deal with energy and the associated implications.

The first and second laws of thermodynamics and their implications

The first law of thermodynamics refers to the conservation of matter and energy. This law states that matter can neither be created nor destroyed, but it can be transformed from one form into another. This same principle holds for energy as well. That is, the energy lost in one process must equal the energy gained by the surrounding environment. Therefore, in terms of *quantity*, the total energy is always constant. This is why, at times, the first law is referred as the law of conservation of energy.

The second law of thermodynamics deals with energy transformations and with the concepts of energy *quality* (useful versus useless energy). Energy can exist in a number of different 'states'. For example, light is a form of energy, as are various types of fossil fuels,

wind, nuclear power sources (fuels), gunpowder and electricity, among others. Energy from fossil fuels can be converted to heat to boil water and produce steam that can turn a turbine to produce electricity that can be converted to make a light bulb work or run an electric motor. We may consider each of these forms of energy to be useful since they can be used to do work—turn a turbine, move an automobile or provide light by which to see.

The second law of thermodynamics states that each time useful energy is converted from one state to another, there always is a lesser amount of *useful* energy available in the second state than there was in the first state. For example, in the case of an incandescent light bulb, electrical energy is converted to 'useful' light energy as well as some useless heat, which you can detect by touching a light bulb that has been turned on for a few minutes. For incandescent light, approximately 5 percent of the electrical energy becomes light and 95 percent becomes heat: a 5 percent energy efficiency. Similarly, the energy of fossil fuel used to do the work of moving an automobile generates a substantial amount of useless heat that must be dissipated through the 'cooling system' (i.e., the radiator and water pump), or it will ruin the motor. Therefore, in any transformation of energy, in terms of energy quality (useful energy) there is an apparent loss of available energy. This phenomenon is often referred to as the principle of energy degradation or *entropy*, and it is universally applicable (Georgescu-Roegen 1993).

As a whole, the significant implications of the second law of thermodynamics are the following:

- ■ Energy varies in its quality (ability to do work);
- ■ In all conversion of energy to work, there will always be a certain loss of energy. Thus, it will be impossible to devise a 'perfect' energy conversion system, or perpetual motion. Hence, there are limits to energy conservation through technological means (see Exhibit 2.1); and
- ■ Since energy moves unidirectionally, from high to low temperature (or from concentrated to dissipated condition), it follows that a highly concentrated source of energy (such as the available

EXHIBIT 2.1 PERPETUAL MOTION, A SORT OF 'ORIGINAL SIN' IN SCIENCE

Garrett Hardin

Perpetual motion is an anti-Epicurean notion. Derek Price argues that it was probable, though not certain, that the pursuit of perpetual motion did not become a 'growth industry' until after A.D. 1088, when 'some medieval traveler . . . made a visit to the circle of Su Sung' in China. At this place there was exhibited a marvelous water clock that seemed to run forever without any motive force being required to replenish the elevated water supply. 'How was the traveler to know that each night there came a band of men to turn the pump handles and force the tons of water from the bottom sump to the upper reservoir, thus winding the clock for another day of apparently powerless activity?'

Such may have been the historical origin of what Price calls 'chimera of perpetual motion machines . . . one of the most severe mechanical delusions of mankind.' The delusion was not put to rest until the late nineteenth century when explicit statements of the conservation of matter and energy were advanced by physicists and accepted by scientists in general. It should be noted that a comparable advance was made in biology at about the same time when Pasteur (and others) demolished the supposed evidence for the spontaneous generation of living organisms. Modern public health theory is based on, and committed to, the belief that Epicurus was right: there is indeed a 'need of seeds,' for disease germs to appear in this world of ours.

The 'conviction of the mind' that limits are real, now firmly established in the natural science, has still to be made an integral part of orthodox economics. As late as 1981 George Gilder, in his best-seller *Wealth and Poverty*, said that 'The United States must overcome

the materialistic fallacy: the illusion that resources and capital are essentially things which can run out, rather than products of the human will and imagination which in freedom are inexhaustible.' Translation: 'Wishing will make it so.'

Six years later at a small closed conference two economists told the environmentalists what was wrong with their Epicurean position. Said one: 'The notion that there are limits that can't be taken care of by capital has to be rejected.' (Does that mean that capital is unlimited?) Said another: 'I think the burden of proof is on your side to show that there are limits and where the limits are.' Shifting the burden of proof is tactically shrewd: but would economists agree that the burden of proof must be placed on the axiom, 'There's no such thing as a free lunch'?

Fortunately for the future progress of economics the wind is shifting. The standard ('neoclassical') system of economics assumes perpetual growth in a world of no limits. 'Thus,' said economist Allen Kneese in 1988, 'the neoclassical system is, in effect, a perpetual motion machine.' The conclusion that follows from this was explicitly laid out by Underwood and King: 'The fact that there are no known exceptions to the laws of thermodynamics should be incorporated into the axiomatic foundation of economics.' But it will no doubt be some time before economics is completely purged of the covert perpetual motion machines that have afflicted it from the time of Malthus to the present.

Source: *Living within Limits: Ecology, Economics, and Population Taboos* (1993: 44–5). Copyright © 1993 by Oxford University Press, Inc. Used by permission.

energy in a piece of coal or wood) can never be reused. That is, energy can never be recycled. *This clearly demonstrates why the natural ecosystem requires continual energy from an external source*, answering the question posed above.

From the first and second laws of thermodynamics, the following lessons can be learned:

■ The human economy, as part of the biosphere, cannot escape the fundamental laws that describe and dictate the transformation of matter and energy. To emphasize this point, Georgescu-

Roegen (1993) actually declared thermodynamics to be the most 'economic of all physical laws'.

■ Since matter is always conserved, the earth's biosphere is composed of a constant amount of matter. From a purely physical perspective, therefore, activity in nature is typified by the transformation of matter and not its *creation*. No activity in the biosphere (including the human economy) creates matter (Georgescu-Roegen 1993). In this respect, the first law clearly states that *natural resources are finite* (Boulding 1993; Georgescu-Roegen 1993).

Furthermore, it informs us that when matter is transformed, we cannot get rid of anything. Thus, *waste* (in the forms of degraded matter and heat energy) is an inevitable byproduct of any dynamic system, including, of course, the human economy, that sustains itself through continuous transformation of matter–energy. Under normal circumstances, this should pose no problem since degraded organic materials are decomposed (recycled) back to their basic elements, and heat energy is ultimately dissipated into the atmosphere and from there into space, unless it is prevented from exiting, for example, by atmospheric CO_2, water vapor or other compounds.

■ Finally, the second law states that energy cannot be recycled. Furthermore, there are definite *limits* to the conservation of energy through technological means: there is no perfect machine. Given this, should the modern human economy rely heavily on fossil fuels—one of the most limiting terrestrial energy resources? This important issue will be extensively discussed in Chapters 11 through 13.

Let us now turn our attention to ecological succession, the third major principle addressed in this chapter. Ecological succession describes the gradual transition in the kinds of species that occupy an area after some disturbance, or that begin to establish themselves on a previously uninhabited site: for example, bare rock. The discussion focuses primarily on changes in species composition and the complex ways in which these changes are manifested through

time. As will be evident shortly, studying ecological succession helps to shed light on our understanding of the significance of *biodiversity* to the health of natural ecosystems. A good understanding of ecological succession is also crucial to assessing the impacts that large-scale human interference may have on natural ecosystems.

2.4 ECOLOGICAL SUCCESSION AND ITS IMPLICATIONS

> While the origin and 'meaning' of life may be unknown, the way nature transforms the non-living to the living, the simple to the complex, the inefficient to the efficient, is better known and understood.
>
> (Hawken 1993: 20)

What is ecological succession?

Ecological succession involves natural changes in the species composition (types of plants, animals and microorganisms) that occupy a given area over a period of time, as well as the changes that occur in ecosystem dynamics, such as energy flow and nutrient cycling. In a given area, with a specific climate and soil type, the stages of succession (typically recognized by the changes in species composition) are somewhat predictable.

At the *pioneer* (or primary) stage, an ecosystem is populated by only a few different species and characterized by uncomplicated interrelationships. This stage tends to be unstable and, as such, highly vulnerable to environmental stress. Barring severe environmental disturbances, however, the system gradually continues to change in species composition and ecosystem dynamics until it reaches a relatively stable dynamic equilibrium, sometimes referred to as the 'climax' stage. At this stage, the ecosystem is stable and supports a large diversity of organisms with complex and diverse interrelationships.

In other words, a 'mature' ecological system is characterized by diversity, yet the dynamic processes of energy flow and nutrient cycling continue although there tends to be no net-change in the amount of matter and energy in the system. This built-in diversity is what makes the ecosystem, at this last stage, quite resilient to changes in the physical environment (Holling 1997). However, it should be pointed out that controversy exists about whether ecological succession would eventually reach a steady-state stage that would persist indefinitely. The argument is that nature is never constant, and that all ecosystems continually undergo change: for example, from severe storms, floods, or fire (Botkin and Keller 2003). Nevertheless, healthy and reasonably mature ecosystems tend to exist over relatively long time-periods and are at least somewhat, if not completely, self-sustainable over a few hundred years.

An illustrative example of ecological succession

In the eastern United States a good example of succession is abandoned farmland. The first year after a cultivated field (such as corn) is abandoned, it tends to be populated by a few aggressive weedy plants that are sparsely distributed, allowing much of the soil to be exposed to precipitation and intense heating (and evaporation) by the sun during the day and maximum cooling at night. The small number of plants allows for the potential removal of soil nutrients through the physical processes of erosion and/or the chemical process of leaching.

If left alone for a few years, this field is likely to become a dense meadow populated by a diversity of grasses, Queen Anne's lace and/or goldenrod. Still later, woody species (shrubs) such as blackberries or sumac begin to appear. These shrubby species typically grow taller than the herbaceous weeds of the meadow and may provide more shade than some meadow species can tolerate. At the same time, these woody shrubby species do not 'die back' to their roots each year, and consequently more of the mineral nutrients in the ecosystem remain in 'standing biomass' (organic material) rather than being returned to the soil through dead biomass.

After a few years, and through a gradual process, deciduous tree species can be seen emerging above some of the shrubby species and patches of open meadow. As these grow above the shrubs, they typically produce more shade than the shrubs can tolerate and the shrubs will begin to die. The larger woody stems of trees also store more nutrients within the ecosystem in standing biomass, with less in the soil, where it may be susceptible to loss by physical or chemical processes. Figure 2.4 provides a photographic image of ecological succession.

In this example, at least four different successional stages have been described: (1) an abandoned 'weedy' field (pioneer stage); (2) a meadow or 'old-field' stage with abundant grasses and other herbs; (3) a shrubby community; and (4) a forest. Over time, the species composition of the forest is likely to change as well. But ultimately a forest will develop, where little change will be evident over long periods of time (centuries) barring major human influence, natural catastrophe or substantial climate change (possibly associated with glaciations or global warming). Such a community type is often referred to as the climax community.

An area that is covered by a given type of 'climax' community is often referred to as a *biome*. Much of the eastern United States is made up of the 'Eastern Deciduous Forest Biome', whether it be the ancient forests of parts of the Appalachian Mountains that have never been cut or the cities of New York or Detroit, which, if abandoned, would eventually become deciduous forests. Other North American biomes include the 'prairies' of the Midwest, the 'conifer forests' of the Rocky Mountains and the 'deserts' of the Southwest.

Prior to the climax stage an ecosystem is continually undergoing changes, and the transitional time between successional changes may be considerable. The important question is, then, once an ecosystem has achieved a certain developmental stage (in particular, the climax stage), how does it maintain its balance or equilibrium?

The dynamics of a matured ecological community (biome)

Within an ecological system, *equilibrium* refers to the apparent lack of visible changes in its biotic components, in spite of the many important interactions

Figure 2.4 *Old-field ecological succession. The abandoned pasture to the left is slowly reverting to forest. Grasses are gradually replaced by other perennials such as milkweeds, goldenrod, and shrubs. Next come small trees adapted to this habitat. These would include sassafras, hawthorns and the like. Larger trees such as oaks, maples, hickories and eventually beeches will begin to come into the picture, and eventually a mature forest such as the old-growth forest shown in the remaining pictures will come into being after hundreds of years. Note the diversity of tree sizes in the mature forest.*

Source: Dave McShaffrey, Marietta College, USA, www.marietta.edu/~biol. Reprinted by permission.

that continue to occur. As discussed in Section 2.2, ecological interrelationships are clear manifestations of the biological interdependencies among organisms. Depending on the ecosystem's stage of development, the biological interdependencies could be simple and represented by a food-chain, or complex and characterized by a food-web.

To illustrate, suppose that due to a random natural event, the population of a certain organism (for example, rabbits) starts to multiply at an above-normal rate. An increase in the population of rabbits follows, which thereby creates an imbalance in the system. However, the disproportionate number of rabbits will eventually be suppressed by the lack of food or an increase in predation. In general, then, organisms within a given ecosystem maintain equilibrium through their reciprocal needs for food and other materials. In addition, in healthy ecosystems, elements and processes in the atmosphere, hydrosphere and lithosphere remain in healthy dynamic equilibrium through various well-known material cycles. However, as will be discussed in Section 2.5, human activities could disrupt these natural processes significantly.

Typically, a mature ecosystem is characterized by diversity, stability and resilience. These interrelated concepts are of major significance in understanding *biodiversity* and its role in increasing the efficacy of a

35

mature ecosystem (biome). Thus, each of these concepts and how they relate to each other is discussed below.

Earlier, succession was defined as the changes that occur naturally in the species composition of an ecosystem over tens or hundreds of years. It was also postulated that succession would eventually (although not necessarily in a linear fashion) lead to a 'climax' community. This is characterized by *diversity*: complex and wide-ranging interrelationships among multitudes of species. Accordingly, at the climax stage both the interrelationships and the number of species are near a maximum. Furthermore, increasing diversity helps maintain ecological stability, especially in the 'climax' stage. If an ecosystem is characterized by wide-ranging interrelationships among a large number of species, the loss of one species will have a smaller effect on the overall structure and functioning of that ecosystem (Holling 1997).

Stability refers to the ability of a natural ecosystem to return to its original condition after a change or disturbance. It is generally defined at the level of *biological populations* (Common and Perrings 1992). A system in dynamic equilibrium tends to be more stable than one in which disequilibrium exists, such as during early successional stages. On the other hand, *resilience* is defined at the *system level* and refers to the rate at which a perturbed system will return to its original state (Holling 1997). In other words, resilience refers to the robustness of a natural ecosystem in the face of considerable exogenous disturbance. Generally, as succession proceeds in an ecosystem, its diversity, stability, resilience and complexity tend to increase. Furthermore, these factors tend to reinforce each other.

However, many ecological controversies seem to sprout from the lack of agreement about these generalizations (Holling 1997). Conclusions resulting from manipulated experiments that differ from natural field-studies fuel these controversies. The differences are exacerbated further by the argument that the more interconnected the components of the system are, the less stable the system is likely to be. A major disturbance to closely connected species, can initiate a 'ripple effect' through the system. Others argue that stability does not always depend on diversity. Some of the more resilient ecosystems—the Arctic tundra, for example—are actually very simple.

Considerably more research is necessary before these controversies can be resolved. We do not clearly understand how these factors are related, nor do we have much knowledge of the kinds or magnitudes of environmental changes that might lead to major ecosystem disruptions (Holling 1997). This is particularly important with regard to actual and potential anthropogenic perturbations such as deforestation and global warming. It will be difficult, if not impossible, to predict what changes might occur as a result of such human activities. This is cause for concern and it is compounded when the scientific uncertainty of the long-term effects of certain environmental problems such as global warming is used to justify inaction. For example, an economic study by Nordhaus (1991) argued for a modest program of international abatement of CO_2 on the basis that many of the long-term effects of global warming are still uncertain (more on this in Chapter 9).

Lessons learned

The discussion in this section underscored the importance of the following ecological dictums:

- If left undisturbed, the natural tendency of ecosystems is to go through 'developmental' stages leading toward a mature ecosystem that supports a large diversity of species with a web of interrelationships.

- Conventional wisdom dictates that mature ecosystems are highly *efficient* and resource conserving (in terms of nutrient recycling and the length of time energy is retained in an ecosystem before being lost). Furthermore, mature ecosystems are stable, have diverse communities with complex interrelationships, and as such are more resistant to major disturbances in their environment.

- However, no ecosystem can remain unchanged forever. In recent years, as the size of the human economy relative to natural ecosystems (for that matter the biosphere) increases, the major threats to (the 'simplification' of) mature ecosystems appear to come from the increasing and disproportionate dominance of a single species, Homo sapiens. To get a better understanding of this phenomenon let us now turn to Section 2.5, which deals with specific human activities intended to modify nature to their advantage and the possible ramifications of these actions.

2.5 HUMANS AS BREAKERS OF CLIMAXES

> For a great many species today, 'fitness' means the ability to get along in a world in which human kind has become the most powerful evolutionary force.
> (Pollan 2001: xxiii)

This last section offers a brief account of the specific ways in which human technology and resource consumption have been contributing towards the simplification of natural ecosystems, and the possible implications of this trend for the survival of the biosphere as it is presently known. More specifically, ever since humankind acquired technology in the form of fire and stone tools, the pace of its domi-

nance and exploitation of nature has been dramatic. Now it is getting to the point, as several studies have suggested, that the world-wide human economy is on an annual basis utilizing approximately 40 percent of the total *net primary production* (NPP)—defined as the sum of all photosynthesis minus the energy required to maintain and support the plants (Vitousek et al. 1986).

In addition, many human activities, such as commercial and residential development, mining and the extraction of minerals, and the production and disposal of large amounts of toxic waste, further degrade natural ecosystems. These activities come with a cost: the increasing loss of biodiversity. The evidence for this is quite clear from even casual observations of the ordinary activities (agriculture, mining, production and consumption of goods and services, transportation, and so on) of modern industrial societies.

In agriculture, with the historical clearing of forestland and the planting of crops or orchards, a complex and mixed flora of native wild plants and the animals that depended on them, which once extended over wide areas, is now replaced in many cases by a single kind of plant or monoculture, for example potato (see Exhibit 2.2). To increase yield, fertilizers

---

EXHIBIT 2.2   THE IRISH POTATO FAMINE

Catharina Japikes

More than a million Irish people—about one in every nine—died in the Great Potato Famine of the 1840s. To the Irish, famine of this magnitude was unprecedented and unimaginable.

When the famine hit in 1845, the Irish had grown potatoes for over 200 years—since the South American plant had first arrived in Ireland. During this time, the lower classes had become increasingly dependent on them. Potatoes provided good nutrition, so diseases like scurvy and pellagra were uncommon. They were easy to grow, requiring a minimum of labor, training, and technology—a spade was the only tool needed. Storage was simple; the tubers were kept in pits in the ground

and dug up as needed. Also, potatoes produce more calories per acre than any other crop that would grow in northern Europe.

To increase their harvest, farmers came to rely heavily on one variety, the lumper. While the lumper was among the worst-tasting types, it was remarkably fertile, with a higher per-acre yield than other varieties. Economist Cormac O Grada estimates that on the eve of the famine, the lumper and one other variety, the cup, accounted for most of the potato crop. For about 3 million people, potatoes were the only significant source of food, rarely supplemented by anything else.

It was this reliance on one crop—and especially one variety of one crop—that made the Irish vulnerable to famine. As we now know, genetic variation helps protect against the decimation of an entire crop by pests, disease or climate conditions. Nothing shows this more poignantly than Ireland's agricultural history.

In 1845, the fungus Phytophthora infestans arrived accidentally from North America. A slight climate variation brought the warm, wet weather in which the blight thrived. Much of the potato crop rotted in the fields. Because potatoes could not be stored longer than 12 months, there was no surplus to fall back on. All those who relied on potatoes had to find something else to eat.

The blight did not destroy all of the crop; one way or another, most people made it through winter. The next spring, farmers planted those tubers that remained. The potatoes seemed sound, but some harbored dormant strains of the fungus. When it rained, the blight began again. Within weeks the entire crop failed.

Although the potatoes were ruined completely, plenty of food grew in Ireland that year. Most of it, however, was intended for export to England. There, it would be sold—at a price higher than most impoverished Irish could pay. In fact, the Irish starved not for lack of food, but for lack of food they could afford.

The Irish planted over two million acres of potatoes in 1845, according to O Grada, but by 1847 potatoes accounted for only 300,000 acres. Many farmers who could turned to other crops. The potato slowly recovered, but the Irish, wary of dependence on one plant, never again planted it as heavily. The Irish had learned a hard lesson—one worth remembering.

Source: *EPA Journal* 20, Fall 1994, p. 44. Reprinted by permission.

---

are applied to the soils, disrupting natural nutrient cycles. Competition by other organisms (insects, weeds and disease pests) is reduced or eliminated through ecological poisoning, such as the use of insecticides, herbicides and fungicides. In addition to crop farming, commercial cattle-ranching contributes to the rapid clear-cutting of old-growth tropical forestlands throughout the globe. The ultimate effect of all this has been the *simplification* of the natural ecosystems to such an extent that their ability to withstand environmental disturbances (their resilience) has been significantly diminished.

Through the mining of mineral ores and the production of goods and services, human society continues to introduce and dispose of industrial wastes that are new and often highly toxic to the natural environment (Commoner 1974). These human-made non-degradable toxic wastes, such as synthetic chemicals (for example, plastics), large doses of radiation, heavy metals, the family of organochlorines (which, among others, includes DDT, Dioxin, PCBs, and CFCs) continue to cause serious stresses on natural ecosystems. The ultimate effect of such environmental stresses has been to reduce the productivity, diversity, stability and resilience of natural ecosystems. For example, Exhibit 2.3 shows how, in Thailand, waste resulting from a boom in commercial shrimp-farming is causing ecological havoc. In other cases, relatively nontoxic wastes such as CO_2 may be produced in such large quantities (largely a result of the dependency of modern society on fossil fuels) that normal ecosystem processes cannot handle them, and they may begin to accumulate—potentially causing global warming and climate change.

Another way in which humanity has contributed to the increasing simplification of natural ecosystems is through the introduction of *invasive alien species* (IAS). What exactly are invasive alien species? At the United Nations Environment Program and the Convention on Biological Diversity (2004), invasive alien species were formally defined as 'non-native species that are introduced deliberately or unintentionally outside their natural habitats where they become established, proliferate, and spread in ways that cause damage to human interests'. This definition indicates that invasive alien species are introduced both intentionally (such as birds and aquarium species, ornamental plants, pets, and so on) and unintentionally (e.g., zebra mussels that entered the waters of the Great Lakes from shipping ballast).

EXHIBIT 2.3   THAILAND'S SHRIMP BOOM COMES AT GREAT ECOLOGICAL COST

John McQuaid

Ban Lang Tha Sao, Thailand—Two years ago, Dulah Kwankha was toiling his life away in a rice paddy on the outskirts of his village, supporting his wife and three children with the $400 he earned each year. Then, in a story worthy of Horatio Alger, he became an entrepreneur and started earning six times that much. Dulah, 46, rode the economic wave that has swept up and down the Thai peninsula during the 1980s and '90s: shrimp farming.

With a $12,000 bank loan, backed by a Thai company, he converted his rice paddy into a shrimp pond that produces three crops a year, earning him $2,400. He now spends most of his time supervising the two villagers he pays to feed the shrimp, maintain the water flow and circulation, and harvest the black tiger prawns when they reach full size.

The succulent prawns, produced cheaply by farms like Dulah's, have flooded the US market in the past ten years and continue to gain popularity. To cash in, Thailand, Ecuador, China, Taiwan and other developing countries have thrown billions of dollars into shrimp farms. The shrimp-farming craze illustrates the power of the global marketplace to alter people's lives on opposite sides of the world, often for the worse.

Farmed shrimp has undercut the price of wild shrimp caught in the Gulf of Mexico, helping send a once-vital industry spiraling into economic decline. And it has brought the forces of capitalism to the doorsteps of subsistence farmers and fishers for the first time in history. Aquaculture has turned thousands of square miles of coastline in Thailand and other countries into humming engines of shrimp production.

But the price of this newfound wealth has been high. Cultures and values have been altered, often with devastating consequences. And in many places, the delicate ecologies that millions of people depend upon for their living are being ravaged by a headlong rush to collect on the world shrimp boom.

Every shrimp crop produces a layer of black sludge on the bottom of the pond—an unhealthy combination of fecal matter, molted shells, decaying food and chemicals. It must be removed somehow—by bulldozer, hose or shovel—before the next crop cycle can begin.

There's no place to put it. So it is piled everywhere—by roadsides, in canals, in wetlands, in the Gulf of Thailand, on the narrow spits of land between the ponds. When it rains, the waste drains into the watershed, causing health problems. All along the coast, fishers say, the sludge, along with untreated or poorly treated shrimp farm waste water, has killed fish close to shore. Over time, a buildup of waste products from the ponds often renders them useless. When that happens, neither shrimp nor rice farming is possible.

The farms have other costs too, which may not become apparent for years. Nearly every tree in the shrimp farm zone has been uprooted or killed by polluted water. Many of those that remain are dying. There is literally nothing holding the land in place, and coastal erosion has increased dramatically in the past 10 years, residents say. The intrusion of salt water has ruined rice paddies where they still exist.

Source: Kalamazoo (MI) Kalamazoo Gazette/Newhouse News Service, Nov. 1996. Copyright © The Times-Picayune Publishing Corporation. Reprinted by permission.

How are the negative ecological impacts of IAS manifested? IAS show their impacts on natural ecosystems by out-competing and displacing native species, preying on or parasitizing native organisms, causing species extinctions, disrupting pollination, altering energy and nutritional flows and cycles, altering the local food-web, and altering the composition and species interactions within ecosystems (Brink et al. 2008; Tallamy 2007). Through some combinations of these processes, the ultimate effect of IAS is to reduce the efficiency with which any given ecosystem functions. This is because, as discussed in the previous section, ecosystems with many types of species use energy more efficiently (with less loss to the surroundings) than energy moving through simplified ecosystems (Tallamy 2007). Furthermore, to the extent that the introduction of IAS contributes to the loss of biodiversity and the disruption of species interactions, in many situations it could have the potential to materially affect the stability and resilience of ecosystems (more on this in Chapter 10).

Finally the rapid growth of human population and per capita consumption of material goods and energy resources, as has been witnessed over the past century, has exerted negative impacts on the stability and resilience of many natural ecosystems. This expands the human ecological footprint and in so doing increases the risk of exceeding the carrying capacity of the biosphere. Carrying capacity refers to the finite environmental resource base upon which all economic activity depends, including ecological systems (see Exhibit 2.4). This suggests that the 'scale'

EXHIBIT 2.4 CARRYING CAPACITY AND ECOSYSTEM RESILIENCE

K. Arrow, B. Bolin, R. Costanza et al.

The environmental resource base upon which all economic activity ultimately depends includes ecological systems that produce a wide variety of services. This resource base is finite. Furthermore, imprudent use of the environmental resource base may irreversibly reduce the capacity for generating material production in the future. All of this implies that there are limits to the carrying capacity of the planet . . .

Carrying capacities in nature are not fixed, static or simple relations. They are contingent on technology, preferences, and the structure of production and consumption. They are also contingent on the ever-changing state of interactions between the physical and the biotic environments. A single number for human carrying capacity would be meaningless because the consequences of both human innovation and biological evolution are inherently unknowable. Nevertheless, a general index of the current scale or intensity of the human economy in relation to that of the biosphere is still useful. For example, Vitousek et al. calculated that the total net terrestrial primary production of the biosphere currently being appropriated for human consumption is around 40 per cent. This does put the scale of the human presence on the planet in perspective.

A more useful index of environmental sustainability is ecosystem resilience. One way of thinking about resilience is to focus on ecosystem dynamics where there are multiple (locally) stable equilibria. Resilience in this sense is a measure of the magnitude of disturbance that can be absorbed before a system centered on one locally stable equilibrium flips to another. Economic activities are sustainable only if the life-support ecosystems on which they depend are resilient. Even though ecological resilience is difficult to measure and even though it varies from system to system and from one kind of disturbance to another, it may be possible to identify indicators and early-warning signals of environmental stress. For example, the diversity of organisms and the heterogeneity of ecological functions have been suggested as signals of ecosystem resilience. But ultimately, the resilience of systems may only be tested by intelligently perturbing them and observing the response with what has been called 'adaptive management.'

The loss of ecosystem resilience is potentially important for at least three reasons. First, the discontinuous change in ecosystem flips from one equilibrium to another could be associated with a sudden loss of biological productivity, and so to a reduced capacity to support human life. Second, it may imply an irreversible change in the set of options open to both present and future generations (examples include soil erosion, depletion of groundwater reservoirs, desertification and loss of biodiversity). Third, discontinuous and irreversible changes from familiar to unfamiliar states increase the uncertainties associated with the environmental effects of economic activities.

If human activities are to be sustainable, we need to ensure that the ecological systems on which our economies depend are resilient. The problem involved in devising environmental policies is to ensure that resilience is maintained, even though the limits on the nature and scale of economic activities thus required are necessarily uncertain.

Source: *Science* 268, 1995, pp. 520–1. Copyright © American Association for the Advancement of Science (AAAS). Reprinted by permission.

of human activities is becoming so disproportionately large that its ecological effects not only threaten the survival of some local and regional ecosystems, but the health and ecological resilience of the entire planet. This is a rather controversial issue as evident from the discussion in Exhibit 2.4. This topic will be further explored in Chapters 10 and 11.

Thus, purely from an ecological viewpoint, the natural disposition of the technological human has been to act as the *breaker of climaxes*. This activity reduces the sustainability of natural ecosystems. An immediate symptom of this is to be found in the alarming increase in the extinction of species (Wilson 1999). According to a recent study approximately a quarter of the global biodiversity on land has already been lost. This is a rather disturbing statistic on biodiversity loss globally, and it is substantiated by several other highly regarded studies (Butchart et al. 2010). This is how Hawken (1993: 27) succinctly summarized the broad implications of the alarming trend in the loss of biodiversity over the past several decades:

> The ecologist who fights for the preservation of bowhead whales, Oregon silverspots, snail darters, Gooding's nodding onion, and periwinkles does so not just for their intrinsic value, but because he or she respects the fact that we remain largely ignorant of how the infinitely complex interconnections between different biotic communities affect the well-being of all

species, including human beings. When species disappear, we can delude ourselves that human life exists independently of grackles and goatfishes, but that is only true to a limited extent. What concerns ecologists is that extinctions are a direct indication of ecosystem health, which bears directly on our own survival.

Furthermore, it is important to note that, even from a narrower perspective pertaining only to the welfare of humanity, the availability and quality of nature's *ecosystem services* (such as pollination, biological control of pests and diseases, water supply and regulation, waste recycling and pollution control, nutrient cycling, soil building and maintenance, climate regulation, atmospheric regulation, recreation, education, spiritual growth, and so on) directly depends on the health of the biosphere (the subject matter of ecosystem services and biodiversity will be covered at some length in Chapter 10).

Finally, it will be worthwhile to end the discussion of this chapter with the following suggestion. Please refer to Appendix B if you wish to see how the ecological principles discussed in this chapter are used as tools for conceptually revealing arguments and analyses in the development of a new sub-discipline in environmental economics, namely, ecological economics – a subject matter thoroughly discussed in Chapter 11.

2.6 CHAPTER SUMMARY

This chapter has established that ecology studies the interrelationships between living organisms and their habitat, the physical environment. Since the key issue is always interrelation, the concept of the system is fundamental in any serious ecological study. Using the ecosystem as a framework, ecologists try to explain the general principles that govern the operation of the biosphere.

The basic lessons of ecology are several, and from a *purely biophysical* perspective (or biocentric view of the world), the most pertinent ones are as follows:

1. No meaningful hierarchical categorizations can be made between the living and non-living components of an ecosystem because the physical environment and living organisms are mutually interdependent.
2. At a fundamental level, what goes on in a 'living' natural ecosystems can be characterized by a continuous transformation of matter and energy. This transformation may be manifested in several forms, such as production, consumption, decomposition, recycling of matter, and the processes of life itself.
3. Any ordinary transformation of matter into energy is governed by certain immutable natural laws, two of which are the first and second laws of thermodynamics. The first law informs us that there are stocks of resources (or a constant amount of matter) in the biosphere. The second law reminds us that, since energy flows in only and from a useful to less useful form, the continuing operation of any ecosystem requires a continuous input of energy from an external source. Usefulness is defined here in terms of the ability to do a task—to move or transform an object.
4. Since matter is essentially constant in the biosphere, but used up in the process of transformation, the continuous functioning of an ecosystem dictates that matter must be recycled. In a natural ecosystem this is accomplished through complex and interacting biogeochemical cycles.
5. The species composition of a natural ecosystem undergoes gradual and evolutionary changes (succession). A mature ecosystem supports a great number of interdependent species. Although controversial, the conventional wisdom suggests that ecosystems attain greater resilience as they continue to mature.
6. Ecosystems, however, are also systems of discontinuous changes. Disruptions resulting from external environmental factors (such as climate change) that affect extensive areas could have significant detrimental effects on species composition and the structure and functioning of the ecosystem.

Furthermore, in this chapter attempts were made to highlight some of the important links between ecology and economics. Among them are the following:

1. At a fundamental level, economics and ecology deal with common problems. That is, both disciplines deal with the transformation of matter and energy.
2. However, this also means that, like that of the natural ecosystem, the operation of the human economy (as a subsystem of the entire earth's ecosystem, or the biosphere) must be subjected to the same natural laws governing natural ecosystems. This implies that the human economy must depend on the earth's ecosystems for its basic material and energy needs.

Beyond this, on the basis of the materials discussed in this chapter, it is possible to conclude the following:

1. Natural resources are finite. More specifically, the human economy is 'bounded' by a non-growing and finite ecological sphere. This may be taken to imply that nature cannot be exploited without limits or without the exis-

tence of a biophysical limit.

2. As implied by the second law of thermodynamics, there are definite limits to the conservation of energy through technological means.

3. Throughout history, the tendency of humanity has been to lessen the resilience of the natural ecosystem, by either a simplification of the ecosystem (for example, modern agricultural practice) and/or the introduction and disposal of industrial wastes that are either persistent or totally foreign to a particular ecosystem(s). In extreme cases, the threat here is loss of biodiversity and climate change.

REVIEW AND DISCUSSION QUESTIONS

1. Carefully review the following ecological concepts: ecosystem, primary producers, consumers, decomposers, photosynthesis, nitrogen fixation, ecological succession, biodiversity, ecological resilience, first and second laws of thermodynamics, entropy, monoculture, carrying capacity, invasive species, and ecosystem services.

2. Regarding the following, state 'True', 'False' or 'Uncertain' and explain why:
   (a) Energy is the ultimate resource.
   (b) In principle, an ecosystem can continue to function without the presence of consumers.
   (c) A mature ecosystem is characterized by a diverse community with complex interrelationships. This makes a mature ecosystem stable and resilient.

3. Ecology and economics deal with the production and distribution of valuable resources among complex networks of producers and consumers. Energy and material transformations and the fundamental constraints imposed by thermodynamics underlie all these processes. Discuss.

4. What is ecological resilience? Provide three specific instances of human-induced loss of ecological resilience.

5. In his classic article 'The Historical Roots of Our Ecological Crisis' (1967), Lynn White, Jr., asserted that 'we shall continue to have a worsening ecological crisis until we reject the Christian axiom that nature has no reason for existence save to serve man'. Do you think the ecological crisis has anything to do with our religious beliefs? Explain your position.

6. Dasgupta et al. (2000: 343) argued that 'the preservation of biodiversity is essential, both to provide unique services and to provide insurance against the loss of similarly functioning species'. Do you agree? Explain.

7. Using your understanding about the second law of thermodynamics, *critically* evaluate the evidence provided below by Ausubel (1996) to support the tremendous potential for energy saving that the US economy can expect from advances in technology. Is Ausubel suggesting that the second law is not a limiting factor to energy availability? Explain.

> Segments of the energy economy have advanced impressively toward local ceilings of 100 percent efficiency. However, modem economies still work far from the limit of system efficiency because system efficiency is multiplicative, not additive. In fact, if we define efficiency as the ratio of the theoretical minimum to the actual energy consumption for the same goods and services, modern economies probably run at less than 5 percent efficiency for the full chain from extracting primary energy to delivery of the service to the final user. So, far from a ceiling, the United States has averaged about 1 percent less energy to produce a good or service each year since about 1800. At that pace of advance, total efficiency will still approach only 15 percent by 2100. Because of some losses difficult to avoid in each link of the chain, the thermodynamic efficiency of the total system in practice could probably never exceed 50 percent. Still, in 1995 we are early in the game.

8. The two paragraphs presented below capture the essence of the ideas that have been discussed in the last two chapters. Read these paragraphs very carefully and then write an essay that shows your understanding of the central message(s) portrayed by these two paragraphs.

In the last section of Chapter 1, a criticism was made about the economic perspective for treating the environment (the natural ecosystems) as *external* to the human economy. On the other hand the arguments presented in the last section of the current chapter, Chapter 2, appear to suggest that the current paradigm in ecology treats humans as being an 'external disturbance' on the natural ecosystem.

Clearly, a parallel exists here between ecology where humans are viewed as an external factor (disturbance) to the natural ecosystem and the modern economic paradigm where the natural environment is viewed as being external to the human economy. In both instances, the all-important *dynamic* links between the natural ecosystem and the human economy are ignored. Rather, human society and nature should be treated as *single dynamic entity* (O'Neal and Khan 2000).

REFERENCES AND FURTHER READING

Arrow, K., Bolin, B., Costanza, R., Dasgupta, P., Folke, C., Holling, C. S., Jansson, B., Levin, S., Maler, K., Perrings, C. and Pimentel, D (1995) 'Economic Growth, Carrying Capacity and the Environment', *Science* 268, 520–1.

Ausubel, J. H. (1996) 'Can Technology Spare the Earth?' *American Scientist* 84, 2: 166–8.

Benyus, J. M. (1997) *Biomimicry: Innovation Inspired by Nature*, New York: Harper Perennial.

Botkin, D. B. and Keller, E. A. (2003) *Environmental Science*, 4th edn., New York: John Wiley & Sons.

Boulding, K. E. (1993) 'The Economics of the Coming Spaceship Earth', in H. E. Daly, and K. N. Townsend (eds.) *Valuing the Earth: Economics, Ecology, Ethics*, Cambridge, MA: MIT Press.

Brink, P., Peralta-Bezerra, N. and Kettune, M (2008) 'Annex III: Invasive Alien Species (IAS) and their Global Impacts', in L. Braat, and P. ten Brink, (eds.) *The Cost of Policy Inaction (COPI): The Case of the 2010 Biodiversity Target*, Wageningen/Brussels: Report for the European Commission.

Butchart S. H., Walpole M., Collen B., van Strien A., Scharlemann J. P., Almond R. E., Baillie J. E., Bomhard B., Brown C., Bruno J., Carpenter K. E., Carr G. M., Chanson J., Chenery A. M., Csirke J., Davidson N. C., Dentener F., Foster M., Galli A., Galloway J. N., Genovesi P., Gregory R. D., Hockings M., Kapos V., Lamarque J. F., Leverington F., Loh J., McGeoch M. A., McRae L., Minasyan A., Hernández Morcillo M., Oldfield T. E., Pauly D., Quader S., Revenga C., Sauer J. R., Skolnik B., Spear D., Stanwell-Smith D., Stuart S. N., Symes A., Tierney M., Tyrrell T. D., Vié J. C. and Watson R. (2010) 'Global Biodiversity Indicators of Recent Declines', *Science* 328: 1164–8.

Common, M. and Perrings, C. (1992) 'Towards an Ecological Economics of Sustainability', *Ecological Economics* 6: 7–34.

Commoner, B. (1974) *The Closing Circle: Nature, Man and Technology*, New York: Bantam Books.

Dasgupta, P., Levin, S. and Lubchenco, J. (2000) 'Economic Pathways to Ecological Sustainability', *BioScience* 54, 4: 339–45.

Georgescu-Roegen, N. (1993) 'The Entropy Law and the Economic Problem', in H. E. Daly and K. N. Townsend (eds.) *Valuing the Earth: Economics, Ecology, Ethics*, Cambridge, MA: MIT Press.

Hawken, P. (1993) *The Ecology of Commerce: A Declaration of Sustainability*, New York: Harper Collins.

Holling, C. S. (1997) 'The Resilience of Terrestrial Ecosystems: Local Surprise and Global Change', in R. Costanza, C. Perrings and C. J. Cleveland (eds.) *The Development of Ecological Economics*, London: Edward Elgar.

Miller, T. G., Jr. and Spoolman, S. (2010) *Environmental Science*, 13th edn., New York: Thomson Brook/Cole.

Moolgavkar, S. and Luebeck, E. G. (2002) 'Dose-response Modeling for Cancer Risk Assessment', in D. J. Paustenback (ed.) *Human and Ecological Risk Assessment: Theory and Practice*, New York: John Wiley & Sons.

Nordhaus, W. D. (1991) 'To Slow or Not to Slow: The Economics of the Greenhouse Effect', *Economic Journal 6*, 101: 920–37.

O' Neill, V. R. and Kahn, J. (2000) 'Homo Economus as a Keystone Species', *BioScience 50*, 4: 333–7.

Pearce, D. W. (1978) *Environmental Economics*, 3rd edn., London: Longman.

Pollan, M. (2001) *The Botany of Desire*, New York: Random House.

Schneider, S. H. (1990) 'Debating Gaia', *Environment 32*, 4: 5–9, 29–30, 32.

Tallamy, D. W. (2007) *Bringing Nature Home*, Portland, OR: Timber Press, Inc.

United Nations Environment Program and the Convention on Biological Diversity (UNEPCBD) (2004) *Decisions Adopted by the 7th Conference of the Parties (COP)*, Kuala Lumpur: Malaysia.

Vitousek, P., Ehrlich, P., Ehrlich, A. and Matson, P. (1986) 'Human Appropriation of the Product of Photosynthesis', *BioScience 36*, 6: 386–73.

White, L., Jr. (1967) 'The Historical Roots of Our Ecological Crisis', *Science 55*: 1203–7.

Wilson, O. E. (1999) *The Diversity of Life*, New York: W.W. Norton and Company.

Chapter 3

Tradeoffs: Economic activity versus environmental quality

LEARNING OBJECTIVES

After reading this chapter you will be familiar with the following:

- The tradeoff between economic activity (i.e., the production of goods and services) and environmental quality (i.e., the degradation of the environment).
- The ecological determinants of the waste-absorptive capacity of the natural environment.
- Specific ways in which the waste-absorptive capacity of the natural environment could be augmented through technological means.
- Why most environmental resources lack clearly defined ownership rights and consequently are subject to abuse.
- Why, in the presence of 'real' externalities, a divergence between social and private costs emerges.
- The economic arguments for why the market, if left alone, would lead to lower environmental quality—the notion of market failure.
- The economic conditions for the socially 'optimal' tradeoffs between economic activities (i.e., the production of goods and services) and environmental degradation.
- What the government can do to improve the results of market failure from:
  (a) The 'neoclassical' economics perspective; and
  (b) The 'new institutional' economics perspective.
- The Coase theorem.
- The notion of government failure

At a fundamental level, economics is said to deal with tradeoffs. This chapter deals with the tradeoff between human economic activity and environmental quality (degradation). It does this by revealing the ecological, technological, economic and institutional factors that are uniquely relevant to environmental economics. In this respect, the materials covered in this chapter represent the foundational concepts of environmental economics.

3.1 INTRODUCTION

In Chapter 1, it was shown (see Figure 1.1: p. 10) that the natural environment serves the human economy in three distinct ways: (1) As a source for both renewable and nonrenewable extractive resources; (2) as a provider of environmental amenities and ecosystem services; and (3) as a decomposer and a place of storage for various types of waste generated from normal economic activities. Furthermore, in Chapter 2 it was revealed through the application of the principles of the first and second laws of thermodynamics that economic activities cannot occur without some degradation of the environment. Thus, there is an apparent tradeoff between environmental quality and economic activity. When viewed broadly, the subject matter of environmental economics deals with the identification and valuation of the tradeoffs between economic goods and services and environmental quality at the *margin*.

In broad terms, the nature of this tradeoff is depicted in Figure 3.1 below. This figure indicates that individual wellbeing or *utility* is derived from two distinct sources, namely goods and services and the condition (quality) of the physical environment. To the individual, increasing amounts of goods and services directly improve wellbeing. However, the production of goods and services necessarily causes the emission of wastes leading to the deterioration of the natural environment and, hence, a negative utility. Therefore, on balance, rational economic behavior requires making a conscious tradeoff between goods and services on the one hand, and environmental quality on the other.

The primary focus of Chapter 3 will be to explore the nature of this tradeoff in terms of the *costs* (degradation of environmental quality) and the *benefits* (the production of more goods and services) resulting from the incremental use of the natural environment as a repository of industrial and municipal waste. In − Section 3.2 the ecological and technological determinants of the tradeoffs between economic activity and environmental quality are explored. This is done using a simple model to systematically identify certain key ecological and technological factors that are essential in determining the relationship between increased economic activities and the waste-absorptive capacity of the environment. One observation that will be readily evident from the discussion in this section is the existence of an ecological threshold— a point beyond which more economic activity leads to incrementally higher levels of deterioration of the environment.

In Section 3.3 a systematic economic analysis is offered to explain the causes and consequences of the divergence between *social* and *private* costs when attempts are made to allocate environmental resources through the private-market system. Key concepts introduced in this section include:

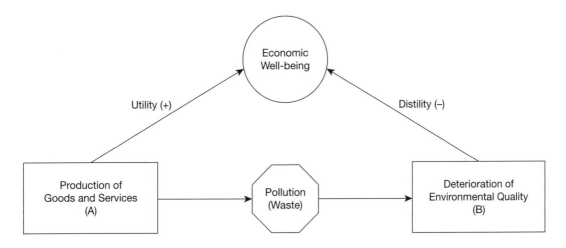

Figure 3.1 *The tradeoff between goods and services and environmental quality. Production of goods and services (Box A) generates utility, and economic wellbeing, when it is eventually consumed by households. At the same time, the deterioration of environmental quality (Box B) resulting from pollution emitted from production activities negatively impact economic wellbeing. Such is the nature of the tradeoff between goods and services and environmental quality.*

externalities, property rights and market failure. The complexity and diversity of institutional arrangements for facilitating market exchange, in particular the critical enforcement of property rights and economic coordination of exchange costs, are highlighted in Section 3.4. The main issues addressed in this section include the extent to which market outcomes can be improved through government intervention within the context of the allocation of environmental resources. In this respect, both the views of mainstream economics and the 'new institutional economics' are presented. Key concepts addressed in this section include: transaction costs, the Coase theorem and government failure. In the last section, Section 3.5, a summary of the chapter is offered.

3.2 ECOLOGICAL AND TECHNOLOGICAL DETERMINANTS OF THE TRADEOFF BETWEEN ECONOMIC ACTIVITY AND ENVIRONMENTAL QUALITY

> The environment can absorb waste, redistributing and transforming it into harmless forms, but just as the earth has a limited capacity to produce renewable resources, its capacity to receive waste is similarly constrained. Its capacity to accept highly toxic waste is practically nonexistent.
> (Hawken 1993:37)

We all want to protect the purity and vitality of our air and water, and the natural landscape. However, despite our desire to do so, as long as we are engaged in transforming material inputs (land, labor, capital and raw materials) into economic goods, we cannot avoid creating residuals (by the second law of thermodynamics) that have the effect of degrading the natural environment. These residuals (low entropic matter–energy) of the economic process are commonly referred to as *pollution*. Pollution is, then, an inevitable byproduct of economic activities.

Furthermore, by the law of conservation of matters, these residuals have to go somewhere. That 'somewhere' consists of the various media of the natural environment—air, water and/or the landscape (although some energy matters may escape into

the outer space). It is in this way that the natural environment is used as a repository of pollution (waste) generated through the economic process.

In general, however, disposal in this way should pose no problem if done up to certain level. This is because, as noted in Chapter 2, the natural environment has a decomposer population which, given adequate time, will transform the waste into harmless material (i.e., through dilution), and/or return it as a nutrient to the ecosystem. This self-degrading ability of the natural environment is commonly referred to as its *assimilative capacity*. It should not be surprising, then, that from the viewpoint of environmental management, the quality of a particular environmental medium (air, water, landmass) is determined by the extent of its capacity to assimilate (degrade) waste.

In further discussing the assimilative capacity of the natural environment, the following *three* important factors should be noted:

1. Like anything else in nature, the assimilative capacity of the environment is *limited*. Thus, the natural environment cannot be viewed as a bottomless sink. With respect to its capacity to degrade waste, the natural environment is, indeed, a *scarce* resource.

2. The assimilative capacity of the natural environment depends on the *flexibility* of the ecosystem(s) under consideration and the *nature* of the waste. That is, the natural environment will not degrade any and all waste with equal efficiency (Benyus 1997; McDonough and Braungart 2002; Pearce 1978). For example, the natural environment can deal with *degradable pollutants*, such as sewage, food waste, papers, etc., with relative ease. On the other hand, it is quite ineffective in dealing with *persistent* or *stock* pollutants, such as plastics, glass, most chemicals and radioactive substances. For most of these waste elements there are no biological organisms in existence that can effectively deal with the degradation process. Thus, a very long period of time is required before these wastes can be rendered harmless.

3. The *rate* and *volume* at which the waste is discharged greatly affects the ability of the environment to degrade residuals. The implication of this is that pollution has a cumulative or dynamic ecological effect. More specifically, pollution *reduces the capacity* of an environmental medium to withstand further pollution, especially when waste is discharged at a high rate and in large fluxes (Pearce 1978).

The obvious lesson is that, in managing the natural environment, it is crucial to give careful consideration to the *quality* (nature) of the waste, its *quantity* and the *rate* at which it is disposed of into the environment per unit of time. To understand the significance of this point, the following simple model can be used. It is assumed that a *linear* relationship exists between pollution emission (waste generation) and economic activity (production of goods and services). Furthermore, this relationship is expected to be *positive*: that is, more waste is generated with increasing levels of economic activity. Mathematically, the general form of the functional relationship between waste emission into the environment and economic activity can be expressed as

$$W = f(X, t) \tag{3.1}$$

Or, in explicit functional form, as

$$W = \alpha + \beta X \tag{3.2}$$

where W is the amount of waste generated in some unspecified unit, and X is the level of economic activity. The variable 't' in Identity 3.1 represents technological and ecological factors that are capable of influencing the relationship of W and X (to be discussed later). In Identity 3.2, the variable 't' is assumed to be constant and captured by the intercept term α.

Identity 3.2 depicts the simple linear relationship that was assumed between waste (W) and economic activity (X), holding the variable 't' at some predetermined level. In this Identity, β represents the slope parameter, and is assumed to be positive. The

relationship shown in Identity 3.2 can be presented graphically, as shown in Figure 3.2a. In this figure, the x-axis shows the level of economic activity (in terms of production of goods or services) and the y-axis represents the quantity (volume) of waste disposed into the environment in some unspecified unit. The broken horizontal line, W_0, represents an additional assumption that was made to complete the basic framework of this simple model. This line is assumed to represent the total amount of waste that the environment could assimilate at a given point in time. Note also that, to the extent that W_0 is positive, the pollutants under consideration are assumed to be *degradable*.

What general conclusions can be reached from this simple model? The following *four* points can be made in response to this question. First, given that the assimilative capacity is invariant at W_0, the maximum amount of economic activity that can be undertaken without materially affecting the natural environment is X_0. The waste generated at this level of economic activity will be completely degraded through a natural process. Thus, from this observation it can be concluded that a certain minimum amount of economic goods, such as X_0 in Figure 3.2a, can be produced without inflicting damage to the natural environment. Thus, X_0 indicates an *ecological threshold* of economic activity.

Second, increased economic activity beyond X_0 would invariably lead to an accumulation of unassimilated waste in the natural environment. Although it may not be fully captured by the above simple model, the effect of this accumulated waste on environmental quality (damage) will be *progressively higher* because, as indicated earlier, pollution reduces the capacity of an environment to withstand further pollution. As shown in Figure 3.2b, the ultimate impact of this dynamic ecological effect would be to shift the assimilative capacity of the environment—the broken horizontal line—downward.

The third point that can be conveyed using the above model is how *technological* factors may affect the ecological threshold of economic activity. The effect of technological change could take the following two forms:

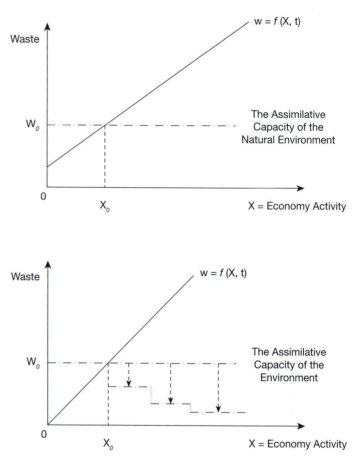

Figure 3.2a *The relationship between economic output and waste discharge. Below X_0 level of economic activity, waste generated through economic activity is less than the natural assimilative capacity of the environment (W_0). Thus, economic activity up to the level of X_0 would not lead to a deterioration of environmental quality. Environmental quality will start to suffer when economic activity is pursued beyond this threshold level of economic activity, X_0.*

Figure 3.2b *The dynamic effects of continued waste disposal beyond the assimilative capacity of the environment. The downward cascading dynamic effect refers to the notion that pollution tends to reduce the capacity of an environment to withstand further pollution.*

1. Through technology the decomposition process may be accelerated (facilitated). Note that in our simple model, this type of change is captured by the variable 't' (see Identity 3.1). For example, adding activated charcoal in a sewage-treatment facility can accelerate the decomposition process of municipal waste. This amounts to an artificial enhancement of the assimilative capacity of the environment. Therefore, in Figure 3.2a the effect of this type of technological change would be to shift the dotted line upward, indicating an increase in the assimilative capacity of the environment. Other factors remaining equal, this would have the effect of increasing the ecological threshold of economic activity to something greater than X_0.

2. A change in technology may also alter the relationship between the level of economic activity, X, and the rate at which waste is discharged into the natural environment. In our simple model this would be indicated by a change in the slope parameter, ß (see Identity 3.2). For example, a switch from high to low sulfur content coal in the production of electricity using a coal-burning power plant would lower the amount of sulfur emitted into the environment per kilowatt hour of electricity produced, X.

   In this case the ultimate effect would be to *lower* the value of the slope parameter, ß. As shown in Figure 3.2c, this entails a clockwise rotation of the line depicting the relationship between waste and economic activity. Again, if other factors are

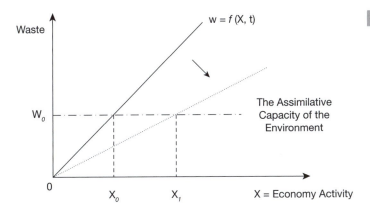

Figure 3.2c *The effect of technology on the relationship between economic output (X) and waste discharge (W) by a decline in the slope parameter, ß; that is, a lower environmental impact on a per unit basis. Hence, it is now possible to engage in more activity without affecting the environment, as shown by the increase in the economic threshold activity from X_0 to X_1.*

held constant, the overall effect of this type of technological change is to increase the ecological threshold of economic activity. Thus, the implication here is that we can, to a certain degree, *augment* the ecological threshold of the natural environment by means of technology. As discussed above, the technological improvement could be triggered by either an improvement in waste processing or input switching.

However, as Commoner et al. (1971) warned us, technological solutions to environmental problems can have harmful side-effects (more on this in Chapter 11). For example, at the local level increasing the height of factory smokestacks can substantially alleviate the problem of acid deposition (acid rain in dry form) arising from sulfur dioxide emission. The intended effect of this is to emit a good share of the pollutants into the higher strata of the atmosphere. This would amount to solving the problem of pollution through *dilution*. However, as it turns out, what this does is to change the local pollution problem into a transboundary acid-rain problem.

The important lesson here is that technological projects intended to address environmental concerns should not be implemented without careful consideration of their *potential side-effects*.

The fourth and final point that should be noted is that, as discussed earlier, the natural environment will not degrade all waste with equal efficiency. In some instances the assimilative capacity of the natural environment could be, if not zero, highly

insignificant. In Figure 3.2, this situation would dictate that the broken horizontal line representing the assimilative capacity of the natural environment would be closer to, or could even coincide with, the x-axis. In this situation, the ecological threshold of economic activity would, for all practical purposes, be zero.

The following important lessons can be drawn from the discussion in this section:

- The natural environment has a limited capacity to degrade waste. The implication of this observation is that, in purely physical (not necessarily economic) terms, the waste-assimilative capacity of the natural environment is a *scarce* resource.
- A certain minimum amount of economic goods can be produced without causing damage to the natural environment. Thus, zero pollution not only is a physical impossibility, but even on purely ecological considerations it is an unnecessary goal to pursue. The exception to this will be when the pollutants are highly toxic.
- Although the above simple model does not adequately capture this, the cumulative effect of waste discharge into the natural environment is *nonlinear*. This is because pollution tends to reduce the capacity of an environment to withstand further pollution.
- The ecological threshold of economic activity (X_0 in Figure 3.2c) can be augmented by technological means.

The above observations are made through a simple but careful conceptual analysis of the various factors affecting the relationships between the level of economic activity and the damage this action inflicts on the natural environment. However, so far nothing specific has been said about the tradeoff between economic activity (the production of goods and services) and environmental quality. This issue becomes relevant when the level of economic activity, as it is often the case, extends beyond a certain *ecological threshold* (for example, X_0 in Figure 3.2a). This is, indeed, a key issue that will occupy much of the next section.

3.3 THE ANATOMY OF MARKET FAILURE

One important lesson that can be learned from the discussion so far is that the natural environment has a limited capacity to degrade waste. To that extent, then, the natural environment is a scarce resource (at least in absolute terms). Given this, it would be in the best interest of any society to manage its natural environment *optimally*. This entails that, as for any other scarce resource, the services of the natural environment as a repository of waste (and a provider of ecosystem services) should be considered taking full account of all the *social* costs and benefits. Could this be done through the normal operations of the market system? A complete response to this question requires, first and foremost, a clear understanding of certain complications associated with assignment of *ownership rights* to environmental resources. This is the subject matter of the next subsection.

Common property resources and the economic problem

As explained in Section A.2 and A.3 of Appendix A, under a *perfectly competitive* market setting, resource allocation through a private market economy would lead to what is considered to be a socially optimal end. It was also demonstrated that the allocation of any scarce resource is socially optimal when, for the last unit of the resource under consideration, the marginal social benefit is equal to the marginal social cost (MSB = MSC).

How could a market economy that is primarily instigated by the decisions of private actors seeking to promote their own self-interest lead to a socially optimal result? In other words, what is the magic at work in transforming self-interest to social interest? To Adam Smith, this magic was 'invisible' yet real, provided the actors in the market have indisputable rights to the use and disposal of all the resources that they are legally entitled to own. In other words, for Adam Smith's 'invisible hand' to operate, resource ownership must be clearly defined.

What exactly does a clearly defined ownership-right entail? From the perspective of resource allocation, the ownership of a resource is said to be clearly defined if it satisfies the following conditions (Randall 1987):

1. The ownership rights of the resource are *completely specified*. That is, its quantitative and qualitative features as well as its boundaries are clearly demarcated.
2. The rights are completely *exclusive* so that all benefits and costs resulting from an action accrue directly to the individual empowered to take actions.
3. The ownership rights of the resource are *transferable*. In other words, resources can be exchanged or simply donated at the 'will' of their owners.
4. Ownership is *enforceable*. That is, ownership of resources is legally protected.

When these four criteria are met, it can be shown that reliance on the self-interest-based behavior of individuals will ensure that resources are used where they are most valued.

An example of a resource that satisfies the above four criteria is the ownership of a private car. The ownership manual, together with the car registration, completely specifies the contents, model, color and other relevant characteristics of the car. On the car's registration document the relevant authority confirms the owner's exclusive legal right to the car. Therefore, no one else is allowed to use this car without proper permission from the owner. Once an exclusive ownership is attained, it is in the owner's interest to adhere to a regularly scheduled maintenance program for the car since failure to do so would cost no-one else but the owner. Last but not least, the owner of the car can enter into voluntary trade or exchange of her or his car at any point in time. Furthermore, should the owner decide to sell the car, it would be in her or his best interest to sell it at the highest possible price. The ultimate effect of this process is to assure that ownership of a car will gravitate toward those individuals who value it the most (or are willing to bid the highest price).

In the real world not all resources satisfy the above ownership specifications. For example, a lake shared by all residents living in the surrounding area will not satisfy the second and third of the conditions set out above. In this case, the lake is a resource that is owned in common by all users living within a given geographic boundary line. Another example is the ambient air of a certain locality or region. In this case, none of the above four conditions could be completely satisfied. Thus, the ambient air is a common property owned by everyone, and on practical grounds it is owned by no-one—a clear case of *res nullius*. As you can see from these two examples, environmental resources, such as the ambient air and water bodies (lake, rivers, ocean shorelines, etc.), tend to be common property resources. By their very nature, the ownership of these resources cannot be clearly defined.

The question, then, is what happens to private markets as a medium for resource allocation in situations where ownership rights of a resource(s) cannot be clearly delineated? The implications of this question can be seen with the hypothetical situation presented in Exhibit 3.1. This exhibit demonstrates how a valuable asset like a car can be reduced to valueless junk when it is perceived as a common property resource. In general, a closer look at a situation of this nature brings two important points into focus.

First, for the commons, economic pursuit on the basis of individual self-interest would not lead to what is best for society as a whole. In other words, the principle of Adam Smith's 'invisible hand' would be violated.

Second, if tragedy is to be averted, the use of commons needs to be regulated by a 'visible hand' (Ciriacy-Wantrup and Bishop 1975; Hardin 1968) in some manner (such as, enforceable legislative mandates, fines, taxes, and so on).

At conceptual level, these two points represent the *core* issues of environmental economics. The next subsection provides the analytical and conceptual framework used to address these core issues at the very fundamental level.

EXHIBIT 3.1   WHEN A CAR TURNS INTO TRASH

Assume for a moment that you are a resident of a small island nation with a population of only 150,000. The families of this nation are economically well off and most of them own at least one car. The nation hardly uses public transportation. Now, imagine that one morning you wake up at your usual time, around 6:30 am, and you hear on the radio that the government has passed a law that completely revokes the private ownership of a car. The public announcement also states that the government has issued a master key that will run any car on the street, and such a key is to be found on the doorstep of each individual household. Of course, your first reaction would be to think that this is just a dream. However, the public announcement is so incessant and firm that it leaves you with no chance of ignoring the event, of taking it as just a dream.

As shocking and disturbing as this event may be, let us assume that the people of this nation are so nonviolent that no visible disturbance occurs as a result of this draconian action. Instead, the people, perhaps grudgingly, make the necessary efforts to deal with the prevailing situation. What is the situation? First, people still need a car to go to work, to shop, to visit friends and relatives, etc. Second, the citizens of this nation have no access to public transportation. Third, by government decree every citizen has free access to the cars that currently exist on the island. What will happen to the use and maintenance of cars in this society under these circumstances?

At first, people will start by driving a car that is within easy reach of them. Once they reach their destination, they will leave the car knowing full well that the same car may not be available for their next use. For how long would this pattern of car use continue? Not for long. This is because people would not have any incentive to properly maintain the cars. Who would fill a car with gasoline knowing that any amount left unused from a one-way trip might never be recouped? What would happen to cars should they run out of gas in the middle of a highway? Furthermore, who would have the incentive to pay for regularly needed maintenance, such as oil changes, tune-ups, etc.?

What would happen to the cars that simply ceased running because of mechanical problems? The answer to all these questions is that in a short while, in this island nation, *cars would be transformed from being commodities of great value to valueless debris scattered all over the traffic arteries of the nation.* Of course, the root cause of this undesirable end is the treatment of cars as common property with free access for all. As Garrett Hardin (1968: 1244) elegantly puts it, 'Ruin is the destination toward which all men rush, each pursuing his own best interest in a society that believes in the freedom of the commons. Freedom in a commons brings ruin to all'. Clearly, from the perspective of environmental and natural resource management, the implications of this conclusion are quite significant. After all, what is at stake is the vitality and integrity of the global commons: the ambient air, most rivers, the sea, the shorelines, the oceans, etc.

Environmental externalities and their economic consequences

It was noted above that Adam Smith's fundamental theorem of the 'invisible hand' would fail when resource ownership is defined in such a way that individuals couldn't take account of the full benefits or costs of their actions. This will happen not because the costs or benefits are *not* real. Instead, in this situation, the costs and benefits would be treated as incidental or external. A technical term used to describe this situation is *externality*. Formally, externalities are defined as conditions arising when the actions of some individuals have direct (negative or positive) effects on the welfare or *utility* of other individuals, none of whom have direct control over that activity. In other words, externalities are incidental benefits or costs to others for whom they are not specifically intended.

Two classic examples of externality are described by the following cases. One is represented by the action of an avid *gardener* who invests in the beautification of her or his own property and, in so doing, raises the property values of the surrounding houses. A second example is represented by a *fish hatchery plant* that has to bear the cleanup costs for wastes discharged by a *paper mill* located upstream. In the first example, the neighbors are gaining *real* external benefits (positive externalities) without sharing the costs of the actions that yielded the beneficial result(s). In the second case, the cleanup cost to the hatchery is external (a negative externality) because it is the result of an action imposed by a third party, in this case the paper mill.

What are the main sources of externalities? Let us use the two classic examples above to answer this question. In the first example, no assumption is made that the benefits to the neighbors have resulted from a benevolent act by the gardener. On the contrary, the assumption is that the gardener's investment, in terms of both time and monetary outlays in the beautification of her or his property, is done on the basis of cost–benefit calculations that are consistent with any investor's self-interest. However, the fruit of this investment is an 'aesthetic enhancement' or 'environmental amenity' which has peculiar characteristics when viewed as an economic commodity. This commodity is *nonrival* in consumption. That is, once it is produced, the consumption of this commodity, say by the neighbors or any passers-by, would not reduce the utility of the gardener. Therefore, when such a commodity is produced, it makes no economic sense to exclude anyone from the use (consumption) of such an activity. Of course, in our simple example, the gardener, if she or he wishes, could exclude the neighbors by building a tall concrete wall around the house. However, this would not be achieved without additional cost.

The most commonly used economic jargon to describe the costs associated with internalizing (remedying) externalities is *transaction cost*. In broad terms, a transaction cost includes any outlay expended for the purpose of specifying properties, excluding non-users and enforcing property rights. This would be the intended effect if, in fact, the gardener in our example decided to erect a concrete wall around her or his clearly identified property line.

It is very important to keep in mind that in any effort to internalize (correct) externalities transaction costs are very important considerations. This is because this cost alone could, in some cases, undermine the viability of correcting the externality due the prohibitive administrative and enforcement costs. The protection of many global commons through international treaties (such as endangered animal and plant species, ocean fisheries, CO_2 emissions into the atmosphere, and so on) are often handicapped by prohibitively high transaction costs (more on this in Chapters 9 and 10).

To summarize, the basic lesson that can be drawn from the first example, a private garden, is that an externality arises when the use of a property (resource) is difficult to exclude. This difficulty may result from one of two possible sources. First, the resource by its very nature may be nonrival in consumption, and hence subject to *joint consumption*. Second, for either natural or technical reasons, the transaction cost of internalizing the externality may be excessively high (Coase 1960; Seneca and Taussig 1984).

While this first example may appear trivial, the same concept explains the externalities associated with *ecosystem services* which, as explained in Chapter 2, includes the benefits that nature (as opposed to the gardener) freely provides to households, communities and economies (Boyd and Banzhaf 2006). Representative examples are: decomposition of

wastes, clean drinking water, nutrient cycles, crop pollination, climate regulation and cultural (e.g., spiritual, recreational and educational) benefits. Costanza et al. (1997) estimated the value of the world's ecosystem services to be, on average, US$33 trillion per year—a huge sum when compared to the global national product of about US$18 trillion a year. Assigning dollar values to ecosystem services is a very controversial subject, mainly because these resources are hard to quantify and their values are not fully captured in markets. This important area will be addressed in Chapter 7.

In the second example, the hatchery, the externality arises from the fact that the owners of the hatchery plant do not have the legal right to stop the operators of the paper mill from dumping their industrial wastes in the river. For that matter, since the river is viewed as a common property no one can be excluded from using it. Thus, in a similar way to our first example, the nonexclusive use of the river is what causes an externality to persist. The only difference is the source of nonexclusiveness.

In the first case, nonexclusiveness resulted from the fact that the resource under consideration is nonrival, and thus subject to joint consumption. In our second example, nonexclusiveness resulted from the fact that the ownership of the resource under consideration (the river) was not clearly defined—that is, it is common property. Hence, from these two examples it can be generalized that, in the final analysis, *lack of excludability* (nonexclusiveness) is the root cause of externality (Randall 1983; Tietenberg 1992).

Most, if not all, environmental resources are externality ridden for this very reason. Furthermore, on practical grounds, the factor that could prevent society from readily dealing with environmental externality is high transaction-cost: the cost of effectively internalizing externalities.

What is the economic consequence of an externality? Given what have been discussed so far, this is a simple question to answer. In the presence of 'real' externalities, there will be a *divergence between private and social evaluations of costs and benefits* (Seneca and Taussig 1984; Turvey 1963). In general, the following relationships can be expected to hold:

1. In a situation where a *positive* externality is present (example one above):

Social benefits = Private benefits + External benefits

and

External benefits > 0

Therefore,

Social benefits > Private benefits.

2. In a case where *negative* externality prevails (example two above):

Social costs = Private costs + External costs

and

External costs > 0

Therefore,

Social costs > Private costs.

What can be inferred from the above series of relationships is that, in the presence of an externality, a *divergence* between social and private benefits and social and private costs are expected to occur. Under these conditions, resource allocation through a market mechanism—that is, one solely based on the consideration of private costs and benefits—would be inefficient when viewed from the perspective of society at large. This constitutes a clear case of *market failure* because the market, if left alone, lacks any mechanism by which it can account for external costs and/or benefits.

Equipped with a clear understanding of the factors contributing to market failure, it is now possible to show why the allocation of environmental goods and services through market mechanisms leads to suboptimal results. This will be demonstrated using the hypothetical case of not just a single paper-mill, but a paper-mill industry. It is assumed that all firms in this industry are located along riverbanks and use rivers as a means of disposing of their industrial waste.

In Figure 3.3, curve D represents the market demand for paper. As discussed in Appendix A

(Section A.3), a demand curve such as D represents the marginal private benefit to consumers (MPB). Furthermore, in a situation where external benefit is zero (i.e., there are no positive externalities), a demand curve represents both the marginal private and the social benefits. This is assumed to be the case in Figure 3.3 (D = MPB = MSB).

The complication arises when considering the supply curve of paper. For the paper industry, the supply curve, S, represents the marginal private costs (MPC) of producing varying levels of paper. These costs represent the firms' expenditures on all priced inputs (i.e., labor, capital, raw materials, and the services of any resources owned by the owners of the firms in this industry). However, in the process of producing paper firms are assumed to use rivers to dispose of their production waste at no cost. Thus, no such cost appears in the balance sheets of the firms in this hypothetical paper industry, and therefore disposal costs do not form any part of the firm's supply curve, S, in Figure 3.3.

However, as explained in Section 3.2, the discharge of waste into a river would cause damage costs beyond a certain threshold level (see X_0 in

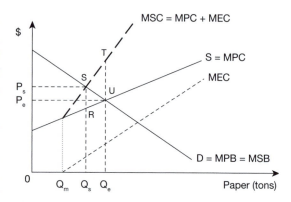

Figure 3.3 Social optimum in the presence of externality: the case of a hypothetical paper industry. Optimality is attained when MSC = MSB and this not at the intersection of the demand and the supply curves. The reason for this is the divergence between the marginal private cost (the ordinary supply curve) and the marginal social cost (MSC)—which explicitly accounts for externality.

Figure 3.2a, p. 50). In Figure 3.3, this damage cost is represented by the broken curve labeled MEC: *marginal external cost*. This cost represents the monetary value of pollution damage imposed on society by the paper-mill industry.

At this stage it is important to note the following two features about the MEC curve in Figure 3.3:

1. The marginal external costs do not start to materialize until the paper industry reaches a production level of Q_m. This is because, consistent with our earlier discussion, a certain minimum amount of output can be produced by the paper industry without materially affecting the quality of the environment (the river).

2. The marginal external cost curve, as shown in Figure 3.3, is expected to be positively sloped. That is, beyond Q_m, further increases in the production of paper (hence, more waste discharge) would be associated with external costs that tend to increase at an increasing rate. This is because, as discussed earlier, pollution reduces the capacity of an environment to withstand further pollution.

As shown in Section A.4 of Appendix A, *efficiency* in resource allocation requires the equating of MSC and MSB. In Figure 3.3 this condition would be met when the level of paper production was Q_s. Note that the marginal social cost curve (MSC) in Figure 3.3 is obtained by the vertical summation of the marginal private and marginal external cost curves (i.e., MPC + MEC). Thus, this condition establishes the necessary condition for attaining the level of output (economic goods) that would be consistent with the socially optimal level of environmental quality—optimal tradeoff between economic goods and environmental quality.

However, if the production decision of paper were made through a freely operating market-mechanism, the market equilibrium level of production would have been Q_e, where MPB = MPC. Clearly, then, the market solution would fail to achieve the level of paper production that is consistent with what is considered to be socially optimal. More specifically, the tendency would be for the market to produce more paper than is socially desired.

What exactly is the implication of the above analysis in terms of environmental quality? The answer is rather straightforward. Assuming the amount of waste dumped in the river is directly proportional to the amount of paper produced, the market solution, Q_e, would be associated with a higher level of pollution than the socially optimal level of output, Q_s. What this suggests is that the market, if left alone, would lead to a *lower environmental quality*. In other words, the market solution is *not* efficient. In fact, as shown in Exhibit 3.2, this can be formally demonstrated by showing that society would stand to gain if, in fact, the production of paper were curtailed from Q_e to Q_s.

EXHIBIT 3.2   SOCIAL OPTIMAL OUTPUT IN THE PRESENCE OF ENVIRONMENTAL EXTERNALITY

In Figure 3.3, if the production of paper were reduced from Q_e to Q_s, the total cost savings as a result of this move would be represented by the area under the social marginal cost curve, $Q_e TSQ_s$. This total social cost is composed of the total private costs as represented by the area under the marginal private cost curve, $Q_e URQ_s$, and the total external costs as indicated by the area UTSR.

On the other hand, in reducing the production of paper from Q_e to Q_s society would incur a loss in benefits. The forgone benefits to society as a result of this particular move would be measured by the area $Q_e USQ_s$—the area under the marginal social-benefit curve. Stated differently, this represents the forgone consumers' benefit resulting from a reduction of paper production from Q_e to Q_s. Clearly, then, in reducing the

57

production of paper from Q_e to Q_s, the total cost saving, area Q_eTSQ_s, exceeds the total forgone benefit area Q_eUSQ_s.

Thus, the final outcome of this move represents a net cost saving measured by the area of the triangle UTS. Furthermore, since a move away from the market solution represents a clear gain to society, the market solution, Q_e, is *not* Pareto optimal. Note that

the market's inability to deliver the socially optimal solution arises from the fact that it has no automatic mechanism to account for the external costs. In Figure 3.3, area UTSR represents the total external costs that would be unaccounted for by the market. This cost is a measure of the imputed value for the additional environmental service (river) required if the production of paper is expanded from Q_s to Q_e.

For those who are well versed in marginal analysis this point is rather obvious, given that at Q_e (the market solution) the MSC > MSB. Hence, it pays to reduce the production of paper until the equality between MSC and MSB is restored.

At this stage it will be instructive to see what general conclusions can be drawn from the analysis presented thus far. In the presence of an externality, resource allocation through the guidance of a free-market system would lead to inefficiency. More specifically, because the market lacks a mechanism through which it accounts for external costs, it tends to favor more production of goods and services from industries inflicting damage to the natural environment. Thus, the presence of real externality creates a misallocation of societal resources.

The question, then, is what can be done to correct the misallocation of resources created by environmental externalities? Does this require a minor or a major modification of the market system? In responding to these questions, the key issue at hand is finding the most effective institutional mechanism(s) to internalize the externality. The next section discusses this issue at some length.

3.4 INSTITUTIONAL ARRANGEMENTS ADDRESSING MARKET FAILURE

As discussed in Section 3.3, in the presence of environmental externality, private markets fail to allocate resources efficiently. In our example above, this entailed the discharge of more pollution (waste) into the river than is considered socially optimal. This occurred because private firms (producers of paper)

neglected to account for the external costs they imposed on a third party (the fish hatchery). This section provides a brief overview of three approaches that can be used to internalize (correct) an externality. As will be evident from the discussion that follows, one feature that the three approaches have in common is the idea that the remedy for market failure requires some form of government intervention. However, significant disagreements exist among these approaches about the specific nature and scope of government intervention. The crucial and unresolved question is what should be the proper role of government in the marketplace.

Garrett Hardin (1968) argued in his classic article 'The Tragedy of the Commons' that, on the whole, there are *no* technical solutions to environmental externality. In other words, externality of this nature cannot be effectively internalized through voluntary private-sector negotiation among the parties involved. Thus, he proposed that the only way to resolve the problem associated with common property resources is through *coercive* methods. This is how Hardin articulated his position on this matter:

The social arrangements that produce responsibility are arrangements that create coercion, of some sort . . . Coercion is a dirty word . . . but it need not forever be so . . . The only kind of coercion I recommend is mutual coercion, mutually agreed upon by the majority of the people affected . . . To say that we mutually agree to coercion is not to say that we are required to enjoy it, or even to pretend we enjoy it. Who enjoys taxes? We all grumble about them. But we accept compulsory taxes because we recognize that voluntary taxes would favor the conscience-less. We institute and (grumblingly) support taxes and other coercive devices to escape the horror of the commons.

(Ibid: 139–40)

Hardin, however, did not go beyond the recognition that government's coercive power can be used to correct externalities arising from free access to common property resources. In this regard, he gives the impression that government intervention would automatically lead to the desired social outcome. The possibility that government *may* malfunction, and as a result fail to do its stated duties, is either overlooked or simply ignored. Furthermore, other than the passing remark given to taxes, Hardin did not attempt to provide policy instruments that are specifically designed for correcting externalities. Simply put, Hardin did not attempt to specifically address the question of what is the proper role of government in the marketplace.

Despite these apparent shortcomings, what makes Hardin's article highly influential is its lucid and forceful articulation of the causes and tragic consequences associated with the unrestrained use of common property resources for private gains. Furthermore, for those who are pro-government regulations, Hardin provided a 'good enough' rationale for government interventions to prevent the misallocation of environmental resources arising from a free access to the commons (such as overfishing, overgrazing, overpopulation and excessive pollution that leads to, among other things, coral bleaching, etc.).

Given that the 'invisible' hand is taken as an article of faith, mainstream economists' reactions to Hardin's proposed remedy for market failure is rather obvious. From their perspective, while government coercive power may be a necessary condition for correcting externalities, concerted and deliberate efforts should be taken to *minimize* coercion (i.e., government intervention). This can be done in various ways. First, the role of government can be reduced to a mere assignment of rights when a property lacks ownership. Once this is accomplished, private negotiation

among the parties involved will allow resources (including the environment) to be allocated efficiently (more on this later). Second, government could create the institutional framework that would allow the design and implementation of market-based regulations, such as pollution taxes. How this is done is extensively discussed in Chapters 4 through 6.

The third approach to address the problem with the commons finds its root in the realm of institutional economics. This subfield in economics focuses primarily on the study of institutions and how institutions interact with organizational arrangements, such as markets—institutional arrangements specifically created to facilitate the production and exchange of goods and services.

Broadly defined institutions are formally the constitutions, laws, contractual rules, and regulations, and informally the unwritten codes of conduct, norms of behavior and belief, that govern a given society. From the perspective of institutional economics, government has the coercive power to enforce formally enacted institutional rules and regulations. Furthermore, within the context of the marketplace, it is perfectly acceptable for governments to use coercive force, provided it is done to reduce risk and transaction costs (North and Thomas 1973). Thus, the proper role of government intervention is strictly defined in terms of *transaction costs*: the costs of enforcing, monitoring and establishing clearly defined property rights. This is how Zerbe and McCurdy (2000: 4) expressed the perceived advantages of government when the focus is placed on transactions costs:

> Transaction cost analysis calls attention to the characteristics of government that give it an advantage relative to other institutions in its ability to lower transaction costs. One important advantage is its power of coercion: governments monopolize the use of force or coercive power over a given territory. The government may change laws and use force to compel compliance with them; it may force payment for a good through taxation and it may use police powers to forbid or compel actions.

It is important to note, however, that coercive rules would yield benefits only to the extent that they reduce transaction costs. Furthermore, as will be discussed shortly, coercive rules also have their own costs. To such an extent 'the issue of government intervention is largely empirical rather than theoretical' (Ibid).

It is the last statement that brings scholars in new institutional economics (NIE) into conflict with neoclassicists. More specifically, proponents of NIE consider the standard economics pursuit—addressing the problem of market failure using a theoretical model that assumes *zero* transaction costs—to be flawed.

For example, in Figure 3.3 neoclassical economists could entertain the idea of imposing a tax on the paper producers in such a way that the supply curve will shift parallel just enough to go through point S; thus, resulting in the desired (efficient) social outcome (since at point S, MSB = MSC). However, this approach has neglected to account for the various transaction-costs that are inherently present in the process of enforcing a specific rule, in this case tax on output. These costs are real and they include, among others, the cost of monitoring and enforcing the rule, and the cost of bringing suits to violators of the rule.

When transaction cost is assumed to be zero, the Coase theorem (named after a Nobel Laureate and distinguished Chicago University law and economic professor) is often used to demonstrate how efficient allocation of resources can be achieved in the presence of externality. When applied to environmental pollution, the Coase theorem can be stated this way: it is possible to achieve an optimal level of pollution reduction by an arbitrary *assignment* of property rights to either the polluters or the pollutees. Thus, the Coase theorem effectively reduces the role of government to the mere assignment of property rights. Once this is accomplished, its immediate effect will be to trigger mutually beneficial trade among the parties affected by externalities.

To demonstrate how this theorem works in the simplest possible manner, in the example of the fish hatchery and the paper mill that have been used earlier (let us assume only two parties are involved:

one paper mill and a single fish hatchery), suppose the rights to the river is assigned by the government to the paper mill. In this situation, it can be shown that the fish hatchery will have the incentive to initiate negotiation with the paper mill provided the damage cost to its hatchery operation is greater than the loss to the paper mill, which is measured by the required reduction in the production of paper.

For example, if the damage cost to the fish hatchery from a discharge of some unspecified units of waste into the river by the paper producer is $1,500, and the expected profit from the production of this unspecified units of output to the paper mill is estimated to be $1,100, the fish hatchery would be able to bribe by offering compensation for lost profit to the paper mill at an amount more than $1,100 but less than $1,500. Thus, within a price range between $1,100 and $1,500, a mutually beneficial trade can occur between these two parties in terms of pollution control. It can also be inferred from this analysis that trade between these two parties will continue to occur until the difference between the costs to the hatchery and the compensation for forgone profit to the paper mill for further reductions in paper production are essentially exhausted; that is, no one can gain from further trade—a condition for Pareto optimality.

Furthermore, it can be easily shown that the same conclusion would be reached even if the initial ownership rights to the river are assigned to the fish hatchery instead of the paper mill. For the above situation (i.e., damage cost of $1,500 and control cost $1,000) the hatchery will be prompted to deny the paper mill access to the river. In other words, the paper mill has to reduce its waste discharge into the river until a situation develops where payment to the hatchery for the rights to get access to the river is at least equal to the damage cost. Thus, for the Coase theorem to work the assignments of rights can be completely arbitrary and this will have no effect on the attainment of the optimal level of pollution.

As stated earlier, the Coase theorem is derived with the assumption of zero transaction costs. However, in the real world, transaction costs are not zero and in some instances can be significantly larger.

For instance, if trade in pollution rights on a river requires a lawyer, who charges $2,000, then the mutually beneficial trade would not take place and an optimal outcome will not be reached.

Another example can be drawn by referring back to our avid gardener. The only way that this gardener can exclude her neighbors from enjoying the fruits of her labor (the beautiful scenery of her flower garden) would be by erecting a tall wall, and it will be a costly proposal. Thus, when situations like this occur, which are often the norm rather than the exception within the context of environmental problems, the focus should be, according to scholars in NIE, to search for alternative institutional arrangements that would reduce transaction costs.

For example, if the reason for our avid gardner to exclude her neighbors is to recoup some of her expenses, it is possible that this can be achieved through an informal institutional arrangement, such as a request for a voluntary donation (perhaps a yearly fee) to compensate for her labor. This strategy may or may not work, but it simply demonstrates that there are always several alternative ways of reducing transaction costs through formal and/or informal institutional arrangements.

Other possible, and closely related, transaction cost concerns develop when dealing with multiple parties. For example, the negotiations for access to a river may involve a number of polluters and residents of several communities along the river's shoreline. In this situation, complications may arise from free-riders (when paying) and holdout problems (from receiving compensation). These kinds of issues can be resolved by institutionalizing charges (for example, tax or some form of mandatory fees to solve free-riding, and eminent domains to solve holdout). *Clearly, when transaction costs are significant no single, general rule works in all cases.* This remains troubling to scholars with a neoclassical ideological bent.

The lesson that emerges from the above discussion regarding the institutional approach to internalizing environmental externalities is this: the internalization of environmental externalities is best resolved, not with a focus on market failure and/or a theoretical framework that is constructed by assuming zero transactions costs. Instead the emphasis should be on providing the appropriate institutional framework for solving problems associated with externalities on a case-by-case basis. As Zerbe and McCurdy (2000: 4) put it, the transactions costs approach 'provides insights into the accumulation of institutional arrangements that exists in practice, and it voids the endless quest for 'failures' in either the private or the public sector that provide a basis for government intervention'.

One last issue that needs to be addressed with regard to the NIE perspective on government intervention is the keen awareness of government failure. The reasons for this could be possible government malfunctioning generally arising from excessive costs in the forms of: information cost, bureaucratic decision cost, implementation cost, enforcement costs (policing, court, collection), political failure (public choice), the public's cost of monitoring the government agency that enforces the rule is too high (Zerbe and McCurdy 2000). These are inherently transaction costs and should be factored into the cost–benefit calculus for assessing the merits of government intervention.

Finally, Case Study 3.1 is presented to show a real-world example where government intervention through coercive means is used to internalize externality. In this case the resource under consideration is the common-pool water that is shared by residents of Austin, Texas. Over the past several years Austin has been experiencing extremely hot and dry weather patterns lasting for a protracted period of time, creating a very serious water shortage during the summer months. One way the city has been trying to resolve this problem has been by imposing water-use restrictions through coercive means. This is done to correct the apparent externality involved in this particular situation. That is, each individual water-user (primarily for automatic sprinkler systems) has the unintended effect of denying the availability of that much water to others because it is drawn from a common pool of water. In this case study the key issue under consideration is what policy the city government of Austin should use to ration the common pool

CASE STUDY 3.1   TRAGEDY OF THE COMMONS: A CASE STUDY OF WATER POLICY IN AUSTIN, TX

James Garven

Since 2007, Austin has been subject to so-called Stage 1 Water Use Restrictions. Under Stage 1, residents are legally entitled to use their automatic sprinkler systems before 10 a.m. and after 7 p.m. two days per week (the actual days of the week depend upon whether one has an even-numbered or odd-numbered residence). Violations of this schedule are Class C misdemeanors, with each instance punishable by a fine of up to $500. Starting August 24, Austin will be under Stage 2 Water Use Restrictions, which limits the use of automatic sprinkler systems to Saturdays (for odd-numbered residential addresses) and Sundays (for at even-numbered residential addresses) before 10 a.m.

The manner in which water use is priced (with a nonlinear pricing schedule that is increasing in the volume of water usage) motivates most consumers to conserve. However, I suspect that the prospect of a $500 fine and Class C misdemeanor citation probably affects the *timing* of water use more than it affects *volume* for most consumers. In spite of the (rather compelling) economic incentives to conserve which derive from nonlinear pricing, apparently the City of Austin still finds it necessary to impose these highly restrictive rationing constraints

... [Instead] the *Austin American Statesman* went so far on Monday as to publicly shame the top 10 users in June and July 2009 in a front page article (cf. http://bit.ly/qMq6I). This seems like a market failure to me, and my 'inner economist' suggests that a better way to mitigate this externality (rather than impose such draconian water use restrictions) would be to make the pricing schedule sufficiently convex so that even members of the top 10 club would sit up and take notice!

I suspect ... Austinites will abide by the timing restrictions on watering. However, it is also very likely that many (if not most) Austinites will set their sprinklers to run longer each session now that watering can only occur once rather than twice per week. The problem with the policy is that it primarily addresses timing incentives, and not the real problem, which is over-consumption. It remains to be seen whether private actions (running sprinkler systems longer per 'legal' session) don't end up making matters even worse than they already are.

Source: http://tragedyofthecommons.garven.com, August 19, 2009, Jim Garven's blog. Reprinted by permission.

of water available to its citizens under severe drought conditions.

The case study is written to show, from the perspective of standard economics, why a scheme that relies on non-linear water pricing is superior to a water-rationing scheme through *time restriction* (that is, the stipulation of the number of hours and the specific days per week that residents of Austin are allowed to use their automatic water-sprinkler system). The conclusion that the author of the case study is offering is this: if over-consumption of water is the real issue, a policy based on water pricing will be more effective than a government-mandated time-restriction on water use.

In this case study no explicit attempt was made to analyze the problem by looking at transactions costs. Market-based policy is favored simply because it provides a more targeted incentive to conserve water. However, the city government rationing policy may have been based not only on water conservation but also on ensuring that water (a basic necessity) is available to all users in a more-or-less equitable manner. This, at least in theory, could be addressed by constructing a more complicated water-pricing mechanism, hence the reference to a non-linear pricing scheme. However, the transaction costs for designing, implementing and enforcing such a complicated water-pricing scheme could be very high, possibly rendering such an effort untenable.

A major lesson to be drawn here is that the search for an institutional framework that would lead to the most effective ways to resolve problems arising from externalities can be a rather difficult and messy affair. One approach that can be taken to deal with a messy real-world affair is to theorize. In the neoclassical school of thought, as will be evident from the discussions in Chapters 5 and 6, this seems to be the preferred route to take. The obvious advantage of this approach is that general rules for internalizing externality can be established through tightly constructed theoretical models.

Finally, as a way of transitioning to the next chapter, it is worthwhile to note that the approach used in this chapter does not directly reveal the amount of waste (pollution) associated with what is considered to be the socially optimal output. This would pose no problem if there existed a stable and predictable relationship between waste emission and output, and if changes in market conditions did not have an independent effect on output. Furthermore, the approach used in this chapter does not say anything about either *pollution-control technology* or the *demand* for environmental quality. However, these are technical and economic considerations that can hardly be taken for granted and are, therefore, the subject matter of the next chapter, Chapter 4.

3.5 CHAPTER SUMMARY

This chapter has dealt with concepts and principles fundamental to understanding standard environmental economics.

It was postulated that the assimilative capacity of the environment (i.e., the ability of the natural environment to degrade waste arising from an economic activity) is in effect *scarce,* and is affected by a number of ecological and technological factors.

It was observed that, for degradable pollutants such as most municipal wastes, a certain minimum amount of economic goods can be produced without causing damage to the natural environment. The exception to this is the emission of a highly toxic and persistent chemical compound such as DDT. In such a case, a *zero* level of pollution may be justified—like the ban on DDT in the United States. Thus, at least for degradable pollutants, *zero* levels of pollution cannot be defended even on purely ecological grounds.

However, given that most economic activities (production and consumption of goods and services) extend beyond the ecological thresholds necessary to keep the integrity of the natural environment intact (beyond X_0 in Figure 3.2a), *tradeoff* between increased economic activity and level of environmental quality become unavoidable.

It was noted that the search for the 'optimal' tradeoff between economic and environmental goods requires full consideration of all the relevant *social* costs and benefits. Unfortunately, for environmental resources, this cannot be done through the normal market mechanism for the reasons outlined below:

1. Environmental resources, such as the atmosphere, all large bodies of water and public lands, are *common property resources,* and access to them has traditionally been open to all users.
2. Consequently, environmental resources tend to be prone to *externalities*—incidental costs imposed by a third party.
3. In the presence of externalities, economic pursuits on the basis of individual self-interest (hence, the private market) do not lead to what is best for society as a whole. This is because a freely operating private market has *no* automatic mechanism to account for external costs. Thus, scarce environmental resources are treated as though they are *free* goods.
4. When external costs are unaccounted for, the production of economic goods and services is in excess of what is socially optimal, and the quality of the environment is compromised. That is, the market, if left alone, tends to favor the production of more economic goods at the expense of the environment.

Alternatively, the above problem could be viewed this way: in the presence of an externality, market prices would fail to reflect 'true' scarcity value. As discussed in this chapter (see Figure 3.3 and Section 4 of Appendix A), price is a measure of 'true' scarcity when the market equilibrium price, P_e, is equal to both marginal *social* cost and marginal social benefit (i.e., $P_e = MSC = MSB$). However, in the presence of an externality, the market equilibrium price, P_e, is equal to marginal private cost but not the marginal social cost ($P_e = MPC < MSC$). This is because the market has no mechanism to capture the external component of the social cost ($MSC = MPC + MEC$). Thus, since $P_e < MSC$, market price fails to reflect 'true' scarcity value.

Once this is understood, a possible solution to this type of externality problem is to find mechanisms that will account for external costs and correct the price distortion. How these are done is the subject matter of Chapters 5 and 6.

Finally, the last section of this chapter showed the various institutional arrangements that should be carefully considered in order to minimize the 'transaction costs' involved in any effort to internalize environmental externalities (i.e. correct market failure).

REVIEW AND DISCUSSION QUESTIONS

1. Briefly review the following concepts: persistent pollutants, assimilative capacity of the environment, common property resources, transaction cost, joint consumption, social cost, private cost, externality, market failure, the polluter-pays principle, Coase theorem, internalization of externality.

2. State the *four* features for a clearly defined ownership rights.

3. Read the following statements. In response, state 'True', 'False' or 'Uncertain' and explain why.
   (a) 'Everybody's property is nobody's property'.
   (b) Waste emissions should not exceed the renewable assimilative capacity of the environment.
   (c) Pollution problems can always be resolved by technological means.

4. What is externality? Provide two examples that are not given in the text? What are the root causes of environmental externality? Be specific. You are encouraged to use demand and supply analysis to answer this question.

5. Clearly delineate the differences and similarities between public goods and common property resources. You may find it helpful to use concepts, such as rival, non-rival, joint consumption, and non-exclusive, to answer this question.

6. It has been shown that the consequence of environmental externality is a divergence between social and private costs. Explain the differences between social and private cost and explain how the difference in these two concepts causes market failure. What exactly is meant by market failure? Be specific.

7. In some instances, consideration of 'transaction costs' alone could make internalizing an externality (positive or negative) economically indefensible. Can you provide three concrete examples of this nature? In answering this question, make sure to provide a clear definition of transaction cost.

8. Questions for discussion: read the material in Exhibit 3.3 below and answer the three questions presented at the end of the exhibit.

EXHIBIT 3.3   WHAT IS THE MOST DESIRABLE LEVEL OF POLLUTION?

Recently, the Society for Zero Pollution sponsored a panel discussion on the topic 'Is zero pollution viable?' The panelists included a well-known environmental economist and a very famous ecologist.

Probably to the dismay of their sponsor, both the economist and the ecologist agreed that zero pollution is neither viable nor desirable. On the other hand, both panelists were quite complimentary about the society's efforts to initiate a timely and well-conceived public debate on general issues concerning the environment, and the genuine concern the society has shown for the growing deterioration of our environment.

In discussing his view against zero pollution, the ecologist stated that we must not forget that the environment has a limited ability to process waste. The concern for environmental pollution arises only when we emit wastes into the environment beyond its assimilative capacity. In his view, therefore, the socially desirable level of waste discharge (pollution) is that which is consistent with the assimilative capacity of the environment. In other words, waste emission should not exceed the renewable assimilative capacity of the environment.

In her turn, the economist disputed the assertion made by the ecologist by stating that it is quite consistent and rational for society to discharge waste (pollute) above and beyond the assimilative capacity of the environment in so far as society collectively values the benefit from the excess pollution (the extra value of the goods and services produced) at more than the cost of the damage to the environmental quality. Hence, the optimal (socially desirable) level of pollution is attained when the marginal social cost (MSC) of waste reduction—in terms of extra output and services sacrificed—is equal to the marginal social benefit (MSB) of waste reduction—in terms of the psychic and tangible benefit society may attain from improved environmental quality.

1. Do you agree that zero pollution is neither viable nor desirable? Why? Be specific.

2. How would you reconcile the views expressed by the ecologist and the economist? If you think they are irreconcilable, why so? Explain.

3. Recently, the Environmental Protection Agency proposed to ban the use of EDB (ethylene dibromide) to spray on domestically produced citrus fruits. Would this be consistent with either one of the above two views? Why, or why not?

REFERENCES AND FURTHER READING

Benyus, J. M. (1997) *Biomimicry: Innovation Inspired by Nature*, New York: HarperCollins Publishers Inc.

Boyd, J. and Banzhaf, S. (2006) 'What are Ecosystem Services?' *Discussion Paper*, Washington, DC: Resources for the Future (RFF)

Ciriacy-Wantrup, S.V. and Bishop, R.C. (1975) '"Common Property" as a Concept in Natural Resource Policy', *Natural Resource Journal* 15: 713–27

Coase, R. (1960) 'The Problem of Social Cost', *Journal of Law and Economics* 3: 1–44.

Commoner, B., Corr, M. and Stamler, P. J. (1971) 'The Causes of Pollution', in T. D. Goldfarb (ed.) *Taking Sides: On Controversial Environmental Issues*, 3rd edn., Sluice Dock, CT: Guilford.

Costanza, R., D'Arge, R., De Groot, R., Farber, S., Grasso, M., Hannon, B., Limburg, K., Naeem, S., O'Neill, R. V., Paruelo, J., Raskin, R. G., Sutton, P. and van den Belt, M. (1997) 'The Values of World's Ecosystem Services and Natural Capital', *Nature* 387: 253–60.

Hawken, P. (1993) *The Ecology of Commerce: A Declaration of Sustainability*, New York: Harper Collins Publishers

Hardin, G. (1968) 'The Tragedy of the Commons', *Science* 162: 1243–8.

McDonough, W. and Braungart, M. (2002) *Cradle to Cradle: Remaking the Way We Make Things*, New York: North Point Press.

North, D. C. (1995) 'The New Institutional Economics and Third World Development', in J. Herris et al. (eds.) *The New Institutional Economics and Third World Development*, London: Routledge.

North, D. C. and Thomas, P. R. (1973) *The Rise of the Western World: A New Economic History*, Cambridge: Cambridge University Press.

Pearce, D. W. (1978) *Environmental Economics*, 3rd edn., London: Longman.

Randall, A. (1983) 'The Problem of Market Failure', *Natural Resource Journal* 23: 131–48.

—— (1987) *Resource Economics: An Economic Approach to Natural Resource and Environmental Policy*, 2nd ed., New York: John Wiley.

Seneca, J. J. and Taussig, M. K. (1984) *Environmental Economics*, 3rd edn., Englewood Cliffs, NJ: Prentice-Hall.

Tietenberg, T. H. (1992) *Environmental and Natural Resource Economics*, 3rd edn., New York: HarperCollins.

Turvey, R. (1963) 'On Divergence between Social Cost and Private Cost', *Economica*, August: 309–13.

Zerbe, R. O. and McCurdy, H. (2000) 'The End of Market Failure', *Regulation* 23, 2: 1–5.

Part II is composed of five chapters (Chapters 4–8). These chapters cover topics normally included in standard texts on 'environmental economics'. Chapter 4 develops the basic theoretical model and economic condition for the optimal level of pollution control. In Chapters 5 and 6 a number of pollution-control policy instruments are thoroughly discussed and evaluated.

Chapter 7 addresses a significant issue in environmental economics, namely the economic valuation of damages inflicted on environmental assets (such as coral reefs, mangroves, wetland ecosystems, etc.). The significance of this chapter lies in the fact that people are more likely to care about the services of the natural environment that are often taken for granted once their values in monetary terms become more apparent to them. However, as will be evident from the discussion in this chapter, attempts to assign dollar values to the environment are often confronted with considerable methodological and practical challenges.

The last chapter in Part II, Chapter 8, is devoted to addressing the evaluation of environmental projects using the framework of standard cost–benefit analysis. This chapter also includes discussions of four other criteria for project evaluation that can be used as either a complement or a substitute to cost–benefit analysis.

It is important to point out that, while the general approaches used in the five chapters covered in Part II have the appearance of following the standard treatment in mainstream environmental economics textbooks, a careful reading of each chapter will reveal a departure of some significance from the norm. This difference stems from the conscious efforts to interject ecological perspectives relevant to the main topics addressed in each chapter. These efforts are not made casually. In general, the topic under consideration is first presented using the standard economic treatment, and is then followed by critical appraisals of the main conclusions on the basis of their conformity or departure from the 'ideal' conclusion that might have been reached if sufficient reflection had been given to the ecological perspectives on this same subject matter.

Chapter 4

The economic theory of pollution control: The optimal level of pollution

LEARNING OBJECTIVES

After reading this chapter you will be familiar with the following:

- The determinants of the pollution-control (abatement) cost function.
- Why abatement cost is expected to increase at an increasing rate as pollution control proceeds.
- The determinants of the pollution-damage cost function.
- Why pollution-damage costs are externalities
- Why the damage cost is expected to increase at an increasing rate with a further incremental accumulation of untreated waste.
- The condition for cost-effective levels of pollution control.
- The economic rationale for environmental regulation.
- The concept of an 'optimal' level of pollution from an ecological perspective.
- The difference between pollution cleanup and pollution prevention strategies.

This chapter offers the theoretical foundation of a standard economics approach to pollution control. When waste emissions are viewed as a 'tradable commodity' in a free-market setting (to be discussed in Chapter 6), the pollution control and pollution-damage cost functions, explored at some length in this chapter, would literally represent the ordinary supply and demand functions for pollution permits (rights), respectively. Furthermore, it is important to develop a very good understanding of the pollution-damage function and its determinants before embarking on the 'valuation' of the environment—a subject to be covered in Chapter 7.

4.1 INTRODUCTION

In Chapter 3 an attempt was made to address the issue of environmental quality by looking at the tradeoff society has to make between economic goods and improved environmental quality. In addition to merely recognizing the existence of this tradeoff, in the same chapter an attempt was made to formally establish the necessary condition for attaining the level of output (economic goods) that would be consistent with the socially optimal level of environmental quality.

This chapter will discuss an alternative approach to the management of environmental quality by looking directly at the nature of *waste disposal costs*. Viewed this way, the economic problem will be to determine the volume of waste (not the production of economic goods as in Chapter 3) that is consistent with the socially optimal level of pollution (or environmental damage). This approach, as will be seen shortly, provides a good many helpful new insights as well as a thorough evaluation of all the economic, technological and ecological factors that are considered significant in assessing pollution prevention (abatement) and pollution-damage cost functions. Furthermore, the materials presented in this chapter provide the basic analytical framework for the evaluations of alternative environmental public-policy instruments (subject matters covered in Chapters 5 and 6).

Finally, it should be noted at the outset that a section of this chapter (Section 4.4) is devoted to an ecological appraisal of the standard economic notion of the 'optimal' level of pollution control. This is done primarily to observe possible inconsistencies that may exist between the economic and ecological notions of optimal pollution (environmental damage).

4.2 THE DETERMINANTS OF POLLUTION-CONTROL AND DAMAGE COSTS

From a purely economic perspective, the management of environmental quality or pollution control is easily understood if the problem is viewed as minimizing *total* waste-disposal costs. Broadly identified, waste-disposal costs originate from two distinct sources. The first component is *pollution-control* (abatement) *cost*: the cost that arises from society's cleanup effort to control pollution using some kind of technology. The second element is the *pollution-damage cost*, which results from damage caused by untreated waste discharged into the environment that is considered to be above and beyond the assimilative capacity of the environment.

Thus

Total waste disposal cost	=	Total pollution-control (abatement) cost
	+	Total pollution-damage cost.

Hence, the economic problem of interest is to minimize the total disposal cost, with full recognition of the implied tradeoff between its two components: control and damage costs. *This is because, from an economic viewpoint, a dollar's worth of investment (expenditure) on pollution-control technology will make sense if, and only if, society is expected to be compensated by the benefits to be realized from the avoidance of environmental damage that is worth more than a dollar.* A good understanding of this economic logic requires, first of all, a clear and in-depth understanding of the nature of these two types of waste-disposal costs, to which we now turn.

The determinants of pollution-control (abatement) costs

Pollution-control (abatement) costs represent direct monetary expenditures by a society for the purpose of procuring resources to improve environmental quality or to control pollution. Expenditures on sewage treatment facilities, smokestacks, soundproof walls and catalytic converters on passenger cars are just a few examples of pollution-control costs.

These expenditures may be incurred exclusively by private individuals, such as expenditures on soundproof walls by residents living in close proximity to an airport. In contrast, sewage-treatment facilities may be undertaken as a joint project by local and federal government agencies. In this case, the expenditure is shared by two government bodies. In some situations a project may be undertaken by a private firm with some subsidy from the public sector. Thus, as these examples illustrate, the bearers of the expenditures on pollution-control projects may vary, and in some instances are difficult to trace. Despite this possible complication, the conventional wisdom is to view pollution-control cost in its entirety. To this extent the specific source of the expenditure is irrelevant. What is relevant is that all components of the expenditures attributable to a specific pollution abatement project are fully accounted for, regardless of the source of the funds.

In general, we would expect the *marginal* pollution-control cost to increase with increased environmental quality or cleanup activities. This is because incrementally higher levels of environmental quality require investments in technologies that are increasingly costly. For example, a certain level of water quality could be achieved through a primary sewage-treatment facility. Such a facility is designed to screen out the solid and visible material wastes, but nothing more. If a higher level of water quality is desired, an additional expenditure on secondary or tertiary treatment may be required. Such additional treatments would require the implementation of new and costly technologies designed to apply either chemical and/or biological treatments to the water. Graphically, we can visualize the marginal control cost (MCC) as follows.

Figure 4.1 represents the *marginal* pollution-control cost in graph form. Before we proceed any further, it is very important to understand the exact reading of this graph. First, the *benchmark* or total number of units of waste that is being considered for treatment is 20. This is evident since the marginal cost of the twentieth unit of waste (i.e., no waste treatment) is indicated to be zero. Second, it is important to note that the marginal pollution-control cost increases at an *increasing rate* as a higher level of cleanup or environmental quality (a movement towards the origin) is desired. The numerical example

in Figure 4.1 clearly indicates this. The marginal cost to control (or treat) the fifth unit of waste is indicated to be $50. However, the marginal cost is increased to $200, a fourfold rise, to treat the fifteenth unit of waste. Note that the units of waste treated are read by starting from the benchmark and moving towards the direction of the origin.

At this stage it is important to specify certain important technological factors that determine the position of any marginal pollution-control cost curve. More specifically, it is important to note that the marginal pollution-control cost curves are constructed by holding constant such factors as the technology of pollution control, the possibility of input switching, residual recycling, production technology, etc. A change in any one of these predetermined factors will cause a shift in the entire marginal pollution-control cost curve.

For instance, an electric power-plant that uses coal as its primary source of input could reduce pollution (sulfur) emissions by switching from coal with high sulfur-content to low-sulfur coal. In this particular case, the effect would be to shift the marginal pollution-control cost downward. Similar results would occur if there was a significant improvement in pollution-control technology, such as the development of a new and more efficient catalytic converter for automobiles.

Finally, since pollution-control costs are explicit or out-of-pocket expenditures, it is assumed that no apparent market distortion occurs as a result of a third-party effect—that is, an externality. In other words, for pollution-control costs, there will be no difference between private and social costs. However, this is not to suggest that market distortion in the assessment of pollution-control costs cannot exist as a result of either market imperfection (monopoly power) or government intervention in the form of subsidies and taxes (more on this in Chapters 5 and 6).

In sum, pollution-control costs are private and public outlays for the purpose of ameliorating environmental damages arising from pollution. As a general rule, these costs would be expected to rise at the margin. That is, efforts to further reduce pollution

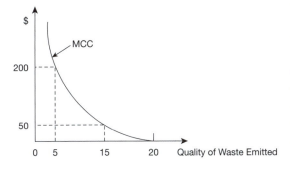

Figure 4.1 *Marginal pollution-control cost as a downward-sloping curve. Note that in the above graph pollution control (i.e., cleanup) implies a movement towards the origin from a benchmark level of waste, which in this case is 20 units. Thus, the cost of controlling pollution increases with the successive increase in pollution cleanup. It costs a lot more to clean up the last unit of pollution than the first.*

are encountered with incrementally rising costs—the MCC is increasing at an increasing rate. Furthermore, it is assumed that there is no externality problem associated with pollution-control costs.

Pollution-control costs account for only one side of the total social costs of pollution. Let us now turn to a detailed examination of the second component of the total pollution-disposal costs: pollution-damage costs.

The determinants of pollution-damage costs

Even if it is technologically feasible to get rid of all pollutants from a given environmental medium, such an undertaking may be difficult to justify on the basis of cost considerations. However, as discussed in Chapter 3, when the volume of waste discharged exceeds the assimilative capacity of the environment, and is left untreated, it can contribute to a deterioration in environmental quality. The total monetary value of all the various damages resulting from the discharge of untreated waste into the environment is referred to as *pollution-damage cost*.

Such damage to environmental quality may be manifested in a variety of ways, largely depending on the *amount* and the *nature* of the untreated waste. For example, when *biodegradable* pollutants, such as sewage, phosphate-containing detergents and feed-lot waste are emitted into a lake, they can lead to the development of a process known as eutrophication. Over time, the outcome of this process is to cover a substantial portion of the lake with green substances composed mainly of algae and weeds. One immediate effect is the reduction of the scenic appeal of the lake. In addition, there is a negative impact on the population of aquatic organisms, because the ability of a body of water to support fish and other organisms depends on how much dissolved oxygen it contains. Thus, if biodegradable pollutants were discharged into a lake and left untreated, the damage to environmental quality would be identified in terms of reduced scenic attraction and decreased population of certain aquatic organisms, such as fish. The monetary value of these adverse environmental effects constitutes pollution-damage cost.

The identification and estimation of pollution-damage costs are even more complicated in the case of *persistent* pollutants. Examples of such pollutants include toxic metals, such as lead and mercury, radioactive wastes and inorganic compounds such as some pesticides and waste products produced by the petrochemical industry. What is particularly significant about these types of pollutants is not the mere fact that they are patently dangerous to living organisms and the ecosystem as a whole, but the fact that because of their very slow decomposition process they tend to persist in the environment for a very long period of time. In other words, their adverse environmental effects *transcend present action*. For example, radioactive elements leaking from nuclear power plants today will have detrimental effects over several generations. This makes the estimation of damage costs arising from persistent pollutants extremely difficult.

In general, then, pollution-damage costs are identified in terms of the losses of, or damage to: plants and animals and their habitats; aesthetic impairments; rapid deterioration to physical infrastructures and assets; and various harmful effects on human health and mortality. In order to estimate damage costs, however, we need to go beyond the physical account of damage. More specifically, as far as possible the damage identified in physical terms needs to be expressed in monetary terms.

As the above discussions indicate, the estimation of pollution-damage costs is a formidable task and requires a good deal of imagination and creative approaches. Furthermore, other factors being equal, the more persistent the pollutants, the harder the task of evaluating damage costs. In fact, as we will see in Chapter 7, some aspects of pollution damage are simply beyond the realm of economic quantification. Regardless of these difficulties, pollution damage does occur. Hence, as a society striving for a better life, we need to develop a procedure that will provide us with a framework designed to enhance our understanding of pollution-damage costs.

Conceptually, Figure 4.2 represents the general characteristics of the marginal pollution-damage cost (MDC). More specifically, as discussed above, the damage cost curve measures the social cost of the damage to the environment in monetary terms, resulting from each additional unit of waste emission. A basic assumption in the construction of this curve is that damage cost is an increasing function of pollution emissions. In other words, the damage caused by a unit of pollution increases progressively as the amount of pollution (untreated waste) emitted increases. As the numerical example in Figure 4.2 indicates, the MDC increases from $125 (the cost of the tenth unit of waste) to $500 (the cost of the fifteenth unit of waste) as the amount of waste emissions increases from ten to 15 units. This is of course, in accord with the ecological principle discussed in Chapter 2, a cumulative (nonlinear) effect of pollution on the environment.

One last issue of considerable significance to be discussed is the fact that pollution-damage costs are *externalities*. By definition these are costs incurred by members of a society after the pollution damages have already occurred.

In sum, pollution-damage costs represent the monetary values of all aspects of the environmental damages arising from untreated waste. The estimation of pollution-damage costs is often complicated by the fact that these costs are externalities. To make matter worse, it is extremely difficult to evaluate all aspects of the damage costs, especially when the pollution under consideration involves irreversible ecological change and the risk of major adverse surprise over a long time-horizon. As a general rule, damage costs are expected to be an increasing function of pollution.

4.3 THE OPTIMAL LEVEL OF POLLUTION

At the outset of this chapter it was stated that the management of environmental quality is easily understood if the problem is viewed as the minimization of total disposal costs. It was also made clear that the total disposal costs are composed of two parts: pollution-control and pollution-damage costs. In subsections 4.2.1 and 4.2.2 we made a considerable effort to understand the nature of these two components. Equipped with this information, we are now in a position to formally specify what exactly is meant by an optimal level of pollution and how it is associated with the minimization of total disposal cost.

In Figure 4.3 the marginal-damage cost (MDC) and the MCC curves are drawn on the same axis. From this graph it is evident that if a pollution-control

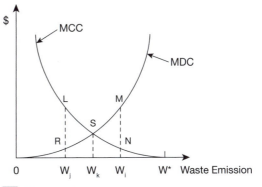

Figure 4.3 *The optimal level of pollution. This is achieved at the emission level of W_k where MDC = MCC. Any deviation from this level of emission in either direction would not be cost-effective. For example, if the emission level is W_j, the fact that MDC > MCC at this level of emission suggests that the total waste disposal cost can be reduced by further controlling emissions—a movement towards W_k. Similar arguments can be made for any emission level to the left of W_k, such as W_j.*

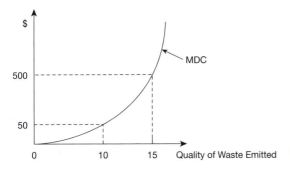

Figure 4.2 *Marginal pollution-damage cost. This graph shows that the damage cost of each successive unit of pollution is incrementally increasing at an increasing rate. The justification for this relies on the notion that pollution has the cumulative effect of reducing the capacity of an environment to withstand further pollution, hence, hastening the process of environmental damage.*

73

measure is not undertaken, the total amount of waste discharged would be W*: the benchmark level of waste. However, the socially optimal level of waste discharge is W_k, where the usual equi-marginal condition is satisfied—that is, MDC is equal to MCC. When this condition is met, the total waste-disposal cost (the sum of total control and damage cost) is minimized.

We can easily demonstrate that W_k is optimal by showing that any attempt to set the level of waste emission either above or below W_k would lead to an increase in the total disposal cost. In other words, any deviation from this level of pollution in either direction would not be cost-effective. For example, if the level of waste emission is set at the W_i level, MDC > MCC, suggesting that the cost of dumping untreated waste in the environment is greater than what it costs to treat the waste through technological means. Thus, there is something to be gained by taking action to clean waste—a movement towards W_k. A

similar argument can be made for the case of waste disposal W_j, which is to the left of W_k. In this situation, at the margin, the cost to controlling waste will be greater than the damage cost of leaving waste untreated. Hence, it does not pay to control waste.

It is actually instructive to note that to say optimality is attained when MDC = MCC is equivalent to the statement made at the beginning of this chapter, that it would be beneficial for society to spend an additional dollar on pollution-control cost (i.e., MCC) only if the incremental benefit arising from the damage avoided by the additional cleanup (i.e., MDC) exceeded or was equal to one dollar.

Can this optimal waste-discharge, W_k, be automatically attained through the operation of a free market? Based on our discussion of market failure that is associated with environmental resources in Chapter 3, the answer to this question is clearly no. A full explanation as to why this is the case is given in Exhibit 4.1.

EXHIBIT 4.1   AN ALTERNATIVE LOOK AT MARKET FAILURE

This exhibit revisits market failure—a subject that was explored extensively in Chapter 3. The main intent is to demonstrate how the phenomenon of market failure can be explained using the theoretical framework developed in Chapter 4. This is done using Figure 4.4. According to this figure, the optimal level of pollution is W_k, where the equality of marginal damage and marginal control costs is satisfied. The question is, could this level of pollution be attained through the free operation of the market?

The answer is rather straightforward once we recognize one important difference between damage and control costs. That is, as already discussed, *damage costs are externalities, while control costs are not.* Given this, what is cheapest (advantageous) for private firms may

not be so for society as a whole. In general, the tendency is for private firms to totally ignore the damage (external) costs. This point is illustrated using Figure 4.4. At the socially optimal level of pollution, W_k, the total waste-disposal cost is represented by area 0SW*. This total cost is composed of the total damage costs, area $0SW_k$, and the total control costs, area W_kSW*.

However, if this were done through the market, it would be in the best interests of private firms to minimize control costs and ignore damage costs altogether (since damage costs are externalities). This would move the market solution in the region of W*, implying a virtually zero level of pollution abatement. Thus, the optimal solution, W_k, could not be attained unless measures were taken to make private firms internalize the externality; a clear case of market failure.

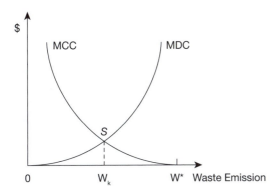

Figure 4.4 *Alternative look at market failure. In the absence of emission control policy, the reluctance of polluters to invest in pollution control technology will cause the final outcome to be near or at W* – further away from W_k (where MDC = MCC)*

4.4 THE OPTIMAL LEVEL OF POLLUTION: AN ECOLOGICAL APPRAISAL

> Pollution cleanup is better than doing nothing, but pollution prevention is the best way to walk more gently on the earth.
> (Miller 1993: 15)

This section addresses whether or not basic ecological realities are consistent with the concept of an economically optimum level of pollution. Let us start by looking at an extreme case where no pollution is permitted, such as DDT in the United States. While the ecological justification for this is easy to see, how can this ban be addressed using the theoretical framework discussed in this chapter? The simple answer to this question would suggest that if a zero level of pollution is deemed socially optimal, then at every level of pollution the MDC is greater than the MCC, and the ban on any substance generating such waste is economically justified. In such an instance, no inconsistency exists between the economic and ecological resolutions of pollution.

Yet that is an extreme case. In most instances, the economic optimum is associated with a positive level of pollution emission. This is to be expected, and it is not necessarily inconsistent with ecological reality (refer to Section 3.2 in Chapter 3). However, there are several reasons why the economic optimum may not be

ecologically desirable. For now, this issue is illustrated using two specific cases. The first case suggests that basing the 'optimum' on damage assessment that solely relies on *human preference* (willingness to pay) is not appropriate, especially when it is applied to the environment. The second case implies that the standard economic approach to pollution control may put more emphasis on *pollution cleanup* than *pollution prevention*.

First, as the discussion so far reveals, in estimating the damage function, only human preferences are considered. What is troubling is the extent to which a purely anthropocentrically based preference-ordering adequately accounts for future human life (i.e., inter-generational equity) and the integrity of the natural ecosystems (Funtowicz and Ravetz 1994). Without such assurance, a divergence between economically and ecologically optimum pollution may be inevitable. In this respect, the bias is expected to be toward more pollution since the economic estimate of the damage function is likely to understate the welfare of the future generations and the diversity and resilience of the natural ecosystem (more on this in Chapter 7).

Second, as is evident from our discussion throughout this chapter, the economic criterion for an optimal level of pollution is developed with the implicit assumption of a predetermined level of waste emission—a benchmark. For example, in each of the cases where the determination of optimal pollution level has been demonstrated, W* was identified as the benchmark—the maximum level of a particular waste under consideration for cleanup. In searching for the optimum level of cleanup, no economic considerations are made concerning the absolute size of the benchmark itself. The focus is simply on the *cheapest* way of disposing a predetermined level of waste. Thus, optimum pollution is calculated without any consideration of what it would be worth to society if a reduction of the benchmark pollution, W*, were to take place. *Given this, the standard economic approach to pollution control is most likely to stress pollution cleanup, rather than pollution prevention.* A strategy of pollution prevention emphasizes waste reduction at source or reducing the amount of waste before it enters any waste system. To the extent that this is ignored or de-emphasized, the economic approach to pollution control may yield a suboptimal ecological outcome. The discussion in Exhibit 4.2 presents some of the difficulties as well as the opportunities involved in applying pollution prevention to manage environmental problems.

In closing, there is actually one more criticism about the cost-effective level of pollution control as discussed in this chapter. When the pollution under consideration involves irreversible ecological change and the risk of major adverse surprises over a long time-horizon, the optimum pollution may not adequately safeguard the interests of future generations and the ecosystem as a whole. In other words, inconsistency between the economic and the ecological optimum may arise when the pollution under consideration is likely to impose environmental damage that is *irreversible* in the long term. This situation will be fully explored in later chapters that specifically deal with the economics of global warming and biodiversity.

EXHIBIT 4.2 AN OUNCE OF POLLUTION PREVENTION?

It is Benjamin Franklin who is usually credited with the maxim an ounce of prevention is worth a pound of cure, although Franklin himself conceded that the sayings in Poor Richard's Almanack were derived from the wisdom of many ages and nations. Poor Richard also said: ''Tis easier to prevent bad habits than to break them.' Was he troubled by the vision thing and trying to tell us something? Forewarn'd forearm'd? The trouble with pollution prevention is that it wears many faces and is not always easily recognized. (What's more—bite thy tongue—it's not always feasible. How, for example, should we apply it to the problem of radon?) Designing an automobile engine to burn gasoline more completely, and thereby emit less carbon monoxide, is pollution prevention; hanging a catalytic converter on the tailpipe is not. Similarly, EPA's 'green' programs, which conserve electricity, prevent pollution (electricity generation accounts for 35 percent of all US emissions of carbon dioxide); planting trees does not.

The Pollution Prevention Act of 1990 sets up a hierarchy of preferred approaches to protecting the environment. First and foremost, pollution should be prevented at the source whenever feasible. Pollution that cannot be prevented should be, in order of preference, recycled, treated or, as a last resort, disposed of in an environmentally safe manner. Operationally speaking, then, pollution prevention is source reduction, which is further defined in the Act as any practice that reduces the amount of any pollutant entering any waste stream. This applies to all activities in our society, including those carried out in the energy, agriculture, consumer and industrial sectors. Restricting development to protect sensitive ecosystems like wetlands is pollution prevention, as is cultivating crops that have a natural resistance to pests. Wrapping a blanket around your water heater is pollution prevention, and so is using energy-efficient light bulbs.

Sounds easy. Pollution prevention is not one of the many tools that can be applied to manage environmental problems (see the May/June 1992 issue of EPA Journal); rather, it is the ideal result that all management programs should try to achieve. The trouble is we've had so little experience pursuing pollution prevention that when we get down to making real choices it sometimes eludes us. We may have to compare products over their entire life cycle—mining, manufacturing, use, reuse, disposal. Now that they are both recyclable, which should we use, paper or plastic grocery bags? Paper biodegrades, but not in most landfills, and it is both bulkier and heavier to handle. Plastic manufacture has an image as a pollution-intensive industry, but papermaking is too. In fact, when pollution prevention has been the result, it has sometimes been inadvertent: It is the rising cost of landfilling, for example, that has persuaded many companies to reduce the solid waste they generate. As Poor Richard advised: Would you persuade, speak of Interest, not of Reason.

Source: *EPA Journal* 19, 3, 1993, p. 8. Reprinted by permission.

4.5 CHAPTER SUMMARY

The primary objective of this chapter was to derive the condition for an 'optimal' level of pollution. This was done by closely examining the tradeoff between two categories of costs associated with pollution: pollution-control and damage costs.

■ Pollution-control cost refers to all the direct or explicit monetary expenditures by society to reduce current levels of pollution: for example, expenditure on sewage-treatment facilities. This cost function primarily reflects the *technology* of pollution control.

■ Pollution-damage costs denote the total monetary value of the damage from discharges of untreated waste into the environment. Pollution-damage costs are difficult to assess since they entail: assigning monetary values to harms done to plants and animals and their habitats; aesthetic impairments; rapid deterioration to physical infrastructure and assets; and various harmful effects on human health and mortality.

■ Furthermore, it was noted that pollution-damage costs are externalities.

■ A tradeoff exists between pollution-control and damage costs. The more spent on pollution control, the lower will be the damage costs, and vice versa.

■ In view of these tradeoffs, it would be beneficial to spend an additional dollar on pollution control only if the incremental benefit arising from the damage avoided by the additional cleanup (waste control) exceeded one dollar. It can then be generalized from this that it would pay to increase expenditure on pollution control provided that at the margin the control cost is less than the damage cost: that is, MCC < MDC.

■ It follows, then, that the optimal level of pollution (waste disposal) is attained when, at the *margin*, there is no difference between control and damage costs: that is, MCC = MDC. When this condition is met, as demonstrated in this chapter, the total waste-disposal cost (the sum of the total control and damage costs) is minimized.

Further analysis of the nature of the two categories of costs of pollution revealed the following:

1. The marginal pollution-control cost (MCC) increases with an increase in pollution cleanup activities. This is because, incrementally, a higher level of environmental quality requires investments in technologies that are increasingly costly. In the extreme case, taking the initial visible waste from a body of water will cost much less than removing the last remaining waste, provided it is even feasible.

2. The marginal pollution-damage cost is an increasing function of pollution emission. This could be explained by an ecological principle that pollution reduces the capacity of a natural ecosystem to withstand further pollution. That is, a gradual loss of ecological resiliency.

Another important issue addressed in this chapter is the possible divergence between economic and ecological optima. Two specific cases were examined to illustrate the significance of this issue:

1. It was observed that, since the economic problem is stated as finding the cheapest way to dispose of a predetermined level of waste W*, in searching for the economic optimum the emphasis has been on *pollution cleanup* rather than *pollution prevention*. This difference matters because the focus on pollution prevention is *reduction of waste at the source* whereas in the case of pollution clean up the goal to find the *cheapest way of disposing a predetermined level of waste*.

2. Because damage costs are anthropocentrically determined, there is no assurance that the economically optimum level of pollution will adequately protect the wellbeing of other forms of life and the ecosystem as a whole.

REVIEW AND DISCUSSION QUESTIONS

1. Briefly identify the following concepts: pollution-control technology, pollution-control cost, pollution-damage cost, cost-effective, eutrophication, pollution prevention.

2. Read the following statements. Respond 'True', 'False' or 'Uncertain' and *explain* why:

    (a) Improvement in pollution-control technology reduces pollution while at the same time allowing society to realize savings in its expenditure for waste control. A 'win–win' situation, indeed! (Hint: A graph and an understanding of what effect technology has on MCC may help in answering this question).

    (b) The MDC is an increasing function with respect to pollution for the simple fact that more pollution means more damage.

3. Fundamentally, the economics of pollution-control attempts to balance the cost of pollution cleanup with the damage cost to the environment at the margin. With this in mind, *explain* what happens under each one of the following situations:

    (a) MCC > MDC

    (b) MCC < MDC

    (c) MCC = MDC

4. Examine the following two statements. Are they equivalent? Why or why not?

    (a) Pollution-damage costs are externalities.

    (b) Not all aspects of pollution-damage costs can be evaluated in monetary terms.

5. Evaluate the relative merit of each of the following environmental-management strategies. Identify a real-world case under which one of these strategies is more appropriate than the others.

    (a) Pollution should be 'controlled' up to a point where the total *social* cost for disposing of it is *minimized*.

    (b) Pollution should be 'prevented' at source.

    (c) Pollution should be controlled to prevent major long-term and irreversible ecological impacts.

REFERENCES AND FURTHER READING

Funtowicz, S. O. and Ravetz, J. R. (1994) 'The Worth of a Songbird: Ecological Economics as a Post-normal Science', *Ecological Economics* 10: 197–207.

Miller, T. G., Jr., (1993) *Environmental Science*, 4th edn., Belmont, CA: Wadsworth.

Chapter 5

The economics of environmental regulations I: Emission standards and effluent charges

---

LEARNING OBJECTIVES

After reading this chapter you will be familiar with the following:

- Four criteria (norms) for evaluating environmental policy instruments.
- Some landmark US environmental legislation mandates.
- How emission standards based on command-and-control approaches are designed and implemented: emission limits; performance standards; and technology-based performance standards.
- Why emission standards are often favored by environmentalist groups.
- Why, when polluting firms are heterogeneous, regulations based on uniform emission standards are not cost-effective.
- Why regulations based on emission standards may not provide sufficient incentives for firms to invest in pollution-control technologies.
- Evaluations of emission standards as regulatory policy instruments: their strengths and weaknesses.
- How effluent charges (fees) are designed and implemented, in theory and practice.
- How effluent charges enable regulators to raise revenue, while at the same time allowing waste emissions to be controlled at levels that are cost-effective.
- How environmental regulations based on effluent charges provide firms with the incentive to invest in pollution-control technology.
- Why a cost-effective outcome at the firm level don't necessarily imply socially 'optimal' outcomes.
- Evaluations of effluent charges as instruments for pollution-control policy: their strengths & weaknesses.

In practice, the choices between emission standards and effluent charges are to some extent influenced by political ideology and the collective moral and ethical positions of a given society. Thus, in practice, the second- and third-best solutions to environmental problems could be unavoidable. If the real world is viewed this way, economic analyses of the kinds provided in this chapter serve an important function by establishing a benchmark against which we can measure how far we may be from achieving the first-best solution.

5.1 INTRODUCTION

One of the major revelations in the previous two chapters has been that environmental resources are externality ridden. For this reason, the socially optimal level of emission control cannot be achieved through the unbridled operation of private markets. As it has been already noted, this is a clear case of market failure and, consequently, a justification for *public intervention*. However, as will be evident throughout the discussion in the next two chapters, on practical grounds, resolving environmental problems requires more than a mere recognition of market failure or the necessity of public intervention to correct an externality.

With this important caveat in mind, in the next two chapters (Chapters 5 and 6) attempts will be made to explain and evaluate *three* policy instruments that have been widely used for regulating waste emissions into the environment. These three instruments are: emission standards, effluent charges and transferable emission credits.

Emission standards are set and enforced through legally mandated laws. Hence, the focus is on the use of the legal system to deter abuse of the environment. By its very nature, emission standards favor a centralized or command-and-control approach to pollution control. On the other hand, effluent charges and transferable emission credits are used to correct *price distortion* arising from environmental externalities. This is done by imposing a financial penalty (such as pollution tax) or by creating artificial market conditions that would allow pollution trading. Since the legal system is only used to enforce the terms of the financial or trade contracts and not the emission level, the effluent charge and transferable emission credits are both a *decentralized* or market-based form of pollution-control policy instruments.

Purely for pedagogical convenience, the discussions of the three pollution-control instruments (i.e., emission standards, effluent charge and transferable emission credits) are covered in two separate chapters. Chapter 5, the current chapter, covers emission standards and effluent charges. Transferable emission credits are discussed in Chapter 6. Chapter 6 also includes discussion on the macroeconomic effects of environmental regulations.

It is important to point out at the outset that the criteria used to evaluate the relative merits of the three policy instruments are cost-effectiveness, compliance (transaction) costs, moral and ethical con-

siderations, fairness or equity considerations, and ecological effects (Sterner 2003).

5.2 EMISSION STANDARDS

An emission standard is a *maximum* rate of effluent discharge that is legally permitted. Emission standards can take a variety of forms. The form that is intuitively most obvious is, of course, a standard expressed in terms of the *quantity* or *volume* of waste material released into the ambient environment per unit time. For example, it might be the case that, in any given week, no more than 100 tons of untreated sewage waste is allowed to be released into a given river stream.

Alternatively, standards could be set in terms of *performance*. Performance standards mandate specific environmental outcomes per unit of product. Furthermore, performance standards may include process changes, reduction in output and changes in fuels or other inputs. The ultimate objective of performance standards is to achieve a predetermined level environmental outcome. For example, in their joint announcement for proposed Greenhouse Gas and Fuel Economy Standards for Passenger Cars and Light Trucks, the US EPA (Environmental Protection Agency) and the US Department of Transportation's National Highway Traffic Safety Administration (NHTSA) are aiming at projected reduction of GHGs by approximately 2 billion metric tons and will save 4 billion barrels of oil over the lifetime of vehicles built between 2017 and 2025 (US EPA, Office of Transportation and Air Quality, May 2010).

In some cases, in setting emission standards the focus is on maintaining the overall quality of a more diffuse environmental medium. This is normally done by setting an *ambient standard* on the basis of an allowable concentration of pollution. For example, the ambient standard for dissolved oxygen in a particular river might specify that the level must not be allowed to drop below three parts per million (ppm). One other commonly used regulatory practice is *technology standards*. Technology-based standards mandate specific pollution-abatement technologies or production methods that polluters must use to meet an emissions standard. In some instances, performance-based standards that are technology based may not specify a particular technology, but rather consider what available and affordable technologies can achieve when establishing a limit on emissions. Technology standards are best used when there are few options open to the polluter for controlling emissions; in this case, the regulator is able to specify the technological steps that a firm should take to control pollution. Technological standards are often used as one of the alternative means of attaining ambient air- and water-quality standards.

In principle, emission standards, regardless of the specific form that they may take, are supposed to reflect the public interest at large; any violators are subjected to legal prosecutions. Moreover, if found guilty violators are punished by a monetary fine and/or imprisonment. In this sense, then, emission standards are environmental policies that are based on 'command-and-control' approaches. On the other hand, it may be said that emission standards are based on the *polluter-pays principle*. That is, the regulatory mandates strictly adhere to the legal philosophy that polluters are accountable for the damages they cause to the environment (Baumol and Oates 1992).

In the United States, the EPA is responsible for implementing environmental laws enacted by Congress. Table 5.1 provides a list of some of these laws. In implementing them, the US EPA, which is a federal agency, works in partnership with state, county and local municipality governments to use a

Table 5.1 *Major environmental laws enacted by the United States Congress since the 1970s*

In the environmental literature, the1970s is often called the environmental decade and this is not without merit. As is evident from the list of some of the more notable environmental laws in the United States since the 1970s, most of them trace their origin to that decade

The Clean Air Act (1970, 1977, 1990)	Established national standards for regulating the emission of pollutants from stationary and mobile sources.
The Clean Water Act (1972, 1977, 1987)	Established water-quality standards; provided for the regulation of the discharge of pollutants into navigable waters and for the protection of wetlands.
Endangered Species Act (1973)	Established to protect and recover endangered and threatened species of fish, wildlife and plants in the United States and beyond. The law works in part by protecting species habitats.
The Safe Drinking Water Act (1974, 1977, 1986)	Set drinking-water standards for levels of pollutants; authorized the regulation of the discharge of pollutants into underground drinking-water sources.
Federal Land Policy and Management Act (1976)	Established for the protection of the scenic, scientific, historic and ecological value of federal lands and for public involvement in their management.
The Toxic Substance Control Act (1976)	Provided for the regulation of chemical substances by the EPA and the safety testing of new chemicals.
The Resource Conservation and Recovery Act (1976)	Established cradle-to-grave regulations for the handling of hazardous wastes.
The Comprehensive Environmental Response, Compensation and Liability Act (1980), also known as the Superfund program	Provided for the cleanup of the worst toxic waste sites.

Source: National Resources Defense Council (NRDC). Extracted from www.nrdc.org/reference/laws.asp

range of tools designed to protect the environment. State and local standards may exceed federal standards, *but cannot be less stringent.* All states have environmental agencies: some are separate agencies and others are part of state health departments. Although the EPA sets the minimum standards, these state agencies are responsible for implementing and monitoring many of the major environmental statutes, such as the Clean Air Acts provisions. Enforcement of the standards is usually a state or local responsibility, but many enforcement actions require the resources of both federal and state authorities.

The basic economics of emission standards can be briefly discussed using the familiar graph presented in Figure 5.1. Suppose that the amount of waste that would have been emitted in the absence of regulation is 300 units. If it is assumed that the public authorities have full information about the damage and control cost-functions, then they will be in a position to recognize that the socially optimal level of pollution is 150 units (where MDC = MCC), which is less than 300. To attain the socially optimal level of pollution, public authorities would now set the emission standard at 150, and strictly enforce it.

The ultimate effects of this are as follows: first, if the standard is successfully implemented, the socially optimal level of pollution is preserved; second, polluters will be forced to internalize the cost of controlling pollution emissions up to the socially optimal level. As shown in Figure 5.1, polluters will be forced to reduce their waste from 300 to 150 units and, given their MCC curve, the total cost of doing this will be area W_eFW^*. Note that if it were not for the emission standards, polluters would have been in a position to *entirely avoid* this cost.

In the discussion so far it has been explicitly assumed that the public authorities somehow have perfect information concerning the damage and control costs. That is a very strong assumption, given what is known about the nature of these two cost-functions, especially the difficulty associated with estimating MDC (see Chapter 4). Is this assumption absolutely necessary? The short answer to this question is *no* (more on this later).

However, without the assumed perfect informa-

tion there is no guarantee that the outcome will be socially optimal. Nevertheless, in the absence of full information on damage and control costs, the public authorities may set the initial emission standard on the basis of what appears to be the *best available information* about these costs at the point in time the decision is made. For example, in Figure 5.1 suppose that the emission standard is initially set at 100—a standard stricter than the socially optimal level, W_e or 150 units. Clearly, this policy is likely to anger the polluters and cause a request for a re-evaluation of the emission standard. If, after a careful re-evaluation of the damage and control costs, the outcome of the initial standard-setting is judged to be too stringent, then the public authorities will revise their standard in such a way that more pollution will be permitted. Similarly, if the authorities set emission standards that are below what is considered to be socially optimal, such as 175 units, this mandate will be vehemently challenged by advocates of the environment. The news account in Exhibit 5.1, although dated still illustrates typical public reactions to proposed changes in emission standards. In this case the specific issue involves public reactions to a stricter air-quality standard proposed by the EPA.

The broader implication of the above analysis is that through trial and error and the competing voices

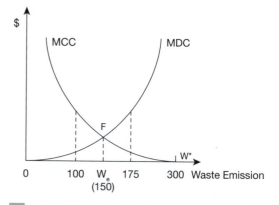

Figure 5.1 *Under ideal emission standards regime the level of pollution tends to gravitate towards W_e (where MDC = MCC) through legislative enactments that are driven by competing special interest groups (see the text for full explanation).*

EXHIBIT 5.1   EPA PROPOSES STRICT NEW AIR-QUALITY STANDARDS

Washington—To the consternation of many state and business leaders, the Environmental Protection Agency proposed stringent new air quality standards Wednesday that would cost more than $6.5 billion a year to meet. The new rules would tighten pollution limits that many cities already fail to meet and regulate more of the tiny particles from smokestacks.

After reviewing more than 200 studies—its most extensive scientific peer review ever—the agency concluded that current standards do not adequately protect public health, especially for children. 'Today, EPA takes an important step for protecting public health and our environment from the harmful effect of air pollution,' said EPA Administrator Carol Browner.

But opponents criticized the agency for failing to consider the high cost of the proposals and said it lacked data to support some assumptions. 'The US EPA is putting a huge mandate on the state, on local governments and on consumers without having fully evaluated the cost, the relative health benefits and the technical feasibility of meeting the standards,' said Donald Schregardus, director of the Ohio Environmental Protection Agency.

But Browner said the EPA's mandate called for it to ensure that health standards meet current science regardless of cost. She estimated that meeting the new standards would cost between $6.5 billion and $8.5 billion annually. However, she claimed that would be offset by up to $120 billion in health benefits, such as fewer hospital stays or missed work. The decision was a setback for industry, which mounted a massive lobbying campaign against the proposal.

A coalition of industry and business groups predicted that states and cities would have to impose drastic pollution controls, including travel restrictions, mandatory car pooling and restrictions on pleasure boats, lawn mowers and outdoor barbecues. Owen Drew of the National Association of Manufacturers predicted that the restrictions would have 'a chilling effect on economic growth.'

But the EPA called that a scare tactic, and said most areas could meet the standards using smog-reduction programs already on the books. Also, in those areas needing changes, most will come in factories and refineries, not in changed driving or other habits, the agency said.

The new standards would require communities to cut ozone levels by one third to 0.08 parts per million cubic feet of air from 0.12 ppm, the current standard. The readings, however, will be taken over an average of eight hours, rather than during a single one-hour period, making it somewhat easier to meet the new standard.

The EPA also wants to regulate tiny particles of dust down to 2.5 microns in diameter. Currently standards apply only to particles of 10 microns or larger. It would take about 8 microns to equal the width of a human hair. Health experts argue that the minuscule particles—many of which come from industrial or utility smokestacks—cause the most harm because they lodge deep in the lungs.

Source: *Kalamazoo Gazette/The Associated Press*, November 28, 1996. Copyright © 1996 The Associated Press. Reprinted by permission.

of various special interest groups, the public authorities gravitate toward setting a standard that will, in the long run, lead to the attainment of the *optimal level of pollution*. In this respect then, at least in principle, emission standards appear to provide room for flexibility. However, despite this presumed *flexibility*, for successful outcomes emission standards require well-informed and responsive regulators (more on this later).

In addition to its presumed flexibility, emission standards are sought to have the following advantages. First, in principle emission standards can be simple and direct—to the extent that they aim at the attainment of clearly defined numerical or technological objectives. Second, they can be effectively used to keep extremely harmful pollution, such as DDT and industrial toxic wastes, below dangerous levels. In other words, when a given pollutant has well-known and long-lasting adverse ecological and human-health effects, command-and-control approaches may be the most cost-effective. Last but not least, they tend to be politically popular because they have a certain *moral appeal*. Pollution is regarded as a 'public bad', and therefore the activities of polluters should be subject to considerable public scrutiny.

However, despite their simplicity, flexibility and political appeal, emission standards as a policy instrument for environmental regulation have several flaws. Moreover, some of these flaws are considered to have serious adverse economic and social implications. First, standards are set solely by government fiat. To this extent they are highly interventionist and signify a major departure from the cherished spirit of the 'free market'. Second, pollution-control practices are applied through administrative laws and generally require the creation of a large bureaucracy to administer the program. The implication here is that the administrative and enforcement costs (i.e., the transaction costs) of emission standards can be considerable.

Third, in setting standards a strong tendency may exist for the regulators and the established firms to cooperate. The end result of this may be a 'regulatory capture' where regulators are influenced to set standards in ways that are likely to benefit the existing firms. Thus, standards have the potential to be used unjustly as barriers to entry. A good recent example of this would be the discovery of the blatantly questionable relationships between government regulators and British Petroleum (BP) that had been going for many years before the oil-drilling accident that has caused so much environmental damage in the Gulf of Mexico, and for that matter in the United States as a whole.

Fourth, while the administrative and enforcement costs of pollution-control laws are real and in some instances considerable, the regulatory agency is not designed to generate its own *revenue*, except for the occasional collection of fines from violators of the law.

A fifth weakness of emission standards deals with a realization that the unintended effect of setting a standard may be to discourage investment in new and improved pollution-control technology. This is because emission standards are generally set on the basis of 'the best available technology' and as such subject to change with changing circumstances. In other words, there is no guarantee that the regulatory authorities will not revise their decision when the new technological condition becomes fully apparent to them. That is, when policymakers become aware of a new waste-processing technology available to the firm, they may decide to change the emission standard (i.e., impose a tighter emission standard) to reflect this change. Hence, this possibility may have the effect of both increasing business *uncertainty* and reducing the expected net savings from implementing the new technology. The implication here is that emission standards could have the potential to *undermine firms' incentives to invest* in new pollution-control equipment. Furthermore, in all likelihood, with emission standards firms would have an *incentive to hide technological changes from the regulatory authorities*.

The sixth and last problem with emission standards to be discussed in this chapter is that the administrative process used to set the standard may neglect the consideration of *economic efficiency*. This situation appears to manifest itself in the following two ways:

1. Economic efficiency requires that, in the setting emission standards, *both* damage and control costs should be taken into account. Public regulators, in their desire to please a particular special-interest group, may be inclined to set standards on the basis of either damage or control cost, but not both. For example, administrators wishing to please their environmentally conscious constituents would be inclined to set emission standards on the basis of damage cost only. This action might overly sensitize regulators to the risk of environmental damage (pollution)—which could ultimately result in a recommendation of excessively stringent emission standards. The opposite would have been the case if emission standards are set by only considering control costs.

2. Typically, emission standards are applied *uniformly* across emission sources. This tends to happen for two practical reasons. First, the administrative and enforcement costs of design-

ing and implementing standards that vary with the different circumstances of each pollution source could be quite costly. Second, from a purely administrative viewpoint, it is much easier to monitor and enforce standards that are uniform across emission sources.

When there are several emitters with a wide range of technological capabilities, however, pollution-control policy based on a uniform emission standard would not be cost-effective (Freeman and Kolstad 2006, Tietenberg 2006). The reason for this is rather straightforward, as is demonstrated using Figure 5.2.

In this example, for the sake of simplicity, the activities of only two firms or sources are considered. As is evident from the curvatures of their respective MCC curves, these firms employ different emission-control technologies. Furthermore, let us assume that the emission standard is set so that a total of 200 units of waste will be controlled by these two firms. In addition, the government authorities have decided to accomplish this through a uniform emission-standard that splits the responsibilities of cleanup equally between the two parties. In Figure 5.2, this suggests that each firm would be responsible for cleaning up 100 units of waste. Under this mandate, the *total* waste-control cost for these two firms would be represented by area K + L + M + N. This total is composed of the waste-control costs of Firms 1 and 2, which are represented by areas M and (K + L + N) respectively. Could this total control-cost be reduced by using a non-uniform assignment of emission-

standard setting? In other words, is a policy based on a uniform emission-standard cost-effective?

The answer to the above question is clearly *yes*, as can easily be demonstrated using Figure 5.2. Suppose the government authorities order Firm 2 to clean up only 75 units of the total waste, and Firm 1 is charged to clean up the rest, which will be 125 units (200 − 75). Under this scenario, the total waste-control cost (the combined cost of both firms) is measured by area K + L + M. Note that this cost is smaller than the cost the two firms incurred when a uniform emission-standard was applied: area K + L + M + N. Furthermore, careful observation indicates that, with the new allocation, the MCCs of the two firms are equal: that is, $MCC_1 = MCC_2$.

This condition is significant because it suggests that area K + L + M is the minimum cost for cleaning up the desired level of total waste-emissions, 200 units. This is the case because, at this level of emission, the MCCs for the two firms are equal, and hence there is no opportunity left to further reduce costs by reallocating resources from one firm to the other. Thus, the following can be concluded: the total cost of controlling (cleaning up) a given amount of waste is minimized when the MCCs are equalized for all emitters. Awareness of this condition clearly reveals that unless the firms under consideration operate using *identical* waste processing technology, pollution-control policy based on a uniform emission control will *not be cost-effective*. This is an important lesson to note for policymakers dealing with environmental pollution-control.

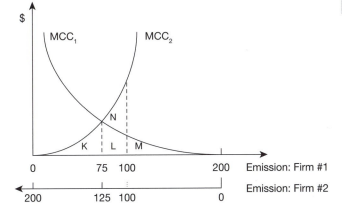

Figure 5.2 *The cost-effectiveness of emission standards. When the technologies firms use to control waste are not the same (MCC_1 is flatter than MCC_2), policy based on a uniform emission control will not be cost-effective.*

Thus, it is largely on efficiency grounds that economists are hesitant to fully endorse the use of emission standards as policy instruments to reduce environmental degradation. As shown above, the main problem with emission standards is that they do not provide polluters with the incentive(s) to search for better approaches to reducing pollution. Thus, they may not perform well in inducing innovation and technological change (Freeman and Kolstad 2006; Sterner 2003). An alternative policy instrument that has the potential to remedy the efficiency problem with emission standards is effluent charges—a subject addressed shortly.

Finally, to make matters more complicated, it is important to point out that there could be several situations in which standards may lead to lower emissions and economically more efficient outcomes than market-based instruments (such as effluent charges and transferable emission credits). Some of these situations arise when: firms under a non-competitive setting are not responsive to price signals, the control costs among firms tend to be homogenous, and waste-monitoring costs tend to be high (Freeman and Kolstad 2006). For example, in many developing countries where markets are not well-developed, regulatory standards are likely to be more effective in dealing with environmental problems than market-based policy instruments. Thus, the debate as to whether emission standards or market-based instruments are preferable for regulating environmental abuse should be looked at on a case-by-case basis (Sterner 2003).

5.3 EFFLUENT CHARGES

An *effluent charge* is a tax or a fee imposed on polluters by government authorities. The fee is specified on the basis of dollars or cents per unit of effluent emitted into an ambient environment. For example, a firm may be required to pay an effluent charge of $0.30 per unit of effluent it is discharging into a lake or a river. The fee on effluent charge could also be based on the quality (the ecological impacts or toxicity) of the waste. In many instances effluent charges are used to protect water quality, and water resources in

general. The way the fee structures are set and implemented varies widely.

For example, according to a report by the US EPA National Center for Environmental Economics (NCEE):

> In California, effluent annual fees are based on the threat to water quality and the complexity of the permit. There are three categories for each characteristic: I, II, and III for water quality threat and a, b, and c for permit complexity. Permittees with an I-a rating, with the greatest threat to water quality and the most complex permits, pay the highest fees, $10,000 a year. III-c permittees pay the lowest fees, $400 a year . . . [On the other hand] The Wisconsin effluent fee system is believed to have potential incentive effects. Since the fee rate per pound of pollutant is inversely related to the permit limit for the pollutant, the most harmful pollutants are taxed at the highest rate. Pollutant loadings are calculated on the basis of flow and concentration information contained in wastewater monitoring reports. Polluters are thereby encouraged to reduce both the quality and the toxicity of pollutant releases.
>
> (2011: 1–2)

As public-policy instruments, effluent charges have a long history and have been used to resolve a wide variety of environmental problems. For example, in recent years, to address the concern of global warming, several prominent scholars have been proposing a global carbon tax (Mankiw 2007; Pearce 1991). As will be evident from the discussions to follow, the major appeals of an effluent charge are: (1) it is less interventionist than emission standards and operates purely on the premise of financial incentive or disincentive, not on a command-and-control principle; (b) it can be relatively easy to administer; and (c) it provides firms with incentives to reduce their pollution through improved technological means—quite the opposite of what have been witnessed in the discussion of emission standards.

How does the effluent-charge approach work? This question is addressed using Figure 5.3, which por-

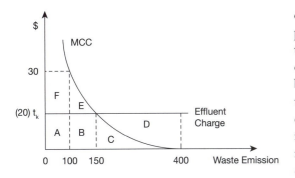

Figure 5.3 *Pollution control through effluent charges. When a profit-maximizing firm is confronted with an effluent charge, such as t_k, it would be in the best interest of the firm to reduce waste emission whenever the cost of controlling an additional unit of waste is less than the effluent tax (i.e., t_k > MCC). The firm would cease its effort to control waste when no gain could be realized from any additional activity of this nature (i.e., t_k = MCC).*

trays a situation in which a firm is discharging waste into a particular environmental medium (air, water or land). This firm is required to pay an effluent tax at the amount t_k, or $20 per unit of waste discharged. In addition, the MCC curve represents the nature of the pollution-control technology of this firm. Given this information, it is fairly easy to draw the conclusion that a private firm interested in minimizing its cost would discharge 150 units of waste. Note that this means that the firm will control 250 units of waste (400 − 150) using its facility (technology) to clean the waste. This is cost minimizing because at 150 units, the usual equi-marginal condition is attained. More specifically, the MCC is equal to the predetermined effluent tax: MCC = t_k = $20.

When this condition is met, the firm has no incentive to reduce its waste discharge to less than 150 units. To see this, suppose the firm decided to reduce its emissions to 100 units. At this level of emission, as shown in Figure 5.3, the MCC = $30 > t_k = $20. Thus, paying the tax to discharge the waste would be cheaper to the firm than using its facility to clean the waste. A similar argument can be presented if the firm decides to increase its waste discharge to a level exceeding 150 units. However, in this case it would be cheaper for the firm to clean the waste using its waste-processing facilities than pay the tax: that is, MCC < t_k. Simply stated, when a profit-maximizing firm is confronted with an effluent charge, it would be in its best interests to treat its waste whenever the cost of treating an additional unit of waste was less than the effluent tax (i.e., t_k > MCC). The firm would cease its effort to control waste when no gain could be realized from any additional activity of this nature (i.e., t_k = MCC).

At this stage, it is important to note the following two points. First, without the effluent charge this firm would have had no incentive to employ its own resources for the purpose of cleaning up waste. In other words, in Figure 5.3, since the service of the environment is considered a free good, this firm would have emitted a total of 400 units of effluent into the environment. This implies that an effluent charge reduces pollution because it makes the firm recognize that *pollution costs the firm money*—in this specific case, $20 per unit of effluent. This shows how an externality is internalized by means of an effluent charge. Second, as shown in Figure 5.3, when the effluent charge is set at t_k, the total expenditure by the firm to control pollution using its own waste-processing technology is represented by area C—the area under the MCC curve when the emission level is 150 units or the firm chooses to control 250 units of its waste (400 − 150). In addition, the firm has to pay a tax ($20 per unit) on the amount (150 units) of untreated waste it decided to emit into the environment, which is indicated by area A + B. In this specific case the tax will be $3,000. Thus, the total cost for this firm to dispose of its 400 units of waste will be the tax plus the total control-cost, i.e., area A + B + C. Note that under an effluent-charge regime, the public authorities will not only make the firm clean up its waste to some desired level, but also enable it to *generate tax revenue that could be used to further clean up the environment or for other social objectives*. This is an important advantage that an effluent charge has over emission standards.

It is important to note that the firm has the option not to engage in any waste-cleanup activity. However, if the firm decides to exercise this option it will end up paying an effluent tax in an amount represented by area A + B + C + D, which will be $8,000 ($20 × 400). Clearly, this will not be desirable, since it entails a net-loss equivalent to area D when compared to the effluent-charge scheme.

So far effluent discharges have been discussed on a purely conceptual level and considering only a single firm. No efforts have yet been made to inquire how the 'optimal' level of effluent discharge is determined. Ideally, effluent charges should represent the *social cost*, on a per unit basis, to the environment (such as the hydrosphere or the atmosphere) when used to assimilate or store waste. In other words, the effluent fees actually represent the shadow prices of the environmental service and as such fully internalize the externalities.

For this to happen, the effluent charge needs to be determined by taking *both the damage and control costs* into consideration at an *aggregate level*. In Figure 5.4 the MCC curve represents the aggregate (sum) of the MCCs for all the relevant firms (or polluting sources). Given this, the optimal effluent charge, t_e, is attained at the point where MCC = MDC. In other words, t_e is the uniform tax per unit of waste discharged that society need to impose on all the firms under consideration, so that collectively they will

emit a total of no more than W_e amount of waste— the optimal level of waste. This level of waste is achieved after a full consideration of all the damage and control costs and from the perspective of society at large.

However, obtaining all the information that is necessary to impute the *ideal* (i.e., socially optimal) effluent charge would be quite costly (Baumol and Oates 1992). Thus, in practice policymakers can only view this ideal as a target to be achieved in the *long run*. In the short run, government authorities determine effluent charges using a trial-and-error process. Initially, they will start the motion by setting an 'arbitrary' effluent-tax rate. This rate may not be totally arbitrary, to the extent that it is based on the best possible information about damage and control costs available at that point in time. Moreover, at least in principle this initial rate could be adjusted continually after observing the reaction of the polluters and as new and refined information on damage and control costs became available. The ultimate objective of the government authorities in charge of setting the tax rate should be to realize the optimal rate as expeditiously as possible. This, more than anything else, requires the use of a carefully crafted trial-and-error process and flexible administrative programs and procedures.

However, Roberts and Spence (1992) basically rejected the idea that the regulatory authorities, simply by means of an iterative process, could arrive at the optimum solution when they are uncertain about the actual costs of pollution control. They showed that, in the presence of *uncertainty*, government authorities base their decision on what they expect to be the MCC of the firm. When control costs turn out to be greater than expected, environmental policy based on effluent taxes would allow waste discharges in excess of what is considered to be socially optimal, and the opposite result (excessive cleanup) will occur if control costs turn out to be less than expected. In either case, optimality is not attained. In addition, in situations where it is very difficult or costly to assess pollution damages, regulatory policy that uses effluent charges may produce socially inefficient outcomes.

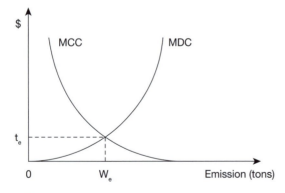

Figure 5.4 *The socially optimal level of effluent charge. This tax rate, t_e, equates the MCC and MDC (i.e., t_e = MCC = MDC). Note that t_e may not be the same as t_k—the effluent charge imposed at the firm level. This is because for various reasons t_k may be set without full consideration of both the damage and control costs.*

One of the most heralded advantages of an effluent charge is that, once it is set, it automatically guides private concerns (all pollutions sources) to allocate their resources in such a way that they are cost-effective (i.e., minimizing pollution-control costs). Earlier, in Section 5.2, the economic criterion for cost-effectiveness was developed. To restate this criterion, when pollution cleanup is performed by several firms (pollution sources) the total cost of cleaning up (pollution control) is minimized when the MCCs are the *same for all the firms engaged in pollution-control activities* (refer to Figure 5.2).

Why is effluent charge cost-effective? Under the effluent charge regime, each firm (polluting source) is charged a uniform tax per unit of waste discharged, such as t_k in Figure 5.3. As discussed earlier, each firm would determine its emission rate independently by equating its MCC cost with the predetermined emission tax, t_k. Suppose there are ten firms; since they all are facing the same effluent charge, then, at equilibrium, $MCC_1 = MCC_2 = MCC_3 = \ldots = MCC_9 = MCC_{10} = t_k$. This, as mentioned earlier, is precisely the condition for a cost-effective allocation of resources, and it results in the effluent charge that automatically minimizes the cost of pollution control among firms. This is indeed a startling and desirable result.

Nonetheless, it is important to note that a *cost-effective allocation* of resources among private concerns *does not necessarily imply social optimality*. This is because a cost-effective allocation of pollution control requires only that all the parties involved in pollution cleanup activities face the same effluent charge, and nothing more. On the other hand, a socially optimal allocation of pollution cleanup presupposes a single and uniquely determined effluent charge after accounting for both control and damage costs. As shown in Figure 5.4, this unique rate, t_e, is attained when the condition MCC = MDC is met. It is important to note, however, that t_e is not necessarily equal to t_k.

At the onset of this section, a claim was made that an effluent charge provides firms with an incentive to improve their waste-control technology. How? Using Figure 5.5, suppose only a single firm (polluter) exists that is subjected to an effluent charge of t_k per unit of emission. The shift of this firm's MCC curve from MCC_0 to MCC_1 is caused by the introduction of a new and improved method of pollution control. Of course, since the innovation and implementation of the new technology costs money, the firm will undertake this project if, and only if, the expected cost savings from the project under consideration are substantial. In general, other factors being equal, the higher the expected cost-savings from a given project, the stronger the firm's incentive to adopt the new and improved pollution-controls technology. Having stated this, using the information in Figure 5.5 the following two points can be vividly illustrated: (1) the potential cost-savings of a hypothetical firm resulting from new pollution-control technology; and (2) the fact that, when compared to emission standards, a

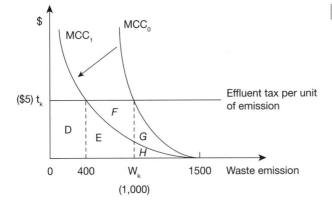

Figure 5.5 *This graph is used to illustrate how, relative to emission standards, effluent charge may promote greater incentive to invest on a new pollution-control technology. Under the effluent tax regime, cost savings include not only the reduction in pollution control costs resulting from the adoption of the new technology (area G) but also from a decrease in tax payment (area F). The tax saving, area F, arises from the additional 600 units of waste that could be controlled using the new technology at a cost of area E while reducing tax payment by area (E + F).*

89

policy based on effluent charge will provide greater financial incentives (cost savings) to investors in pollution-control technology.

Given that t_k represents the effluent charge per unit of emission, before the introduction of the new technology the firm is discharging 1,000 units of its waste. This means that the firm is controlling or cleaning up 500 units (1,500 − 1,000) of its waste. For discharging 1,000 units, the regulatory agency would be able to collect effluent tax (revenue) of $5,000, which is represented by area D + E + F. In addition, this firm incurs a further expenditure for cleaning up or processing 500 units of its waste. The expenditure for controlling this amount of waste is measured by area G + H. Thus, area D + E + F + G + H represents the combined expenditure of effluent tax and waste processing for this firm.

By applying a logic similar to that above, it can be shown that if the new waste-processing technology is adopted, area D + E + H represents the total (effluent charge plus waste processing) expenditure of this firm. Note that the relevant MCC curve is MCC_1. Thus, *area F + G represents the cost saving directly attributable to the adoption of the new technology*. Is this cost saving large enough to warrant the adoption of the new technology? Unfortunately, the answer to this question cannot be addressed here. However, what can be demonstrated at this stage is that this cost saving from the new technology would have been smaller if the firm's activity had been regulated using a policy instrument that is based on emission standards instead of an effluent charge. In other words, an effluent charge provides stronger financial incentives to the firm to adopt new technology than does an emission standard.

To see this clearly, suppose the emission standard is set at 1,000—that is, at the level of the firm's operation prior to introducing the new technology. To process the required waste, 500 units, the firm's total expenditure for controlling its waste is represented by area G + H. However, provided the emission standard remains unchanged, this cost can be reduced to area H if the firm decides to adopt the new technology. Thus, the area G represents the cost saving to this firm as a result of adopting the new waste-processing

plant. Clearly, the magnitude of this saving is smaller than the cost saving that was gained under the effluent-charge system: area F + G. Thus, under the effluent-tax regime the saving is greater by area F.

Of course, there is no great mystery about this result. Under the effluent-charge regime the firm's cost saving is limited not only to the *efficiency gains* in its waste processing plants, but also by what the firm is obliged to pay to the government authorities in the form of *effluent tax*. To see this, first note that, with the new technology, the firm is able to reduce its waste from 1,000 to 400 units—a reduction of 600 units. In doing this, the firm is able to reduce its tax by $3,000 (5 × 600). This tax saving corresponds to area E + F. However, the firm's expenditure to clean up the 600 units using the new technology is only area E. Thus, the net saving to the firm is area F. Note that under emission standards, there is no saving from tax.

The discussion so far clearly indicates that, as a public-policy instrument, an effluent charge has many attractive features. However, no policy tool can be free of weaknesses, and effluent charge is no exception. The following are some of the major weaknesses of an effluent charge.

First, the waste monitoring and enforcement costs of a pollution-control policy based on an effluent charge could be high, especially when a large number of polluters are scattered over a wide geographical area. That is, when compared to an emission-standard setting, an effluent charge requires the gathering and monitoring of more refined and detailed information from each pollution source, since the effluent charge requires the processing of both financial and technological information. Unlike emission standards, it is not based on a purely physical consideration.

Second, an effluent charge can be, and rightly so, viewed as an emission tax. The question is, then, who actually ends up paying this tax? This is a relevant issue because firms could pass this tax on to consumers by charging a higher price for their products. Furthermore, how does the tax impact consumers in a variety of socioeconomic conditions: for example, the poor versus the rich, and ethnic minorities versus the ethnic majority?

What this clearly suggests is that the need for recognizing the *income-distribution* effect of effluent charge (Baumol and Oates 1992). It is important to note, however, that an effluent charge generates revenue. If a government adopts a policy that is fiscally neutral, the revenue raised by taxes on pollution can be used to correct the income distribution or any other negative effects caused by the tax. Some argue that it is important to be mindful about the *double dividend feature of pollution tax*. That is, pollution tax can be used to correct market distortion (i.e., externalities arising from the excessive use of environmental services) and raise revenues which could be used to finance worthwhile social projects, such as helping the poor, providing an incentive to firms to undertake environmentally friendly projects, etc. (Pearce 1991).

Third, earlier it was shown that an effluent charge automatically leads to the minimization of pollution-control costs. However, while an effluent charge is cost-effective in this specific way, this result in itself does not imply *social optimality*. Whether an effluent charge produces a socially optimal outcome or not depends entirely on the choice of the 'appropriate' effluent tax. The determination of this tax requires not just pollution control, but the simultaneous consideration of both control and damage costs.

Fourth, because of the amount of detailed information needed to estimate the appropriate charge, in practice an effluent charge is set on a trial-and-error basis. If nothing else, this definitely increases the uncertainty of private business-ventures concerning pollution-control technology. Furthermore, in some situations (e.g., where significant regional differences in ecological conditions exist) *optimality may require imposing a non-uniform effluent charge policy* (Sterner 2003; Tietenberg 2006) For example, the correct level of carbon tax imposed to control GHG emissions may vary in different countries of the European Union. Situations of this nature clearly add to the complexities of imposing the appropriate absolute level of charges in relation to the level and nature of emissions caused by each source.

Fifth, effluent charge is a financial disincentive given to polluters. This system of charge does not say that it is *morally* wrong to knowingly engage in the pollution of the environment. It simply states that it is okay to pollute provided that one pays the assessed penalty for such an activity. Of course, the justification for this is that damage to the environment can be restored using the money generated by penalizing polluters (Pearce 1991). To some people, this conveys a perverse logic. There is a big difference between protecting the natural environment from harm and repairing it after it has been damaged.

The fact that effluent charges necessitate a prior knowledge of the approximate magnitude of the charges has been a source of considerable concern to economists (Baumol and Oates 1992). The upshot of this concern has been the development of an alternative policy instrument to control pollution, namely transferable emission credits. This policy tool, the subject of the next chapter, has all the advantages of effluent charges, and it treats pollution as a commodity to be traded piecemeal using the *market*.

91

5.4 CHAPTER SUMMARY

This chapter discussed two alternative policy approaches used to internalize environmental externalities: emission standards and effluent charges.

Emission standards represent a form of 'command-and-control' environmental regulations. The basic idea involves restricting polluters to a certain predetermined amount of effluent discharge. Exceeding this limit subjects polluters to legal prosecution resulting in monetary fines and/or imprisonment. This has been a widely used method of environmental regulation in many countries of the world.

The main advantages of emission standards are:

1.   Generally, less information is needed to introduce regulations. As a standard represents a government fiat, it is simple and direct to apply;
2.   They are effective in curbing or controlling harmful pollution, such as DDT;
3.   They are morally appealing and politically popular since the act of polluting is declared a 'public bad'; and
4.   Environmental groups favor them because standards are generally aimed at achieving a predetermined policy target.

The primary disadvantages of emission standards are:

1.   They are highly interventionist;
2.   They do not generate revenue;
3.   They may require the establishment of a large bureaucracy to administer programs;
4.   They are generally *not* cost-effective;
5.   They do not provide firms with sufficient incentive to invest in new pollution-control technology; and
6.   There is a strong tendency for regulatory capture: cooperation between the regulators and polluters in ways that provide unfair advantages to established firms.

Effluent charges represent a tax per unit of waste emitted. Ideally, a tax of this nature reflects the imputed value or shadow price (on a per-unit basis) of the services of an environment as a repository for untreated waste. Thus, the idea of the tax is to account for external costs so that price distortion will be corrected. For some philosophical and cultural reasons, effluent charges seem to be used more widely in Europe than in the United States. In general, Americans seems to exhibit considerable intolerance to any form of taxes.

The principal advantages of the effluent charges are:

1.   They are relatively easy to administer;
2.   They are generally cost-effective;
3.   They generate revenues while correcting price distortions—the double-dividend feature of effluent charges; and
4.   They tend to provide firms with incentives to invest in pollution-control technology.

The main disadvantages of the effluent charges are:

1.   Monitoring and enforcement costs could be high;
2.   They could have a disproportionate effect on income distribution;
3.   They do not condemn the act of polluting on purely moral grounds—it is okay to pollute, provided one pays for it;

4. Firms are philosophically against taxes of any form, especially when they are perceived to cause increased prices and an uncertain business environment; and
5. Environmental organizations generally oppose effluent charges for both practical and philosophical reasons. Pollution taxes are 'licenses to pollute'. Taxes are generally difficult to tighten once implemented.

REVIEW AND DISCUSSION QUESTIONS

1. Quickly review the following concepts: the polluter-pays principle, regulatory capture, emission standards, effluent charge, and the double-dividend feature of pollution tax.
2. Read the following statements. In response, state 'True', 'False' or 'Uncertain' and explain why:
    (a) Public intervention is *both* a necessary and sufficient condition for internalizing environmental externality.
    (b) Environmental advocacy groups generally favor the command-and-control approach to pollution abatement because they believe that polluters should be overtly punished.
    (c) The so-called double-dividend feature of pollution tax is a theoretical myth.
    (d) While most taxes distort incentives, an environmental tax corrects a market distortion.
3. Provide *four* reasons why economists generally don't favor a policy that is based on a command-and-control approach to environmental regulation.
4. To say that an effluent charge is cost-effective does not necessarily mean that it is *socially* optimal. Discuss. (Hint: base your answer on the possible inconsistent outcome between these two equilibrium conditions: t_k = MCC, and MCC = MDC.)
5. The core problem of a command-and-control approach to environmental policy is its inherent bias or tendency to standard-setting practice that is *uniformly* applicable to all situations. For example, the ambient-air-quality standards in the United States are basically national. This may have serious efficiency and ecological implications because regional differences in terms of the factors affecting damage- and control-cost relationships are *not* effectively captured. Comment. Would considerations of transaction costs have a bearing to your response to this question? Why or why not?
6. Refer back to Figure 5.3, p. 87. Let t_k now represent, not effluent tax, but subsidies. In other words, the firm will be paid by the regulators t_k (i.e., $20) for each unit of waste cleaned up.
    (a) Demonstrate that the final outcome will be the same (cleanup 250 units of waste or control 150 units of waste) regardless whether the firm is charged tax or paid a subsidy.
    (b) If the firm is paid a subsidy, it stands to earn a net gain of area D in Figure 5.3, and the government loss will be area A +B in terms of tax receipt.
    (c) If the above outcomes are true, what does it suggest about a 'cost-effective' outcome of pollution control in terms of income distribution and fairness?
7. It is often argued that effluent charge (not subsidy) may have a regressive effect on income distribution (i.e., lower-income households may end up paying more tax relative to their income). However, some economists have argued that effluent charge should not be dismissed on the basis of 'fairness' alone. The issue of fairness can always be addressed separately through income redistribution. For example, the tax revenue from effluent charges can be used to compensate the losses of the damaged parties. Are you convinced by this argument? Explain.

REFERENCES AND FURTHER READING

Baumol, W. J. and Oates, W. E. (1992) 'The Use of Standards and Prices for Protection of the Environment', in A. Markandya and J. Richardson (eds.) *Environmental Economics: A Reader*, New York: St. Martin's Press.

Freeman, J. and Kolstad, D. C. (2006) *Moving to Markets in Environmental Regulations: Lessons from Thirty Years of Experience*, London: Oxford University Press.

Mankiw, G. (2007) 'One Answer to Global Warming: A New Tax', *The New York Times*, September 16, 2007.

Pearce, D. W. (1991) 'The Role of Carbon Taxes in Adjusting to Global Warming', *Economic Journal* 101: 938–48.

Roberts, M. J. and Spence, M. (1992) 'Effluent Charges and Licenses under Uncertainty', in A. Markandya and J. Richardson (eds.) *Environmental Economics: A Reader*, New York: St. Martin's Press.

Sterner, T. (2003) *Policy Instruments for Environmental and Natural Resource Management*, Washington, DC: Resource for the Future (RFF) Press

Tietenberg, T. (2006) *Environmental and Natural Resource Economics*, 5th edn., New York: HarperCollins.

US EPA (United States Environmental Protection Agency) (1994) *EPA Journal*, Fall issue.

—— (1995) *EPA Journal*, Winter issue.

US EPA (United States Environmental Protection Agency's National Center for Environmental Economics) (2011) 'Examples of State Effluent Fees: Louisiana, California, and Wisconsin', http://yosemite.epa.gov/ee/epa/eed.nsf/a8aa55f234e6571a852577420067397e/b0c30e95a082047585257746000aff3c!OpenDocument, accessed 08/15/2011.

US EPA (United States Environmental Protection Agency's Regulatory Announcement) (2010) 'EPA and NHTSA to Propose Greenhouse Gas and Fuel Efficiency Standards for Heavy-Duty Truck; Begin Process for Further Light-Duty Standard', www.naseo.org/news/newsletter/documents/2011-05-20/EPA&NHTSA.pdf, accessed 11/09/2011.

Chapter 6

The economics of environmental regulation II: Transferable emission credits and the macroeconomic effects of environmental regulation

---

LEARNING OBJECTIVES

After reading this chapter you will be familiar with the following:

- The concept of transferable emissions credits (TECs).
- How TECs, as a market-based approach to control pollution, are designed and implemented.
- Alternative mechanisms for rationing initial emission credits.
- The arguments for why TECs are cost-effective and how they provide firms with incentives to invest in pollution-control technology.
- How the efficacy of TECs can be enhanced by emission banking, offsets, and bubbles.
- The major shortcomings of TECs.
- Real world application of TECs: the sulfur emissions trading programs in the United State as established under Title VI of the 1990 Clean Air Act Amendment.
- The macroeconomic effects of environmental regulations: environmental protection, the economy, and jobs.

Transferable emissions control is a relatively new market-based pollution-control policy instrument. The ingenuity behind this policy instrument is the creation of 'artificial' markets for pollution rights that are traded as commodities. The growing appeal of TECs arise from their applicability, not only in regulating pollution, but also in the management of common property resources under free access such as ocean fisheries and tropical forests. A TEC is a regulatory tool with tremendous potential for the management of wide-ranging environmental resources provided they are used *appropriately*. To do so, one need to have a good understanding of both the strengths and limitations of this rather novel policy tool, and it is with this in mind that the materials in this chapter presented.

6.1 INTRODUCTION

This chapter deals with the economics of environmental regulation and as such is a continuation of Chapter 5. In Section 6.2 the concept of TEC is discussed at some length. The academic interest in the concept of emissions trading goes as far back as the 1960s. However, its actual use as a policy instrument to control pollution on a large-scale basis did not occur until the mid-1970s when it was used to facilitate the regulatory process for the United States' ambient air pollution standards in *non-attainment* areas—the areas in which the level of a given air pollutant exceeds the level permitted by the federal standards (Atkinson and Tietenberg 1984). However, since the mid-1980s it has been gaining widespread acceptance and been implemented in a wide variety of applications.

To see some of the reasons of its growing popularity, in Section 6.3 an attempt will be made to evaluate the efficacy of TEC using the United States' acid-rain program, established under Title IV of the 1990 Clean Air Act Amendment. This program requires a major reduction in emissions of sulfur dioxide and nitrogen oxide, the primary precursors of acid rain, from the electric-power industry. The acid-rain program makes an ideal case-study because it has been in existence since 1995 and the regulatory mandates explicitly include provisions for trading emission-allowances.

The topic covered in the last section of this chapter, Section 6.4, is the macroeconomic effects of environmental regulations. The main issue here is the extent to which environmental regulation affects employment, price and productivity at national (aggregate) level. This topic remains very controversial and as such contains several important unresolved issues about the impacts of environmental regulations on key macroeconomic variables.

A final remark to make before ending the discussion in this section is the consistent use of 'emission credits' instead of 'emission permits'. This is done intentionally because the use of the term 'permits' may be confused with the broader concept of air- or water-pollution permits. However, in the broader environmental economic literature, the term credits and permits are used interchangeably.

6.2 TRANSFERABLE EMISSION CREDITS

The main idea behind emission credits is to create a market for *pollution rights*. In this instance, a pollution right simply signifies a *credit* that consists of a unit (pounds or tons per year) of a specific pollutant. It is important to note that the conceptualization of tradable rights in this specific way literally permits pollution to be a fungible commodity that can be exchanged in the marketplace. Under the tradable emission-credit system, government authorities have three functions: they determine the *total credits* that would be consistent with the broader environmental

target(s) or objective(s) under consideration; they decide the mechanism to be used to *allocate* (distribute) the initial emission credits among polluters; and they *monitor* and *enforce* activities to ensure compliance with all the relevant regulatory mandates.

How do regulatory authorities determine the total number of credits or units of pollutants? Ideally, as discussed in Chapter 4, this total should be set through a consideration of *both* the damage and the control costs from the perspective of society at large. In practice, however, accurate estimates of damage and control costs may not be readily available because of cost considerations. Thus, normally, the total number of credits is determined by regulatory agencies on the basis of best available emission-control technology standards. It is important to note, however, that what is involved here is an effort to determine the level of pollution that is considered to be consistent with the attainment of the *socially 'ideal' level of environmental quality*. Thus, this is not a decision that should be taken lightly.

Once the total emission-credits (i.e., environmental quality target) are determined, the next step requires finding a mechanism by which the total credits are initially distributed among polluters. No single magic formula exists that can be used to distribute the initial rights among polluters, especially if equity (fairness) is an important consideration. Notwithstanding the concern for equity, the *efficient* allocation of the total credits will be independent of the initial distribution of pollution rights, provided credits are freely transferable. Is this the Coase theorem in disguise? The discussion of this theorem in the last section of Chapter 3 may provide an important clue to this question.

From the discussion so far, it is important to observe that a system of transferable emission credits operates on the basis of the following basic postulates:

1. It is possible to obtain a legally sanctioned right to pollute.
2. These rights (credits) are clearly defined.
3. The total number of credits and the initial distribution of the total credits among the various polluters are assigned by regulatory agencies. In

addition, polluters emitting in excess of their credit allotments are subject to a stiff monetary penalty. The monitoring and enforcement responsibilities are bestowed to the pollution-controlling authorities.

4. Pollution credits are freely transferable. That is, they can be freely traded in the marketplace.

Efficient credit allocation: a theoretical framework

To provide a theoretical framework on how a resource allocation system that is based on transferable credits is supposed to work, let us consider the following simple examples. Suppose that, after careful consideration of all the relevant information, government agencies of some hypothetical place issue a total of 300 credits for a period of one year. Each credit entitles the holder to emit a ton of sulfur dioxide. There are only two firms (Firm 1 and Firm 2) emitting sulfur dioxide. Using a criterion that is considered to be 'fair', government authorities issue an equal number of emission credits to both firms. That is, the maximum that each firm can emit into the air is 150 tons of sulfur dioxide per year. Finally,

let us suppose that in the absence of government regulation *each* firm would have emitted 300 tons of sulfur dioxide (or a total of 600 tons of sulfur dioxide for both firms). Thus, by issuing a total of 300 credits, the ultimate objective of the government policy is to reduce the current level of total sulfur emissions in the region by half (300 tons). Figure 6.1 incorporates the hypothetical data presented so far. Furthermore, in this figure the MCCs for these two firms are assumed to be different. Specifically, it is assumed that Firm 1 uses a more efficient waste-processing technology than Firm 2.

Given the conditions described above, these two firms can engage in some form of mutually beneficial negotiations. To begin, let us look at the situation that Firm 1 is facing. Given that it can discharge a maximum of 150 units of its sulfur emission, Firm 1 is operating at point R of its MCC. At this point it is controlling 150 units of its sulfur emission. For this firm, the MCC for the last unit of the SO_2 (sulfur dioxide) is $500. On the other hand, Firm 2 is operating at point S of its MCC, and it is controlling 150 units of its waste and releasing the other 150 units into the environment. At this level of operation, point S, the MCC of Firm 2, is $2,500.

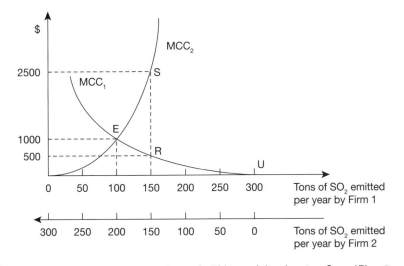

Figure 6.1 *How transferable emission permits work. This graph involves two firms (Firm 1 and 2) with pollution control technologies that are different in their efficiency—as indicated by the slope of the two MCCs. Furthermore, it is assumed that the two firms are initially allotted equal amount of permits, 150 tons of SO_2. At this initial stage, $MCC_2 > MCC_1$. The question is, can these two firms do better? Read the text for answer to this question.*

What is evident here is that, at their current level of operations, the MCCs of these two firms are different. More specifically, to treat the last unit of emission it costs Firm 2 five times as much as Firm 1 ($500 versus $2,500). Since emission credits are freely tradable commodities, it would be in the best interest of Firm 2 to buy an emission credit from Firm 1 provided its price is less than $2,500. Similarly, Firm 1 will be willing to sell an emission credit provided its price is greater than $500. This kind of mutually beneficial exchange of credits will continue to persist as long as, at each stage of the negotiation between the two parties, $MCC_2 > MCC_1$. That is, as long as the MCC of Firm 2 exceeds that of Firm 1, Firm 1 will be in a position to supply pollution credits to Firm 2. This relationship will cease to occur when the MCC of the two firms attain equality—that is, $MCC_2 = MCC_1$.

In Figure 6.1, this equilibrium condition is reached at point E. At this equilibrium point, Firm 1 is emitting 100 tons of sulfur (or controlling 200 tons of sulfur). This means that Firm 1 is emitting 50 tons of sulfur less than its maximum allowable emission credits. On the other hand, at the equilibrium point, Firm 2 is emitting 200 tons of sulfur, 50 tons more than its maximum allowable emission credits. However, Firm 2 is able to fill this deficit by purchasing 50 tons worth of pollution credits from Firm 1. Note also that, at equilibrium, the total amount of sulfur emitted by these two firms is 300 tons, which is exactly equal to the total pollution credits issued by government authorities.

What exactly is the difference between the initial situation of these two firms (points R and S) and the new equilibrium condition established through a system of transferable pollution credits (point E)? In both instances, the total units of sulfur emission are the same: 300 tons of sulfur. However, what is desirable about the new equilibrium position (point E) is that it is *cost-effective* (i.e., the same air-quality goal—a reduction of 300 tons of sulfur—can be achieved at a lower cost).

This can be demonstrated in two ways. First, at point E, the usual condition for the cost-effective allocation of resources—that is, the *MCCs of the firms under consideration are equal*, is satisfied (see Chapter 5). Alternatively, using Figure 6.1 it is possible to show that both firms are better off at the new position. At the initial level of operation (points R and S), the *total* pollution-control cost for these two firms is represented by area 0ESRU. The *total* pollution-control cost at the new equilibrium position (point E) is measured by area 0EU. Therefore, by moving to the new equilibrium, the total control-cost is reduced by area ERS. This clearly constitutes a Pareto improvement since—by moving from the old to the new position—no one is made worse off. This is because the movement is done through a voluntary and mutually beneficial exchange between the two firms.

Furthermore, like the effluent charge system, the use of tradable emission credits would provide strong incentives to encourage investment in new pollution-control technologies. For those who are curious, this can be easily demonstrated using an approach similar to that used in the previous chapter, in Figure 5.5. The intuitive explanation relies on the notion that a regulatory regime that allows the free exchange of emission credits is likely to provide the flexibility and incentives needed for firms to find low-cost compliance (i.e., pollution-control technology) options.

As a public-policy instrument, perhaps the most remarkable feature of transferable credits is that, once the size of the total credits is determined, the allocation of these credits among competing users is based entirely on the market system. This was demonstrated above using a rather simple case of only two firms. However, an interesting feature of the emissions trading system is that it *works even better when the number of parties (pollution sources) involved in the exchange of credit increases*.

The only thing that this regulatory system requires, as discussed earlier, is the creation of clearly defined new property rights: pollution credits. Once this is accomplished, as in the case for the markets for goods and services (see Appendix A), individual firms will be guided, via an 'invisible hand', to use environmental resources in a manner that is considered 'socially' optimal. Furthermore, this system of allocation creates an *actual market price* for the environmental commodities under consideration. For example, in Figure 6.1 the market equilibrium price is $1,000 per emission credit.

Furthermore, a well-functioning emissions trading program with large number of participants (pollution sources) can also add policy features that could further enhance efficiency. Three different types of emissions trading policies that can be used to add flexibility within a given regulatory mechanism—*bubble*, *banking* and *offset*—are briefly mentioned here. The practical applications of these three policies will be further evident in the next section along with the discussion of the United States' acid-rain program.

The *bubble policy* is generally used by a company with several sources. A source in this case refers each vent and smokestack. The bubble policy would allow a factory to form an imaginary 'bubble' by treating all of its sources as a single source. Thus, based on economic considerations, the company is then able to adjust the emissions of each individual source within the bubble (i.e., some can emit more than others) so that the factory as a whole remains in compliance with the emission standard. The obvious benefit of this strategy is that by pooling together all of a factory's emissions as one source, a company does not need to meet standards for each source, therefore, reducing costs.

The *banking policy* allows pollution credits to be saved (but not borrowed) for later use. The effect of this policy is to add flexibility to how companies use their initial credit allotment over time. For example, a company can save the emissions that became available when an existing source is retired and use them to meet its expected future need, such as adding a new source(s). The main advantage of this policy is that it relieves companies from making a hasty decision regarding what to do about their emission credits immediately upon the retirement of an existing source (facility). Note, however, that the saved emissions credits cannot be borrowed by other companies.

The *offset policy* is often used when adding new sources into given areas or regions that is already under environmental stress is under consideration. For example, in the United States the offset policy is used to regulate the air quality of non-attainment areas—the areas or regions in which the level of a given air pollutant exceeds the level permitted by the federal standards. The main objective here is to find ways to allow the addition of new sources (expansion of economic activity) in such a way that the adverse environmental impacts of the new addition is offset by environmental gains, with the overall aim of achieving a net neutral or beneficial outcome (McKinney 2005).

This is generally accomplished by subjecting that new source in non-attainment areas to a requirement that is consistent with the lowest emissions rate achievable by a similar source in any other parts of the country or region. Although the offset policy is also applicable at factory level, it is finding increasing use worldwide as a policy tool to conserve wetlands, forested areas and biodiversity (Ibid.).

Given these efficiency centered features of the tradable emissions credit system, it is not difficult to see why such a system should command the enthusiastic support of economists. Since the early 1980s, economists have been strongly lobbying the EPA to adopt transferable pollution credits as the primary policy tool for regulating the environment. As a result of this effort, in recent years there has been an increasing application of transferable pollution credits in a wide variety of situations. In some sense, the growing application of transferable pollution credits is creating what amounts to a revolutionary reform, not only of the way the US EPA has been formulating its regulatory statutes, but also of how the general public is reacting to environmental concerns. The reading in Case Study 6.1, while it may appear trivial, is a good illustration of this. The interesting aspect of this case study is that even environmental groups are willing to participate in such a market-based environmental regulation instrument because it provides opportunities to purchase and retire emission credits.

It is also important to point out that the growth in the adoption and applications of emissions trading programs have not been entirely confined to the United States. Over the past two decades there have been notable and steady increases in the application of emissions trading program particularly in the member states of the European Union (EU) and some Latin

CASE STUDY 6.1   PURCHASING POLLUTION

Meg Sommerfeld

What can $20,500 buy?

More than 1,800 reams of photocopier paper, 6,833 pints of Ben and Jerry's ice cream, or a new car, among other things.

How about 290 tons of sulfur dioxide? At least that's what students at Glens Falls (N.Y.) Middle School want to buy with money they have raised.

The students have raised $20,500 to buy so-called pollution allowances at the US Environmental Protection Agency's annual auction at the Chicago Board of Trade this week.

Each credit allows the purchaser to emit a ton of sulfur dioxide, a colorless, suffocating gas. The students would retire the allowances they buy, thereby reducing the amount of sulfur dioxide that is released into the air. The EPA will auction about 22,000 credits this year.

The school in upstate New York raised about $13,640 from a community auction, more than $4,000 from a letter-writing campaign, and $3,860 through 25-cent 'gum allowances' and 50-cent bubble-blowing permits.

While gum is usually verboten, a Glens Falls teacher had permission to sell gum for one day. The teacher sold 1,000 pieces of gum before 8:30 a.m.

Leading the charge was sixth-grade teacher Rod Johnson.

'We study the problem, and buying the pollution allowances gives us a solution,' he said.

Glens Falls and fifteen other elementary, middle and secondary schools participating in the pollution auction got involved with the help of the National Healthy Air License Exchange, a Cleveland-based nonprofit environmental group. Most of the other schools have raised a few hundred dollars.

Last year, Glens Falls Middle School was the first K-12 school to buy allowances, raising $3,200 to buy 21 tons. And though the 290 tons of emissions the school hopes to buy this year is small relative to the total being auctioned, Mr. Johnson says it's a significant learning experience for his students.

Source: Education Week Library, March 27, 1996. Copyright © 1996 Editorial Projects in Education. Reprinted by permission.

American countries. In fact, several of the most recent and exciting applications of emissions trading have been developed by the EU in their effort to comply with their collective commitment to control GHG emissions as mandated by the Kyoto Protocol (more on this in Chapter 9).

Major drawbacks of emission trading programs

Is such a worldwide and enthusiastic endorsement of emissions trading justified? It would be all right, provided that the enthusiasm was tempered with proper qualifications. In other words, notwithstanding the important positive attributes of the emissions trading system that have been already discussed, it is important to recognize some of the major weaknesses

associated with this regulatory scheme. These drawbacks are identified and explained in the rest of this section.

Transaction costs: although it has not been stated explicitly, the theoretical analysis presented so far was done with the assumption of zero transaction costs. When transaction costs are significant, however, emission trade markets may not be cost-effective (Stavins 1995). This concern is not entirely groundless given the costs of finding an appropriate trading partner, establishing the terms of the trade, and completing the arrangements could be significant. In fact, in the 1980s high transaction cost was used as one of the reasons for the slow start of the emissions trading programs (Hahn and Hester 1989; Tietenberg 1990). Most recently, transaction costs (in particular, concern over compliance costs) has been cited as being one of the major reasons for the reluctance of many countries (including the US) to develop market-based mechanisms for reducing greenhouse gases (more on this in Chapter 9).

Cost-effectiveness and social optimality: it is important to note that what a system of TEC guarantees is, at most, a cost-effective allocation of the total credits that are issued by the government authorities. Whether such a system leads to a *socially optimal* use of environmental resources depends largely on how the regulatory authorities determine the *total* credits to be issued, hence, the environmental target. However, under the tradable credit system the total credits are based primarily on technological standards (i.e., pollution-control costs). This approach, therefore, may not adequately consider *damage costs* that are essential for the determination of the socially optimal level of environmental target (quality) or total credits. More specifically, as discussed in Chapter 4, social optimality requires considerations of both the pollution damage and control costs. What this suggests is that, to the extent that regulatory authorities largely base the environmental objective(s) on primarily technological standards, the outcomes of market-based trading approaches can not represent a global improvement in efficiency (i.e., the first-best).

Furthermore, even when control costs are considered, as Roberts and Spence (1992) demonstrated, in the presence of *uncertainty* a regulatory scheme based on transferable pollution credits would yield results that differ from the socially optimal outcome. When control costs turn out to be higher than expected, a policy based on transferable credits will tend to yield an outcome that suggests a cleanup costing more than the socially optimal level and vice versa.

Equity issues associated with the allocation methods of the initial credits: at the beginning of this section it was stated that the regulatory authorities have the responsibility to decide on the allocation methods for the initial total credits. Evidently, the mechanisms by which government agencies eventually decide to distribute the *total* credits among potential users can have significant equity implications. Should credits

be distributed *equally* among the potential users (sources)? Should they be distributed in proportion to the size of the firms under consideration? Should they be distributed by means of a lottery? Should credits be publicly auctioned? Since each one of these allocation systems has varying impacts among the various users of the credits, it will be impossible to completely avoid the issue of fairness or equity.

For example, in the United States, credits are allocated on what is known as the *grandfathering principle*, where credits are allocated relative to the size of a firm's historical level of emissions. Under this emission-rationing rule, existing firms only have to purchase any additional credits they may need over and above the initial allocation (as oppose to purchasing *all* credits in an auction market). This scheme is used mainly because it is politically convenient. Obviously, grandfathered rules can be judged as being 'unfair' given that new firms are asked to pay for all the credits they purchase while existing firms receive the initial credits at no cost.

Market power and price distortion: the contention here is that emission credit markets could be susceptible to the development of market power. First, existing firms tend to have advantage in the initial allocation of credits where the grandfathering rules are applied to the initial allocation of credits. Under this, and other similar circumstances, the potential exists that the existing firms could refuse to sell credits to new firms to limit competition, creating a barrier to entry (Misiolek and Elder 1989).

Another source of potential price distortion that is uniquely associated with emission credit markets arises from the fact that environmental groups are allowed to buy and retire credits (see Case Study 6.1). Of course, this action may serve conservation-minded souls very well, but will this be true for society at large? Most importantly, what this entails is that any group with a considerable amount of money can influence the market price for emission credits.

Ultimately, unless suitable mechanisms are used to deal with market distortions of the above nature, the notion of protecting the environment through marketable pollution credits may be far less satisfactory than theory suggests.

101

The moral dilemma of using markets to do some good for the environment: within the environmental community, there are many who take the position that the very idea of pollution rights conveys reprehensible moral and ethical values. More specifically, their objections are based on the notion that to view the environment as just another commodity to be owned privately and traded in a piecemeal fashion using the marketplace is morally indefensible. Furthermore, on practical grounds, since market prices normally fail to include the values of several aspects of environmental services (a subject matter to be discussed in Chapter 7), it would amount being at the very least disingenuous to consider markets as the panacea for environmental problems.

Relocation effect and hot-spots: the relocation effect refers to the possibility that firms could have the incentive to sell all their initial credit allotments and then relocate to a region or a country where pollution regulation is less stringent. Activities of this nature are likely to persist where the costs of effectively monitoring the amount of pollution leaving a source are very costly. Under this condition, there would be a high probability that firms could avoid detection of their illegal acts—by selling or avoiding buying credits and relocating their operations to areas with less stringent pollution regulation.

Another problem associated with emissions trading programs is a phenomenon known as *hot-spots*—a high local-concentration of pollution. Emissions trading programs provide firms with the legal rights to pollute as long as they don't exceed their initial credit allocations. However, the spatial considerations of how these rights are exercised could give rise to environmental justice concerns. For example, firms with multiple facilities located in different locations may choose to emit greater amounts of pollution in one location provided they can offset it using a reduction in emissions from other locations. This clearly leads to the hot-spots—the particular location or area where a pollution emission is allowed to increase. The concern for hot-spots is often associated with *environmental justice* concerns (more on this in Chapter 8). These concerns are based on the economic vulnerability of low-income communities to environmental hot-spots.

6.3 APPLYING THE THEORY: THE SULFUR EMISSIONS TRADING PROGRAM IN THE UNITED STATES

In this section, the real-world application of emissions trading programs is examined using, as a case study, the United States' experience with the acid-rain program (ARP), established under Title IV of the 1990 Clean Air Act Amendment. The ARP has been in existence since 1995 and as such provides plenty of information with which to understand and appreciate the complexities involved when a market-based emissions trading mechanism is used for compliance with environmental mandates at a national level. It is important to point out, right from the outset, that while the ARP requires major emission reductions of both sulfur dioxide (SO_2) and nitrogen oxide (NO_x), the focus of this case study will be primarily on SO_2.

The acid rain program (1995–2010)

The first large-scale use of tradable pollution credits in the United States was introduced with the passage of the 1990 Clean Air Act Amendments. More specifically, Title IV of this Act was responsible for initiating a nationwide use of market-based approaches primarily designed to reduce sulfur dioxide (SO_2) emissions from power plants to about half the amount of the 1980 levels by 2010 (US EPA Report, 2010).

In the 1980s, acid rain was a hotly debated worldwide environmental concern, including in the US. Emissions of sulfur dioxide (SO_2) from power plants were the chief precursor of *acid rain*. Sulfur dioxide emissions were steadily increasing during the 1970s and the 1980s. By the late 1980s, in the United States alone the *total* SO_2 emissions were approaching 25 million tons per year. Accumulated over time, acid rain depositions on lakes, streams, forests, buildings and people are believed to cause substantial damage to aquatic organisms and trees, erode and disfigure stone buildings and historical monuments, and impair the lungs of people (for more on the causes and consequences of acid rain see Exhibit 6.1).

Confronted with the prospect of growing acid rain-related problems, the United States government started Phase I of its ambitious sulfur-emissions reduction program in 1995. The goal of the program has been to cut the annual sulfur dioxide emissions from power plants by ten million tons from 1980

EXHIBIT 6.1 CAUSES AND CONSEQUENCES OF ACID RAIN

Acid rain is a term commonly used to refer to several processes through which human-generated pollutants increase levels of acidity in the environment. The problem arises when pollutants such as sulfur dioxide and nitrogen oxides are released into the atmosphere, primarily from power plants, metal smelters, factories and motorized vehicles. Some of these pollutants, which are known as precursors of acid deposition, quickly precipitate to the earth in a dry form near their source, where they combine with surface moisture to form acidic solutions. Under certain circumstances, however, these pollutants remain in the atmosphere for periods of up to several days, during which they may be carried by wind sources over considerable distances. While in the atmosphere, the pollutants may undergo a complex series of chemical reactions in the presence of sunlight and other gases, such as ammonia and low-level ozone, which are also generated by human activities. The resulting chemicals may be absorbed by water vapor to form tiny droplets of sulfuric and nitric acids that are washed out of the atmosphere in the form of rain, snow, mist or fog (Parker 1987: 40–8).

Acid rain was largely a localized problem near the source of the pollutants until well into the twentieth century. The problem became increasingly regional as governments began mandating taller smokestacks to disperse pollutants more widely as a strategy for relieving local air pollution problems. Originally, it was thought the pollutants would become so diluted as they were dispersed that they would pose no further problems. By the 1960s, however, it had become apparent that pollutants from the industrial centers of Great Britain and mainland Europe were causing an increasingly serious condition of acidification in southern Sweden and Norway. Subsequent studies soon revealed that large amounts of air pollution were flowing across national frontiers throughout the European region, and between the United States and Canada as well. More recently, much of the pollution responsible for Japan's acid rain has been traced to China and Korea.

Acid rain has several harmful effects. The most visible of its consequences is corrosion of the stone surfaces of buildings and monuments, as well as of metals in structures such as bridges and railroad tracks. In Scandinavia and eastern North America, the heightened acidity of rivers and lakes has been linked to the disappearance of fish and other forms of aquatic life. The severity of the impact of acid rain on freshwater environments varies considerably depending on the extent to which the rocks and soils of the region neutralize the acids. Acid rain also appears to have been a cause of the widespread damage to trees that was observed in the forests of Central Europe by the early 1980s, a phenomenon known by the German word Waldsterben, which means 'forest death'. A similar pattern of forest decline has been observed in eastern North America, especially at the higher levels of the Appalachian Mountains. Scientists have had difficulty, however, isolating the natural processes through which pollution causes widespread damage to trees (Schutt and Cowling 1985).

Acid rain has several potential impacts on human health. Humans get exposed to acidic substances from ambient air during the pre-deposition (dry form) of acid rain. However, the most harmful effects of acid rain to human health arise from the deposition of acidic materials on water and soil that causes the mobilization, transportation and even chemical transformation of toxic metals. Acidification increases the bioconversion of mercury to methylmercury, which accumulates in fish, increasing the risk of toxicity in people who eat fish. Increases in the lead and cadmium content of water and soil raises the human exposure to these metals, in addition to other sources presently under regulatory control (Parker 1987; Soroos 1997).

levels by the year 2000. The acid rain reduction programs in Phase I involved 110 mostly coal-burning plants. Phase II started in the year 2000, immediately following the end of Phase I. In Phase II, the goal was to further reduce sulfur dioxide emissions by another ten million tons per year by 2010. This was supposed to be achieved by increasing the number of power plants participating in the acid rain reduction programs and by further tightening emissions standards—sulfur dioxide emitted per million British thermal units. The projection was that, by 2010, total sulfur dioxide emissions in the United States will dwindle to 8.95 million tons per year.

However, when Congress passed the 1990 Clean Air Act Amendments, the cost of the acid rain control programs was a major concern. The cost estimates for Phase I alone were running as high as $10 billion a year, which is equivalent to $1,000 per ton of sulfur dioxide controlled (Kerr 1998). This cost estimate was based on the assumption that sulfur dioxide emissions will continue to be regulated through 'command-and-control' approaches. Given this, considerable attention was given to searching for cost-effective ways of operationalizing the acid-rain control programs. One outcome of this was the adoption of a flexible system of emissions trading.

Under the system of emissions trading, the EPA still retains the power to set the upper limits on the annual levels of sulfur dioxide emissions for the nation. Furthermore, to achieve the total annual emissions goal, the EPA limits individual power plants under the acid-rain programs by issuing a fixed number of tradable allowances on the basis of historical emissions and fuel use. Each allowance is worth one ton of sulfur dioxide released from the smokestack, and to obtain reductions in emissions the number of allowances declines yearly.

A small number of additional allowances (less than 2 percent of the total allowances) are auctioned annually by the EPA (Tietenberg 1998). At the end of each year, utilities that have emitted more than their pollution credits allow them will be subjected to a stiff penalty, $2,000 per ton. In addition, all power plants under the acid-rain program are required to install continuous emission monitoring systems (CEMS), machines that keep track of how much sulfur dioxide the plant is emitting.

However, although each participant in the acid-rain reduction program is given a fixed number of allowances, power-plant operators are given complete freedom on how to cut their emissions. On the basis of cost considerations alone, a plant operator might install scrubbers (desulfurization facilities that reduce the amount of SO_2 exiting from the stack), switch to a coal with a lower sulfur content, buy or sell allowances, or save allowances for future use. As will be shown shortly, these are the unique features that greatly contributed to the overall flexibility and cost-effectiveness of the United States' acid-rain reduction programs. Note that the overall flexibility of the acid rain reduction programs is not limited to a consideration of allowance trading. The options provided to plant operators with regard to the types of scrubber and the different qualities of coal that they can purchase are significant contributors to the overall flexibility and cost-effectiveness of the acid-rain reduction programs.

Allowance trading can be effected using the *offset*, the *bubble* or the *banking* policies. As discussed in the previous section, the *offset policy* is designed to permit credit in a geographic region known as a non-attainment area—a region in which the level of a given air pollutant (sulfur dioxide, in the case of the acid-rain reduction program) exceeds the level permitted by the federal standards. Under this policy, an increase in sulfur dioxide emissions from a given smokestack can be offset by a reduction in the same pollutant from any other smokestack owned by the purchase of allowances, equal to the offset amount, from other companies in the nonattainment area. Hence, trading offset among companies is permitted, provided the permit requirements are met and the nonattainment area keeps moving towards attainment. This is feasible because companies are required to more than offset (by an extra 20 percent) any pollution they will add to the nonattainment area through new sources. Under the offset policy, the new sources could be new firms entering into the non-attainment area—hence allowing economic growth (Tietenberg 1998).

By contrast, the *bubble policy* allows emissions trading opportunities among multiple emission sources (collectively recognized as forming a bubble) to be controlled by existing emitters. Provided the total pollutants leaving the bubble are within the federal standards, polluters are free to pursue a cost-effective strategy for controlling pollution. In other words, not all sources are held to a uniform emission standard; thus, within a given bubble, emitters are allowed to control some pollution sources less stringently than others, provided a sufficient amount of emission reduction is realized from the other sources within the same bubble.

The emissions *banking policy* simply allows polluters to save their emission allowances for use in some future year. These saved allowances can be used in offset, bubble or for sale to other firms. This is an important feature of the United States' sulfur dioxide reduction program, as it allows firms an opportunity for intertemporal trading and optimization (Schmalensee et al. 1998).

A major study by Chestnut and Mills (2005) estimated the annual benefits in 2010 to be $122 billion (in 2000). For the same year, the total annualized cost is projected to be about $3 billion: $2 billion for reducing SO_2 and $1 billion for reducing NO_x. This indicates a 40 to 1 benefit to cost ratio—a strong endorsement of the ARP program on financial grounds.

In this study, most of the benefits (over $100 billion) in 2010 are attributed to significant reductions in human mortality and morbidity arising from improvements in air quality. The other sources of benefits are associated with reduction in acid deposition, improvements in visibility and damages avoided to forests, materials and structures (see Exhibit 6.1).

The emission reductions attributed to Title IV in 2010 are estimated to be eight million tons of SO_2, 2.7 million tons of NO_x, and ten tons of mercury. The SO_2 emissions in 2010 are expected to be about 50 percent lower than they would have been without Title IV (eight versus 17.3 million tons) (Ibid). The finding by Chestnut and Mills also envisioned a scenario in which the same level of in SO_2 and NO_x reductions could have been achieved without Title IV,

but it would have been only at a substantially higher cost.

The average annual cost of each ton reduction is estimated to be about $250 for SO_2. Previous estimates by the National Acid Precipitation Assessment Program (NAPAP) provided the average annual cost-reduction to be within the range of about $370 to over $800 (NAPAP, 1991). Thus, the estimated average annual cost reduction in 2010 for SO_2 under the ARP is less than expected—about 50 percent of the Program's cost estimated by EPA in 1990 (Ibid). The pertinent question for the purpose of this case study is how much of this cost reduction can be attributed to the ARP SO_2 trading program.

Chestnut and Mills (2005: 255) suggest that:

> costs are lower than originally predicted primarily because flexibility occurred in areas that were thought to be inflexible and technical improvements were made that were not anticipated. Factors contributing to the lower costs include lower transportation costs for low-sulfur coal (attributed to railroad deregulation), productivity increases in coal production leading to favorable prices for low-sulfur and mid-sulfur coal, cheaper than expected installation and operation costs for smokestack scrubbers, and new boiler adaptation to allow use of different types of coal.

None of the above factors explicitly include the ARP SO_2 trading program. This should not be surprising given the expected impacts of this program on costs occur somewhat indirectly. The impacts of the SO_2 trading program would come from the flexibility and incentives it provides for facilities managers to find low-cost compliance operations.

There is strong, although circumstantial, evidence to indicate that the ARP SO_2 trading program has played a major role as a catalyst for improved operational efficiencies and, therefore, for the predicted outcome of lower than expected costs. According to the EPA report in 2010, the allowance market for SO_2 in 2009 was quite robust. There were 2,716 private allowance transfers involving approximately 15.1

million allowances of past, current and future vintages. The total value of the SO_2 allowance market was $1.1 billion and the year-end price for SO_2 was $61 per ton (US EPA 2010). Furthermore, all 3,572 units at ARP facilities complied in 2009 with the requirement to hold enough allowances to cover SO_2 emissions. Sources emitted 5.7 million tons of SO_2 in 2009 (this figure was 15.7 in 1990), well below the current annual emission cap of 9.5 million tons, and already below the statuary annual permanent cap of 8.95 million tons set for compliance in 2010 (US EPA 2010).

Finally, it is also important to note that there have been several other successful applications of emissions trading programs undertaken in the United States. The most notable of these programs have been the programs to phase out leaded gasoline and ozone-depleting chlorofluorocarbons (CFCs) (Nussbaum 1992; Stavins 1998). Furthermore, in recent years, there have been serious efforts by the countries of the European Union (EU) to experiment with carbon trading as a way of fulfilling their commitments to the Kyoto Protocol in ways that would be cost-effective. The preliminary indications of the EU's success are, although somewhat encouraging, too early to evaluate. Thus, the evidence to support the contention that market-based emissions trading systems can assist policymakers to cost-effectively reduce pollution and address environmental damages is not limited to the acid-rain program, established under Title IV of the 1990 Clean Air Act Amendment.

6.4 THE MACROECONOMIC EFFECTS OF ENVIRONMENTAL REGULATIONS: IS THERE A TRADEOFF BETWEEN EMPLOYMENT AND ENVIRONMENTAL PROTECTION?

Introduction

In Chapter 5, and so far in Chapter 6, the focus of the discussion has been on government regulatory policies specifically designed to protect the environment. It was observed that environmental protection entails costs in the form of pollution-abatement capital expenditures. It is important to note that these are expenditures that firms would have been able to avoid

in the absence of government regulations. Thus, when viewed at the aggregate (national) level, environmental regulations could cause a diversion in firms' capital expenditures with potential implications for economy-wide productivity and employment. This section attempts to examine the impacts of environmental protection expenditures (EPE) on jobs.

There exists what appears to be a long-standing public perception that EPE has a negative effect on jobs. In other words, a tradeoff exists between jobs and EPE. It may be difficult to discern the actual reason(s) for why such a perception exists. In part it may be psychological—general fears and anxieties people may have about losing jobs (i.e., job insecurities), especially during periods of economic downturn (i.e., recessions). It may also be the result of misinformation resulting from reports by the news media of stories regarding job losses and factory closures in a given locality or region. In many instances, such reports tend to be sensationalized, which is understandable given the devastating effects that job losses often have on people's lives even when they are confined to a small locality. However, more than anything else, the problems with this kind of reporting are: (1) factory relocations are the normal and frequently occurring events of a dynamic capitalist economy; (2) factory relocations and their associated job losses are caused by several factors, environmental regulation being just one of them; and (3) job losses at a given locality or region may not inform the public of the effect on economy wide employment resulting from the very factor that caused the reported local or regional job loss.

With this as a background, the rest of this section will investigate both the theoretical explanations and empirical evidence for why there may or may not exist a tradeoff between EPE and jobs.

Theoretical arguments for why tradeoff between jobs and EPE may or may not exist

In this subsection, the cases for and against EPE with respect to its impacts on employment are outlined. The fact that this is done suggests that, contrary to conventional wisdom, EPE may actually have a positive *net* impact on jobs.

A. Negative tradeoff exists

This position holds that EPE has adverse impacts on the economy and causes a net loss of jobs. Here are some of the major reasons given by those who support this position:

1. *EPE displaces investment in new plants and equipment*: this refers to the fact that environmental regulations force firms to invest less on 'conventional' capital because they are required by law to invest more on technologies and design standards specifically targeted to control pollution. This has two possible negative implications on firms' investment options. First, firms are not free to make decisions on their entire capital budgets solely on the basis of what they consider to be the most productive use for their primary operations—the production of either intermediate or final goods and services. Second, whether firms have any choice on the part of the capital investment expenditures specifically intended for pollution abatement depends on the policy instruments used by the regulators. For example, a performance-based emission standard may not always allow firms (polluters) to choose any available method to meet the standard.

   These kinds of restrictions on capital expenditures can have detrimental implications for productivity, especially for industries where the ratio of pollution-abatement capital expenditures to total capital outlays is large. For some manufacturing and mining industries in the United States (such as pulp and paper, plastics, petroleum refining, primary metals, electric utilities, and so on) the ratio of pollution-abatement expenditures to total capital outlays could fall in the range of 5 to 15 percent (US Department of Commerce 1993). However, even in this situation, the empirical evidence does not suggest that EPE is associated with net job-loss (Morgenstern et al. 1998).

2. *Environmental regulations require the use of additional labor and capital for compliance purposes*: this refers to the fact that regulated firms have to spend additional money on record keeping and other administrative needs to ensure compliance with the law.

Furthermore, it is also suspected that environmental regulations increase the energy and waste-disposal costs of companies (Goodstein 1994). These additional direct costs to regulated firms may have the effect of reducing productivity (to the extent that it affects expenditure on capital) and profitability.

3. *Environmental regulations cause plant closures and relocations*: the most compelling argument for this claim is the notion that regulated firms make decisions to locate plants in parts of the world where environmental regulations are lax—*pollution havens*. The empirical evidence for this claim has been rather weak (Bezdek et al. 2008; Goodstein 1994). The primary reasons for firms to relocate may have been lower wages and benefits. However, this does not rule out that, in some instances, environmental regulations may have contributed to factory relocations.

4. *Environmental regulations cause increased business uncertainty*: it is often said that while entrepreneurs are risk takers by their nature, they despise uncertainty. In an uncertain environment the probabilities for success or failure are unknown and this often leads to paralysis in the decision-making process of business concerns. Environmental regulations are often accused of contributing to business uncertainty.

   First, working with regulators tends to frustrate business managers because of delays resulting from bureaucratic red tape and slow political decision-making processes. Second, while investment in plants and equipment entail long-term financial commitments, government policies on environmental regulations are subject to change at short notice since environmental standards are often set on the basis of the 'best available technologies'. The overall effect of uncertainty will be to make businesses invest less in new plants and equipment, which is not good for either employment or the economy as whole.

5. *Jobs created by environmental regulations are often low paying and manual*: no question is raised here in recognizing that EPE create more job opportunities in the sectors of the economy that are involved in the production of pollution control

and monitoring devices (such as scrubbers, catalytic converters, etc.) and services (such as the cleanup of coastal ecosystems that have been contaminated by oil spills, recycling, etc.). However, critics argue that jobs in environmental industries tend to be rather low paying manual-labor work. The implication, then, is that these gains cannot offset the loss of highly skilled and highly paid jobs in the manufacturing sector—a sector that, according to some critics, has been adversely and disproportionately impacted by environmental regulations.

6. *Environmental regulations contribute to economy-wide productivity slow-down and in so doing dampen economic growth and job creation*: on the basis of the above five arguments presented against environmental regulations, it is not unreasonable to suspect that EPE, through its capital diversion effects, is likely to contribute to the slow-down of productivity. This is, of course, an empirical question.

Since the 1980s, a number of studies have been conducted to test the extent to which environmental regulations have actually contributed to productivity slow-down in the US and other countries around the world. However, the findings of these studies have been, at best, inconclusive (Crandall 1981; Denison 1979; Gary 1987; Goodstein 1994; Jaffe et al. 1995; Meyer 1992; Portney 1981). One of the major difficulties with research efforts of this nature has been the ability to isolate the independent effects of environmental regulations on productivity. For example, in the 1980s, when the concern for excessive environmental regulations was at its zenith, much of the research that was done in this area had problems with isolating the effect of the environmental regulations from that of the oil price-shocks of the early and late 1970s. In recent years, the challenge has been isolating the independent effects of globalization and environmental regulations on plant closures and job losses in general.

B. Positive tradeoff exists

According to this position, EPE is good for the economy and creates a gain in jobs. Here are some of the major reasons given by those who support this position:

1. *EPE allows the creation of new industries that provide new sources of environmental employment*: over the past four decades, 'technology-forcing regulation'—regulation that pressures the private economy to create new, cleaner technologies that will not only clean up the environment, but also generate whole new businesses and industries—has been growing rapidly. The following are just a few examples of new business opportunities that are likely to emerge when strictly enforced environmental regulations are put in place:

> Removing pollutants from smokestacks means you must install scrubbers. Capturing wind or solar energy means you have to build and install turbines or solar panels. Reducing overall energy consumption means a whole variety of capital investments ranging from weatherization to replacing old HVAC systems. Reducing water use means installing drip irrigation. Reducing polluted storm-water runoff means building greener storm-water facilities-bioswales instead of culverts, for example.
>
> (Fulton 2010)

Clearly EPE generates new job opportunities with a potential to renew the economy. Furthermore, environmental companies are, to varying degrees, located throughout the United States. According to a report by the Management Information Service, Inc. (MISI), EPE for the United States was $301 billion in 2003. It was estimated that, at this level of spending, environmental companies were able to generate about 5 million jobs nationwide (Bezdek et al. 2008). By 2010, EPE was expected to reach $357 billion (in 2003 dollars)—an average annual growth-rate increase of about 2.7 percent during the years between 2003 and 2010. This is a rate of growth greater than the US economy as a whole for the same period of time.

Furthermore, it is argued that, despite the unwarranted claims by the opponents of environmental regulations, a recent study by Bezdek et al. (2008: 70) shows that environmental companies 'employ a wide range of workers at all education and skills levels and at widely differing earnings'.

Despite this empirical evidence, proponents of environmental regulations are disturbed by the fact that few people fully realize the size and job-creating potential of the environmental industry.

2. *Pollution cleanup is a labor-intensive activity*: pollution cleanup is an important aspect of the services performed by environmental companies and it represents a sizeable part of the EP expenditures. Representative EP expenditures of this nature include: cleanup expenditures at Superfund sites, cleaning dirty or contaminated soil, scrubbing oily rocks, uprooting invasive species, and so on. These activities are clearly labor-intensive as they involve slow and meticulous work (Goodstein 1994). These kinds of jobs also require special skills and are likely to be high-paying jobs because of the inherent health-risk factors involved in the workplace for this type of position.

On a theoretical level, it should not be surprising to realize that cleaning an already polluted environment takes more human labor and energy because the effort is intended to reverse entropy (i.e., to go in the direction from high to low entropy). The second law of thermodynamics informs us that any effort to move from disorder to order always comes at a greater cost. This is why pollution prevention (reducing pollution emissions at the source), as argued earlier in Chapter 4, is considered more cost-effective than end-of-pipe pollution-control.

3. *Environmental regulations could have the unintended effect of inducing firms to lower costs and provide a competitive edge*: as argued earlier, technology forcing regulations pressure private companies to be innovative in many ways. One argument to support this point of view is articulated by Goodstein and Hodges (1997: 67): 'When industry is required to lower pollution output, it usually does not just slap a new filter on an existing process; it often invents new technology. Frequently the new technology turns out to have higher productivity benefits'.

Another line of argument that complements the above position is ascribed to a notion that was first articulated by Michael Porter (1990) of the Harvard Business School and it is commonly referred to as the *Porter Hypothesis*. The Porter Hypothesis is based on the recognition that the market for pollution-abatement technology is expanding rapidly both at home and abroad. Thus, firms that have a lead in the development of new pollution-technologies will have *competitive advantages* in these growing domestic and international markets. The Porter Hypothesis, therefore, invokes the idea that strictly enforced environmental policy would have the effect of forcing firms to adopt efficient pollution-abatement technology and production process with long-term benefits in the enhancement of competitive advantage (Porter 1991; Porter and van der Linde 1995). Several empirical studies appear to support this hypothesis (Jaffe et al. 1995; Renner 2000; Repetto 1995; World Resource Institute 1992).

It is also argued that new circumstances are emerging that appear to support strong future growth in global environmental markets. Concerns about global warming and the growing interest within the business community to embrace environmental sustainability (Barrett and Hoerner 2002) are two prime examples that can be cited to support the outlook for healthy and robust growth in global environmental markets. In such an environment, consistent with the Porter Hypothesis, strictly enforced environmental regulations are likely to induce companies to take the lead in the development of relevant and cutting-edge technologies.

4. *EPE and its impact on the economy are exaggerated*: this refers to the tendency to overestimate envi-

ronmental control costs during the public-debate phases (stages) of environmental regulation. Goodstein and Hodge (1997: 64) pointed out the flaw associated with such a position by offering this observation: 'When forecasting the costs for new environmental regulation, economic analysts routinely ignore a primary economic lesson: Market cut costs through innovation. And innovation can be promoted through regulation'. The important lesson here is that *environmental regulations*, when they are implemented, *create situations that will help offset the cost of regulations*. A prime example of this is the strict regulation of CFC emissions that led to the development of affordable substitutes for these substances.

Overestimation of the cost of environmental regulations remains a serious concern despite the fact that examples abound to show that pollution-control costs to firms have been, on average, far less than their initial estimates. This is how Goodstein and Hodge (1997: 69) portrayed this situation:

> Researchers at Resources for the Future recently conducted a study asking how much $1 spent on environmental protection really costs an industry. For some industries, specifically steel, the answer was little more than $1, due to the diversion effect. For others, notably plastics, the industry actually saved money as productivity was boosted. On average, the study concluded $1 spent on environmental pollution-control reflected a real expense of 13 cents. In general then, even when cost estimates are 'correct,' this new research suggests that the reported values often overestimate the true costs to the firms, on average by a factor of seven.

The empirical evidence

In the previous subsection, the seemingly contentious theoretical arguments concerning the relationships between environmental protection, the economy, and jobs have been presented. The central issue in this debate is the existence or absence of tradeoffs between environmental protection and jobs at the aggregate level. In this regard, as indicated earlier, the conventional wisdom has been that the impact of environmental regulations (i.e., environmental protection) on jobs is a *net* loss. On the other hand, as shown in Table 6.1, the empirical evidence accumulated over the past three decades strongly indicates that EPE has created more jobs than it has destroyed. In other words, a tradeoff between environmental protection and employment does *not* exist and, if it does, it has been *positive*. Surprisingly, there were similar findings at regional and state levels. Several studies have indicated that there is no evidence to link job losses with state environmentalism (Meyer 1992; Bezdek et al. 2008).

How can these empirical findings—the absence of a tradeoff between the environment and jobs at both the national and state levels—be reconciled with the conventional wisdom that holds the opposite view? Does this suggest that the conventional wisdom concerning the tradeoff between the environment

Table 6.1 The employment effects of environmental protection expenditures (EPE)

Author(s)[1]	Year	Employment Impact
Hamrin	1975	Positive
Hollenbeck	1978	Negative
Data Resources Inc.	1981	Positive
Bezdek and Wendling	1989	Positive
Meyer	1992, 1993	Positive
Bezdek	1993	Positive
MISI	1993	Positive
Goodstein	1994	Positive
Templet	1995	Positive
Repetto	1995	Positive
Bliese	1999	Positive
Yapijakis	1999	Positive
Jergensen and Wilcoxen	1990	Negative
Bezdek and Wending	2005	Positive

1 These are representative examples of studies that have been done on the tradeoff between the environment and jobs. For more studies of this nature refer to the article by Bezdek et al. (2008).

and employment is simply a 'myth'? If it is a myth, what factors could account for its persistent presence in the minds of the public?

First, it is important to note that the absence of tradeoffs between the environment and jobs at the national or state level does not mean that environmental regulations do not cause job losses and plant closures at local levels. Prime examples in the United States can be found in small communities that rely on jobs in the textile, mining and paper industries for their livelihood. The media reports on plant closures and the resulting job losses in these communities remind the public that environmental regulations can have serious negative impacts on people's livelihoods and ways of life. Events of this nature, depending on how the stories are reported, have the potential to leave permanent psychological scars on the minds of the public about the human costs of environmental protection.

Second, environmental regulations entail coercing private companies to do something that they would have normally avoided doing. Furthermore, environmental regulations, regardless of their economic merits, have the effect of expanding the domain and reaches of government into private affairs. These perceived traits of environmental regulations are often used by special-interest groups (such as industry lobbyists, conservative-leaning policy institutes or think tanks) to reinforce and strengthen the negative public-perception of environmental regulations, regardless of their merits.

Third, in the United States there exists a strong lack of confidence in the government's ability to do something that would actually improve market performance. Thus, it is not inconceivable to imagine that, in the public's mind, the concern of market failure (the real reasons for environmental regulation) may be outweighed by an equally important fear of government failure.

Therefore, taking all of the above factors into consideration, it is not difficult to see why the myth that environmental protection entails a net loss in jobs persists in the public mind. This remains true despite the transformative and often positive impacts of environmental regulation on society at large. There is no better place to see these mixed feelings that society appears to have about environmental regulations than in California—a state known for its large outlays on environmental protection and numerous progressive environmental initiatives. This is presented in Case Study 6.2—a must-read if one wants to fully capture the essence of what has been discussed in this last section of this chapter: the macroeconomic effect of environmental regulations.

CASE STUDY 6.2   DO ENVIRONMENTAL REGULATIONS HURT THE ECONOMY?

William Fulton (March 2010)

Here in California, we are in the middle of not just a recession, but also one of the deepest and most disturbing crises in government finance since the Great Depression. Our state spending is chronically 20 percent above our state revenue. Government services up and down the state are disrupted on a regular basis, followed quickly by a Keystone Cops effort to restore things. And it's never clear from one week to the next whether Wall Street will buy our bonds.

Yet all through this crisis, one aspect of governmental life in California has moved forward unabated: We are constantly creating ever-more-rigorous environmental regulation. Right now, we are implementing one of the world's most aggressive climate change laws—an effort that could fundamentally alter the way we live our lives. We are ramping up our water-quality regulations in a way that will surely cost developers and cities a lot of money. And we continue to push forward on a variety of other fronts, from wetlands to endangered species to coastal protection.

The question that arises from all this is not about environmental protection or quality of life; it's a question about economic development. Is this kind of aggressive regulation a drag on our economy? Or is it the basis for our emerging green economy—and hence the foundation of our future prosperity?

For decades, environmentalists and others on the left have argued that our heavy regulation has actually fueled economic growth—and this argument has only gotten stronger in the last couple of years. Sometimes this has been known as 'technology-forcing regulation'—regulation that pressures the private economy to create new, cleaner technologies that will not only clean up the environment, but also generate whole new businesses and industries that will renew the economy.

Over the past few decades, regulation has transformed the California economy in many ways, but it's not always clear that the result has been positive. Restrictions on oil drilling, for example, have led to less drilling and more environmentally responsible drilling when it occurs—but the reduction in oil production has contributed toward America's ongoing dependence on foreign oil. A net plus? Maybe for somebody like me who lives near the beach, but not necessarily for anybody who drives.

Similarly air-pollution regulations have cleaned up the air—but they have done so partly by driving 'dirty' industries to Arizona, Nevada and Mexico. The air's cleaner here, but it's not clear that this has had a net benefit either to California's economy or the world's environment.

Yet you can't dismiss regulation-driven change as a way to stimulate a more innovative and greener economy. Although environmental protection is often airily advertised as a matter of making different personal choices or forcing corporations to be more responsible, the down-and-dirty fact is that it's mostly a matter of capital investment.

Removing pollutants from smokestacks means you must install scrubbers. Capturing wind or solar energy means you to have to build and install turbines or solar panels. Reducing overall energy consumption means a whole variety of capital investments, ranging from weatherization to replacing old HVAC systems. Reducing water use means installing drip irrigation—not too hard for the average homeowner, but an enormous cost for the average farmer. Reducing polluted storm-water runoff means building greener storm-water facilities—bioswales instead of culverts, for example.

Inevitably many of these capital investments will be made over the course of time—smokestacks will be replaced, as will irrigation systems, storm-water systems and HVAC systems. The trick to environmental protection and prosperity is to use both the sticks and carrots government has available to drive those capital investments in a certain direction on a certain timeline.

A smokestack or an HVAC system will be replaced sooner or later—but if the private market is left to its own devices, these new capital investments may be no greener or efficient than the old ones. An aggressive regulation can force technological innovation by requiring that new capital investments, in fact, be greener than old ones. Oftentimes, however, that's not enough because the payback period on green capital investments can be so long. Low-cost financing programs—from the government or water purveyors or electrical utilities—may also be necessary to bridge the gap.

That's what's happening in California with the energy efficiency financing programs being created under a law known as AB 811. Under the provisions of AB 811, local governments can create assessment districts that will help provide low-cost, long-term financing for homeowners who wish to green their homes, whether through solar panels or HVAC upgrades.

The AB 811 program has been successful and popular in places as diverse as Berkeley, where the climate is moderate but the voters are not, and Palm Desert, where things are more or less the other way around. It wouldn't work without the government carrot of low-cost financing (assuming anybody will buy the AB 811 bonds, but that's another story)—but it also wouldn't be moving as fast if it weren't for California's climate change bill, which essentially forces reductions in energy consumption. Sometimes the carrots and sticks actually do help California through an economic transition—one that protects the environment and creates new economic opportunity in the process.

Source: www.governing.com/columns/eco-engines/Do-Environmental-Regulations-Hurt.html. Permission granted by the Author.

6.5 CHAPTER SUMMARY

The transferable emission credit approach to pollution control requires, first and foremost, the creation of *artificial* markets for pollution rights. A pollution right represents a permit that consists of a unit of a specific pollutant. The role of the regulator is limited to setting the total number of credits and the mechanism(s) by which these credits are distributed among polluters. Once they receive their initial allocation, polluters are allowed to freely exchange credits on the basis of market-established prices. This pollution-control instrument is gaining popularity in recent years, especially in the United States of America.

The primary advantages of transferable emission credits are:

1. They are least interventionist;
2. They are cost-effective, especially when the number of parties involved in the exchange of credits is large;
3. They provide observable market prices for environmental services; and
4. They can be applied to a wide range of environmental problems.

The principal disadvantages of transferable emission credits are:

1. The mechanisms used to distribute credits among potential users could have significant equity implications;
2. The idea of credits to pollute conveys, to some, a reprehensible moral and ethical value;
3. Their applicability is questionable for pollution problems with an international scope, such as global warming;
4. They are ineffective when there are not enough participants to make the market function; and
5. Credits can be accumulated by firms for the purpose of deterring entrants, or by environmental groups for the purpose of attaining the groups' environmental objectives.

Preliminary empirical evidence indicates that the United States' sulfur dioxide emissions trading program has performed successfully. Targeted emissions reductions have been achieved and exceeded, and at costs significantly less than what they would have been in the absence of the trading provisions.

This success would not necessarily apply in cases of international pollution. For example, could an emissions trading program be effective in cutting CO_2 emissions intended to reduce the risk of global warming? It will most likely be less effective than the United States' experiment in sulfur dioxide emissions reduction programs because of the high enforcement and monitoring costs of a pollution problem with a global dimension. Despite this, during the Kyoto summit on climate change one of the most contentious events was the insistence by the United States government to allow the use of TEC as an instrument to control global CO_2 emissions.

Finally, it was shown that taking any action to regulate the market to take into account environmental externalities implies a tradeoff. Therefore, one concern that is often raised is the *macroeconomic* effect of environmental regulations.

In general, environmental regulations are suspected to have a negative effect on the economy for two reasons. First, they increase the private costs to firms. Second, they reduce the productivity of the economy because resources are diverted from the production of goods and services to investment in pollution control. Despite these claims, studies of the effects of environmental policies on macro variables such as productivity and unemployment have been inconclusive. In general, the empirical evidence tends to suggest that environmental regulations have, if anything, a net *positive* effect on employment.

This is not to say, however, that effect of environmental regulation is evenly spread throughout an economy. Indeed, the main source of continued controversies in this area stems from the very fact that some industries (such as textiles and chemicals) are significantly affected by measures taken to regulate the use of the environment. To make matters worse, in the United States the business sector (and for that matter the public at large) seem to have inherent aversion to regulations—even if they are intended to protect the environment. For this reason the myth that there is a tradeoff between job and the environment persists.

REVIEW AND DISCUSSION QUESTIONS

1. Briefly describe the following concepts: emission credits, the grandfathering principle, the emissions bubble policy, the emissions offsets policy, the emissions banking policy, pollution havens, hot-spots, the jobs–environment tradeoff myth, the Porter Hypothesis.

2. As you have read in this chapter, since the mid-1980s the Environmental Protection Agency (EPA) in the United States has seemingly come to increasingly rely on transferable emissions control (TEC) as an instrument to regulate pollution.

    (a) Do you support this fundamental shift in policy from the traditional 'command-and-control' regulation regime to the market-based trading of pollution allowances? Explain.

    (b) Why do you think the rest of the world has been somewhat slow, or not as enthusiastic, in adopting this type of pollution-control policy instrument as the US? For example, it was at the insistence of the US that the rest of the world reluctantly agreed to incorporate emissions trading as part of the Kyoto accord on climate change. Speculate.

3. Environmental organizations have opposed market-based pollution-control policies out of a fear that permit levels and tax rates, once implemented, would be more difficult to tighten over time than command-and-control standards. Is this fear justifiable? Why, or why not?

4. Which of the environmental policy options discussed in this and previous chapters would you recommend if a hypothetical society were facing the following environmental problems? In each case, briefly explain the justification(s) for your choice.

    (a) Pollution of an estuary from multiple source irrigation runoffs;

    (b) Air pollution of a major metropolitan area;

    (c) The clean up of a toxic waste dump;

    (d) Damage to lakes, streams, forests and soil resulting from acid rain;

    (e) A threat to human health due to stratospheric ozone depletion; and

    (f) A well-founded fear for the gradual extinction of endangered species, for example rhinos.

5. Are the following three statements reconcilable? Give reasons for your answers.

    (a) Uncertainty arising from environmental regulation is crippling job creation.

    (b) Environmental regulations enhance innovation and competitiveness.

    (c) Market-based approaches to pollution control provide incentives for continuous inducements seek new technologies.

6. Environmental regulation creates more jobs that it destroys. Do you agree? Discuss.

7. As discussed in this chapter, by all accounts the US acid-rain program has been hailed a success at reducing emissions of SO_2 and NO_x from power plants. The reason for its success is largely attributed for its use of market-based instruments; namely, the emissions trading scheme. Furthermore, the emissions trading program has been enhanced by the use of the offset, the bubble, and emission-banking policies. (a) Do you agree with the overall assessment that the US acid-rain program has been successful? (b) Explain how the offset, the bubble and the emission-banking policies, taken separately and in combination, might have contributed to the further enhancement of the overall efficiency the US sulfur emissions trading program. Be specific.

REFERENCES AND FURTHER READING

Atkinson, S. E. and Tietenbeg, T. H. (1984) 'Approaches for Reaching Ambient Standards in Non-attainment Areas: Financial Burden and Efficiency Consideration', *Land Economics* 60, 2: 148.

Barrett, J. P. and Hoerner, J. A. (2002) 'Clean Energy and Jobs: A Comprehensive Approach to Climate Change and Energy Policy', Economic Policy Institute, Washington, DC.

Bezdek, R. H. (1993) 'Environment and Economy: What's the Bottom Line?', *Environment*, 35 7: 7–32.

Bezdek, R. H., Jones, J. D. and Wendling, R. M. (1989) 'The Economic and Employment Effects of Investments in Pollution Abatement and Control Technologies', *Ambio*, 18, 5: 274–9.

Bezdek, R. H., Wendling, R. M. and DiPerna, P. (2008) 'Environmental Protection, the Economy, and Jobs: National and Regional Analysis', *Journal of Environmental Management* 86: 63–79.

Bezdek, R. H. and Wendling R. M. (2005) 'Potential Long-term Impacts of Changes in US Vehicle Fuel Efficiency Standards', *Energy Policy* 33, 3: 407–19.

Chestnut, G. L. and Mills, M. D. (2005) 'Fresh Look at the Benefits and Costs of the US Acid Rain Program', *Journal of Environmental Management* 77: 255–66.

Crandall, R. W. (1981) 'Pollution Controls and Productivity Growth in Basic Industries', in T. G. Cowing and R. E. Stevenson (eds.) *Productivity Measurement in Regulated Industries*, New York: Academic Press.

Denison, E. P. (1979) *Accounting for Slower Economic Growth: The United States in the 1970s*, Washington, DC: Brookings Institution.

Gary, W. (1987) 'The Cost of Regulation: OSHA, EPA and Productivity Slowdown', *American Economic Review* 5: 998–1006.

Goodstein, E. (1994) 'Jobs and the Environment: The Myth of a National Trade-Off', Washington, DC: Economic Policy Institute.

—— (1995) 'Jobs or the Environment? No Trade-off', *Challenge*, Jan–Feb.

Hahn, R. W. and Hester G. L. (1989) 'Marketable Permits: Lessons for Theory and Practice', *Ecology Law Quarterly* 16: 361–406.

Hollenbeck, K. (1978) 'The Employment and Earnings Impacts of the Regulation of Stationary Source Air Pollution', *Journal of Environmental Economics and Management* 6, 2: 208–21.

Jaffe, A., Peterson, S., Portney, P., and Stavins, R. (1995) 'Environmental Regulation and the Competitiveness of U.S. Manufacturing: What Does the Evidence Tell Us?', *Journal of Economic Literature*, 33, 1: 132–63.

Jergensen, D. and Wilcoxen, P. (1990) 'Environmental Regulation and US Economic Growth, *RAND Journal of Economics* 21, 2: 153–67.

Kerr, R. A. (1998), 'Acid Rain Control: Success on the Cheap', *Science* 282: 1024–7.

Management Information Services, Inc. (MISI) (1993) 'Potential Economic and Employment Impact on the US Economy of Increased Exports of Environmental and Energy Efficiency Technologies under NAFTA', Report Prepared for the White House.

McKinney, B. (2005) 'Environmental Offset Policies, Principles, and Methods: A Review of Selected Legislative Frameworks', Biodiversity Neutral Initiative, www.biodiversityneutral.org/EnvironmentalOffsetLegislative Frameworks.pdf, accessed 6/16/2011.

Meyer, S. (1992) 'Environmentalism and Prosperity: Testing the Environmental Impact Hypothesis', Cambridge, MA: MIT Project on Environmental Politics and Policy.

—— (1993) 'Environmentalism and Prosperity: An Update', Cambridge, MA: MIT Project on Environmental Politics and Policy.

Misiolek, W. S. and Elder, H. W. (1989) 'Exclusionary Manipulation of Markets for Pollution Rights', *Journal of Environmental Economic and Management* 16, 2: 156.

Morgenstern, R. D., Pizer, W. A., Ahih, J. S. (1998) 'Job Versus Environment: An Industry-lever Perspective', Washington, DC: Resources for the Future.

NAPAP (1991) '1990 Integrated Assessment Report', Washington, DC: National Acid Precipitation Assessment Program.

Nussbaum, B. D. (1992) 'Phasing Down Lead and Gasoline in the U.S.: Mandates, Incentives, Trading and Banking', in T. Jones and J. Corfee-Morlot (eds.) *Climate Change: Designing a Tradable Permit System*, Paris: OECD.

Parker, C. C. (1987) *Acid Rain: Rhetoric and Reality*, London: Routledge.

Porter, M. A. (1990) *The Competitive Advantage of Nations*, New York: Free Press.

—— (1991) 'America's Green Strategy', *Scientific American* 263, 4: 168.

Porter, M. A. and van der Linde, C. (1995) 'Toward a New Conception of the Environment–Competitiveness Relationship', *Journal of Economic Perspectives*, Fall: 97–118

Portney, P. (1981) 'The Macroeconomic Impacts of Federal Environmental Regulation', in H. M. Peskin, P. R. Portney and A. V. Knees (eds.) *Environmental Regulation and the U.S. Economy*, Baltimore, MD: Johns Hopkins University Press.

Renner, M. (2000) 'Working for the Environment: A Growing Source of Jobs', Worldwatch Paper 252, Washington, DC: Worldwatch Institute.

Repetto, R. (1995) 'Jobs, Competitiveness, and Environmental Regulations: What are the Real Issues?', Washington, DC: World Resources Institute.

Roberts, M. J. and Spence, M. (1992) 'Effluent Charges and Licenses under Uncertainity', in A. Markandya and J. Richardson (eds.) *Environmental Economics: A Reader*, New York: St Martin Press.

Schmalensee, R., Joskow, P. L., Ellerman, A. D., Montero, J. P. and Baily, E. M. (1998) 'An Interim Evaluation of Sulfur Dioxide Emissions Trading', *Journal of Economic Perspectives* 2, 12: 53–68.

Schutt, P. and Cowling, E. B. (1985) 'Waldsterben, A General Decline of Forests in Central Europe: Symptoms, Development, and Possible Causes', *Plant Disease* 69: 548–58.

Soroos, M. S. (1997) *The Endangered Atmosphere: Preserving Global Commons*, Columbia, SC: University of South Carolina Press.

Stavins, R. N. (1995) 'Transaction Costs and Tradable Permits', *Journal of Environmental Economics and Management* 29, 2: 133.

—— (1998) 'What Can We Learn from the Grand Policy Experiment? Lessons from SO2 Allowance Trading', *Journal of Economic Perspectives* 2, 12: 69–88.

Templet, P. H. (1995) 'The Positive Relationships Between Jobs, Environment, an Economy', Spectrum of the Institute of Electrical and Electronics Engineers.

Tietenberg, T. H. (1990) 'Economic Instruments for Environmental Regulation', *Oxford Review of Economic Policy* 6, 1: 17.

—— (1998) 'Ethical Influences on the Evolution of the US Tradable Permit Approach to Air Pollution Control', *Ecological Economics* 24: 241–57.

US Department of Commerce (1993) 'US Statistical Abstract, Table 1256': 12-13.

US EPA (2010) '2009 Environmental Results', www.epa.gov/airmarkets/progress/ARP09_3.html, accessed 6/15/2011.

World Resource Institute (1992) *World Resources 1992–93*, New York: Oxford University Press.

Yapijakis, C. (1999) 'The Myth of Job Versus the Environment', New York: Environmental Research Laboratory, Cooper Union School of Engineering.

Chapter 7

Economic valuation of environmental goods and services

According to the current paradigm in economics 'The ecosystem is viewed as external to society, providing goods and services, unoccupied territory in which to expand, and assimilative capacity to handle by-products . . . Economics seeks to integrate this externalized environment into its own paradigm through the concept of 'valuation.' This approach sounds reasonable on the surface. Society should place a monetary value on the goods and services provided by the ecosystem and also on the effects of human activity on the ability of the ecosystem to provide these goods and services. Values for these 'externalities' can then be inserted into the economic model. Within the economic model, these externalities would provide the self-regulation needed to manage society's use of the environment.

(O'Neill and Kahn 2000: 333)

LEARNING OBJECTIVES

After reading this chapter you will be familiar with the following:

- ■ How the environmental-damage function actually represents the demand function for improved environmental quality or avoided damage cost.
- ■ Methodological issues in the valuation of environmental benefits or avoided damages:
  - (a) Valuation yardstick: willingness to pay (WTP) versus willingness to accept (WTA);
  - (b) What is actually being measured: the value of the 'environment' or something else; and
  - (c) The scope of measurement: incremental changes in ecosystem services.
- ■ Revealed preference valuations methods: why the attempt to elicit willingness to pay for ecosystem services requires not one, but several 'indirect' valuation techniques.
- ■ The notions of 'non-use' and 'total' values of ecosystem services.
- ■ Stated preference valuation methods: the challenges of measuring the non-use values ecosystem services.
- ■ The contingent valuation method.
- ■ Critical assessments of the economic approach to environmental valuation.

This chapter addresses the most challenging and critically important subject in environmental economics. The challenge arises from the arduous conceptual and methodological tasks involved in imputing values to many aspects of the environmental services that lack observable market prices. Despite this, as presented in some detail throughout this chapter, in recent years economists have been making measurable advances in environmental valuation techniques. This is a very important progress, as it will potentially make the justifications for the conservation of environmental resources easier.

7.1 INTRODUCTION

Humans continuously draw benefits (utility) from environmental goods and services (such as clean air, clean water, scenic views, harvesting of animals and plants, provision of wildlife habitats, carbon cycling, prevention of soil erosion, biological diversity, and so on). However, as discussed in Chapters 3 and 4, because most of the goods and services provided by nature are not traded in the market it is, if not impossible, difficult to put a price tag on them. Yet, it would be hard to justify the implementation of public policies that would prevent the excessive use (or abuse) of environmental goods and services without some ideas about their benefits. These benefits, if they can be measured in monetary terms, would provide society with not only an estimate of the value of these resources but also the opportunity costs of failing to act to avoid environmental damage (such as excessive soil erosion, excessive levels of air and water pollution, loss of biodiversity, etc.).

Thus, Chapter 7 deals with the various ways in which economists approach the valuation of ecosystem services. This is a very important topic in environmental economics as it provides the much-needed information on the 'benefit' side of cost–benefit analysis of environmental projects (e.g., a government mandate for stricter hazardous-waste disposal or the preservation of wilderness areas). In Section 7.2 the methodological issue of valuing the environment will be addressed. More specifically, an attempt will be made to clarify what specific measuring-stick economists use to value the environment and what exactly economists mean by the 'value' of an environment.

Section 7.3 explores the various environmental valuation methods economists use, that rely on the observation of people's actual market behavior, whether directly or indirectly revealed. Section 7.4 deals with environmental valuation methods where

values are inferred from individuals' *stated* responses to hypothetical market-like situations. Section 7.5 provides critical assessment of the standard economics approach to environmental valuation. A summary of the chapter is given in the last section, Section 7.6.

Please note before starting to read the next section that *willingness to pay*, *consumer surplus*, and *producer surplus* are three key concepts that will be repeatedly used in this chapter. The material in Section A.3 of Appendix A will be helpful for a quick review of these concepts.

7.2 VALUATION OF ENVIRONMENTAL AMENITIES AND AVOIDED DAMAGES: THE METHODOLOGICAL ISSUE

Economists use willingness to pay (WTP) as the standard measuring stick of benefit. WTP is measured by the demand price at the margin. For example, in Figure 7.1 P_1 represents what consumers are willing to pay for the 10th unit of a given good or service, Q. Similarly, P_e would be a measure of consumers' willingness to pay for the twentieth unit of output. For products where a market exists, individuals exercise choice by comparing their WTP with the price of the product under consideration. They purchase the good or service when their WTP equals or exceeds the price, and not otherwise. For example, in Figure 7.1, if P_e is assumed to be the market equilibrium price, all those consumers whose WTP is represented by P_1 will be expected to decide to purchase this good or service. Thus, viewed this way, *decision-making based on WTP must reflect individuals' preferences for the good in question*. What does this mean to our task at hand, the measurement of social benefits from an environmental project?

To answer this question more clearly, let us assume that the specific project under consideration is a government mandate to control sulfur emissions from electric power plants located in certain regions of a nation. In this case, the benefit is derived from improved air quality or the environmental damage avoided as a result of reduced sulfur emissions—a precursor of acid rain. Benefits of this nature are measured using WTP once it is realized that the MDC curve actually represents the demand curve for environmental quality. To demonstrate this, in Figure 7.2 the MDC is drawn in a slightly different way than it has been displayed in the previous three chapters. The x-axis in this case measures the reduction of sulfur emission (i.e., environmental cleanup) instead of the amount of sulfur emitted into the environment.

Thus, a rightward movement along the x-axis starting from the origin (which represents zero cleanup effort or the benchmark level of SO_2 emissions, Q^*) signals the improvement in environmental quality resulting from the SO_2 pollution damage that is avoided. Once this is understood, the MDC curve in Figure 7.2 depicts the amount society is willing to pay to avoid damage (or cleanup) at the margin. In other words, it measures society's WTP for improved environmental quality on an incremental basis, hence the demand curve for environmental quality. Note that this demand curve is negatively sloped, indicating that society's WTP declines as higher levels of environmental quality (more cleanup) are sought—

an observation that is consistent with the law of demand (see Section A.3 of Appendix A).

Going back to our earlier question, how does this help us to develop a general framework for the measurement of social benefit from an environmental project? To answer this question more clearly, suppose point A on the demand curve represents the situation that prevailed before the project was initiated. Note that the project here is the legislative mandate to control sulfur emissions. Thus, before the mandate, individuals were willing to pay the price P_1 to avoid the last unit of sulfur emission, Q_1. Now, suppose that due to the new mandate, sulfur emission is reduced from Q_1 to Q_2. That is, with the stricter sulfur-pollution control (more cleanup), society is allowed to move from point A to C along its demand curve for environmental quality. At the new position, point C, individuals are willing to pay the price P_2 in order to avoid the last unit of emission; that is, Q_2. Given this, what is the *total* social benefit of this project?

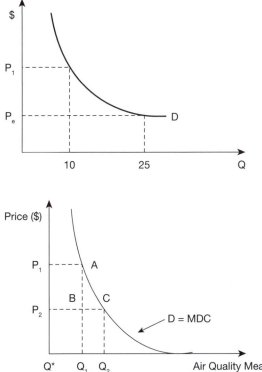

Figure 7.1 *Demand price as a measure of consumers' willingness-to-pay. Demand measures the price, P, households are willing to pay for a specified quantity of goods, Q, provided in the market at a point in time, holding all other factors affecting demand constant.*

Figure 7.2 *Given the MDC curve represents the demand for environmental quality, the total value of an environmental project that is expected to reduce SO_2 emission from Q_1 to Q_2 will be measured (imputed) by the area Q_1ACQ_2. The sum of the marginal WTP (Prices) on emission of SO_2 is reduced from Q_1 to Q_2.*

119

This total benefit is represented by the area under the demand curve—area Q_1ACQ_2, which represents the sum of society's willingness to pay for moving from its initial position, point A, to the new position, point C. A total benefit derived in this fashion is subject to several interesting interpretations. One interpretation is to view it as a measure of the *maximum* sum of money members of a given society are willing to pay to reduce sulfur emission from Q_1 to Q_2. Hence, viewed this way, it is a measure of WTP. Alternatively, it could be interpreted as the *minimum* monetary compensation that members of a given society need to voluntarily accept if the proposed project (reduction in sulfur emission from Q_1 to Q_2) is *not* undertaken. This is a measure of *willingness to accept* (WTA).

To consider that WTP and WTA are *equivalent* would suggest that people value gains and losses similarly. If people do not in fact do this, if they weigh losses more heavily than gains for example, there may be a higher value on preserving environmental amenities than the economic estimates based purely on WTP would indicate. This would also be a result consistent with the usual assumption of the convexity (absence of discontinuity) of the consumers' preference function (for a detailed discussion on this subject matter see Hanemann (1991)).

Furthermore, it is important to note that since economic valuation of benefit is based on the concept of WTP, the area Q_1ACQ_2, measures people's 'preferences' for changes in the state of their environment (Pearce 1993). What this suggests is that when economists attempt to measure the benefits from improved environmental quality, they are measuring not the *value* of the environment but the *preferences of people for an environmental good or environmental bad*.

To further clarify this, consider the following: one effect of a higher air-quality standard may be an improvement in human health, which causes a decrease in the average mortality rate. Thus, in this particular case, benefit is synonymous with increased 'life' expectancy. Despite this, the economic measure of benefit makes no pretension of valuing 'life' as such. Instead, the measure is of people's preferences for a healthier and longer life. Essentially, then, *economists*

do not and cannot measure the value of life or the environment as such. Instead, what they attempt to measure is the *preferences* of people for a healthier life or for a preservation of environmental amenities. This, indeed, represents one of the key methodological foundations of the economic valuation of environmental quality.

At this stage it is very important to note the following three salient points when benefits from avoided environmental damages are derived using the above valuation methodology:

1. Valuation of the environment is based on human preferences alone, and it is assumed that all aspects of environmental damage can be valued in monetary terms. This means that a dollar value should be assigned to species and ecosystems that are considered to be irreplaceable. The alternative is, of course, to assume that nothing in life is irreplaceable (or everything has substitutes).

2. As shown in Figure 7.2, the estimation of benefit is not time-specific. This approach either assumes perfect foresight or simply neglects to address the *uncertainty* involved in environmental damage. This is an important point to keep in mind since many relevant environmental concerns (such as acid rain, ozone depletion, climate change, species preservation, etc.) involve a considerable degree of uncertainty (Krutilla 1967).

3. This approach assumes that the changes in environmental quality (such as the move from A to C in Figure 7.2), are reasonably *small*. In other words, what is being treated as measureable is the value (benefit) of incremental change in environmental service. Thus, when viewed from a larger perspective, losses from environmental damage are too small to count (Johansson 1990). It is important to understand, however, that small changes would not precipitate major disturbance only if one assumes a convex world (i.e., absence of extremes and discontinuity)—in both its economic and ecological contexts (O'Neill and Kahn 2000).

Thus far the discussion has focused on the methodological basis for measuring environmental benefits.

This methodology measures economic benefits on the basis of individuals' WTP. However, to measure benefit by WTP is not sufficient by itself, since the actual measurement of WTP requires *information on the prices* (i.e., demand) which—in the case of environmental assets—are, if not impossible, difficult to obtain directly through the usual market mechanism. Therefore, economists have no choice but to look for various *alternative techniques* of directly and indirectly eliciting WTP for environmental assets. In recent years considerable advances have been made in this area and a fairly wide range of techniques are now available for eliciting WTP for various aspects of environmental assets, which is the subject of the next section.

Please note that this chapter goes beyond the presentation of the various techniques standard economists use to measure the value of environmental services that are based on the elicitation of WTP. Section 7.5, consistent with what has been the main feature of this book, presents a critical assessment of the standard approaches of environmental valuation.

7.3 ALTERNATIVE METHODS FOR ELICITING WILLINGNESS TO PAY FOR ENVIRONMENTAL GOODS AND SERVICES: REVEALED PREFERENCE VALUATION METHODS

In the previous section we explored the methodological issues pertaining to the measurement of benefits from environmental improvement. Economists appear to agree that such benefits or avoided-damage costs should be measured by eliciting individuals' *WTP for incremental changes in environmental quality*. Once the issue is identified this way, then the challenge lies in discovering methods of eliciting this information when market failure is the rule rather than the exception. This section discusses the techniques most commonly used by economists to elicit people's WTP for changes in the quality of environmental services or assets.

The choice of the specific technique to elicit WTP depends on the types of environmental damages that

are avoided in order to achieve the desired environmental quality. Among others, these may include:

- Impairment to human health—a higher risk of mortality and morbidity;
- Loss of economic outputs, such as fish harvest and extraction of certain minerals;
- Increased exposure to environmental nuisances, such as noise, odor and debris;
- Amenity and aesthetic losses;
- Simplification of natural habitats; and
- Irreversible damage to an ecosystem.

While several techniques may be used to elicit a WTP to avoid a particular type of environmental damage (for example, noise), *economists have yet to develop a single technique that could be used effectively in all circumstances*. Also, in a specific situation some techniques tend to be better than others. Thus, as will be evident from the discussion in the rest of this chapter, economists use several valuation methods. Furthermore, in many cases the choice of technique could be an important issue in itself.

Finally, the various valuation methods presented in this section share two very important common elements. First, WTP is elicited by using market prices either explicitly or implicitly (such as prices of substitutes and complementary goods and services). A phrase often used to describe the valuation methods that are covered in this section is *revealed preference*. Revealed preference works on the notion that WTP should be elicited by observing the *actual* purchasing behavior of resource users in real market settings. Four distinctly different approaches that follow the underlying logic of the revealed-preference methodology are discussed in this section, namely, market pricing, replacement cost, hedonic pricing and household-production function (which includes aversive expenditures and travel-costs) approaches. In Section 7.4 non-market valuation methods will be presented.

The market-pricing approach

The market-pricing approach is used when the environmental improvement under consideration causes an increase or decrease in real outputs and/or inputs. Examples may include a decrease in timber harvest and/or extraction of minerals from a legislative enactment that effectively expands the acreage set aside as a wilderness area; the expected increase in fish harvest due to the implementation of a new water-pollution control technology; or an increase in crop yield arising from a legislative mandate of a higher air-quality standard.

In the above examples, benefits from environmental improvement (avoided damage) are identified in terms of changes in outputs or inputs; more specifically, in timber, minerals, fish and crops. These outputs or inputs are expected to have market prices that accurately reflect their scarcity values or, where this is not the case, shadow prices (i.e., values of similar goods in private markets). Thus, where environmental improvement is directly associated with changes in the *quantity or price of marketed outputs or inputs*, the benefit directly attributable to the environmental improvement in question can be measured by changes in *social surplus* (composed of consumers and producers). In the analysis to follow only consumers' surplus is considered, mainly to make the analysis simple. This is also why the supply curve in Figure 7.3 is drawn as a horizontal line—it is perfectly elastic.

Consumers' surplus refers to the difference between what consumers are willing to pay and what they have actually paid at the prevailing market price and quantity. The main idea is that consumers would stand to benefit (gain surplus) when market prices are lower than what they are actually willing to pay (for more on this concept see Section A.3 of Appendix A). To illustrate how consumers' surplus can be used in the evaluation of benefit arising from an environmental policy mandate, consider a hypothetical case where a significant increase in crop yield has been realized due to an improved air-quality standard. As shown in Figure 7.3, the actual effect of the higher air-pollution standard is a shift in the supply curve from S_0 to S_1, indicating an improvement in crop yield. In other words, since improved air quality enhances crop yield, other things equal, at every level of output farmers are now willing to sell their crop at a lower

price than prior to the legislative enactment to improve environmental quality. As a result of the shift in the supply curve, the market equilibrium price for the agricultural commodity will fall from P_0 to P_1.

As shown in Figure 7.3, at the original equilibrium position (P_0, Q_0), the consumers' surplus is indicated by the area of the triangle $P_m BP_0$. On the other hand, at the new equilibrium, (P_1, Q_1), the new consumers' surplus is now represented by the area of the triangle $P_m CP_1$. Thus, the net effect of the new environmental policy is to increase consumers' surplus (i.e., the benefit to society) by the area $P_0 BCP_1$ (area $P_m CP_1$ − $P_m BP_0$). What is significant about this is that the benefit from the environmental project is measured entirely using WTP—the standard measuring-stick of benefit.

For an excellent case study that uses the market-pricing approach see Dixon and Hufschmidt (1986: 102–20). These authors estimated a value for the loss of the fishery resource caused by the coastal development of Tokyo Bay using the market value of lost marine products (shrimp and crab, seaweed and fish) production.

Another variation of the market-pricing approach is the use of the *opportunity cost* scenario. For example, Kremen et al. (2000) used the opportunity cost

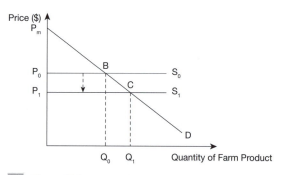

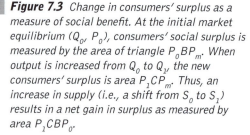

Figure 7.3 Change in consumers' surplus as a measure of social benefit. At the initial market equilibrium (Q_0, P_0), consumers' social surplus is measured by the area of triangle $P_0 BP_m$. When output is increased from Q_0 to Q_1, the new consumers' surplus is area $P_1 CP_m$. Thus, an increase in supply (i.e., a shift from S_0 to S_1) results in a net gain in surplus as measured by area $P_1 CBP_0$.

method in a case study that dealt with forest conservation and development programs in Madagascar. The case study specifically dealt with preserving a 33,000 hectare area of tropical forest (Masoala National Park and surrounding buffer zone). The opportunity cost approach simply looks at the land use that produces the highest alternative return. At the national level, it was estimated that the highest return would result from large-scale industrial logging concessions—implying that the Masoala Peninsula should become a forestry concession instead of a national park. How does the opportunity cost approach approximate the WTP as measuring-stick of value? The opportunity cost approach performs the magic by using *shadow prices*—values of similar products in the private market. In this particular case study, the value from large-scale industrial logging concessions (in other words the commercial value of forest products) is used to impute the forgone benefit of conserving the land so that it can be used as a national park.

The market-pricing approach has several limitations. Among them, the major ones are: (1) few ecosystem services are bought and sold in the markets, hence its application is very limited; (2) prices may be distorted due to market imperfections and government interventions (such as farm subsidies); and (3) net benefit that depends on empirically estimated consumers and producer surpluses are likely to be compromised due to errors in the specifications of demand and supply functions.

The replacement cost approach

The replacement cost approach is used as a measure of benefit when the damage that has been avoided by improved environmental conditions can be approximated by the market value of what it would have cost to *restore* or *replace* the damage in question. For example, acid rain, among its other effects, is known to accelerate the deterioration of a nation's infrastructure, such as highways, bridges and historic monuments. Suppose a given nation passed a bill that reduces the emissions of acid rain precursors (sulfur and nitrates) by 50 percent. For the sake of simplicity,

assume that all the sources of these pollutants emanate from within the boundary of the nation. One obvious outcome of a mandate of this nature is to slow down the deterioration of the nation's physical infrastructure. If the replacement cost approach is used to measure this gain from avoided environmental damage, the benefit will be assessed on the basis of the savings realized from reduced expenditures on repairing, restoring and replacing the nation's infrastructure.

In exactly what way does the replacement cost approach measure people's WTP? It can elicit people's WTP to the extent that the reduction in replacement and restoration costs (due to improved environmental conditions) closely reflects people's WTP to avoid environmental damage (Pearce 1993). This response is qualified because *replacing lost services rests on the assumption that the public will accept a one-to-one tradeoff between a unit of services lost due to damage and a unit of service gained due to restoration.*

However, in some cases it may be impossible to completely repair or replicate environmental damage. Even if it could be replicated, the replicas would probably be of little worth compared to the original. An example of this would be an attempt to estimate the value of a wetland area that is earmarked for housing development by what it would cost to restore or replicate it somewhere else in the vicinity of the original site. In this instance, other non-market-based methods of benefit assessment, such as contingent valuation (to be discussed in the next section), would be more appropriate. For this reason, the replacement cost approach should be used with some care. The use of this method could be quite tempting because it is generally easy to find what *appear to be* rough but fairly adequate estimates of replacement costs.

As an example, in one case study (Dixon and Hufschmidt 1986: 63–82) the replacement cost approach was used to estimate the cost of recovering and replacing eroded soil from an agricultural project in Korea. The productive asset that had been damaged was the soil in the upland areas. The costs of physically replacing lost soil and nutrients were used as a benchmark by which to measure the replacement costs. These costs were then the minimum benefits to be realized from preventive steps (new soil management techniques) that could be undertaken to restore and maintain the original productivity of the damaged soil.

An area where the replacement cost approach is most commonly used is in the assessment of the economic values of a specific service (or services) provided by wetland ecosystems, such as flood and flow control, storm buffering, sediment retention, groundwater recharge/discharge, water-quality maintenance, and water-quality retention. Alternatively, if a specific wetland ecosystem service can be achieved using technical substitutes (such as dams to control flooding or flood plains as nutrient sinks to improve water quality), then the cost of this substitute to replace the specific ecosystem service can be regarded as the economic value of the wetland's service.

It is important to note that what the replacement cost is measuring here is the *indirect use* of the specific wetland ecosystem functions. Furthermore, the substitute may not provide exactly the same service(s) as the natural resources that are to be valued. With this as a caveat, several studies have found that valuation using replacement cost approach to be quite appropriate in several instances (Brander et al. 2006). However, if the interest is to assess the monetary value of *ecosystem functions* then, as will be shown in Section 7.4, other valuation methods are needed. This is because a dam or flood plain can only replace a specific service (or services) of an ecosystem but not the ecosystem function(s). The important lesson here is that great care must be taken in applying the replacement cost valuation method and the interpretation of the estimated avoided-damage cost (hence, benefit) arrived at through the application of this method.

Hedonic pricing methods

A. Environmental amenities associated with property values

Environmental features can increase land and house values if they are viewed as attractive or desirable, or they can reduce values if they are viewed as being dangerous or a nuisance, and therefore undesirable. For example, because of the associated odor, noise, debris and health risk, people in search of housing sites would tend to equate a landfill site's proximity with diminished environmental quality (Milla et al. 2005; Nelson et al. 1992; Sander and Polasky 2009). Given a choice between two houses offered for the same price, and that are identical in every respect other than the fact that one is closer to a landfill site, home buyers will choose the house that is further away. Only when the closer house is offered for less money will families consider it a suitable alternative. At some lower market price for the closer house, homebuyers will become indifferent in choosing between that house and a higher-priced one further away from the landfill site.

In this way, then, people are *implicitly* revealing their WTP for avoiding the nuisances associated with a landfill by paying higher prices for houses located further away from such a site. This is the typical case of a *hedonic price* where the value or price of an environmental feature (neighborhood amenities, clean air, clean water, serenity, etc.) is imputed by looking at the *effect that its presence has on a relevant market-priced goods* (such as, property value). Other examples where hedonic prices can be used effectively include noise pollution by a point source (an airport, say), which can reduce the nearby residential property values; the effect of the construction of a nuclear plant on the property values of nearby residential areas; and urban residential development and its effect on nearby agricultural land value. How is hedonic valuation carried out in practice?

Hedonic valuation uses statistical methods to estimate how much of the overall price (say of housing) is due to a given environmental attribute or amenity. The analysis starts by establishing a functional relationship between a set of *independent* and *dependent* variables (Ekeland et al. 2004). In the case of housing, the attributes constituting the independent variables may include location, lot size, scenery, number of rooms, floor space, mechanical systems, age, school district, property tax level, and so on. The dependent variables are observed market prices for housing. The analyst collects data for these variables on as many parcels of property as is practical. These data are fitted statistically to produce estimated coefficients for an identity called the *hedonic price function* (see Figure 7.4 for a prototype hedonic demand function). The coefficients of the price function express a unit dollar value (marginal price) associated with a unit of measurement for each attribute.

For example, Nelson et al. (1992) conducted an empirical study to estimate the price effects of landfill sites on house values. Using a sample of 708 single-family homes in Ramsey, Minnesota, that were located near a landfill site, they found that the site adversely affected home values. More specifically, according to the empirical results of this study, 'house value rises by nearly $5,000 for each mile it is located away from the landfill. On a percentage basis, house value rises by about 6.2 percent per mile from the landfill' (1992: 362).

A problem with the above finding is that it assumes that the unit dollar value revealed by the hedonic price function will remain constant regardless of the level of the environmental quality, in the above example, at $5,000 for each mile away from the landfill site. However, in many instance, one would expect the unit value to be higher for homes closer to the landfill site. Economists approach this problem by applying a statistical technique known as a *second stage of the hedonic valuation methods* (a discussion of this method is beyond the scope of this text). Thus, the two-stage hedonic valuation method produces values for both a one-unit change and a multi-unit change from the sample average value of the environmental amenity (Songhen 2001).

In our earlier example, Nelson et al. (1992) applied the second stage of the hedonic valuation methods and reported the following. As would be expected, the effect of a landfill site on house values varies with distance. The adverse effect on home values was 12 percent for homes located at the landfill boundary and 6 percent at about one mile. The adverse effect on home values was negligible for homes that were located beyond two miles from the landfill site.

In another more recent study, Sander and Polasky (2009) examined how environmental amenities, particularly views and access to open space, impacted on the sale price of residential homes in Ramsey County, Minnesota, using a hedonic pricing model. Their findings showed that home sale-prices increase with closer proximity to parks, trails, lakes and streams. Proximity to lakes produced the greatest impact on home sales, followed by parks, trails and streams.

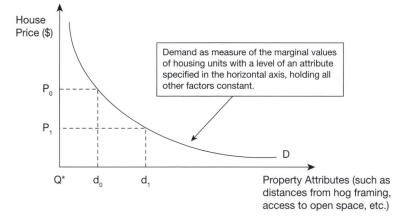

Figure 7.4 *The hedonic housing price method. Indicates the marginal values, P_y, of housing units associated with different levels of the attribute specified on the horizontal axis. It is important to note that hedonic pricing method of this nature has been used to place a value to environmental quality, climate change, and urban policies, such as traffic calming and pedestrian zone schemes.*

The above discussions focused the application of a hedonic price approach on cases where environmental attributes can be inferred by looking at the market prices for housing and/or land or, in general, property values. In cases where such data are easily available, a hedonic price approach can be of great utility because it is based on people's *actual* behavior. In other words, the derived values reflect real commitments of consumer resources to achieve specific environmental quality improvement. Hedonic valuation of this nature is also significant because the purchase price of a house represents a large share of most consumers' income (welfare). Thus, the value attached to the residential environment should represent a large share of the overall value attached to environmental quality.

Although the above discussions appear to limit the use of hedonic pricing to property values, the approach has been used, among others, to estimate the demand for environmentally friendly products, such as organic food, clothing outfits, etc. (Huang and Biing-Hwan 2007). Thus, in applying the hedonic pricing approach the *key requirement* is that the market goods and services under consideration are affected by *changes in the quantity of environmental goods and services*. In other words, the prices (values) for houses, organic foods, and environmentally friendly clothing outfits are all affected by changes in people's preferences about some environmentally induced attributes (such as less noise, improved nutritional quality, lower health-risk, and so on).

Another area where a hedonic pricing approach can be effectively applied is in the economic valuation of changes in human-health conditions, such as *mortality* (premature death) and *morbidity* (illness), primarily associated with exposure to workplace environmental hazards or pollution. In these cases, as will be explained in the next subsection, WTP is inferred from available data on medical expenditures and income or wages.

B. Valuation of health risks from exposure to workplace environmental pollution and hazards

Pollution is often perceived as an environmental factor that exposes humans to some degree of health risk. For example, groundwater contamination that is caused by toxic-waste disposal on a landfill site that is not properly sealed may be a serious human-health hazard. This health hazard, over time, may result in a significantly higher than average incidence of disease and premature death among the population in the nearby community. Similar results can occur from workplace exposure to toxic chemicals, carcinogens, or other environmental hazards. How can one measure, in monetary terms, an environmental effect that increases the mortality and morbidity rates of a community? Are we not here implicitly measuring such things as human 'life', pain and suffering? After all, is not life priceless?

These are all legitimate questions. However, as stated in Section 7.2, if benefits from avoiding environmental damage are to be measured by means of individuals' WTP, what is being measured is not values of 'life' or 'pain' but *people's preferences for health risk*—how much damage they are willing to avoid. People take risks of this nature on a daily basis. What else can explain people's behavior when they drive a car, especially on congested highways such as the Los Angeles freeways? Accordingly, then, the 'life' that is measured is a 'statistical life'. With this caveat, how can one measure morbidity and mortality using the hedonic price approach?

When applying the hedonic price approach, *morbidity* risks associated with workplace environmental hazards are assumed to be factored into wages paid by different occupations. That is, jobs which are associated with a higher than average health risk, such as mining, tend to pay risk premiums in the form of higher wages. Such wage–risk differentials can be used for measuring changes in morbidity resulting from environmental pollution. For example, let us assume that the average wage of coal miners is $25 an hour, whereas the average wage of blue-collar workers in the manufacturing sector is only $15 an hour. The $10 wage premium offered in the mining industry can be used as a measure of the relatively higher health risk associated with this industry. In other words, the compensating wage differential, in our example $10, is presumed to be sufficient to entice a worker to accept a less desirable or more hazardous job such as mining, rather than work on an assembly line with less risk to the worker's safety. One obvious problem with this approach is that it assumes that workers have the economic freedom to choose among occupation alternatives.

Similar to what was done to analyze the adverse effects of landfills on home values in the previous subsection, statistical methods are used to construct a functional relationship between environmental risk and the level of workers' compensation. In this case, the dependent variables are wage rates for similar occupational categories and the independent variable are attributes of risk, such as different levels of exposure to environmental hazards. The major challenge here is being able to control statistically for all the non-safety-related differences between the different occupational categories in order to isolate the difference in wages associated with the difference in safety. If this is successfully accomplished, the final statistically fitted *hedonic wage function* would reveal how much compensation, on average, workers require to accept more environmental risk.

Another health-related area where hedonic valuation is considered is in the economic evaluation of *premature mortality*, in general. Here, the economic value of interest is approximated by society's loss of labor productivity (lost real income) as a result of an individual's premature death caused by specific pollution-related ailments. The valuation approach used in this case relies on calculating the *present discounted value* (to be discussed in the next chapter) of future earnings that were lost due to premature mortality. An empirical study conduced by Peterson (1977) should help clarify how this method actually works in a fairly straightforward manner.

This study dealt with estimating the social cost of Reserve Mining Corporation discharges of non-magnetic rock or tailings into Lake Superior. The tailings contaminated the lake's water with asbestos-form fibers—a known carcinogen. This incidence exposed the North Shore citizens to serious health risks since these communities draw their public water from the lake. It was estimated that contamination of the lake water would increase the average annual number of deaths in the North Shore region by 274 over the 25 years of remaining operation of the plant. It was also determined that the mean age at death of the North Shore victims would be 54 years of age, or 12.8 years less than the average life expectancy of a US male, which was 66.8 years.

In addition, the social cost caused by each individual premature death was computed by estimating the annual present value of the lost productivity society suffers from each victim. This was estimated to be $38,849 (at 1975 prices) per victim. Then, given the projected 274 deaths per year, the total social cost imposed by Reserve's pollution to the North Shore community was estimated to be $10,644,626.

At this point, note that the estimate of $38,849 (the equivalent of about $163,166 in 2011) does not represent the value of the 12.8 extra years of life to an individual. Can you imagine anyone willing to sacrifice 12.8 years of her or his life for as little as $39,849 (in 1975) or even ten times that figure? To an individual, life, however short, cannot be given a price. Therefore, what the above estimate measures is the economic value of 12.8 years of statistical life and nothing else (Mishan 1971).

In 2008 the US EPA estimated the value of a statistical life to be $6.9 million. This value was arrived at on the basis of insurance claims and wrongful death lawsuits (i.e., claims for job-related fatalities). Thus, unlike the example above, this estimate is not based on people's earning capacity or potential contributions to society based on data drawn from payroll statistics (The Associated Press 2008). What should be evident here is that the value of a statistical life could vary considerably depending on, among others things, the methodologies used to estimate the final figure.

Measuring the economic value of changes in morbidity and mortality resulting from environmental pollution is much more involved, however. Prior to even starting the economic valuation process, it is necessary to establish a clear understanding of the various ways in which the specific pollutant(s) in question impair human health. Formally, this is done by using a technique known as the *dose–response* approach. In general, the steps required to carry out an effective dose–response analysis include measuring emissions and determining the resulting ambient quality, estimating human exposure and measuring impacts on human health (more on this in Section 8.6 of the next chapter). These are biological and ecological relationships that need to be established before estimating the economic value of changes in mortality and morbidity arising from environmental pollution. In several situations, dose–response could be, although necessary, a very involved and expensive procedure to undertake.

This ends the discussion of hedonic pricing and its wide-ranging applications as a method of undertaking economic valuations of environmental goods and services. The next subsection examines yet another valuation method, this time by looking at the behavior of household expenditures, to avoid environmental damage from contaminated groundwater for example. Valuation techniques that rely on eliciting WTP based on the observed behavior of household expenditures often refer to the household production function methods. In the next subsections two variations of the households production functions are discussed, namely, *aversive expenditure* and *travel-cost* methods.

The household production function approaches

A. Aversive (defensive) expenditures

In the household production function approach, benefits from improvements in environmental quality are measured by looking at households' expenditures on goods and/or services that are *substitutes* for, or *complements* to, avoiding environmental damage. Examples of such household expenditures include installing soundproofing to reduce noise; purchasing radon-monitoring equipment to protect oneself from radon gas exposure; purchasing water filters to reduce the risk of drinking contaminated water; frequent hospital visits to reduce the chance of serious ailments from prolonged exposure to air pollution; frequent painting of residential dwellings due to smoke emissions from a nearby factory, and so on. In each of these cases, what is evident is that households are willing to pay a certain amount of money (price) to avert specific environmental damage(s). Therefore, these expenditures, commonly known as aversive expenditures, can be used as a measure of households' WTP for a certain level (standard) of environmental quality (quietness, clean water, clean air, etc.).

Note that in many cases, to attain a given change in environmental quality several types of aversive expenditures may be undertaken simultaneously. In this situation, total benefit is measured by summing the various expenditures needed to attain the desired level of environmental attributes.

At the macroeconomic level, the amount of defensive expenditures by a given nation on *activities* directed to mitigate or avoid damages caused by pollution (created in the goods and services production process) can be quite substantial. In the United States estimates for defensive environmental expenditure range from 5 to 10 percent of total GDP. Some economists argue that this amount should be subtracted out from GDP because defensive expenditures actually represent a loss of income that cannot be spent again for consumption or investment but can be spent only to repair or prevent environmental damage caused by current production of goods and services.

B. Travel-cost method

Another variation of the household production function approach involves the valuation of environmental services from *recreational sites*, such as national parks. A special technique that is used to estimate the benefit from changes in the environmental amenities of recreational sites is known as the travel-cost method. This method measures the benefit (willingness to pay), stemming from a recreational experience, by looking at households' *expenditures on the cost of travel to a desired recreational site*. The basic idea behind the approach is this: the services of a recreation site, for example a camping ground, cannot be adequately measured by the gate price, which is usually very low. However, users of this campsite come from various locations. Therefore, instead of the gate price, the price or the WTP of each user can be approximated by her or his travel cost. This method originated in the 1950s, and ever since then it has been used widely, and with considerable success, to empirically estimate the demand (hence willingness to pay) for recreational sites.

For example, in one study (Dixon and Hufschmidt 1986), the recreational value of Lumpinee Park in Bangkok was estimated using the travel-cost approach. Lumpinee is a public park located in the middle of Bangkok, the capital of Thailand. As the population and the economic activities around this city continued to grow, the opportunity cost (the commercial value of the park for other activities) of maintaining this park had been increasing steadily. What this prompted was a doubt in the minds of the public about the economic viability of the park. How would the recreational and amenity value of the park compare with the commercial value for other activities?

If the value of the park were to be assessed on the basis of the entrance fee (which was zero or nominal),

its value would be virtually nothing. The alternative was to use the travel-cost approach, and this was done to get a more accurate measure of consumers' surplus for the park. This approach basically entails the constructing of an empirical demand function for the public park. As discussed above, this was done by hypothesizing that the costs in money and time spent traveling to a free, or nominally priced, recreational site could be used to approximate consumers' willingness to pay for the site. For people living close to the recreational site the travel cost was low, and the expectation was that they would tend to visit the site more often. The opposite would be the case for those visitors traveling to the site from more distant places. Thus, other things remaining constant, the general expectation would be that an *inverse relationship* between the travel cost and the number of visits to the given recreational site would be observed. In essence, this would represent the demand for a recreational site (see Figure 7.5 for a prototype recreational demand function).

There are two types of travel-cost model: single-site and multiple-site models. The multiple-site model differs from the single-site model by explicitly considering that individuals are able to make trips to alternative recreational sites. This consideration is very important as omitting the prices and quantities

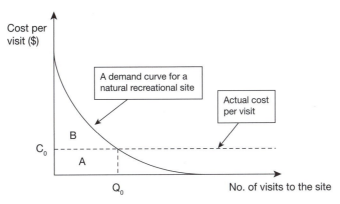

Figure 7.5 *The travel-cost method. Shows the relationship between the number of visits and the cost per visit, other factors affecting demand held constant. Normally, the get price for a natural recreational site is low (near zero) giving no use value to the site. However, by discovering the demand for recreational sites using the travel-cost method, it can be shown that the use value will include the consumers' surplus associated with the user of the recreational site as indicated in the above figure by area B—which can be quite significant.*

of relevant substitutes will bias the resource valuations.

The basic data needed to use the travel-cost methods includes: the characteristics of individuals, the number of visits they make to the site and their travel costs. As would be expected more data are needed in the multiple-site models. In addition to the characteristics above, data are needed to delineate the sites that will be included in the model. Furthermore, if the travel-cost method is to be used to value changes in environmental quality, then site-quality data are needed that vary over or across individual park users.

In our earlier example, the demand for Lumpinee Park was estimated using *single-site* survey data. Interviews of 187 randomly selected visitors, arriving from 17 different administrative districts, were conducted to obtain the basic data. The actual interviews took place at the park in August and November 1980. Afterwards, from this survey data and using a statistical demand analysis, the demand for Lumpinee Park was estimated. This demand estimate set the consumers' surplus enjoyed by the visitors of the park at 13,204,588 baht annually. This was equivalent to $660,230 at the 1980 exchange rate of US$1 = 20 baht. At 10 percent the capitalized value of the park would be $6.6 million. Thus, even though visitors did not pay an admission fee, the large consumers' surplus realized by its users clearly indicated that Lumpinee Park was a very valuable environmental asset.

However, the travel-cost method has the following two glaring drawbacks. First, the application of the method is limited to the valuation of recreational sites. Second, the valuation itself is incomplete, since this method does not account for a recreational site's *existence or conservationvalue*. People may still value a recreational area even if they themselves have never been there. A simple example would be people who value the Grand Canyon even though they have never been there and have no plans to visit this site in the near future. For them the primary motivation to protect it may be for future use by themselves or their offspring. Motivation could also be derived from the strong ethical and moral commitment that some people have to preserve nature. As important as it is

to ascertain the preservation value of environmental resources, such as the tropical rainforest in Malaysia, the travel-cost method does not capture it. For example, for Lumpinee Park, when an explicit effort was made to account for the existence-value of the park, the capitalized value was increased from $6.6 million to $58 million. The various methods used to capture the 'non-use value' of an environmental asset such as preservation of Lumpinee Park is the subject of the next section.

Another case study (Carr and Mendelsohn 2003) that is worth mentioning briefly used the travel-cost method to estimate the annual recreational value of the Great Barrier Reef to Australia (domestic visitors) and other distant countries (international visitors). For Australia alone the estimated value was found to be in the range between US$700 million to 1.6 billion. The general conclusion reached by this study was that there are considerable benefits associated with conservation policies that protect high-quality coral reef systems.

7.4 METHODS FOR ELICITING WILLINGNESS TO PAY FOR ENVIRONMENTAL GOODS AND SERVICES: STATED PREFERENCE VALUATION METHODS

The valuation approaches considered so far (such as, replacement, hedonic, aversive expenditure, and travel-cost) are collectively identified as revealed preference valuation methods. The unique feature of revealed preference methods is that values are inferred from the actual choices (behavior) of resource users. The limitation of these methods is that they can only measure *use values* (i.e., values determined by the 'utility' of those who are making the actual choices). This is a limiting factor because for many ecosystems and environmental resources non-use values are quite significant. For example, earlier it was shown that the non-use value (i.e., preservation value) of the Lumpinee Park was almost nine times higher than its use value (i.e., recreational value of the park). The main message here is that valuation methods that don't account for non-use values could severely underestimate the preservation values of many ecosystem services, such as the biodiversity conservation value of forest ecosystems.

Valuation methods that are used to estimate the non-use values of ecosystem services are referred to as 'stated preference' valuation methods. Stated preference valuation methods differ from revealed preference valuation methods in one important respect. Under the stated preference valuation method, WTP is elicited by asking people to directly *state* their preference (choices) by using survey methods, rather than by observing the behavior of people who are making actual choices in real market settings, as the revealed preference methods do. Stated preference valuation methods are controversial because they use nonmarket valuation techniques. On the other hand, stated preference valuation methods are flexible and can be used to estimate the non-use values of many valuable ecosystem services. How this is done is the subject matter of this section.

At both the conceptual and application phases of stated preference valuation methods, to have a clear understanding of the nature and scope of non-use values is very important. With this in mind, Exhibit 7.1 presents a detailed explanation of non-use values. This exhibit shows that non-use values are composed of three components, namely, option, bequest and existence values. A definition of each one of these three parts of non-use values is offered. Furthermore, the discussion in Exhibit 7.1 clearly indicates that the attainment of non-use values would require resource conservation and/or preservation. For this reason, in the environmental and economic literature, non-use values are often referred to as conservation values or preservation values. Another term often used to describe non-use values is existence values—by virtue of the fact that it often entails the largest component of non-use values. It is important to understand from the outset that these four terms (non-use values, conservation values, preservation values and existence values) are used interchangeably. Exhibit 7.1 is a 'must read' prior to proceeding to the next section.

EXHIBIT 7.1   THE PRINCIPAL COMPONENTS OF NON-USE VALUES AND THE CONCEPT OF TOTAL VALUE

This exhibit is designed to explain the principal components of non-use values associated with environmental assets, such as wilderness areas. In the environmental and resource economics literature, non-use values are hypothesized to have *three* separable components, namely option, bequest and existence values.

Option value refers to a sort of insurance premium individuals may be willing to pay to retain the option of possible future use. For example, people will be willing to pay some amount of money to preserve wilderness or to protect a unique site—such as the Grand Canyon or Yosemite—not because they are currently using them, but because they want to reserve an option that would guarantee their future access to these resources. Note here that people behave this way because of their uncertainty regarding the future demand for or supply of these natural resources (Johansson 1990; Krutilla 1967). In this sense, option value is important to consider when uncertainty is prevalent (Johansson 1990).

Bequest value refers to the satisfaction that people gain from the knowledge that a natural resource is being preserved for future generations. Strictly speaking, bequest value is an intergenerational component of option value. Bequest value would have considerable relevance in a situation where the natural resources under consideration are unique and irreversible, and there exists uncertainty regarding the supply of these resources and future generations' demand for them. Examples are national parks, wilderness, tropical forests, aquifers, blue whales, coastal wetlands, coral reefs, and so on. Basically, bequest demand exists *to the extent that the present generation is willing to pay for preserving natural resources for the use of future generations.*

Existence value refers to the satisfaction that some people derive from the preservation of natural resources so that there remains a habitat for fish, plants, wildlife and so on. In other words, it refers to what people are willing to pay (demand) for preserving the ecological integrity and resilience of the natural environment— stewardship. Examples of this activity are recent *debt-for-nature swaps* by several internationally renowned conservation organizations, such as the Nature Conservancy, to protect the tropical forest. Debt-for-nature swaps allow developing countries to have some of their foreign debt forgiven in exchange for undertaking conservation measures within their countries. The main rationale behind this program is to allow poor nations to be liberated from their debt without destroying their natural resources, such as a forest ecosystem with diverse species of animals and plants.

The following identities present a general conceptual model that captures the essence of the above discussion:

(a) Total value = Use value + Non-use value,

and

(b) Non-use value = Option value + Bequest value + Existence value.

Thus, the *total value* of an environmental asset is composed of *not one, but several willingness to pay.*

Direct and indirect stated preference valuation methods

Economists use stated preference (SP) valuation methods to elicit willingness to pay for the non-use values of ecosystem services. SP valuation methods rely on asking people *hypothetical* questions to elicit willingness to pay for a particular ecosystem service (such as carbon sequestration) or the preservation of an ecosystem as a whole (such as a local nature center). In other words, SP is based on what people say rather than what they do. In this respect SP is clearly different from revealed preference (discussed before) where elicitation of willingness to pay is based on observed evidence of how people behave in the face of real (not hypothetical) market choice.

SP valuation methods have two major components: direct and indirect SP valuation methods. A common feature of these two methods of SP valuation is that they both use a survey instrument in which a hypothetical market for an environmental resource (such as a wetland ecosystem) is created (more on this later). Once this is done, people will then be asked to *state* their preference within the context of the hypothetical market under consideration, and how much they are willing to pay for either avoiding a degradation of the environment or how much they would ask as compensation for the degradation.

Direct SP valuation is commonly referred to as a contingent valuation method (CVM). CVM directly asks people to provide the *monetary* value of the environmental resources under consideration. In other words, this method aims to elicit monetary willingness to pay and in this respect it has the same objective as revealed preference valuation methods. CVM is the traditional SP valuation method and it is extensively covered in this chapter

On the other hand, the indirect SP valuation methods use a choice-based elicitation mechanism and the choices are *not* necessarily expressed in monetary terms. The two variations of indirect SP valuation methods are: *conjoint choice* and *choice-modeling methods*. These choice-based valuation methods use a hypothetical market to ask people to either rank or rate (in the case of conjoint choice), or choose among alternative bundles of environmental goods and services that include several attributes (Louviere et al. 2000).

For example, in a hypothetical study of a mountain-range preservation, a conjoint rating survey may ask respondents to *rank* a set of hypothetical bundles of environmental goods and services (such as snow cover, wildlife population, vegetation, cost, etc.) and the attributes associated with each one of the environmental commodities (such as the thickness of the average winter snow cover, the amount of wildlife, the size of forest cover, the cost to the public, etc.) from 'most preferred' to 'least preferred'. Similarly, for conjoint *rating* a numerical scale may be used (such as, from zero to five, zero being the lowest rating). It is important to note that each respondent will be asked to rank or rate each environmental commodity along with his or her corresponding attribute(s). The task of conjoint analysis is to integrate (hence, join) all of these individual pieces of information from all of the respondents in order to develop an overall ranking or rating that can be used to offer a qualitative valuation of the environmental resource under consideration (Stevens et al. 2000).

In the case of choice modeling the same principle of conjoint analysis remains, namely, that this is a method of eliciting qualitative data by offering hypothetical choices, except that here respondents will be given several alternative to choice from. In the above example of a hypothetical mountain-range preservation study, several alternatives choice categories (options) may be formed by varying the thickness of the average winter snow cover, the estimate of wildlife population, the size of forest cover, and the cost to the public in each of the environmental commodity categories. Hence, the available alternatives are differentiated by the variations in the nature of the attributes. Then, respondents will be asked to choose their most preferred resource option from the given alternatives. This information is then used to estimate respondents' willingness to pay using some estimation technique (Hanley et al. 2002).

There are several variations of conjoint analysis and related choice-modeling methods. The key characteristic of all of these models is that the 'tradeoffs' are evaluated by jointly considering a number of important attributes. These kinds of models have been used for many years in marketing research and other related areas. However, in recent years, there have been numerous and growing applications of these so-called *indirect* SP valuation techniques. In good part, the reason for their increasing

use as an alternative to CVM is because these methods do not require people to state their preference exclusively in *monetary* terms. In other words, preferences are expressed *qualitatively*.

A recent publication evaluated a total of 84 studies of conjoint analysis and related choice-modeling (Alriksson and Oberg 2008). This paper affirmed the usefulness of the indirect SP valuation methods in eliciting preferences concerning environmental assets, especially in areas where the monetary valuation of resources is difficult to ascertain, such as in the preservation of large forest ecosystems. Furthermore, choice-based elicitation mechanisms are shown to reduce some of the biases associated CVM, the traditional valuation method.

The discussion in the rest of this section deals with an expanded discussion of CVM both in theory and applications. Thus, discussions of choice-based valuation methods (i.e., conjoined and choice-modeling) are presented only to indicate their use as potential 'remedy' to some of the major biases associated with CVM. This is done for no other reasons except to keep the chapter to a manageable size.

The contingent valuation method: theoretical framework

The contingent valuation is a *survey-based* method where people are asked directly how much money they would be willing to pay, within a context of a hypothetical market-like choice, to maintain the existence of some environmental features such as biodiversity. Like any other survey-based method, the design of the questionnaire is crucial. It requires an in-depth knowledge of statistical survey methods, economics and ecology and, most importantly, a good deal of creativity and imagination. Hence, normally, a good contingent-valuation survey involves a collaborative effort of people from different fields of study: environmental scientists, economists, policy analysts and statisticians (Carson and Mitchell 1991).

Normally, a contingent valuation survey is composed of two major phases—the *scenario* and the *valuation questions*. The main objective of the scenario phase is to explain to study participants the exact nature of the environmental goods or services, including the changes in the resource(s) to be valued. For example, in a case involving a local nature center, the contingent valuation scenario would describe the attributes of the particular nature center in detail, including the services it provides, the habitats and species it protects, as well as available alternative recreation sites. Photographs and maps should be provided as supplements to this information to make sure each respondent has the same basic knowledge of the center. The scenario should also include current conditions of the nature center, and conditions that might result if a proposed action is or is not implemented. For instance, the scenario might describe what the center is like now, and what would happen to the area if the nature center had to close or substantially reduce services due to lack of funds. The scenario should give respondents enough information about the relevant effects of the proposed actions so they are able to consider how valuable those effects are to them.

After completing the scenario, next come the valuation questions. This phase of the contingent valuation survey deals with the design of the specific format(s) of the questions to be posed to the respondents for the purpose of eliciting the respondent's willingness to pay. Two issues are involved here—the context of the payment mechanism and the format of the valuation question.

How payments would be collected is an important issue within the context of valuation. Would the payment be in the form of taxes, increased fees, increased utility bills, or voluntary donations? If taxes, what kind of tax? Income or property taxes? In general, the question's objective is to seek payment mechanisms that will seem *realistic* to respondents yet be *neutral* in their effects on responding to the valuation question. As will be shown soon, these are not necessarily easy conditions to satisfy.

Because of its familiarity to respondents, valuation questions are often framed as a *referendum*. For instance, respondents may be asked if they would vote *yes* or *no* on a ballot that would increase their taxes in order to keep the nature center in their locality. The increase in taxes may vary from respondent to respondent in order to understand willingness to pay across a wide range of possible values. An alternative format to this is to ask *open-ended questions* where respondents are asked to record the maximum increase in taxes they would accept and still vote for the proposed change. In general, given the unfamiliarity of most people with placing a monetary value on an environmental amenity, the result of the valuation exercise would be more accurate if a *closed-ended* choice (such as, a referendum) of willingness to pay is used (Arrow et al. 1993). Exhibit 7.2 offers a simple illustration of how a valuation question might actually be framed. The material in this exhibit is extracted from a class project written by one of my students. The project under consideration was the Kalamazoo Nature Center.

EXHIBIT 7.2   VALUATION QUESTIONNAIRE: THE CASE OF THE KALAMAZOO NATURE CENTER

When answering the questions provided in this survey, please make sure to keep in mind the following three situations: (i) The Kalamazoo Nature Center is only one among many recreational opportunities in the Kalamazoo Area. (ii) Your income is limited and has several alternative uses. (iii) The following set of questions asks you to focus solely on KNC and not on other environmental issues or other parks and nature centers in the state.

1. What aspects of Kalamazoo Nature Center do you value?
    (a) Quietude/Get-away from the city
    (b) Aesthetic/Scenic Beauty
    (c) Protection of native plants and animals, including some rare habitats and species
    (d) Availability to next generation
    (e) Educational value
    (f) I benefit from just knowing it exists
    (g) I hope to visit KNC in the future

2. How concerned are you about the possibility of the KNC's closure?
   (a) very concerned (b) a little concerned (c) not concerned at all
3. As a taxpayer, how much of an increase in your annual taxes would you be willing to pay to support the continuation of the services currently provided by the KNC?
   (a) $50 (b) $100 (c) $500 (d) other (please specify) $
4. What is the maximum annual amount that you would be willing to pay to prevent closure of KNC?
5. Have you ever considered bequesting money to KNC to ensure its continued existence? If so, how much are you willing to give?

6. Would you be willing to act as a volunteer at the Nature Center in one of its educational programs, secretarial duties, maintenance, animal care, or other? If so, how many hours per week are you willing to spend?

You may revise your willingness to pay value at any point. Please tell me now if you wish to do so.

Thank you Sir/Madam. The Kalamazoo Nature Center thanks you for taking the time complete this survey as your responses will help their research efforts greatly. (Sarah Rockwell)

Finally, although they have not been discussed so far, a good contingent valuation survey would ideally incorporate the following *four* important issues (all of which can make contingent valuation studies expensive):

1. Most contingent surveys incorporate additional questions that provide data on the respondents' demographic characteristics and socioeconomic conditions that are considered relevant to elicit their willingness to pay.
2. Contingent valuation surveys may include questions specifically designed to determine the actual motivation of a respondent's vote. Is the vote of a respondent to a valuation question an expression of *preference*, *opinion* or *protest*? This matters because the primary goal of contingent survey is to elicit an individual preference (i.e., willingness to pay) and nothing else.
3. Properly identifying the relevant population and determining sample size are also important issues.
4. Whether the survey should be conducted in personal or telephone interviews or mail surveys (or in some combination of these three survey mechanisms) is also another important and unavoidable decision to be considered.

The final step of the contingent valuation study is the statistical analysis. The willingness-to-pay responses are normally regressed against the socioeconomic and attitudinal characteristics and the final estimated identity is used to provide aggregate estimates of the average consumer's surplus.

Biases associated with the contingent valuation method

On technical grounds alone, several potential biases may arise that could undermine the validity of the preference information gathered by using the contingent valuation method. Among others, the biases include:

1. *Strategic bias*: respondents may refuse to respond to survey questions or may not reveal their 'true' willingness to pay for strategic reasons. They may do this if they think there is a 'free rider' situation (i.e., use a resource without paying for it, or pay less than the full cost). However, there appears to be limited evidence of strategic bias (Bohm 1979). In some instances, however, people may refuse to respond to survey question(s) based, not on a 'free rider' consideration, but on the fact that they simply refuse to put a monetary value

on environmental services that they considered to be priceless, or on ethical/moral grounds (more on this later).

2. *Information bias*: the survey result is not independent of the information provided to respondents and their interpretation of the survey questions. For example, it matters a great deal whether respondents are asked how much they are willing to pay to preserve a wilderness in its pristine condition, or how much they are willing to accept in compensation for its loss. In general, empirical studies indicated that WTA estimates tend to be higher than WTP estimates. In another situation, respondents may express their WTP on the basis of paying of what they consider to be their fair share instead of what the resource under consideration is worth to them.

Furthermore, information bias with regard to 'existence value' could be more pronounced and entails a considerable risk because, as Gatto and De Leo (2000: 350) pointed out, 'species with very low or no aesthetic appeal or whose biological role has not been properly advertised will be given a low value, even if they play a fundamental ecological function'. For example, protecting 'the Big Five' (lions, elephants, buffalo, hippos and tigers) is the major driving-force in the wilderness conservation movements in many African countries. However, protecting these animals is prompted because they are perceived as having commercial values and as being a locus of people's emotional attachments rather than on their roles in maintaining the dynamic balance of the ecosystems of which they are a part.

3. *Hypothetical bias*: bias introduced because respondents are not making 'real' transactions. In this situation respondents tend to be sensitive to the instruments used for payment (such as entrance fee, sales tax, payroll tax, income tax, and so on.) Economists express considerable doubt regarding the extent to which a simulated market can fully capture the dynamic feedback that characterizes real competitive markets. Is it then possible to generate efficient price information from an artificially constructed market?

The most likely answer to the above question is no. Several studies (List and Galler 2001; Murphy et al. 2005) suggest that mean hypothetical values are about 2.5 to three times greater than actual cash payments. Possible reasons for hypothetical bias include lack of consequence associated with an individual's response, desire to increase the likelihood that the good is provided at little or no personal cost, and respondent uncertainty or ambivalence (Stevens 2005: 191–2).

4. *Difficulties with the reference group for pricing*: valuation of environmental damage based on contingent valuation methods could be significantly influenced by the group of people that is taken as a reference for valuation—particularly on their income (Gatto and De Leo 2000). For instance, using the population of the United States as a reference group, the existence value of the affected species and ecosystems from the 1989 Exxon Valdez oil-spill incident in Alaska was calculated to be in the region of $5 billion—a figure that was used to compensate the people of Alaska for their losses (Van der Straaten 1998). Could this level of compensation have been warranted if this same incident had occurred in a country with similar ecological conditions but whose people had an income much lower than that of the United States? This question has very important implications on how contingent valuation methods are used to evaluate the existence values of fragile, but *globally* important, natural resources (such as tropical forests) that are largely found in the poorest regions of the world.

Contingent valuation method: applications

In this subsection, attempts will be made to demonstrate how the contingent valuation method is used in a real-world situation. The first case study deals with wilderness designations in Colorado. This case study (although somewhat dated) will be used to illustrate the application of contingent valuation analysis in a very comprehensive and illuminating manner. Following this, several case studies are cited to show more recent, and wide-ranging, successful applications of contingent valuation analysis

Walsh et al. (1983) sought to estimate the preservation value of incremental increases in wilderness designations in Colorado. For this case study, during the summer of 1980, a mail survey was sent to 218 Colorado households. The participants were shown four maps of the State of Colorado, and on each map a different acreage was designated as wilderness. One of the maps showed the 1.2 million acres of land currently (in 1980) designated as wilderness in Colorado. This represented 2 percent of the state land. The other three maps showed hypothetical wilderness designations that were respectively 2.6, five and ten million acres. As far as possible, every effort was taken to provide the respondents of the survey with credible information about the contingent market. This information was intended to offer a solid background on the scientific, historical and economic significance of wilderness areas for the current and future citizens of Colorado.

With the above information in hand, each respondent was asked to write down the maximum amount of money she/he would be willing to pay annually for the preservation of the four increments of wilderness depicted on four maps. Then the survey asked the respondents to allocate their reported willingness to pay among the four categories of value: recreational use, option, existence and bequest demands. Note that option, existence and bequest values are measures of non-use, hence the preservation value of wilderness. Viewed in this way, total preservation value is the residual after recreational-use benefits have been subtracted from the total willingness to pay for wilderness. (Please refer to Exhibit 7.1 on page 131 if you wish to make a quick review of the components of non-use value and the concept of total value.)

Once all the necessary survey data had been gathered and processed, Walsh performed a statistical demand analysis to estimate preservation values. This involved estimating a separate demand for each component of the preservation value, namely option, existence and bequest values. It would be beyond the scope of this text to go into the details of the procedures used to estimate these demand functions. The final result of the study is presented in Table 7.1.

The last row of Table 7.1 shows the estimate of the total values for each of the four wilderness designations. For example, for the existing (1980) level of wilderness areas of 1.2 million acres, the total value was estimated to be $28.5 million. The total values of each designation are split into two parts, namely use value (which represents the recreational use of the wilderness) and non-use value (which corresponds to the preservation value of the wilderness). For example, for the existing wilderness designation area of 1.2 million acres, the total value ($28.5 million) was obtained by summing recreational-use value ($13.2 million) and the preservation or non-use value ($15.3 million). The preservation value was further broken down into its three major components, namely the option, existence and bequest values. For the existing wilderness area, these values were 4.4, 5.4 and 5.5 million dollars, respectively. All categories of the preservation value are reported for a household and as a total.

Several inferences can be drawn from these results. For example, increasing the number of acres for wilderness designation from 1.2 to 2.6 (which amounted to slightly more than a doubling of the existing wilderness designation areas) was shown to increase the total value by 46 percent (from $28.5 to $41.6 million). Thus, doubling the areas of the wilderness designation does not double the total value. As interesting as this observation may seem, however, for our purpose it is important to note that for all four wilderness designation categories, the non-use or preservation values represented a significant portion of the total value. At the higher end (which was associated with the wilderness areas of 10 million acres), the non-use value was more than one-third of the total value. What this shows is, at least in principle, the significance of valuation techniques (such as the contingent valuation method) that deliberately incorporate the estimation of non-use values (benefits) to the analysis. Obviously, failure to account for such benefits may lead society to take decisions that could cause irreversible damage to wilderness areas and other similar environmental resources.

Table 7.1 *Total annual consumer surplus (US$) from recreation use and preservation value to Colorado households from increments in wilderness designation, Colorado, 1980*

Value Categories	Wilderness areas, 1980 1.2 million acres	Wilderness areas, 1981, 2.6 million acres	Double 1981 Wilderness areas 5 million acres	All Potential Wilderness areas 10 million acres
Recreation use value				
Per visitor day	14.00	14.00	14.00	14.00
Total, million	13.2	21.0	33.1	58.2
Preservation value to Colorado residents				
Per household	13.92	18.75	25.30	31.83
Total, million	15.3	20.6	27.8	35.0
Option value				
Per household	4.04	5.44	7.34	9.23
Total, million	4.4	6.0	8.1	10.2
Existence value				
Per household	4.87	6.56	8.86	11.14
Total, million	5.4	7.2	9.7	12.3
Bequest value				
Per household	5.01	6.75	9.10	11.46
Total, million	5.5	7.4	10.0	12.5
Total annual recreation use value And preservation value to Colorado households, million	28.5	41.6	60.9	93.2

Source: Land Economics 60, 1, February 1984. © 1984. Reprinted by permission of the University of Wisconsin Press.

The contingent valuation method is used widely and in many different situations. Exhibit 7.3 cites several representative situations where contingent valuation methods have been applied. If a lesson is to be drawn from this, it is that the CV method has been used for environmental valuation with considerable success and for a fairly long period of time.

This concludes the discussion of the various techniques economists have been using in recent years to assess benefits arising from an improvement in the condition of the natural environment (clean air, water, etc.). Before embarking to the next section—a critical appraisal of the economic approach to environmental valuation—Table 7.2 (see p. 140) summarizes the salient characteristics and functions of the valuation techniques discussed in this chapter.

7.5 THE STANDARD ECONOMIC APPROACH TO ENVIRONMENTAL VALUATION: A CRITICAL ASSESSMENT

In the previous section a concerted effort was made to point out some of the major drawbacks associated with each of the techniques that economists use to assess the benefits of environmental assets (such as coastal coral reefs, atmospheric visibility, wilderness, and so on). However, this was done without questioning the fundamental premises of the neoclassical economic valuation methodology. In this section, an attempt will be made to highlight *four* of the most serious criticisms of the neoclassical approaches to valuing the environment. These are as follows:

EXHIBIT 7.3 APPLICATIONS OF STATED PREFERENCE VALUATIONS

By Thomas H. Stevens

One measure of the importance of stated preferences, SP, in decision-making is the extent to which this method has successfully been used for that purpose. A review of the literature indicates that SP has been used for more than 40 years and during this time well over 2,000 SP studies have been conducted (Carson 2000). This method has been applied to a wide range of real world problems including water quality, wilderness, and wildlife preservation, air quality, health care, and food safety.

Contingent valuation studies have also influenced decisions about the reintroduction of Gray Wolves to Yellowstone National Park and salmon restoration in New England. The net economic value of Gray Wolf reintroduction to Yellowstone National Park was estimated to total between 6.6 and 9.9 million dollars per year. This value which consists entirely of existence value, represented between 22 and 29% of the estimated total economic impact associated with wolf reintroduction (USFWS).

Atlantic salmon were virtually extinct in southern New England by the early 1800s. The Anadromous Fish Conservation Act (PL89-304) provided federal funds for salmon restoration, the first Atlantic salmon to return to this region was spotted in 1974. Since then annual returns have ranged between 100 and about 500 per year and critics of the restoration program have noted that the cost of returning salmon is about $3,000 per pound. However, it turns out that Atlantic salmon produce substantial existence value. SP studies suggest that this value is about 16 million dollars per year for residents of Massachusetts and as much as 81 million dollars per year for New England as a whole. The latter value is about twice that of annualized restoration program costs.

The Elwha River Restoration Project (ERRP) in the Olympic National Park is another example where existence values played an important role in decision-making about wildlife. This study included estimates of nonmarket benefits associated with dam removal and salmon restoration. An SP survey asked each respondent if they would vote in favor of an increase in federal taxes over a ten year period to remove two dams

and restore both the river and fish populations. Results for the US totaled about 6.3 billion dollars per year; an amount that substantially exceeds market benefits, as well as program costs (Loomis 1996).

Other applications of SP focus on environmental quality. For example, Krupnick and Portney (1991) used willingness to pay data to evaluate the health benefits of reducing volatile organic compound emissions. Since considerable debate surrounds the problem of atmospheric pollution and visibility in wilderness areas and national parks, several SP studies of the value of visibility have been conducted (Smith & Osborne 1996). One study (Halstead, Stevens, Harper, & Hill 2004) examined the relationship between electricity deregulation and willingness to pay for atmospheric visibility to the Great Gulf Wildness in New Hampshire's White Mountains. Visibility in this area is now about one-third of natural conditions, and visibility may get worse with electricity deregulation if consumers switch to lower cost coal fired generation. The SP question in this study presented each respondent with two pictures. One picture represented the status quo visibility, while the other represented reduced visibility with option to pay a higher electricity bill to avoid this loss in visibility.

From a much broader perspective, SP has been frequently used to value entire ecosystems and wilderness areas. One recent example is a study of National Parks in Portugal (Nunes 2002). Photo simulation was used to show alternative development/preservation scenarios and a total of 28 survey versions were used to test the effects of information, payment vehicle (a national tax or voluntary contribution), and level of park protection. SP has also been successfully applied to the problem of rain forest preservation, biodiversity, ecosystem management of forestland and wilderness, and open space preservation.

Source: Stevens, T. (2005) 'Can Stated Preference Valuations Help Improve Environmental Decision Making?', *Choices: The Magazine of Food, Farm, and Resource Issues,* a publication of the American Agricultural and Applied Economic Association (AAEA), 20, 3, 189–91.

Table 7.2 A grand summary of the economic methods for valuing ecosystem services discussed in this chapter

Specific Nature of the Environmental Damage	Examples	Primary Economic Method(s) Used for Valuations	Type of Uses
1. Loss of economic outputs & inputs	Fish, crops, & wood products	Market valuation approach	Use value
2. Increased exposure to environmental nuisance	Noise, odor, & debris	Hedonic pricing & household production approaches	Use value
3. Impairment to human health	Risk of mortality & morbidity	Hedonic pricing approach	Use value
4. Recreational, amenity & aesthetic losses	Bird watching, camping, etc.	Travel cost & contingent valuation methods	Use value
5. Simplification of natural habitats	Loss of biodiversity	Contingent valuation (?) & precautionary approach	Non-use value
6. Irreversible damage to an ecosystem function and/or structure	Species extent & climate change	Precautionary approach[1]	Non-use value

1. There is extensive discussion of the precautionary approach in Chapter 9.

1. Environmental values should not be reducible to a single one-dimensional standard that is ultimately expressed only in monetary terms.
2. High levels of uncertainty make the measurement and the very concept of *total value* meaningless.
3. Survey techniques used to elicit willingness to pay confuse preferences with beliefs.
4. Important ecological connections may be missed when valuing components of a system separately.

The rest of this section discusses these four issues.

First, *environmental values should not be reducible to a single one-dimensional standard that is only expressed in monetary terms*.

The conventional approaches to valuations assume that a monetary value can be assigned to all aspects of environmental amenities. Furthermore, as Funtowicz and Ravetz (1994: 199) put it: the issue is not whether it is only the marketplace that can determine value, for economists have long debated other means of valuation. Our concern is with the assumption that, in any dialogue, all valuations or 'numeraires' should be reducible to a single one-dimensional standard.

They described this whole effort as a 'commodification of environmental goods'.

It is argued that this principle should not be accepted because it blatantly *denies the existence of certain intangible values* of the natural environment that are *beyond the economic*. These values are immeasurable and can be described only in qualitative terms that are noneconomic in nature. Improved quality of life, the protection of endangered species and ecosystems, the preservation of scenic or historic sites (such as the Grand Canyon), and the aesthetic and symbolic properties of wilderness are examples of non-economic values. It would be wrong and misleading to ignore intangibles in an effort to obtain a single dollar-value estimate for benefits. There are irreplaceable and priceless environmental assets whose values cannot be captured either through the market or by survey methods designed to elicit people's willingness to pay. However, it is important to note that *to describe an environmental asset as priceless cannot mean that such a resource has an infinite value*. This would imply that it would be worth devoting the whole of a nation's GNP (and beyond) to the preservation of its environmental assets.

It is also important to point out that the use of indirect stated preference valuation (contingent ranking/rating and choice modeling) methods, may have the potential to mitigate the above concern. This is because the valuation is done in qualitative (not monetary) terms.

Second, *high levels of uncertainty make the measurement and concept of total value meaningless.*

The conventional measure of environmental damage stems from the difficulties associated with the *uncertainty* inherent in the ways that certain environmental resources are used. Uncertainties of this nature are particularly important when the resources in question are difficult or impossible to replace and for which no close substitute is available (Arrow and Fisher 1974; Krutilla 1967). Under these circumstances the potential costs of current activities could be very high. This is particularly significant where the outcomes are expected to be *irreversible.* Contemporary examples are global warming, biodiversity loss, ozone destruction, and so forth. Several important implications follow from these uncertainties. Among them are the following:

- Uncertainty compounds the difficulty of evaluating environmental damage.
- Where irreversibility is a serious concern, the damage may be immeasurable or infinitely high (Johansson 1990). In such a case, the very notion of *total* value may be meaningless.
- As Krutilla (1967) effectively argued, the maximum willingness to pay could be less than the minimum amount that would be necessary to compensate for the loss of the natural phenomenon in question. This is because the more difficult it is to replace a loss of environmental goods with other goods, the higher the compensation needed for people to accept the loss. Under this condition, attempts to determine individuals' willingness to pay for non-use values (i.e., existence, option and bequest values) using the contingent valuation method could have misleading outcomes.
- When the potential for catastrophic outcomes in the future is a major concern, proper manage-

ment of the underlying uncertainty requires explicit consideration of the interest of the future generations—intergenerational equity. According to Perrings (1991), this can be done using the *precautionary principle* as a guide for decision-making. This approach assigns a worst-case value to the uncertain outcome of current activities. The 'optimal' policy is then the one that minimizes the worst imaginable outcome. Under this approach it makes perfect sense to opt for the preservation of the natural environment if costs are potentially large and very long-term (more on this in Chapter 8).

Third, *survey techniques used to elicit willingness to pay confuse preferences with beliefs.*

Sagoff (1988b) wrote a stinging criticism of the whole approach of evaluating environmental damage on the basis of survey data that purports to reflect the respondents' willingness to pay. His main objection is based on what is or is not conveyed by people's preferences, which are used as a means of eliciting willingness to pay. More specifically, he argued that the conventional wisdom in economics is to treat judgments (or beliefs) expressed about the environment as if they are preferences (or desires). According to Sagoff (1988b: 94), judgments (ethical or otherwise) involve:

> not desires or wants but opinions or views. They state what a person believes is right or best for the community or group as a whole. These opinions may be true or false, and we may meaningfully ask that person for the reasons that he or she holds them. But an analyst who asks how much citizens would pay to satisfy opinions that they advocate through political association commits a category mistake. The analyst asks of beliefs about objective facts a question that is appropriate only to subjective interests and desires.

This consideration is especially significant when property rights are not clearly delineated (such as in the case of the environment). The main reason for this is that people's preferences for these resources include aspects of their feelings that are *not purely economic*. These feelings may be based on aesthetic, cultural, ethical, moral and political considerations. Therefore, under this condition, it is quite possible that some people may prefer not to sell publicly owned resources at any price. This perhaps explains why some respondents in contingent valuation surveys refuse to indicate the price at which they are willing to buy or sell environmental resources; not, as often claimed, for strategic reasons.

The implication is that environmental policy should be based not only on market information (prices) but also on a decision-making process that includes open dialogues on the basis of democratic principles (see Sagoff 1988a). In this way, the various dimensions of environmental policy (aesthetic, cultural, moral and ethical) are adequately incorporated.

Fourth, *important ecological connections may be missed when valuing components of a system separately*.

Another drawback, particularly relevant to the contingent valuation method, results from a potential failure to account for certain ecological factors. More specifically, to the extent that *total* value (use values plus non-use values) is based on economic values, it may fail to account for *primary values*—'system

characteristics upon which all ecological functions are contingent" (Pearce 1993). In this sense, total value may not really be total after all.

As discussed in Chapter 2, one of the lessons of ecology is that all parts of a natural ecosystem are mutually interrelated. Therefore, strictly from an ecological viewpoint, the value of a particular entity in the natural environment (an animal species, a valley, a river, humans, etc.) should be assessed on the basis of its overall contribution to the sustainability (health) of the ecosystem as a whole. Essentially, assessing the total value of a natural environment (such as wilderness) as the sum of the values of the parts or individual attributes does not account for the whole (Van der Straatan 1998). However, this is the underlying premise of the contingent valuation approach (see Exhibit 7.4).

Using a similar line of reasoning, O'Neill and Kahn (2000: 333) also argued that the current economic concept of *valuation* is of limited use because the *dynamic* responses of the ecosystem itself are not included within the economic model. The economic model assumes, incorrectly, that the environment is the constant and stable background for economic activity. The feedback loop between the human species and its ecosystem remains incomplete.

EXHIBIT 7.4   TOWARDS ECOLOGICAL PRICING

Alan Thein Durning

Ecological pricing is [a] . . . necessary condition of a sustainable forest economy. Virgin timber is currently priced far below its full costs. For instance, the price of teak does not reflect the costs of flooding that rapacious teak logging has caused in Myanmar; nor does the price of old-growth fir from the US Pacific Northwest include losses suffered by the fishing industry because logging destroys salmon habitat. Those losses are estimated at $2,150 per wild Chinook salmon in the Columbia River, when future benefits to sports and commercial fishers are counted.

Few attempts have been made to calculate the full ecological prices of forest products but they

would undoubtedly be astronomical for some goods. A mature forest tree in India, for example, is worth $50,000, estimates the Center for Science and Environment in New Delhi. The full value of a hamburger produced on pasture cleared from rain forest is about $200, according to an exploratory study conducted at New York University's School of Business. These figures, of course, are speculative. Calculating them requires making assumptions about how many dollars, for instance, a species is worth—perhaps an imponderable question. But the alternative to trying—failing to reflect the loss of ecological functions at all in the price of wood and other forest products—ensures that the economy will continue to destroy forests.

The full economic value of a forest ecosystem is clearly huge. Forests provide a source of medicines worth billions of dollars. Their flood prevention, watershed stabilization and fisheries protection functions are each worth billions more. Their scenic and recreational benefits also have billion-dollar values for both the world's growing nature tourism industry and local residents.

The full value of forests includes each of these components, from sources of medicines to pest controls. But, again, market prices count only the direct costs of extracting goods, not the full ecological costs. In accounting terms, the money economy is depleting its natural capital without recording that depreciation on its balance sheet. Consequently, annual losses come out looking like profits, and cash flow looks artificially healthy. For a business to do this—liquidate its plant and equipment and call the resulting revenue income— would be both self-destructive and, in many countries, illegal. For the money economy overall, however, self-destruction generally goes unquestioned.

How can we move toward ecological pricing? By changing government policies. A primary responsibility of governments is to correct the failures of the money economy, and global deforestation is surely a glaring one. Yet forest policies in most nations do the opposite: They accelerate forest loss. The first order of business for government, therefore, is to stop subsidizing deforestation. The second is to use taxes, user fees and tariffs to make ecological costs apparent in the money economy. Until the money economy is corrected in these ways, forest conservation will remain an uphill battle.

Source: Worldwatch Institute, *States of the World 1993*, Copyright © 1993. Reprinted by permission.

7.6 CHAPTER SUMMARY

This chapter dealt with the economic approaches to the assessment of benefits arising from improvement in environmental quality or avoided environmental damage.

Following the standard practice in economics, theoretically, the benefit (or avoided-damage cost) from a project to improve environmental quality is captured by individuals' willingness to pay at the margin. Total benefit is then measured by the sum of society's willingness to pay—the area under the relevant range of the demand curve for an environmental good or, more specifically, the MDC curve.

When environmental benefit is measured in this manner, *three* important issues require particular attention:

1. The benefit from improved environmental quality is not intended to measure the 'value' of the environment as such. Instead, what is measured is people's preferences or willingness to pay for an environmental good or to avoid an environmental bad (damage).
2. The estimation of the total benefit includes consumers' surplus. In other words, total benefit is not computed by simply multiplying equilibrium market price and quantity.
3. It is understood that the motivation of estimating environmental benefit is not to value the environment as a whole, but to evaluate the benefits and/or costs associated with changes made to the environment due to human activities. Most importantly, the changes are assumed not to be large enough to cause a major modification to the future circumstances of humanity—life, as we know it, will go on.

Because measuring the area under the MDC curve entails assessing the benefits (as far as possible in monetary terms) of environmental services normally not traded through ordinary markets, mechanisms must be developed to *implicitly* measure willingness to pay. This is done using shadow prices, that is, the prices of substitutes and complementary goods and services that are traded through the ordinary market.

In this chapter, we examined the *three* most common approaches to measuring *implicit* willingness to pay, namely the replacement cost approach, the hedonic price approach and the household production approach—which incorporates, among other things, the travel-cost method. Considerable efforts were made not only to explain these alternative measures of the value of environmental services but also their apparent strengths and weaknesses. In addition, some case studies illustrated how the estimates of values are done empirically.

These approaches have one common feature: they measure benefits on the basis of *use values*. These are benefits or satisfactions received by individuals who are directly utilizing the services or amenities provided by the natural environment. But some environmental assets, such as wilderness, have *non-use values*: for example, the value of preserving wilderness so that it will be available for the use of future generations. Three distinctively different features of future uses were discussed in this chapter, namely option, bequest and existence values.

The economic value of the natural environment goes beyond what can be captured by direct and/or indirect observations of market information or use value. Thus, the total benefit of environmental assets (such as wilderness) should reflect *total* value—the sum of use and non-use values. (Please note that total value is not the value of the flow of environmental services on a global scale.)

However, techniques designed to estimate non-use values could *not* use real market information, which means that willingness to pay for non-use values must be estimated by means of a *hypothetical* market condition. This is done using the contingent valuation method. The main feature of this method is that it elicits willingness to pay by conducting an extensive *survey*. The use of contingent valuation by economists is increasing and appears to hold the key for further advancement in estimating *total* values of environmental services.

In general, the economic approaches to environmental valuation have been criticized for a number of reasons. Chief among them are:

1. The 'commodification' of environmental goods—the idea that environmental values are reducible to a single one-dimensional standard that is ultimately expressed only in monetary terms—is objectionable to some.
2. Survey techniques used to elicit willingness to pay confuse preferences with beliefs. This is a serious criticism given that economists (as serious 'scientists' who are engaged in an effort to measure value as objectively as possible) never have the desire to enter into the realm of measuring belief, even unintentionally.
3. Where uncertainty and irreversibility are serious concerns, the damage may be immeasurable or infinitely high. In this case, the very notion of *total* value may be meaningless.
4. Important ecological connections may be missed when valuing components of a system separately. In this case, the *total* value may not be total after all.

REVIEW AND DISCUSSION QUESTIONS

1. Briefly explain the following concepts: consumers' surplus, revealed preference valuation methods, stated preference valuation methods, conjoint rating analysis, statistical life, aversive expenditure, use values, option values, bequest values, existence value, total value, commodification of environmental goods, debt-for-nature swaps, and the precautionary principle.
2. Read the following statements. In response, state 'True', 'False' or 'Uncertain' and explain why:
    (a) To describe an environmental asset as 'priceless' does not mean that it has an infinite value.
    (b) Economists do not attempt to measure the value of the environment. What they attempt to measure are the preferences of people for an environmental good or environmental bad.
    (c) The estimation of the benefits of environmental assets would be unaffected by whether the method used to measure benefit is based on willingness-to-pay (WTP) or willingness-to-accept (WTA).
3. On April 20 2010, an oil rig leased by oil giant BP exploded in the Gulf of Mexico, killing 11 workers and releasing approximately 200 million gallons of oil, tens of millions of gallons of natural gas and 1.8 million gallons of chemicals. The ecological, economic and human impacts of this oil spill have been devastating and widespread throughout the Gulf of Mexico (more specifically in Louisiana, Alabama, Mississippi and Florida). Among the obvious impacts have been those on: commercial fishing; recreational fishing; tourism; coral formation; turtles, birds and other endangered and threatened species of wildlife and their habitats; human health; and property values along the coastal areas.

    Identify the specific environmental valuation method(s) that would be appropriate to use for each one of the impacts mentioned above. Provide a brief rationale for your choice.
4. With respect to the contingent valuation method, explain why is hypothetical bias a more serious problem than strategic bias?
5. Are the two comments below equivalent? Do you agree with the ideas conveyed by these comments? Explain.
    (a) Putting real economic value on *components* of nature will help protect the environment and promote biodiversity. (Hint: notice the emphasis on components.)
    (b) The reason we are losing natural capital is because it is free.
6. How would you respond to a skeptic who asked the following question: Should we put a dollar value on nature? (Hint: Is this what economists are attempting to do?)

7. Carefully explain the differences and similarities between the following pairs of concepts as environmental valuation methods:

    (a) Aversive expenditure versus travel-cost.

    (b) Conjoint analysis versus choice-modeling.

    (c) Contingent valuation versus choice-modeling.

    (d) Contingent valuation versus hedonic price.

8. In this chapter we discussed five commonly used techniques for measuring the *monetary values* of avoided environmental damages (benefits): market pricing; replacement cost; hedonic price; household production function (which includes the travel-cost and aversive expenditures); and contingent valuation. Below, you are given a hypothetical situation in which environmental damage of some aspect of the natural world has occurred. For each of these cases choose the best technique(s) to estimate the cost of the damage in question, and provide a brief justification for your choice of the particular technique(s).

    (a) Excessive soil erosion due to deforestation.

    (b) Decline in property values due to groundwater contamination.

    (c) Excessive noise from a nearby industrial complex.

    (d) Damage to the scenic value of a lakeshore due to eutrophication.

    (e) The provision of flood control services by wetland ecosystems.

    (f) Loss of habitats for rare plant species due to a development project affecting ecologically sensitive wetlands.

9. A colleague said to me,

    I have my own personal doubts about contingent valuation when respondents are ethically committed to environmental preservation. If they are asked a willingness-to-accept question, then they may respond with an infinite or very large price. In essence, they see the resource as priceless or incommensurable with respect to monetary values. If they are asked a willingness-to-pay question, they may object on grounds that they are being forced to pay for something that has ethical standing and on moral grounds should not be damaged or destroyed; or they might simply offer what they can afford in order to meet what they see as their moral obligation to save the environment. The point is that contingent valuation analysis, while interesting, could be conceptually problematic.

    Do you agree or disagree with my colleague? Why, or why not?

10. Economists are difficult to understand. They claim that they can put a monetary value on premature death, but not on human life. They also claim that they can value ecosystem services (such as a wetland area) in a certain locality, but not the value of the world's ecosystem services. How could this be? Discuss, and be specific.

REFERENCES AND FURTHER READING

Alriksson, S. and Oberg, T. (2008) 'Conjoint Analysis for Environmental Evaluation: A Review of Methods and Applications', *Environmental Science and Pollution Research* 15, 3: 244–57.

Arrow, K. and Fisher, A. C. (1974) 'Environmental Preservation, Uncertainty, and Irreversibility', *Quarterly Journal of Economics* 88: 312–19.

Arrow, K. J., Solow, R., Leamer, E., Portney, P., Randner, R. and Schuman, H. (1993) 'Report of the NOAA Panel on Contingent Valuation', *Federal Register* 58, 10: 4602–14.

Bohm, P. (1979) 'Estimating Willingness to Pay: Why and How?' *Scandinavian Journal of Economics* 84: 142–53.

Brander, L., Raymond, J. G., Florax, M. and Vermaat, J. (2006) 'The Empirics of Wetland Valuation: A Comprehensive Summary and a Meta-Analysis of the Literature', *Environmental Resource Economics* 33, 2: 223–50.

Carr, L. and Mendelsohn, R. (2003) 'Valuing Coral Reefs: A Travel Cost Analysis of the Great Barrier Reef', *AMBIO* 32, 5: 353–7.

Carson, R. (2000) 'Contingent Valuation: A User's Guide', *Environmental Science & Technology* 34, 8: 1413–19.

Carson, R. and Mitchell, R. (1991) *Using Surveys to Value Public Goods: The Contingent Valuation Method*, Baltimore, MD: Resources for the Future.

Costanza, R., D'Arge, R., De Groot, R., Farber, S., Grasso, M., Hannon, B., Limburg, K., Naeem, S., O'Neill, R. V., Paruelo, J., Raskin, R. G., Sutton, P. and van den Belt, M. (1997) 'The Value of the World's Ecosystem Services and Natural Capital', *Nature* 387: 253–60.

Dixon, J. A. and Hufschmidt, M. M. (eds.) (1986) *Economic Valuation Techniques for the Environment: A Case Study Workbook*, Baltimore, MD: Johns Hopkins University Press.

Ekeland, I., Heckman, J. and Nesheim, L. (2004), 'Identification and Estimation of Hedonic Models', *Journal of Political Economy* 112: 60–109.

Funtowicz, S. O. and Ravetz, J. R. (1994) 'The Worth of a Songbird: Ecological Economics as a Post-normal Science', *Ecological Economics* 10: 197–207.

Gatto, M. and De Leo, A. G. (2000) 'Pricing Biodiversity and Ecosystem Services: The Never-ending Story', *BioScience* 50, 4: 347–55.

Halstead, J., Stevens, T., Harper, W. and Hill, B. (2004) 'Electricity Deregulation and the Valuation of Visibility Loss in Wilderness Areas: A Research Note', *The Journal of Regional Analysis and Policy* 34, 1: 85–95.

Hanemann, W. M. (1991) 'Willingness-to-pay and Willingness-to-accept: How Much Do they Differ?' *American Economic Review* 81: 635–47.

Hanley, N. and Mourato, S., and Wright, R. E. (2002) 'Choice-modeling Approaches: A Superior Alternative for Environmental Valuation?' *Journal of Economic Surveys* 15, 3: 435–62.

Huang, C. and Biing-Hwan L. (2007) 'A Hedonic Analysis of Fresh Tomato Prices among Regional Markets', *Review of Agricultural Economics* 29, 4: 783–800.

Johansson, P-O. (1990) 'Valuing Environmental Damage', *Oxford Review of Economic Policy* 6, 1: 34–50.

Kremen, C., Niles, J. O., Dalton, M. G., Daly, G. C., Ehrlich, P. R., Fay, J. P., Grewal, D. and Guillery, R. P. (2000) 'Economic Incentives for Rain Forest Conservation Across Scales', *Science* 288: 1828–31.

Krutilla, J. V. (1967) 'Conservation Reconsidered', *American Economic Review* 57: 787–96.

List, J. and Galler, C. (2001) 'What Experimental Protocols Influence Disparities between Actual and Hypothetical Stated Values?' *Environmental and Resource Economics* 20: 241–54.

Loomis, J. and White, D. (1996) *Economic Benefits of Rare and Endangered Species: Summary and Meta-analysis*, Fort Collins, CO: Colorado State University.

Louviere, J., Hensher, D. and Swait, J. (2000) *Stated Choice Methods: Analysis and Applications*, Cambridge: Cambridge University Press.

Milla, K., Thomas, M. and Winsbert, A. (2005) 'Evaluating the Effect of Proximity to Hog Farms on Residential Property Values: A GIS-based Hedonic Price Model Approach', *URISA Journal* 17: 1.

Mishan, E. J. (1971) 'Evaluation of Life and Limb: A Theoretical Approach', *Journal of Political Economy* 79: 687–705.

Murphy, J., Allen, G., Stevens, T. and Weatherhead, D. (2005) 'A Meta-analysis of Hypothetical Bias in Stated Preference Valuation', *Environmental and Resource Economics* 30: 313–25.

Nelson, A. C., Genereux, J. and Genereux, M. (1992) 'Price Effects of Landfills on House Values', *Land Economics* 68, 4: 359–65.

O'Neill, V. R. and Kahn, J. (2000) 'Homo Economus as a Keystone Species', *BioScience* 50, 4: 333–7.

Pearce, D. W. (1993) *Economic Values and the Natural World*, Cambridge, MA: MIT Press.

Perrings, C. (1991) 'Reserved Rationality and the Precautionary Principle: Technological Change, Time, and Uncertainty in Environmental Decision Making', in R. Costanza (ed.) *Ecological Economics: The Science and Management of Sustainability*, New York: Columbia University Press.

Peterson, J. M. (1977) 'Estimating an Effluent Charge: The Reserve Mining Case', *Land Economics* 53, 3: 328–40.

Sagoff, M. (1988a) 'Some Problems with Environmental Economics', *Environmental Ethics* 10, 1: 55–74.

—— (1988b) *The Economy of the Earth*, Cambridge: Cambridge University Press.

Sander, H. and Polasky, S. (2009) 'The Value of Views on Open Space: Estimates from Hedonic Pricing-model for Ramsey County, Minnesota, USA', *Land Use Policy* 26, 3: 837–45.

Schulze, W. D., d'Arge, R. C. and Brookshire, D. S. (1981) 'Valuing Environmental Commodities: Some Recent Experiments', *Land Economics* 57: 11–72.

Songhen, J. F. (2001) 'Case Study of a Market-Based Analysis: Soil Erosion in the Maumee River Basin', in Alegra Cangelosi (ed.) *Revealing the Economic Value of Protecting the Great Lakes*, Washington, DC: Northeast-Midwest Institute and National Oceanic and Atmospheric Administration.

Stevens, T. (2005) 'Can Stated Preference Valuations Help Improve Environmental Decision Making?' *Choices: The Magazine of Food, Farm, and Resource Issues*, a publication of the American Agricultural and Applied Economic Association (AAEA) 20, 3: 189–191.

Stevens, T., Belkner, R., Dennis, D., Kittredge, D. and Willis, C. (2000) 'Comparison of Contingent Valuation and Conjoint Analysis in Ecosystem Management', *Ecological Economics* 32: 63–74.

The Associated Press (2008) 'How to Value Life? EPA Devalues Its Estimate: $900,000 is Taken Off in What Critics Say is Way to Weaken Pollution Rules', *The Associated Press*, Washington, DC: USA, July 10.

Van der Straaten J. (1998) 'Is Economic Value the Same as Ecological Value?' Paper presented at the Seventh International Congress of Ecology (INTECOL), 19–25 July, Florence, Italy.

Walsh, R. G., Miller, N. P. and Gilliam, L. O. (1983) 'Congestion and Willingness to Pay for Expansion of Skiing Capacity', *Land Economics* 59, 2: 195–210.

Walsh, R. G., Lommis, J. B. and Gillman, R. A. (1984) 'Valuing Option, Existence, and Bequest Demands for Wilderness', *Land Economics* 60, 1: 14–29.

Chapter 8

Frameworks for the economic appraisal of environmental projects: Cost–benefit analysis and others

LEARNING OBJECTIVES

After reading this chapter you will be familiar with the following:

- A formal definition of an environmental project.
- The welfare economics foundation of cost–benefit analysis: 'actual' and 'potential' Pareto improvements.
- The net present value criterion.
- Private versus public project appraisals: a comparative analysis of how costs and benefits are assessed for private versus public projects.
- The risk of double-counting the costs of environmental projects.
- The choice of the discount rate and the issue of intergenerational equity.
- Major shortcomings of standard cost–benefit analysis (CBA).
- Other environmental project evaluation criteria, such as:
  (a) The precautionary principles versus CBA;
  (b) Cost-effectiveness analysis (CEA) versus CBA;
  (c) Environmental impact analysis (EIA) versus CBA;
  (d) Environmental risk assessment and risk management; and
  (e) Distributive justice (environmental justice).

This chapter will demonstrate that assessing the worthiness of environmental projects is often a very difficult task. The difficulty is not confined to measuring the benefits of environmental assets that have been addressed already in Chapter 7. As will be discussed in this chapter, efforts to account for all the 'social' costs of an environmental project may lead to double-counting costs. Another complication arises from the choice of the discount rates that may have important intergenerational ethical implications. Social justice is also an important issue that should be considered when environmental projects are assessed using the framework of CBA. Despite these challenges, CBA (especially when it is used in combination with other evaluation criteria) can be a very powerful technique for assessing the viability of environmental projects.

8.1 INTRODUCTION

In Section 7.3 of the previous chapter, we discussed at some length the various techniques that economists employ to assess the benefits of a project implemented to avoid environmental damage. A *project* in this case is defined as a concrete action taken to alter the state of the natural environment—usually against its deterioration. A case in point is an intentional plan taken by a given society to control the sulfur dioxide emissions from an electric power plant. As shown in Figure 8.1 (which is a replica of Figure 7.2), undertaking this project allows society to move from the status quo, point A, to a new position, point C. Furthermore, in this particular case, the total benefit resulting from the implementation of the project is identified by area ACQ_2Q_1 under the society's demand curve for environmental quality.

However, if a society wants to evaluate the worthiness of this project, information about a project's benefit alone will not be sufficient. Undertaking a project requires the use of scarce societal resources. Thus, to determine a project's worthiness, the benefit of the project has to be weighed against its cost. The basic technique economists use to appraise *public* projects is popularly known as *cost–benefit analysis* (CBA).

CBA is commonly used to appraise a wider range of public projects. Highways, bridges, airports, dams, recycling centers, emission control technology, and a legislative mandate to conserve or preserve resources, are just a few examples of projects that can be evaluated using CBA (see Mishan and Euston Quah 2007). In general, a full-scale CBA uses *four* steps as presented in Exhibit 8.1. It is important to note, however, that these are suggested steps and, as such, subject for some variations.

From the beginning, it is important to know that CBA involves making a *value judgment*. This is because, in assessing the relative worthiness of a project, it is necessary to declare that a given state of nature is either 'better' or 'worse' than another. For example, in Figure 8.1 there is a move from state A (the status quo) to state B (a position attained after the sulfur emission control technology has been implemented). In CBA, the objective is to develop a 'norm' by which one can judge that state A is 'better' or 'worse' than state B. Thus, CBA falls directly into the province of what is known as *normative (welfare) economics* (more on this in the next section).

It is very important to know from the onset that this chapter is not limited to a discussion of CBA. Section 8.6 discusses several alternative methods that can be used either as a complement or a substitute to the traditional CBA for assessing the worthiness of environmental projects. More specifically, the discussion in Section 8.6 includes the following well-known environmental project evaluation criteria: the precautionary principle, cost-effectiveness analysis, environmental impact analysis, risk assessment and risk management, and environmental justice and ethics. In addition, as far as possible, this section discusses the compatibility of each one of these alternative environmental project evaluation methods with traditional CBA procedure.

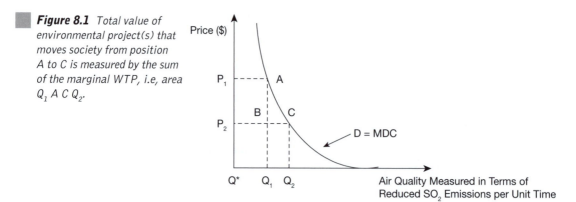

Figure 8.1 *Total value of environmental project(s) that moves society from position A to C is measured by the sum of the marginal WTP, i.e, area $Q_1 A C Q_2$.*

EXHIBIT 8.1   THE FOUR STEPS INVOLVED IN CONDUCTING COST–BENEFIT ANALYSIS (CBA)

1. Specify the social values of concern. There are actually many public and many social values. The first step in CBA is to decide on the values and perspectives of concern to the decision-makers . . . If one is conducting a CBA for a national agency, the public normally would be the population of the entire country. But if an employee of a city or regional planning agency conducts a CBA of a local environmental program, a more appropriate focus would be on the costs and benefits accruing to people living locally in those areas. The first step also includes a complete specification of the main elements of the project or program: location, timing, groups involved, connections with other programs, and the like.

2. Identify and measure the physical and biological changes that should be measured. All that public money for environmental monitoring could really pay off if quality data could be fed into CBAs in this step. For some projects, determining the changes for concern including both input and output flows, can be reasonably easy. For example, in planning a water treatment facility, the engineering staff will be able to provide a full physical specification of the plant, together with the inputs required to build it and keep it running. For other types of programs, such determinations can be much harder. For example, a restriction on development in a particular region can be expected to reduce runoff locally. But what could be the actual environmental consequences? Could the restrictions deflect development into surrounding 'green fields?' In this step, we become acutely aware of the time it can take to complete large environmental projects and the even greater time involved as their impacts play out. Uncertainty

management becomes a major factor in the process because the job of specifying inputs and outputs involves predictions of future events, sometimes many years after an intervention begins.

3. Estimate the costs and benefits of changes resulting from the program. Assigning economic values to inputs and outputs flows is done to measure social costs and benefits. Typically, costs and benefits are measured in monetary terms. This does not mean relying on market value because in many cases, particularly on the benefit side, the effects are not registered directly in markets. Neither does it imply that only monetary values count. It means we need a single metric to translate all of the effects on an intervention to make them comparable among themselves and with other public activities. When we cannot find a way to measure how much people value these effects, it is important to supplement monetary results of a CBA with estimates of intangible effects.

4. Compare costs and benefits. In this final step, total estimated costs are compared with total estimated benefits. However, if benefits are not to be realized until some time in the future, first they must be converted to the present-day value, factoring in the selected discount rate . . . This judgement call deserves special examination and discussion and is closely linked to Step 1, in which social values of concern are identified. The present value of the stream of benefits minus the present value of costs give the present value of net benefits.

Source: *Revealing the Ecological Economic Value of Protecting the Great Lakes*, Northeast-Midwest Institute and National Oceanic and Atmospheric Administration (2001), pp. 60–61.

8.2 THE WELFARE FOUNDATION OF COST–BENEFIT ANALYSIS

Welfare economics deals with economic methodologies and principles that are indispensable to policymakers engaged in designing and implementing collective decisions. The following two principles of welfare economics are especially important since they form the foundation on which economists base their judgments regarding the relative desirability of varying economic states of nature:

- *Principle I*: 'Actual' Pareto improvement states that if, by undertaking a project, no members of a society become worse off and at least one becomes better off, the project should be accepted.
- *Principle II*: 'Potential' Pareto improvement states that a project should be considered if, by undertaking it, the gainers from the project can compensate the losers and still remain better off in their economic conditions than they were before.

Let us examine the implications of these two principles by using Figure 8.2. The hypothetical production possibility frontier curve describes the choices that a given nation is facing between *conservation* (setting aside more land for wilderness) and *development* (using land to produce consumption goods and services or to increase the production capacity of the economy). Suppose that point M on the production possibility frontier represents the status quo. Recently, the government of this hypothetical nation has passed legislation that mandates the expansion of the public land that is specifically designated for wilderness. The expected effect of this mandate on the economy of this nation is shown by a movement along the production possibility frontier from point M to N.

According to the criterion outlined in Principle I, the move from point M to N should be accepted if, and only if, not one single member of this hypothetical nation becomes worse off and at least one becomes better off as a result of such a move.

However, it is highly unlikely that a situation of this nature could occur in the real world. For our hypothetical nation, some pro-development individuals are likely to be made worse off by the move from M to N. This is because such a move could be attained only through the sacrifice of goods and services (the move from G_0 to G_1) that are appealing to these particular members of this nation. '*Actual*' *Pareto improvement* would be possible if, and only if, our hypothetical nation has been operating *inefficiently* to begin with, such as at point K. In this case, it is possible to move from K to N without violating Principle I.

On the other hand, according to Principle II, the move from M to N should be acceptable if, and only if, the gain by the pro-conservation individuals (the monetary value of $F_1 - F_0$) is greater than the loss by the pro-development individuals (the monetary value of $G_0 - G_1$). Thus, at least conceptually, the gainers could be able to compensate the losers and still remain ahead. It should be noted, however, that, *Principle II does not require that compensation actually has to occur*. What is stressed is that the 'potential' for compensation exists. Essentially, then, Principle II states that the move from M to N would be

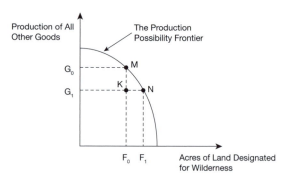

Figure 8.2 *A production possibility frontier representing alternative choices between conservation and economic development. An increase in the land designated for wilderness from F_0 to F_1 would require a decrease in the availability of other goods from G_0 to G_1 unless the initial position of an economy is inefficient, such as point K.*

considered economically 'efficient' provided that the aggregate benefit from such a move exceeded the aggregate cost. That is, the net benefit of the project is positive. In other words, if we let the letters B and C represent aggregate benefit and cost, respectively, then, according to Principle II, the move from M to N would be economically *efficient* provided B – C > 0. In short, real income is higher at point N than at M.

However, it is important to note that *this criterion does not even pretend to address the income distribution effect* of a project. That is, who gains or loses from undertaking a project is considered irrelevant (or something to be addressed after the fact), provided that the net benefit from the project in question is positive (Mishan and Euston Quah 2007).

8.3 THE NET PRESENT VALUE CRITERION

The fundamental normative (welfare) criterion of CBA is actually based on 'potential' Pareto improvement. To understand this, let us see how a project appraisal is performed ordinarily using a CBA approach.

First, CBA requires information on the flow of expected benefits and costs of the project in question. Let B_t and C_t represent the streams of benefits and costs in year t, where t = 0, 1, 2, 3, . . . , n – 1, n. Thus, for example, B_1 and C_1 would represent the benefit and the cost of the project in year 1, and similarly B_5 and C_5 are the benefit and the cost relating

to year 5. The letter n represents the expected lifetime of the project under consideration. If n = 30, the project has an expected lifetime of 30 years, and B_{30} and C_{30} would represent the benefit and the cost of the project in its final year.

Second, we need to know what the *discount rate* is, and what the rate at which the streams of time-dated benefits and costs are weighted is. Let the variable r represent the discount factor, and assume that 0 < r < 1.

Given the streams of the expected benefits and costs from a project and the discount rate, a typical CBA arrives at a decision using the following rule: (1) Compute the *net* present value (NPV) using the formula

$$NPV = \Sigma \{(B_t - C_t)\,[1/(1 + r)^t]\}$$

(2) A decision rule: a project should be *accepted* if its NPV is greater than 0.

The present value formula above is composed of two components: the *net* benefit for year t, $(B_t - C_t)$, and an expression used for weighing the benefit of year t, $[1/(1 + r)^t]$. Thus, accordingly, net present value is calculated by summing (Σ) the weighted net benefits of a project over its entire lifetime. (The formula used to weight the flow of future benefits, $1/(1 + r)^t$, and the rationale behind it may require further explanation. The write-up in Exhibit 8.2 is designed for this purpose and it is a 'must read'.)

EXHIBIT 8.2 THE DISCOUNT FACTOR AND THE RATIONALE BEHIND IT

This exhibit is specifically designed to probe a bit deeper into the nature of the weighing factor, i.e., the expression $1/(1 + r)^t$ and the rationale behind it. It can be shown that what this expression represents is *the present value of a dollar of net benefit coming at the end of t years*. Let us demonstrate what this concept entails using a simple numerical example.

Suppose the value of the discount rate, r, is given to be 0.05 or 5 percent, and let t = 5. This would suggest that the present value of $1 of net benefit coming five

years from now would be $1/(1.05)^5$, or roughly 78 cents. It can be also shown, with the same discount rate, that the present value of a $1 net benefit coming ten and 15 years from now would be 61 and 48 cents, respectively. Consistent with the results in this numerical demonstration, it can be shown that as long as the discount rate is positive, r > 0, the present value of a dollar *net* benefit declines as time passes. If this is the case, a positive discount rate would suggest putting less weight on the value of net benefit in the future relative to present, hence, *discounting* the future. This has a very important implication for the subject matter in this chapter since a *positive discount rate means giving less weight to environmental benefits (amenities) that accrue in the long term* (more on this later).

What economic rationales can be given for discounting future benefits? According to conventional wisdom, this behavior depicts a simple fact that people typically have *a positive time preference*—that is, other things remaining equal, people prefer their benefit now rather than later. In fact, this preference is evidenced by the fact that financial institutions must offer interest payments in order to get people to deposit money, thereby foregoing current consumption. Viewed in this way, discounting reflects the *opportunity cost* of not having access to

money or any other immediate benefits. What does this all mean for the *intertemporal* choice of environmental amenities, a subject that is of particular interest to us? Taken literally, discounting suggests that people would value environmental amenities (for example, recreational experiences such as water-rafting, fishing, skiing, etc.) more highly now than if they were provided with the *same* experience 20 years from now. Why so?

Two explanations are given for this behavior: (1) people tend to discount the future because they are *myopic* or impatient (Mishan 1988); and (2) people are *uncertain* about the future (Mishan 1988; Pearce and Nash 1981). Discounting is an important issue in cost–benefit analysis, and it will be discussed further in Section 8.5.

As mentioned above, according to the NPV criterion a project is declared acceptable if the *sum of the net discounted benefit over the lifetime of the project is positive*. This result is, in fact, consistent with potential Pareto improvement, according to which a project is worthy of consideration provided the net benefit from the project is positive—that is, B –C > 0. It is in this sense, then, that potential Pareto improvement serves as the *theoretical foundation for CBA* that is based on the *net present value criterion*. However, this also means that a CBA that is based on the net present value criterion has the same pitfalls as the potential Pareto improvement (see 1 and 2 below):

1. When a *net* present value criterion is used for a project appraisal, the acceptability of the project is based purely on *economic efficiency*. In other words, a positive net present value means nothing more than an improvement in real income (Arrow et al. 1996; Dasgupta et al. 1999).
2. The *net* present value criterion does not address the issue of *income distribution*. It focuses exclusively on the project's contribution to the aggregate real income of a society. In other words, the impact that the project may have on income distribution is simply ignored (Mishan and Euston Quah 2007).

As is evident from the above discussion, the use of NPV for project appraisal requires three concrete pieces of information, namely estimates for both the annual *benefits* and *costs* over the expected lifetime of the project and the *discount rate*. Since the net present value criterion is used to assess public projects, these three variables need to be assessed from the perspective of *society* at large. To fully understand what this actually entails, it would be a worthwhile exercise to compare and contrast how benefits, costs and discount rates are treated in project appraisals in the *private* and *public* sectors.

8.4 PRIVATE VERSUS PUBLIC PROJECT APPRAISAL

As noted above, CBA is used primarily for project appraisal in the public sector. An analogous approach used in the private sector is called *financial appraisal* or *capital budgeting*. When the net present value is used, both CBA and financial appraisals follow the same criterion for accepting or rejecting a project. That is, a project is accepted if NPV > 0. However, the two approaches *differ significantly* in the methods used to estimate the costs and benefits of a project and the choice of the discount rate. This section explains why this is so.

Estimation of benefits

In the private sector, benefit is identified as *revenue or cash flow*, and it is obtained by simply multiplying market price and quantity. However, for public projects benefit is measured by the *sum of individuals' willingness to pay (WTP)* along the relevant range of the demand curve for a product or a service under consideration.

These two approaches to measuring benefit could result in markedly different outcomes. To see this, let us revisit our earlier example of a project designed to control sulfur dioxide emissions from electric power plants located in a certain region. As shown in Figure 8.1, for society at large in any given year, the total benefit from this project is represented by the area ACQ_2Q_1. This value is obtained by summing the WTP (the prices) along the relevant range (Q_1 to Q_2) of the demand curve for environmental quality.

However, if the project's benefit is to be evaluated using the demand price, P_2, associated with the Q_2 level of environmental quality, the incremental benefit of increasing the environmental quality from Q_1 to Q_2 would be $P_2 (Q_2 - Q_1)$ or the area of the rectangle Q_1BCQ_2 (the revenue or cash flow from the project). This would have been the case if the project had been viewed as a private concern. Accordingly, the benefit estimate by the public sector would be greater than for the private concern by the area of the triangle ABC—the consumers' surplus realized by this particular society as a result of improving its environmental quality from Q_1 to Q_2. In summary, the estimate of benefit from a public project includes the *cash flows plus consumers' and producers' surpluses*, whereas in the private sector the estimate of benefit from a project includes *only cash flows received by private concerns*. Thus, unless the size of the project is *very small*, the difference in the estimates of benefits using these two approaches could be quite significant.

It is worthwhile mentioning one other important issue regarding the nature of the benefits of a public versus private project. As discussed in Chapter 7, because most public projects, especially those associated with the environment, tend to be *externality ridden*, an estimation of their benefits poses a major challenge and often requires the use of valuation techniques that are subject to major controversies. Exhibit 8.3 shows general guidelines for CBA that incorporates environmental valuation—the valuation of benefits that are indirectly traded in markets or not traded at all. In contrast, the estimation of the benefits from private projects tend to be a straightforward exercise because it is based on actual observable market information of price and quantity changes.

EXHIBIT 8.3 GUIDELINES FOR COST–BENEFIT ANALYSIS THAT INCORPORATE ENVIRONMENTAL VALUATION

Principles for valuing benefits that are indirectly traded in markets (i.e., reduction in health and safety risks, the use values of environmental amenities, and scenic vistas):

1. To estimate the monetary value of such an indirectly traded good, the willingness-to-pay valuation methodology is considered the conceptually superior approach.
2. Alternative methods may be used when there are practical obstacles to the accurate application of direct willingness-to-pay methodologies.

3. A variety of methods have been developed for estimating indirectly traded benefits. Generally these methods apply statistical techniques to distill from observable market transactions the portion of willingness to pay that can be attributed to the benefit in question. Examples include estimates of the value of environmental amenities derived from travel-cost studies, hedonic price models that measure differences or changes in the value of land, and statistical studies of occupational risk premium in wage rates.

4. For all these methods, care is needed in designing protocols for reliably estimating benefits in adapting the results of previous studies to new applications.

5. Reliance on contingent valuation methods depends on hypothetical scenarios, and complexities of the goods being valued by this technique raises issues about its accuracy in estimating willingness to pay compared to methods based on (indirect) revealed preferences.

6. Accordingly, value estimates derived from contingent valuation studies require greater analytical care than studies based on observable behavior. For example, the contingent valuation instrument must portray a realistic choice situation for respondents—where the hypothetical choice situation corresponds closely with the policy context to which the estimates will be applied.

Principles and methods for valuing goods that are not traded, directly or indirectly in markets (e.g. goods such as preserving environmental or cultural amenities apart from their use and direct enjoyment by people):

1. For many of these goods, particularly goods providing non-use values, contingent valuation methods may provide the only analytical approaches currently available for estimating values.

2. The absence of observable and replicable behavior with respect to the good in question, combined with the complex and often unfamiliar nature of the goods being valued, argues for great care in the design and execution of surveys, rigorous analysis of the results, and a full characterization of the estimates to meet best practices in the use of this method.

Source: *Revealing the Ecological Economic Value of Protecting the Great Lakes,* Northeast-Midwest Institute and National Oceanic and Atmospheric Administration (2001), pp. 59–60.

Estimation of costs

The approaches used to assess the costs of a project are also materially different between the private and public sectors. In the private sector, the cost estimate of a project reflects all of the *direct* costs associated with the implementation and operation of the project in question. In other words, in the private sector cost estimates include all the monetary expenditures by private firms on acquiring resources to make the project operational. Costs that directly affect the interests of the private firms under consideration are considered relevant. Furthermore, these costs are 'financial' to the extent that their estimate is based on market prices; therefore, they *may or may not reflect opportunity costs* (the value of alternatives not chosen).

On the other hand, in the public sector costs are measured in terms of forgone opportunities (see Case Study 8.1). Moreover, both the internal and the external costs of the project should be included. In short, an estimate of a cost for a public project should

reflect *social costs*—which include both the internal and the external costs of a project evaluated in terms of opportunity costs (Mishan and Euston Quah 2007).

However, one has to be extremely cautious in evaluating the social cost of a project. In an attempt to include all of the relevant internal and external costs, it is quite easy to count some costs more than once. *Double counting* is, therefore, a very serious problem in the CBA of public projects (Ibid).

To illustrate this let us go back once more to the example dealing with a legislative mandate enacted for the purpose of conserving wilderness. As shown in Figure 8.2, the effect of this project or legislative mandate has been to move this society from its initial position, M, to a new position, N. The new position is associated with less consumption of goods and services and more wilderness. More specifically, the opportunity cost of expanding the acreage allotted to wilderness from F_0 to F_1 is measured by a decrease in the production of conventional economic goods and services from G_0 to G_1.

CASE STUDY 8.1 ECONOMICS AND THE ENDANGERED SPECIES ACT: COSTS OF SPECIES PROTECTION

Jason F. Shogren

When Congress passed the Endangered Species Act (ESA) of 1973, it was explicit in stating that economic criteria should play no role in species listings or in the designation of critical habitat. It was not until the amendments to the ESA in 1978 that economics first entered into the ESA.

Today it does not take an economist to see that economic issues are critical to the ESA debate. With a large fraction of endangered or threatened species inhabiting private land (75 percent according to a 1993 estimate by The Nature Conservancy), a significant portion of the ESA costs are borne by private property owners, while the ESA benefits accrue to the entire nation. Assessing costs and benefits in endangered species protection, however, is not simple. This exhibit illustrates the difficulties associated with assessing the costs of species preservation. These costs include the transaction costs of species protection, opportunity costs to property owners of restricted property rights, and opportunity costs of public funds used in species recovery.

The best measure of economic loss is opportunity cost. Opportunity costs include the reduced economic profit from restricted or altered development projects including agriculture production, timber harvesting, minerals extraction and recreation activities; wages lost by displaced workers who remain unemployed or who are re-employed at lower pay; lower consumer surplus due to higher prices; and lower county property and severance tax revenue.

Opportunity costs have been estimated for a few high-profile, regional ESA conflicts such as the northern spotted owl. One study estimated that an owl recovery plan would decrease economic welfare by between $33 and $46 billion (Montgomery et al. 1994). Another study estimated the short-run and long-run opportunity costs of owl protection to Washington and Oregon at $1.2 billion and $450 million (Rubin et al. 1991).

Opportunity costs also exist with public programs, because resources devoted to species conservation could have been spent on something else viewed as potentially more valuable to the general public. The US Department of the Interior estimated that the potential direct costs from the recovery plans of all listed species were about $4.6 billion (US Fish and Wildlife Service 1990).

The General Accounting Office (1995) compiled estimates of the predicted direct outlays needed to recover selected species, including the costs of implementing the most important, 'high-priority' recovery actions. The total for the 34 plans with complete cost estimates was approximately $700 million.

Of the money actually expended on endangered species recovery by federal and state agencies between 1989 and 1991 (1989 was the first year data were published), over 50 percent was spent on the top ten species including the bald eagle, northern spotted owl, and Florida scrub (Metrick and Weitzman 1996).

In addition to direct public spending, private expenditures add to the cost of ESA implementation. These expenditures include the time and money spent on applications for permits and licenses, redesign of plans, and legal fees. National estimates for these expenditures do not exist for the ESA. As a possible benchmark, private firms fighting over Superfund spent an estimated $4 billion through 1991 (Dixon 1995).

Source: *Endangered Species UPDATE Vol. 14*, 1997, pp. 4–6. Copyright © 1997 School of Natural Resources and Environment, University of Michigan. Reprinted by permission.

To illustrate the problem of double counting, let us suppose that lumber is one of the conventional goods that are affected negatively. That is, one effect of the new conservation initiative is a decline in lumber production. How should we measure this as part of the social cost to the conservation initiative? One way to do this would be to impute the market value of the decline in lumber that is directly attributable to this particular conservation initiative.

To show more clearly how this can be done, let the variables L_0 and L_1 represent the output of lumber (in cubic feet) before and after the conservation project is implemented. Since we have already postulated that $L_0 > L_1$, $(L_0 - L_1)$ represents the amount in cubic feet by which lumber output is reduced. Then, let P_0 and P_1 represent the real prices of lumber (in cubic feet) before and after the conservation initiative. Other things being equal, we expect that $P_1 > P_0$. Given this information on the changes of the prices and outputs for lumber, we can impute the market value of the decline in lumber that is directly attributable to the wilderness conservation project to be $P_1(L_0 - L_1)$.

However, the decline in lumber from L_0 to L_1 may have additional economy wide effects. For example, a shortage of lumber may cause an increase in the prices for new housing constructions, and household and office furniture. Should cost increases of this nature be imputed as part of the overall costs for the decline in lumber output? In other words, the social cost of the wilderness conservation project should include not only the market value of the decline in lumber, namely $P_1(L_0 - L_1)$, but also the increases in the costs of new houses and household and office furniture. Although at first glance this idea may seem to make sense, a closer look would suggest that *only the market value of the decline in real output of lumber should be counted*. The *inflationary* impact of lumber shortages on the construction of new houses and office furniture should not be counted as part of the costs of the new conservation initiative. Otherwise, it would amount to counting cost twice: once by the increase in the price of lumber (from P_0 to P_1), and then again by the *inflationary* or *secondary* effects of this same price increase throughout the economy.

It is important not to confuse secondary effects of the above nature with externalities or external effects. Unlike environmental externalities (see Chapter 3), secondary effects are not associated with changes in output. For instance, in the example above no indication is given that the increase in price for lumber is causing a decline in new housing and/or the output of the furniture industry.

On the other hand, if the decrease in lumber production has caused an actual decline in new housing construction and/or the output of the furniture industry, then the market value of these real output effects should be a part of the overall cost attributable to the wilderness conservation project. To sum up, in imputing the costs of a public project, all real output effects should be included. However, in CBA, *special care should be taken not to include inflationary or secondary effects of price changes as part of the cost of a project*. Otherwise, for reasons already stated above, we will be double-counting costs.

Choice of the discount rate

A third and final difference between public and private project appraisal is the choice of the discount rate. Both the private and public sectors use positive discount rates: that is, $r > 0$. The difference is that, in general, the public or social discount rate, r_s, is lower than the private discount rate, r_p. There are *two* justifications for this difference:

1. Individuals (or private concerns) will not view the future in the same way as society, which represents the collective concern of individuals. In general, individuals are seen as being *selfish* and *shortsighted* (Mishan and Euston Quah 2007). They seem to be mostly concerned with their own welfare in the present or in the very near future. Hence they do not assign much importance to benefits or costs that might be forthcoming in the future. That is, they tend to heavily discount benefit or cost coming at some future date (Daly 1996). On the other hand, the public sector, which represents society as a whole, is believed to have a longer-term perspective. Thus,

the discount rate used in the public project should be lower than that used in the private sector (Dasgupta et al. 1999).

2. Individuals are more *risk averse* or *uncertain* about the future than society at large. After all, for all practical purposes society can be viewed as having an eternal life. What this means is that private projects are exposed to more risk while public projects are virtually immune. Under this circumstance, efficient allocation of societal resources would dictate that a relatively higher discount rate should be applied to private investment projects (Ibid; Pearce and Nash 1981). In other words, the discount rate should be adjusted upward to reflect the greater risk associated with undertaking private projects.

A pertinent question, then, is how big should the difference between *social* and *private* discount rates be? From past empirical studies, both in the United States and elsewhere, the difference between these two discount rates can range between 3 and 5 percentage points. For social projects, although no consensus view exists, a discount rate of 4 percent (net of inflation) is generally recommended. On the other hand, the private discount rate (net of inflation) could be as high as 10 percent. If this is the case, would a difference of 3 to 5 percentage points matter much? From the viewpoint of resource allocation over time, the answer to this question depends on the *time horizon* of the project under consideration. For more on this read Exhibit 8.4—a 'must read' for those who want to understand the pervasive nature of discounting.

EXHIBIT 8.4   THE PERVASIVE NATURE OF DISCOUNTING

This exhibit shows how project appraisal is sensitive to changes in the discount rate, r, when the time horizon of the project under consideration is long. This is a very relevant issue to consider because most environmental projects (such as the rehabilitation of damaged ecosystems, slowing the trend in global warming, and investing in solar or some other soft-energy projects) require high upfront costs for benefits that are anticipated as being realized in the far distant future. In some cases, the investment(s) may entail costs to an existing generation for benefits to be realized by future generations. How these types of investments are sensitive to the discount rate can be demonstrated through a close examination of the terms and expressions of the NPV formula in the following manner:

$$NPV = \Sigma \, (B_t - C_t) \, a_t$$

where, $a_t = 1/(1 + r)^t$ or the present value of a dollar (i.e., net benefit) coming at time t and for a given discount rate, r. Table 8.1 is constructed to show how the a_t values change for varying durations of time, t, and discount rate, r. For example, when t =10 years and r = 4 percent, $a_{10} = \$0.675$; the present value of a dollar of net benefit coming ten years from now.

Table 8.1 *Computing the value of a_t*

t = Time	r = 0.01	r = 0.04	r = 0.05	r = 0.10
1	0.990	0.961	0.952	0.909
5	0.951	0.822	0.783	0.620
10	0.905	0.675	0.614	0.385
15	0.861	0.555	0.481	0.239
20	0.820	0.456	0.377	0.149
25	0.780	0.375	0.295	0.092
50	0.608	0.141	0.087	0.0085
85	0.429	0.036	0.016	0.0003

Where t is time in year, r is discount rate, $a_t = 1/(1 + r)^t$ or the present value of a dollar coming in time t. In other words, a_t is the weighting factor for the flow of benefit or cost occurring in time, t.

The expression $(B_t - C_t)$, as discussed already, represents the flow of net benefit per unit time, t. Thus, the net present value of a project is obtained by the *sum* of all the *weighted* net benefits of a project over its lifetime. Clearly, the weighing factor is a_t and it has a significant impact on the assessment of environmental projects. This is shown by further observations regarding the entries in Table 8.1 as follows:

1. As shown by the column entries of this table, for any given discount rate, the longer the time horizon, t, the lower the value of a_t. For example, for a discount rate of 4 percent the a_t values range from $0.961 at the end of one year to $0.036 at the end of 85 years. In other words, when the discount rate is 4 percent, a dollar of net benefit coming at the end of a year from today would be worth 96 cents, but merely 3.6 cents if the flow of benefit is occurring at the end of 85 years from now.

2. As shown by the raw entries of Table 8.1, for any given time-period, the higher the discount rate, the lower the value of a_t. For example, at the end of five years (t = 5), the value of a_t will be $0.951 if the discount rate is 1 percent but only $0.62 if the discount rate is 10 percent.

3. If both the discount rate and time increase at the same time, the impact on a_t will be *non-linear*. For example, when the discount rate is 1 percent, at the end of the first year, the value of a_t is $0.99 and at the end of 85 years is $0.429. Suppose the discount rate is increased to 4 percent, the corresponding a_t values at the end of 1 and 85 years will be $0.961 and $0.036, respectively. As can be seen, the impact of increasing the discount rate from 1 to 4 percent causes a reduction in the value of a_t by a factor of 1.03 (0.99/0.961). On the other hand, the impact of the same percentage change in discount rate is shown to have an impact on the a_t value by a factor of 11.9 (0.429/0.036). (Note: If the change has been linear, the value of a_t would have changed by only a factor of 2.55 (85 × 0.03).) Such is the pervasive nature of discounting.

This is an extremely important result since it suggests that when the time duration of a project under consideration is fairly long, the fact that discounting is done at 1 or 4 percent matters a great deal. This is because, as demonstrated above, the impact of discounting is non-linear. In fact, it can be generalized that discounting reduces benefits coming in the far-distant future to virtually zero within a finite time. This is shown in Table 8.1 by the a_t values for years 50 and 85 at interest rates above 4 percent.

Finally, in the above illustration interest rates of 1 and 4 percent are highlighted because, as will be discussed in Chapter 9, one of the ongoing debates in climate change has been what discount rate to use to evaluate the future benefits arising from investments intended to slow global warming. For example, the Stern Review used a discount rate of 1 percent to discount net-benefits arising from projects associated with mitigating future global warming, while several others consider 4 percent or even higher to be quite appropriate. Clearly, these choices are not inconsequential. Eighty-five years is used simply to limit the discussion to within the expected lifetime of humans (at least in the developed nations).

8.5 DISCOUNTING AND INTERGENERATIONAL EQUITY

In our discussions in the previous section, we noted that projects dealing with the conservation of environmental assets (such as coastal wetlands, wilderness, national parks, estuaries, etc.) are highly sensitive to discounting because their benefits are realized in the distant future (see Exhibit 8.4). Moreover, while the decision about project appraisal is done on the basis of the preferences of the current generation, a particular feature of environmental costs and benefits is that they often *accrue to people in generations yet to come*. Under these circumstances, since discounting implies that gains and losses to society are given less value the more distant they are in the future, can the use of a positive discount rate be ethically and morally justifiable? What restraints, if any, should the current generation voluntarily accept for the benefit of the future? As would be expected, even within the economics profession the responses to this question vary widely depending on one's point of view about humankind's future predicament (Daly 1996; De Shalit 1995).

For many economists, the use of a positive discount rate is not an issue of significance *per se*. It simply reflects that people have a *positive time preference*, which is considered to be normal (for more on this refer to back to Exhibit 8.2). The implication is, if present consumption is preferred to later consumption for any reason then positive discounting is appropriate.

A variation of this argument is that discount rates should be positive on the grounds that the rate of return on investment is positive (Dasgupta et al. 1999). Thus, for most economists (primarily neo-classicist ones), what is important in appraising any project is choosing the appropriate discount rate (Ibid). More specifically, for public projects, which include most of the projects of an environmental nature, the *social* discount rate should be used (Ibid; Mishan and Euston Quah 2007). For reasons that have been discussed in the previous section, in most instances the social discount rate tends to be *smaller* than its private counterpart. In this sense, then, preferring *social to private discount rates* of itself constitutes an *intentional step towards allowing distributional fairness among generations* (Mueller 1974).

However, will this be adequate? In other words, since discounting, however small, implies unequal weighting of costs and benefits over time, can there be distributional fairness when the discount rate is not reduced to zero? Those professionals who uphold the position that intergenerational fairness need not demand a zero discount rate support their position with the following line of reasoning:

1. Generations do overlap. The current population includes three generations: grandparents, parents and children. Parents care for their children and grandchildren. Current children care for their children and grandchildren, etc. Thus, this chain of generational caring clearly indicates that *the preference function of the current generation takes the interest of the future generation into account* (Baumol 1968).
2. To argue for a zero social discount rate when market conditions indicate otherwise would lead to an inefficient allocation of resources; the current generation would be operating inside its

production possibility frontier. Concern for intergenerational fairness can be addressed through public policy measures that have no effect on prices, such as some sort of lump-sum tax. In other words, *addressing the concern for intergenerational equity need not impoverish the current generation unnecessarily* (Arrow et al. 1996; Nordhaus 1994).

3. Historically the average wealth (income) of the current generation has been higher than that of its immediate predecessor. Given this historical trend of upward mobility in standard of living, why should the current generation voluntarily accept such a condition (such as a zero discount rate), thinking that it might benefit the future? This sentiment is eloquently expressed by Baumol (1968: 800), a prominent economist, who states that:

    > in our economy if past trends and current developments are any guide, a redistribution to provide more for the future may be described as a Robin Hood activity stood on its head—it takes from the poor to give to the rich. Average real per capita income a century hence is likely to be a sizable multiple of its present value. Why should I give up part of my income to help support someone else with an income several times my own?

4. Using the so-called Ramsey-Koopmans theory, it is argued that investment projects with long-run effects should be evaluated using the same conceptual decision rules as those that affect only the near future (Dasgupta et al. 1999). Hence, this particular view prescribes to the notion that there should not be a difference between the social and private discount rate. Furthermore, given that the rate of return on investment is positive, both the private and social discount rates cannot be zero.

On the other hand, there are a few economists (Sen 1982; Stern 2007) who oppose the use of positive discount rates when appraising public projects (especially projects designed to conserve the amenities of the natural environment). The reasoning behind this position is that, as shown in Exhibit 8.4, for projects with long time-horizons discounting effectively *reduces future benefits and costs to zero after a finite number of years*.

This has the effect of favoring projects associated with either short-term benefits (such as development projects instead of projects designed to conserve environmental amenities) or long-term costs (such as the construction of a nuclear plant). In either case, the wellbeing of future generations is put at risk. Given this, there are economists who argue that intergenerational fairness justifies no discounting at all—a *zero* discount rate (Stern 2007). Some economists have gone even further and argued for *negative* discounting to reflect the need for greater protection of the interest of future generations in natural resource management decisions dealing with either irreplaceable amenities (such as the Grand Canyon) and/or irreversible outcomes, such as global warming and species extinction (Dasgupta et al. 1999).

However, it should be pointed out that the *risk* of considering a zero or negative discount rate is the possibility that it may *hinder important technological advances*. Of course such an outcome, if realized, would have negative welfare implications to both current and future generations—an economically inefficient (or Pareto inferior) position, indeed (Arrow et al. 1996).

Clearly, what the analysis in this section indicates is the intractable nature of the task of resolving the contradiction between efficiency and the concern for the future generations (Arrow et al. 1995; Dasgupta et al. 1999). However, intractability need not suggest paralysis. It simply indicates that the consideration of intergenerational equity, although a subject that defies clear-cut answers, requires the thoughtful and serious application of all the relevant economic, ecological, moral and ethical concerns to the issue in hand. Are there alternative methods of environmental project assessments that are likely to be more sensitive or accommodating to these issues than the traditional CBA? This question anticipates the discussions in the next section.

8.6 OTHER ENVIRONMENTAL PROJECT EVALUATION CRITERIA

So far, the discussion has been confined to key issues normally raised in the standard economic appraisal of environmental projects: CBA. Using CBA has been criticized for a number of reasons. Most importantly, the focus of CBA on things that can be measured and quantified in money terms is considered its major flaw. The fact that intangibles (ecosystem services that cannot reasonably be assigned a monetary value) are included in the decision process as ancillary information has not provided any consolation to the ardent critics of CBA. In this section, an effort will be made to provide a brief account of a number of alternative methods for the appraising of environmental projects that are used either to supplement or, under certain circumstances, replace the conventional CBA.

The precautionary principle

In broad terms, and applicable to environmental resources, precautionary principles convey the idea that society should take action against certain practices when there is potential for *irreversible* consequences or for severe limits on the options for future generations—even when there is as yet no incontrovertible scientific proof that serious consequences will ensue. Global warming, ozone depletion, the introduction of new species and protection for rare, threatened or endangered ecosystems and habitats are examples of environmental concerns where precautionary principles may be applicable.

In the case of global warming, the ongoing policy debate has been the rate at which greenhouse gas (GHG) emissions should be curtailed to avert environmental damage from climate change in the future. For example, one study recommended a 71 percent reduction from baseline (i.e., the 1990 level of global carbon emission) by 2050 (Cline 1992). This implies that if no aggressive action of this nature is taken, the damages arising from climate change (such as flooded coastal cities, diminished food production, loss of biodiversity, land lost to oceans, increased storm damages and so on), despite the scientific uncertainty, are expected to be quite significant (Ibid; Stern 2007). There is more on this in Chapter 9.

On the other hand, Nordhaus's study (1994) of this same subject matter, but using a standard CBA approach, recommended policy actions that were far too modest—an abatement of 11 percent of total GHG emissions (see Chapter 9). It is also important to note that there are some academics and industry groups who are reluctant to consider the precautionary principle seriously because it may have serious effects such as discouraging economic growth and scientific discovery (Holm and Harris 1999)

The main reason for the difference in the policy recommendation between the above two empirical studies is simply this: when precautionary principles are applied, in the case of global warming, the high social opportunity costs that are associated with anticipated large-scale and irreversible degradation of natural capital are sufficient to warrant aggressive action to slow down GHG emissions (Cline 1992; Stern 2007). This conclusion would be reached despite the scientific uncertainty about the outcomes of future damages. In other words, precautionary principles take the position that, in order to safeguard against the large-scale, irreversible degradation of natural capital, the prudent course of action entails *erring on the side of the unknown* (Cline 1992; Krutilla 1967; Stern 2007) This is, indeed, the essence of the precautionary principle.

It is important to note that the precautionary principle is different from the traditional CBA because the decision is based *exclusively* on avoiding damages to generations of people living in the far distant future. In other words, the fact that a policy to slow global warming could reduce current consumption (GDP) is not considered at all. Obviously, the basic premise of the precautionary principle is not *efficiency*, since no claim is made that a dollar spent on projects to slow global warming today must be justified by benefits of a dollar or more that are expected to be realized from avoiding future environmental and ecological damages (Ibid). Essentially, precautionary principles favor *prudence* over efficiency, and prudence is the justification for the bias that precautionary principles exhibit towards protecting future generations.

The Endangered Species Act of 1973 (amended in 1988) in the United States is another public policy provision where precautionary principles have been successfully applied (Rubin et al. 1991; Shogren 1997). According to this Act, individual areas can be excluded from the designation of critical habitat. Therefore extinction of species is allowed if, and only if, the economic impacts of preservation are judged to be *extremely severe* or *intolerable*. In other words, exemption from species protection cannot be allowed just because the overall economic impact (in terms of changes in output and employment) of such action is found to be *negative*, as conventional CBA would have suggested (more on this in Chapter 13). In the Act, this seemingly precautionary condition is stipulated with an intention to diminish the likelihood of accepting a project or policy action with an outcome that is irreversible—the extinction of species in this case.

Cost-effectiveness analysis

Cost-effectiveness analysis (CEA) deals with least-cost methods of achieving a stated environmental goal. An example would be a project to clean up a river in a certain specified location with an objective to attain a clearly specified water quality. Here, the desired water quality may be based on factors other than economic reasons: for example, political pressure from a certain special-interest group, consideration of a well-documented health risk, or consideration of social justice or ethics.

In CEA, the *benefits from a project are taken for granted and considered important*. Hence, the *emphasis is on costs*. Operationally, CEA analysis entails ranking the various technological approaches designed to accomplish the desired environmental objective. This ranking is done purely on the basis of cost-effectiveness—the biggest bang for the buck. Clearly, CEA differs from traditional CBA, where both the costs and benefits of a project are considered. Using CEA is often justified when *identifying benefits is difficult or too costly*.

It is important to note that this methodology, CEA, was used in Chapters 5 and 6 to develop a theoretical framework for pollution control. Thus, the discussion here is intended to show how this methodology is related to standard CBA and to indicate its broader applications. Critics of CEA very much doubt if analysis of this nature adequately considers hidden ecological costs. This is because it completely omits consideration of environmental benefits, and in so doing consideration of environmental damages. Remember that environmental benefits are avoided environmental damages.

Environmental impact analysis (EIA)

The primary focus of EIA is on tracing all the relevant physical or ecological *linkages* through which environmental impacts of given projects are manifested or spread. Since the emphasis is on ecological rather than economic linkages, EIA is primarily performed by natural scientists. In the United States, the National Environmental Policy Act (NEPA) of 1969 requires that all federal agencies file an environmental impact statement (EIS) for any proposed legislation or project having a significant effect on environmental quality. The NEPA also created the Council on Environmental Quality (CEQ), an executive agency, among others, that establishes guidelines for preparing environmental impact statements. Each EIS must include (Miller 1991: 576):

1. The purpose and need for the proposed action;
2. The probable environmental impact (positive, negative, direct and indirect) of the proposed action, and possible alternatives;
3. Any adverse environmental effects that could not be avoided should the project be implemented;
4. Relationships between the probable short-term and long-term impacts of the proposal on environmental quality;
5. Irreversible and irretrievable commitments of resources that would be involved should the project be implemented;
6. Objections raised by reviewers of the preliminary draft of the statement;
7. The names and qualifications of the people primarily responsible for preparing the EIS; and

8. References to back up all statements and conclusions.

The EIA process has been successful in forcing government agencies to carefully scrutinize the side-effects of publicly funded environmental projects at all governmental levels—local, regional, state or national. It has also had the effect of forcing government agencies to evaluate projects by considering the possible alternatives. Because of its success in the United States, several nations worldwide have adopted the use of EIA (for example, France 1976 and the European Union in 1985).

EIA is not without its own shortcomings. EIAs are retrospective: that is, they are often prepared to justify a decision that has already been made. Most EIAs do not receive careful scrutiny because of costs. Also, EIAs do not make any attempt to directly impute *social values* on the impacts identified as relevant for evaluating the project, hence it is far removed from CBA.

Environmental risk assessment and risk management

Risk assessment and risk management are valuable in the area of environmental regulations, and they are extensively used by the US EPA (US EPA 1999). Other areas where information obtained from risk assessment and risk management would be invaluable are, as discussed in Section 7.3, in the attempts that environmental economists often make to impute monetary values to occupational risk, mortality and morbidity (placing a value on human life and health). In this sense risk assessment, and risk management in general, provides significant contributions towards assessing environmental damage and formulating environmental regulatory policies. This process also contributes to assessing environmental benefits—a key variable in conventional CBA. So then, what do we mean by environmental risk assessment and risk management? How is risk assessment performed? Is there a radical difference between risk assessment and risk management?

Risk assessment is the scientific foundation for most EPA regulatory actions (US EPA 2007). It is the process by which scientific data are analyzed to describe the form, dimension and characteristics of risk—that is, the likelihood of harm to humans or the environment (Paustenbach 2002). The scope and nature of risk assessment range widely—from broadly based scientific conclusions about air pollutants such as lead or arsenic affecting the nation as a whole, to site-specific findings concerning these same chemicals in a local water supply (Ibid). Some assessments are retrospective, focusing on injury after the fact—for example, the kind and extent of risks at a particular toxic landfill site (US EPA 1999). Others seek to predict possible future harm to human health or the environment—for example, the risks expected if a newly developed pesticide is approved for use on food crops.

By its very nature environmental risk assessment is a *multidisciplinary* process (to a varying degree this is also the case for many of topics addressed in this section). It draws on data, information and principles from many scientific disciplines including biology, chemistry, physics, medicine, geology, epidemiology and statistics, among others (US EPA 2007).

For human-health risk assessment, the process takes place in a series of steps that begins by identifying the particular hazard(s) of the substance: hazard identification. Subsequent steps examine 'dose-response' patterns and human exposure considerations, and the conclusion is a 'risk characterization' that is both qualitative and quantitative (Moolgavkar and Luebeck 2002). As an example, when expressed numerically, the risk for cancer from pollutant $\times$ may be presented as 1×10^{-6} or 0.000001, or one in a million—meaning one additional case of cancer projected in a population of one million people exposed to a certain level of pollutant $\times$ over their lifetimes. It is important to note that the quantitative result of risk is a *worse case* estimate and indicates an *average* attributed risk—it applies to no one in particular and to everyone on average (Ibid; US EPA 2007).

As would be expected, risk assessments are not infallible. For one thing, information regarding the effects of small amounts of a substance in the environment is often not available, and data from animal experiments must be extrapolated to humans. Such extrapolation cannot be made with absolute *certainty* (Paustenbach 2002). Therefore, scientific uncertainty is a customary and expected factor in all environmental risk assessment. As much as possible, it is important to identify uncertainties and present them as part of risk characterization.

On the other hand, *risk management* is the process by which the risk assessment is used with other information to make regulatory decisions. The other information includes data on technological feasibility, on costs, and on the economic and social consequences (e.g., employment impacts) of possible regulatory decisions (AIRMIC et al. 2002). In most instances, risk managers consider this additional socioeconomic and technological information together with the outcome of the risk assessment when evaluating risk management options and making environmental decisions (Ibid; US EPA 1999).

Risk assessment and risk management are closely related and equally important but different processes, with different objectives, information content, and results. Risk assessment asks 'How risky is the situation?' and risk management then asks 'What shall we do about it?'

The risk management decision often influences the scope and depth of a risk assessment (Ibid). A question often raised is 'Should risk management (what we wish to do about risk) be allowed to influence risk assessment (what we know about risk)?' This is similar to asking whether politics should control science. However this issue may be interpreted, a nagging concern remains about whether risk management objectives override the risk assessor's impartial evaluation of scientific data. This concern should be taken seriously if it has implications that go beyond the acknowledgement that the application of the results of risk assessment should be sensitive to the policy context.

Rawlsian ethics and environmental justice

Considerations of social justice and ethics in environmental matters arise from two distinct sources. The first emerges from the concern about the distribution of environmental amenities (benefits) or damages (costs) across society within a given generation: *intragenerational equity*. The second source of concern stems from the distribution of environmental benefits and costs across generations: *intergenerational equity*.

Both concerns, while relevant to environmental management issues, are not adequately addressed in traditional CBA—where consideration of economic efficiency is stressed and the distributional or equity considerations given little or no attention. This subsection will attempt to address both intra- and intergenerational equities within the context of environmental issues. Furthermore, it will look at whether including these concerns when making environmental decisions is justified on the basis of social justice (fairness) considerations and ethical theory.

A. Distribution of benefits or costs across generations: Rawlsian justice

Actually, the issue of *intergenerational* equity was already discussed at some length in Section 8.5. At that point, the discussion focused on the effect of *discounting* on the distribution of benefits across generations. Several arguments were made about selecting the appropriate discount rate, and these arguments were presented using a purely economic logic. We now add the case for a discount rate (i.e., valuing the benefit in the future equally with today's benefit) and unlike our previous discussion its justification is solely based on a particular ethical theory: *Rawlsian justice*.

Philosopher John Rawls, in his highly acclaimed book *A Theory of Justice* (1971), attempted to construct a general principle of justice using the following preconditions. Let us hypothesize that every person in an original position is placed behind a 'veil of ignorance' so that no one would have prior knowledge about his or her eventual position in society. For example, in the case of intergenerational decision-making, because of the veil of ignorance people are prevented from knowing the generation to which they will belong. Once placed behind this veil, people

would be asked to develop rules to govern the society (generation) that they would, after the decision, be forced to live in.

Under such a hypothetical setting, it would be in the best interest of the decision-makers to act *impartially* and favor *equal* sharing of resources across generations. Viewed broadly, this so-called Rawlsian justice may be interpreted as suggesting that current generations should use environmental assets in a way that preserves the ability of future generations to enjoy these assets. Some economists have used this ethical principle, sometimes referred to as 'the sustainability criterion', to argue for a zero discount rate. Are they correct in doing so?

From a purely utilitarian perspective, they would be correct if, and only if, placing equal values on time-dated benefits and costs (which are implied by zero discount rate) would ensure equal enjoyment (or standard of living) across generations. However, equal sharing of physical assets may or may not guarantee outcomes that are proportionally enjoyable (measured either in terms of income or utility). Thus, using Rawlsian justice as a justification for zero discounting can be defended only on a purely 'fairness' or moral basis.

Mueller (1974: 1) further stressed the importance of this feature of Rawlsian justice by stating that the social discount rate question is to be viewed as 'one of justice between generations under conditions of individual uncertainty over position, rather than as one generation's paternalism or altruism for the next generation'.

B. Distribution of benefits and costs across current generations: environmental justice

Is it by accident that waste sites and other noxious facilities (i.e., landfills, incinerators and hazardous waste treatment, storage and disposal facilities) are not randomly scattered across the landscape? Waste generation is directly correlated with per capita income, but few garbage dumps and toxic sites are located in affluent suburbs. Waste facilities are often located in communities that have high percentages of poor, elderly, young and minority residents. Is this fair or just? This question points to a very important environmental issue discussed under the heading of *environmental justice*.

Standard economic theory would predict that poverty plays a role in the spatial distribution of environmental hazards. Because of limited income and wealth, poor people do not have the means to buy their way out of polluted neighborhoods. Also, land values tend to be lower in poor neighborhoods, and the neighborhoods attract polluting industries seeking to reduce the costs of doing business. Furthermore, as discussed in Chapter 6, the adoption of specific policies to control pollution (such as tradable emission credits) may tend towards 'hot spots', with social justice implications of the nature discussed here. In recent years, an additional issue has been raised suggesting that *race* is as important a factor as poverty (income) in determining the location of hazardous waste facilities. What this clearly implies is the existence of 'environmental racism'.

Could the claims that poverty and race are two important determinants in the distribution of environmental hazards be empirically verified? Given that poverty and race are highly correlated, is it possible to assess the relative influence of income and race on the distribution of pollution? In other words, are not minorities disproportionately impacted because they are disproportionately poor? If the claim of 'environmental racism' is to be accepted we need to know that race has an impact on the distribution of environmental hazards that is independent of income.

Since the early 1990s a number of studies have been done to answer the questions raised above. In one instance, the results of 15 studies were pooled and analyzed to see what common factual (empirically verifiable) observations could be distilled from their findings. Although these studies vary considerably in their scope and the methodologies employed, the findings point to a consistent pattern. Taken together, the findings from these studies indicate clear and unequivocal class and racial biases in the distribution of environmental hazards. Further, they support the

argument that race has an additional effect on the distribution of environmental hazards that is independent of class. Indeed, the racial biases found in these studies have tended to be greater than class biases (Bryant and Mohai 1992; US EPA 1994).

Although the empirical evidence may not be as complete or conclusive as the bias in the distribution of commercial hazardous-waste facilities, minority groups and the poor, in general, appear to be disproportionately exposed to other types of environmental hazards, such as water pollution, pesticide exposure, asbestos and lead exposures, and so on. Even in the absence of strong empirical evidence, such as that shown in Exhibit 8.5, a convincing theoretical economic argument can be made to show that environmental justice is a valid concern that warrants action (US EPA 1994). At the minimum, environmental justice should be given an *explicit and serious consideration* in the CBA of public projects and the EPA's risk assessment and risk management efforts. If these are done, perhaps the voices of poor and underrepresented minorities will be adequately incorporated such that environmental decisions that have harmful consequences for these groups are avoided.

The issue of environmental justice is not limited to the United States. Although there have not been well-documented empirical studies to support this claim, to a varying degree environmental justice is a very relevant issue in most economically advanced nations. Furthermore, in recent years environmental justice has been a hot and contested international issue as several enterprises from the world's rich nations have been caught shipping toxic waste to dump in the territories of some poor countries (Olurominiyi 2008). These incidents are, of course, in addition to the growing trends of companies from developed nations preferring to locate parts of their industrial operations (mostly in less developed nations) primarily on the basis of environmental considerations—from very lenient, to the almost total absence of, environmental regulations; the so-called *pollution havens* (more on this in Chapter 11).

EXHIBIT 8.5 DISTRIBUTION OF BENEFITS ACROSS SOCIETY

Jay Coggins

It is well know that the distribution of environmental costs and benefits resulting from an environmental intervention, such as the siting of a waste disposal facility, is often geographically uneven, with most of the costs concentrated on neighbors and most of the benefits on more distant users of the facility. Economists have historically neutralized these geographic variables by, as a first step, defining the population affected by an intervention, both local and distant, and sampling from that population in a representative way. The end result is an average measure of willingness to pay for the intervention. If the sample is truly representative, this average should be a good measure of value for the population.

Problem arise, however, when the differential impacts sustained by subpopulations directly correspond with gross differences in income. In these cases, environmental costs averaged over the entire population may not reflect the effect that the intervention would have on wealth (i.e., the opportunity costs) within the individual subpopulations.

If the communities are studied separately, economists can clarify the differences in impacts reflected in each community's willingness to pay for environmental quality. However, interpreting these findings will also be tricky. Based on these findings, economists might falsely conclude that the low-income, near-neighbors are less willing to pay for environmental quality simply because they would have to sacrifice more meaningful goods and services (such as food or health care) to do so than would rich community. *In these cases, economists must attempt to differentiate willingness to pay from ability to pay.*

The key question economists should ask is whether the effect of a given environmental problem is felt most strongly by a low-income subpopulation. *If so, the average willingness to pay obtained by an economic study could be biased downward, precisely because the group most severely affected by the problem has low income and therefore relatively low willingness to pay.*

Source: The Northeast-Midwest Institute and the National Oceanic and Atmospheric Administration (2001), pp. 51–53.

8.7 CHAPTER SUMMARY

Cost benefit analysis (CBA), the main topic of this chapter, is one of the techniques most widely used by economists for appraising environmental projects in the public domain. A project is defined here rather broadly, and it entails any intentional action undertaken by the public to move from the status quo to an alternative state, for example, a legislative mandate to increase the amount of land allocated as wilderness. Another example would be damming a river to divert the water flow of the river in a certain desired direction.

In conducting CBA, both costs and benefits have to be estimated in certain ways, and evaluated from the perspective of *society* as a whole. As discussed in Section 8.4, in considering social costs both the *internal* and the *external* costs of the environmental project under investigation should be carefully evaluated. In fact, CBA differs from capital budgeting or private project appraisal simply because the latter may not include external costs.

However, in an attempt to include *all* of the relevant internal and external costs, it is quite easy to count some costs more than once, and this *double counting* is a serious problem in assessing the costs of environmental projects, forcing one to be very cautious in estimating social costs. Furthermore, as discussed in Section 7.2, the benefits of environmental projects are measured using the concept of WTP. This entails not only knowledge of prices but also measuring an area along the relevant segment of the demand for environmental services (see Figure 8.1). Not an easy thing to do, by any means.

Once both the social benefits and costs of a project are evaluated, the next step in project appraisal is to develop a criterion (a norm) for weighing the benefits of a project against its costs: CBA. For an appraisal of public projects, the fundamental normative (welfare) criterion of CBA is based on potential Pareto improvement. This means, as demonstrated in this chapter, that the sum of the *net* discounted benefits over the lifetime of the project (or net present value) must be *positive*. This is done using the net present value criterion. This criterion leads to the economically *efficient* outcome, but positive net present value focuses only on the project's contribution to aggregate *real* income. CBA does not explicitly consider the effect that the project may have on *income distribution*.

The choice of the *discount rate* is critical when the net present-value method is used as a norm for project appraisal. For public projects (which include most environmental projects) the standard procedure is to use the *social* discount rate, which is *lower* than the *private* discount rate. In general, compared to individuals, society is predisposed to view environmental projects from a long-term perspective. This is important because the flow of benefits from environmental projects tends to stretch over a long time-horizon, and most of the benefits tend to appear towards the later part of the projects' expected lifetime. At the same time, the short-term costs (sacrifice) are considered to be considerable. A good example of this would be a reforestation project (a re-establishment of forest cover either naturally or artificially). The alternative use of this land (cost) might have been its possible use for cash-crop farming or cattle ranching. The benefits from reforestation will be slow, only being fully realized when the forested area reaches its mature stage. Furthermore, the benefits are hard to measure because most of the forest ecosystem services (such as climate regulation, wildlife habitat, scenic beauty, carbon sequestration, and so on) are not exchanged in the marketplace.

However, when the time horizon of a project under consideration is fairly long, as is the case for many environmental projects, the difference between private and social discount rates that are within the range of 3 to 5 percent appears to be *irrelevant*. This is because discounting reduces benefits coming in the far distant future to virtually zero within a finite time, as long as the discounting rate is positive—however small it may be. Thus, what matters is the very fact that a positive discount rate is used.

Furthermore, since discounting implies that gains and losses to society are valued less the more distant they are in the future, can the use of a positive discount rate be morally and ethically justified? This question points to the unsettling issue of intergenerational equity. Furthermore, since the choice of discount rate is made entirely by the current generation, the responsibility of resolving this moral and ethical dilemma cannot be shifted to future generations. What is significant is the one-sided nature of this intergenerational dependency.

What is unsettling here is that, in principle, the current generation could take actions that have the potential to adversely affect the wellbeing of future generations without any fear of retaliation. Should we care (on moral and ethical grounds) about the wellbeing of future generations? The answer to this question is clearly beyond the realm of economics unless, of course, the current generation wishes to identify itself with posterity to such an extent that its preference function is markedly influenced. If this is to happen then, as Boulding (1993: 306) put it, 'posterity has a voice, even if it does not have a vote; and in this sense, if it can influence votes, it has votes too'. By and large, neoclassical economists tend to believe that this is actually possible on the premise that casual observation of generational caring seem to indicate that the preference function of the current generation takes the interest of the future generations into account.

On the other hand, another school of thought (composed of scholars from diverse disciplinary backgrounds) views discounting as being unjust and, as such, should be reduced to *zero*. This position is defended, as explained in the chapter, by a moral principle known as Rawlsian justice. According to this principle, the social discount rate is an issue of *justice* between generations under conditions of individual uncertainty over position, rather than as one generation's paternalism or altruism for the next generation. The intention of this principle is to ensure that current generations are acting in a way that preserves the *ability* of future generations to maintain a living standard that is enjoyed by current generations.

Another method that is advocated as a way of expressing concern about the welfare of future generations is the precautionary principle. The application of this principle is confined to a situation where the action taken by current generations have, or are suspected to have, irreversible consequences with the potential (although uncertain) for large-scale degradation of natural capital that severely limits the options of future generations (e.g., global warming). In this instance, the prudent course of action would be to err on the side of the unknown—entailing a clear bias towards the protection of future generations. Note that, under this circumstance (where the potential for irreversible outcome, although uncertain, exists), CBA is rendered irrelevant.

At the outset of this chapter it was discussed that CBA, using the net present value criterion, does not account for income distribution. Thus, strict application of CBA for selecting waste sites and other noxious facilities (landfills, incinerators and hazardous waste treatment, storage and disposal facilities) is likely to favor outcomes where these facilities are located in communities with a high percentage of poor, elderly, young and minority residents. In fact, several empirical studies support the premise that race and poverty are two factors that are often used when locating hazardous waste sites: for example, a high concentration of low-income housing within close proximity to hazardous waste sites. This issue of *environmental justice* is a significant moral and ethical dilemma facing nations of the world. This problem is not confined to one nation because there have been many accounts of rich nations intentionally exporting pollution and hazardous waste materials to poor nations whose environmental laws are very weak.

Three other methods used to evaluate public projects that are discussed in this chapter are cost-effective analysis (CEA), environmental impact assessment (EIA), and environmental risk assessment and risk management:

1. CEA is used for environmental projects whose benefits are assumed to be large (but where there is difficulty in measuring in monetary terms), and the purpose of the analysis is confined to evaluating the alternative technologies required to undertake the projects based on their costs. In CEA, the objective is to choose the technologies that would accomplish the objective of project(s) under consideration at minimum cost. CEA differs from CBA because it considers only costs.
2. EIA avoids placing monetary values on the costs and benefits of environmental projects entirely. Instead, EIA attempts to trace all the key physical and ecological factors (impacts) involved in an environmental project under

consideration. EIA is performed by natural scientists and, if done well, can provide invaluable information to authorized public agents enabling them to make informed decisions regarding public projects.

3. Environmental assessment and risk management are two related instruments widely used in the area of environmental regulations. In environmental *risk assessment*, scientific data are analyzed to determine the nature of the risk or the likelihood of harm to humans or the environment. It asks the question 'How do we determine how risky the situation under consideration is?''. As discussed in Chapter 7, economists often use results from risk assessment to impute monetary values to occupational risk, mortality and morbidity—important information for assessing the benefits of certain environmental projects. On the other hand, *risk management* entails the actual decision-making process after fully considering the outcomes from risk assessments and in conjunction with other relevant socioeconomic and technological information. It asks the question 'What should we do about it?'

REVIEW AND DISCUSSION QUESTIONS

1. Briefly identify the following concepts: 'actual' Pareto improvement, 'potential' Pareto improvement, capital budgeting, double counting, net present value, private discount rates, social discount rates, the discount factor, positive time preference, the precautionary principle, cost-effective analysis, environmental impact assessment, Rawlsian justice, environmental justice, risk assessment, risk management and pollution havens.

2. Read the following statements. In response, state 'True', 'False' or 'Uncertain' and explain why.
   (a) Double counting is a potentially serious problem often encountered in assessing both social and private projects.
   (b) Addressing the concern for intergenerational fairness need not impoverish the current generation.
   (c) There really is no difference between risk assessment and risk management.

3. Carefully explain the differences and/or similarities between the following pairs of concepts:
   (a) Capital budgeting and cost–benefit analysis.
   (b) Net present value criterion and potential Pareto improvement.
   (c) Private and social discount rates.

4. A hypothetical country has a surplus of $200 million in its budget for the fiscal year just ended. Several proposals have been examined for the use of this money, two of which are emerging as leading candidates for serious consideration. One of the favored projects is to use the entire surplus money for countrywide road repairs. This project is assumed to have an expected life of ten years. The alternative is a proposal to invest the entire $200 million in a long-overdue hazardous waste cleanup.

The table shows estimates of the flow of the net benefits for these two projects

Project 1: road repair		Project 2: hazardous cleanup	
Years	Benefit/year	Years	Benefit/year
1–5	$40 million	1–5	$5 million
6–10	$25 million	6–10	$15 million
		11–20	$45 million

    (a) Using the net present value (NPV) approach, evaluate the two projects using a 5 percent and 10 percent discount rate.

    (b) Would it make any difference which discount rate is used in the final selection between these two projects? Why, or why not?

    (c) If the discount rate is reduced to zero, project 2 will be automatically chosen. Why? Does this provide a clue as to why discounting may be unfair? Explain.

5. The Stern Review on the Economics of Climate Change (to be discussed in the next chapter), a report commissioned by the British government in 2005, argued for *zero* discounting of future generations. What could be the rationale for this? Speculate.

6. Imagine that an environmental regulatory body is in the process of attempting to decide on the level of a toxic substance that can be safely released into an estuary that provides shelter and food for a variety of birds, fish and other animals. This estuary is also located in a very close proximity to a city with a population of about 150,000.

    (a) Given the above hypothetical scenario, explain what specific factors (information) the environmental regulatory body needs to consider in order to evaluate the permissible level of toxic waste to be discharged into the estuary using a standard *risk assessment* strategy.

    (b) What additional information is needed if *risk management* is going to be an integral part of the final risk analysis of the environmental regulatory body? Be specific.

7. If a company locates a plastic recycling facility in a predominantly poor neighborhood of a city, would this be sufficient to place the action in the realm of environmental justice? Discuss.

8. How would you reconcile the two observations below regarding the precautionary approach as a decision-making framework (Russell 2005):

    (a) Making the precautionary principle the norm would encourage scientific responsibility in developing new technologies, rather than encouraging the economic interests of large corporations from dictating what is and is not safe. Particularly given how much is now documented about the harms various chemicals and activities can cause, it makes sense for all scientific research to consider fully its potential adverse impacts.

    (b) The precautionary principle would merely discourage research and development, rendering it costly and impractical. Innovation and experimentation is the lifeblood of the American economy and value system. Stymieing these efforts is in no one's best interests, and if adopted unilaterally it will merely give other countries a lead in technology.

REFERENCES AND FURTHER READING

AIRMIC, ALARM and IRM. (2002) 'A Risk Management Standard', London: The Institute of Risk Management (IRM); ALARM The National Forum for Risk Management in the Public Sector; The Association of Insurance and Risk Managers (AIRMIC), www.theirm.org/publications/documents/Risk_Management_Standard_030 820.pdf, accessed 06/21/2011.

Arrow, K. J., Cline, W.R., Maler, K.-G., Munasinghe, M., Squitieri, R. and Stiglitz, J. E. (1996) 'Intertemporal Equity, Discounting, and Economic Efficiency', in J. P. Bruce, H. Lee, and E. F. Haites (eds.), *Climate Change 1995— Economic and Social Dimensions of Climate Change*, Cambridge: Cambridge University Press: 125–44.

Baumol, W. J. (1968) 'On the Social Rate of Discount', *American Economic Review* 58: 788–802.

Boulding, K. E. (1993) 'The Economics of the Coming Spaceship Earth', in H. E. Daly and K. N. Townsend (eds.) *Valuing the Earth: Economics, Ecology, Ethics,* Cambridge, MA: MIT Press.

Bryant, B. and Mohai, P. (1992) *Race and the Incidence of Environmental Hazards: A Time for Discourse*, Boulder, CO: Westview Press.

Cline, W. R. (1992), *The Economics of Global Warming*, Washington, DC: Institute for International Economics.

Daly, H. E. (1996) *Beyond Growth: The Economics of Sustainable Development*, Boston, MA: Beacon Press.

Dasgupta, P., Maler, K. and Barrett, S. (1999) 'Intergenerational Equity, Social Discount Rates and Global Warming', in P. Portney and J. Weyant (eds.), *Discounting and Intergenerational Equity*, Washington, DC: Resources for the Future.

De Shalit, A. (1995) *Why Posterity Matters: Environmental Policies and Future Generations*, London: Routledge.

Dixon, L. (1995) 'The Transaction Costs Generated by Superfund's Liability Approach', in R. Revesz and R. Stewart (eds.) *Analyzing Superfund: Economics, Science, and Law*, Washington, DC: Resources for the Future.

Holm, S. and Harris, J. (1999) 'Precautionary Principle Stifles Discovery', *Nature*, 400: 398.

General Accounting Office (1995) *Correspondence to Representative Don Young on Estimated Recovery Costs of Endangered Species*, Washington, DC: General Accounting Office.

Krutilla, J. V. (1967) 'Conservation Reconsidered', *American Economic Review* 57: 787–96.

Metrick, A. and Weitzman, M. (1996) 'Patterns of Behavior in Endangered Species Preservation', *Land Economics* 72: 1–16.

Miller, T. G., Jr. (1991) *Environmental Science*, 3rd edn., Belmont, CA: Wadsworth.

Mishan E, (1988) *Cost Benefit Analysis*, London: Allen and Unwin.

Mishan, E. J., and Euston Quah (2007) *Cost Benefit Analysis*, 5th edn., London: Routledge.

Montgomery, C., Brown, G. Jr., and Darius, M. (1994) 'The Marginal Cost of Species Preservation: The Northern Spotted Owl', *Journal of Environmental Economics and Management* 26: 111–28.

Moolgavkar, S., Luebeck, E. G. (2002) 'Dose-response Modeling for Cancer Risk Assessment', in D. J. Paustenback (ed.) *Human and Ecological Risk Assessment: Theory and Practice*, New York: John Wiley & Sons: 151–88.

Mueller, C. D. (1974) 'Intergenerational Justice and the Social Discount Rate', *Theory and Decision* 5, 3: 263–73.

Nature Conservancy (1993) *Perspective on Species Imperilment: A Report from the Natural Heritage Data Center Network*, Arlington, VA: The Nature Conservancy.

Nordhaus, W. D. (1994), *Managing the Global Commons: The Economics of Climate Change*, Cambridge, MA: MIT Press.

Norgaard, R. B. and Howarth, R. B. (1992) 'Economics, Ethics, and the Environment', in J. M. Hollander (ed.) *The Energy–Environment Connection*, Washington, DC: Island Press.

Northeast-Midwest Institute and National Oceanic & Atmospheric Administration (2001), *Revealing the Economic Value of Protecting the Great Lakes*, Washington, DC.

Olurominiyi, L. (2008) *Transboundary Dumping of Hazardous Waste*, Boston, MA: The Encyclopedia of Earth, www.eoearth.org/article/Transboundary_dumping_of_hazardous_waste

Paustenbach, D. J. (2002) 'Primer on Human and Environmental Risk Assessment', in D. J. Paustenbach (ed.) *Human and Ecological Risk Assessment: Theory and Practice*, New York: John Wiley & Sons: 3–84.

Pearce, D. W. and Nash, C. A. (1981) *The Social Appraisal of Projects: A Text in Cost–benefit Analysis*, New York: John Wiley.

Rawls, J. (1971) A *Theory of Justice*, Oxford: Oxford University Press.

Rubin, J., Helfand, G. and Loomis, J. (1991), 'A Benefit–Cost Analysis of the Northern Spotted Owl', *Journal of Forestry* 89: 25–30.

Russell, J. (2005) 'Precautionary Principle', International Debate Education Association (IDEA), www.idebate. org/debatabase/topic_details.php?topicID=357

Sen, A. K. (1982) 'Approaches to the Choice of Discount Rates for Social Benefit–Cost Analysis', in R. Lind, et al. (eds.) *Discounting for Time and Risk in Energy Policy*, Washington, DC: Resources for the Future.

Shogren, J. F. (1997) 'Economics and the Endangered Species Act: Endangered Species Update', Ann Arbor: University of Michigan Press, School of Natural Resources and Environment.

Stern, N. (2007) *The Economics of Climate Change: The Stern Review*, Cambridge: Cambridge University Press.

US EPA (1992) 'Environmental Protection—Has It Been Fair?' *EPA Journal* 18, 1: 1–68.

—— (1994) 'Executive Order #12898 on Environmental Justice: Memorandum for President Clinton', *EPA-175-N-94-001*, Washington DC: EPA, www.epa.gov/fedfac/documents/executive_order_12898.htm, accessed 06/13/2011.

—— (1999) *Ecological Risk Assessment and Risk Management Principles for Super Fund Sites*, Washington, DC: EPA, www.epa.gov/oswer/riskassessment/ecorisk/pdf/final99.pdf

—— (2007). *Integrated Risk Assessment System (IRIS)*, Washington, DC: EPA, www.epa.gov/iris/intro.htm

US Fish and Wildlife Service (1990) *Report to Congress: Endangered and Threatened Species Recovery Program*, Washington, DC: US Government Printing Office.

Part III

The New Scarcity

With the book *Silent Spring* (1962), Rachel Carson was responsible in initiating the modern phase of the environmental movement by warning the public about the long-term effects of misusing pesticides. Half a century later, humanity appears to be confronted with a new warning of environmental disasters of even greater magnitudes. These warnings are coming in the form of climate change, losses in the stratospheric ozone layer, and massive species extinction.

Part III, consists of two chapters (Chapters 9 and 10). Chapter 9 presents the economics of climate change. Here, the scarcity issue refers to the atmospheric capacity to absorb CO_2—the most important of the GHGs. Evidence abounds to suggest that this is caused by steady increases in carbon emissions from fossil-fuel burning since the beginning of the industrial revolution. The economic and ecological impacts of climate change (through its global warming effect) are considered to be quite large in both magnitude and scope, as will be discussed at some length in this chapter.

Chapter 10 covers the economics of biodiversity. Recent interest in this subject has been prompted by empirically verifiable trends in losses of biodiversity on a global scale. This development is disturbing because biodiversity plays important roles in ecosystem stability and resilience, and in the efficiency (productivity) of ecosystems to produce ecosystem services. Biodiversity is, therefore, an important natural capital asset that is becoming increasingly scarce.

Biodiversity and climate change share three common elements that represent a 'new scarcity' reality. First, both biodiversity and climate change provide 'global' public goods. Without question, everyone on earth will be affected by changes in climate and any large-scale loss in biodiversity. Second, both climate change and biodiversity take a very long time to reverse. In the case of climate change, alterations in atmospheric chemistry are slow to reverse because GHGs are a cumulative (persistent) pollutant. Of course, losses in biological diversity are completely irreversible as they involve species extinctions, and could be quite devastating depending on the magnitude and scope of the losses.

Third, from policy perspectives these two environmental concerns require the additional challenges of explicit consideration of uncertainty and a call for unified involvements and actions of the world community through the various United Nations agencies and/or non-governmental organizations (NGOs).

Part III will not include a discussion of the stratospheric ozone layer depletion. This is because, since the mid-1980s, there have been significant technological breakthroughs in the search for substitutes for many of the major ozone-depleting substances, such as chlorofluorocarbons (CFCs).

Chapter 9

The economics of climate change

LEARNING OBJECTIVES

After reading this chapter you will be familiar with the following:

- The science of global warming, including:
  - (a) The chemistry of the atmosphere relevant to global warming;
  - (b) The anthropogenic contribution to global warming;
  - (c) Climate model predictions of future global and regional mean surface-temperature scenarios; and
  - (d) The scientific controversies of climate change.
- The economics of global warming: the specific nature of greenhouse gas (GHG) abatement and damage costs.
- The economic debates on global warming and its impacts on the economy, including:
  - (a) The 'business as usual' approach to global warming and policy implications;
  - (b) The 'gradualist' approach to global warming and policy implications; and
  - (c) The 'precautionary' approach to global warming and policy implications.
- The responses of the international community to global warming concerns, including:
  - (a) The slow but persistent journey of international climate treaties—from the signing of the 1992 Framework Convention on Climate Change to the adoption of the Kyoto Protocol;
  - (b) Key features of the Kyoto Protocol;
  - (c) The Kyoto Protocol: its achievements and setbacks; and
  - (d) The prospect of international climate treaties post-Kyoto Protocol.
- The efficacy of market-based policy instruments to control greenhouse gas emissions: carbon-taxes versus carbon-trading.

This chapter offers a detailed account of both the scientific and economic aspects of global warming. This is the environmental problem of the twenty-first century, and as Sir Nicolas Stern, the highly noted British economist, put it 'climate change is a result of the greatest market failure the world has seen'. This chapter is written to fully capture the essence of this highly consequential claim. The chapter is rather long, the unintended outcome of my effort to provide a balanced and comprehensive coverage of the scientific, economic and international treaties aspects of global warming.

9.1 INTRODUCTION

This chapter attempts to provide a comprehensive treatment of climate change—the most daunting contemporary environmental problem—from an economic perspective. As will be evident from the discussions in this chapter, what makes climate change daunting is not so much that the problem is not well understood, but rather that viable solutions to the problem, first and foremost, requires a unified global commitment for actions. This is the biggest challenge humanity is facing at this very moment, and addressing it requires not just the usual search for technological fixes but also, and most importantly, a commitment for an unprecedented display of human cooperation and political will. It is also important to add that an enduring solution to climate change demands that humanity has the fortitude and foresight to avoid taking actions that will unduly inflict harm on future generations.

With this in mind, the discussions in this chapter are organized in the following ways: Section 9.2 presents the scientific foundation of global warming. This section attempts to clearly, and at some length, lay out the scientific consensus on the causes and consequences of global warming (GW). It also highlights some of the key elements of the criticisms against this consensus scientific view.

This is followed in Section 9.3 with a discussion of the basic theoretical framework that economists use to gain insights into the costs and benefits of actions taken to slow future GW trends. As will be evident from the discussion in this section, the estimation of these two social costs clearly depends on the scientific understanding of climate change and climate modeling.

Section 9.4, provides a survey of the empirical studies that have been performed by economists since the early 1980s. Most of these empirical studies are based on simulation models that incorporate different scenarios for GW trends and its future economic impacts. For this reason, there is a lack of consensus on policy measures that need to be taken to slow future warming trends. To get a better sense of these policy controversies the discussion is organized by grouping the economic studies that have been done in

this area over the past two decades into three broadly defined categories—each category associated with a particular worldview about GW and its future economic and ecological effects.

Section 9.5, presents the various attempts that world governments have made through international treaties and agreements to limit global emissions of GHGs. The last section, 9.6, provides a discussion on the extent to which emissions trading and/or carbon taxes have been effective in controlling global carbon emissions. This is discussed within the context of global climate treaties, primarily the Kyoto Protocol.

9.2 THE SCIENTIFIC EVIDENCE FOR CLIMATE CHANGE AND ITS ECOLOGICAL IMPACTS

In this section an attempt will be made to provide a brief and balanced account of the scientific understanding of the causes and consequences of climate change. This is done in the following order:

1. A working definition of climate change is outlined;
2. The major molecular elements of the earth's atmosphere are identified. This is followed by the discussion of the conditions under which changes in the concentrations of certain molecular elements of the atmosphere would tend to raise the temperature near the earth's surface (i.e., contribute to GW);
3. An attempt is made to document the evidence for the anthropogenic (human) perturbation of the atmospheric composition of the earth since the time of the industrial revolution, mainly due to the combustion of fossil fuels and deforestation;
4. The challenges associated with predicting future warming trends extending over a century or more are discussed; and finally
5. A brief discussion of scenario-based climate modeling is offered. This is important because it generates the basic information needed to estimate the cost of the damages associated with future GW trends.

What is climate change?

It will be instructive to start this chapter with a working definition of climate and climate change. First, since the terms weather and climate are often used as though they mean the same thing, clarifying the differences between these two related concepts will be a good starting point to discussing climate.

Both weather and climate describe the behavior of the atmosphere over a period of time. *Weather* refers to conditions of the atmosphere over a short period of time. It fluctuates rapidly and is primarily characterized by changes in the temperature, humidity, atmospheric pressure, wind, precipitation, clouds, and so on. Weather is hard to predict beyond a week or two because change is caused by rapidly changing atmospheric conditions (IPCC 2007). On the other hand, *climate* refers to the long-term *average* of daily weather in a particular area. Thus, climate varies from place to place, depending on latitude, distance to the sea, vegetation, and the presence or absence of mountains or other geographical factors. Climate varies also in time, from season to season, year to year, decade to decade and on much longer time-scales (Ibid). In this chapter, the emphasis is on climate changes that pertain to the entire globe and extend over a long time-horizon of a century or more.

Thus, *climate change* refers to any change (cooling or warming) in climate over time, whether due to *natural* variability or as a result of *human* activity (IPCC 1996). What should be immediately evident from this definition are the following points:

1. The factors causing climate change could be *natural or human*. It is true that humans have always influenced the condition of their environment (primarily by introducing change in the ways they use land and other terrestrial resources) since at least the beginning of human settlement as an agrarian society. However, as we will see shortly, until the mid-eighteenth century or so, the effects of human-induced factors on climate have been limited mainly to local or regional geographic regions. Thus, as will be evident shortly, for much of the earth's history, the causes of climate changes with global dimensions came from natural factors.

2. The concept of climate change applies either to the *cooling or warming* of global average temperature although the concern of this chapter happens to be GW. Historical records indicate that our planet has gone through several warming and cooling trends during its long history (Barnola et al. 1987). For example, since the mid-ninth century the earth has undergone one warming and one cooling period. During the period from 850 to 1350, the earth's atmosphere experienced a sharp and pronounced warming with an average surface temperature increase of as much as 2.5 degrees Celsius. There was also a cooling period, historically known as the 'little ice age' that occurred between 1550 and 1850 (Taylor 1998). Accordingly, climate change appears to be a repeated (cyclical) event that has occurred several times throughout the earth's history, although the cause(s) for each change may differ. Furthermore, it is important to note from the two examples above that climate change refers to an increase or decrease of the average global temperature extending over a long period of time. Even the so-called 'little ice age' lasted for about three centuries.

According to the currently available scientific evidence (more on this later) the average temperature of the earth has risen between 0.5 to 0.8 degrees Celsius since the industrial revolution (IPCC 2007). Furthermore, this rise in global temperature was observed to coincide with the unprecedented increase in carbon emissions into the atmosphere primarily arising from human-induced activities. Recent evidence based on sophisticated climate modeling (more on this later) appears to indicate that the atmospheric concentration of carbon has been increasing steadily since the beginning of the industrial revolution, from about 280 parts per million (ppm) carbon-dioxide equivalent to about 370 ppm carbon-dioxide equivalent by 2001 (Keeling and Whorf 2002).

The latest figure for the atmospheric concentration of carbon is 394 ppm, a worrisome trend given its potentially dire implication to the future GW trend. To understand how increased atmospheric concentration of CO_2 would cause GW, it is important to have some understanding of the various molecular elements of the earth's atmosphere and the interactions that are prevalent among these elements.

The causes of global warming

How does an increase in the atmospheric concentration of carbon cause GW? To answer this question adequately a closer look at the components of the atmosphere is needed. In terms of its molecular elements, the atmosphere is composed of Nitrogen (N), Oxygen (O_2), Argon (Ar) and various *trace* gases. The three elements, that is, Nitrogen (78 percent), Oxygen (21 percent) and Argon (0.9 percent) constitute the bulk of the atmosphere: 99.9 percent. However, when it comes to understanding GW, it will be a sub-set of the trace gases commonly known as the Greenhouse gases (GHGs) that are going to be of paramount significance (Anthes 1992).

GHGs are composed of carbon dioxide (CO_2), methane (CH_4), nitric oxide (N_2O), ozone (O), and hydroflurocarbons (HFCs). These gases are vital to life on earth in many respects. For example, photosynthesis cannot occur without CO_2 and no one can underestimate the importance of the shielding effect of ozone from ultraviolet light that could cause cancer and blindness in humans. However, the focus here is the ability of these gases to trap or block long wavelengths of heat energy, which can also be referred to as infrared radiation or outgoing heat energy from the earth.

Because of their ability to trap this outgoing heat energy, these gases act as a 'greenhouse' circulating between the earth and the open space. However, as they trap the heat these gases become unstable and eventually release the heat, some of which radiates back to earth (Anthes 1992). Thus, GHGs may be rare, but their impact could be significant since by trapping heat near the planet's surface, they warm our world. To underscore the significance of this, without the presence of GHGs in the atmosphere, it is estimated that the average temperature of the earth (which is around 15 degrees Celsius or 57 degrees Fahrenheit) would be reduced to −18 degrees Celsius

—which would have far-reaching implications for life on earth (Flannery 2005). In other words, without the GHGs, the earth would most likely be a frozen wasteland. When viewed in this way, what humanity is doing right now is polluting the atmosphere with too much of a good thing (Gillis 2010).

It is important to recognize the following properties of the GHGs:

1. Among the GHGs, CO_2 is by far the most abundant. However, each GHG has a different thermal warming potential (TWP)—how much a given mass of a particular GHG contributes to GW over a given time-period compared to the same mass of CO_2. In terms of TWP, ozone and some hydroflurocarbons have considerably higher heat-trapping scores than CO_2 and methane.

2. Even after accounting for its relatively weak TWP, it is estimated that CO_2 accounts for about two-thirds of GW. On the other hand, although very scarce, because of their high potency to trap heat energy approximately ten percent of the GW is attributed to hydroflurocarbons which are entirely created by humans (IPCC 2007).

3. Each GHG has different life cycles (staying power) in the atmosphere. For example, CO_2 and ozone are very long-lived in the atmosphere lasting as long as a century or more, whereas methane is known to stay in the atmosphere for a relatively short time-span of about 12 years. This is a very important point to note because it indicates that some GHGs, such as CO_2 released today will have an impact on global temperatures lasting as long as a century or more (IPCC 1996).

From the above discussion, at least in theory the accumulation of GHGs in the atmosphere over an extended period of time could by itself contribute to an increase in the average global temperature (i.e. GW). However, this may not be as straightforward as it first appears because of other complicating factors.

Most importantly, scientists have noted the existence of other atmospheric factors that could significantly affect the temperature of the earth. Most notable of these factors are water vapor, clouds and aerosol gases—small particles in the atmosphere—from smoke, dust, manufacturing and other sources (Flannery 2005). It is the inclusion of water vapor, clouds and aerosol gases as factors influencing temperature change that have greatly contributed to the ongoing scientific controversies on climate change (more on this later). Furthermore, as will be discussed later, other factors to consider are those associated with climate dynamics—the complex interactions among the various elements of the *climate system* that, in addition to the atmosphere, includes the oceans, the parts of the earth that are covered with ice and snow, the surface of the earth, and the biosphere.

Human factors

There is growing evidence that suggests GW is largely caused by human activities, most notably the increased use of fossil fuels since the beginning of the industrial revolution. What has been the scientific evidence for such an assertion? The earliest and most notable scientific experiment to support this claim goes as far back as the late 1950s. A climatologist named Charles Keeling climbed Mt. Mauna Loa in Hawaii to record the CO_2 concentration in the atmosphere. He then created a graph, the Keeling curve, which plotted the concentration of CO_2 in the atmosphere (as measured at the top of Mt. Mauna Loa) over 40 years (1958–2000). What the Keeling graph showed, among other trends, was a steady increase in CO_2 concentration in the atmosphere. It is the contention of many climate scientists that the fact that the rise in CO_2 concentrations occurred at the same time as an exponential increase in the use of fossil fuels cannot be dismissed as being a mere coincidence (Keeling 2005).

Since the early 1990s, primarily arising from the works of the Intergovernmental Panel on Climate Change (IPCC), there has been additional scientific evidence to support the links between the burning of fossil fuels and the increased concentration of GHGs in the atmosphere. The IPCC was created in 1988 by the World Metrological Organization (WMO) and the United Nations Environmental Programme (UNEP).

The role of the IPCC has been to periodically assess the state of climate science as a basis for informed policy actions. These assessments are done on the basis of experts' peer-reviewed and published scientific literature. So far, the IPCC has completed four major assessment reports with an interval of approximately five years between each one. The latest IPCC report was released in April 2007. Using a highly sophisticated form of climate modeling, the IPCC has been able to affirm with increasing confidence that the cause of GW has been the anthropogenic emissions of GHGs, most notably CO_2. In fact, in its latest report the IPCC has gone as far as attaching a probability figure of 95 percent that the cause for GW is the emission of heat-trapping GHGs arising primarily from human activities. Furthermore, it is observed that over two-thirds of the CO_2 build-up in the atmosphere has occurred since World War II, paralleling the recent era of incredible global economic expansion.

Humans have affected the composition of the atmosphere in several other ways (i.e., in addition to increased emissions of CO_2). The following is a list of some of the major human activities that have contributed to climate change:

1. The industrial age has been responsible for emitting a large amount of an entirely human-made GHGs into the atmosphere; namely, the hydroflurocarbon compounds. These compounds are not only very potent absorbers of infrared radiation, but are also known for causing the depletion of the stratospheric (i.e., the upper atmosphere) ozone layers.

2. Steady economic progress over the past century has been accompanied by a change in the use and management of land. More specifically, it entailed changes in agricultural and forestry practices and a steady increase in urbanization. In many instances, these changes have had a significant effect on the *physical* (i.e., surface roughness and albedo—the average solar energy reflecting power of the earth) and *biological* (i.e., terrestrial vegetation) properties of the earth's surface. The consequence of this has been to change the *balance* of the incoming and outgoing solar radiation in ways that have had momentous impacts on regional and global climatic condi-

tions. Most notably, land-use changes that have caused deforestation (as has been the case in recent human history) have materially affected the carbon cycle. This is because terrestrial plants, such as forests, store significant amount of carbon derived from CO_2.

3. Human industrial and land-use activities have also caused increases in the amounts of aerosol in the atmosphere, in the form of mineral dust, sulfates, nitrates and soot. As discussed earlier, aerosols play an important role in determining the energy balance of the earth's atmosphere system, although their atmospheric lifetime is short.

In summary, what is evident from the discussion so far is that, since the beginning of the industrial revolution, humans have altered the chemistry (i.e., the molecular concentration and composition of the elements) of the earth's atmosphere in various ways. The ultimate effect of this has been to cause a warming trend in the earth's atmosphere and, in recent years, worldwide attention on this development has grown. However, as will be discussed in the remaining parts of this section, this is not in any way to suggest that the concern for GW including its anthropogenic origin is shared by everyone.

Uncertainty regarding climate model predictions

The existence of a scientific 'consensus' on the anthropogenic sources for climate change, as discussed above, should not imply that we now know all we need to know about climate change and its consequences. This is because many details about *climate interactions* (i.e., the interaction of the atmosphere, the oceans, the land surfaces and the biosphere) are still not well understood. What this means is that, while there appears to be ample evidence that increased concentrations of GHGs in the atmosphere has contributed to recent GW, there still remains a great deal of *uncertainty* surrounding the nature, severity, time horizon and regional impacts of future warming trend (Stevens 1999). This is because predictions of future trends in global temperature do not only depend on the atmospheric concentration of

GHGs but also on a host of several other highly interactive factors.

For instance water vapor, which is always present in the atmosphere, is a very potent absorber of heat energy. Hence, the presence of water vapor in the atmosphere reinforces (amplifies) the impacts of GHGs on GW. Aerosol gases, on the other hand, other things being equal, may actually contribute to 'global cooling'. This is because aerosol gases block (reflect back) the heat energy from the sun (shortwave radiation) and in doing so reduce the amount of radiation reaching the surface of the earth. In general, clouds in the upper region of the atmosphere are known to reflect back shortwave radiation which, other things being equal, will have the effect of reducing the surface temperature of the earth. On the other hand, cloud formation that is close to the surface of the earth has the opposite effect, increasing the temperature of the earth (Soroos 1997)

Furthermore, the situation becomes even more complicated when one considers not only the atmosphere but also the dynamic interactions of all components of the climate system: the atmosphere, the oceans, the cryosphere (i.e., the ice and snow cover), the land surface and the biosphere. While it is beyond the scope of this chapter to go into a detailed discussion of the dynamic interactions among all the components of the climate system, it is important to provide a brief mention of the important roles the oceans and cryosphere play in regulating the earth's climate. These are two components of the climate system that have not been addressed so far and yet play a significant role in the heat exchange and carbon circulation of the earth.

The oceans cover approximately 70 percent of the earth's surface. They store and transport a large amount of energy and dissolve and store great quantities of CO_2. This is how they can influence the flux in the global carbon cycle. Furthermore, mainly due to the large thermal inertia of the oceans, they dampen potentially huge temperature changes and in so doing function as a regulator of the earth's climate (Ibid). Thus, while it is important to consider the effect the oceans have on the earth's climate, it also complicates matters when the issue under consideration is to isolate the anthropogenic factors that contribute to GW (Ibid).

Another major influence of the oceans in climate variability comes from the hydrological cycle, which begins with the evaporation of water from the surface of the ocean. This cycle, among others, plays a major role in determining the atmosphere's moisture content and the formation of clouds. Clouds, as discussed earlier, play an important role in the earth's energy balance. They absorb and emit infrared radiation and thus contribute to warming in the earth's surface, just like the GHGs (IPCC 2007).

Another complicating factor that has significant influence in the energy balance of the earth (i.e., the balance between the incoming and outgoing energy in the earth's atmosphere system) is the cryosphere—the portions of the earth's surface that are covered with ice and/or snow. This includes the ice sheets of Greenland and Antarctica, continental glaciers and snow-fields, sea ice and permafrost. Its significance to the climate system comes from, among other things, the fact that it is highly reflective with regard to solar radiation (it has a high albedo), and thus has a significant ability to transfer heat (Soroos 1997). For this reason, it plays an important role in the determination of the earth's surface energy balance.

The upshot is clear. Future trends of global average temperatures may not be influenced by any one single factor. This suggests that models used to project future global temperature trends must account for all the relevant physical processes, the dynamic interactions of climate system (the atmospheres, the oceans, the cryosphere, the surface of the earth) and biogeo-chemical factors affecting the earth's atmosphere (Moffatt 2004).

In addition, the regional impacts of GW, which tend to be highly uncertain, can be sufficiently explained only when adequate consideration is given to the effects of the oceans, clouds and other factors of this nature on surface temperatures. Global warming is *not just about the increase in the average surface temperature of the earth*. It also implies that there will be variations of temperatures and weather patterns on a regional basis. In fact, some have used global 'weirding' instead of warming to indicate that one

outcome of GW is the unpredictable and often intense (hence damaging) regional weather patterns (Calvin 1998; Friedman 2008).

The discussion in this subsection shows that the earth maintains its equilibrium climate state by balancing incoming and outgoing energy through feedback mechanisms that in some way involves all the components of the climate system (the atmosphere, the oceans, the cryosphere, the surface of the earth and the biosphere). This exchange of energy between the surface and the atmosphere maintains, under present conditions, a global mean temperature near the earth's surface of 57 degrees Fahrenheit or 14 degrees Celsius, decreasing rapidly with height (IPCC 2007). Other things held constant, a significant increase in CO_2 and other GHGs in the atmosphere could cause a measureable increase in the global mean temperature near the surface of the earth. As discussed before, this is because these gases have the ability to absorb (trap) infrared or outgoing radiation, effectively causing an imbalance in the heat exchange. In this particular case, there will be more energy radiating down on the earth than there is radiating back out into space. When this happens, something has to heat up. If this trend continues over a long period of time, then GW (or increase in the mean temperature of the earth) would be sustained.

However, projecting future climate change is an extremely difficult task. It gets even harder when there is a need to link the changes in the global mean surface temperature with changes in the emissions of GHGs *extending over a century or more*. This is because the temperature near the surface of the earth is influenced by the interactions of the components of the climate system that include: the oceans, the cryosphere and the biosphere. In other words, to predict the changes of the climate brought about by human activities, one cannot entirely ignore any of these other contributory factors that determine the climate system as a whole.

Despite this apparent difficulty, rough estimates of future global temperature changes resulting from anthropogenic factors are essential in order to identify and assess the physical and ecological damages associated with future GW trends.

183

The potential future effects of global climate change: scenario-based projections

Despite the uncertainty involved in forecasting future temperature trends at both the global and regional level, scientists have been making efforts to explore the likely environmental, ecological, economic and human-health effects of GW on the basis of several scenarios (Moffatt 2004). Each scenario embodies specific assumptions about GHG emissions targets, the range of the projected future temperature increase, changes in demography, social and economic development as well as energy technology.

For instance, the 'business as usual' scenario may be based on the assumption that observed increases in GHGs will continue and the carbon concentrations will be double the pre-industrial levels by 2020. This scenario predicts a warming of 1.6 to 2.6 degrees Celsius above pre-industrial levels by 2030 (Moffatt 2004). Other scenarios are developed by assuming different time-periods for the doubling of the carbon concentration from pre-industrial levels, and this is done by assuming that there will be progressively increasing levels of control over the emission of GHGs.

For example, three scenarios could be developed by delineating the effective doubling of CO_2 to occur by 2040, 2050 and 2100. Once the various scenarios are identified this way, the next step involves assessing the potential future impacts that GW may actually have on the natural environment and socioeconomic wellbeing of humans. As would be expected, this is not a simple matter and involves a great deal of guesswork regardless of the level of the sophistication of the specific scientific models used to arrive at the final projections of any given GW scenarios.

The IPCC reports (1996, 2001, and 2007) have been very valuable sources for these kinds of scenario-specific projections. As will be observed in the next section, these projections are the essential raw materials for economic assessment of future damages (costs) arising from GW. According to the IPCC reports, under the 'business as usual' scenarios the potential impacts of GW may include: glaciers melting, rising sea-levels and the risk of land being lost to coastal flooding; salinity in water supplies and the effect this may have on aquatic plants and animal species; changes in ocean currents and fish supplies; melting of mountain ice-caps and alteration of the seasonal flow of inland watersheds and rivers; changes to natural vegetation belts and to agricultural production; increased risks of storms and hurricane damages; water shortages in some regions and flooding in other regions of the world; increased human morbidity and mortality arising from heat stress and the expansion of the range of tropical diseases such as malaria, dengue fever, and so on; increased risk of forest fires in some regions of the world; and increased risk of hunger and mass migrations.

As implied by our discussion in the previous section, it is not difficult to expect that the environmental and socioeconomic impacts of GW will vary regionally, and in some cases by quite a considerable margin. For that matter, some areas of the globe may actually benefit from GW. For example, regions with colder climates like those in Siberia will have longer growing seasons. However, as will be discussed later, it could be rather dangerous to use this fact to undermine or downplay the significance of the wide-reaching negative impacts of GW (Oreskes 2004).

Summary

This concludes the discussion of the scientific foundation of GW. This section started by offering a simple but concrete definition of climate change. This was followed by detailed investigations of the causes and consequences of GW. In recent years, the scientific consensus has stated that the main cause for GW is the unprecedented burning of fossil fuels that started at the beginning of the industrial revolution. Taken at face value, this fact clearly validates the significance of the anthropogenic contribution to GW. However, there are still a few well-known and highly respected scientists (Dyson 2007; Lindzen 2009; Singer 2007) who continue to disagree with 'consensus' views (see Exhibit 9.1) largely because they give more weight to factors other than GHGs (such as aerosols) that have a cooling instead of a warming effect.

EXHIBIT 9.1 THE ORIGINS OF SCIENTIFIC CONTROVERSIES OF CLIMATE CHANGE

There are many critics of global warming. They range from those who would like to argue that the hype on global warming is nothing but political propaganda orchestrated for the purpose of influencing energy policies, to those who are simply skeptical about the 'consensus' positions on scientific evidence for the causes and consequences of global warming. This exhibit presents the essence of these skepticisms by focusing on the views expressed by three highly distinguished scientists; namely, Professors Fred Singer (a physicist), Richard Lindzen (a climatologist), and Freeman Dyson (a physicist).

None of these three scientists can be accused of being climate change deniers. They all agree with the conventional wisdom that the atmospheric concentration in carbon dioxide has been rising steadily. Furthermore, they do not dispute the slight increase in the average temperature of the earth that has occurred over the past two centuries or so. Furthermore, Professor Lindzen, one of the world's most renowned climatologists, has done several collaborative works with the IPCC.

Where these three scientists appear to diverge from the conventional wisdom on climate change can be identified in the following three specific ways: (1) the extent to which human activities have contributed to the atmospheric concentrations of carbon dioxide; (2) the extent to which changes in average global temperature have been associated with the rising atmospheric concentration of carbon dioxide (CO_2); and (3) the way in which the assessment and projection of ecological and environmental damages has been done based on large-scale climate change modeling that relies on positive feedback mechanisms.

To start with, contrary to the conventional wisdom, all three scientists appear to take the position, that *human activities are not influencing global climate in any discernable way*. They argue that there are other 'natural' factors that may be causing the current warming. Thus, until we can scientifically isolate the human from the natural factors it will be, if not wrong, premature to say that human activities are the causes for the warming trends observed since the beginning of the industrial revolution.

Furthermore, even when they don't dispute the steady increases in CO_2, these scientists remain adamant in their position that the observed correlation between the increases in average global temperatures and the atmospheric concentration of CO_2 over the relevant period under consideration should *not* in any way warrant the view that *the cause for global warming is the burning of fossil fuels*. According to them, correlation is not causation. In other words, science is not based on simple correlation; it is a question of data. Hence, more evidence is needed.

Professors Lindzen and Singer have been very critical of the greenhouse computer models that are used by the IPCC. According to them, these models have not been able to properly evaluate important feedback arising from the interaction of water vapor and CO_2 and the effect of clouds. Furthermore, no considerations have been made regarding other feedbacks from within the models and the natural factors that have regularly warmed the climate prior to the industrial revolution, such as continental drift and mountain-building, changes in the earth's orbit, volcanic eruptions and solar variability. According to these two scientists, *models that include these omitted natural factors are likely to show that man-made greenhouse contribution to current temperature change is likely to be insignificant*. Given this, they conclude that the recent hypes on climate change are dangerous because they would have the effect of distorting energy policies in ways that would have detrimental effects on the world economy.

In slightly different way, Professor Dyson has criticized the conventional climate models by observing that 'climate models take into account atmospheric motion and water levels but have no feeling for the chemistry and biology of sky, soil and trees. The biologists have essentially been pushed aside'. For Dyson this is an important omission given his vision of humans' capability of cultivating 'carbon-eating trees' on a massive scale as a last resort to slow a future global warming trend.

Even if this kind of criticism is considered to be rather minor and somewhat irrelevant, serious considerations of climate dynamics (the interactions among the components of the climate system) indicate that there exists a high degree of uncertainty in the projections of future temperature increases and the environmental and socioeconomic impacts of GW. With this much understanding about the science of GW, it is now time to proceed to the economics of GW.

9.3 THE ECONOMICS OF GLOBAL WARMING: BASIC THEORETICAL CONCEPTS AND FRAMEWORK OF ANALYSIS

The main economic problem associated with climate change deals with the extent to which society should allocate its scarce resources to control GHG emissions into the atmosphere with the objective of *slowing* future GW trends. However, on practical grounds this turns out to be a very complicated matter for several reasons:

1. Because the atmosphere is a common-property resource it is very difficult, if not impossible, to deny access to anyone. Thus, the abuse of the atmosphere would be inevitable if the decision to emit GHGs were left to individual actors—the tragedy of the commons (Hardin 1968).
2. GHG emissions that occur in one part of the world can quickly move to any other part of the globe since movement in the atmosphere occurs without a material connection—the *telekinesis* property of the atmosphere (Flannery 2005). Thus, by its very nature, the problem associated with climate change has global dimensions.
3. Since GHGs have a long lifecycle in the atmosphere, emissions that occur at a given point in time have effects lasting over a long period of time. In the case of CO_2, by far the largest component of the GHGs, the effect may extend over a century (IPCC 2001). The implication of this is that addressing the problems associated with climate change involves long-run economic analy-

sis looking as far ahead into the future as 50, 100, 200, or even more, years.
4. As is evident from the discussion in Section 9.2, several important aspects of climate change are still *uncertain*. Hence, a serious economic analysis of climate change has to explicitly consider risk and uncertainty (Schelling 2007). In addition, the economic analysis needs to incorporate non-marginal changes since irreversible outcomes may not be ruled out (Cline 1992).

Indeed, viewed this way climate change confronts economists, as Sir Nicholas Stern (2007) put it, with 'the biggest case of market failure' ever known. Despite these challenges, in the next section, an attempt will be made to analyze the economic problem of climate change using a slightly modified version of the analytical framework that has been already presented in Chapter 4.

Tradeoffs between two social costs

At its basic level, and from a purely standard economic perspective, concern for climate change is a resource allocation problem. It deals with how much of a reduction in consumption society is willing to sacrifice today to mitigate environmental damages arising from global temperature increases in the future.

More specifically, at any given point in time society is confronted with the need to ration its scarce resources (land, labor, capital, environmental assets, etc.) to satisfy competing ends. Thus, if a society decides to use more of its resources to invest in projects intended to avoid future environmental damages arising from GW (such as investment in renewable energy resources, preservation of forest ecosystems, higher fuel-efficiency standards on passenger cars, etc.) it means that less resources will be available to produce goods and services for current consumption (such as food, cars, housing, apparels, furniture settings, public recreational facilities, etc.).

Viewed in this way, the economics of GW starts with the recognition of the tradeoff that exists between two social costs: *greenhouse–damage cost* (i.e., the costs of *not* reducing GHG emissions beyond the current level and maintaining the status quo) and *greenhouse–abatement costs* (the costs of cutting the level of GHG emissions below the current level in order to slow future GW). The tradeoff between these two costs is quite apparent since a higher *abatement cost* (i.e., a reduction in GHG emissions) would be expected to cause lower *damage cost*, and a lower abatement cost would have the opposite effect.

Once the tradeoff between greenhouse damage and abatement costs is clearly recognized, applying the same logic used in previous chapters, a standard *cost–benefit analysis* dictates that *a rational decision regarding climate change would warrant that a dollar spent on projects to slow GW today (i.e., the abatement cost) must be justified by a dollar or more of benefit expected to be realized from avoiding future economic, human health, environmental and ecological damages (i.e., damage cost).* However, the complexity of this decision-making rule cannot be appreciated without a fair amount of knowledge about the nature and key determining factors of greenhouse-abatement and greenhouse-damage cost functions. The next two subsections will provide detailed analyses of these two costs.

Greenhouse-damage costs

The greenhouse-damage costs arise from the fact that, if no action is taken today, GW, despite the scientific uncertainties, is predicted to inflict significant economic, human health and ecological damages. Damage costs, therefore, represent the estimated dollar values of all these expected damages. As discussed in Section 9.2, these damages could be physically manifested in various forms, such as flooded cities, diminished food production, loss of biodiversity, land lost to oceans, increased storm damages, increased human morbidity and mortality arising from heat stress and the expansion of the range of tropical diseases, and so on. These are, therefore, the *costs of doing nothing to slow GW.* They measure the costs to the economy, human health and the natural environment at some future time due to a higher atmospheric concentration of GHGs (Cline 1992; Nordhaus

1991). It is also important to recognize that, while these costs arise from the side-effects of activities undertaken by the present generation, future generations have no say in the matter directly. Hence, these are 'external' costs imposed on future generations.

The salient characteristics of the greenhouse-damage cost function can be explained using Figure 9.1. The graph is segmented into three parts purely for analytical convenience. The horizontal axis represents the concentration of GHGs in the atmosphere in parts per million (ppm) CO_2 equivalents. As discussed in Section 9.2, GHGs are *stock* pollutants because of the long lifecycle these gases have once they enter the atmosphere. Hence, the damage function is not only affected by the current level of GHG emissions, but also by the cumulative effect of past emissions extending over a long period of time (as long as 100 years or more).

The vertical axis is the dollar value of the expected future damages arising from GW associated with any given atmospheric concentration of GHGs. The estimation of the monetary values of the damages from future GW is extremely difficult to undertake for a number of reasons. First, future damages from GW are clouded with uncertainty (Cline 1992; Schelling 2007; Stern 2007). Second, as discussed in Chapter 4, damage costs are externalities, hence reliable market information on these costs are not readily available—the case of market failure. Last but not least, as discussed in Chapter 7, damage costs are not easily quantifiable since they include intangible ecosystem services (such as the possible extinction of species) that are impossible to capture in monetary terms. As Nordhaus (1990) put it, the effort to quantify damage costs is 'the terra incognita of the social and economic impacts of climate change'.

Despite the difficult practical issues involved in estimating damage costs, as shown in Figure 9.1 above, it is theorized that the incremental (marginal) damage cost is an increasing function of the atmospheric concentration of GHGs. The rationale for this argument comes from the simple fact that GHGs have cumulative effects that extend over a long period of time. The GW effect of GHGs is not only determined by what happens at a point in time but also, and most

costs at all levels of GHG emissions that must have resulted from the lower increase in the average global temperature (i.e., slower GW) achieved due to the steps taken to cut GHG emissions. The important lesson here is this: although GW cannot be stopped, measures can be taken to *slow the future warming trend* and in so doing avoid major future environmental catastrophes. This is, of course, the impetus for a binding international agreement to cut the emissions of GHGs, such as the Kyoto Protocol (more on this later in the last section of this chapter). However, this comes at a cost which is addressed next.

Greenhouse-abatement costs

Greenhouse-abatement costs represent the *social* costs arising from the use of resources for projects that are intended to reduce GHG emissions. Costs of this nature may include investment in: carbon emission control devices; energy conserving technologies; the development of alternative energy sources; raising coastal structures to prevent flooding; research projects to develop drought-tolerant crops; afforestation projects for expanded carbon sequestration capacity; and so on.

A helpful way to look at abatement costs is to view them as an *investment* by the current generation to benefit future generations by preventing future environmental damages. When abatement costs are viewed this way, they may raise ethical considerations of the following nature:

1. Why should the current generation be obligated to care for future generations, especially given that the impacts of GW on the wellbeing of future generations remain *uncertain*?
2. Why worry about future generations when their living standard (per capita GDP), based on the empirical evidence of the past 200 years, is expected to be three to four times higher on average than people living today (Baumol 1968 Taylor 1998)?
3. Investments to avoid future environmental damages often compete with current expenditure budget allocations to improve the conditions of

today's poor. Given this, would it be *fair* to care for the environment that stands to benefit future generations, at the expense of today's poor? For example, increased investment to slow GW by the developed nations may mean providing less money for international assistance to mitigate child malnutrition in parts of Africa, Asia and Latin America (Dawidoff 2009; Singer 2007).

Setting aside these ethical considerations, Figure 9.3 is a graphic depiction of the abatement cost function. The horizontal axis can be read in two ways: (1) reading from left to right, it indicates the amount of GHGs emitted, in ppm of CO_2 equivalent. The values range from 390 ppm, the current level of emissions (status quo), all the way to zero; (2) reading from right to left, it represents the percentage reduction in GHG emissions. A zero percent reduction is associated with the current level of emissions (i.e., 390 ppm). Thus, a move from the current level of emissions towards the origin represents successively higher percentage reductions in GHG emissions. Viewed in this way, at least theoretically, the origin represents a 100 percent reduction in GHGs emissions.

It is evident from Figure 9.3 that the abatement cost for each successive percentage reduction of GHG emissions is considered to be increasing at an increasing rate. The reason for this is that a successive reduction in GHGs requires the use or implementation of more sophisticated and expensive technologies. For example, as indicated in Figure 9.3 the first 10 percent reduction in GHG emissions may require no more than minor changes in lifestyle (such as the use of more energy efficient light bulbs, stricter enforcement of existing industrial pollution regulations, planting trees and minor changes in the way we transport people (such as carpooling) and commodities (such as the use of trains instead of tracks). On the other hand, the second 10 percent reduction in GHGs may require the development and use of alternative energy fuels (such as ethanol, wind and solar energy) and investment in new public transportation infrastructures on a massive scale, such as light passenger railway systems in the major cities of the United States. Note that as shown in Figure 9.3,

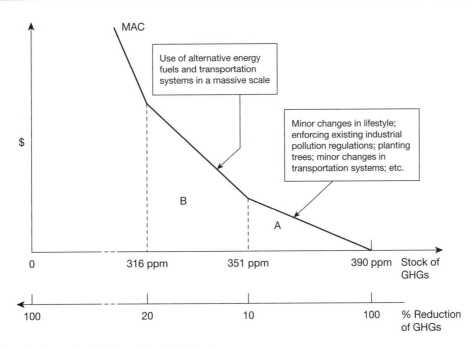

Figure 9.3 *Marginal abatement cost for GHGs*

the total abatement cost increases dramatically from area A to B if a cut in emission is raised from 10 to 20 percent. The expectation of this kind of increase in abatement cost, as will be evident from the discussion in the next section, is used against a policy initiative that would favor to cut GHG emissions beyond ten percent.

What would happen if advances in GHG emission abatement technologies were realized? This is an important issue to consider since the effect of technological advances, when realized, would be to precipitate a downward *shift* of the entire curve in Figure 9.3. This means a lower abatement cost for each percentage reduction in GHG emissions. As will be evident shortly, it is due to the anticipation of this kind of cost reduction, mainly arising from advances in emissions abatement technology, that some economists continue to support a guarded (or 'wait and see') approach to emissions mitigation policies in the near-term (Taylor 1998).

What has been discussed so far is the anatomy (structure) of two important cost functions—damage and abatement costs—which economists use to

perform cost–benefit analyses relevant to GW. Since the early 1990s, with various assumed conditions about these two cost functions, economists have been conducting empirical studies that allowed them to offer policy recommendations relevant to GW—the annual reduction of GHG emissions needed to slow GW. The analyses in these studies have been undertaken using large simulation models of various natures and a framework of standard cost–benefit analysis that was thoroughly discussed in Chapter 8. The next section will explore the nature and policy implications of these empirical studies.

9.4 GLOBAL WARMING: THE ECONOMIC DEBATES AND POLICY IMPLICATIONS

In the last two sections an attempt was made to present the scientific and economic foundations of GW. This was done with the belief that any effective policy response intended to mitigate climate risk by curtailing GHG emissions cannot be done without a good understanding and serious consideration of both the scientific and economic basis of GW.

major GHG emitters among developing nations, to justify the continuation of the high rate of growth in GDP that they have been experiencing over the past two decades (more on this later).

Finally, it is important to note that the positions taken by nations (developed or developing) that continue to advocate the BAU approach are based on economic analyses that fail to provide explicit accounting of *damage costs*. Thus, intergenerational equity (i.e., the wellbeing of future generations) has not been considered adequately. To the extent that 'fairness' or 'justice' are considered, it tends to be limited to the 'poor' within the existing generation— intragenerational equity. The question then becomes: Should this blatant neglect to consider the wellbeing of future generations be tolerated given that the biggest share or burden of the cost of GW is likely to fall on those who will be living in the far distant future? This question will be the central issue of the next two subsections.

The 'gradualist' approach

The economic analyses in this situation are different from the BAU approach discussed above, in two important ways. First, proponents of the gradualist approach do not intentionally attempt to discredit or distort what appears to be the scientific consensus on GW. Second, at least in principle, they accept that a cost–benefit analysis intended to evaluate the desirability of proposed projects or policy actions to slow climate change should explicitly consider both the *damage* and *abatement* costs.

Once a decision is made to include damage costs in the cost–benefit calculus of GW, the major challenge becomes finding reliable methods to estimate these costs. This is because such an endeavor involves the estimations of several anticipated economic impacts of climate change. As discussed in Section 9.2, chief among them are: agricultural losses from heat stress and drought; losses from sea-level rise; increased demand for space cooling; losses from runoff in water basins; increased urban pollution associated with warmer weather; increased incidence of mortality with heat stress; loss in amenity values of

everyday life and leisure; increased hurricane and forest damage; loss of biological diversity; and deterioration of environmental quality. Of course, not all of these costs are easily *quantifiable*. Furthermore, the fact that damage costs are externalities makes market information, even if it exists, unreliable.

However, despite these apparent difficulties several estimates of damage costs exist although, as would be expected, they differ widely (by a factor of two to three). These estimates are made using simulation models that explicitly attempt to integrate both economic and climate factors. More specifically, as discussed in Section 9.2, atmospheric general circulation models (AGCMs) are used first in order to develop scenarios of the greenhouse effects on global average temperatures and the expected environmental and infrastructural damages for an extended period of time. Generally, the scenarios are presented under three categories: high estimates, best estimates and low estimates. Finally, using the damage estimates from the 'best estimates' scenarios, economic simulation models are used to project the impacts of GW on macroeconomic variables, especially GDP. It is beyond the scope of this chapter to go into more details of either the atmospheric or economic simulation models. However, in general the simulation models used by followers of the 'gradualist approach' incorporate the following underlying assumptions concerning future warming trends, economic conditions and time horizons:

1. By about 2050 the global emissions of GHGs will plateau, which will eventually lead to the stabilization of the warming impacts of industrial activities.

2. The impacts (damages) of GW on the economy, human health and natural ecosystems will be limited to the next 100 years. That is, by 2100, the global average temperature will be in a steady state, at which point full adaptation to warming effects will occur. Furthermore, it is assumed that the likelihood that irreversible catastrophic environmental damage could occur between now and the end of the twenty-first century is negligible or simply zero.

3. When the steady state or full adaptation to GW is achieved (about 100 years from now) the median global surface temperature will have increased by about 2.5 degrees Celsius and the rise would be highly unlikely to exceed 3 degrees Celsius.

4. A *discount rate* of 4 percent is used to perform cost–benefit analysis. This assumption is not to be taken lightly since, as discussed in Chapter 8, the effect of a high discount-rate is to reduce (compress) benefits or costs coming in the distant future. In the case of GW, significant portions of the damage costs occur in the distant future (50 or 100 years from now). If the discount rate is high, the value of these projected damage costs will be considerably reduced. This factor alone could be sufficient to cause the rejection of investment projects intended to abate GHG emissions on the basis of cost–benefit analysis. As will be discussed below, this is one of the fundamental issues that differentiate the 'gradualist' and the 'precautionary' approaches to GW.

Among economists, William Nordhaus is noted for his pioneering works on the economic consequences of GW. Based on the above set of assumptions, and using a simulation model known as the Dynamic Integrated Model of Climate and the Economy (DICE), over the years (1991, 1992, 2006, and 2008) Nordhaus and his associates have done several academic studies on GW. The most representative outcomes of the economic studies performed by these economists can be summarised as follows.

First, by 2100 the *net* damage costs of a 2.5 to 3 degree temperature increase will be approximately 1 to 2 percent of global GDP. The word 'net' implies that both the positive and negative effects of GW are considered in calculating damage cost at a global level. Thus, the loss in some parts of the world (such as the continent of Africa) is compensated fully or in part by the gains realized in some other parts of the globe (such as Greenland, Siberia, etc.)

Second, abatement costs are shown to vary considerably depending on the level of emissions reductions sought in the following ways:

■ About 10 percent of GHG emissions can be reduced at extremely low cost; however

■ Above this level, the incremental (marginal) cost of GHG emissions reduction is expected to rise *sharply* (See Figure 9.3).

Thus, in light of these sharply rising marginal abatement cost estimates and given that the estimate of the damage cost is not that high (only 1 to 2 percent of global GDP), the conclusions reached by Nordhaus and his associates were to recommend only a reduction in GHG emissions—*between 8 and 10 percent in the near term* (or by about 2015). Nordhaus and his associates also recommend the *gradual* tightening of GHG emissions through increased carbon taxes as the scientific evidence for increased future GW becomes more evident (hence, the label of the 'gradualist approach').

According to the proponents of the gradualist approach to GW, therefore, to go beyond a *modest* cut in GHG emissions suggests a very pessimistic assessment of damages, and this will be unnecessary given that, in the long run, GW is unlikely to be *catastrophic* to the extent of reducing world income sharply below today's levels (Nordhaus 2008). Furthermore, it was argued that if a *drastic* cut in emissions is to be recommended, the necessary reductions in near-term consumption would come from today's poor. If this is the case, to reduce current consumption sharply in order to prevent a decline in the wellbeing of future generations would hardly seem equitable or ethically defensible, especially given that future generations are expected to be much richer than today (Nordhaus 2008).

The gradualists are aware of the criticisms often voiced by various environmental groups for recommending what are considered to be modest and incremental policy measures to slow GW. Nordhaus responded to these critics by echoing his sentiment this way: 'while the findings of such mainstream economic assessments may not satisfy the most ardent environmentalists, if followed, they would go far beyond current global emissions reductions and would be a good first step on a journey of many miles' (Nordhaus 2007). Of course, this seemingly con-

today or in the near future, to taking aggressive action now to avoid irreversible and catastrophic impacts on future generations. This should hardly be surprising, given that economic impact assessments of GW rely on scientific information that is subject to disputes. Furthermore, the assessment of damage costs involves the consideration of normative issues that require making subjective judgments, particularly regarding the extent to which present generations should be concerned about the wellbeing of future generations.

Since the early 1990s there has been a growing call for strong and binding international actions to mitigate climate risk. This call for action has been prompted largely by the growing scientific evidence that the IPCC has been able to provide on future GW trends and their ominous environmental, human health and economic implications. The next and the last section of this chapter will address the successes and failures of the international policy initiatives on climate change that have been on display over the past two decades.

9.5 TOWARDS THE FORMULATION OF INTERNATIONALLY BINDING GHG EMISSIONS TARGETS

As discussed in Section 9.2, the movement of GHGs in the atmosphere knows no boundary. This being the case, it will be impossible to link specific damages done by GHG emissions in one region to specific emissions in another region. This problem is further compounded when it is realized that the atmosphere is a common-property resource, and as such is subject to abuse if its use (in this case as a sink for GHGs) is determined by the unrestrained actions of a self-interested private party (whether the party involved happens to be an individual person, a business entity or a nation)—the tragedy of the commons. The key issue then, is what can be done to deal with the worldwide anthropogenic GHG emissions given that no 'world government' with the authority to legislate and enforce mitigating actions exists?

Normally, problems of this nature are left to the community of nations, which currently numbers more than 190, to enter voluntarily into agreements with one another to limit the flow of pollutants that contribute to environmental problems of international and global scope. Such agreements usually take the form of *multilateral treaties* that are negotiated through conventions among interested countries, often under the auspices of an international institution such as the United Nations (Soroos 2004). Only those countries that formally become parties to a treaty, in accordance with their constitutionally specified ratification procedures, are legally obligated to comply with its provisions. This was, indeed, the spirit under which the 1992 Framework Convention on Climate Change (FCCC) at the Earth Summit in Rio de Janeiro evolved.

From the signing of the FCCC to the adoption of the Kyoto Protocol

The threat of significant GW was first taken up at high-level international conferences in the late 1980s, following a series of years with unusually warm global average temperatures (Ibid). Negotiations began in 1991 and led to the signing of the FCCC at the Earth Summit in Rio de Janeiro the next year. At this convention no schedule for mandatory limits on GHG emissions was formally established. However, the convention was able to establish an ambitious framework for stabilizing concentrations of GHGs in the atmosphere at a level that would prevent dangerous anthropogenic interference with the climate system. The convention entered into force on March 21, 1994 and enjoys near universal membership, with 192 countries having already ratified.

The nations that have ratified the FCCC meet each year as the Conference of the Parties (COP), the governing body of the convention, to the treaty. The nations attending COP1, which was held in Berlin in 1995, and agreed that the original treaty did not go far enough and committed themselves to negotiate a schedule for binding reductions that would be ready for adoption when they gathered for COP3 in Kyoto in 1997. Surprisingly, this landmark international treaty actually materialized as scheduled, and COP3 adopted a protocol (more specifically, the Kyoto Protocol) committing the developed countries to achieving an average 5.2 percent reduction in their GHG emissions from 1990 levels in the commitment period, 2008 to 2012. Initially, the developed countries (more specifically the parties included in Annex I) are called upon, but not required, to limit their GHG emissions to 1990 levels by the year 2000. However, by 2005 each party included in Annex I was expected to 'have made demonstrable progress in achieving its commitments' under Article 3 of the Protocol (Grubb 2004). The Kyoto Protocol does not call upon developing countries to restrain their emissions of GHGs, which are on course to exceed those of the developed countries by about 2025 (Grubb 2004). Naturally, this particular provision continues to be one of the most contentious and unresolved issues of the Kyoto Protocol.

Flexible mechanisms to control GHG emissions

One other major contentious issue of the Kyoto Protocol has been the mechanisms by which Annex I parties, those committed to binding emissions limitation targets, are allowed to meet their obligations (individually or jointly). To this end, the Kyoto Protocol included several so-called 'flexible mechanisms', which offer Annex I parties several options that could make it easier for them to achieve their emissions targets (Grubb 2004).

First, the Protocol permits the use of a wide range of strategies to offset mandated emissions reductions through either: (1) increased carbon sinks (such as the expansion of forest cover by means of afforestation, reforestation and land-use changes); and/or (2) reductions of GHG emissions through technological means such as the enhancement of energy efficiency, carbon capture and storage, and so on.

Second, under Article 17 the Kyoto Protocol Parties are allowed to engage in the trading of their emissions allowances. This would allow nations to offset mandated emissions reductions by purchasing emissions credits from countries whose emissions are below their Kyoto targets. Third, Annex I parties could agree to allocate reduction, but among themselves agree on differentiated targets (an option that has been adopted by the European Union). Fourth, under

Article 6, Annex I parties are allowed to transfer emissions reduction units (ERUs) from projects undertaken within Annex I. This project-based mechanism is commonly referred to as 'joint implementation'.

Finally, under Article 12 the 'joint implementation' scheme is also extended to investment on projects in developing countries that would achieve a net savings in GHG emissions. This scheme, known as the Clean Development Mechanism (CDM), allows emissions reductions to be earned within non-Annex parties and used towards meeting an Annex I party's commitment (Markandya and Halsnaes 2004). An example of this would be a reforestation project in a developing country that is financed, say, in Germany. In general, the primary purpose of the 'flexible mechanisms' is to achieve emissions reductions as *cost-effectively* as possible.

The Kyoto Protocol: its achievements and setbacks

The last year of the first Kyoto commitment period, the year 2012, is fast approaching. The Conference of the Parties for this year (2011) was held in Durban, South Africa. Two years ago, with much more fanfare than this year, the same conference was held at Copenhagen and marked the fifteenth anniversary of the Kyoto Protocol. What can be said about the achievements and setbacks of this landmark international environmental treaty since the time of its inception? As would be expected, the implementation of the Kyoto protocol has had a rather rocky start. For several years, little progress was made at the annual Conference of the Parties meetings. The treaty's ambitious goal of reducing emissions to 1990 levels by the year 2000 was not met. Instead, GHG emissions in most Annex I countries continue to increase to this day. The major unresolved issues have been the continued reluctance of the United States to ratify the treaty let alone comply with it, while China and India continue to resist emissions reductions even on a voluntary basis. This is a serious issue given that China and the United States are the number one and two GHG emitters in the world, respectively (Markandya and Halsnaes 2004).

199

not only is the carbon dioxide level rising relentlessly, the pace of that rise is accelerating over time . . . [on the day the climate talks at Cancun, Mexico ended] at midnight Mauna Loa time, the carbon dioxide level hit 390—and rising.

The most recent UN climate change conference before the publication of this book was held in Durban, South Africa, November 28 to December 9, 2011. The negotiations in this conference were contentious but ended with outcomes that exceeded many people's expectations. Both developed and developing countries agreed to work towards a new treaty with 'legal force' under which all countries would take on emissions targets by 2015, although it will not come into effect until 2020. This so-called the 'Durban Platform' is considered to be a historic breakthrough in the climate-change negotiations since it directly confronts the most contentious aspect of the Kyoto Protocol (i.e., the exclusion of China and India from a legally binding carbon emissions cut). Understandably, the fact the 'big three' (the US, China and India) would agree to cut carbon emissions was a moment to celebrate. In addition, it was agreed to prolong the life of the Kyoto Protocol beyond 2012 and to set up the Green Climate Fund, a major new climate finance facility.

However, much detail remains to be clarified, Canada has withdrawn from the Kyoto agreement and current emission reduction commitments remain inadequate to prevent the average global temperature rising by more than 2 degrees Centigrade, which scientists say would cause dramatic climate change. Given this development, it seems rather extraordinarily unfortunate that it took fifteen years to arrive at no substantive and effectively binding agreements in climate negotiations. Worst yet, given the current global economic conditions, it will be very difficult to envision a major break through in climate negotiations as we are about to end the Kyoto Protocol's first commitment period (December, 2012).

9.6 MARKET-BASED GHG EMISSIONS CONTROL POLICY INSTRUMENTS

As discussed above, one feature of the Kyoto Protocol that has received a great deal of attention from economists is the 'flexible mechanisms' that incorporate, among other things, the use of carbon taxes and emissions trading by Annex I parties to fulfill their commitments to specific quantitative emissions targets. The rest of this chapter will discuss the relative merits of these two policy instruments within the context of their applications to climate change. The discussion will be relatively brief, given that the basic definitions and theoretical explanations for why these two policy instruments (tax and emissions trading) are cost-effective means with which to control environmental pollution have been already provided in Chapters 5 and 6.

From the outset, it is important to consider the following three issues when carbon tax and emissions trading that are designed to reach internationally agreed upon emissions targets are used:

1. GHGs are transboundary pollutants with a truly international scope. Thus, specific damages in one region cannot be linked to specific emissions in another region. From a policy perspective, a piecemeal approach, that is, a country-by-country use of either a carbon tax and/or emissions trading, will not necessarily imply cost-effectiveness at a global level. Hence, when these two policy instruments are offered as an option (as suggested by the Kyoto Protocol), what may be guaranteed, at best, will be the cost-effective control of GHG emissions at only a country or regional level—perhaps a second-best solution.

2. Unlike other transboundary pollutants, such as acid rain (due to SO_2 emissions), emissions of GHGs are not measured 'end-of-pipe', that is, at the chimney or exhaust level. This is because the cost of capturing GHG emissions through technological means is currently very high. This has a very important policy implication since, as discussed in Chapters 5 and 6, one of the advantages of both a carbon tax and emissions trading is the

incentive they provide to promote pollution-control technology. It is also important to keep in mind that carbon sequestration through technological means may be a feat that is very challenging to accomplish.

3. Both carbon taxes and emissions trading are very sensitive to 'transaction costs' (which includes search and information, bargaining and decision, and monitoring and enforcement costs) and 'uncertainty'. These two factors are greatly amplified when the applications of carbon tax and emissions trading at the international level are considered.

The discussions above proceeded as though both carbon tax and emissions trading are equally effective in controlling GHG emissions. This would be difficult to defend given the huge number of academic articles that have been written in recent years that are mainly intended to delineate the relative merits of these two policy instruments.

Those who would like to take a position in favor of *carbon tax* for controlling GHG emissions argue that a carbon tax is relatively easy to implement and administer. It essentially represents a 'shadow' price (fine) for a 'public bad': in this particular case the emissions of GHGs into the atmosphere and the harm it imposes on the public through its GW effects (Mankiw 2007; Pearce 1991). As shown in Chapter 5, effluent tax is cost-effective—it controls a given emissions target at minimum cost. Furthermore, at the firm level it encourages technological innovation related to pollution-control devices—the development of technological devices (capital stocks) that are less GHG intensive. Last but not least, a carbon tax generates revenues that can be used to finance other pollution-control projects. For example, in the case of greenhouse emissions control, the revenue could be used to cover administrative costs and/or sponsor projects that are taking place in developing countries under the auspices of the Kyoto Protocol that are certified, such as the Certified Development Mechanism (CDM).

On the other hand, those who are less inclined to favor carbon tax as a policy instrument to control GHG emissions generally argue against it because its enactment and implementations are largely based on political considerations. Given this, how feasible would it be to design an 'international' carbon tax in a world that is characterized by diverse political and economic systems as well as economic conditions? This question is relevant because, in a world where globalization is on a fast track, differences in pollution tax may result in the development of 'pollution havens'—places to which firms may have incentives to move their operations because carbon taxes are low. This could potentially make many countries reluctant to use carbon tax as means of controlling their emission targets. Thus, 'although the implementation of an international carbon tax has been discussed extensively in recent years, politically it has never been acceptable to a wide range of countries' (Missfeldt and Hauff 2004: 136).

In the absence of the above types of political considerations, *emissions trading* has become popular as a policy instrument to control GHG emissions in recent years (Solomon 2007). As demonstrated in Chapter 6, emissions trading has the advantages of the carbon tax with respect to cost-effectiveness and the incentives to encourage the development of improved pollution technologies, but its operation is based on very limited government roles. The only two functions of government are to set the emissions cap and decide whether the initial rationing of the caps on pollution permits to firms (or other parties involved) is going to be through *grandfathering*, an *auction* or a combination of the two. Once this is done, the exchange of permits (popularly known as cap-and-trade) through private markets will allow a price for carbon to emerge that is 'actually' based on consumers' willingness to pay (Solomon 2007).

While this is a standard claim made by the proponents of emissions trading, it is important not to overlook the difficulties involved in developing market mechanisms that are designed for such a purpose. This is clearly supported by the recent European Union experiment in emissions trading. This concern is even more acute when considerations are made about the potential use of emissions trading by countries with underdeveloped private-market institutions. Thus, those who are skeptical about the use of emissions trading are quick to point out its very limited applications (Mankiw 2007; Pearce 1991). Furthermore, although strictly an academic argument, 'recent literature on technological change shows that the least cost property of emissions trading is not always maintained when strategic interaction of trading participants and the fact that firms may imitate patented technology is taken into account' (Missfeldt and Hauff 2004: 142).

Finally, some economists, at least in theory, argue that under certain conditions a combined use of carbon tax and emissions trading may actually result in a gain in efficiency. More specifically, as Missfeldt and Hauff (2004: 142) point out that:

> Carbon taxes provide greater certainty with respect to the price attached to emitting greenhouse gases than emissions trading, while emissions trading provides greater certainty regarding the capacity to meet the targeted emission reductions. The combination of the two could result in improved efficiency.

Let me end this section by noting the following. The public discourses and the media headlines on climate change appear to give the impression that the policy instruments by themselves (in particular cap-and-trade) are a panacea for dealing with global concerns on climate change. This is a rather misleading position to take and has the potential for harm, since it may cause global communities to lose focus on the real issue.

As discussed in Section 9.3, the main focus should be the determination of the caps—the total allowable emissions of GHGs on an annual basis. These total caps are ideally determined on the basis of a cost–benefit analysis and should be independent of the considerations of policy instruments. Policy instruments (such as carbon tax and emissions trading) can only play a very important secondary role to the extent that they provide society, when they are applied correctly, with ways of controlling the total greenhouse emissions targets (caps) at the minimum cost. In the final analysis, the two important questions we need to ask should be:

1. Is the total annual global reduction of GHG emissions (the cap) commensurate with our best estimates of the damages to be avoided from the amelioration of future climate risks?
2. Are we using policy instruments that would allow us to control the annual global GHG emissions target at minimum cost?

Unfortunately in political arenas, the popular media (including, magazines, TV, radio, etc.) and even in academic journals, the effort frequently seems to be directed towards answering question 2. If taken to the extreme, which seems to be the case in recent years, this has the effect of obscuring (or even ignoring) question 1, which is the one that needs to be addressed most urgently.

9.7 CHAPTER SUMMARY

This chapter started with an extended discussion on the current scientific understanding of the causes and consequences of climate change. From this discussion, the following scientific 'consensus' views appear to emerge:

1. There is strong empirical evidence to support the view that the main cause for global warming is the unprecedented burning of fossil fuels that started at the beginning of the industrial revolution.

2. While there appears to be ample evidence that increased concentrations of GHGs in the atmosphere have contributed to recent global warming, there still remains a great deal of uncertainty surrounding the nature, severity, time horizon and regional impacts of future warming trends. This is because many details about climate interactions (the effects of water vapor, clouds, aerosols, ocean currents, forest ecosystems, etc.) are still not well understood. Thus, predictions of future trends in global temperature do not only depend on the atmospheric concentration of GHGs but also on a host of other highly interactive factors.

Economics is about tradeoff. Following this logic, the economics of global warming starts with the recognition of the tradeoff that exists between two social costs: greenhouse-damage cost (i.e., the costs of not reducing GHG emissions beyond the current level—maintaining the status quo) and greenhouse-abatement costs (i.e., the costs of cutting the level of GHG emissions beyond the current level in order to slow future GW). The tradeoff between these two costs is quite apparent since a higher *abatement cost* (i.e., a reduction in GHG emissions) would be expected to cause a lower *damage cost,* and a lower abatement cost would have the opposite effect.

Once the tradeoff between greenhouse damage and abatement costs is clearly recognized, applying the same logic used in previous chapters, a standard cost–benefit analysis dictates that a rational decision regarding climate change would warrant that a dollar spent on projects to slow GW today (i.e., abatement cost) must be justified by a dollar or more of benefit expected to be realized from avoiding future economic, human health, environmental and ecological damages (i.e., damage cost).

However, putting the seemingly basic economic principles above into practice faces major impediments, because the estimation of the monetary values of the damages from future GW is an extremely difficult undertaking for several reasons discussed in some detail in Section 9.3.

Economists are renowned for expressing divergent views on public-policy matters. With respect to GW, the economists' view on what to do to slow future warming trends varies from maintaining the status quo (i.e., doing nothing) to taking a very aggressive program of international abatement of GHGs in the near-term.

In Section 9.4 three economic approaches to GW are identified, namely, the 'business as usual', the 'gradualist', and the 'precautionary' approaches. This was done mainly to understand the reasons for why economists uphold such a widely divergent set of policy prescriptions for the reductions of GHG emissions needed to slow future GW trends.

Section 9.5 was an attempt to understand the nature, complexity and development of several landmark climate conventions that the world has witnessed since the Earth Summit in Rio de Janeiro in 1992. Some of the notable conventions (treaties) discussed in this chapter are: The Framework Convention on Climate Change (1992), the Kyoto Protocol (1997), the Marrakesh Accord (2001), and most recently the Copenhagen Summit. So far, the primary objectives of these international treaties have been to gradually and systematically develop the social, economic and political frameworks that would allow world governments to meet their treaty obligations to cut carbon emissions that have been ratified by the Kyoto Protocol.

After almost two decades of seemingly endless negotiations, are world governments any closer to achieving their commitments as specified by the Kyoto Protocol? Unfortunately it is very difficult to find evidence that would allow an affirmative response to this question. On the other hand, one would hope that these past efforts are not without their merits. If one is to be optimistic, they can be seen as crucially important building blocks for future climate treaties.

REVIEW AND DISCUSSION QUESTIONS

1. Briefly explain the meaning of the following concepts and terms: greenhouse gases (GHGs), the IPCC, the 'little ice age', the Keeling graph, telekinetic property of the atmosphere, global 'weirding', greenhouse-damage costs, greenhouse-abatement costs, clean development mechanism (CDM), and Annex I parties.

2. Read the following statements. In response, state 'True', 'False' or 'Uncertain' and explain why.
   (a) Climate change and GW are two perfectly interchangeable terms.
   (b) It is more effective to control global carbon emissions using a carbon tax than tradable emissions permits.
   (c) The scientific evidence supports the theory that GW is caused by the unprecedented amount of fossil-fuel burning since the dawning of the industrial revolution.
   (d) It is fair to say that the 'business as usual' approach to GW treats the concern for future generations as though it is irrelevant, a secondary issue.

3. Explain how the combined effects of clouds, aerosols, forest ecosystems and ocean currents contribute to the difficulty of estimating future GW trends.

4. Do you agree with the distinguished British economist Sir Nicholas Stern's claim that climate change confronts economists with 'the biggest case of market failure'? Explain.

5. Suppose you are someone who really feels that something serious has to be done to slow the GW trend.
   (a) Would you support the 'gradualist' or the 'precautionary' approach? Explain.
   (b) If you are not convinced by either of these approaches, is there a different approach that you would suggest? If so, please explain.

6. It is very dangerous to put too much faith in agreements reached through international conventions to address a problem like GW. Look how insignificant the accomplishments of the Kyoto Protocol have been after 15 years of its existence and only a few years left before its mandate officially expires. Comment.

7. To safeguard the interest of future generations, studies done by the proponents of 'the precautionary approach to GW (such as, Cline and the Stern Report) strongly advocate the use of a discount rate that is very close to zero. However, a very highly regarded British economist, Sir Partha Dasgupta, pointed out that the use of an almost zero (in the case of the Stern Report, 0.1 percent) discount rate carries its own risk. This is because of the possibility that a discount rate close to zero may *hinder important technological advances in the near-term*. The adverse effects on technological advances will not only be limited to present but also future generations. In this regard, very low discount rates are seen as having an unintended adverse effect on future generations—which counters the intended motivation of those who advocate the precautionary approach to GW. How do you reconcile these two markedly different interpretations on the impact(s) discount rates may have on future generations? Be specific.

8. Identify the significance of the following international treaties and organizations:
   (a) The Framework Convention on Climate Change (FCCC) (1992)
   (b) The Kyoto Protocol (1997)
   (c) The Marrakesh Accords (2001)
   (d) The Copenhagen Summit (2009)
   (e) The World Metrological Organization (WMO)
   (f) The United Nations Environmental Programme (UNEP).

REFERENCES AND FURTHER READING

Alder, H.J. (1996) 'The Absurdity of Trying to Control Climate', www.ourcivilisation.com/aginatur/cool.htm. Accessed 02/16/2007.

Anthes, R. A. (1992) *Meteorology*, 6th edn., New York: Macmillan.

Barnola, J. M., Raynaud, D., Korotkevich, Y. S. and Lorius, C. (1987) 'Vostok Ice Core Provides 160,000-year Record of Atmospheric CO2', *Nature* 329: 408–14.

Baumol, W. J. (1968) 'On the Social Rate of Discount', *American Economic Review* 58: 788–802

Boulding, K. E. (1966) 'The Economics of the Coming Spaceship Earth', in H. Jarrett (ed.) *Environmental Quality in a Growing Economy*, Washington, DC: Johns Hopkins University Press.

Calvin, W. H. (1998) 'The Great Climate Flip-flop', *Atlantic Monthly* 281, 1: 47–64.

Carson, R. (1962) *Silent Spring*, New York: Houghton Mifflin.

Cline, W. R. (1992) *The Economics of Global Warming*, Washington, DC: Institute of International Economics.

—— (2004) 'Meeting the Challenge of Global Warming: Reply to Manne and Mendelson', *Copenhagen Consensus Challenge Paper*, May.

Dawidoff, N. (2009) 'The Civil Heretic: Freeman Dyson', *New York Times*, March 25.

Desgupta, P. (2006) 'Comments on the Stern Review's Economics of Climate Change', *The Foundation for Science and Technology at the Royal Society*, London, November 8.

Dyson, F. (2007) 'Heretical Thoughts About Science And Society', Edge Foundation Inc., www.edge.org/3rd_culutre/dysonf07/dysonf07_index.html.

Flannery, T. (2005) *The Weather Makers*, New York: Atlantic Monthly Press.

Friedman, T. L. (2008) *Hot, Flat, and Crowded*, New York: Farrar, Straus and Giroux (FSC).

Gillis, J. (2010) 'A Scientist, His Work and a Climate Reckoning', *New York Times*, December 12.

Grubb, M. (2004) 'The Economics of the Kyoto Protocol', in A. D. Own and N. Hanley (eds.) *The Economics of Climate Change*, London: Routledge.

Hardin, G. (1968) 'The Tragedy of the Commons', *Science* 162: 1243–8.

IISD (International Institute for Sustainable Development) (2009) 'A Brief Analysis of the Copenhagen Climate Change Conference', IISD Reporting Services, www.iisd.org. Accessed December, 2009.

IPCC (1996) *Climate Change 1995: The Science of Climate Change*, The World Meteorological Organization— United Nations Environmental Program, Cambridge: Cambridge University Press.

—— (2001) *Climate Change 2001: The Scientific Basis, Summary for Policy Makers*, New York: IPCC (Intergovernmental Panel on Climate Change), http://www.ipcc.ch/pub/spm22-01.pdf, accessed 11/08/2010.

—— (2004) *16 Years of Scientific Assessment in Support of the Climate Convention*, UNEP and WHO, December 2004.

—— (2007) *Climate Change 2007: The Physical Scientific Basis*, Cambridge: Cambridge University Press.

Keeling, C. D., Piper, S. C., Bacastow, R. B., Wahlen M., Whorf, T. P., Heimann, M. and Meijer, H. A. (2005) 'Atmospheric CO2 and CO2 Exchange with the Terrestrial Biosphere and Oceans from 1978 to 2000: Observation and Carbon Cycle Implication', in J. R. Ehleringer, T.E. Cerling, and M.D. Dearing (eds.), *A History of Atmospheric CO2 and its Effects on Plants, Animals, and Ecosystems*, New York: Springer Verlag: 83–113.

Keeling, C. D. and Whorf, T. P. (2002) 'Atmospheric Carbon Dioxide Record from Mona Loa', Oak Ridge, TN: The Carbon Dioxide Information Analysis Center (CDIAC) http://cdiac.esd.ornl.gov/trends/co2/sio-mlo.htm, accessed 11/22/2010.

Lindzen, R. (2005) 'Is There a Basis for Global Warming Alarm?' New Haven, CT: Yale Center for the Study of Globalization, October 21.

—— (2009) 'The Climate Science isn't Settled', *Wall Street Journal*, November 30.

Mankiw, N.G. (2007) 'One Answer to Global Warming: A New Tax', *New York Times*, September 16.

Markandya, A. and Halsnaes, K. (2004) 'Developing Countries and Climate Change', in A. D. Own and N. Hanley (eds.) *The Economics of Climate Change*, London: Routledge.

Mendelsohn, R. (2004) 'Opponents Paper on Climate Change', *Copenhagen Consensus*, Denmark: Copenhagen Consensus Center.

Missfeldt, F. and Hauff J. (2004) 'The Role of Economic Instruments', in A. D. Own and N. Hanley (eds.) *The Economics of Climate Change*, London: Routledge.

Moffatt, I. (2004) 'Global Warming: Scientific Modeling and its Relationship to the Economic Dimensions of Policy', in A. D. Own and N. Hanley (eds.) *The Economics of Climate Change*, London: Routledge.

Nordhaus, W. D. (1990) 'Greenhouse Economics: Count before you Leap', *Economist*, July 7.

—— (1991) 'To Slow or Not to Slow: The Economics of Greenhouse Effect', *Economic Journal* 6, 101: 920–48.

—— (1992) 'An Optimal Transition Path for Controlling Greenhouse Gases', *Science* 258: 1315–19.

—— (2006) 'After Kyoto: Alternative Mechanisms to Control Global Warming', *Foreign Policy In Focus Discussion Paper*, March 27.

—— (2007) 'The Challenge of Global Warming: Economic Models and Environmental Policy', http://nordhaus.econ.yale.edu/dicemss072407all.pdf.

—— (2008) *A Question of Balance: Weighing the Options on Global Warming Policies*, New Haven, CT: Yale University Press.

Oeschger, H. and Mintzer, I. M. (1992) 'Lessons from the Ice Cores: Rapid Climate Changes during the Last 160,000 Years', in I. M. Mintzer (ed.) *Confronting Climate Change: Risks, Implications and Responses*, Cambridge: Cambridge University Press.

Oreskes, N. (2004) 'The Scientific Consensus on Climate Change', *Science* 306, December 3.

Pearce, D. (1991) 'The Role of Carbon Taxes in Adjusting to Global Warming', *The Economic Journal* 101, 407: 938–48.

Schelling, T. C. (2007) 'Climate Change: The Uncertainties, the Certainties, and What They Imply About Action', *Economists' Voice*, Berkeley, CA: The Berkeley Electronic Press.

Sheehan, M. J. (1996) 'United Nations' Experts Doctor Evidence', www.ourcivilisation.com/aginatur/hot.htm. Accessed 02/16/2007.

Shogren, J. 'From Negotiation to Implementation: The UN Framework Convention on Climate Change and its Kyoto Protocol', in A. D. Own and N. Hanley (eds.) *The Economics of Climate Change*, London: Routledge.

Shushan, A., (2007) 'World Agriculture May Suffer Under Global Warming', www.yaledailynews.com/articles/view/19906. Accessed 02/16/2007.

Singer, F. S. (2007) 'Global Warming: Man-Made or Natural?' *Imprimis* (publication of Hillsdale College) 36, 8.

Solomon, D. (2007) 'Climate Change's Great Divide, Lawmakers Favor Carbon Caps, Trading; Economists Prefer a Tax', *Wall Street Journal*, September 12.

Soroos, M.S. (1997) *The Endangered Atmosphere: Preserving a Global Commons*, Columbia, SC: University of South Carolina Press.

—— (2004) 'Global Environmental Pollution: Acid Rain, Ozone Depletion and Global Warming', in A. Hussen, *Principles of Environmental Economics*, 2nd edn., London: Routledge.

Stern, N. (2007) *The Economics of Climate Change: The Stern Review*, Cambridge: Cambridge University Press.

Stevens, W. K. (1999) *The Change in the Weather: People, Weather, and the Science of Climate*, New York: Delacorte Press.

Taylor, J. (1998) 'Global Warming: The Anatomy of a Debate', Presentation before the Johns Hopkins University Applied Physics Laboratory, January 16. (Jerry Taylor, Director of the Cato Institute's Natural Resource Studies).

UNFCCC (1997) *Kyoto Protocol to the United Nations Framework Convention on Climate Change*, Bonn: UNFCCC.

Varian, H.R. (2006) 'Recalculating the Costs of Global Climate Change', *New York Times*, December 14.

Wigley, T. M. (1989) 'Possible Climate Change Due to Sulfur Dioxide-derived Cloud Condensation Nuclei', 339: 365–67.

Wigley, T. M., Ramaswamy, V., Christy, J. R., Lanzante, J. R., Mears, C.A., Snater, B. D. and Folland, C.K. (2006) 'Executive Summary', in T. R. Karl, S. J. Hassol, C. D. Miller. and W. L. Murray (eds.) in *Temperature Trends in the Lower Atmosphere: Steps for Understanding and Reconciling Differences*, Washington, DC: US Climate Change Science Program.

Chapter 10

The economics of biodiversity and ecosystem services

Biodiversity is a national treasure that we have abused terribly, partly because we have not understood the consequences of doing so. Our understanding of such consequences is far from perfect, but we now know enough to behave responsibly toward the plants and animals on which we ourselves depend. We must manage our biodiversity just as we manage our water resources, our clean air, and our energy.

(Tallamy 2007: 41)

LEARNING OBJECTIVES

After reading this chapter you will be familiar with the following:

- Worldwide trends in biological diversity loss.
- Drivers of biodiversity loss.
- The economic rationale for biodiversity conservation, including:
  - (a) The link between biodiversity loss and the flow of ecosystem services; and
  - (b) A formal model that links biodiversity, ecosystem conservation and the flow of ecosystem services.
- Non-economic reasons for biodiversity conservation.
- Identifying the costs and benefits of biodiversity conservation and the conditions for 'optimal' levels of biodiversity conservation.
- Important clues as to why the worldwide investment in biodiversity conservation may be at sub-optimal levels.
- International responses to mitigate the rapidly growing threat of biodiversity loss.
- The evidence for overstressed natural ecosystem and mass species-extinctions.
- The tenuous nature of the general framework that economic models use to understand and analyze biodiversity loss.

Heightened concern for biodiversity loss on a global scale is a fairly recent phenomenon. This problem is becoming increasingly evident as the appropriation of the products of photosynthesis by humans (a single species) has grown so markedly that it accounts now for nearly 40 percent of the total. The ramifications of this increasingly human-dominated biosphere are difficult to grasp fully, given that they may entail irreversible changes in ecosystem structures and functions on a global scale. Given the uniqueness, complexity and scope of this problem, the economic analyses and observations of this chapter are understandably of a somewhat sketchy and tentative nature, but are highly relevant nonetheless. This chapter is designed more to raise awareness of this critically important emerging global environmental concern than to show the application of sophisticated economic models.

10.1 INTRODUCTION: THE EVIDENCE FOR WORRISOME TRENDS IN BIODIVERSITY LOSS

In Chapter 2 our discussion was primarily focused on a comprehensive understanding of the basic principles of the structures and functions of ecosystems, from a biocentric perspective. That chapter (especially in Section 2.5) also outlined some of the major negative impacts of human-induced pressures on natural ecosystems. In Chapter 10, the focus will be primarily on biodiversity—the diversity of species, populations, genes, communities and ecosystems.

At the 1992 Convention on Biological Diversity (CBD), where the first global agreement on the conservation and sustainable use of biological diversity was framed, biodiversity was formally defined as 'the variability among living organisms from all sources including, inter alia, terrestrial, marine and other aquatic ecosystems and the ecological complexes of which they are part; this includes diversity within species, between species and of ecosystems' (CBD 1992).

It is worth saying a few words on the significance of the above definition of biodiversity. First, it indicates that the emphasis is not on a single or a few arbitrarily selected species, but all the native species of a given ecosystem. Second, concern about population size is not limited to a single species but the ecological system as a whole (i.e., the group of species that live and interact together in one place). In other words, the focus is on the diversity of species not just abundance or large populations of each. Third, biodiversity is best understood when the spatial interdependencies between various ecosystems (for example, the relationships between a coral-reef ecosystem and the mangrove ecosystems on the nearby shore) are given maximum clarity. These are three important factors to keep in mind throughout the discussions in this chapter.

Why should humanity care about biological diversity? An effort will be made to provide answers to this difficult but very important question in the next section. For now, it suffices to say that the benefit of biological diversity to humans can be inferred from the basic ecological principle that biodiversity positively impacts the *productivity* and *resilience* of natural ecosystems (Tallamy 2007). Viewed in this way, not only can biodiversity be used as an *indicator* of the overall health of ecosystems' functions, but it can be viewed as something that is important for the sustainability of all forms of life on earth, including humans. If this is the case, biodiversity loss, regardless of its origins, must be a cause of great concern.

Concern for the loss of biological diversity has been more pronounced and quite alarming over the past few decades. For example, in one study it was concluded that 'by the year 2000, about 73 percent of the original global biodiversity on land remained. The largest declines have occurred in the temperate and tropical grasslands and forests, the biomes where human civilizations developed first. There is a projected further biodiversity loss on land of about 11 percent worldwide between 2000 and 2050' (Oarschot 2008: 53).

Another expression of concern at the alarming rate of biodiversity loss was given by the Millennium Ecosystem Assessment (2005: 15) when a report based on the collective wisdom of over 1,000 leading biological scientists claimed that 'the human-caused rate of species extinction is estimated to be 1,000 times more rapid than the "natural" extinction rate typical of the earth's long-term history'.

These are disturbing statistics on the state of global biodiversity loss. The question is, what have been the *drivers*, the various causes of extinction and the subsequent loss of biodiversity of this magnitude, over the past five decades or so? Experts in this field identify two categories of driver: (1) *direct* divers that affect ecosystem function and processes; and (2) *indirect* drivers that affect the rate at which some of the direct drivers impact ecosystem functions. The implication here is that indirect drivers have the effect of accelerating loss in ecosystem *resilience*. The direct drivers of biodiversity loss generally manifest themselves in the forms of natural disasters with potentials to cause extreme environmental stress, large environmental disturbances, severe limitations of resources, geographic isolations, and extreme habitat degradation and fragmentation.

The indirect drivers of biodiversity loss are not necessarily limited to human factors, although it is the primary focus of this chapter. The human factors that have been responsible for habitat loss and destruction are, in large part, attributable to a combination of the dramatic increase in human *population* (more on this in Chapter 16, Section 16.2), *economic development* and the reliance on *technology* to fix environmental problems (i.e., technological fix).

It is argued that the pressures from these three factors (human population, economic development and technology) have caused the following outcomes: (1) the over-exploitation of natural resources as manifested by growing deforestation, desertification and overfishing and hunting activities on a global scale; (2) the degradation and fragmentation of ecosystems (i.e., habitat loss) primarily arising from changes in land-use that were encouraged by the rapid growth in agriculture, urbanization, highway construction, commercial and industrial development,

and other similar human endeavors; and (3) the introduction of invasive alien species arising from increases in international commerce, tourism and transcontinental commodity transportation through air and water. Most recently, as discussed in Chapter 9, climate change threatens to become a major contributing factor to future biodiversity loss.

There are still many unresolved and unknown scientific issues regarding how each direct and indirect driver affects biodiversity loss, independently and in combination. While delving into this subject matter in any meaningful depth is beyond the scope of this chapter, this much is clear. First, biodiversity loss is real and it is occurring because of the alarming rate of habitat loss caused by both natural and human factors (see Exhibit 10.1). Second, from a policy perspective it is the unknown elements of biodiversity loss (especially when it is viewed within the context of the current trend in biodiversity loss) that should prompt the world community to act with some urgency to take serious steps to understand and protect 'our biological resources while balancing the risks and tradeoffs inherent in environmental decision making' (ELC n.d.).

EXHIBIT 10.1   EVIDENCE OF PAST AND PROJECTED LOSSES ON BIODIVERSITY

- In the last 300 years, global forest has shrunk by approximately 40 percent. Forests have completely disappeared in 25 countries, and another 29 countries have lost more than 90 percent of their forest cover. The decline continues. (UN Forest and Agriculture Organization, 2001 & 2005, Global Forest Resources Assessment 2000 & 2006)

- Since 1900, the world has lost about 50 percent of its wetlands. While much of this occurred in countries in the temperate zone during the first 50 years of the last century, there has been increasing pressure since the 1950s for conversion of tropical and subtropical wetlands to alternative land uses. (http://www.ramsar.org/about/about_wetland_loss.htm)

- Some 20 percent of the world's coral reefs have been effectively destroyed by fishing, pollution, disease and coral bleaching and approximately 24 percent of the remaining reefs in the world are under imminent risk of collapse through human pressures. (Wilkinson C., 2004: Status of Coral Reefs of the World: 2004 report)

- In the past two decades, 34 percent of mangroves have disappeared. Some countries have lost up to 80 percent through conversion for aquaculture, over exploitation and storms (Millennium Ecosystem Assessment 2005)

- The human-caused rate of species extinction is estimated to be 1,000 times more rapid than the 'natural' extinction rate typical of the earth's long-term history. (Millennium Ecosystem Assessment, 2005 . . . p. 15)

■ Fishing pressure has been such in the past century that the biomass of larger high-value fish and those caught incidentally has been reduced to 10 percent or less of the level that existed before industrial fishing started. The loss of biomass and fragmented

habitats has led to local extinctions. (Millennium Ecosystem Assessment, 2005 . . .)

Source: The Cost of Policy Inaction (COPI): The Case of Not Meeting the 2010 Biodiversity Target, Wageningen/Brussels: Report for the European Commission, pp. 173–4. Reprinted by permission.

The past two centuries have been characterized by a rapid loss in biodiversity mainly arising from increasingly dominant human disruption and the alteration of nature. Human appropriation of *net primary production* (i.e., the amount of solar energy converted to plant organic matter through photosynthesis) has now reached to around a third or more of potential vegetation (Vitousek et al. 1986, 1997). That is, one third of the earth's resources are eventually consumed by humans. Undoubtedly, this *disproportionate share* of net primary production going to a single species (i.e., humans) has had a marked impact on biodiversity, flows of carbon, water and energy, and ecosystem services (ESS) on a global scale.

The above statement suggests that human dominance over nature has not only been causing a *loss in biological diversity*, but also affecting *ecosystem functions* (through its effects on the flows of carbon, water and energy) and the supply of ESS—the very thing upon which human welfare directly depends (see Exhibit 10.2). To fully understand the human welfare implications of biodiversity loss, the interrelationships (links) among these three inter-related concepts; namely, biodiversity, ecosystem functions and ESS, have to be formally established. This is done in the next section.

10.2 THE ECONOMICS RATIONALE FOR BIODIVERSITY CONSERVATION

[B]iodiversity also plays an important role in the efficiency with which ecosystems function. Ecosystem efficiency can be determined by measuring how long energy is retained in an ecosystem before being lost. Not all species use energy with equal efficiency. When a community has many different species, the chance that some of those species will be efficient energy-users increases. Energy flowing through ecosystems with many types of species is therefore used more efficiently, and with less loss to the surrounding environment, than energy entering simplified ecosystems. More energy

---

EXHIBIT 10.2 ECOSYSTEM SERVICES

■ Raw materials production:
   (food, fisheries, timber and building materials, non-timber forest products, fodder, genetic resources, medicines, dyes)
■ Pollination
■ Biological control of pests and diseases
■ Habitat and refuge
■ Water supply and regulation
■ Waste recycling and pollution control

■ Nutrient cycling
■ Soil building and maintenance
■ Disturbance regulation
■ Climate regulation
■ Atmospheric regulation
■ Recreation, cultural, educational/scientific.

Source: Worldwatch Institute, *State of the World 1997,* p. 96. Copyright © 1997. Reprinted by permission.

in the system means that the system will be more productive (it will produce more plant and animal biomass, that is, weight) and, from a selfish human perspective, produce more ESS for us (make more fish, more lumber, and more oxygen, filter more water, sequester more carbon dioxide, buffer larger weather systems, and so on).

(Tallamy 2007:38)

The simple message of Tallamy's remark is this: ecosystems and the communities within them function better when they are more *diverse*. That is, in general ecosystems with more species function with increased *efficiency* (as measured by the increase in energy retained within the systems) and are better able to *withstand external disturbances* (hence they are more stable and resilient). More specifically, a diversity of species is better able to utilize the inputs of water, sun and nutrients than a single or small number of species, which leads to higher levels of biomass and less soil erosion and nutrient loss. Furthermore, diversity gives the natural system the ability to resist and adapt to disease, severe weather and climate change. Thus, biodiversity leads to *increases in the flow of ESS* and also plays an essential role in the *sustainable use of these services*.

Figure 10.1 is a schematic representation of these perceived links between biodiversity, ecosystem functions and the flow (supply) of ESS. This is not to imply that the interactions from biodiversity to ecosystem functions to ecosystem services are *linear*. On the contrary, the dynamic nature of ecological interactions may yield significant secondary and tertiary effects. For example, one important secondary effect of biodiversity is the decrease in the *variability* of ESS. This is an important consideration, because it suggests that biodiversity not only contributes to an increased flow of ESS but also to increasing the reliability (or decreasing the variability) of this flow over time.

By having several species that perform similar roles, nature creates *ecological redundancy*. If one species suddenly disappears in a diverse ecosystem others may be able to hold the functioning of the ecosystem together. In other words, as the number of species increases, the range of conditions that at least some species do well in also increases. When perturbations do occur, it is more likely that some of the species present will be able to do well, and these species will protect the community as a whole. Viewed in this way, biodiversity may provide significant 'insurance value' (Baumgartner 2007).

In Exhibit 10.3, it is shown that wild bees are under threat of extinction in the United States mainly because of the failure to recognize their insurance value. As discussed in this exhibit, honey bees are favored over wild bees because, unlike honey bees, wild bees do not produce honey or beeswax. However, they offer more diversity in pollination, are more likely to work in weather conditions honey bees would find unfavorable, and have been found on some occasions to be more effective pollinators. Thus, depending solely on honey bees is risky, as honey bees alone are ineffective in terms of biodiversity. A number of pollinators—not just one—are necessary, because that will ensure more redundancy in pollination. That is, even if one group of pollinators were to disappear or be badly affected by conditions, other groups could make up for their decreased pollination.

Admittedly it will be, if not impossible, very difficult to fully and explicitly capture secondary effects of the above nature through a simple diagrammatic representation. Despite this, Figure 10.1 can still help demonstrate the *positive* feedback mechanisms among

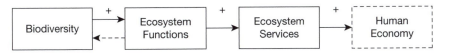

Figure 10.1 *The linkages between biodiversity, ecosystem functions, and ecosytem services. Biodiversity, by enhancing the productivity and stability of natural ecosystems would ultimately lead to increases in the flow of ecosystem services. Ecosystem services represent the last link between the natural ecosystems and the human economy where 'values' are determined.*

EXHIBIT 10.3   HONEYED ECONOMICS: DRAW OF HONEY BEES AND WHY NATIVE BEES MATTER

In the US both the non-native honey bee and also some species of wild bees are utilized for the pollination of crops. Both managed honey bees and wild bees are appraised differently by the growers who benefit from their presence. Commercialized honey bees are easy to work with and produce measurable economic products, honey and beeswax, as well as pollination services. They are more costly than native bees because they require upkeep by beekeepers; however, their presence (and therefore crop pollination) is easy to ensure, as growers can rent bees for the duration of their crop's bloom. Honey bees are not necessarily the best pollinators, however; they are less likely than wild bees to visit flowers in inclement weather and are not always efficient pollinators.

There are a wealth of native bees that also pollinate crops. These bees include mining, leafcutter, sweat and bumble bees, among many others. Unlike honey bees, wild bees do not produce honey or beeswax. However, they offer more diversity in pollination, are more likely to work in weather conditions that honey bees would find unfavorable, and have been found on some occasions to be more effective pollinators. A good example of the importance of wild bees can be seen in a 2004 study by Ricketts, who found that a higher diversity of native bees stabilized pollinator activity in coffee crops even as honey bee populations declined. Wild bees generally provide 'free' pollination, pollinating crops without necessarily costing the grower. It has actually been found that leaving a certain amount of uncultivated land around a field may increase agricultural yield due to an increase in native bees (Morandin and Winston 2006).

Wild bees essentially provide a free ecosystem service to farmers. So why do many farmers depend exclusively on honey bees, even when encouraging wild bee abundance for pollination is a viable and possibly less expensive option? The answer may lie in the economic uncertainty of wild bee availability. Wild bees are not as readily marketable as commercialized ones and their worth in terms of pollination are therefore grossly undervalued (Allsopp et al. 2008). It may be difficult for growers to risk a dependence on wild bees when bringing in honey bees will ensure fruit pollination. This is especially so if the alternative is decreasing agricultural land to conserve wild bee habitat, which would be a costly effort if native bees did not supply the hoped-for pollination. As many people tend to associate more intensified agriculture with higher profit, giving up even a small amount of land to try to encourage native bees may seem counter-intuitive.

However, depending solely on honey bees is dangerous, as honey bees alone are ineffective in terms of biodiversity. A number of pollinators—not just one—are necessary, because that will insure more redundancy in pollination. That is, even if one group of pollinators were to disappear or be badly affected by conditions, other groups could make up for their decreased pollination. Biodiversity is extremely important now, as honey bees are being subjected to a myriad of problems that are threatening their population. Possibly because many honey bees are regularly transported instead of being kept stationary, they are exposed to a number of diseases and pests that negatively affect honey bee numbers. Worse still, now honey bees are disappearing in great numbers in what has been termed Colony Collapse Disorder (CCD), whose cause is unknown (van Engelsdorp et al. 2009).

Essentially, while wild bees are an important consideration for pollination, their contributions to both human agriculture and ecosystem health are ignored in favor of the honey bee. Depending solely upon honey bees for pollination could end disastrously if their population continues to fall; ignoring wild bees could result in the loss of supplemental or even replacement pollination on their part as increasingly intensified agriculture eliminates their natural habitat. In situations where wild bees are scarce and honey bees are not an option, growers may find that they will experience either a loss in harvest or be forced to pollinate through the use of human labor. This can be seen in the case of the vanilla plant, which, due to the limited range of its traditional bee pollinators, often has to be hand pollinated (Pollination Canada 2008). This could potentially be costly.

Acknowledgement: I am grateful to the support I received from my student Ms. Molly Waytes (Class of 2012) in researching and writing this exhibit.

these three variables. It is also evident from this diagram that ESS represents the most important link between natural ecosystems and the human economy.

As discussed in Section 10.1, in recent years the trends in biodiversity loss have been rather unsettling. Furthermore, the discussion in this section so far affirms the *positive* correlation between biodiversity and ESS. Taken together these two observations would suggest that humans may actually be able to mitigate the alarming biodiversity loss and protect ESS through investment in *conserving biodiversity*.

Conserving biodiversity does not occur without a cost. It entails the use of scarce resources, such as land, labor, capital and managerial resources, for the purpose of reducing biodiversity loss and ecosystem degradation. An investment of this nature is expected to have two mutually reinforcing outcomes: a healthier ecosystem and more ecosystems services.

The first outcome, a healthier and more diverse ecosystem, can be measured by some kind of ecological diversity *index*. While it is admittedly very difficult to do this, it is assumed that the simplest way to measure diversity, the one that will be used in this textbook, is through an index of *species richness*, R, which could vary in value from zero to one. A zero value for R would imply that the given ecosystem is populated by a single species (a complete lack of biological diversity, for example a pioneer ecosystem or a dense urban area). On the other hand, an R value of one may suggest a highly matured ecosystem characterized by a considerable degree of diversity, stability and resilience, for example an old-growth forest ecosystem that is hardly impacted by human activities.

It would be nonsensical to claim that humans, through investment, can transform a natural ecosystem from pioneering to mature stage. However, at the margin, investment in biodiversity conservation or ecosystem restoration could mitigate or even increase

species richness through its effect on the population and interactions of the existing species. Understood in this way, a specific level of R could be associated with a specific level of human effort (i.e., investment) to conserve species. Normally, it is progressively more difficult to increase species richness. Thus, as a general rule, *higher R value would require incrementally more investment in biodiversity conservation*.

Of course, investment to preserve ecosystems cannot be done without expecting some beneficial outcomes. In this case, the return for investment is measured by the expected increase in the *flow* (supply) of *ESS*. The unit used to measure ESS, S, may be difficult to delineate. This is because ESS often represents heterogeneous 'bundles' of multiple goods and services (see Exhibit 10.2). For our purpose here the flow of ESS, S, is assumed to be measured in terms of a physical unit (tons of fish, cubic feet of lumber, gallons of freshwater, and so on). Furthermore, the value of the variable S is assumed to vary from zero to infinity.

Figure 10.2 shows the relationship between the index of biodiversity, R, and the flow of ESS, S. It is important to note that R is measured in terms of species richness (expressed as an index that ranges in value from 0 to 1). It is evident from this figure that an increase in R would invariably lead to an increase in S. Moreover, it is further postulated that the *rate of the increase in S diminishes as 'R' increases*.

Alternatively, the relationship in Figure 10.2 can be seen as depicting the functional relationships of *output* (i.e., ESS, S) with a composite *input* (i.e., the use of land, labor, capital and management to attain a certain level of biodiversity, R). In other words, Figure 10.2 actually represents a *production function*— a relationship of inputs (i.e., land, labor and capital) and output. Following convention, this graph shows that, beyond certain point, additional ESS, S, can be attained though increased investment in biodiversity,

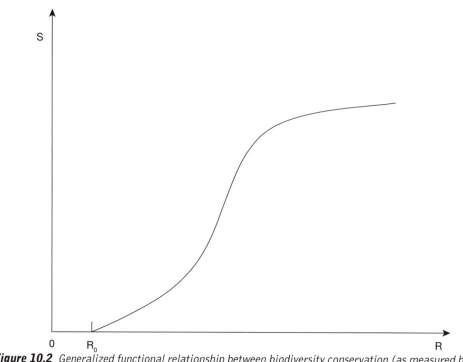

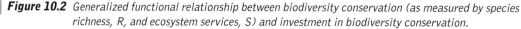

Figure 10.2 *Generalized functional relationship between biodiversity conservation (as measured by species richness, R, and ecosystem services, S) and investment in biodiversity conservation.*

R, but at an ever increasing rate of resources use—such as land, labor, capital and management—suggesting the prevalence of *the law of diminishing marginal product*. This, as we shall see shortly, will be an important factor to consider in determining the 'optimal' level of biodiversity (or biodiversity conservation effort)—a core concept of the economics of biodiversity.

It is important to note that Figure 10.2 does not start at the origin. This is simply to acknowledge that, for most ecosystems, the *critical thresholds* for species extinction would have an R-value greater than zero. That is, *beyond these thresholds ecosystems functionally collapse and their ESS would be virtually reduced to zero once species richness, R, is reduced to a certain critical minimum*.

To clearly understand the essence of the variables R and S, it may be helpful to offer two real-world examples. The first example is an award-winning project in South Africa called 'Working for Water'. This project started in the mid-1980s in response to the multiple problems arising from the introduction

of alien invasive species in the western region of South Africa. Many of the invasive species in this region consume vast quantities of water, significantly decreasing the level of water flow in the major rivers in the area. Working for Water is a public project that employs thousands of people to clear away alien vegetation on a fulltime basis. In addition, this project involves developing education and awareness campaigns, conducting research, introducing stricter measures at airports, ports and other border posts and devising a solid legal framework. The ultimate goal of the project has been to restore the native biodiversity of the region, R, and in so doing prevent further depletion or even increase the flow of fresh water, S, in the region (www.southafrica.info).

For our second example, refer back to Case Study 1.1 in Chapter 1, p. 14. Here, investment to protect and preserve the watershed in the Catskill Mountains is expected to increase the freshwater supply to New York City by a significant amount. This is because the investment to protect the watershed (i.e., to protect natural capital) would increase the capacity of the

Catskill Mountains forest ecosystem to purify water through a natural filtration process involving root systems and soil microorganisms. Thus, in this case, the biodiversity variable R of this model represents not only the absolute number of species in the region, but also the diverse biological, chemical and geological processes that are either maintained or enhanced as a result of increased biodiversity. In this example, the service variable S simply represents the increase in the flow and quality of freshwater (in gallons) to the city of New York.

So far the arguments for the conservation of biodiversity have been based strictly on an economic (i.e., ESS) and ecological (i.e., ecosystem functions) basis. However, it is important to note that the conservation of biodiversity is also defended on other grounds too, the following being the most notable:

- *The potential for the discovery of new drugs*: this expectation has emerged from the observation that many drugs in use today were originally from plants. As such, it is not just wishful thinking to argue that the potential exists for biochemical and genetic resources that have considerable medicinal value in diverse and mature forest ecosystems. This kind of argument provides a strong case for the conservation of the world's forest regions, especially the tropical rainforest ecosystems.
- *Protection against evolving pathogens*: this is based on the theory that the more biodiverse a population is the less likely it is to be eliminated when a powerful pathogen evolves. The converse of this argument is that ruinous outcomes are often encountered when a society relies on a single or genetically uniform crop variety for food. A well-known example of this, as has been already discussed in Chapter 2 (Exhibit 2.2, p. 37), was the Irish reliance on one variety of potato, the lumper, for reasons of efficiency (i.e., yield per acre). When the fungus *Phytophthora infestans* arrived in 1845, like most other pathogens it took no time for the blight to thrive and cause much of the potato crop to rot in the fields. More than a million Irish people—about one in every nine—died in the Great Potato Famine of the 1840s.

- *Ethical considerations*: it is argued that being good stewards to nature is a human responsibility. This responsibility is based on the notion that future generations should not be denied the opportunity to interact and enjoy nature to the same extent as the generations before them.
- *Aesthetic considerations*: Diversity has a value in itself, in that it is aesthetically desirable.

10.3 THE 'OPTIMAL' LEVEL OF ECOSYSTEM SERVICES AND BIODIVERSITY CONSERVATION

In this section, an attempt will be made to establish a theoretical framework that will allow us to identify the conditions for the 'optimal' amount of biodiversity conservation at a given point in time. Optimality implies the attainment of biodiversity as measured by species richness, R^*, that is consistent with the provision of ecological services, S^*, such that societal *net* benefit is maximized. As is often the case, this requires weighing the benefits and costs of all the steps taken to enhance biodiversity through increased biodiversity conservation at the *margin*.

From the outset, it is important to note the following three axiomatic assumptions about the standard economic optimization model under consideration. First, the theoretical analysis is *static* (i.e., economic conditions are evaluated at a fixed point in time). Second, what is being assessed is the *anthropocentric* value of biodiversity loss or gain. Third, no allowance is given for *uncertainty*. The position taken here is that, at the theoretical level the tradeoffs (i.e., costs and benefits) that need to be considered for the purpose of deriving the condition for the 'optimal' level of biodiversity conservation can be realized with a simple, but carefully crafted, economic model. (Exhibit 10.4 is a 'must read' for those who would like to have a full picture of the shortcomings associated with the simple theoretical model presented in this chapter.)

Identifying the benefits and costs of biodiversity conservation projects

As is evident from the discussion in Section 10.2, the *benefit* of biodiversity conservation projects is

EXHIBIT 10.4   CAVEATS TO SIMPLE ANALYTICAL ECONOMIC MODEL OF BIODIVERSITY AND ECOSYSTEM SERVICE CONSERVATION

In this chapter, to make the analysis simple, a number of simplifying assumptions were intentionally introduced. The objective of this exhibit is to present a list of some of the key assumptions that were made in this chapter. This is done primarily to acknowledge the limitations of some of the models as well as the arguments presented.

First, most of the discussion about the biodiversity of ecosystems has been in very broad terms without being specific about its components. No attempt has been made to say whether the situation under consideration deals with the conservation of species biodiversity, conservation of genetic biodiversity or conservation of biological diversity of ecosystems, habitats and biomes. Furthermore, no effort was made to delineate between the diversity of terrestrial and marine biomes and ecosystems.

Second, the definition of ecosystem services has been kept intentionally vague and broad. More specifically, it was treated as though it represents a service with distinctly defined properties and units of measurement. In reality, however, ecosystem services are heterogeneous bundles of multiple goods and services provided by an ecosystem(s).

Third, most ecosystem services are public goods and/or commons and as such, markets are not available to provide prices and clear units of account. Therefore the issues of pricing, units of measurement, and valuations are addressed on a rather ad hoc basis

and cannot be known. However, an in-depth discussion of these important issues has been already offered in Chapter 7.

Fourth, it was assumed that biodiversity is always positively correlated with ecosystem services. That is, investment in biodiversity conservation will always lead to the increased provisioning of ecosystem services, hence increased human welfare. However, the economic importance of natural ecosystems may not rely solely on *variability* (e.g. species and genetic diversity). Indeed, many of the benefits obtained from nature rely heavily on the abundance of particular species.

However, we don't always know what that species is, or how it is interconnected with other species. Stressing ecosystems can lead to unpleasant surprises where a species of interest is harmed incidentally. Nevertheless, the view that biodiversity automatically leads to increased human welfare is difficult to confirm in all situations. For example, the human experience of tinkering with natural systems through over-hunting, and then with plant and animal species through agriculture, has caused an increased abundance of humans and their crops, but reduced habitat for wild species. Finding a balance between cultivating the earth and leaving it alone is sustainability—a difficult task to accomplish with the human population growing exponentially in a century of rising expectations for developing countries (more on this in Chapter 15).

realized from the expected increase in the supply of ESS it generates, S. However, by their nature ESS are composed of a heterogeneous group of goods and services (see Exhibit 10.2). Despite this complication, in this section an assumption will be made that classifies ESS into two broad categories depending on whether or not the *marginal willingness to pay* (i.e., the demand price) for the services can be entirely captured through the normal market mechanism. As shown in Figure 10.3, the two categories of willing-

ness to pay are represented by the demand curves D_1 and D_2. In this figure, it is important to note that the vertical axis represents the monetary value of ESS, S.

The reading of the horizontal axis is not entirely straightforward since it represents two interrelated variables. In one respect, it can be viewed as representing the quantity or volume of ESS, S, measured in some physical unit (such as the weight of plant and animal biomass). At the same time, it can also represent the level of biodiversity as measured by the index

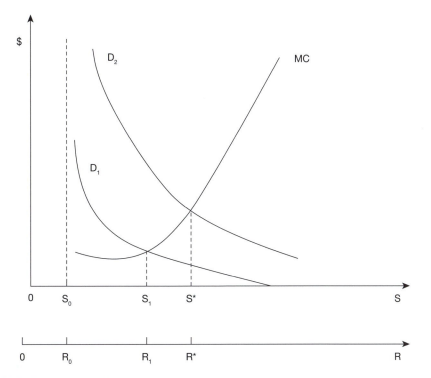

Figure 10.3 *Optimal level of biodiversity conservation and ecosystem services occurred at R* & S*, respectively, where MC = D$_2$*

of the species richness, R, which in turn directly corresponds to each level of S. This is because, as shown in Section 2, R and S are *positively* correlated. That is, an increase in R arising from measures taken to protect biodiversity would cause a corresponding increase in S, although at a diminishing rate (see Figure 10.2). With this understanding of the interpretations of the variables in the vertical and horizontal axis of Figure 10.3, we are now in a position to further analyze the two demand curves for ESS.

The first demand curve, D$_1$, represents the marginal willingness to pay for ESS that can be readily captured through normal market operation, such as food crops, timber, tourism, and so on. The second demand curve, D$_2$, represents people's marginal willingness to pay for ESS including those that have no readily available market values (prices), such as soil formation, pollination, climate regulation, water purification, flood control, and so on. Presenting the demand curves for ESS in this manner would suggest that *willingness to pay (as measured by the total demand D$_2$)*

could differ from actual payments (as represented by D$_1$) by several orders of magnitude (Pearce 2007). However, to the extent that D$_2$ remains a hypothetical construct, it remains a major unresolved problem in ecosystem 'valuation' that economists working in this field have to contend with (for more on this refer back to Chapter 7).

Setting aside the valuation problem for a moment, we observe that both demand curves (D$_1$ and D$_2$) are negatively sloped—which follows the *law of demand*. The important implication of this is that the marginal values (or willingness to pay) attached to ESS will decline monotonically with each incremental increase in ESS, S. An alternative way to look at this same phenomenon is to observe what happens to people's willingness to pay as society moves from a situation approaching a 'pristine' stage (a very high value of R) to a virtual 'extinction' of species (i.e., as the value of R approaches close to zero). This illustrates that people's *willingness to pay to conserve biodiversity (as measured by increases in species richness) increases steadily*

219

as extinction of species becomes increasingly imminent. In fact, as shown in Figure 10.3, the marginal willingness to pay is likely to be *infinitely large* (or unbounded) before extinction of all species occurs; that is, before the value of R approaches zero. This observation has *significant policy implications*. Most importantly, it illustrates the *enormous foregone social benefit* associated with not taking biodiversity conservation measures until it is too late to do any good.

Let us now turn to the *cost* side of the issue. Costs are incurred because it takes resources to obtain a high level of biodiversity, R. In Figure 10.3, the marginal cost, MC, of biodiversity conservation is drawn as an upward sloping curve. The positive slope of MC is to be expected given that the production function of R is governed by the law of diminishing marginal product, as shown in Figure 10.2. This cost curve represents the monetary values of all the expenses incurred to acquire the necessary land, labor, capital and management resources for the purpose of biodiversity conservation (or amelioration of biodiversity loss). This cost represents an *opportunity cost* to the extent that the resources that are used to reduce the loss of biodiversity would preclude the use of these same resources to undertake other projects that are of some value to society. For example, if a large tract of land is set aside as a 'wilderness area' by some legislative measure for the purpose of protecting certain animal and plant species, it would preclude the use of this area for other purposes, such as cattle ranching or growing crops.

The optimal level of biodiversity conservation

Given the demand (benefit) and supply (cost) information provided by Figure 10.3, it is a simple matter to identify the theoretically 'optimal' level of ESS. This condition occurs at S^* where the marginal benefit of ESS (as represented by D_2) is equal to the marginal cost curve, MC. It is important to note that the optimal amount of ESS, S^*, is simultaneously determined with the optimal level of biodiversity conservation (index of species richness), R^*. In what way does S^* or R^* represent an optimal outcome? To answer this question, it will be worthwhile examining

the outcomes (in terms of cost and benefits) of slight deviations from R^* in either direction. Keep in mind that whatever is said about R applies equally to S in this model.

From Figure 10.3, it is obvious that any situation to the left of R^* is associated with biodiversity conservation effort where marginal social benefit is greater than marginal cost. This would clearly suggest that increased biodiversity conservation (i.e., measures taken to enhance species richness) is worthwhile because at this level the marginal benefit outweighs the marginal cost. Similarly, any outcome to the right of R^* would imply a marginal cost that is greater than the marginal benefit, hence, a reduction in biodiversity conservation effort would be justified. Given this optimality condition, is there evidence to suggest that the world is currently operating at suboptimal level? The answer to this question is the primary focus of the next section.

10.4 WHY THE SOCIAL BENEFITS OF ECOSYSTEM SERVICES MAY BE UNDERSTATED: POLICY IMPLICATIONS

A quick look at Figure 10.3 would suggest that there are actually two ways in which the marginal willingness to pay for ESS, S, can be read, depending on which of the two demand curves (D_1 or D_2) is considered relevant. As discussed earlier, the *total* demand curve, D_2, is mainly a theoretical construct since it includes the value of ESS that has *no* observable market prices. This being the case, in practice the value for ESS is measured by the prices (marginal willingness to pay) observed along the demand curve D_1. Hence, given that D_1 is the relevant demand, other things equal, the market equilibrium level of ESS will be S_1, where D_1 intersects with MC. This outcome is clearly suboptimal since it is located to the left of S^*. The message of this outcome should be clear. Failing to account for the marginal benefits of the ESS that are not exchanged in the market leads to *inadequate provision of ESS* (S_1 instead of S^*) which also suggests a *deficiency in ecosystem conservation* (R_1 instead of R^*).

Clearly, the above conclusion has public-policy implications. Given that the values of many aspects of

ESS are not captured by market prices, a move towards optimality, S^* (or R^* in term of ecosystem conservation), cannot be achieved without binding regulations and/or monetary fines that are intended to close the gap between the two demand curves (D_1 and D_2). Furthermore, the cost of policy inaction could be quite significant. For example, a recent study (Brink et al. 2008: 119) described the loss to the European Union (EU) countries for failing to meet the 2010 global biodiversity target in this way:

> we are currently losing each year land-based ESS worth around 50 billion Euros (this is a welfare loss, not GDP loss, as a large part of these benefits is currently not included in GDP). These losses continue over time, and are added to by losses in subsequent years of more biodiversity. They could be equivalent in scale to 7 percent of GDP by 2050. This is a conservative estimate.

Until the last two decades there was a lack of internationally coordinated and effective public policy to mitigate the rapidly growing threat of biodiversity loss worldwide. Pro-biodiversity policies, to the extent that they existed, were limited in their scope and applied in piecemeal fashion (such as to the protection of wetlands, migratory species of wild animals, etc.).

The Convention on Biological Diversity (CBD) was formally convened at the 1992 Earth Summit with the goal of forming comprehensive global strategies to address biodiversity concerns. This Convention produced the first global agreement on the conservation and sustainable use of biodiversity, which was signed by 150 government leaders. All the parties to the Convention have committed themselves to achieving some broadly defined biodiversity targets.

What emerged from this Convention, among other things, was the 2010 Biodiversity Target which was formally enacted in 2002. In terms of its scope and specificity, the 2010 Biodiversity Target has been the most ambitious as it aims for a significant reduction in the rate of biodiversity loss at all levels and globally (see Exhibit 10.5a). A comprehensive discussion of all the pro-biodiversity international and national agreements is beyond the scope of this textbook. However, Exhibit 10.5b provides a list of some of the major legally binding international

EXHIBIT 10.5A   2010 BIODIVERSITY TARGETS

- Target 1.1: At least 10 percent of each of the world's ecological regions effectively conserved. Target 1.2: Areas of particular importance to biodiversity protected.

- Target 2.1: Restore, maintain, or reduce the decline of populations of species of selected taxonomic groups. Target 2.2: Status of threatened species improved.

- Target 3.1: Genetic diversity of crops, livestock, and of harvested species of trees, fish and wildlife and other valuable species conserved, and associated indigenous and local knowledge maintained.

- Target 4.1: Biodiversity-based products derived from sources that are sustainably managed, and production areas managed consistent with the conservation of biodiversity. Target 4.2: Unsustainable

consumption, of biological resources, or that impact upon biodiversity, reduced. Target 4.3: No species of wild flora or fauna endangered by international trade.

- Target 5.1: Rate of loss and degradation of natural habitats decreased.

- Target 6.1: Pathways for major potential alien invasive species controlled. Target 6.2: Management plans in place for major alien species that threaten ecosystems, habitats or species.

- Target 7.1: Maintain and enhance resilience of the components of biodiversity to adapt to climate change. Target 7.2: Reduce pollution and its impacts on biodiversity

- Target 8.1: Capacity of ecosystems to deliver goods and services maintained. Target 8.2: Biological resources that support sustainable livelihoods, local food security and health care, especially of poor people maintained.

■ Target 9.1 Protect traditional knowledge, innovations and practices. Target 9.2: Protect the rights of indigenous and local communities over their traditional knowledge, innovations and practices, including their rights to benefit sharing.

■ Target 10.1: All transfers of genetic resources are in line with the Convention on Biological Diversity, the International Treaty on Plant Genetic Resources for Food and Agriculture and other applicable agreements. Target 10.2: Benefits arising from the commercial and other utilization of genetic resources shared with the countries providing such resources.

■ Target 11.1: New and additional financial resources are transferred to developing country Parties, to allow for the effective implementation of their commitments under the Convention, in accordance with Article 20. Target 11.2: Technology is transferred to developing country Parties, to allow for the effective implementation of their commitments under the Convention, in accordance with its Article 20, paragraph 4.

Source: www.cbd.int/2010. (Reproduced with permission.)

EXHIBIT 10.5B SOME NOTABLE INTERNATIONAL BIODIVERSITY TREATIES

■ UN Convention on Biological Diversity (CBD): Signed by 150 government leaders at the 1992 Rio Earth Summit. The broader objectives of this 'convention are the conservation of biological diversity, the sustainable use of its components and the fair and equitable sharing of the benefits arising out of its utilization of genetic resources' (UNDP 2000: 3).

■ Cartagena Protocol on Biosafety to the Convention on Biological (BCB) Diversity: Adopted in 2000 and entered into force in 2003. The main aims of this international agreement are the protection of human health and the natural ecosystems from the possible adverse effects of the products (i.e., modified living organisms) of modern biotechnology.

■ Ramsar Convention of Wetlands: adopted in 1971 and came into force in 1975. This convention is an intergovernmental treaty but not affiliated with the United Nations system of Multilateral Environmental Agreements. The primary mission of this convention has been 'the conservation and wise use of all wetlands through local and national actions and international cooperation, as a contribution towards achieving sustainable development throughout the world' (Ramsar 1971).

■ Convention on the Conservation of Migratory Species of Wild Animals (also known as CMS). The convention was signed in 1979 and entered into force in 1983. The objectives of this intergovernmental treaty have been the conservation of migratory species, their habitats and migration routes on a global scale. As of 2011, 116 countries have signed the treaty. The signed agreements may range from legally binding treaties to less formal instruments, such as Memoranda of Understanding.

■ Convention on International Trade in Endangered Species of Wild Fauna and Flora (CITES): The convention was adopted in 1973 and entered into force in 1975. The primary aim of the convention has been to regulate the international trade in animals and plants that may be threatened by trade, through binding international treaties. As one of the signs of the success of this treaty, no species listed under CITES has gone extinct in the last 30 years.

Note: The above treaties undergo regular amendments on the basis of the specific bylaws of the convention under which the treaties have been enacted. Furthermore, the above international treaties have been adopted in national- and regional-level legislations such as the Convention on the Conservation of European Wildlife and National Habitat of 1979 and the US Endangered Species Act of 1973.

agreements that have been enacted over the past four decades. The primary aims of these international treaties have been to promote the sustainable use of natural ecosystems, which in turn contribute to furthering the promotion of biodiversity conservation.

Sadly, however, the majority of the existing international pro-biodiversity treaties lack legal force even when they are based on binding agreements. This situation is even more evident in those policies aimed at protecting biodiversity and ESS outside of 'protected areas'. Lack of political will and inadequate financial resources for policy implementation appear to be the major causes of failing to fulfill the commitments to biodiversity targets. In the final analysis, for those who have studied this issue closely it appears that the actual positive contributions of existing international and regional agreements to biodiversity conservation have been quite modest (Brink et al. 2008).

However, there have been some observable successes at the national and local levels in promoting the sustainable use of natural resources through efforts to protect ecosystems that are highly sensitive to human exploitation. At the national level, many countries have policies that set aside large pieces of land as 'protected areas'. These land conservation and preservation measures have been prominent in many developed nations even when the opportunity costs of doing so have been quite significant. On the other hand, mainly due to cost considerations, 'protected areas' in developing nations are not effectively managed, and rules governing their use are not adequately enforced, such that the goals for ecological protection are unlikely to be achieved (more on this in Chapter 16). The implication of new protected areas also encounters social justice and/or moral complications when it involves the displacement of indigenous or local peoples. This situation signals a serious setback in global biodiversity conservation initiatives since a disproportionately large portion of ecologically sensitive landmasses (the tropical zones) are under the jurisdictions of governments from the developing nations.

Understandably, due to their economic circumstances developing countries cannot be expected to undertake measures to reduce biodiversity loss without significant financial compensation from the developed nations. Furthermore, it would be unfair to expect these countries to shoulder the burden of the full costs of biodiversity conservation measures when the benefits from such initiatives are shared by the entire global community, and much of the biodiversity loss is a result of the heavy resource consumption of the developed nations.

For example, it would be very difficult for the Brazilian government to absorb the entire cost for preserving a large tract of land in the Amazon Basin when one of the major benefits from a conservation measure of this nature is carbon sequestration—a key factor in mitigating the threat of climate change worldwide. The same situation applies when relatively poor countries like Costa Rica, Madagascar, Malaysia, Ecuador, Congo and the Philippines are asked to set aside large areas of tropical forest to preserve the genetic pools of certain plants and animals. Evidently, negotiating equitable shares of the costs and benefits among all the parties involved in international and regional treaties on biological diversity is a difficult task. This factor alone has been a major impediment to international and regional treaties in biodiversity.

However, despite this it is important to point out that there have been some successful biodiversity conservation programs in developing countries. Some have emerged from collaborative work with non-governmental organizations (NGOs). A good example of this has been the *debt-for-nature swaps*. The idea here is to forgive (swap) the debt of a particular developing nation, usually through a local conservation NGO, with a commitment to protect an environmentally sensitive area (or areas). Some of the early applications of this kind of conservation program have been in tropical rainforest regions such as Bolivia, Costa Rica, Ecuador and the Philippines.

In addition, in some developed countries there have been many *environmental organizations* at both the national and local levels with long histories of successful accomplishments in protecting various kinds of animal and plant species and preserving land for wilderness. Since these are not-for-profit organizations, their operations are financed through money collected from membership dues and competitive grants they may receive from government agencies. In the United States, the Audubon Society and the Nature Conservancy function this way. There are also many nature conservancies that operate strictly at the local level. These local environmental organizations have been quite effective in persuading private owners of large areas of land to limit the rights for the future uses of their properties. What is being sought in this kind of local agreement is the 'sustainable' use of the 'acquired' properties in perpetuity. The principal parties in the negotiation are provided with tax advantages (easement) in exchange for the limits placed on their rights for the future use of their properties, and they also gain a certain moral satisfaction of contributing to ecological and biodiversity conservation.

As discussed above, while there have been many successful biodiversity conservation measures taken at local, regional and national levels throughout the world, these efforts lack coordination to make them more effective. More specifically, the duplication of efforts and a lack of global perspective can greatly undermine the effectiveness of many of these well-intentioned but narrowly defined biodiversity initiatives.

So far, we have discussed biodiversity conservation policies that have been implemented through binding international agreements, regional treaties and legislative enactments provided by national and local government bodies. While these efforts have shown some measurable positive outcomes, there are economists who still believe that global concerns regarding biodiversity losses can be addressed effectively through the normal operations of the market system. Exhibit 10.6 provides an overview of this particular perspective. The main argument is based on that notion that markets emerge, although gradually, for ESS as the things that were treated

EXHIBIT 10.6 CAN MARKETS BE TRUSTED TO ADDRESS BIODIVERSITY LOSS EFFECTIVELY?

While not disputing the growing human-induced pressures on biodiversity, some economists (Lomborg 1998; Simon and Kahn 1984) have argued against premature public interventions to move society from a situation resembling S_1 towards S^* in Figure 10.3. Their argument is based on the notion that S_1 actually represents a 'transitional' equilibrium market outcome. This is because of the belief by pro-market economists that D_1 will start to shift upward as ecosystem services become increasingly valuable in the future, mainly due the expected increases in global population and economic growth.

More specifically, according to Simon and Lomborg, in the future an upward shift in D_1 will automatically occur as some ecosystem services that are now treated as 'free goods' become scarce and start to be appropriated and assigned well-defined ownership rights. A good example of this kind of transformation would be the recent effort to capture the 'scarcity' value of forest ecosystem services for carbon sequestration through market mechanisms—the price for carbon. In the European Union (EU) there are emerging markets in which carbon is traded like any other commodity with delineated ownership rights. What prompted this development has been the growing scientific evidence for the human-induced causes of climate change—the emission of greenhouse gases.

Another example is a case already discussed in Chapter 1—the scarcity of potable water in the New York City area. The water that quenches the thirst of millions of New Yorkers comes entirely from an ecosystem that is still functional: the forested Catskill Mountains north of the city. However, in recent years, pollution (i.e., sewage and pesticides) has degraded the water quality to the point where New York's water no longer met EPA standards.

This problem could be remedied in two ways: by investing in capital equipment (such as water-treatment facilities) or by investing in 'natural' capital—the conservation of the forested Catskill Mountains watersheds. The latter option requires buying lands in-and-around the watersheds in order to restrict its use. As discussed in Case Study 1.1 (see p. 14), this could be done through securitization—by assigning to corporations the obligation to manage and conserve natural capital in exchange for the right to the benefits from selling the services provided.

The conclusion one can draw from these two examples is that, *as natural ecosystems become scarce, many*

of their services would be effectively priced through normal market mechanisms. The effect of this process will be to continually narrow the gaps between the two demand curves in Figure 10.3, D$_1$ and D$_2$. Hence, in the long-run, an optimal outcome (such as S* in Figure 10.3) is achievable without undue interference with the normal operation of the market. However, *what is not clear is how long it will take for the market to accomplish the necessary adjustment.* In the case of biodiversity conservation, this is a crucial issue given the long lag-times involved in ecosystem responses.

as 'free goods' become scarce and start to be appropriated and assigned well-defined ownership rights. A good example of this is the recent development in carbon trading markets. The broader implication would suggest that, in Figure 10.3, the gap between D$_1$ and D$_2$ will, in the course of time, diminish.

In this section, we discussed why market prices for ESS understate the 'true' scarcity values of these resources. As shown using Figure 10.3, the ultimate outcome of this has been to reduce the estimates of the flow of future benefits arising from investment projects intended for biodiversity conservation. This is continuing to occur while the pressure on global ecosystems continues to mount due to the unabated growth of both human population and the economy. Under this circumstance, as discussed in the next section, the recent trends of accelerated species extinctions may not cease if investment projects that are likely to contribute to biodiversity conservation continue to be based on standard cost–benefit analysis.

10.5 THE PHYSICAL EVIDENCE FOR OVERSTRESSED GLOBAL NATURAL ECOSYSTEMS: MASS SPECIES EXTINCTIONS

Extinction is just the last step in a long degradation process. Countless local extinction precedes a potentially final global extinction. As a result, many different ecosystem types are becoming more and more alike, the so-called homogenization process.

(Brink 2008: 56)

The quotation above suggests that high rates of species extinctions could be taken as an ominous sign of unhealthy or overexploited natural ecosystems. The implication of this observation for the sustainable use of ESS is rather serious given that a growing number of scientists expect that the rate of species extinctions is likely to increase in the foreseeable future.

Ecologists make their estimates by comparing trends of species extinctions between different time-periods or by comparing current extinctions with past mass-extinction events. According to a recent report, 'scientists estimate there are 10 to 30 million plant and animal species on the planet, most of them unidentified. Each year as many as 50,000 species disappear. Most die off because of human activity' (Tallamy 2007). Another publication put the situation for species extinctions this way:

Over the past few centuries humans may have increased the species extinction rate by as much as three orders of magnitude. The available information, based on recorded extinctions of known species over the past 100 years, indicates extinction rates are at least 100 times if not 1000 times greater than rates characteristic of species in the fossil record.

(Millennium Species Assessment, 2005).

How valid are the above estimates of species extinctions? As would be expected, species extinction is very difficult to estimate since verifying extinction is an extremely time-consuming and expensive process, and only a fraction of all the species on earth have even been scientifically identified. Furthermore, there are important differences in the assumptions and methodologies used to come up with the various estimates that have been reported about the rates of species extinctions over the past three decades. Thus, no 'consensus' estimates on species extinctions exist. Despite this, recent publications on species extinctions suggest that extinctions are rising at rates that justify taking serious policy actions (Bakkes et al. 2006; Vitousek et al. 1997; Wilson 1992).

Species extinctions of the above magnitude signal the widespread degradation of natural ecosystems that accompany significant biodiversity loss. This also suggests that, from a global perspective, we are losing our supply of ESS, by operating at a suboptimal level of biodiversity conservation. This will imply a loss of social and economic wellbeing in the long run.

Finally, it is important to contemplate the consequences of failing to take actions intended to address the emerging concern of species extinctions. In this case, the concern amounts to the possibility of transgressing *critical ecological thresholds*—points beyond which *irreversible* changes in ecosystem functions may occur. When critical thresholds are crossed, it becomes very (infinitely) costly, because at this stage the changes tend to be irrevocable.

In Figure 10.3, this is illustrated in a situation where society is operating at or to the left of R_0 (or S_0). As evident from this figure, the normal cost–benefit analysis would not apply once this *ecologically critical threshold* is crossed—the forgone benefit (as measured by consumers' willingness to pay) is *unbounded or infinite*. That is, where irreversibility is apparent, marginal analysis of the type used in this chapter is totally inadequate. In this case, as will be discussed in Chapter 13, the appropriate approach for evaluating biodiversity conservation projects dealing with threatened or endangered species would be the *Safe Minimum Standard*, which holds that each species is irreplaceable and worthy of preservation for its own sake (more on this in Chapter 13).

The emergence of new plants and animals is an ongoing process. However, as Olson (2005) put it, 'that is sort of a 1 million to 4 million year process, and yet we are causing species to be lost at rates of 100 to 1000 times faster'. What this indicates, as many scientists have already declared, is that unless something drastic is done to reverse recent trends of species extinctions, human activity is destined to cause a 'sixth extinction'. That is, a mass extinction of a severity equivalent to any of the previous five large-scale extinctions that are evident through surveys of the fossil record. Almost all of the past large-scale species extinctions appear to be due to geological processes or possibly the impact of asteroids. For the first time, humans (a single species) are on the verge of creating an unimagined calamity of epic proportions.

10.6 CHAPTER SUMMARY

Chapter 10 started by providing a definition of biodiversity and an overview of some of the facts and figures that indicated the current worrisome trends in biodiversity loss throughout the world. For example, according to one study it was estimated that, by the year 2000, approximately 27 percent of the original global biodiversity on land was lost forever. Worse yet, under the 'business as usual' scenario, this same study projected a further biodiversity loss on land of about 11 percent worldwide between 2000 and 2050. Clearly, the cost of inaction appears to be very high indeed.

The conventional wisdom in ecology supports the idea that biodiversity contributes to human welfare by enhancing the productivity of natural ecosystems (i.e., the production of more plant and animal biomass: that is, weight) which in turn leads to the production of more ESS (i.e., more fish, more lumber, more oxygen, more water filtered, more CO_2 sequestered, larger weather systems buffering, and so on). Hence, it is the flow of ESS that, in the end, link biodiversity with human economies.

Once the benefits of ESS in the human economy are acknowledged, the next logical step is to find ways of assessing the social costs of realizing these benefits. To do this, it is important to understand the functional relationships between biodiversity and ESS. In this chapter, this was done by using a simple production function model. Production function relates inputs (i.e., factors of production) and output. In this case, the inputs are identified as the amount of labor and capital and other resources used by society to increase biodiversity through investment in the protection and conservation of natural ecosystems. The output is the associated yield from such an investment in terms of ESS. The relationship between inputs and outputs are assumed to be positive: the increased investment in biodiversity conservation would lead to increased ESS, but at a diminishing rate. In other words, the production function adheres to the law of diminishing marginal productivity. In terms of production costs, this implies that increased ESS are realized at incrementally higher costs—increasing marginal cost.

The next step is to understand the nature of the 'benefits' that society receives from the availability of ESS. In standard economics, the ideal measure of benefit is willingness to pay which, under certain conditions, can be approximated though prices or points along a demand curve (see Chapter 7). Thus, to obtain estimates of social benefits, information about the demand for ESS is needed.

Conceptually, determining demand is done by deconstructing the demand for ESS into two components. The first component (D_1 in Figure 10.3) represents that portion of the demand curve with observable (through market prices) willingness to pay. The second component (D_2 in Figure 10.3) includes both the market and nonmarket values of the ESS. Thus, because several aspects of ESS are not captured by market prices, at each level of ecosystem provisions the willingness to pay associated with D_2 will be greater than with D_1. An important observation that can be drawn from this is that the valuation of ESS solely on the basis of market information could have the effect of unduly underestimating the social benefits of ESS.

Once the nature of the benefits and costs for ESS are identified, the theoretically optimal level of ESS would be at the point where marginal social benefit (D_2) equals to marginal cost (MC), as shown in Figure 10.3. Given the valuation problem associated with the social benefits derived from ESS, this unique outcome remains purely theoretical.

However, one important insight that can be deduced from the above theoretical outcome is the strong likelihood of a suboptimal outcome in a world that relies heavily on market signals (observable market prices) to determine the level of investment in the protection of nature or the flow of ESS. This is because benefits measured using market prices significantly underestimate the social values of ESS and in so doing undermine the urgency for undertaking projects that are intended to augment biodiversity.

Consistent with the above observation, in recent years several empirical studies (see Exhibit 10.1) indicate that the world abounds with overstressed ecosystems, clearly suggesting that global investment to protect natural ecosystems in order to promote biodiversity are lacking.

227

Over the past three decades, the responses of the global communities to the biodiversity crisis have been rather mixed and not particularly effective. However, at the global level the United Nations have ratified many treaties primarily intended to decelerate biodiversity loss. Notable treaties among these include the Convention on International Trade in Endangered Species of Wild Fauna and Flora, CITES (1973), the UN Convention on Biological Diversity (1992), the International Plant Protection Convention, IPPC (1997) and the 2010 Biodiversity Targets. In addition to the UN treaties, there have been, as discussed in Section 10.4, several national, regional and local government initiatives to address specific aspects of biodiversity related concerns. Furthermore, initiatives that have been undertaken to promote biological diversity by private and corporate philanthropists and NGOs should not be overlooked.

As discussed in Section 10.4, the problems with most of the above efforts have been a lack of coordination and repeated failure to enforce even the treaties that are considered to be binding. Another issue that is making international treaties on biological diversity ineffective has been the lack of mechanisms for the equitable sharing of benefits and costs among countries of the world. What makes this kind of problem particularly difficult to resolve is that often negotiations on biological diversity involve nations at different stages of economic development: developed (rich) and developing (poor) nations.

Lastly, as discussed in Section 10.5, from a global perspective the statistical evidence for species extinction is quite disturbing. Considering the rate of biodiversity loss, the cost of inaction is intolerably high. In these circumstances the prudent policy is to act without delay even in the presence of uncertainty about costs and benefits.

REVIEW AND DISCUSSION QUESTIONS

1. Carefully review the following key concepts discussed in this chapter: ESS, biodiversity conservation, species richness, critical thresholds for species extinction, debt-for-nature swaps, protected areas, and the insurance value of biodiversity.

2. Provide the ecological argument for why increases in species diversity would lead to increases in ecosystem productivity, and hence an increase in the production of ESS.

3. Do you think it is reasonable to assume that the production of ESS follows the law of diminishing marginal product? Explain.

4. In your own words, explain the arguments given in this chapter regarding why the demand for ESS should be separated into two distinct segments.

5. Provide three economic reasons why, from a global perspective, there appears to be underinvestment in projects that would lead to the reversal of the current trends in biodiversity loss.

6. Read Exhibit 10.6 carefully and answer the following question: Can a free-market system be trusted to effectively address the global concern in biodiversity loss? Why or why not?

7. Read the following statements. In response, state 'True', 'False' or 'Uncertain' and explain why:
   (a) Biological diversity contributes to an increase in the stability of the supply of ecosystems services.
   (b) Human population growth, economic growth and increased use of technology (technological fix) are the root causes for the current malaise in the state of global biodiversity.
   (c) Growing concerns for mass extinctions of biological species clearly indicate that the cost of policy inaction could become intolerably high.

8. Provide brief but critical comments on the following major UN biodiversity related treaties and policy guidelines:
   (a) The 1973 Convention on International Trade in Endangered Species of Wild Fauna and Flora, CITES (and the subsequent amendments).

(b)   The 1992 Convention on Biological Diversity, CBD

(c)   The Millennium Ecosystem Assessment (2005)

(d)   The 2010 Biodiversity Targets.

REFERENCES AND FURTHER READING

Allsopp M. H., de Lange W. J. and Veldtman, R. (2008) 'Valuing Insect Pollination Services with Cost of Replacement', *PLoS ONE* 3, 9: e3128.

Bakkes, J. A., Bräue, I., Brink, P., Görlach, B., Kuik, O. J. and Medhurst, J. (2006) 'Cost of Policy Inaction—A Scoping Study', *Final Report for the European Commission, Germany*, Brussels: European Commission.

Balmford A., Bruner, A., Cooper, P., Costanza, R., Farber, S., Green, R., Jenkins, M., Jefferiss, P., Jessamy, V., Madden, J., Munro, K., Myers, N., Naeem, S., Paovola, S., Rayment, M., Rosendo, S., Roughgarden, J., Trumper, K. and Turner, K. R. (2002) 'Economic Reasons for Conserving Wild Nature', *Science* 2979: 50–95.

Baumgartner, S. (2007) 'The Insurance Value of Biodiversity in the Provision of Ecosystem Services', Department of Economics, University of Heidelberg, Germany.

Bishop, R. C. (1978) 'Endangered Species and Uncertainty: The Economics of a Safe Minimum Standard', *American Journal of Agricultural Economics* 60: 10–18.

Boyd, J. and Spencer, B. (2006) 'What are Ecosystem Services?' Discussion Paper: 1–24, Washington DC: Resources for the Future.

Braat, L., Klok, C., Walpole, M., Kettunen, M., Peralta-Bezerra, N. and Brink, P. (2008) 'Changes in Ecosystem Services', in L. Braat, and P. ten Brink (eds.) *The Cost of Policy Inaction: The Case of Not Meeting the 2010 Biodiversity Target*, Brussels: European Commission.

Brink, P., Chiabai, A., Rayment, M., Braeuer, I., Peralta-Bezerra, N., Kettunen M. and Braat, L.(2008) 'The Cost of Policy Inaction in Monetary Terms', in L. Braat and P. ten Brink (eds.) *The Cost of Policy Inaction: The Case of Not Meeting the 2010 Biodiversity Target*, Brussels: European Commission.

CBD (1992) *Article 2: Use of Terms*, Convention on Biological Diversity, http://www.cbd.int/convention/articles/?a=cbd-02, accessed 07/02/2012.

—— (2006) *Global Biodiversity Outlook 2*, Montreal: Convention on Biological Diversity.

Chichilnisky, G. and Heal, G. (1998) 'Economic Returns from the Biosphere', *Journal of Nature* 391: 629–30.

Ciriacy-Wantrup, S. (1952) *Resource Conservation: Economics and Policy*, Berkeley, CA: University of California Press.

ELC (n.d.) *Driver of Biodiversity Loss*, http://www.enviroliteracy.org/subcategory.php?id=352&print=1, accessed 07/02/2012.

Gaston, J. and Balmford, A. (2001) 'Can we Afford to Conserve Biodiversity?' *Bioscience* 51, 1:43–52.

Lomborg, B. (1998) *The Skeptical Environmentalist: Measuring the Real State of the World*, Cambridge: Cambridge University Press.

Markandya, A., Nune, P., Brauer, I., Brink P., Kuik, O. and Rayment, M. (2008) 'The Economics of Ecosystems and Biodiversity-Phase I (Scoping) Economic Analysis and Synthesis', *Final Report for the European Commission*, Venice.

Millennium Ecosystem Assessment (2005) *Living Beyond Our Means: Natural Assets and Human Well-being*, Washington, DC: Island Press.

Millennium Ecosystem Assessment (2005) *Millennium Ecosystem Assessment: Ecosystems and Human Well-Being, Current State and Trend*, Volume I, Washington, DC: Island Press, www.millenniumassessment.org/documents/document.331.aspx.pdf.

Morandin, L. and Winston, M. (2006) 'Pollinators Provide Economic Incentive to Preserve Natural Land in Agroecosystems', *Agricultural Ecosystem Environment* 116: 289–92.

O'Neil, V. R. and Kahn, J. (2000) 'Homo Economus as a Keystone Species', *BioScience* 50, 4: 33–7.

Olson, D. (2005) 'Species Extinction Rate Speeding Up', *Minnesota Public Radio*, http://news.minnesota.publicradio.org/features/2005/01/31_olsond_biodiversity/, accessed 07/02/2012.

Oorschot, M. van, Braat, L., Brink, B. ten, Walpole, M., Kettunen, M., Peralta-Bezerra, N. and Jeuken M.(2008) 'Chapter 4: Changes in Biodiversity', in L. Braat and P. ten Brink (eds.) *The Cost of Policy Inaction: The Case of Not Meeting the 2010 Biodiversity Target,* Brussels: European Commission.

Pearce, D. (2007) 'Do we Really Care about Biodiversity?' *Environmental Resource Economics* 37: 313–33.

Pollan, M. (2002) *The Botany of Desire*, New York: Random House.

Pollination Canada (2008) *The Dying Bees*, Toronto: Pollination Canada, http://www.pollinationcanada.ca/index.php?k=86.

Prementel, D. (2001) 'Economic and Environmental Threats of Alien Plant, Animal, and Microbe Invasions', *Agriculture, Ecosystems and Environment* 84:1–20.

Ramsar (1971) *The Ramsar Convention on Wetlands*, Ramsar: Iran, http://www.ramsar.org/cda/en/ramsar-home/main/ramsar/1_4000_0__, accessed 06/08/2012.

Simon, J. I. and Khan, H. (1984) *The Resourceful Earth: A Response to Global 2000 Report,* Oxford: Basil Blackwell

Tallamy, D. (2007) *Bringing Nature Home: How Native Plants Sustain Wildlife in Our Gardens*, Portland, OR: Timber Press.

Tilman, D. (1999) 'The Ecological Consequences of Changes in Biodiversity: A Search for General Principles', *Ecology* 80: 1455–74.

UNDP (2000) 'Sustaining Life on Earth: How the Convention on Biodiversity Promotes Nature and Human Well-being', New York: The Secretariat of the Convention on Biodiversity.

van Engelsdorp, D., Evans, J. D., Saegerman, C., Mullin, C., Haubruge, E., Nguyen, B. K., Frazier, M., Frazier, J., Cox-Foster, D., Chen, Y., Underwood, R., Tarpy, D. R. and Pettis, J. S. (2009) 'Colony Collapse Disorder: A Descriptive Study', *PLoS ONE* 4: e6481.

Vitousek, P., Ehrlich, P., Ehrlich, A. and Matson, P. (1986) 'Human Appropriation of the Products of Photosynthesis', *BioScience* 36: 268–373.

Vitousek, P., Mooney, H., Lubchenco, J. and Mellillo, J. (1997) 'Human Domination of Earth's Ecosystems', *Science* 277: 494–9.

Wilson, E. O. (1992) *The Diversity of Life*, Cambridge, MA: Harvard University Press.

Part IV

Sustainable development and the limits to growth

In the academic world, the extent to which human material progress could eventually be retarded by biophysical limits has been a subject of controversy since 1798. This was the year that marked the publication of the book *An Essay on the Principles of Population as it Affects the Future Improvement of Mankind*, by Thomas Malthus—a highly celebrated British economist. For Malthus, the core problem was the growth of the human population since, if unchecked, it was postulated to confront humanity with lasting misery. While the Malthusian 'gloomy' human predicament persists even to this day, it has not been for a lack of ideas and schools of thought that support the prospect of boundless economic growth.

Part IV consists of five chapters (Chapters 11–15). The unifying theme of these chapters is how to cope with the possible limits to economic growth resulting from large-scale resource scarcity. Chapter 11 explores the arguments for impending limits on growth based on the Malthusian tradition. This is followed in Chapter 12 by the responses of the proponents of neoclassical economics to the Malthusian perspectives on limits to growth. These two chapters provide debates on limits to growth that have a long history and represent fascinating and lively intellectual discourses on the fate of human material progress.

The other three chapters in Part IV (Chapters 13, 14 and 15) approach the issue of limits from the perspective of sustainability. In these chapters limits are taken as a biophysical reality. The focus then shifts to addressing the biophysical constraints on growth, with sustainability being a core principle. Chapter 13 develops three conceptual criteria for the sustainable use of natural resources, including the environment. The discussions in Chapter 13 are theoretical.

In Chapter 14 attempts are made to show how environmentally adjusted gross domestic product (GDP) can be constructed within the framework of the system of national accounts (SNA). Furthermore, this chapter develops four aggregate sustainability indicators with practical relevance. Chapter 15 examines both the opportunities and challenges associated with making environmental sustainability one of the core missions of commerce—the practice of business. This is an important sustainability issue because, as Paul Hawkin (1993: 17) aptly put it 'Business is the problem and it must be a part of the solution. Its power is more crucial than ever if we are to organize and efficiently meet the world's need'.

Chapter 11

Biophysical limits to economic growth: Malthusian perspectives

---

LEARNING OBJECTIVES

After reading this chapter you will be familiar with the following:

- Malthus' original thesis on population and the limits to human economic progress.
- The nature of the debate regarding the association between population growth and natural resource scarcity within the classical school of economics.
- An overview of the nature of the 'early' environmental movement: the debate between conservation and preservation, and environmental activism.
- The 'modern' environmental movement that began in the early 1960s.
- The dawning of the neo-Malthusians' theory on limits to economic growth: overpopulation, pollution and overconsumption (affluence).
- The contributions of neo-Malthusians to public environmental awareness and the enactment of major environmental policies.
- The emergence of ecological economics as a 'new' economic paradigm and its contributions to the debates on limits to growth.
- Critical appraisal of the general arguments regarding limits to growth.

This chapter is about worldviews that at some fundamental levels are rooted in the Malthusian prognosis regarding the prospects of continued human material progress within the confines of a finite earth. In this regard, Malthusians of all stripes take limits to economic growth seriously, although they may differ on the principal causes for the limits. This 'pessimistic' tradition regarding the possibilities of unabated economic growth has a long history and is founded on strong and intellectually fascinating arguments. In addition, the Malthusian worldviews have been responsible for galvanizing social and environmental movements that have left significant marks on human history since the mid-eighteenth century. This chapter is about the intellectual legacies and the social and environmental movements that have been created by the various Malthusian and neo-Malthusian creeds.

11.1 INTRODUCTION

In this chapter, 'Malthusian' refers to a particular perspective to which scholars attribute the association of resource scarcity and the prospect for long-run human economic growth. This perspective traces its origin to the work of an English economist Thomas R. Malthus (1766–1834)—hence the word Malthusian. Although several variations have evolved over time, at the fundamental level the basic postulates of the Malthusian perspective on resource scarcity and economic growth are as follows:

1. Resources are scarce in *absolute* terms. That is, humanity is endowed with a finite amount of material resources;

2. If uncontrolled, the tendency of human populations is to grow exponentially; and

3. Technology should not be perceived as the 'ultimate' solution to the problem of resource scarcity. First, technology can only serve as a temporary solution to resource scarcity because it will eventually be hampered by the law of diminishing returns. Second, if not designed and applied properly, technology may have ill effects on the environment or allow the excessive and unwarranted exploitation of certain resources, further aggravating their scarcity.

Given this perspective, Malthusians argue that economic activity cannot be expected to grow indefinitely unless the rate of population growth and/or the rate of resource utilization are effectively controlled. Limits to economic growth arise through the depletion of key resources and/or large-scale degradation of the natural environment (Meadows et al. 1974).

This chapter offers a detailed examination of three general approaches scholars have used to explain 'limits to growth': the Malthusian (in reference to its origin); the neo-Malthusian; and the ecological economic. These three approaches, although they may differ in specifics and emphases, at the fundamental level consider population growth, resource scarcity (including the environment) and technology to be significant limiting factors to long-term human material wellbeing. The rest of this chapter will discuss these three conceptions of 'biophysical' limits to economic growth in some detail. Section 11.2 begins with the work of Malthus. It also includes brief discussions of the scholarly contributions of a few well-known economists from the classical economics era to the advancement of the Malthusian perspective to growth.

Section 11.3 provides an explanation of limits to growth from the perspective of scholars who, as a group, are known as neo-Malthusians. The neo-Malthusian era was at its prime during the 1960s and early 1970s due to an interesting confluence of various events, such as a new conceptualization of pollution and the environment, a dramatic increase in world population, and a new awareness of the critical need for energy conservation. This section also includes a brief discussion of the resource conservation versus preservation movement in the United States during the late nineteenth century. This is done as a prelude to the main focus of the section—the neo-Malthusian perspective on limits to growth.

In Section 11.4 the 'ecological economics' perspective on limits to growth is presented. At the fundamental level, ecological economics looks at the human economy as being an integral part of the natural ecological system, and as such sees its functioning as governed by the same immutable physical laws and biological principles. What emerged from this has been an increasing use of these laws (especially the first and second laws of thermodynamics) to explain physical and biological systems in terms of energy and material flows. Respect and attention to the reality of biophysical limits to growth is one of the core principles of the ecological economic orthodoxy. It is perhaps to convey this message that ecological economics is at times refered to as 'biophysical economics'. (Read Appendix B for a brief sketch of the historical development of the basic tenets of ecological economics.) The last section, Section 11.5, provides a summary of the chapter.

11.2 POPULATION, RESOURCE SCARCITY, AND LIMITS TO GROWTH: THE SIMPLE MALTHUSIAN MODEL

> Thomas Malthus developed a formal model of a dynamic growth process in which each country converged toward a stationary per capita income. According to this model, death rates fall and fertility rises when incomes exceed the equilibrium level, and the opposite occurs when incomes are less than that level.
>
> (Becker et al. 1990)

In 1798 Malthus published his book *An Essay on the Principle of Population as It Affects the Future Improvement of Mankind*, possibly the first formal theoretical underpinning concerned with the human population problem. In expounding his population–resource theory, Malthus made the following three postulates: (1) the total amount of land available for agriculture (arable land) is immutably fixed; (2) the growth of population is limited by the amount of food available for subsistence; and (c) the human population will invariably grow where the means of subsistence increase.

He then stated that, if not prevented by some checks, population will tend to grow *geometrically* (2, 4, 8, 16, etc.) while the means of subsistence continues to increase *arithmetically* (1, 2, 3, 4, etc.). Malthus then argued that the ever-increasing imbalance between population growth rates and the means of subsistence needed to be resolved through moral restraints (*preventive checks* such as the postponement of marriage, abstinence from sex, etc.). Otherwise, in the long-run, vice and misery (*positive checks*) will ultimately repress the superior power of a population to reach a level consistent with the means of subsistence. In other words, population growth, if left unchecked, will lead to the eventual downfall of living standards to a point barely sufficient for survival. Malthus had envisioned a scenario in which human population growth would eventually exceed the growth in food production. This has been called the 'dismal doctrine' of Malthus.

The essence of this doctrine can be further captured using a simple graphical approach as shown in Figure 11.1. If we assume that quantity of labor, L, can be used as a proxy for population size, and real output, Q/L, as a measure of per capita income, Figure 11.1 can be viewed as depicting the relationship between population size and per capita income. This relationship is constructed assuming a fixed amount of resources (i.e., land) and technology. Since the intent here is to offer a graphical explanation to the simple Malthusian model discussed above, let output, Q, represent agricultural or food products in general.

In Figure 11.1, per capita food output, Q/L, was initially rising with an increase in population. This positive association between population and per capita food production continued until the population size (labor force) reached L_1. Beyond this point, however, farm-labor productivity (measured

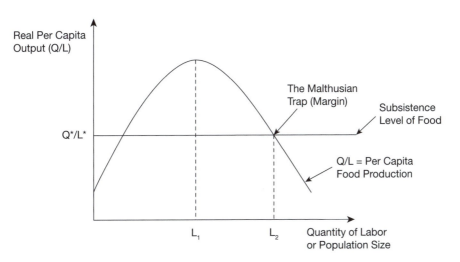

Figure 11.1 A simple Malthusian growth model. This model suggests if no action is taken to control population, the natural tendency is for the population to grow to L_2 at which point per capita food production is reduced to a level just sufficient for subsistence. According to this model, L_1 may be considered the optimal level of population.

235

in terms of output per unit of labor service) began to decline with each successive addition of labor service in accordance with the *law of diminishing marginal product*. That is, since fertile land is assumed to be fixed in supply, more labor applied to a given plot of a homogeneous quality of land or to a successively less fertile plot of land, yields a proportionately smaller return. Hence, as population and the accompanying demand for food and fiber increases, progressively larger quantities of resources, L, are required for the production of additional units of farm output.

In Figure 11.1, Q^*/L^*—the thick horizontal line—represents the output per unit of labor (or real wage rates) barely sufficient for survival, i.e., the subsistence level of food. Thus, when the labor force (i.e., the population) has increased to level L_2, the Malthusian trap (margin) is attained. This will be a stable long-run equilibrium.

According to Malthus, for a population below L_2, unless enforceable public-policy measures are taken to limit population growth (i.e., preventive checks), the natural tendency of the human population is to continue growing as long as the per capita food exceeds the minimum food required for a subsistence life: Q^*/L^*. On the other hand, any increase of population beyond L_2 would be prevented by positive checks, or, to use Malthus' terms, by 'vice and misery'. Therefore, in the long run disease, malnutrition and famine will bring growth to a halt at L_2. Finally, one interesting feature of this simple model is its suggestion of an *optimum* population size (labor force), attained at L_1, where the per capita food level (or real income) is at its maximum.

Of course, Malthus' original population–resource theory has been subjected to criticism since its pronouncement. His own contemporary, David Ricardo (1772–1823), another highly celebrated classical economist, objected not to Malthus' gloomy prophecy of the future condition of human material progress, but to the emphasis that Malthus had given to population in reaching this conclusion. For Ricardo, human material progress would not be hampered in the long-run by the explosive growth of human population as Malthus had envisioned, but by the *progressive decline in the quality and quantity of extractive resources*, most importantly agricultural land.

This development would trigger a steady increase in *rent* (i.e., the difference in the price between different grades of land) over time as quality of land declines. According to Ricardo, it is the steady increase in rent as land-use expands or intensifies that will ultimately stifle long-term human economic progress (an expanded discussion of Ricardian rent and its effect on economic growth is presented in Section 5 of Appendix A).

To Ricardo, in this particular context, population is only relevant to the extent that it affects demand. In other words, the major impediment to human material progress would emerge because resources are in short supply rather than from a population (demand) increase. This issue was hotly debated between Malthus and Ricardo, resulting in several written exchanges that are of significant interest to economic historians.

Ricardo supplemented his theory of rent with another very important economic principle, the *law of diminishing returns*, leading him to a dismal outlook about the future. This law simply states that the *productivity* of variable inputs (such as, labor and capital) will eventually decline as long as resources (such as land) are available in fixed supply (some economists give credit to Ricardo for the clear articulation of this law). This implies that when a society is confronted with a fixed amount of land and other natural resources, it is destined for economic stagnation. Malthus anticipated an even gloomier ending of human material progress because he combined the impacts of the law of diminishing returns with the pressure that exponential growth of the human population would have on a fixed supply of resources.

Another famous classical economist, John Stuart Mill (1806–1873), wrote on population and human material progress from a perspective that was quite different from Malthus in both tone and substance. Mill's book *The Principles of Political Economy* (1848) included a section entitled, 'Of the Stationary State', in which he forcefully argued that unlimited economic growth would lead to the destruction of the environment and a lower quality of life.

Mill had a romantic view of nature and his major concern was the destruction of nature and people's way of life in the name of material progress. About this he said:

> If the earth must lose that great proportion of its pleasantness which it owes to things that the limited increase of wealth and population would extirpate from it, for the mere purpose of enabling it to support a larger, but not a better or a happier population, I sincerely hope, for the sake of posterity, that they will be content to be *stationary*, long before necessity compel them to it.
>
> (Population Council 1986: 321)

Although this may not read as a grand general theory of population and resources, Mill's resignation to a 'stationary state' could be taken as an implicit endorsement of Malthus' prophecy on the 'dismal' nature of human economic progress.

However, Mill's vision of the stationary state economy was hardly gloomy as evident in his statement that:

> It is scarcely necessary to remark that a stationary condition of capital and population implies no stationary state of human improvement. There would be as much scope as ever for all kinds of mental culture, and moral and social progress; as much room for improving the Art of Living and much more likelihood of its being improved, when minds ceased to be engrossed by the art of getting on.
>
> (Population Council 1986: 321)

Thus, for Mill, the overriding concern in envisioning a 'stationary state' economy was to warn humans about the value of preserving the ecological integrity of nature and people's way of life. In this sense Mill was adding an element missing in Malthus' original theory on limits to growth. Mill was actually presenting an 'environmentalist' argument for limits to growth.

In addition to Ricardo and Mill, many other eminently accomplished classical economists, starting from Adam Smith (1723–1790) all the way to William Stanley Jevons (1835–1882), more or less appeared to share Malthus' 'dismal' outlook on the economic progress of human society, but without giving much credence to the 'Malthus doctrine on population'.

William Stanley Jevons claimed in his well-known book, *The Coal Question* (1865), that Britain's industrial might depends on coal and therefore, inevitably, would decline as the resource was depleted. Here is how Jevons expressed his concern about the British economy's heavy dependence on coal:

> A farm, however far pushed, will under proper cultivation continue to yield forever a constant crop in a mine there is no reproduction, and the produce once pushed to the utmost will soon begin to fail and sink towards zero. So far then as our wealth and progress depend upon the superior command of coal we must not only stop— we must go back.
>
> (Jevons 1865: Ix.19–Ix.20)

Thus, unlike Malthus and Ricardo, for Jevons it was coal (a nonrenewable natural resource), not agricultural land, that would ultimately determine the future economic prosperity or decline of a nation or nations.

However, Jevons was keenly aware of the fact that technological advances could ameliorate the scarcity of coal. More specifically, he understood that advances in coal mining and the efficient use of coal could significantly extend the life of coal mines and the availability of coal for industrial use in general. However, Jevons theorized that, over time, the rate of growth in coal consumption will tend to outstrip the rate of growth in technological advances in coal mining and utilization. Thus, in the final analysis, the exhaustion of coal will be inevitable.

This idea, that the advantages gained by advances in technology will inevitably be offset (or more than offset) by the rate of increase in consumption, is known as the *Jevons paradox*. Clearly, Jevons is Malthusian, but he is also neo-Malthusian (a topic to be discussed in the next sub-section) to the extent that he is making the rate of growth in per capita 'material' consumption part of the Malthusian arguments for the enviable stagnation of economic growth in the very long-run.

Finally, present-day criticism of Malthus' theory on population and resource scarcity takes the following forms:

1. It ignores the *institutional* factors that influence population growth. Humans do not just multiply like rabbits. Under adverse conditions social and economic factors influence humans to check their own population growth (Cole et al. 1973; Simon 1996).

2. Malthus' theory simply overlooks the very important role that *technology* plays in ameliorating resource scarcity (Ausubel 1996; Cole et al. 1973; Simon 1996). Factor substitutions and technological advances can alleviate resource scarcities (see Chapter 1). This issue will be further discussed in Chapter 12.

3. Malthus' model is considered to be ecologically naive. That is, it only recognizes the existence of absolute limits to natural resources (mainly land), and thereby fails to explain the effect of economic growth on the natural ecosystem and its inhabitants as a whole (more on this issue in Section 11.4).

Thus, the simple Malthusian theory on population and resources is viewed as incomplete from economic, technological and ecological perspectives.

Despite its simplicity, however, Malthus' theory on population and resource scarcity and the gloomy outlook it portrays for the long-term economic progress of humankind, in particular, is vigorously argued even today.

On the one hand it would be easy to dismiss the theory and its predictions, since over 200 years have passed since Malthus first announced his gloomy prophecy, and yet the world has experienced a rapid growth in resource use and population growth, along with significant improvements in material standards of living on a per capita basis (Simon 1996).

On the other hand, it is difficult to completely discredit Malthus because the main thrust of his dismal forecast is still a recurring concern in many poor nations of the world. In this sense, the Malthusian 'specter' is still relevant for events that are occurring after virtually 200 years of the first publication of Malthus's essay on population and resource scarcity (see Exhibit 11.1). Given this, it is not difficult to understand the presence of scholarly

EXHIBIT 11.1 FEEDING THE WORLD: LESS SUPPLY, MORE DEMAND AS SUMMIT CONVENES

Charles J. Hanley

Decade by decade, the land has provided—wheat fields, rice paddies, bulging silos of corn keeping pace with a growing world population. But now the grain harvests have leveled off, the people have not, and the world is left to wonder where next century's meals will come from. The blip in the upward slope of grain production in the 1990s has ready explanations: Economics, politics and weather conspired to hold down global output.

But some specialists believe longer-range forces, from the Kansas prairie to China's river deltas, are also at work—and the outlook is troubling. Troubling enough, in Africa particularly, for the Food and Agriculture Organization to hold a global summit in Rome this week to search for new approaches to help poor nations grow, buy or otherwise get more food.

'We are in a crisis situation,' said FAO chief Jacques Diouf. His UN agency projects world agricultural production must expand by 75 percent by 2025 to match population growth. It's not off to a good start. New FAO figures show that the global grain harvest—forecast at 1,821 million tons for 1996–97—will have increased by 2.3 percent since 1990, while population was growing 10 percent . . . Because of this lag in production, grain prices rose and the world's buffer stocks of wheat, rice and other grains were drawn down. Reserves now stand at 277 million tons—some 40 million below what is needed to meet emergencies. A mix of factors helped stunt the decade's crops.

Lester Brown of Washington's Worldwatch Institute maintains that fertilizers and high-yield grain varieties have been pushed to their limit in many places . . . [In addition] Worldwatch sees China as a huge problem. Shrinking croplands, rising incomes and a growing appetite for meat—an inefficient means for passing along the calories of grain—have combined to turn China, almost overnight, into the world's No. 2 grain importer, behind Japan. 'It is only a matter of time until China's grain import needs overwhelm the export capacity of the United States and other exporting countries,' Brown contends.

On the broader, global point, the World Resource Institute, a Washington think tank, finds some agreement among major studies that birth rates may slow enough to allow a plodding agriculture to keep up with 'effective' demand—the demand from consumers with the money to buy. But that projection comes with asterisks attached: In Africa and other poor regions without that money, hundreds of millions will remain underfed.

To Luther Tweeten, the outcome is far from clear. Looking ahead to 2030, the Ohio State University agricultural economist stacked the global trend in per-acre yield—rising ever more slowly—up against UN population projections. The yields lose out. 'I don't want to take a Lester Brown approach on this,' Tweeten said, but the world cannot be complacent. 'It's daunting.'

The FAO estimates 800 million people are undernourished worldwide, at a time when high prices have undercut international food aid, slicing it in half since 1993 to today's 7.7 million tons of grain a year. The summit will try to encourage increased aid, stepped-up research and pro-agriculture policies in Africa and other food-short regions.

But Brown sees another solution—population control. 'I think we're now in a new situation where the primary responsibility for balancing food and people lies with family planners, rather than fishermen and farmers,' he said. 'And I don't think the world has quite grasped that yet.'

Source: Kalamazoo, MI: *Kalamazoo Gazette/The Associated Press*, November 10, 1996. Copyright © 1996 The Associated Press. Reprinted by permission.

---

interest in this particular area of inquiry even to this day. The next two sections explore the enduring legacy of Malthus in the continuing scholarly debates about the extent to which human material progress may be hindered by the 'niggardliness' of nature and the growth of human population.

11.3 POPULATION, THE ENVIRONMENT, TECHNOLOGY AND LIMITS TO GROWTH: THE NEO-MALTHUSIAN VARIATION

Around the 1960s the neo-Malthusian theory of human population and resource scarcity emerged. The academic backgrounds of the proponents of the neo-Malthusian worldviews are quite eclectic. This being the case, neo-Malthusians use several variations of competing formal theoretical approaches to explain the adverse effects that the human aspiration for boundless economic growth has on the scarcity of conventional resources and the health of the natural environment. Before exploring some of the well-

known neo-Malthusian models on limits to growth, it will be instructive to take a very brief detour to describe the 'early' environmental movement, starting with the period from the early part of the nineteenth century to about 1960.

Throughout much of the nineteenth and early twentieth centuries, an increasing concern arose about the capacity of humans to cause lasting destruction to the environment. Many scholars who cannot be neatly categorized as Malthusians put serious thought into this issue. In America, these scholars included Henry David Thoreau (1817–1862), John Muir (1838–1914), and Aldo Leopold (1886–1948).

Through their literary and philosophical writing they expressed their love for nature and lamented its destruction by the rapid expansion of industrialization and urbanization. Their objectives were never to formulate a grand theory on how humans should relate with nature, but rather to raise the general public's awareness about the need for the preservation and the conservation of nature. Nothing could convey this sentiment better than Thoreau's powerful proclamation that 'in wilderness is the preservation of the world'.

Of course, this does not undermine the debate between 'preservationists' (led by Muir) and 'conservationists' (led by Aldo Leopold) about wilderness management philosophy, an important and highly consequential subject. Aldo-Leopold for example, forcefully advocated the novel idea of the 'scientific' management of forestlands held under government protection.

In the United States, this was the nature of the early environmental movement eventually responsible for the formation of several well-known conservation societies, such as the Sierra Club and the Wilderness Society. This was when America's *national parks* were conceived and enacted by laws to preserve natural treasures, such as Yosemite, Yellowstone, Grand Canyon and Crater Lake, along with many other wilderness areas. It is important to point out that around the same period similar environmental movements appeared around the world, although not necessarily with the same level of intensity.

During this first phase of the environmental movement in the United States, as a whole, the primary challenge focused on saving nature from the assault of mankind by setting aside sizeable areas of land as wilderness preserves. As America continued to advance economically, the environmental movement shifted its focus from preserving wilderness areas to environmental woes closely associated with the new industrial age, such as toxic-waste pollution.

It is reasonable to argue that the 'modern' environmental movement began in the early 1960s with the publication of Rachel Carson's *Silent Spring* (1962). Carson's defense of nature was not based on the romantic feeling she might have had towards nature. She was a scientist who studiously collected the necessary data to clearly and systematically explain the insidious, damaging effects that human-made chemicals—particularly pesticides such as DDT—have on the natural world. Most importantly, it was Carson's vividly imaginative portrayal of a barren landscape that made this publication so instrumental in establishing the modern environmental movement: *the landscape where no birds sang.*

In addition to concerns about industrial toxic waste and their devastating effects on the environment, in the 1960s scholars began to notice the rapid rate of human population growth, exceeding 2 percent annually in many parts of the world (resulting in a doubling of population in 35 years or less). A human population that stood at two billion in 1930 had reached three billion by 1960. This was a startling increase in population when one noticed that the human population first hit one billion in about 1800. In other words, it took many thousands of years for the world population to reach its first billion, 130 years to reach its second billion, and 30 years for the next billion.

This era was also the beginning of the 'space age', where humans started to vividly visualize the earth as a 'finite sphere'. Kenneth Boulding, an economist and humanist, expressed this new awareness in his widely read essay 'The Economics of the Coming Spaceship Earth' (1966: 303), in which he wrote that

> The Earth has become a single spaceship, without unlimited reservoirs of anything either for extraction or for pollution, and in which, therefore, man must find his place in a cyclical ecological system that is capable of continuous reproduction of materials even though it cannot escape having inputs of energy.

As a matter of fact, this marked the end of what Kenneth Boulding aptly called 'a frontier mentality', that is, 'the strongly held belief that there is always a new place to discover when things got too difficult, either for reason of the deterioration of the natural environment and/or a deterioration of the social structure in places where people happened to live' (p. 297).

The Ehrlich–Commoner model: population, affluence, technology

It was during the social settings of industrial development and scientific awareness described above that Paul Ehrlich, an eminent biologist from Stanford University, published *The Population Bomb* (1968). This book was Malthusian in almost all of its aspects, with the central theme of the book being human population. Its prediction of the future material wellbeing of humans was alarmingly bleak: a future of resource shortage and famine. Ehrlich's work on human population marked the beginning of the neo-Malthusian era.

Distinguishing him from other neo-Malthusians, Ehrlich takes an unwavering position that human population-growth is the primary culprit in a period of continued resource depletion and environmental degradation. This is explained below using a general conceptual framework hereafter referred to as the Ehrlich–Commoner Model (Commoner et al. 1971a; Ehrlich and Holdren 1971).

The Ehrlich–Commoner model begins with the postulate that all human activities modify the natural environment to some extent. In its simplest form, this model can be mathematically expressed as follows:

$$I = P \times F \qquad (11.1)$$

Here, the variable I is the total environmental effect or damage measured in some standard unit. It can be expressed in a variety of ways, such as: the amount of resources extracted or harvested annually; the total land area subjected to deforestation in a given year; the amount of waste discharged into the environment yearly; the surface area of the land inundated by mining activities in a given year; the rate at which some key nonrenewable resources (such as fossil fuels) are depleted; the rate of species extinction; and so on.

Although the variable I is assumed to be measurable, given the above examples, we see that it is difficult to construct an index (or a single measuring unit) that is expected to capture all the various types of environmental damages caused by human activities.

The variable P is the population size in terms of head count. From the outset, it is assumed that more people cause more environmental damage; or mathematically, $\Delta I / \Delta P > 0$; i.e., a positive correlation between population size and environmental damages.

Finally, the variable F is an index that measures the per capita impact on (or damage to) the environment. In the above Identity it enters simply as I/P. As will be discussed shortly, the variable F is assigned several different designations. Among others, it is interpreted to indicate: (1) affluence, given by either GDP/P (i.e., per capita income) or AC/P (i.e., aggregate per capita consumption); (2) per capita resource use, that is, throughput/P or the *ecological footprint* of the *average* person (more on this concept in Chapter 14).

What exactly does Identity 11.1 tell us? This identity states that, at any given point in time, the total environmental impact of human activities is a product of the underlying population size, P, and the per capita damage to the environment, F. In other words, *total environmental impact equals total population multiplied by the average impact that each person has on the environment.* The proxy for the average impact is affluence (as measured by GDP/P) or by per capita resource use (as measured by throughput used in the production process/P).

Most importantly, Ehrlich used the above model to demonstrate his main thesis that population plays the primary role in explaining the impact that human activities have on the environment and resource use. He argued that when population grows the total impact, I, increases for two reasons. First, the size of the population, P, will increase. Second, for reasons to be explained below, the per capita impact, F, increases with successive additions to population, P. That is, an increase in population has a *secondary effect* on per capita impact, F. (Mathematically this implies that $F = (f(P)$ and $\Delta F / \Delta P > 0$.) Therefore, according to Identity (11.1), the total impact increases since both P and F grow with expansions in population. This, as shown below, is illustrated in Figure 11.2.

Why is the per capita damage, F, an increasing function of population? Ehrlich gave the *law of diminishing marginal returns* as a plausible explanation of this phenomenon. He argued that most of the developed nations' economies are already operating at high levels of production capacity. These nations are, therefore, on the diminishing returns part of their production activities. Under these circumstances, if other factors are held constant, *successive additions of*

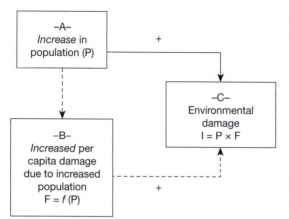

Figure 11.2 *Graphic illustration of Ehrlich's model of population and its impact on the environment. According to the above graph, increase in population (Box A) impacts the environment directly (Box C). Population growth (Box A) also triggers a secondary impact on the environment (Box C) though its impact on per capita damage (Box B), suggesting that the negative impact of population growth is far greater than what it may appear to be when only factors associated with the primary impact (Box A) are considered.*

people would require the increased use of resources, such as energy, water, fertilizer, pesticides and other renewable and nonrenewable resources. Thus, as a population continues to grow, the per capita impact, in terms of resource depletion and environmental deterioration, will increase successively.

Furthermore, the same argument can be made for the agricultural sectors of most developing countries. For most of these nations, the agricultural sector accounts for a significant percentage of their economy, and diminishing returns would be encountered because of the limited availability (in both quality and quantity) of farmland.

In the final analysis, Ehrlich and his followers would contend that a rising human population is the predominant factor for accelerating pollution and other resource problems in both the developed and developing nations of the world. There have been several empirical studies that support this hypothesis (Allen and Barnes 1995; Repetto and Holmes 1983; Rudel 1989). For example, in his empirical investigation on

the causes of deforestation, Thomas K. Rudel (1989: 336) reported the following as one of his findings:

> The analysis provides empirical support for the Malthusian idea that population growth contributes to high rates of deforestation both directly (by increasing the population which clears the land) and indirectly (by increasing the demand for wood products in a country).

However, some well-known neo-Malthusians were quick in criticizing Ehrlich for not *explicitly* considering several other factors, most notably per capita consumption of resources (i.e., affluence) and technology. Critics argued that these factors have independent effects on the per capita impact variable, F, in Identity 11.1. Would explicit consideration of these two factors (affluence and technology) materially challenge Ehrlich's position on the primacy of population in explaining total environmental damages, I, in Identity 11.1? The discussion in the next two subsections will attempt to answer this question.

A. Affluence and its contribution to environmental degradation

Per capita consumption is one conventional measure of affluence. It refers to the amount of goods and services consumed per person, per unit of time (generally a calendar year). At the aggregate level, consumption can be viewed as being equivalent to production or gross domestic product (GDP). Thus, per capita consumption, GDP/P, may be used as a measure of the wellbeing or affluence of the average person. Would a change in per capita consumption directly and significantly affect the per capita impact, F, in Identity 11.1?

The first step in answering the above question would require a clear understanding of the expected positive relationship between per capita consumption, GDP/P, and per capita impact, F. The argument is as follows. If population and technology are held constant, an increase in per capita consumption, GDP/P, could only result from an increased use of resources. Increased resource use implies increased production. In the absence of technological progress, this would translate into increased pollution and possible resource depletion. Furthermore, holding other factors constant, an increase in per capita consumption (income) may encourage a change in consumption patterns that are characterized by an incrementally higher level of material and energy intensity, F. Thus, in general we would expect an increase in per capita consumption to be associated with increased per capita damage, F. This observation has a number of interesting implications.

First, suppose that, as proposed by Ehrlich, the per capita damage, F, is an increasing function of population, P. Then, an increase in per capita consumption or income *reinforces* the negative impact that a population increase has on per capita damage to the environment. In this case, because increases in both population and per capita consumption affect the per capita damage function, F, in the same direction, it would be difficult to isolate the independent effects of these two variables on the per capita damage function, F, without undertaking a full-blown empirical test. This poses *a serious challenge to Ehrlich's unequivocal assertion that population growth is the single most dominant factor in explaining the total environmental impact, I.* In other words, one cannot relegate the impact of per capita consumption (income) to a minor role, as Ehrlich seems to have done, without solid empirical evidence.

Second, as stated above, if an increase in per capita consumption (income) leads to an increase in per capita damage to the environment, F, it is easy to envision a situation in which the *total environmental impact, I, may be increasing, while population, P, remains unchanged or even declining.* In other words, in Identity 11.1, P and F may move in opposite directions, causing uncertainty in the direction of the total impact, I. This supports the argument often made by some scholars that *the main culprit of environmental deterioration and resource depletion is overconsumption or affluence* (Durning 1992).

Alan Thein Durning, a noted researcher and founder of Sightline Institute—a non-profit research center in Seattle—is one of the leading advocates of this position. If this has any validity, it suggests that some of the most serious global environmental problems have been caused by the phenomenal growth in per capita resource consumption in the developed nations (see Table 11.1).

B. Technology and its contribution to environmental degradation: Commoner's perspective

Although not stated explicitly up to this point, what actually differentiates Barry Commoner, a noted biologist and eco-socialist, from Ehrlich, is the tacit assumption he makes that the per capita environmental damage variable, F, in Identity 11.1, is affected by technology. This variable is introduced in the environmental damage model to affirm the widely held belief by some neo-Malthusian scholars that technology negatively affects the environment.

Barry Commoner has been the leading advocate among those who view modern technology as ill-conceived and poorly applied in the production of goods and services, and the extraction and harvest of materials. More specifically, Commoner's concern is centered on the assortment of economic activities

Table 11.1 Share of population, resource consumption, and waste production in percentages

Country	Population	Fossil fuel consumption	Metal	Paper	Hazardous waste
USA	5	25	20	33	72
Other Developed Countries	17	35	60	42	18
Developing Countries	78	40	20	25	10

Source: World Population and the Environment: a data sheet for the Population Reference Bureau, Copyright 1997. Reprinted by permission of the Population Reference Bureau.

pursued by a nation, and the resulting composition of production and consumption in response to population pressure that, according to him, has had the effect of significantly intensifying the resource and environmental problems for a country. Why does Commoner take this position, and what evidence does he rely upon?

To understand Commoner's anti-technological position, it is important to understand that technical progress is often attained by changing the composition, or mix, of inputs and outputs for an economy. According to Commoner, the decision to change the composition of economic inputs and outputs is made purely for profit motives. Therefore, input and output decisions are made on the basis of technical efficiency (increased per capita production, which increases profit), rather than the impacts these decisions may have on the environment. To illustrate this, consider how Commoner et al. (1971: 101) depicted the outcome of technical progress in industrial nations: in their rush to increase productivity, industrial nations have been engaged in the excessive use of

> synthetic organic chemicals and the products made from them, such as detergents, plastics, synthetic fibers, rubbers, pesticide and herbicide, wood pulp and paper products; total production of energy, especially electric power; total horsepower of prime movers, especially petroleum-driven vehicles; cements; aluminum; mercury used for chlorine production; petroleum and petroleum products.

This suggests that changes in the composition of material inputs and outputs as a result of specific technological choice have the effect of increasing the per capita damage to the environment, F, in Identity 11.1. Thus, according to Commoner, technological responses to population pressure (an increase in P) invariably lead to increased total environmental damage, I (since I = P × F). Furthermore, to Commoner, the most significant portion of the total environmental damage in contemporary industrial nations arises, not from population increases, P, but from *increases in per capita impact, F, resulting from changes*

in *the mix of inputs and outputs*. To show this more vividly, Commoner (1972) reformulated Identity 11.1 as follows:

$$I = PAT \qquad\qquad (11.2)$$

where, P = population, A = affluence (economic good/P), and T = technology (pollution/economic good).

Thus, in Identity 11.2 the variable F is decomposed into two components, affluence, A, and technology, T. It is important to note that, according to Commoner as expressed in Identity 11.2 , total impact, I, is equal to pollution. On the other hand, for Ehrlich and his associates I represents a broader measure of environmental impact, such as the damage created by pollution on ecosystem structure and function including the amount of resource depletion caused by pollution.

The controversial aspect of Commoner's reformation of Identity 11.1 (to what is popularly known as the IPAT identity) was not so much the explicit recognition of technology as an independent explanatory variable that should be used to derive total environmental impact, I, but rather the claim that technology, T, exerts more pressure on the environment, I, than either P or A. This claim by Commoner represented not only a direct challenge to Ehrlich and his associates, but also symbolized a grave indictment of modern technology, and as such required further empirical justifications.

Aware of this, Commoner made a serious effort to substantiate his thesis on technology and the environment using data from the United States from 1946–68. On the basis of this data analysis, he determined that

> the predominant factor in our industrial society's increased environmental degradation is neither population, nor affluence (per capita consumption), but the increasing environmental impact per unit of production due to technological changes.
> (Commoner et al. 1971a: 107)

Moreover, Commoner made the following general observations:

On these grounds it might be argued as well that the stress of a rising human population on the environment is especially intense in a country such as the United States, which has an advanced technology. For it is modern technology which extends man's effects on the environments for air, food, and water. It is technology that produces smog and smoke; synthetic pesticide, herbicides, detergent, plastics; rising environmental concentrations of metals such as mercury and lead; radiation, heat; accumulating rubbish and junk.

(Ibid: 97)

Furthermore, in terms of the relative contribution of technology to total environmental impact, I, Commoner's empirical study indicated that

> population accounted for 12–20 per cent of the increase. Affluence accounted for 1–5 per cent except for the component of passenger travel, where the contribution rises to 40 per cent of the total. In contrast, technology accounted for about 95 per cent of the total pollution except in passenger travel where it only accounts for 40 per cent. So T, is far more significant than P or A.
>
> (Gaia Watch n.d.)

Of course, the above observation is somewhat dated, and for this reason its relevance to our current situation may be questioned. However, even today there exists a widely held belief that modern technology has been more successful in shifting the environmental impact than in removing it.

Indeed, over the past two decades most industrial nations have been able to ameliorate some of their environmental problems, especially at the local and regional levels. No doubt stricter environmental regulations and advances in emission control technologies have played a major part in making such environmental improvements possible. However, some of the technological solutions that brought relief to local pollution problems seem to have caused pollution problems that cross regional and international boundaries.

For example, requiring coal-burning electric power-plants in the Midwest to install smokestacks might alleviate local pollution problems, but improvement in the local environment would be achieved at the expense of increased acid precipitation in the northeastern United States and in Canada (Soroos 1997).

In essence, then, the scope of environmental and resource concerns are becoming increasingly global, as are issues such as holes in the ozone layer, global warming, tropical deforestation and the depletion of well-known commercial fish species. Furthermore, in 1998 a report by the US President's Committee of Advisors on Science and Technology (PCAST) expressed a concern similar to Commoner's view this way:

> [That] the composition and scale of economic activities in the United States are changing the chemistry of the nation's land, water, and atmosphere so dramatically that some of these changes are adversely affecting its natural capital and, thus, the ecosystem services required to support its population.
>
> (Dasgupta et al. 2000: 339)

Other contemporary examples of technological applications with potential to cause additional harm to natural resources and environments are: genetically modified organisms in agriculture; nuclear power to generate electricity; and new fishing gear that has led to a more rapid depletion of fish stocks.

The neo-Malthusians and their contributions to environmental policy

The Ehrlich–Commoner model is introduced to identify, at the fundamental level, the variables with significant powers in explaining the impacts of continued economic growth on the natural environment. According to this model, neo-Malthusians would be inclined to contend that the steady increases in population, per capita consumption (or affluence), and the proliferation of products that are harmful to the environment, are three major factors contributing to continued global environmental degradation.

In spite of this, as observed in the discussion above, there seems to be no consensus on the relative effects these three key variables have on the environment. For example, Ehrlich and his followers would contend that growth in human population is the predominant factor for accelerating pollution and other resource problems in both the developed and the developing nations of the world. On the other hand, to Commoner and his associates, population growth plays only a minor role in explaining the environmental and resource conditions of the modern era, especially in the economically advanced regions of the world. Instead, Commoner believes that a major part of environmental damage results from the inappropriate application of modern technologies in the extraction, production and consumption sectors of the economy. This is because technological choices are often made purely on the basis of profitability rather than environmental sustainability.

Finally, for others such as Alan Durning (the founder of the Sightline Institute, a non-profit research center in Seattle, and formerly an environmental analyst at the Worldwatch Institute), it is 'wasteful' consumption habits supported by raising per capita income (affluence) that are the major culprits for worsening global environmental condition.

Based on the above discussions, the policy implications of the neo-Malthusians are quite evident. In general, their policy goals are directed to achieving some combination of the following: (1) controlled population growth; (2) moderated or reduced per capita resource use; and (3) the development of technologies that are environmentally benign.

To achieve these ends, the natural inclination of neo-Malthusians has been to favor policy instruments that permit *direct* government intervention. The intellectual support for this position was articulated by Garrett Hardin, a noted ecologist, in his famed essay entitled 'The Tragedy of the Commons' (1968). In this essay, Hardin forcefully argued that overpopulation and environmental pollution cannot be remedied through institutional mechanisms that are guided by individual actions intended to promote self-interest, such as private markets.

Instead, he argued, problems like overpopulation and environmental pollution are most effec-

tively addressed through 'coercive' means. These could include taxes and regulations accompanied by effectively enforced legal sanctions such as fines or imprisonment. In the 1960s and 1970s economists were also questioning the efficacy of the private market to deal with problems of overpopulation and environmental pollution (Coase 1960; Randall 1972; Turvey 1963). At the same time, air and water pollution emerged as major problems in many large industrial cities in the United States and elsewhere in the world.

Given this reality and the urgency of the pollution problem, neo-Malthusians understandably advocated policy instruments that economists would like to characterize as command-and-control. These were meant to curb pollution, conserve resources and even slow the rate of population growth through government fiats. Specific policy measures of this nature include: emission standards; ending environmentally damaging subsidies by government decree; penalizing wasteful consumption habits by means of income redistribution; implementing family planning programs with considerable government supervision; providing subsidies to promote the development of environmentally benign technology; placing strict quotas on the amount of fish to be harvested or forest area to be cleared on an annual basis; and so on.

Even to this day, neo-Malthusians remain skeptical of market- or extra-market-based policy instruments to deal with the environment. This is because, in general, it is perceived that private markets allocate resources on the basis of short-term gains and losses. Furthermore, as discussed in Chapter 8, private markets use high discount rates that ultimately have the effect of working against the environment in various ways, including the decision of what technologies to use in the production and delivery of goods and services. For neo-Malthusians, technology is a double-edged sword, and if we are not careful the application of ill-conceived technology could harm, rather than solve environmental and resource problems (see Exhibit 11.2).

In addition to their contributions to the development of specific policy instruments used to 'effectively' regulate environmental abuse, neo-

EXHIBIT 11.2 BEYOND SHIVA

Garrett Hardin

If, as European folk wisdom has it, each new mouth brings with it a pair of hands, how are we to view the fantastic changes brought about by the industrial–scientific revolution of the past two hundred years or so? Have we not now reached a stage at which each new mouth comes into the world with more than a single pair of hands? The woolgathering mind may recall statues of the Indian god Shiva, with his many (most commonly four) lively arms and busy hands.

If scientists were inclined to take up new gods (which they are not), Shiva would be a fine one for representing science and technology ('custom' in Bacon's language). Even before Malthus, technology began to increase the output of human hands (through such inventions as the wheelbarrow), but the change did not catch people's attention for a long time. Everyone is aware of it now. Especially in the developed world it has become obvious that material income per capita has increased greatly. The Shiva of Western technology is indeed a many-handed god.

As the beneficiaries of more than two centuries of rapid growth of science and technology, the masses cannot easily be persuaded that they should be worried about the future of population and the environment. Yet we would do well to remember that the Hindus' Shiva is a god of both creation and destruction. It is not without reason that we perceive a many-handed god as uncanny and frightening.

Source: Living within Limits: Ecology, Economics, and Population Taboos (1993: 100–1). Copyright © 1993 by Oxford University Press, Inc. Reprinted by permission.

Malthusians have also played a major role in initiating, as well as sustaining, the momentum of the 'modern' environmental movement, both in the United States and throughout the world. Scholars of a neo-Malthusian persuasion have published a voluminous number of books and articles that eventually led to greater public awareness and sensitivity on the 'state' of the environment. In this respect, the neo-Malthusians' 'alarm' of doom and gloom has not been without its merits.

The environmental movement of the 1960s and 1970s rightfully claims a number of landmark legislative victories noted for their lasting impacts on resource conservation and the protection of the environment from pollution damage. In the United States the establishment of the Environmental Protection Agency (EPA) would not have been possible without public awareness of the harms that modern industrial production facilities have been inflicting on the environment. It is through the EPA that the regulation and monitoring of environmental pollutants of all sorts have routinely and systematically been synchronized at both the federal, state and local levels. Furthermore, the environmental movement of the 1960s and 1970s has been responsible for the emergence of a number of non-government organizations (NGOs)—such as the Environmental Defense Fund (EDF), Friends of the Earth (FoE), the Worldwatch Institute and the Natural Resource Defense Council (NRDC)—whose primary missions have been to advance changes in public policy that are considered to be consistent with building an environmentally sustainable society. These non-profit environmental advocacy groups and research organizations also play an important role in the regulation and timely dissemination of information to the public regarding the state of the environment.

Despite the above positive contributions, neo-Malthusians have been criticized for a number of reasons. Among them, the most prominent have been that:

1. Their predictions about the growth rate of the world population have been repeatedly wrong. The growth rate of world population peaked in

1972 at an annual rate of 2.06 percent. Ever since, the growth in world population has been declining steadily and in 2011 it was 1.1 percent. This is an important issue given the weight neo-Malthusians, such as Ehrlich, attach to population growth in the assessment of environmental damages. Note, however, that this is the world average and that in some developing countries the rate of population growth exceeds 3 percent. This disparity in the population growth among nations of the world, more specifically between the rich and poor nations, creates its own special problems that will be addressed in Chapter 16.

2. It is argued that neo-Malthusian conceptual models and empirical analyses are based on an understanding of resources, consumption and population at an *aggregate* level. Given this, they tend to underestimate the resource savings potential of factor substitution and technological advances (Goeller and Weinberg 1976). Davidson (2000: 438) even went on to indicate that 'viewing technology, consumption, and all social variables as fixed is implicit in the limits perspective'. A case in point is the neo-Malthusian application of the concept of (the maximum population that can be sustained on the available resource in any given area) to human society (i.e., carrying capacity as discussed in Exhibit 2.4, p. 40).

3. The neo-Malthusian perspective on physical limits and the forthcoming catastrophe if the limits are transgressed has not been politically useful. This is how Davidson expressed his viewpoint on the matter:

> Environmentalists have often predicted impending catastrophe (e.g., oil depletion, absolute food shortages and mass starvation, or biological collapse). This catastrophism is ultimately damaging to the cause of environmental protection. First, predictions of catastrophe, like the boy who cries wolf, at first motivate people's concern, but when the threat repeatedly turns out to be less

severe than predicted, people ignore future warnings. Secondly, the belief in impending catastrophe has in the past led some environmentalists to report withholding food and medical aid to poor nations (Hardin 1972), forced sterilization (Ehrlich and Ehrlich 1968), and other repressive measures. Not only are these positions repulsive from a social justice perspective, they also misdirect energy away from real solutions.
> (2000: 438)

To get a good sense of Davidson's criticism above, read Exhibit 11.3 entitled 'Has Malthus been discredited?'

11.4 BIOPHYSICAL LIMITS ON GROWTH AND THE CONCEPT OF OPTIMAL SCALE: THE ECOLOGICAL ECONOMIC VARIATION

In this last section of the chapter, the unique features of the ecological economic perspective on limits to economic growth will be discussed briefly. (See Appendix B for a brief background on the history of the development of ecological economics.) This discussion will delineate the specific elements that make the ecological economic perspective on limits different from that of the neo-Malthusians.

At the fundamental level these two perspectives on biophysical limits begin with many of the same assumptions about human population, the finiteness of the earth's resources and technology. More specifically, they both uphold the belief that an assessment of sustained economic growth on a global scale cannot be fully understood without careful consideration of the finiteness of the earth's resources, the growth of human population and the design and application of technology. It is also important to point out that both perspectives see the virtue of limiting the growth of human population and have a cautious view of technology. Thus, in this respect, the ecological economic perspective of biophysical limits is inherently Malthusian.

The ecological economics perspective differs from the neo-Malthusians in how certain earth's resources

EXHIBIT 11.3   HAS MALTHUS BEEN DISCREDITED?

Malthus and his followers are often labeled as doomsayers because of their persistent pronouncements of gloom and doom regarding human economic conditions in the distant future. More specifically, Malthusians of all stripes are of one mind in their belief that biophysical limits to economic growth are real, and they continue to support this hypothesis through numerous studies.

In the early 1970s, using a computer simulation, the authors of a highly controversial book, *The Limits to Growth* (Meadows et al. 1974), clearly demonstrated the various scenarios under which the industrial world would encounter limits. The basic conclusion read this way:

> If the present growth trends in world population, industrialization, pollution, food production, and resource depletion continue unchanged, the limits to growth on this planet will be reached some-time within the next one hundred years. The most probable result will be a rather sudden and uncontrollable decline in both population and industrial capacity.
>
> (Ibid: 29)

Although controversial, the frightful warning of the book was taken seriously, as it reflected the consensus view of a group of influential scientists and world leaders. A decade later, in response to the energy crisis of the late 1970s, a study was commissioned by the administration of President Carter in order to conduct a thorough and comprehensive assessment of global resource adequacy. The final outcome of this study was published under the heading *The Global 2000 Report to the President* (Council on Environmental Quality and Department of State 1980: 1). The major conclusions of this report read as follows:

If present trends continue, the world in 2000 will be more crowded, more polluted, less stable ecologically, and more vulnerable to disruption than the world we live in now. Serious stresses involving population, resources, and environment are clearly visible ahead. Despite greater material output, the world's people will be poorer in many ways than they are today. For hundreds of millions of the desperately poor, the outlook for food and other necessities of life will be no better. For many it will be worse . . . unless the nations of the world act decisively to alter current trends.

Clearly, this report echoed the conclusion pronounced a decade earlier by *The Limits to Growth*. In addition, there are a number of other recent empirical studies that reinforce the general conclusions reached by *The Global 2000 Report to the President*. In particular, it is worth mentioning the various publications periodically issued by the Worldwatch Institute — an independent nonprofit environmental resource organization. The annual report on progress to sustainable society, *State of the World*, is now published in 27 languages.

Furthermore, a recent update of the projection by Limits to Growth affirms the conclusions that 'the world is on track for disaster.' What this empirical study actually found is that the 'trend predicted' in the 1972 Study on non-renewable resources, food per capita consumption, population, global pollution, and industrial output per capita remarkably follows the 'observed trend' from 1970 to 2000 (Strauss 2012). To see the chart use this website link: http://www.smithsonianmag.com/science-nature/Looking-Back-on-the-Limits-of-Growth.html#

Based on the above evidence, some may argue that it is quite difficult to reject Malthus' prophecy of doom and gloom entirely. Do you think this is the case? Why or why not?

are perceived to be and how they are understood as a limiting factor to economic growth in the long-run. In this regard, proponents of the ecological perspective give the scarcity of *energy* and *natural capital* special emphasis. In addition, the ecological economics perspective assigns considerable weight to ecological resilience as a condition for sustainable economic activities. The rest of this chapter explains why, from the perspective of ecological economics, energy, natural capital and *ecological resilience* are considered to be the fundamental limiting factors for sustained economic growth.

A. Ecological resilience

One fundamental issue addressed in ecological economics is the issue of *scale*. Here, scale refers to the size of a human economic subsystem relative to the global natural ecosystem (Daly 1992). Ecological economists believe that, under the present conditions, the size of the human economy relative to the global ecosystem is large enough to cause significant stress on the limited capacity of the natural global ecosystem to support the economic subsystem (Goodland 1992).

As evidence of this, they cite some of the major environmental and resource concerns that have made headlines since the early 1980s: the alarming increase in the rate of the generation and release of toxic wastes; the rapid acceleration of the tropical rain forest deforestation; the compelling evidence of the rapid rate of species extinction (both animals and plants); the increased evidence of atmospheric ozone depletion; the unrestrained exploitation (both for waste dumping and resource extraction) of the ocean; the growing evidence of global warming, and so on.

The key inference that can be drawn from the issue of scale is that, as the scale of economic activity continues to increase, 'the economic and ecological systems become *dynamically linked* into a single integrated system. As a result, there is an increasing *risk* that economic activity will precipitate instability in the total combined system, with immediate implications for society' (O'Neill and Kahn 2000: 335).

In other words, unrestrained growth of the eco-

nomic subsystem could ignite a loss in *ecosystem resilience*—the ability to resist and/or recover from disturbance events that periodically disturb normal ecosystem functioning (see Exhibit 2.4: p.40). This, according to the current paradigm of ecological economics, is one way in which possible biophysical limits to economic growth manifest themselves. Furthermore, even though it is uncertain whether outcomes associated with a loss in ecosystem resilience are irreversible, uncertainty does not imply that it will not happen (more on this in Chapter 13).

B. Energy

As discussed in Chapter 2, from a purely physical viewpoint both the human economy and natural ecosystems are characterized by continuous 'exchanges' of matter and energy, and the functioning of all ecosystems (including the human economy) requires a continuous flow of energy from an external source (or sources). The second law of thermodynamics supports this proposition. Using this law, Georgescu-Roegen forcefully argued for the significance of energy as a limiting factor, not only in the growth of material standards of living, but also ultimately to the economic process as a whole:

> [That] environmental low entropy is scarce in a different sense than Ricardian land. Both Ricardian land and the coal deposits are available in limited amounts. The difference is that a piece of coal can be used only once. The economic process is solidly anchored to a material base, which is subject to definite constraints. It is because of this constraint that the economic process has a unidirectional irrevocable evolution.
>
> (1971: 80)

In other words, energy's role as a constraint of economic growth (as conventionally conceived) is uniquely significant because *all transformations require energy, its flow is unidirectional (hence, cannot be recycled), and there is no substitute for it*. The implications of this to the human economy that is largely dependent on fossil fuels is obvious.

C. Natural capital

The ecological perspective to growth also operates with a worldview that the natural world is not only finite, but also non-growing and materially closed. Given this reality, the sustainability of economic growth is increasingly doubtful, especially if it is based on an increasing use of throughput from the natural ecosystem. Why is this so?

In the 'full-world' scenario, natural capital (such as the waste absorptive capacity of the atmosphere, forest ecosystems, biodiversity, mineral deposits, etc.) and human-made capital (such as factories, tools, highways, etc.) can no longer be viewed as *substitutes*. In fact, a more realistic way to view the future relation between these two components of capital is as *complements*.

This suggests that both natural and human-made capital are needed in the production process. Thus, contrary to the widely held view of mainstream economics (see Chapter 1), *an economy cannot continue to function without natural capital*. Furthermore, it is expected that natural capital will be the limiting factor in the future. That is, fishing will be limited not by the number of fishing boats but by the remaining fish stocks; petroleum use will be limited not by refining capacity but by the geologic deposits and by the atmospheric capacity to absorb CO_2 (Dieren 1995). Thus, natural capital is increasingly becoming a limiting factor to future economic growth. From this comes a 'new scarcity' paradigm (more on this in Chapter 14).

To summarize, according to the ecological economic perspective, limits to economic growth can no longer be argued solely on the possibility of running out of conventional resources (such as the supply of agricultural land, or nonrenewable mineral resources including fossil fuels, etc.), as suggested by the traditional Malthusian approach.

Nor can technology be viewed as the ultimate means of circumventing ecological limits, as neoclassical economists would like to argue (to be discussed in the next chapter). Instead, the finite availability of high-quality energy, the growing scarcity of natural capital and the loss of ecosystem resilience are quickly emerging as the three key limiting factors in

humanity's pursuit for continued material progress (economic growth). Proponents of the ecological perspective of limits warn that this reality should be taken seriously if humanity is to avoid a sudden economic and ecological collapse. What can be done to avoid a catastrophe of this magnitude?

Responses to this question vary. However, Kenneth Boulding's classic essay, 'The Economics of the Coming Spaceship Earth' (1966), offers what appears to be the consensus response to this query. The economy of the future, which Boulding referred to as the 'spaceman' economy, requires economic principles that are different from those of the 'open' earth of the past:

> In the spaceman economy, throughput (matter and energy) is by no means a desideratum, and is indeed to be regarded as something to be minimized rather than maximized. Hence, the essential measure of the success of the economy is not production and consumption, but the nature, extent, quality and complexity of the total capital stock, including the state of the human bodies and minds included in the system.

Boulding's message is quite clear. Current human conditions, with respect to population, technology and habits of consumption and production, warrant a fresh look at our social values and economic systems. We need to espouse social values and build economic systems that reinforce the idea that—in the material sense—more is not necessarily better. In the final analysis, what this amounts to is the awareness that the future of humankind depends on our *ability to design an economic system that regulates the flow of throughput with full recognition of ecological limits* in order to establish a sustainable economy.

In his earnest attempt to capture the essential elements of this message Herman Daly, an eminent ecological economist, wrote a book entitled *Toward a Steady-state Economy* (1973). In this book, and in several of his subsequent publications, Daly attempted to design a theoretical model where it is possible to 'develop' even in the total absence of traditional economic growth. In other words, Daly envisioned circumstances under which an economy can grow qualitatively (i.e., develop), without necessitating quantitative growth in its physical dimensions.

According to Daly, this can be achieved through what he called 'stock maintenance efficiency'. This requires reducing the use of throughput (the low entropy matter–energy needed to produce goods and services) to its lowest level. This can be done by producing goods and services that are durable and/or easily recyclable (see Case Study 11.1 for a good illustration of this issue). In this respect, Daly's vision of 'the steady state economy' has served as a frontrunner in the recent growing interest in the theoretical and practical issues of 'sustainable development'—a subject to be discussed in Chapters 13 and 14.

CASE STUDY 11.1 ASSET RECYCLING AT XEROX

Jack Azar

In the industrial society, the proliferation of solid waste in the face of diminishing landfill space continues to be a major concern. Reacting to this challenge, in some countries legislation is in the works that could significantly affect marketplace demands. In Germany, legislation has been proposed that would require manufacturers and distributors to take back and recycle or dispose of used electronic equipment. The European Community is considering similar legislation. In Canada, too, interest in such legislation has been expressed. And in Japan, a 1991 regulation issued by the Ministry of International Trade and Industry promotes not only the use of recycled materials in certain durable items but also the recyclability of those items themselves.

In response to what seems to be a future trend in worldwide movement toward recycling, in 1990 Xerox began a corporate environmental strategy that encompasses equipment and parts recycling. The cornerstone of this strategy is the Asset Recycle Management program. As the name implies, it entails treating all products and components owned by the company—whether out on rental or on the company's premises—as physical 'assets.'

The key feature of the Asset Recycle Management program at Xerox is the emphasis on a rather 'unconventional' approach that machines should be designed from concept with the remanufacturing process and the recapture of parts and materials in mind. This meant getting the company's design and manufacturing engineers to bring an entirely new perspective to their work. To facilitate this the company instituted an Asset Recycle Management organization. The principal charge of this organization is to continually identify areas where significant opportunities to optimize the use of equipment and parts, even for existing products, could be captured.

Early on, it was recognized that company engineers needed design guidelines to enhance remanufacturing and materials recycling . . . Specifically, the guidelines reflect the following design criteria: extended product and component life—i.e., use of more robust materials and design to make asset recovery practical; selection of materials that are relatively easy to recycle at the end of product life; simplification of materials to facilitate recycling; easy disassembly as well as easy assembly; remanufacturing convertibility, meaning that a basic product configuration is convertible to a different use—e.g., a copier to an electronic printer; and use of common parts to enable future reuse in different models and configurations.

Xerox's first environmental design to reach the market was a customer-replaceable copy cartridge, which has many of the characteristics of a complete xerographic copier. Designed for use in the company's smaller convenience copiers, the copy cartridge contains the main xerographic elements critical to the copying process: photoreceptor, electrical charging devices and a cleaning mechanism.

Copy cartridges designed for older convenience copiers posed a special challenge. They had not been designed for recycling. In fact, their plastic housings were assembled by ultrasonic welding. The company had to break them open to get at the components within, thereby destroying the plastic housings. While it was usually possible to reclaim the photoreceptor-transport assemblies, all that could be done with the housings was to grind them down for reuse as injection-molding raw materials.

The new 5300 series of convenience copiers has a new design: a cartridge that is assembled with a few fasteners. It is totally remanufacturable, a process that costs far less than building one with all new parts, and more than 90 percent of the material is recoverable. It also meets all product quality specifications and carries the same warranty as newly manufactured cartridges.

To date, the Asset Recycling Program at Xerox has been a big success from the standpoint of both environmental and business considerations. On the business side, the company saved a total of $50 million the first year in logistics, inventory and the cost of raw materials. These savings are to increase greatly as design-for-environment Xerox products enter the market. In addition, only a minimal amount of material has been scrapped compared with previous years.

Source: *EPA Journal*, 19 (1993), pp. 15–16. Reprinted with permission.

Of course, the ecological economic perspective to limits has not been without critics. Therefore, this section will end by briefly mentioning the three most pointed criticisms of this perspective on biophysical limits.

First, as mentioned earlier, most neoclassical economists are inclined to view the thermodynamic-ecological perspective to limits as nothing more than a new spin on the old-fashioned neo-Malthusian way of thinking. Its prognosis on the predicament of humans does not depart materially from the Malthusian apocalypse in either tone or substance.

Second, ecological economics, by focusing too much on the material basis of human economy, seems to overlook the social and political context by which resources are used. This is considered a serious deficiency as it undermines the adaptive capacity of human institutions to deal with resource scarcity (more on this in the next chapter).

Third, Davidson (2000: 433) disputed the whole notion of biophysical limits to economic growth this way:

biological and physical systems underlie all economic activity and form constraints to which the human economy must adapt. However, I argue, contrary to the limits perspective, the biological or physical limits are seldom actually limiting to economic growth, such that reaching limits causes economic collapse or even stops growth. In most cases, the human economy is extremely adaptable and ways are found to adapt and continue to expand. Furthermore, in most cases, *continued economic growth results not in ecological collapse but rather in continuous environmental degradation without clear limit points* [emphasis added].

Exhibit 11.4 details how Davidson used tapestry as a metaphor to describe his alternative view of environmental degradation.

In essence Davidson is challenging the core assumption of ecological economics; that is, increases in the *scale* of the economy will contribute to greater environmental damage and eventually to the inevitability of ecological collapse. He contends that environmental degradation is often gradual and continuous rather than catastrophic. This implies that catastrophic events can be averted by human intervention in the political process. As he put it, 'A political-ecological analysis often reveals that levels of consumption and destructive production processes are not fixed and inevitable but rather the result of political, economic, and cultural decisions that are subject to change' (Davidson 2000: 439).

EXHIBIT 11.4   THE TAPESTRY METAPHOR FOR ENVIRONMENTAL DEGRADATION

Carlos Davidson

A metaphor based on a tapestry provides a more accurate and useful view of the relationship between economic activity and the environment than either the limits metaphors of rivets and cliffs (i.e., neo-Malthusian and ecological economics) or the technological optimist model of neoclassical economics. Tapestries have long been used as metaphors for the richness and complexity of biological systems (e.g., the tapestry of life). As a metaphor for environmental degradation, each small act of destruction . . . is like pulling a thread from the tapestry. At first, the results are almost imperceptible. The function and beauty of the tapestry is slightly diminished with the removal of each thread. If too many threads are pulled—especially if they are pulled from the same area—the tapestry will begin to look worn and may tear locally. There is no way to know ahead of time whether pulling a thread will cause a tear or not. In the tapestry metaphor, as in the cliff and rivet metaphors, environmental damage can have unforeseen negative consequences; therefore, the metaphor agues for the use of the precautionary principle. The tapestry is not just an aesthetic object. Like the airplane wing in the rivet metaphor, the tapestry (i.e., biophysical systems) sustains human life.

However, the tapestry metaphor differs from the rivet and cliff metaphors in several important aspects. First, in most cases there are not limits. As threads are pulled from the tapestry, there is a continuum of degradation rather than any clear threshold. Each thread that is pulled slightly reduces the function and beauty of the tapestry. Second, impacts consist of multiple small losses and occasional larger rips (nonlinearities) rather than overall collapse. Catastrophes are not impossible, but they are rare and local (e.g., collapse of a fishery) rather than global. The function and beauty of the tapestry are diminished long before the possibility of a catastrophic rip. Third, there is always a choice about the desired condition of the world—anywhere along the continuum of degradation is feasible, from a world rich in biodiversity to a threadbare remnant with fewer species, fewer natural places, less beauty, and reduced ecosystem services. With the rivet and cliff metaphors, there are no choices: no sane person would choose to crash the plane or go over the cliff. This difference is key for the political implications of the metaphors. Finally, in the rivet or cliff metaphors, environmental destruction may be seen primarily as loss of utilitarian values (ecosystem services to humans). In the tapestry metaphor, environmental destruction is viewed as loss of utilitarian as well as aesthetic, option, and amenity consideration.

Source: BioScience: Economic Growth and the Environment: Alternatives to the Limits Paradigm, May 2000, 5, 5: 434–5.

11.5 CHAPTER SUMMARY

This chapter has dealt with analyses of the Malthusian perspective on 'general' resource scarcity and its implications for the long-term material wellbeing of humanity. This perspective has a long history and it starts with the premise that natural resources are finite and, therefore, will eventually limit the progress of the human economy. This assertion is explained using theoretical models envisioned by Thomas Malthus.

The general ideas espoused by recent followers of Malthus, neo-Malthusians, were illustrated using the so-called Ehrlich–Commoner model. As a whole, this model considers population, technology and per capita consumption as the main determinants of environmental degradation and eventually limits to economic growth. A lively debate exists among present-day Malthusians (or neo-Malthusians) regarding which of these three variables is the most important culprit for modern-day environmental crises and/or rapid depletion of some key, but conventionally identified, natural resources (such as oil, gas, arable land, uranium, etc.), and the natural ecosystem as a whole.

In general, Malthusians are skeptical about the ability of technology to circumvent biophysical limits for two reasons:

1. They believe that technological progress is subject to diminishing returns; and
2. They are mindful of the long-run costs of technological cures. Some, such as Commoner, even take the position that ill-conceived technologies are the major culprits in the modern environmental crisis.

In terms of public policy measures, Malthusians tend to consider population control as the key variable. They advocate offering subsidies to encourage the development of production techniques and consumer products that are environmentally friendly. They encourage investment to educate the public to be aware of wasteful resource use and the insidious nature of overconsumption.

In general, Malthusians tend to be suspicious about regulatory programs that are entirely market-based, such as transferable emission permits. For them equity and sustainability considerations are more important than a single-minded focus on efficient outcomes.

Finally, Malthusians are criticized for their tendency to undermine the potential contributions of technology to continued material progress of humanity and for their continued prophecy of doom and gloom. Critics consider that the perennial Malthusian prediction of economic collapse is unwarranted and moreover, not helpful politically.

This chapter also discussed the ecological perspective on 'general' resource scarcity and its implications for the long-run material wellbeing of humanity. The distinctive feature of the ecological economics school of thought is the extensive application of thermodynamic laws and ecological principles as the building blocks for their argument on the existence of biophysical limits.

Ecological economists do not view the human economy as being isolated from the natural ecosystem. In fact, the human economy is regarded as nothing but a small (albeit important) subset of natural ecosystems. Furthermore, since these two systems are considered to be interdependent, ecological economists focus on understanding the linkages and interactions between economic and ecological systems.

From such a perspective, the scale of human activities (in terms of population size and aggregate use of low-entropy matter–energy) becomes an important issue. Furthermore, in ecological economics the consensus view seems to be that the scale of economic growth is already approaching the limits of the finite natural world—the full worldview. This has several implications. Among them are:

1. It is imperative that limits be put on the total resources used for either production and/or consumption purposes— stock maintenance.

2. 'The essential measure of the success of the human economy is not production and consumption at all, but the nature, extent, quality and complexity of the total capital stock, including the state of human bodies and minds included in the system' (Boulding 1966: 304).

3. As far as possible, throughput should be minimized, which implies the production of goods and services that are long-lasting and easily recyclable.

REVIEW AND DISCUSSION QUESTIONS

1. Briefly identify the following concepts: preventive and positive checks to population growth, exponential growth, the Malthusian trap, Ricardian rent, neo-Malthusian, real per capita output, throughput, the spaceship economy, and ecological resilience.

2. Read the following statements. In response, state 'True', 'False' or 'Uncertain' and explain why.

    (a) The connection between population growth and environmental damage is undeniable. More people cause increasing damage to the environment.

    (b) It is inadequate to identify the 'optimal' level of population solely in terms of its correspondence to the maximum real per capita output (such as L_1 in, p. 97 Figure 6.1).

    (c) The modern environmental crisis is predominantly a consequence of affluence or increased level of per capita consumption.

3. More than any other factor, as human population increases it causes a rise in the demand for food and other extractive resources. It is the gradual decline in the quality of arable land and the difficulty of mining increasingly poor-quality mineral deposits that eventually halt human material progress. Discuss.

4. Ill-conceived technology, not population growth or affluence, has been primarily responsible for today's global population problems. Critically comment. Support your comments with specific examples.

5. The isolated and sporadic instances of hunger that we continue to witness in parts of our contemporary world do not support the Malthusian theory as some would like to claim. These events are caused not by population pressure but by the poor global distribution of resources. Do you agree? Why, or why not?

6. Garrett Hardin (1993: 94) wrote:

    [even though] John Maynard Keynes had the highest opinion of his contributions to economics, Malthus continues to be bad-mouthed by many of today's sociologists and economists. The passion displayed by some of his detractors is grossly disproportionate to the magnitude of his errors. A conscientious listing of the explicit statements made by Malthus would, I am sure, show that far more than 95 percent of them are correct. But for any writer who becomes notorious for voicing unwelcome 'home truths' a correctness score of 95 percent is not enough.

    In your opinion, is this a convincing and substantive defense of Malthus? Discuss.

7. Davidson (2000) suggested that Malthusians' repeated predictions about the inevitability of impending economic and ecological catastrophe are ultimately damaging to the cause of environmental protection. How could this be? Explain.

8. Identify what you consider to be the three most important features of the ecological economics perspective about biophysical limits. How are these different from the Malthusian perspective about limits?

9. It is argued that all transformations require energy, that energy flow is unidirectional and that there is no substitute for energy. It therefore makes sense to use energy as a numeraire—a denominator by which the value of all resources can be weighed. That is, energy is the ultimate resource. Critically comment.

10. Compare and contrast the neo-Malthusian and the ecological economic perspectives of the biophysical limits to growth.

REFERENCES AND FURTHER READING

Allen, J. C. and Barnes, D. F. (1995) 'The Causes of Deforestation in Developed Countries', *Annals of the Association of American Geographers* 75, 2: 163–84.

Arrow, K., Bolin, B., Costanza, R., Dasgupta, P., Folke, C., Holling, C. S., Jansson, B., Levin, S., Maler, K., Perrings. and C. Pimentel, D. (1995) 'Economic Growth, Carrying Capacity, and the Environment', *Science* 268: 520–1.

Ausubel, J. H. (1996) 'Can Technology Spare the Earth?' *American Scientist* 84: 166–77.

Ayres, R. U. (1978) 'Application of Physical Principles to Economics', in R. U. Ayres (ed.) *Resources, Environment, and Economics: Applications of the Materials/Energy Balance Principle*, New York: John Wiley.

Ayres, R. U. and Nair, I. (1984) 'Thermodynamics and Economics', *Physics Today* 37: 63–8.

Becker, G. S., and Murphy, K. M. (1990) 'Human Capital, Fertility, and Economic Growth', *Journal of Political Economy* 98, 5: 12–36.

Boulding, K. E. (1966) 'The Economics of the Coming Spaceship Earth', in H.E. Daly, and K.N. Townsend (eds.) *Valuing the Earth: Economics, Ecology, Ethics*, Cambridge, MA: The MIT Press.

Burness, S., Cummings, R., Morris, G. and Paik, I. (1980) 'Thermodynamics and Economic Concepts Related to Resource-use Policies', *Land Economics* 56: 1–9.

Carson, R. M. (1962) *Silent Spring*, Boston: Houghton Mifflin.

Coase, R. (1960) 'The Problem of Social Cost', *Journal of Law and Economics* 3: 1–44.

Cohen J. (1996) *How Many People Can the Earth Support?* New York: W. W. Norton.

Cole, H. S. D., Freeman, C., Jahoda, M. and Pavitt, K. L. R. (1973) *Model of Doom: A Critique of the Limits to Growth*, New York: Universe Books.

Commoner, B. (1972) 'A Bulletin Dialogue on "The Closing Circle": Response', *Bulletin of the Atomic Scientists* 28, 5: 17, 42–56.

Commoner, B., Corr, M. and Stamler, P. (1971a) 'The Causes of Pollution', in T. D. Goldfarb (edn.) *Taking Sides: Clashing Views on Controversial Environmental Issues*, 3rd edn., Sluice Dock, CT: Guilford.

—— (1971b) *The Closing Circle: Nature, Man, and Technology*, New York: Knopf.Council on Environmental Quality and the Department of State (1980) *The Global 2000 Report to the President: Entering the Twenty-first Century*, Washington, DC: US Government Printing Office.

Daly, H. E. (1973) 'Introduction', in H. E. Daly (ed.) *Toward a Steady-State Economy*, San Francisco: W. H. Freeman.

—— (1992) 'Allocation, Distribution, and Scale: Towards an Economics that is Efficient, Just, and Sustainable', *Ecological Economics* 6: 185–93.

—— (1993) 'Valuing the Earth: Economics, Ecology, Ethics', in H. E. Daly and K. Townsend (eds.) *Valuing the Earth: Economics, Ecology, Ethics*, Cambridge, MA: MIT Press.

—— (1996) *Beyond Growth*, Boston, MA: Beacon Press.

Dasgupta, P., Levin, S. and Lubchenco, J. (2000) 'Economic Pathways to Ecological Sustainability', *BioScience* 50, 4: 339–45.

Davidson, C. (2000) 'Economic Growth and the Environment: Alternatives to the Limits Paradigm', *BioScience* 50, 4: 433–9.

Dieren, W. (ed.) (1995) *Taking Nature into Account: A Report to the Club of Rome*, New York: Springer-Verlag.

Durning, A. T. (1992) *How Much Is Enough?* Worldwatch Environmental Alert Series, New York: W. W. Norton.

Ehrlich, P. and Ehrlich A. (1968) *The Population Bomb*, New York: Ballantine Books.

—— (1990) *The Population Explosion*, New York: Simon and Schuster.

Ehrlich, P. and Holdren, J. P. (1971) 'Impact of Population Growth', *Science* 171: 1212–17.

—— (1972) 'A Bulletin Dialogue on the "Closing Circle": Critique: One Dimensional Ecology', *Bulletin of the Atomic Scientists* 28, 5: 16–27.

257

Gaia Watch (n.d.) *I=PAT. An Introduction*, Cardiff: Gaia Watch, http://www.population-growth-migration.info/essays/IPAT.html, accessed 06/05/2012.

Georgescu-Roegen, N. (1971) *The Entropy Law and the Economic Process*, Cambridge, MA: Harvard University Press.

—— (1993) 'The Entropy Law and the Economic Problem', in H. E. Daly and K. Townsend (eds.) *Valuing the Earth: Economics, Ecology, Ethics*, Cambridge, MA: MIT Press.

Goeller, H. E. and Weinberg, A. B. (1976) 'The Age of Substitutability: What Do We Do When the Mercury Runs Out?' *Science* 191: 683–9.

Goodland, R. (1992) 'The Case that the World has Reached Limits', in R. Goodland, H. E. Daly and S. El Sarafy (eds.) *Population, Technology and Lifestyle: The Transition to Sustainability*, Washington, DC: Island Press.

Hardin, G. (1968) 'The Tragedy of the Commons', *Science* 162: 1243–8.

Hardin, G. (1972) *Exploring New Ethics for Survival: The Voyage of the Spaceship Beagle*, New York: Viking Press.

—— (1993) *Living Within Limits: Ecology, Economics, and Population Taboos*, New York: Oxford University Press.

Hawkin, P. (1993) *The Ecology of Commerce: A Declaration of Sustainability*, New York: HarperCollins.

Jevons, S. (1865) *The Coal Question : An Inquiry Concerning the Progress of the Nation, and the Probable Exhaustion of Our Coal-mines*, London: Macmillan and Co.

Lomborg, B. (2001) *The Skeptical Environmentalist*, Cambridge: Cambridge University Press.

Malthus, (1798) *An Essay on the Principle of Population As It Affects the Future Improvement of Society*, 1st ed., London: J. Johnson, in St. Paul's Church-yard.

Martinez-Alier, J. (1987) *Ecological Economics: Energy, Environment, and Society*, Cambridge, MA: Basil Blackwell.

Meadows, D. H., Meadows, D. L., Randers, J. and Behrens, W. W. III (1974) *The Limits to Growth: A Report for the Club of Rome's Project on the Predicament of Mankind*, 2nd edn., New York: Universe Books.

Mill, S. (1848), *The Principles of Political Economy*. London: John W. Park, West Strand.

Odum, H. and Odum, E. (1976) *Energy Basis for Man and Nature*, New York: McGraw-Hill.

Pearce, D. W. (1987) 'Foundation of Ecological Economics', *Ecological Modelling* 38: 9–18.

Population Council (1986) 'John Stuart Mill on Stationary State', *Population and Development Review* 12, 2: 317–22.

Randall, A. (1972) 'Market Solutions to Externality Problems: Theory and Practice', *American Journal of Agricultural Economics* 54, 2: 175–83.

Repetto, R. and Holmes, T. (1983) 'The Role of Population in Resource Depletion in Developing Countries', *Population and Development Review* 9 4: 609–32.

Rudel, T. K. (1989) 'Population, Development, and Tropical Deforestation: A Cross-national Study', *Rural Sociology* 54, 3: 327–37.

Simon, J. L. (1996) *The Ultimate Resource 2*, Princeton, NJ: Princeton University Press.

Soroos, M. S. (1997) *The Endangered Atmosphere: Preserving a Global Commons*, Columbia, SC: University of South Carolina Press.

Turvey, R. (1963) 'On the Divergence between Social and Private Costs', *Economica*, August: 309–13.

United Nations (2002) UN Secretary-General Kofi Annan addressing the World Summit on Sustainable Development, August 26 to September 4, 2002, Johannesburg: SA, http://www.un.org/events/wssd/pressreleases/highlevel-open.pdf

Worldwatch Institute (1997) *Vital Signs 1997*, New York: W. W. Norton.

Young, J. T. (1991) 'Is the Entropy Law Relevant to the Economics of Natural Resource Scarcity?' *Journal of Environmental Economics and Management* 21: 169–79.

Chapter 12

Biophysical limits to economic growth: The neoclassical perspective

LEARNING OBJECTIVES

After reading this chapter you will be familiar with the following:

- Basic postulates of the neoclassical economic worldview on 'general' resource scarcity.
- The neoclassical responses to the Malthusian worldviews on limits to growth.
- Scarcity and growth—the empirical evidence (1860 to 1980).
- Scarcity and growth revisited—the empirical evidence (1980 to the present day).
- The associations of economic growth, the environment and population:
    (a) The environmental Kuznets curve (EKC);
    (b) The theory of demographic transition; and
    (c) The microeconomic theory of human fertility: the cost of children, human capital, fertility and income.
- The policy implications of the neoclassical worldviews on population and the environment.
- Critical assessments of the neoclassical worldviews on population, environment and economic growth.

This chapter is also about the long view of the future of humanity and the biosphere. In direct contradiction of the Malthusians' worldviews, neoclassical economists appear to portray themselves as 'eternal optimists'. Their optimism is grounded on their unwavering beliefs regarding continued human ingenuity, the smooth functioning of the market system and the possibilities for unabated technological progress. This chapter presents the theoretical arguments for the neoclassical worldview on resource scarcity and economic growth—an extension of the subject matter addressed in Chapter 1. It also provides formal neoclassical responses to the Malthusian prognosis of impending doom. Furthermore, the chapter includes critical appraisal of the neoclassical worldviews on scarcity and growth.

12.1 INTRODUCTION

In the preceding chapter, we explored the perspectives on limits to growth put forward by scholars from various Malthusian persuasions. These perspectives evolved over time to reflect shifts in society's understanding of the natural environment, social and cultural conditions, institutional capacity and setting, and technology. In general, Malthusians share the belief that biophysical limits are real and ultimately constrain humans' material progress, or limit 'economic growth' as it is conventionally understood. Thus, in general, Malthusians have a rather pessimistic outlook on the future material progress of humanity and their policy prescriptions to avoid pending catastrophe may appear quite draconian to some. For Malthusians, 'business as usual' is a flawed and dangerous policy option.

This chapter examines the scarcity and growth paradigm of neoclassical (mainstream) economics. Unlike Malthusians, proponents of the neoclassical school of thought are known for their optimistic outlook on the economic progress of human society. This is also quite a departure from their own predecessors, the classical economists, who were known for their 'dismal' worldview. As will be evident throughout this chapter, it is not difficult to see why mainstream economists are such an optimistic bunch once their core assumptions about human institutions and technology are understood. But what are those assumptions?

As discussed in Chapter 1, the neoclassical economic perspective of natural resource scarcity, allocation and measurement is based on the following postulates: (1) nothing rivals the market as a medium for resource allocation; (2) only individual 'preferences' and initial endowments determine resource prices; (3) for privately owned resources, market prices are 'true' measures of resource scarcity (see Section A.4 of Appendix A); (4) as discussed in Chapters 5 and 6, price distortions arising from externalities can be effectively remedied through appropriate institutional adjustments; (5) resource scarcity can be continually augmented by technological means (see Chapter 1); and (6) human-made capital (such as machines, buildings, roads, etc.) and natural capital (such as forests, coal deposits, wetland preserves, wilderness, etc.) are substitutes for each other.

On the basis of these premises, most neoclassical economists have traditionally maintained a strong skepticism toward doom-and-gloom prophecies about the future economic condition of humanity. In fact, since resources are assumed to be available in geologically fixed quantities while the population continues to grow, neoclassical economics would contend that it is tautological, and therefore redun-

dant, to say that resources are becoming increasingly scarce (Rosenberg 1973).

Instead, the really significant issue should be to understand the *circumstances under which technological progress will continue to ameliorate resource scarcity*. And this should be done with a belief that, under the right circumstances, *technology will continue not only to spare resources but also to expand our niche* (Ausubel 1996). Indeed, this view is in sharp contrast to the characteristically gloomy Malthusian position on technology and resource scarcity discussed in the previous chapter. What general explanations could be offered to counter the pessimistic Malthusian disposition?

Mainstream economists provide the following *three* explanations against the traditional Malthusian prophecies of doom-and-gloom:

1. Malthusians are generally predisposed to view humankind as having a natural propensity to exploit (conquer) nature so far that self-destruction is the unavoidable ultimate outcome. As a result of this, Malthusians tend to underestimate human wisdom (creativity) and the human capability for self-preservation (Cole et al. 1973; Lomborg 2001; Simon 1980). Malthusians also tend to underestimate the flexibility and resilience of human economic and social institutions, especially a well-functioning market system (Simon and Khan 1984).

2. Malthusian scholars have the strong tendency to lump resources together without regard to their importance, ultimate abundance, or substitutability (Simon 1996). When these factors are considered, absolute scarcity does not matter (for an expanded discussion on this issue read Exhibit 12.1). Malthusians simply do not comprehend that there is an infinite amount of resource substitutability, even in a world with finite resources. (Goeller and Weinberg 1976; Solow 1974). Accordingly, it is not at all relevant to say that energy has no substitutes. Instead, a meaningful topic of discourse about energy should be the substitution possibilities that exist among different energy sources, such as fossil fuels, wind, solar, bio-diesel, and so on. Even

EXHIBIT 12.1 RESOURCES, POPULATION, ENVIRONMENT: AN OVERSUPPLY OF FALSE BAD NEWS

Julian Simon

The supplies of natural resources are finite. This apparently self-evident proposition is the starting point and the all-determining assumption of such models as *The Limits to Growth* [Meadows et al. 1974] and of much popular discussion.

Incredible as it may seem at first, the term 'finite' is not only inappropriate but downright misleading in the context of natural resources, from both the practical and the philosophical points of view. As with so many of the important arguments in this world, this one is 'just semantic.' Yet the semantics of resource scarcity muddle public discussion and bring about wrongheaded policy decisions.

A definition of resource quantity must be operational to be useful. It must tell us how the quantity of the resource that might be available in the future could be calculated. But the future quantities of a natural resource such as copper cannot be calculated even in principle, because of new lodes, new methods of mining copper, and variations in grades of copper lodes; because copper can be made from other metals, and because of the vagueness of the boundaries within which copper might be found—including the sea, and other planets. Even less possible is a reasonable calculation of the amount of future services of the sort we are now accustomed to get from copper, because of recycling and because of the substitution of other materials for copper, as in the case of the communications satellite.

With respect to energy, it is particularly obvious that the earth does not bound the quantity available to us; our sun (and perhaps other suns) is our basic source of energy in the long run, from vegetation (including fossilized vegetation) as well as from solar energy. As to the practical finiteness and scarcity of resources— that brings us back to cost and price, and by these measures history shows progressively decreasing rather than increasing scarcity.

Why does the word 'finite' catch us up? That is an interesting question in psychology, education and philosophy; unfortunately there is no space to explore it here.

In summary, because we find new lodes, invent better production methods and discover new substitutes, the ultimate constraint upon our capacity to enjoy unlimited raw materials at acceptable prices is knowledge. And the source of knowledge is the human mind. Ultimately, then, the key constraint is human imagination and the exercise of educated skills. Hence an increase of human beings constitutes an addition to the crucial stock of resources, along with causing additional consumption of resources.

Source: *Science* (1980) 268, pp. 1435–6. Copyright © American Association for the Advancement of Science, 1980. Reprinted by permission.

when discussion is limited to only one form of energy, such as fossil fuels, it is important to note that substitutions exist between fossil fuels, such as liquid petroleum and natural gas for space heating or even running motor vehicles.

3. Malthusians are predisposed to believe that economic growth automatically causes environmental degradation and may eventually precipitate serious material shortages and ecological collapse. From the perspective of mainstream economists, this is flawed reasoning because economic growth seldom causes ecological collapse but rather a continuous environmental degradation without clear limit points (Davidson 2000). This may sometimes cause temporary large-scale problems, but not necessarily 'irreversible' environmental damage. For example, agricultural land that has been degraded by excessive soil erosion and/or poor farming practices can be gradually restored to its full

261

productive potential through improved farming practices, such as terrace farming, crop rotation, leaving land fallow for some years, and so on.

These positions of mainstream economists against Malthusians actually reveal the lack of a coherent theory of biophysical limits within the neoclassical economics paradigm. This is not, however, perceived as a shortcoming because the longstanding position of neoclassical economics has been that if economic collapse is to occur it is more likely to be because of deficiencies in the functioning of the economic system and human ingenuity and not because of 'general' (as opposed to specific) resource scarcity.

Thus, this chapter does not present an alternative paradigm of 'biophysical limits' that is uniquely attributable to the neoclassical economics school of thought. However, this is not to suggest that the events of the environmental movement of the 1960s and early 1970s did not cause any realignment in the conceptualizations and analytical approaches used to address environmental problems within the perspective of standard economics. To the contrary, it was during this period that externality and market failure started to be given considerable attention, although these ideas and their policy implications were initially introduced by an English economist, Arthur Pigou (1920), several decades earlier.

It was in the late 1960s that Ayres and Kneese (1969), in their groundbreaking paper on 'Production, Consumption and Externalities', ignited fresh interest in externality and the management of residuals and pollution based on a material balance approach. This approach adheres to the notion that the residuals at the end of the materials flow are determined by materials entering the flow as well as by all the transformation processes in production and consumption activities. 'The entire materials flow is therefore at the core of explaining environmental degradation whose feedback effects on the economy take the form of large-scale multi-party externalities due to missing markets' (Ayres and Kneese 1969: 283). This clearly indicates the pervasive nature of pollution.

Furthermore, the material balance approach to pollution subjects environmental management to the law of conservation, and its corollary the mass balance principle (MBP). It is interesting to note that the development of this idea (i.e., the material balance approach to pollution) by Ayres and Kneese coincided with the application of the laws of thermodynamics to economic problems by Herman Daly and Georgesu-Roegen who, as discussed in Chapter 11 and Appendix B, are known for their pioneering work in ecological economics.

However, perhaps because of its over-reliance on physical laws, the interest of neoclassical economists in the material balance approach to pollution faded away with time. On the other hand, externality and market failure still remain, as shown in Chapters 3 to 6, the cornerstone of the basic tenets of standard environmental economics. At this fundamental level, therefore, the contributions of neoclassical economics to the management and allocation of environmental resources remain strong and quite valuable, as evident by the material covered in Chapters 3 through 8.

This chapter is not a discussion about most recent advances in the standard theories of environmental economics (i.e., externality and market failure). Instead, it deals with the neoclassical economists' responses to limits to growth arguments as manifested by scholars with a Malthusian perspective. This is done in the following two specific ways: first, by offering combined theoretical and empirical evidence to show the fallacies of several key Malthusian positions on limits to growth; and second, by showing how economic growth and technological advances could be viewed *not as problems in themselves*, the way Malthusians tend to view them, but as *cures to stresses* caused by population, resources, pollution and other environmental damages.

The next section will provide several studies conducted by mainstream economists in order to empirically refute the hypothesis of an increasing 'general' scarcity of 'extractive resources'. The empirical evidence suggests that many extractive resources are getting less scarce with the passage of time. Section 12.3 examines the problem of environmental pollution. There, based on a theory that has been partially validated by some empirical studies, it will be argued that the best cure against environmental degradation is sustained economic growth. Section 12.4 shows why economic growth is not only good for the environment, but is also a cure for any nation's population problem. Each section of the chapter also offers substantive criticisms of the methodologies used, and conclusions reached, by neoclassical economists. Section 12.5 provides the chapter summary.

12.2 INCREASING RESOURCE SCARCITY: THE EMPIRICAL EVIDENCE

As discussed in Chapter 11, Malthusians often argue that, in the long-run, the depletion of some key material resources (for example, a prolonged shortage of global petroleum supply, water shortage, or large-scale degradation of land due to erosion and desertification) would act as a bottleneck to further economic growth (Meadows et al. 1974). This section presents several empirical studies that argue against the Malthusian thesis which promotes the inevitability of increasing resource scarcity in the long-run. In fact, the evidence over the past 130 years suggests that resources are becoming more abundant rather than scarcer.

Scarcity and growth: the empirical evidence before the 1970s

The earliest attempt to empirically analyze the condition of resource scarcity was made in a book published in 1963, *Scarcity and Growth: The Economics of Natural Resource Availability*. The authors of this classic and highly influential book, Howard J. Barnett and Chandler Morse (B&M), were members of President Truman's Commission on Materials Policy, whose mission was to investigate the validity of a widespread public perception of future material shortage in the United States following World War II. This study was based on a carefully and ingeniously designed statistical trend analysis for the United States (Potter and Christy 1962), and it encompasses the period dating from the Civil War (1870) to 1957. B&M used this data to test the validity of a core principle of the Malthusian-Ricardian doctrine: the

inevitability of 'increasing resource scarcity with a passage of time'.

In their analysis, B&M defined increasing scarcity as increasing *real cost*, which is measured by the amount of labor and capital required to produce a unit of extractive resources (for a fuller understanding of 'real cost' refer to Section A.5 of Appendix A). They then put forward the following hypothesis:

> The real cost of extractive products per unit will increase through time due to limitations in the available quantities and qualities of natural resources. Real cost in this case is measured in terms of labor (man-days, man-hours) or labor plus capital per unit of extractive output.
>
> (Barnett 1979: 165)

B&M refer to this postulate as the *strong* hypothesis of increasing economic scarcity. It suggests that increasing resource scarcity will be evident if an increasing cost of labor and capital per unit of extractive output, $(\alpha L_E + \beta K_E)/Q_E$, is observed, over time, (see Figure 12.1). Note that L_E and K_E represent the labor and capital used in the extractive sectors of the economy, and Q_E represents the aggregate output of the extractive sectors (which include agriculture, fishing, forestry and mining). The parameters α and β are the weight factors of labor and capital, respectively.

Note the striking similarity between the Ricardian scarcity, discussed in Section 5 of Appendix A, and the strong hypothesis. In both instances the idea is to find a *physical measure of resource scarcity*. In some respect, the strong hypothesis can be viewed as an empirical test for Ricardian scarcity. Note also that, under certain conditions, prices for extractive outputs (as often used in empirical studies) may be used as proxy for real cost per unit of extractive resources. When using prices as proxy for real unit costs, it is important to note how much monopoly and government regulation exists in the markets for both inputs and outputs in the resource markets. Furthermore, externalities are another important consideration to take into account.

Using the above model, B&M proceeded with their extensive statistical trend analysis, and concluded the following:

263

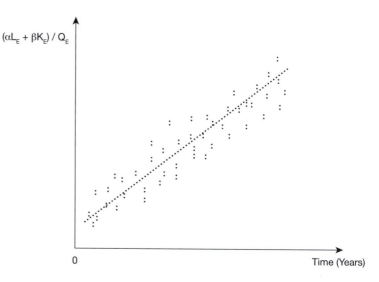

Figure 12.1 *A graphic illustration of the strong hypothesis of increasing natural resource scarcity. The amount of labor and capital used to get a unit of extractive output (the unit in the y-axis) is increasing with a passage of time.*

$(\alpha L_E + \beta K_E) / Q_E$

0

Time (Years)

The U.S. output in extractive sectors (which includes agriculture, forestry, fishing, and mining) increased markedly from the Civil War to 1957, yet the statistical record fails to support, and in fact is contradictory to, the classical hypothesis. Real costs per unit of extractive goods, measured in units of labor plus capital, did not rise. They fell, except in forestry (which is less than 10 percent of extraction). In fact, the pace of decline in real cost . . . accelerated following World War I, compared with the preceding period.

(Barnett 1979: 166)

Moreover, this happened at a time when, according to Potter and Christy (1962: 1), the United States' 'population increased four-fold; land appropriation for agricultural use almost tripled; timber output more than tripled; mining of bituminous coal increased 18-fold; and extraction of iron ore increased 26-fold'. How can a nation that has experienced such strong economic and population growth have not yet experienced increasing economic scarcity of natural resources? It was even more startling to observe a declining trend of resource scarcity during the period under consideration. Four reasons were given in answer to this question (Smith 1979:2):

First, as higher grade sources are exhausted, lower grade sources are found in greater abundance.

Moreover, the qualitative differences among various stocks diminish as the grade of the materials declines. Second, as a particular extractive resource becomes more scarce, continued increases in the rate of appreciation in its price tend to be offset by substitution of other resources. That is, users seek alternatives with more favorable cost relationships and all but the more insistent demands for the resource are reduced or eliminated. Third, increases in prices stimulate exploration for new deposits and provide incentives for increased recycling, which can reduce the pressure on sources of virgin materials. Fourth, technical change reduces the costs of providing natural resource commodities either by reducing the extraction costs for existing deposits or introducing methods which make previously uneconomic resources a part of the effective reserves at current or short-term future prices.

Thus, according to the above explanations, it is through the interplay of scarcity, markets (prices) and technology that the problem of resource scarcity is continually alleviated. As resources become scarce, their prices will increase to reflect that scarcity. These events will set off the following chain reactions: consumers will cut down on their use; substitutes will be identified and put into use; and further technological advances will take place to conserve resources (such as increased recycling of waste) and find more substitutes. It seems quite appropriate to use the old adage here: 'necessity (scarcity) is the mother of invention'.

A further look at the explanation given above by Smith shows the peculiar nature of how mainstream economists perceive the availability of extractive resources. Geologically, these resources don't get exhausted. Scarcity of these resources simply implies qualitative decline towards some uniform grade materials. Furthermore, these uniform grade materials are found in abundant quantities. Thus, with advances in mining technology it is possible to extract these abundantly available but uniformly poor-grade materials (ores) at low cost. How far the cost of extraction will decline primarily depends on the progress made in mining technology.

These are the explanations given to validate the empirical evidence for decreasing resource scarcity with the passage of time. However, even setting aside the doubts one may have about these explanations (more on this later), the limited scope of the B&M study raises a separate and significant issue of concern. That is, it is important to note that the conclusion of the study is strictly applicable only to the United States at a specific moment in its history. As such, it would be inappropriate to generalize global resource conditions from the results of this case study. In addition, this study said nothing about the quality of the natural environment—a subject matter of perhaps little concern at this early stage of economic development in the United States.

Despite its limited scope, and other shortcomings (to be discussed later), this study by B&M holds a special significance because it sets a framework for analyzing 'general' resource scarcity. Some economists even consider it to be 'one of the most famous and influential books ever published on resources and the human prospect' (Simpson et al. 2005).

Scarcity and growth reconsidered: the empirical evidence since the 1970s

The 1970s were, in many ways, watershed years for public awareness of ecological limits and their implications. During this period a number of books and articles were published warning the public about impending natural resource scarcity in the not too distant future. The most influential of these publications was, as discussed in the previous chapter (see Exhibit 11.3, p. 249), *The Limits to Growth,* first published in 1971. Although controversial, the frightful warning of the book was taken seriously because the study was supported by the Club of Rome, which is composed of a large group of well-reputed scientists, businesses and government leaders from around the world. In addition, both the Arab oil embargo of 1973 (a result of the Arab–Israeli War) and the 1978 energy shortage (a result of a unilateral decision by OPEC, the Organization of Petroleum Exporting Countries, to limit petroleum supply), clearly demonstrated the vulnerability of industrial nations' economies to a prolonged shortage of a key, but finite, resource: petroleum.

The events of the 1970s encouraged practitioners of standard economics in the B&M approach to empirically test for evidence of alleged emerging global resource scarcity. In the late 1970s, several attempts were made to empirically study recent trends of resource scarcity. Johnson et al. (1980) updated the original findings of B&M and re-examined the strong hypotheses by extending the period under consideration from the Civil War up to 1970. Kerry Smith (1979) analyzed the United States data from 1900 to 1973, using a more sophisticated statistical technique.

While Smith was somewhat critical of B&M's work on purely methodological grounds, the overall results and conclusions of the above studies were quite consistent with the findings of B&M. Namely, that the United States' experience is still indicative of decreasing resource scarcity with the passage of time. But again, these studies are confined to the economic performance of one nation. The question that still remains unanswered is: Can the United States' experience be generalized to other nations?

Smith's paper, mentioned above, was just one of the many papers that were presented at a conference sponsored by the Resources for the Future and later published in *Scarcity and Growth Reconsidered* (1979). In a paper presented at that conference Barnett, using the published time-series data from the United Nations, made similar studies for various nations of the world. For each specific nation, on the basis of the available data, the trend analysis failed to support the strong hypothesis of increasing scarcity for minerals. In fact, all the results pertaining to the strong hypothesis are consistent with the opposite hypothesis: that is, of increasing resource availability.

However, as Barnett (1979: 185) himself suggested, 'these international results should be regarded as preliminary, since the series involved are only available for short periods (since post World War II) and, in several of the cases, of questionable quality'. Again, in 1982, Barnett et al. examined data through 1979. At this time, there was some evidence of increasing scarcity in the 1970s, but this was attributed to the changing market structure in general and the OPEC cartel in particular.

The overall implication of the above studies is that aggregate global and United States economic trends are improving. Thus, the bad news of the 1970s (pollution, energy crises, acceleration in the rates of soil erosion, desertification, deforestation, etc.) was not indicative of emerging resource scarcity. If anything, such events have to be taken as a temporary setback. Common beliefs assert that these problems, if envisioned properly, would be solved through institutional adjustments and technological means. This particular belief is reaffirmed in, *The Resourceful Earth: A Response to Global 2000*, in which Julian L. Simon and Herman Kahn assert that they

> are confident that the nature of the physical world permits continued improvement in humankind's economic lot in the long run, indefinitely. Of course there are always newly arising local problems, shortages and pollution, due to climate or to increased population and income. Sometimes temporary large-scale problems arise. But the nature of the world's physical conditions and the resilience in a well-functioning economic and social system enable us to overcome such problems, and the solutions usually leave us better off than if the problem had never

arisen; that is the great lesson to be learned from human history.

(Simon and Kahn 1984: 3)

The Resourceful Earth, as indicated by its subtitle, is written as a critical response to *The Global 2000 Report to the President* (Council on Environmental Quality and Department of State 1980). As discussed in Exhibit 11.3, p. 249, the conclusions of this report were very frightening as they represented the reaffirmation of the findings reached by *The Limits to Growth* (1972) almost a decade earlier. Simon and Kahn's response to such gloomy conclusions was quite drastic. Mostly relying on statistical trend analyses similar to those developed by B&M, their general conclusion was that 'for the most relevant matters we have examined, aggregate global and U.S. trends are improving rather than deteriorating'.

Over the past two decades, there were a number of published papers that attempted to either update the original work done by B&M or simply examine certain aspects of its findings (Cleveland 1993; Hall and Hall 1984). One finding that was commonly shared by these studies was the evidence for increasing scarcity of energy during the 1970s and 1980s. However, it is still difficult to know from these studies whether the increasing scarcity of energy observed during this period is a signal of a future trend.

Finally, the most recent comprehensive published work on scarcity and growth appeared in 2005: *Scarcity and Growth Revisited: Natural Resources and the Environment in the New Millennium* (Simpson et al. 2005). This book was the final product of a conference sponsored by Resources for the Future in 2002, almost 40 years after the publication of the original *Scarcity and Growth* by B&M. *Scarcity and Growth Revisited* consists of papers written and presented by distinguished economists at this conference.

These papers deal with wide-ranging topics in the scarcity and growth debates. The basic positions taken in these papers can be organized into two broadly defined categories of resource scarcity debates—the 'old' and 'new' scarcity debates. In the 'old scarcity' debate the focus has been on the adequacy of stock resources (such as minerals, fossil fuels, fisheries, and so on) that are basically traded in markets. On the other hand, in the 'new scarcity' debate the focus is on how to resolve long-term environmental pollution and the depletion of global ecological assets (such as climate change, biodiversity, ecological services, and so on). These resources are not traded in markets and the global dimension of these problems creates tremendous challenges for policy.

The following emerged as consensus views from these conference papers: first, if the focus of the 'original' *Scarcity and Growth* is recognized as dealing with stock resources that are traded in markets (i.e., the 'old scarcity'), no clear evidence exists to indicate that these resources are affecting economic growth.

> Yet, causes for concern persist. While abundant quantities of many resources remain, they are becoming progressively remote. It is only natural that mineral (and fuel and biological) resource stocks were most intensively exploited first in the area closest to where they were used. As demands increased, exploration and eventually extraction took place across oceans, in inhospitable climates, and for minerals and fossil fuels especially, deeper and deeper beneath land and water.
>
> (Simpson et al. 2005: 11)

Second, the papers expressed heightened concern over the state of the global environment (i.e., air, water, climate and biological diversity). Themes that are widely explored by the various contributors to *Scarcity and Growth Revisited* are the challenges that a global society must face in order to address a new set of environmental problems, such as climate change, biodiversity and ecological services—the 'new scarcity'.

This new reality of resource scarcity poses a major problem because its impact on long-term economic growth will not be understood using price trend analysis similar to the one used by the 'original' *Scarcity and Growth*. This is because, as discussed above, the new reality deals with global ecological assets that are not traded in markets. Furthermore, there appears to be increasing evidence that these kinds of resources are getting scarce. In the 'new scarcity' debate, it is argued, the depletions of ecological assets (natural capital) are starting to emerge as the limiting factor in the future. For example, fishing will be limited, not by the number of fishing boats, but by remaining fishing stocks; petroleum use will not be limited by refining capacity but by geologic deposits and the atmospheric capacity to absorb CO_2.

Thus, essentially, the authors of *Scarcity and Growth Revisited* suggest that the claim of declining resource scarcity based on studies and the methodology of the past (i.e., the 'original' *Scarcity and Growth*) is outdated because of its exclusive reliance on market-traded stock resources—the 'old scarcity' paradigm. With this in mind, they make a number of recommendations to remedy this situation without the dire Malthusian warning of catastrophe if these recommendations are not acted upon.

However, even though they may not view the future as being doomed, the authors do express heightened concerns about the adequacy of global ecological assets if a policy of 'business as usual' is pursued. These concerns arise from the awareness of the complexity of emerging environmental issues (such as, climate change, and the degradation of biodiversity and ecological services) under consideration. The challenges are formidable and entail fundamental changes in institutional, technological and policy focuses (arrangements).

When the problems are viewed this way, addressing these challenges in a comprehensive manner demands: (1) major breakthroughs in the economic 'valuation' of environmental services so that externalities arising from global environmental problems can be dealt with through ordinary market mechanisms; (2) the willingness of global society to cooperate so that negative spillovers (such as carbon emissions) are effectively controlled; (3) promoting innovations that generate positive spillovers through the augmentation of knowledge and the implementation of new technologies with full consideration of the potential harms they may induce to natural resources and the environment; and (4) assessing natural resource adequacy with the explicit consideration of both intra- and intergenerational fairness equities.

267

Finally, while the above challenges and their policy implications may appear to signal a significant departure from the mainstream economic worldview, at the fundamental level the belief remains that the *future scarcity of resources can be resolved within the confines of the existing economic paradigm*. Furthermore, with an increasing awareness of the 'new scarcity' reality, mainstream economists are starting to make serious efforts to understand the effects of uncertainty and ecological irreversibility on future economic growth. In fact, many of the 'cutting-edge' research studies in economics include these very topics. However, while these studies deal with very important environmental problems, there is lingering skepticism about the lessons that can be drawn from them. This is because these studies, while they may be interesting, are at this stage either too theoretical and/or limited in scope. Yet, they certainly indicate steps in the right direction.

Scarcity and growth: criticisms

While the empirical studies of B&M, among others, are vividly suggestive of *decreasing* scarcity with the passage of time, can these studies allow us to generalize about the impending scarcity of natural resources in the foreseeable future? This subsection offers *three* reasons why the answer to this question may be *no*. In other words, these are reasons why past trends of decreasing scarcity may not be sustainable.

■ First, during the period when the above-mentioned empirical studies were conducted, major transformations in the use of *energy* had occurred. More specifically, higher-quality fuels displaced the use of lower-quality fuels—first coal replaced wood, and then oil and natural gas replaced coal. According to Cleveland (1991; 1993), it was the substitution of high-quality fuels that reduced the labor–capital costs of extractive sectors in the United States, as depicted in the B&M study. In other words, the decline in real costs of resource extraction observed by empirical studies of the B&M type was not due to technological changes per se, but rather due to the *substitution of higher-quality energy resources for labor and capital in the extraction of resources*.

To verify this, Cleveland conducted an empirical study analogous to that of B&M. More specifically, he calculated the quantities of direct and indirect fuels used to produce a unit of resource in the United States extractive sectors (mining, agriculture, forest products and fisheries industries) using this approach: $Q_E / (E_d + E_I)$, where Q_E is the total extractive output and E_d and E_I are the *direct* and *indirect* energy used to extract the resource in question.

Thus, a general trend that showed a decline in the output per unit of energy input (i.e., the productivity of energy input) would indicate an increase in physical scarcity or an increase in energy cost per unit of output (see Figure 12.2). This is because, as high-quality resources were depleted, more energy would be needed to further extract a unit of resource. For most recent years, between 1970 and 1988, the results of Cleveland's empirical findings indicated increasing scarcity in the metal mining, energy extraction, forestry and fishery sectors of the United States economy. The exceptions to this have been non-metal industries (such as hydrogen, helium, oxygen, carbon, etc.).

■ Second, the pace of technological progress in the past has been uneven. In fact, 'a disproportionate fraction of technological improvements during the past 5,000 years has been concentrated over the last 300 years or so' (Dasgupta and Heal 1979: 206). Given this, it would be dangerous to use past evidence to merely extrapolate into the future. If this point is taken seriously, *rapid resource-saving technical progress* of the kind experienced in the past 200 years does not necessarily imply *continued technical progress at the same pace in the future*.

■ Third, in the past studies based on statistical trends did make explicit environmental quality considerations. This is because the prices for environmental goods might have been significantly undervalued due to externalities (see Chapters 3 and 4). Thus, because of this omission, one might argue that—over the past century—the changes in the patterns of extraction have increased the effective supply of the material input components

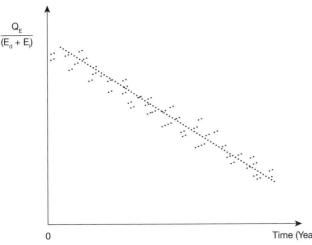

Figure 12.2 *Extractive output per unit of energy input over time. The amount of extractive output obtained from the use of a unit of energy inputs is declining over time—implying a decline in the efficiency of energy as a factor of production.*

The y-axis is labeled $\dfrac{Q_E}{(E_d + E_i)}$ and the x-axis is labeled Time (Years), with origin at 0.

of natural resources (i.e., natural resource commodities), while reducing amenity and life-support services (such as climate regulation and the maintenance of genetic diversity) of these same resources. That is, the *greater degree of technological substitution possibilities* observed in the past might have come from the *increasing replacement of priced goods and services for unpriced goods, services, and amenities* (Brown and Field 1979). Some view this process as being unsustainable, especially when the issue under consideration is loss of biodiversity. Here is what Dasgupta and Heal (1979: 343) have to say on this subject:

> To rely on substitutability among natural resources in commodity production to minimize the utilitarian importance of biodiversity, as is frequently done (e.g., Simon 1981, 1994), is scientifically flawed. First, without biodiversity, substitutability is lost entirely. And, more fundamentally, certain species and groups of species play unique roles in the functioning of ecosystems and thus have no substitutes. Preservation of biodiversity is hence important, both to provide unique services and to provide insurance against the loss of similarly functioning species.

The implication is that if ecological simplification is the outcome of continued economic growth, the neoclassical treatment of natural and human capital as substitutes will not be sustainable. In other words, economic progress has been accomplished at the cost of continued environmental degradation. Has it been so? As will be explained in the next section, the neoclassical economists' response to this question will be a categorical *no*.

12.3 ECONOMIC GROWTH AND THE ENVIRONMENT: THE ENVIRONMENTAL KUZNETS CURVE (EKC)

In Chapter 11, we saw that some neo-Malthusians argue that affluence (or a higher standard of living that is associated with increased income) is one of the primary contributing factors to environmental deterioration. In this section, we will examine the arguments presented by neoclassical economists that economic growth (increase in income) is good for the environment, which seems to turn the neo-Malthusian argument, that affluence contributes to environmental deterioration, upside down. In other words, neoclassical economists argue that significant improvements in environmental quality are fully compatible with economic growth. Why is this so?

In the first instance, one of the outcomes of economic growth is an increase in *real per capita income*. Higher per capita income will increase the demand for improved environmental quality. This means increased expenditure on environmental cleanup operations. Accordingly, economic growth is more likely to be good than bad for the environment. The generalized form of this environment–income hypothesis is depicted by an 'inverted-U' curve as shown by Figure 12.3.

Put into words, this graph portrays how a population with an increasing per capita income initially encounters worsening environmental conditions and, after a certain point, is followed by an improvement in environmental quality. Taken at face value, what this suggests is that a country has to attain a certain standard of living before it starts to respond to its concern for improved environmental quality. The 'inverted U' is commonly referred to as the environmental Kuznets curve (EKC) because of its similarity to the relationship between per capita income and income inequality first postulated by Simon Kuznets (1955).

The EKC hypothesis has a far-reaching implication to the extent that it presumes the eventual decoupling of economic growth and environmental degradation. However, since this hypothesis is based on empirical generalizations, it offers no systematic explana-

tions about the causes for the inverted-U shaped relationship of income and environmental degradation. For this reason, over the past two decades there has been a growing scholarly interest in offering explanations for the shape of the EKC and testing its existence empirically. These attempts are explained at some length in the next two subsections.

Possible causes of the EKC

Several reasons are given to explain the shape of the EKC. The following are the five that are most commonly cited:

1. *The scale effect*: this is a factor used to explain the rising segment of the EKC where increase in per capita income is associated with rising environmental pollution. Such a phenomenon is expected to occur at the early stage of economic development when, other things being constant, increase in output is attained by transforming incrementally growing amounts of throughput (i.e., material and energy resources). Thus, a

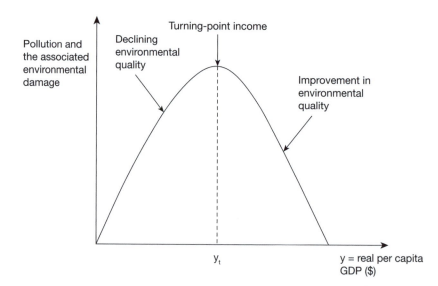

Figure 12.3 *Environmental Kuznets curve. The vertical axis measures environmental damage. The above graph suggests that after a country attains a certain level of per capita income (y_t), increased income is associated with lower environmental damage or higher environmental quality. The turning-point income is y_t.*

larger scale of economic activity (i.e., output production) causes more pollution (Grossman and Krueger 1995). Thus, in the initial stage of economic development, economic growth is expected to be bad for the environment. This is further reinforced by the fact that the institutional priority of low-income countries favors increases in output even at the cost of further degradation of the environment. In other words, at this early stage of economic development, since pollution is externalized, it grows unabated due to the scale effect.

2. *The composition effect*: is used to explain the shape of the EKC by looking at the evolution of the structural changes of an economy over the course of various stages of economic development. More specifically, under this scenario, the EKC depicts the relationship between economic growth and environmental quality as a country progresses from agrarian to industrial and finally to service economy. Initially, environmental degradation tends to increase as the economy makes the transition from an agrarian to an industrial economy. In particular, at the early stage of industrialization, the composition of the manufacturing sector of the economy changes from light industries (such as food and textiles) to heavy industries (such as chemicals, minerals, metal smelting, etc.), which contributes to the decline of the environmental quality (Panayotou 1995).

However, continued economic growth starts to have a positive impact on environmental quality. This occurs when the economy finally enters into another structural change moving from an industrial to a service economy. The service economy is characterized by knowledge-based, technology-intensive industry (Dinda 2004). Thus, the composition effect suggests that the EKC is a manifestation of the structural changes that are inherent along the transformative path of a burgeoning economy: the movement from an agrarian, to an industrial, and finally to a service, economy, wherein economic growth gradually shifts to sectors that pollute less (Grossman and Krueger 1995). Some have argued that, while

structural change helps to explain the gradual reduction in emissions, it is not sufficient to cause the downturn of the EKC (Cole 2000; Lieb 2003).

3. *The technique effect*: this effect is used to explain the downturn of the EKC, that is, the eventual delinking of pollution and economic growth. The technique effect postulates that, as a country increases its wealth through continued economic growth, it can afford to invest more on research and development. This inevitably leads to further technological progress, which will be instrumental in the discovery and implementation of new and cleaner production processes, thereby improving the quality of the environment (Panayotou 1995).

In taking these three effects together, it is argued that the initial increase in environmental pressure due to the scale effect will eventually be more than offset by the combined forces of the two other effects (composition and technique) to eventually cause the delinking of economic growth and environmental pollution (Grossman and Krueger 1995; Selden and Song 1994).

4. *Environmental quality as normal good*: empirical studies have shown that the demand for environmental quality increases with income, that is, environmental quality is a normal good (Kristrom and Riera 1996). This notion of environmental quality as a normal good can be used to explain the downturn segment of the EKC (i.e., why pollution continues to fall after a certain income threshold is attained) by applying the following three interrelated arguments.

First, it is argued that resources are devoted to pollution cleanup only after basic needs have been met. That is, countries have to attain certain levels of income (i.e., basic needs have to be met) before starting to care for the environment (McConnell 1997). Second, as a country becomes richer, the desire for an incrementally cleaner environment will continue to increase. In part, this can be explained by increased environmental awareness arising from increases in educational attainment, which are associated with growth in average income (Selden and Song 1994). Third, continued economic growth would lead to improvements in environmental quality because with higher income people are willing to push for legislative mandates that are specifically intended to protect the environment (Hettige et al. 2000). Thus, for all of these reasons, sustained increases in per capita income beyond a certain threshold level will enable a country to maintain steady improvement in environmental quality.

5. *International trade and environmental quality*: another factor that is used to explain the shape of the EKC is international trade. International trade appears to have contradictory impacts on the environment. First, the effect of free trade is to increase the size of an economy (Bhagawati 1993). For low-income countries (i.e., countries at the initial stage of industrialization), a growing economy entails an increasing use of material and energy resources which, other factors holding constant, leads to increased pollution. In other words, for countries at an early stage of industrialization, the effect of international trade is, through the scale effect, to worsen environmental quality, at least in the short run.

Furthermore, low-income countries with lax or no pollution-control policies tend to attract pollution intensive industries, which is further encouraged by trade liberalization (Cole 2004; Eskeland and Harrison 2003). This so-called displacement effect or pollution haven hypothesis suggests that the high environmental regulations in place within the developed nations enhance the comparative advantage of poor nations in the production of goods and services that are produced by heavy polluters. Based on the discussion thus far, international trade can be used as an explanation for the increasing association of pollution and economic growth at the early stage of economic development.

However, contrary to the above conclusion, international trade is also used to explain the downturn of the EKC. In this case, it is argued that over the

long-run, *ceteris paribus*, international trade will be good for the environment because its ultimate effect is to increase real income. In other words, sustained increases in real income through trade will eventually create demand for stricter environmental regulations and a cleaner environment (Antweiler et al. 2001).

Thus trade liberalization, through the displacement effect (i.e., the migration of dirty industries from the developed countries into emerging countries) could explain the EKC findings obtained in cross-country studies. An inverted U-shaped relationship found by cross-country or panel data estimations would then indicate the combined observation of a positive relationship between pollution and income in developing countries with a negative one in developed countries, and not a single relationship that applies to both categories of country (Vincent 1997).

What should be clear from the above discussion is that a combination of several factors can be used to explain the shape of the EKC. These factors, among others, include income, structural changes of an economy, technology and international trade. Identifying these key factors allows economists to get a step closer to specifying a model that would allow them to empirically test the existence of an EKC, which is the subject of the next subsection.

Empirical evidence for EKC

Over the past two decades, numerous studies have been conducted in an attempt to empirically validate the existence of the EKC. Most of these studies used the following cubic model specification to show the relationships between pollution and income:

$$E_{it} = \beta_0 + \beta_1 Y_{it} + \beta_2 Y^2_{it} + \beta_3 Y^3_{it} + \beta_4 Z_{it} + \varepsilon \tag{12.1}$$

where E represents environmental indicators (such as SO_2 emissions, suspended particulate matters, biological oxygen demand, deforestation, etc.), Y is per capita income, Z represents other variables of influence on environmental degradation (for example, population density, time trend, dummy variables, etc.), and ε is the random error term. The subscripts 'i' and 't' represent a country and time, respectively. Note that 12.1 is a reduced form. The explanatory variable, income, is presumed to incorporate the effects of structural changes, technology and international trade. The reduced form that treats income as a catch-all variable is used mainly because of lack of data (Lieb 2003). In some instances, dummy variables (as part of Z variables) are used to capture technological factors that are presumed to be independent of income.

Using the above model specification, the following three possible outcomes can be anticipated, depending on the signs of the parameters β_1, β_2, and β_3:

- An EKC or inverted U-shaped relationship is implied when $\beta_1 > 0$, $\beta_2 < 0$, and $\beta_3 = 0$. The turning-point income (TPI) of EKC is attained at $Y^* = -\beta_1/2\beta_2$.
- An N-shaped relationship between income and pollution is obtained when $\beta_1 > 0$, $\beta_2 < 0$, and $\beta_3 > 0$. This implies that a second turning-point exists, after which pollution rises again with increasing income.
- A monotonically increasing relationship between income and environmental quality is encountered if $\beta_1 > 0$, and $\beta_2 = \beta_3 = 0$. This case would suggest that the EKC hypothesis does not hold. Similarly, a monotonically decreasing relationship between income and environmental quality is observed if $\beta_1 < 0$, and $\beta_2 = \beta_3 = 0$.

Other dominant characteristics of the empirical studies used to test the EKC hypothesis over the past two decades have been:

- *The nature of the data*: most empirical studies on the EKC hypothesis use cross-country or cross-sectional panel data from as many countries and years as possible. This is based on an implicit assumption that all countries in cross-country or panel data studies follow the same development path. Thus, an inverted U-shaped relationship found by cross-country or panel data estimations

indicates the combined observation of a positive relationship between pollution and income in developing countries with a negative one in developed countries, and not a single relationship that applies to both categories of countries (Vincent 1997).

As will be discussed later, the appropriateness of the assumption that all of the pooled countries follow the same development path (i.e., all of the pooled countries reach the turning point at the same income level) remains controversial. Some have made the argument that only single-country studies using time-series data could be used to test whether EKCs for different pollutants really exist (Huang et al. 2008; List and Gallet 1999; Roberts and Grimes 1997). However, the use of cross-section panel data has one important advantage. It is much easier to get a reasonably large data set, and this is a very important consideration given that good quality and comparable pollution data are very difficult to find.

- *The focus of the EKC studies*: the two main focuses of empirical analyses of the EKC studies have been: (1) the existence of an inverted-U relationship with levels of per capita income and a given environmental indicator (or indicators); and (2) the estimation of the turning-point income associated with a given environmental indicator(s). It is important to point out that no serious attention is given to the level of pollution at the turning-point income (more on this later).

Taking into consideration the aforementioned observations concerning the model specification, nature of data and focus of analysis that have been uniquely relevant to the EKC studies, we now turn to a brief review of the growing body of literature investigating this topic.

The first attempt to empirically verify the EKC hypothesis was undertaken by Grossman and Krueger in 1991. Using cross-country analysis, this study affirmed the existence of an EKC relation for both the atmospheric concentration of sulfur dioxide (SO_2) and suspended particulate matter (SPM). The turning-point income for SO_2 was estimated to occur when per capita GDP was estimated to be between $4,000 and $5,000 measured in 1985 US dollars. The turning-point income represents the threshold income level at which people, on average, start to be concerned about the quality of their environment. Shortly afterwards, another study by Shafik and Bandopadhyay (1992) reached a similar conclusion. In this study, the turning-point income in 1985 US dollars for SO_2 and SPM were given to be $3,700 and $3,300, respectively.

Over the next several years, a number of other studies (Carson et al. 1997; Cole et al. 1997; List and Gallet 1999; Panayotou 1995; Selden and Song 1994) further investigated the relationship between per capita income and a wide range of local air pollutants by using cross-country panel data. The findings of these studies suggested that an EKC exists for local air pollutants (such as SO_2, SPM, CO_2, NO_x, lead, and volatile organic compounds). The existence of an EKC for these pollutants should not be surprising because these pollutants are known to cause local health risks and can be treated without great expense (Selden and Song 1994).

However, the turning-point estimates for the above set of local air pollutants vary widely and in some instances quite significantly. For example, as discussed earlier, the turning-point income for SO_2 in the Grossman and Krueger (1991) study was in the range of $4,000 to $5,000 (in 1985 US dollars). On the other hand, Selden and Song (1994) estimated the turning-point income for SO_2 to be between $8,700 and $10,700 (in 1985 US dollars), and List and Gallet (1999) gave, for the same pollutant, an income figure of $22,600 (in 1985 US dollars). Similar variations in turning-point estimates are evident for other pollutants. This is a significant observation as it suggests that we *cannot make simple generalizations about the turning-point income for local air pollutants* even when the evidence for the EKC relationship is not in question (Lieb 2003).

Grossman and Krueger (1995) did another study on the relationship between per capita income and environmental degradation, this time with a focus on river. Among the pollutants they considered in

their study were: biological oxygen demand (BOD), chemical oxygen demand (COD), fecal coliform (FCOL), total coliform (TCOL), nitrates, dissolved oxygen demand (DOD), and heavy metal pollutants, such as lead, mercury, nickel, arsenic and cadmium in water. Their analyses revealed an EKC relationship for several of the indicators that were considered in this study. Despite this, however, empirical evidence of EKC has been quite *mixed* for water quality with conflicting results about both the shape and turning-point income of the inverted-U curve (Dinda 2004). In other words, there is little empirical support for an inverted-U relationship between income and several important water pollutants (Hettige et al. 2000; Harbaugh et al. 2002).

In addition to environmental factors associated with air and water pollution, other empirical studies that have been conducted to test the existence of the EKC relationship include, among others, municipal waste, CO_2 emissions, carbon monoxide, energy consumption and traffic volume (Cole et al. 1997; Goklany 1999; Holtz-Eakin and Selden 1995; Horvath 1997; Shafik 1994). In most of these cases the results have been either inconsistent or simply failed to confirm the inverted-U relationship with income. For example, several studies found that the relationship between per capita income and CO_2 emissions (a global pollutant) followed an N-shaped curve (Galeotti et al. 2006; Huang et al. 2008; Moomaw and Unruh 1997,). These findings provide further evidence that the EKC relationships are not likely to hold for pollutants with more global, indirect and long-term impacts.

Since it represents a significant environmental concern in developing countries, deforestation has been another environmental factors subjected to EKC empirical studies. Unfortunately, the empirical evidence of EKC for deforestation remains rather controversial (Bhattarai and Hammig 2001; Bulte and van Soest 2001; Koop and Tole 1999; Panayotou 1995; Shafik 1994). Other studies with particular relevance to developing countries have dealt with investigations into the existence of the EKC hypothesis for property rights using several proxy variables. These studies appear to suggest that more secure property rights under a rule of law, better enforcement of contracts and effective environmental regulations can help flatten the EKC (Norton 2002; Panayotou 1997). Clearly, these findings underscore the importance of effectively enforced environmental regulations.

General criticisms of the EKC hypothesis

There have been several criticisms of the EKC hypothesis. These criticisms arise from controversies pertaining to: (1) the EKC's basic methodological foundation and estimation procedures; (2) its inconsistent outcomes from empirical studies; and (3) its policy relevance. What follows is a brief summary of the major criticisms of EKC:

1. *Questions on the conceptual and methodological foundation of EKC*: several of the deficiencies of the EKC hypothesis find their root in its underlying conceptual and methodological foundations. The major deficiency can be found in the fact that:

    (a) The EKC hypothesis has no theoretical foundation, as such. Instead, it represents an empirical generalization (i.e., a belief about reality) based on the observable long-term trajectory of the relationship between income and pollution in a given country. Thus, while an EKC relation must fit the facts upon which the empirical generalization is made, it may do so without offering theoretical explanations for the underlying causes of its occurrence. For example, while the existence of an EKC relation suggests a turning-point income, it offers no theoretical explanation(s) for what causes this particular phenomenon to occur. This has significant implications for the policy relevance of EKC (more on this later).

    (b) An EKC hypothesis neglects to consider several social, physical and economic factors that induce environmental improvements. In this regard, an empirical study by Torras and Boyce (1998), which includes more explanatory variables than income alone, found that social factors such as income

equality, wider literacy and greater political liberties tend to have a significant positive effect on environmental quality, especially in low-income countries.

In another study, Lopez and Mitra (2000) developed a model to show that in a more corrupt country the turning point occurs at a higher pollution and income level. A similar study by Panayotou (1997) that included several proxy variables for the quality of institutions (such as, respect/enforcement of contracts, efficiency of the bureaucracy, the efficacy of the rule of law, the extent of government corruption, and the risk of appropriation) found that 'the quality of policies and institutions in a country can significantly reduce environmental degradation at low-income levels and speed up improvements at higher-income levels'.

Bhattarai and Hammig (2001) studied the EKC relationship for tropical deforestation across 66 countries in Latin America, Asia and Africa. They found that property rights enforcement does matter. Findings of this nature suggest that the omission of important institutional variables may be responsible for why the results from several empirical studies inconclusively show no clear relationship between per capita incomes and deforestation (Ekins 2000). The important implication here is that EKC analysis gains considerable policy relevance when it incorporates relevant social, political and institutional factors.

(c) The EKC hypothesis assumes that while, at a point in time, countries may be in different stages of economic development, all countries follow a similar pattern of pollution–income relationship throughout the course of economic growth. In fact, as pointed out earlier, it is this assumption that justifies pooling the data of different countries into one panel for the purpose of empirical studies (Dinda 2004). However, critics point out that this assumption may not hold because in reality large cross-country variations are observed in social, economic, political and biophysical factors that may materially affect environmental quality. To address this problem, some have suggested the use of cross-regional and preferably time-series data for empirical studies of EKC relation (Huang et al. 2008; List and Gallet 1999; Roberts and Grimes 1997).

2. *The EKC cannot be generalized for all types of pollutants*: first, as discussed earlier, the EKC relationship has been found for only a few pollutants, mainly those that have local health effects and can be abated without great expense. Furthermore, even when local air pollutants are found to follow an EKC, different countries produce different pollution–income relationships. Critics attribute this discrepancy to a lack of explicit consideration of policy differences between countries (Cole et al. 1997; Lieb 2003).

Second, as discussed before, most empirical studies have shown that global and stock pollutants (such as CO_2 emissions and other GHGs) do not follow an EKC relationship and exhibit a monotonically rising pollution–income relationship. Critics argue that this observation should not be surprising given that global and stock pollutants involve intergenerational externalities where a greater part of the damage can be passed to future generations (Lieb 2003). A general observation that can be deduced from the discussion so far is that 'an EKC only emerges for pollutants for which policy measures have been taken, whereas for other pollutants the pollution–income-relation is monotonically rising when the regulator remains inactive' (Ibid: 43).

3. *The EKC may not hold in the long-run*: critics of the EKC hypothesis point out that the possibility that an upturn may occur in the EKC relationship at high-income levels, an N-shaped pollution–income relation, is not considered. For example, a study by Ekins (2000) using data from the OECD and European Commission (high-income countries) indicated that 'despite improvements in some indicators, notably of some air pollutants, these rich countries seem to be experi-

encing continuing serious environmental degradation on all fronts'.

Results of this nature support the plausibility of the so-called *re-linking hypothesis*, in which environmental degradation is, eventually, positively re-linked to income level (de Bruyn and Opschoor 1997; Pezzes 1989). The important implication of this observation is that the *de-linking between economic growth and environmental degradation*, a claim made on the basis of the EKC hypothesis, *may not persist in the long-run*. The high cost of pollution-control resulting from eventual limitations (mainly due to diseconomies of scale) in abatement technology is given as the root cause for the eventual up-tick in pollution at high levels of income (Lieb 2003).

4. *The existence of an EKC relationship does not guarantee that global environmental degradation will not occur*: Why so? First, even when emissions are falling, they could still be above the assimilative capacity of the environment. Thus, for stock pollutants, this situation poses real possibilities for irreversible environmental damage in the long run (Ibid). Second, the concept of EKC is difficult to apply, or simply ineffective, for certain environmental factors that are vulnerable to irreversibility, such as soil erosion, desertification, biodiversity loss, and so on (Dinda 2004; Lieb 2003).

Furthermore, it is argued that trade liberalization within the context of the current globalization movement may be putting the 'global' environmental quality at a greater risk since developing counties (where pollution-intensive industries are migrating) generally have less efficient technologies to abate pollution. Thus, *supporting the EKC pattern portrayed by cross-country experience may impede sustainable development in both the developing countries and the world at large* (Ekins 1997).

5. *The EKC pattern is not inevitable*: taken at face value, the EKC hypothesis appears to suggest that the delinking of environmental degradation and economic growth is inevitable in the long-run. Furthermore, it presupposes that this phenom-

enon will be encountered by all countries at the same income threshold, that is, turning-point income. This can be seen as casting an optimistic view on the long-term economic and environmental predicament of humanity.

On the other hand, since the hypothesis expects such outcomes to occur irrespective of policy considerations, it pretty much locks every country to a predetermined trajectory of economic development. The possibilities of either *flattening* the EKC (i.e., the possibility of reducing the environmental price of economic growth) or *tunneling* through the EKC (i.e., the possibility of developing countries using newer, eco-friendlier technologies and thereby avoiding some of the environmental degradation that often accompanies economic growth) are overlooked (Panayotou 1997). That is, developing countries do not have to grow along the same path that developed nations have taken (Lieb 2003).

As Ekins (2000: 210) explains, the most important lesson to be learned from the discussion above is that 'any improvements in environmental quality as income increase is likely to be due to the enactment of environmental policy rather than endogenous changes in economic structure or technology'. In other words, environmental policy is a major driving force behind the EKC.

6. *The empirical testing for the existence of the EKC hypothesis is based on weak data and econometric framework*: arguments for this criticism run as follows. First, as discussed earlier, finding reliable and comparable environmental data is difficult, especially from developing countries. This is an important issue given that the results of any statistically based empirical analysis are as good as the data used to estimate the parameters of interest.

Second, for those who are versed in econometrics, the standard functional form (i.e., polynomial of degree 3) used to specify the relationship between income and pollution is plagued with a number of well-known estimation biases. The most relevant among these

biases are: *simultaneity bias* (i.e., the fact that income and pollution affect one another); *estimation bias* arising from *multicolinearity* (i.e., the fact that the independent variables are highly correlated); and *homogeneity* (the fact that the slope coefficients are not identical in all countries). While it is beyond the scope of this book to go into the details of the econometric problems, the underlying message is simple. The efficacy and reliability of the estimated parameters (the β's) that are essential for the determination of the existence of the EKC are undermined when problems of the above nature prevail.

In what appears to be a rather sobering note, this is how Stern (2004: 135) concluded his survey of the EKCs statistical findings:

> the statistical analysis on which the environmental Kuznets curve is based is not robust. There is little evidence for a common inverted U-shaped pathway that countries follow as their income rises. There may be an inverted U-shaped relation between urban ambient concentrations of some pollutants and income, although this should be tested with more rigorous time series or panel data methods. It seems unlikely that the EKC is a complete model of emissions or concentration.

Despite the doubts that have been raised above regarding the validity of the EKC hypothesis, the conviction that the long-term effect of economic growth is to improve environmental quality remains strong among the practitioners of neoclassical economics. As the discussion in the next section shows, a similar belief is held about the link between economic growth and population, that is, the deeply held notion that economic growth could serve as an effective way to control population growth.

12.4 ECONOMIC GROWTH AND POPULATION

The theory of demographic transition

Clearly, uncontrolled population growth can be a major problem. For neoclassical economists, the solution to this problem is simply more economic growth. In other words, economic growth is not only good for the environment (as discussed in the previous section), but is also a cure for a nation's population problem. One explanation for this assertion is based on the *theory of demographic transition* (TDT).

This theory is based on an empirical generalization and it claims that, as nations develop, they eventually reach a point where the birthrate falls. Basically, as shown in Figure 12.4, society progresses from a pre-modern regime (Stage I) of high fertility and high mortality to a post-modern regime (Stage III) of low fertility and low mortality. The decline in fertility actually starts in Stage II. However, at this so-called 'transitional stage', the decline in the fertility rate is accompanied by an even bigger decline in the death rate causing a high rate of population growth. The population growth eventually levels off at a low rate in Stage III, in which both fertility and mortality rates are low. It is important to note that the steady decline in the rate of population growth occurs as a country transitions from an industrial to a post-industrial society.

The TDT attempts to provide plausible explanations for why the decline in both the fertility and death rates follow the pattern depicted by Stages II and III. Several socioeconomic factors are given to explain the declining trends in both fertility and mortality and the

eventual decline in population growth, the most important being: rise in level of income per capita; decline in infant and child mortality; decline in child labor; the declining value of children for old-age security; and increasing participation of females in traditionally male-dominated sectors of the economy (Doepke 2004). Exhibit 12.2 offers an expanded discussion of how these socioeconomic factors contribute to the decline in fertility and death rates that eventually lead to low rates in population growth.

From the very inception of the TDT in 1929 (attributed to the work of the American demographer Warren Thomason) until 1960, the explanation for fertility decline was understood in broad generalities and relied on broadly accepted changes in the socioeconomic system (see Exhibit 12.2). In 1960 Gary Becker, a Nobel Laureate from the University of Chicago, published the ground-breaking paper entitled 'An Economic Analysis of Fertility'.

He used standard microeconomic theory to provide a theoretical explanation for the decline in fertility. His theory offered an explanation for the decline in fertility by examining how parents make decisions about childbearing, and how this choice is influenced by the income of the family. For Becker, as will be discussed below, a decline in fertility happens because children become more costly as a result of the modernization that is associated with a rising

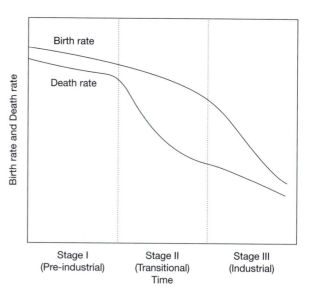

Figure 12.4 *The demographic transition. The pre-industrial stage, Stage I, indicates high birth and death rate. Life is short and population growth is low. Rapid deceleration in death rate due to medical breakthrough that reduces infant mortality and infectious disease creates a big gap between birth and death rates in Stage II—the transitional period towards industrialization. This is the period where population grows at a very high rate. Stage III is characterized by a low level of both birth and death rates. Life is long and population growth is low.*

EXHIBIT 12.2   THE THEORY OF THE DEMOGRAPHIC TRANSITION

In studying the reproductive decisions of humans at the macro level, one view that has been most popular among social scientists is the theory of the demographic transition. This theory derives its appeal from its simplicity and the considerable empirical support for its basic conclusions (Leibenstein 1974).

Briefly stated, as shown in Figure 12.4, the theory of the demographic transition is a generalization advanced to explain the transitional stages of fertility and mortality for a nation over time, as it modernizes. The claim of the demographic transition theory, that as nations develop they eventually reach a point where the birthrate falls, is relevant for our purpose. In other words, in the long-run industrialization is accompanied by a sustained reduction in population growth.

However, this theory does not suggest that there is no cross-country variation in the timing and speed of the demographic transition (Doepke 2004). It simply attempts to ascertain that the economic transition from pre-industrial stagnation to modern growth was accompanied by a demographic transition from high to low fertility. One important implication of this theory is, of course, that industrialization (which is generally associated with increased GDP) is a possible solution to the population problem (Leibenstein 1974). Why so?

First, industrialization implies a shift from an economy that is primarily based on agriculture (which is labor-intensive) to one based on industry (which is capital-intensive). This structural change in the economy increasingly reduces the productivity (hence, the income-generating capacity) of children in the agricultural sector. Furthermore, as often occurs with industrialization and modernization, child labor laws are instituted as a sign of social progress (Doepke 2004; Doepke and Zilibotti 2005). The combined effect of these two factors reduces parental desire to have more children to supplement the household income.

Second, since industrialization is often associated with an increase in the average per capita income of a nation, the increasing affluence of the average family in the course of industrialization reduces the desire for more children. This is because the need for having children as a hedge for security in old age becomes less and less important as families become increasingly wealthy (Caldwell 1976). In addition, this tendency for smaller family size will be reinforced because industrialization is generally associated with declining infant and child mortality. Advances in medicine, public health and hygiene in modernized societies have enabled mortality decline.

Finally, other socioeconomic factors associated with modernization further contribute to a decline in fertility rates. Among them are the rise in the education of women, urbanization and its secularizing influence, the increasing participation of females in traditionally male-dominated sectors of the economy, advances in birth-control methods and family planning.

---

standard of living. In recent years, arguments have been made to suggest that the rise in the demand for human capital is a key factor in explaining a decline in the fertility rate. In this respect, fertility decisions cannot be fully understood without good knowledge of what induces parents to invest in the human capital of their offspring.

To economists, this careful examination of decision-making at the micro (or household) level is extremely significant, not just because it provides alternative explanations to fertility decline, but because it also helps uncover the determinants of fertility decline that

are essential in designing effective population-control policies. As a result, economists have sought alternative theories to explain fertility decline that focus on the cost of children and the formation of human capital, which are discussed below.

Cost of children, human capital, fertility and economic growth

A. Cost of children

Becker (1960), relying on basic microeconomic theory of consumers' choice, set out to explain how parents make decisions about childbearing, and how this choice is influenced by the family's income and the cost of raising children. The economic analysis begins by viewing children as *durable* consumption goods (Becker 1960; Blake 1968).

Children are classified as consumption goods because they provide direct psychic utilities to their parents. There are three basic sources of benefits (utilities) that parents can expect from having a child: (1) consumption or psychic utility—a child is wanted for her- or himself rather than for services or income she or he may provide; (2) work or income utility; and (3) security or old-age benefit. However, it is important to note that the utility derived from (1) and (2) is expected to decline as household income rises.

On the other hand, the costs, or disutility, of having children are composed of the following two broad categories: (1) the direct costs of providing necessities such as food, housing, clothing, and basic education; and (2) the indirect costs of raising children, such as opportunities forgone by parents in terms of time and money (Becker 1960; Becker and Murphy 1990; Leibenstein 1974).

With this identification of the costs and benefits of having children, and on the premise that human fertility decisions are made primarily on a rational basis, the microeconomics theory of fertility gives an explanation for a seemingly negative relationship between household income and family size. This is paradoxical because the theory suggests that children are *inferior* consumption goods (i.e., higher household income leads to a decline in fertility, thereby leading to fewer children).

However, what actually happens is this: as income increases, parents start to desire fewer children but of *superior* quality (well nourished, clothed and highly educated). In other words, increased income allows parents to choose both the quality as well as the quantity of their children, with a stronger emphasis on quality as income increases. Thus, increases in family income *per se* do not drive the desire for fewer children. Instead, it is the increased *cost* of raising high quality children, that is prompted by the increase in parents' income, which ultimately precipitates the decline in fertility (i.e., the choice to have fewer

children). The income effect (which, holding other things constant, would have allowed households' to have more children) is more than offset by the price (cost) effect (which is a result of the deliberate decision made by parents to substitute quality for quantity of children). Consequently, the net effect of increases in parental income will be a decline in fertility (i.e., number of children).

B. The rise in the demand for human capital

In this particular instance, the basic argument recognizes a link between investment in human capital, economic growth and fertility. Human capital is defined here as embodied knowledge and skills that are generally acquired through education and experience. Empirical observation would suggest that countries grow more rapidly when education and other skills are more abundant (Denison 1985). Furthermore, it appears that where human capital is low fertility tends to be high, and vice versa (Becker and Murphy 1990). What explanations can be provided to understand these linkages between investment in human capital, fertility and economic (income) growth?

As discussed throughout this chapter, over the past 150 years the rate of technological progress has been accelerating (Ausubel 1996). This has lead to an increase in the demand for both human and physical capital. Furthermore, Becker and Murphy (1990: S13) argue that

> the rates of return on investment in human capital rise rather than decline as the stock of human capital increases, at least until the stock becomes large. The reason is that education and other sectors that produce human capital use educated and other skilled inputs more intensively than sectors that produce consumption goods and physical capital.

This scenario implies a monotonically increasing rate of return on human capital which, holding other factors constant, will have the effect of inducing parents to invest in the human capital of their off-spring. Thus, in advanced economies where technological progress is the mainstay and the rate of return on human capital is high, parents will gravitate towards allocating more resources for the quality (i.e., human capital formation) of their child. Conversely, higher stocks of capital reduce the demand for children because, as argued earlier, it increases the cost of raising a child. Thus, fertility tends to be low where human capital is widespread and perhaps growing over time (Ibid). In a developed economy, therefore, one is likely to observe a decline in population growth along with a further increases in human capital accumulation (Becker and Murphy 1990; Doepke 2004).

Increase in the demand for human capital has also been instrumental in closing the gender gap during the past century. An economy characterized by high technological progress and human capital accumulation is necessarily favorable to education-intensive tasks. Unlike physically-intensive tasks, women are in a favorable position to compete with men in mentally-intensive and/or less physically demanding tasks, which ultimately has the effect of weakening the traditional division of labor between the sexes. Thus, during the normal progress of growing from an industrial to a service economy, the wage differential between men and women tends to decline (Galor and Weil 1996). An increase in the relative wage rates of women not only induces an increase in labor force participation, but also increases the opportunity costs of a mother if having an additional child entails taking an extended period of time off work. Since accounting for mothers' opportunity costs further increases the cost of child rearing, such an increase ultimately induces a decline in fertility.

Policy implications

The above discussions suggest that a country can use economic incentives to control the rate of its population growth in a variety of ways. Once the determinants of demand for children are known (such as the costs of education, opportunity costs for mothers, the costs of health care, pensions and other retire-ment plans, and so on), policy measures can be formulated to trigger desirable change(s) in the demand schedules for children. However, this should be approached with caution, for reasons that will be explained below.

The discussion of population control through economic incentives is based on the general premise that human fertility decisions are made primarily on a purely *rational* basis. Furthermore, the underlying motive of the individual family is to promote its self-interest, thereby maximizing the *net* benefits from having children (Becker 1960). However, under normal circumstances not all the costs of children are *fully* borne by parents. Education in public-sector schools is almost universally free. In many countries food is subsidized by holding prices below market levels. Even in cases where education and food subsidies are financed through tax revenues, the individual household will not have an incentive to reduce its family size, because normally tax is not based on the number of children. Clearly, then, since not all costs are borne by parents, the private costs for raising children will be less than the social costs (Blake 1968). What this suggests is the presence of some form of *externalities*. As discussed in Chapter 3, in the presence of externalities, decisions reached by individual actors will not lead to the 'best' or optimal outcome for society at large.

Of course, this recognition that *real* externalities are involved in the parents' decisions concerning childbearing underscores the need for adopting a population-control policy. Unfortunately, for reasons that will be evident in Chapter 16, most countries in the developing world (where the population problem appears to be pressing and formidable) lack the institutional structures, political systems and economic resources that are necessary to effectively correct both market and government failures. Until these social infrastructural problems are adequately addressed, the use of economic incentives to control population will continue to be inadequate and, hence, ineffective.

However, the situation will be even worse if the alternatives are *laissez-faire* policies toward reproduction, since these would surely confront society

281

with a ruinous problem of overpopulation. Or, to use Hardin's (1968: 1244) words 'ruin is the destination toward which all men rush, each pursuing his own best interest in a society that believes in the freedom of the commons. Freedom in commons brings ruin to all'. This observation should not be taken lightly, given that the right to bear children is a universally held and UN-sanctioned inalienable human right.

12.5 CHAPTER SUMMARY

In this chapter, we examined the neoclassical perspective of 'biophysical limits' to economic growth. What we have observed is that biophysical limits are treated as nothing more than a generalized resource scarcity problem. According to this worldview, population, environmental degradation and resource depletion problems can be solved through normal (and if needs be through artificial) market mechanisms.

Furthermore, concern for impending biophysical limits need not suggest applying a brake to the pace of economic growth (as measured by increases in per capita income). To the contrary, to alleviate the stresses of population and environmental pollution on the global ecosystem, what is needed is increased economic growth. The conventional wisdom in economics is, therefore, that *limits to growth are more likely to arise due to social and technological failures than environmental or biophysical limits*. This is dramatically different, as discussed in the last chapter, from the perspectives Malthusians hold on this same subject.

We discussed the neoclassical economic perspective on 'general' resource scarcity and its implications for the long-term material well being of humanity. Neoclassical economists do not reject outright the notion that natural resources are *finite*. However, unlike the Malthusians, they do not believe that this fact implies that economic growth is limited. Neoclassical economists uphold this position for five reasons:

1. They believe that technology—by finding substitutes through the discovery of new resources, and by increasing the efficiency of resource utilization—has almost no bounds in ameliorating natural resource scarcity.
2. They differentiate between 'general' and 'specific' natural resource scarcity. To them, general or absolute scarcity (that is, the awareness that there is 'only one earth' and that it is a closed system with regard to its material needs) is tautological and, therefore, irrelevant. What is relevant is scarcity of specific resources, or relative scarcity.
3. However, relative scarcity does not limit growth, due to the possibility of factor substitution.
4. In sharp contrast to the Malthusians, neoclassicists believe that economic growth, through increases in per capita income and improvements in technology, provides solutions to both environmental and population problems. In other words, the solution to environmental and population problems is increased economic growth.
4. They also believe in the effectiveness of the market system to provide signals of emerging resource scarcity in a timely fashion. Price distortions arising from externalities simply require a minor fine-tuning of the market.

Given that societal resources are allocated by smoothly functioning and forward-looking markets, the key resource for continued human material progress is knowledge. It is through knowledge that human technological progress (a necessary ingredient for circumventing biophysical limits) will be sustained indefinitely. The growth of human knowledge is not subjected to any known physical laws.

Thus, the best inheritance to leave to posterity is knowledge in the form of education (stored information about past discoveries) and human-made capital (which has stored knowledge embedded in it). This would raise no problem because of the belief that human-made capital (roads, factories, and so on) and natural capital (forest, coal deposits, wilderness, etc.) are substitutes. Much human progress, especially during the past two centuries, has stemmed from the substitution of human-made capital for natural capital.

According to the neoclassical growth paradigm, this process will continue into the future, as long as the pace of technological growth follows the trend of recent centuries. Given the evidence of the past two centuries, the expectation is for a brighter future. Furthermore, this prognosis is independent of the fact that natural resources are finite.

According to its most ardent critics, the biggest weakness of the neoclassical economic worldview is its assertion of unabated economic growth as extrapolated from past trends. Most importantly, critics argue, past trends of technological growth cannot predict that the same trend will continue in the future; in fact, there are good reasons to suggest that the pace of technological progress may decrease. Another major criticism of the neoclassical view on biophysical limits is its outright denial (or lack of consideration) about the effect of an infinitely growing human economy on the biosphere. Neoclassical economics asserts that the human economy can grow without ever transgressing its ecological bounds. The question of *scale* is not addressed at all.

REVIEW AND DISCUSSION QUESTIONS

1. Briefly identify the following concepts: absolute scarcity, relative scarcity, material balance approach to pollution, extractive resources, real cost, the strong hypotheses of increasing natural resource scarcity, the environmental Kuznets curve, the theory of demographic transition.

2. Provide a list of what you consider to be the three most important features of the neoclassical perspective of biophysical limits. Why are they important?

3. Read the following statements. In response, state 'True', 'False' or 'Uncertain' and explain why:

    (a) Since resources have substitutes, 'nature imposes particular scarcities, not an inescapable general scarcity'.

    (b) Improved social and economic status for women is the key to controlling population growth.

    (c) Countries with a raising EKC are, by definition, underdeveloped.

4. Provide three factors that contribute to each of the following situations:

    (a) The declining portion of the EKC.

    (b) The rising portion of the EKC.

    (c) The high rate of population growth at the beginning of Stage II of the Demographic Transition

5. 'The major constraint upon the human capacity to enjoy unlimited minerals, energy, and other raw materials at acceptable price is *knowledge*. And the source of knowledge is the human mind. Ultimately, then, the key constraint is human imagination acting together with educated skills. This is why an increase in human beings, along with causing additional consumption of resources, constitutes a crucial addition to the stock of natural resources' (Simon 1996: 408). Write a critical comment.

6. Studies of long-running natural resource scarcity trends of the B&M variety are primarily criticized for the following reasons: (a) they fail to explicitly consider environmental quality concerns; and (b) they fail to account for the substitution of high-quality energy resources for labor and capital that has been taking place in the extraction sectors. Are these valid criticisms? Explain.

7. The conventional wisdom in economics holds that limits to growth are more likely to arise due to social and technological failures than environmental or biophysical limits. Comment.

8. What possible implication(s) can you draw from the following empirical findings:

    (a) An N-shaped EKC for energy consumption in high income countries.

    (b) A monotonically increasing EKC for CO_2 emission.

    (c) A U-shaped EKC for deforestation on the Indian subcontinent.

    (d) A monotonically declining EKC for water-borne pathogens in Africa.

9. *Laissez-faire* policies in reproduction would surely confront society with a ruinous problem of overpopulation. Evaluate.

10. Continued economic growth is the panacea for both the population and the environmental problems. Provide a critical evaluation of this assertion.

REFERENCES AND FURTHER READING

Antweiler, W., Copeland, B. R., Taylor, M. S. (2001) 'Is Free Trade Good for the Environment?' *American Economic Review* 91, 4:877–908.

Ausubel, J. H. (1996) 'Can Technology Spare the Earth?' *American Scientist* 84: 166–77.

Ayres, U. R. and Kneese, V. A. (1969) 'Production, Consumption and Externalities', *American Economic Review*, 59, 3: 282–97.

Barnett, H. J. (1979) 'Scarcity and Growth Revisited', in K. V. Smith (ed.) *Scarcity and Growth Reconsidered*, Baltimore, MD: Johns Hopkins University Press.

Barnett, H. J. and Morse, C. (1963) *Scarcity and Growth: The Economics of Natural Resource Availability*, Baltimore, MD: Johns Hopkins University Press.

Barnett, H. J., van Muiswinkel, G. M. and Schechter, M. (1982) 'Are Minerals Costing More?' *Resource Management Optimization* 2: 121–48.

Becker, G. (1960) 'An Economic Analysis of Fertility', in National Bureau of Economic Research, *Demographic and Economic Changes in Developing Countries*, Princeton, NJ: Princeton University Press.

Becker, G. and Murphy, K. M. (1990) 'Human Capital, Fertility, and Economic Growth', *Journal of Political Economy* 98, 5: 12–36.

Bhagawati, J. (1993) 'The Case for Free Trade', *Scientific American* 269: 42–9.

Bhattarai, M. and Hammig, M. (2001) 'Institutions and the Environmental Kuznets Curve for Deforestation: A Cross-country Analysis for Latin America, Africa, and Asia', *World Development* 29, 6: 995–1010.

Blake, J. (1968) 'Are Babies Consumer Durables? A Critique of the Economic Theory of Reproductive Motivation', *Population Studies* 22, 1: 5–25.

Brown, G., Jr. and Field, B. (1979) 'The Adequacy of Measures of Signaling the Scarcity of Natural Resources', in K. V. Smith (ed.) *Scarcity and Growth Reconsidered*, Baltimore, MD: Johns Hopkins University Press.

Bulte, E. H., van Soest, D. P. (2001) 'Environmental Degradation in Developing Countries: Households and the (Reverse) Environmental Kuznets Curve', *Journal of Development Economics* 65: 225–35.

Caldwell, J. C. (1976) 'Toward a Restatement of Demographic Transition Theory', *Population and Development Review* 2: 321–66.

Carson, R. T., Yongil, J. and McCubbin, D. R, (1997) 'The Relationship Between Air Pollution and Income: U.S. Data', *Environmental and Development Economics* 2, 4: 433–50.

Cleveland, C. J. (1991) 'Natural Resource Scarcity and Economic Growth Revisited: Economic and Biophysical Perspective', in R. Costanza (ed.) *Ecological Economics: The Science and Management of Sustainability*, New York: Columbia University Press.

—— (1993) 'An Exploration of Alternative Measures of Natural Resource Scarcity: The Case of Petroleum Resources in the U.S.', *Ecological Economics* 7: 123–57.

Cole, H. S. D., Freeman, C., Jahoda, M. and Pavitt, K. L. R. (1973) *Models of Doom: A Critique of the Limits to Growth*, New York: Universe Books.

Cole, M. A. (2000) 'Air Pollution and "Dirty" Industries: How and Why Does the Composition of Manufacturing Output Change with Economic Development?', *Environmental and Resource Economics* 17: 109–23.

—— (2004) 'Trade, the Pollution Haven Hypothesis and Environmental Kuznets Curve: Examining the Linkages', *Ecological Economics* 48: 71–81.

Cole, M. A., Rayner, Y. and McCubbin, D. R. (1997) 'The Environmental Kuznets Curve: An Empirical Analysis', *Environment and Development Economics* 2, 4: 401–16.

Council on Environmental Quality and Department of State (1980) *The Global 2000 Report to the President: Entering the Twenty-first Century,* Washington, DC: US Government Printing Office.

Dasgupta, P. S. and Heal, G. M. (1979) *Economic Theory and Exhaustible Resources,* Cambridge: Cambridge University Press.

Davidson, C. (2000) 'Economic Growth and the Environment: Alternatives to the Limits Paradigm', *BioScience* 50, 4: 433–9.

De Bruyn, S. M. and Opschoor, J. B. (1997) 'Developments in the Throughput–Income Relationship: Theoretical and Empirical Observation', *Ecological Economics* 20: 255–68.

Denison, E. F. (1985) *Trends in American Economics Growth, 1929–1982,* Washington, DC: Brookings Institute.

Dinda, S. (2004) 'Environmental Kuznets Curve Hypothesis: A Survey', *Ecological Economics* 49: 431–55.

Doepke, M. (2004) 'Accounting for Fertility Decline During the Transition to Growth', *Journal of Economic Growth* 9: 347–83.

Doepke, M. and Zilibotti, F. (2005) 'The Macroeconomics of Child Labor Regulation', *American Economic Review* 95, 5: 1492–524.

Ekins, P. (1997) 'The Kuznets Curve for the Environment and Economic Growth: Examining the Evidence', *Environmental Policy and Planning A* 29: 805–30.

—— (2000) *Economic Growth and Environmental Sustainability,* London: Routledge.

Eskeland, G. S. and Harrison, A. E. (2003) 'Moving to Greener Pasture? Multinationals and the Pollution Haven Hypothesis', *Journal of Development Economics* 70, 1: 1–23.

Galeotti, M., Lanza, A. and Pauli, F. (2006) 'Reassessing the Environmental Kuznets Curve for CO_2 Emissions: A Robustness Exercise', *Ecological Economics* 57: 152–63.

Galor, O. and Weil, D. N. (1996) 'The Gender Gap, Fertility, and Growth', *American Economic Review* 86: 374–87.

Goeller, H. E. and Weinberg, A. M. (1976) 'The Age of Substitutability: What Do We Do When the Mercury Runs Out?' *Science* 191: 683–9.

Goklany, I. M. (1999) *Clearing the Air: The Real Story of the War on Air Pollution,* Washington, DC: Cato Institute.

Grossman, G. M. and Krueger, A. B. (1991) 'Environmental Impacts of a North American Free Trade Agreement', *Discussion Paper 158,* Princeton, NJ: Woodrow Wilson School, Princeton University.

Grossman, G. M. and Krueger, A. B. (1995) 'Economic Growth and the Environment', *Quarterly Journal of Economics* 110: 353–77.

Hall, D. C. and Hall, J. V. (1984) 'Concepts and Measures of Natural Resource Scarcity with a Summary of Recent Trends', *Journal of Environmental Economics and Management* 11: 363–79.

Harbaugh, W., Levinson, A. and Wilson, D. (2002) 'Reexamining the Empirical Evidence for an Environmental Kuznets Curve', *The Review of Economics and Statistics* 84, 3: 541–51.

Hardin, G. (1968) 'The Tragedy of the Commons', *Science* 162: 1243–8.

Hettige, H., Mani, M. and Wheeler, D. (2000) 'Industrial Pollution in Economic Development: The Environmental Kuznets Curve Revisited', *Journal of Development Economics* 62: 445–76.

Holtz-Eakin, D. and Selden, T. M. (1995) 'Stoking the Fires? CO_2 Emissions and Economic Growth', *Journal of Public Economics* 57: 85–101.

Horvath, R. J. (1997) 'Energy Consumption and the Environmental Kuznets Curve Debate', *Mimeo,* Sydney: Department of Geography, University of Sydney, Australia.

Hotelling, H. (1931) 'The Economics of Exhaustible Resources', *Journal of Political Economy* 39: 137–75.

Huang W. M., Lee, G. W. M. and Wu, C. C. (2008) 'GHG Emissions, GDP Growth and the Kyoto Protocol: A Revisit of Environmental Kuznets Curve Hypothesis', *Energy Policy* 36: 239–47.

Johnson, M. and Bennett, J. T. (1980) 'Increasing Resource Scarcity: Further Evidence', *Quarterly Review of Economics and Business* 20: 42–8.

Johnson, M., Bell, F. and Bennett, J. (1980) 'Natural Resource Scarcity: Empirical Evidence and Public Policy', *Journal of Economic and Environmental Management* 7: 256–71.

Koop, G. and Tole, L. (1999) 'Is There an Environmental Kuznets Curve for Deforestation?' *Journal of Development Economics* 58: 231–44.

Kristrom, B. and Riera, P. (1996) 'Is the Income Elasticity of Environmental Improvement Less than One?' *Environmental and Resource Economics* 7, 45–55.

Kuznets, S. (1955) 'Economic Growth and Income Inequality', *American Economic Review* 45: 1–28.

Leibenstein, H. (1974) 'An Interpretation of the Economic Theory of Fertility: Promising Path or Blind Alley?' *Journal of Economic Literature* 22: 457–79.

Lieb, C. M. (2003) 'The Environmental Kuznets Curve: A Survey of the Empirical Evidence and of Possible Causes', *Discussion Paper Series 391*, University of Heidelberg, Department of Economics, Bern: Switzerland: 1–56.

List, J. A. and Gallet, C. A. (1999) 'The Environmental Kuznets Curve: Does One Size Fit All?' *Ecological Economics* 31: 409–23.

Lomborg, B. (2001) *The Skeptical Environmentalist*, Cambridge: Cambridge University Press.

Lopez, R. and Mitra, S. (2000) 'Corruption, Pollution, and the Kuznets Environmental Curve', *Journal of Environmental Economics and Management* 40: 137–50.

McConnell, K. E. (1997) 'Income and the Demand for Environmental Quality', *Environment and Development Economics* 2: 383–99.

Meadows, D. H., Meadows, D. L. Randers, J. and Behrens, W. W., III (1974) *The Limits to Growth: A Report for the Club of Rome's Project on the Predicament of Mankind*, 2nd edn., New York: Universe Books.

Moomaw, W. R. and Unruh, G. C. (1997) 'Are Environmental Kuznets Curves Misleading Us? The Case of CO_2 Emissions', *Environmental and Development Economics* 2, 4: 451–63.

Norgaard, R. B. (1990) 'Economic Indicators of Resource Scarcity: A Critical Essay', *Journal of Environmental Economics and Management* 19: 19–25.

Norton, S. (2002) 'Population Growth, Economic Freedom, and the Rule of Law', *PERC Policy Series*, PS-24, Bozman, MT: PERC.

Panayotou, T. (1995) 'Environmental Degradation at Different Stages of Economic Development', in A. Iftikhar and J.A. Doeleman (eds.) *Beyond Rio: The Environmental Crisis and Sustainable Livelihoods in the Third World*, ILO Study Series, New York: St. Martin's Press: 13–36.

—— (1997) 'Demystifying the Environmental Kuznets Curve: Turning a Black Box into a Policy Tool', *Environment and Development Economics* 2: 465–84.

Pezzes, J. (1989) 'Economic Analysis of Sustainable Growth and Sustainable Development', *Environment Department Working Paper 15*, Washington, DC: World Bank.

Pigou, C. A. (1932) *The Economics of Welfare*. 4th edn., London: Macmillan. (The first edition appeared in 1920.)

Potter, N. and Christy, F.T., Jr. (1962) *Trends in Natural Resource Commodities: Statistics of Prices, Output, Consumption, Foreign Trade and Employment in the United States, 1870-1957*, Baltimore, MD: Johns Hopkins University Press.

Roberts, J.T. and Grimes, P. E. (1997) 'Carbon Intensity and Economic Development 1962–91: A Brief Exploration of the Environmental Kuznets Curve', *World Development* 25, 2: 191–8.

Rosenberg, N. (1973) 'Innovative Responses to Materials Shortages', *American Economic Review* 63: 111–18.

Rothman, D. S. and de Bruyn, S. M. (1998) 'Probing into the Environmental Kuznets Curve Hypothesis', *Ecological Economics* 25: 143–5.

Selden, T. and Song, D. (1994) 'Environmental Quality and Development: Is there a Kuznets Curve for Air Pollution Emission?' *Journal of Environmental Economics and Management* 27: 147–62.

Shafik, N. (1994) 'Economic Development and Environmental Quality: An Econometric Analysis', *Oxford Economic Papers* 46: 757–73.

Shafik, N. and Bandyopadhyay, S. (1992) *Economic Growth and Environmental Quality: Time Series and Cross-Country Evidence*, World Bank Policy Research Paper WPS 904, Washington, DC: World Bank.

Simon, J. L. (1980) 'Resources, Population, Environment: An Oversupply of False Bad News', *Science* 208: 1431–7.

—— (1981) *The Ultimate Resource*, Princeton, NJ: Princeton University Press.

—— (1994) 'Post-debate Statement', in N. Myers and J. L. Simon (eds.) *Scarcity or Abundance? A Debate on the Environment*, New York: W.W. Norton.

—— (1996) *The Ultimate Resource 2*, Princeton, NJ: Princeton University Press.

Simon, J. L. and Kahn, H. (1984) *The Resourceful Earth: A Response to Global 2000*, Oxford: Basil Blackwell.

Simpson D. R., Toman, M. A. and Ayres, R. U. (2005) *Scarcity and Growth Revisited: Natural Resources and the Environment in the New Millennium*, Washington, DC: Resources for the Future.

Smith, K. V. (1978) 'Measuring Natural Resource Scarcity: Theory and Practice', *Journal of Environmental and Economic Management* 5: 150–71.

—— (1979) 'Natural Resource Scarcity: A Statistical Analysis', *Review of Economic Statistics* 61: 423–7.

—— (1981) 'Increasing Resource Scarcity: Another Perspective', *Quarterly Review of Economics and Business* 21: 120–5.

Solow, R. M. (1974) 'The Economics of Resources or the Resources of Economics', *American Economic Review* 24: 1–14.

Stern, D. (2004) 'The Rise and Fall of the Environmental Kuznets Curve', *World Development* 32, 8: 1429–39.

Stern, D. and Common, M. S. (2001) 'Is There an Environmental Kuznets Curve for Sulfur', *Journal of Environmental and Economic Management* 41, 2: 162–78.

Torras, M. and Boyce, J. K. (1998) 'Income, Inequality, and Pollution: A Reassessment of the Environmental Kuznets Curve', *Ecological Economics* 25: 147–60.

Vincent, J.R. (1997) 'Testing for Environmental Kuznets Curves within a Developing Country', *Environment and Development Economics* 2: 417–31.

Yandle, B., Vijayaraghavan, M. and Bhattarai, M. (2004) 'The Environmental Kuznets Curve: A Review of Findings, Methods, and Policy Implications', *PERC Research Study*, Montana: Property and Environment Research Center.

Chapter 13

The economics of sustainability

LEARNING OBJECTIVES

After reading this chapter you will be familiar with the following:

- The transition from the perennial debates on limits to growth to sustainability or sustainable economic development.
- The conceptual problem of defining sustainability and the Brundtland Report on sustainability (WCED 1987).
- The weak sustainability criteria: in theory and practice.
- The strong sustainability criteria: in theory and practice.
- The safe minimum standard (SMS) approach to sustainability: in theory and practice.

When the focus of the discussion is the environment and the economy on a global scale, 'sustainability', by definition, implies the existence of biophysical limits. Given this, the key issues addressed in this chapter are about the alternative paths society may follow in order to achieve economic development that is judged to be sustainable (lasting) and equitable. In this respect sustainability deals with concerns about intergenerational wellbeing, the sharing of resources involving several generations in an equitable manner. The emphasis of Chapter 13 is on the theoretical underpinnings of environmental sustainability in general.

13.1 INTRODUCTION: FROM 'LIMITS TO GROWTH' DEBATES TO SUSTAINABILITY

The old scarcity paradigm

In the last two chapters, the primary focus of the discussion has been on biophysical limits and the extent to which they can be viewed as constraints on economic growth. Currently, little controversy is present concerning the existence of biophysical limits to growth, provided the reference to such concern is confined to the mere recognition that nature's bounties have absolute limits, namely, that there is only one earth. Differences appear to emerge when the main point of the discussion pertains to the extent to which, and the circumstances under which, biophysical limits manifest themselves as independent forces capable of causing economic collapse.

For scholars of a Malthusian persuasion, biophysical limits not only exist, but also present themselves in various ways. Given this reality, if it is in the interests of humanity to avoid an economic calamity with lasting dire consequences, it is imperative that both the size of the human population and the use of material resources (including the life-support systems of the natural environment) should be maintained to such levels that the possibility of transgressing critically important biophysical limits (thresholds) will not ensue (Perrings 1991). According to this worldview, therefore, a scenario of catastrophic economic collapse cannot be ruled out. As discussed in Chapter 11, this so-called Malthusian perspective of 'scarcity and growth' is explained using concepts such as the law of diminishing returns, the first and second laws of thermodynamics, carrying capacity and ecological resilience (Ayres 1999; Ekins 1993; Perrings 1995).

On the other hand, for scholars from the neoclassical school of economic thought, biophysical limits have no practical significance if what they convey is confined to the mere fact that the earth is finite (or, materially, a closed system). In other words, it is tautological to say that resources are becoming increasingly scarce (and hence impairing economic growth) given that they are assumed to be available in a geologically fixed quantity while the population continues to grow.

Instead, it is argued, a good understanding of the association between biophysical limits and economic growth is gained when attention is placed on factor-substitution possibilities and the opportunities available for technological progress are explored (Solow 1974, 1993). When this is done, as discussed in Chapter 12, the very existence of biophysical limits *per se* are neither necessary nor sufficient conditions for predicting the fate of humanity's material progress.

The formal defenses for this so-called neoclassical worldview of 'scarcity and growth' are based on two factors: (1) the flexibility and resilience of human institutions, most importantly the market system; and (2) the claim that the growth of human knowledge is not subject to any known physical laws. According to this worldview, the scenario of perpetual economic growth cannot be ruled out.

The new scarcity paradigm: ecological resilience and biotic diversity

In the 1980s, scholarly debates on 'scarcity and growth' began to change in a significant way. As discussed in the last four chapters, it has become increasingly evident that both the scope and nature of environmental problems, as well as other problems related to natural resources, are changing in a rather dramatic manner. The problems are becoming not only serious, but global in their scope and far reaching (i.e., extending over several generations) in their impacts. The issues of concern were expressed using previously unfamiliar phrases, such as 'climate change', depletion of the 'ozone layer' in the upper atmosphere (more specifically the stratosphere), 'biodiversity loss', deforestation of tropical forests, and so on (Maler 2008; Pearce 2005).

What these problems have in common is the fact that they result from the use of 'global commons', which by their nature are externality ridden. Thus, their solutions demand, as discussed in Chapters 9 and 10, an unprecedented level of human wisdom and international cooperation. This, therefore, is the nature of the 'new scarcity' paradigm.

An important outcome of this emerging scarcity paradigm has been to redirect the nature of the 'old' scarcity and growth debates in a significant way. This is because economists from both the Malthusian and neoclassical camps appear to share common understandings about the nature and complexity of the constraints imposed by the 'new resource scarcity' view (Simpson et al. 2005).

Suddenly, academic papers appeared in many highly regarded mainstream economic journals and other publications on subject matters such as ecological resilience, endangered species, biodiversity loss, intergenerational equity, and so on. This research was reminiscent of the landmark papers produced by Siegfiel von Ciriacy-Wantrup (1952) and John V. Krutilla (1967) on the general topic of resource conservation. The works of these two eminent natural-resource economists were the first to deal with endangered species, irreversibility, biodiversity and resource conservation within the context of the mainstream economic paradigm.

It was Ciriacy-Wantrup who first introduced the concept of the 'safe minimum standard', which conveys the idea that a threshold exists for some ecological resources, below which loss is catastrophic (more on this later). Thus, this movement in the

1980s was a resurrection of interest in the general area of resource conservation, including the function of the environment as a life-support system. Was this development enough to change the neoclassical view of biophysical limits to growth?

Clearly, there were many prominent economists from within the neoclassical school, such as Nobel laureate Kenneth Arrow (Arrow et al. 1995) and the distinguished British economist Sir Partha Dasgupta (Dasgupta et al. 2000), who took the position that pursuing economic growth with no heed to its ill effects on the environment and future generations would be indefensible on both economic and ethical grounds.

To make their points, these economists were using concepts such as ecological resilience, biodiversity and even a possible decline in the rate of technological growth. What appeared to evolve within the mainstream economic profession was a growing interest in 'sustainable economic development'. To cope with the 'new scarcity', it became evident that economic and/or ecological calamity could be avoided only by pursuing patterns of economic growth that would be sustainable into the indefinite future (Freedman et al. 2000). As will be discussed shortly, neoclassical economists have been able to develop a theoretical framework for the sustainable use of resources (i.e., weak sustainability) that is consistent with their worldview on resource scarcity, technology and social institutions (Hartwick 1978; Solow 1986).

It was also around the mid-1980s that ecological economics started to gain popularity and widespread acceptance within the economics profession. As discussed in Chapter 11 and Appendix B, the contributions of ecological economics in the conceptual development of sustainability have been far reaching in many respects (Daly 2007). This should not come as a surprise, given that the main focus of this particular academic discipline is to study the ecological (biophysical) and economic systems in an integrated and systematic manner.

The earliest attempt to construct a theoretical model of a sustainable economy with an explicit account of biophysical limits traces its roots to Herman Daly (1973), who published his ground-

breaking book *Towards a Steady-state Economy* about three decades ago. To be sure, Daly's conceptual model of the 'steady-state economy' (SSE) is not a totally new idea, since it shares common themes and concerns with John Stuart Mill's vision of a 'stationary state' of over a century ago. However, a vision is not the same as a model, and one of the distinguishing features of the SSE is its attempt to explicitly incorporate the biophysical and ethical conditions that are uniquely attributable to ecological economics (Daly 2007). In this respect, the SSE essentially laid out the groundwork for the theoretical framework of what is now known as the *strong* sustainability criteria—a subject that will be discussed later in greater detail.

The emergence of environmental sustainability as a global concern

Towards the end of the 1980s, interest in sustainability was not confined to the academic world. As discussed earlier, one of the lessons conveyed by the 'new scarcity' paradigm has been the recognition of the global dimensions of resource and environmental problems (such as climate change, biodiversity loss, depletion of the ozone layer, deforestation of tropical forests, etc.) and the tremendous policy challenges they imply.

Given this situation, there arose an urgent need for the global community to address these new challenges. It was with this in mind that, in 1982, the World Commission on Environment and Development, a United Nations agency, commissioned a study on the subject of sustainable development (SD). This culminated five years later in the publication of the Brundtland Commission Report (named after the Chair of the Commission, Gro Brundtland, then Norwegian Prime Minster), *Our Common Future*.

Overall, this report was about the goals and aspirations that global society needed to use as a guide in order to pursue sustainable and equitable economic development projects at both the national and global levels. Furthermore, this report attempted to define sustainable development as *development which meets the needs of the present without sacrificing the ability of the future to meet its needs*. This definition is not only well known, but is, in many instances, accepted as the standard definition of SD. Later in this chapter, we will observe to what extent this definition is consistent with the theoretical frameworks for sustainability developed by followers of the neoclassical and ecological schools of economics: namely, the *weak* and *strong* sustainability criteria.

This section has offered a brief discussion on how the interest in SD evolved over the past three decades in both the academic and policy arenas. This development appeared to have the effect of bridging differences in the traditional debates between Malthusian and neoclassical economists. This was done by emphasizing sustainability, and by so doing the focus of attention was no longer on 'running out' of resources (as Malthusians often do) or on 'declining resource scarcity' with a passage of time (as neoclassical economists believe). That is, what sustainability conveys is neither a gloomy nor rosy picture about the wellbeing of humanity in the distant future, but a hopeful one. However, as will be evident from the discussion in this chapter and the next, the realization of this 'hope' is confronted with many conceptual and operational challenges (Ekins 1993; Howarth 1997).

The rest of the chapter is organized in the following way. In the next section, an attempt will be made to clarify the definition of sustainability. In Section 13.3 the neoclassical model of sustainability, *weak sustainability*, will be discussed. This will be followed in Section 13.4 by a discussion of the ecological economics approach to sustainability, that is, *strong sustainability*. Section 13.5 deals with the *safe minimum standard* (SMS) approach to sustainability. As will be evident from the discussion in this section, the SMS is a special case of the neoclassical approach to sustainability. At the same time, it contains an element that is consistent with the ecological economic approach to sustainability. The last section summarizes the chapter.

13.2 SUSTAINABLE DEVELOPMENT: HELPFUL TERM OR VAGUE AND ANALYTICALLY EMPTY CONCEPT?

Since the early 1980s, the term sustainable development (SD) has been used widely but without much

effort being made to explain what it actually entails. For example, is SD the same thing as sustainable economic growth? To what ends should sustainability be pursued? Should sustainability be perceived as an economic or a moral imperative, or both? Furthermore, what are the nature of the resource constraints and tradeoffs that have to be recognized in any consideration of sustainability?

The above questions are raised to indicate the possibility that the phrase 'sustainable development' could be used in many different contexts with the possibility of being rendered a vague and misleading concept (Pezzey and Toman 2005). It was with this in mind that the World Commission on Environment and Development (WCED), a United Nations agency, commissioned a study on the subject of SD. As discussed earlier, the WCED published a report in 1987 known as the Brundtland Report, which defined SD as '*development which meets the needs of the present without sacrificing the ability of the future to meet its needs*'.

There are several key features of the above definition worth pointing out. First, the definition clearly establishes SD as an *equity* issue. As such, it conveys the idea that the economics of SD have, principally, a normative goal. Second, the Brundtland Report's definition of SD offers a specific ethical criterion: the needs of the present are not to be satisfied at the expense of future needs (wellbeing). It therefore deals with equity across generations—intergenerational equity. Third, the Brundtland Report, by emphasizing equity, raises a question concerning the validity of standard economic analysis that is based exclusively on efficiency.

Indeed, the Brundtland Report's definition of sustainability has been quite helpful in establishing a clear consensus that *SD is principally an ethical issue*. Yet a number of important features of SD that were implied by the questions raised at the beginning of this section are not *explicitly* captured by the Brundtland Report definition.

First, the Brundtland Report's definition of SD is not explicit about the physical and technological dimensions of the resource constraints required for sustainability (Pearce and Atkinson 1998). In other words, what is the specific nature of the resource constraints required for sustainability? Is human-made capital considered a substitute for, or a complement to, natural capital? What are the assumptions about the role of technology in ameliorating or circumventing resource scarcity? How should the various resource constraints be measured—that is, in physical or in monetary terms? Would this matter?

Second, it is not clear from the Brundtland Report definition what the term 'development' implies, or how it is (or should be) measured if it is going to be used as an indicator of intergenerational 'wellbeing'. Does development refer to the conventional conception of economic growth: an increase in the *quantity* of goods and services? Or does it refer to the kind of *qualitative* economic growth that includes goods and services that are not traded in the market but are important for gauging quality of life, such as leisure, friendship, environmental stewardship, and so on? Is development measured using the conventional national accounting system (GDP)? Does it matter how the depreciation of human and natural capital stocks are maintained or replaced?

Third, the Brundtland Report definition does not make clear the *exact nature of the tradeoff between equity and efficiency*. The report simply emphasizes the importance of equity in any consideration of SD. This is clearly a departure from economic analyses that are based on the premise of the neoclassical economic paradigm (Solow 1993), but does this mean that the efficiency consideration is irrelevant?

Figure 13.1 is used to illustrate the significance of this question. This figure is constructed assuming a number of simplifying conditions. The curve represents a production possibility frontier measured in terms of GNP—the monetary value of all goods and services produced by a country in a given year. This production possibility frontier is constructed for given tastes, technologies and resource endowments across two generations. It also assumes that market prices reflect 'true' scarcity values, and that markets exist for all goods and services.

What can be said about the tradeoff between efficiency and equity from Figure 13.1? Let us assume that our starting point is point G. Clearly, this point

is inefficient because it is located inside the production possibility frontier. A move to point J or I, or any point between these two, would lead to Pareto improved outcomes. That is, such a move would benefit at least one of the generations without affecting the wellbeing of the other generation. The discussion so far clearly suggests that efficiency (which is reflected by points along the production possibility frontier) can be relevant *even when the focus of attention is intergenerational equity*. This, of course, will be the case provided the economy is operating inefficiently to begin with—which is not necessarily an unusual situation.

On the other hand, what if a move was made from point G to H? Clearly, point H is efficient since it is on the production possibility frontier. But the move to point H makes the future generation worse off. Thus, equity considerations may preclude such a move. In this case, therefore, the point that needs to be stressed is this: *if equity is an important issue in considering SD, not all efficient points are desirable*.

The upshot of the above discussion is clear. Despite the gallant efforts of the Brundtland Report, it is very difficult, if not impossible, to define SD in ways

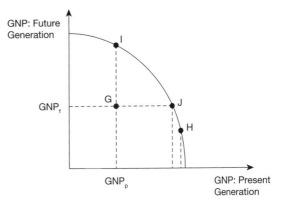

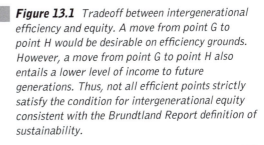

Figure 13.1 *Tradeoff between intergenerational efficiency and equity. A move from point G to point H would be desirable on efficiency grounds. However, a move from point G to point H also entails a lower level of income to future generations. Thus, not all efficient points strictly satisfy the condition for intergenerational equity consistent with the Brundtland Report definition of sustainability.*

293

that are both unambiguous and comprehensive enough to include all the attributes essential to a clear understanding of the full implication(s) of the concept (Pearce and Atkinson 1998). However, as indicated in the above discussions, the concept of SD has far-reaching implications that go beyond making a statement about the significance of intergenerational equity. These include careful considerations of the: exact nature of the resource (capital) constraints; technological options and their limits; economic efficiency; intergenerational equity; and aspects of human values and institutions consistent with SD. These are, indeed, the key issues that will be addressed as we move from the definition to the theoretical conceptualization of sustainability, which is the subject of the rest of this chapter.

13.3 THE NEOCLASSICAL APPROACH TO SUSTAINABILITY: WEAK SUSTAINABILITY

The neoclassical economics conception of sustainability starts with the idea that what is to be sustained is *income* to be used for the consumption of goods and services. Hence, in this respect, income and consumption are regarded as equivalent (more on this later). Income is then defined following the Hicksian tradition as *that amount which can be spent while keeping capital intact*. Or, using Hicks' own words (1946: 172): 'The purpose of income calculations in practical affairs is to give people an indication of the amount which they can consume without impoverishing themselves.' Justifying this definition, Hicks further stated that 'the practical purpose of income is to serve as a guide for prudent conduct, I think it is fairly clear that this is what the central meaning must be'. Accordingly, sustainability implies prudent conduct because to guard oneself from impoverishment requires the avoidance of overconsumption. Failure to do this would decrease capital assets for generating future income. Hence, *non-decreasing consumption can only be ensured by keeping capital intact at all time* (Ayres et al. 2001).

Thus, when viewed in a broader context, what Hicks has in mind is sustainable net (national) income: the amount that can be spent on a regular basis

without causing impoverishment in some future period. Note that this can only be achieved if the total capital stock of a nation is held at a constant level. But, how can we achieve this given that capital is a depreciable asset? This question suggests that *sustainable net income* is calculated after subtracting out the cost for capital consumption (i.e., depreciation), which is imputed to capture the declining income-generating potential of a capital asset over time. In other words, the depreciation allowance represents the level of investment necessary for a nation to maintain its productive capacity.

It is also important to note that a nation's capital portfolio generally includes several types of capital assets, for example, human-made and 'natural' capital stock. How are these two broadly defined categories of capital assets treated in conceptualizing sustainability? Are they considered substitutes, or complements? These are important questions with significant implications.

A defining characteristic of the neoclassical approach to sustainability is that human-made and natural capital assets are assumed to be *substitutes* (Solow 1993). This means that the costs of environmental deterioration (e.g., depleted oil fields) can be compensated by benefit from human-made capital (i.e., income). This is a critical assumption since it has the far-reaching implication of making natural capital a nonbinding constraint on sustainability.

This is because, as discussed in Chapters 1 and 12, if human-made and natural capital stocks are substitutes, the depletion of natural resources and large-scale degradation of environmental quality need not be a major source of concern. According to this view, SD simply requires the *maintenance* of a constant capital stock, but the *composition* of the capital stock is not, as such, relevant.

Primarily to stress this point, the neoclassical economics variation of sustainability is most commonly referred to as *weak sustainability*: weak in the sense that it does not render natural capital an absolute necessity for sustaining net national income (real consumption of goods and services) over an indefinite period. However, this by no means implies that the neoclassical model of sustainability excludes considerations of natural capital. In fact, conceptually, sustainability is generally seen by neoclassical economists as a problem of managing a nation's portfolio of capital to maintain a constant level (Ayres et al. 2001).

A very popular model that represents a special case of the neoclassical sustainability approach is the Hartwick–Solow model of sustainability (Hartwick 1977; Solow 1986). In this case, sustainability was conceptualized as a dynamic optimization where the objective was to trace the 'optimal' consumption path of goods and services that could be maintained over several generations, given that some of the capital assets are potentially *exhaustible*.

After conceptualizing the problem in this manner, Hartwick (1977) was able to generate a 'general' rule of sustainability criterion that still carries his name: the Hartwick sustainability rule. This rule states that maintaining a constant real consumption of goods and services, or real income (in the Hicksian sense), is possible *even in the presence of exhaustible resources*, provided that the rent (i.e., income) derived from an intertemporally efficient use of these resources is reinvested in renewable capital assets. Thus, the focus of concern is on the prudent use of the returns on, or savings of, exhaustible resources, rather than the depletion of these resources (see Exhibit 13.1— necessary reading for a clear understanding of the Hartwick sustainability rule).

EXHIBIT 13.1 WHAT WILL HAPPEN TO SAUDI ARABIA WHEN ITS OIL RESERVE ARE EXHAUSTED?

It is widely accepted that Saudi Arabia possesses the largest share of the total known petroleum reserves in the world. This is also a nation whose people depend solely on this one commodity for their livelihood. The revenue from petroleum exports accounts for a significant share of the country's GNP. This is because most of Saudi Arabia is desert and unsuitable for conventional agricultural pursuits. Furthermore, Saudi Arabia has an insignificant amount of mineral deposits apart from petroleum. There is therefore good reason for Saudi Arabia to be concerned about what happens when the petroleum is exhausted.

This is a fundamental concern that goes beyond Saudi Arabia. It pertains to the sustainability of an economy that depends solely on exhaustible mineral resources. If a fundamental concern of this nature is addressed within the context of the Hartwick–Solow sustainability approach, the following will be the course of action that Saudi Arabia may need to take in order to assure a reasonable standard of living for its citizens beyond the petroleum age.

First, the extraction rates of the country's petroleum deposits are determined in such a way as to maximize the present value of the rent from the intertemporal use of its total petroleum deposits. In general,

this intertemporally efficient use of resources is not consistent with maximizing current extraction rates, and as such dictates that certain principles of resource conservation be observed. Thus, Saudi Arabia cannot simply pump more oil at any price just to raise the standard of living of the current generation.

Second, sustainability requires that the rent derived from the current extraction of petroleum be reinvested into other forms of renewable capital assets. For example, in the case of Saudi Arabia, this may entail investing in large-scale water desalination projects. If successful, this may allow Saudi Arabia to irrigate its land and produce agricultural products in sufficient amounts to feed its people and even export on a sustainable basis. This is just one of the many options that Saudi Arabia has with regard to using an exhaustible resource, petroleum, without jeopardizing the wellbeing of its future citizens.

The clear message is that the people of Saudi Arabia can sustain a reasonable standard of living into the indefinite future provided they are able to use their rich deposits of petroleum efficiently at all times. Of course, this will not occur automatically or without some difficulty. It requires prudent long-term planning, self-discipline and astuteness in using the proceeds from oil.

In other words, the relevant issue is then whether 'adequate' compensatory investments are made to protect the interests of future generations. Strictly speaking, then, the Hartwick rule is more of a condition of intergenerational efficiency than for sustainability (Hamilton and Hartwick 2005).

At this point, it may be instructive to recap the essential features of weak sustainability and its implications:

1. This approach to sustainability maintains that it is possible to envision a situation in which a nation could maintain a *non-declining* income (consumption) over several generations, provided the productive capacity (i.e., capital stock) of the nation is held intact. This can be achieved provided that allowances for capital consumption are kept proportionate to the level of investment necessary for the country to maintain its productive capacity.
2. Weak sustainability allows a country to manage its portfolio of capital (which is composed of various types of human-made and natural capital stock) with a great deal of flexibility since the various types of capital stocks are considered to be close substitutes.
3. Because weak sustainability is formulated with the explicit assumption that human-made and natural capital are close substitutes, it suggests that a country could potentially deplete some of its natural resources (such as petroleum reserves), or harvest its renewable resources, at a rate faster than its natural regenerative capacity (such as forest products) and still maintain a constant flow of income year on year, provided the proceeds from these resources are reinvested in some form other than renewable resources or human-made capital stock.
4. A 'development' is said to be weakly sustainable if the development is non-diminishing from generation to generation. This condition is satisfied as long as net investment is equal to, or exceeds, zero across generations. This is the sort of intergenerational equity (or generational caring) implied by weak sustainability. All that is required from each generation is to ensure that

their actions do not compromise the productive capacity (capital stock) of the generations to follow. But the transfer of the capital stock can be in any form.

5. It is important to note that weak sustainability does not preclude a particular generation from gaining or making income if they happen to use their allotted capital stock in a more productive manner. Thus, if one should assume a steady technological growth-rate over time, the possibility exists that each succeeding generation will be richer than the previous one (Solow 1974).

What now remains is to briefly discuss some of the major criticisms of weak sustainability. First, weak sustainability uses income as a proxy for consumption. Furthermore, income and consumption are equated with utility or even social welfare (Ayres et al. 2001). However, if the welfare of society is the issue of concern, consumption would be the appropriate indicator of wellbeing (as measured by the grand utility function of a given society) rather than income (Daly 1996). Thus, in using income as proxy for consumption, the underlying preference function assumes that people are 'rational' (i.e., their preferences for goods and services are transitive, or ordered in consistent manner), and that these preferences are fixed and stable overtime.

Second, as discussed above, *intergenerational efficiency* (the focus of the Hartwick–Solow sustainability model) requires the prices of all goods and services (including environmental goods) to reflect their social values. However, the practical problems of arranging this are not explicitly addressed. In other words, price distortions due to environmental externalities are, or are assumed to be, remedied with little or no difficulty. Furthermore, the whole issue of 'valuation', that is, imputing the 'non-use values' of environmental services (such as the carbon sequestration of forest ecosystems) is simply ignored. As discussed in Chapter 7, imputing the non-use value of environmental services is an extremely arduous task, but essential if the 'total value' (i.e., use plus non-use values) of environmental resources is to be considered.

Third, although it is not stated explicitly, the neo-classical approach to sustainability does not rule out discounting. As discussed in Chapter 9, some economists and ecologists would argue that the very idea of positive discounting is wrong because it would allot a declining net income to future generations (Common and Perrings 1992). For this reason alone, they view the Hartwick–Solow sustainability model as being insufficiently concerned with the wellbeing of future generations and, as such, ethically questionable.

Fourth, weak sustainability is based on the assumption that the initial size of an economy (as measured by the size of the initial capital stock) is irrelevant, and what matters are only changes in the initial capital stock (Daly 1996). This suggests that the neoclassical approach to sustainability does not explicitly consider *scale*—the size of the existing human economy relative to natural ecosystems. For that matter, neoclassical models do not incorporate information about actual ecosystem structures (Ayres et al. 2001). To this extent, weak sustainability is incomplete in the sense that it only refers to *economic sustainability* or the sustainability of an economic system. However, the fact that the sustainability of an economic system may be linked with, or influenced by, the *ecological system* (of which the economic system is only a part) does not seem to be formally acknowledged by the neoclassical approach of sustainability.

Fifth, weak sustainability is specifically criticized for its inadequate treatment of the nature of the *uncertainty* associated with long-term natural resource assessment and management. It is not recognized that beyond a certain threshold the scale of human economic activities could cause *irreversible* damage to the natural environment or ecosystems (Perrings 1995). This could be a serious omission, possibly resulting in the irrevocable loss of systems that support human life or major reductions in the quality of human life (such as an increase in cancer diagnoses due to the depletion of ozone from the upper strata of the atmosphere). Uncertainty associated with irreversible environmental damage and its implications for long-term resource management will be the central theme of the discussion in Section 13.5, which deals with the safe minimum standard (SMS) approach to sustainability.

Finally, weak sustainability assumes that, overall, human-generated and natural capital assets are *substitutes*. As we observed in Chapter 11, this assumption has been a source of lively dispute between neoclassical and ecological economists. Ecological economists believe that, at the current level and pattern of human economic activity, it is more appropriate to view human and natural capital as complements, not substitutes (Costanza et al. 1997; Daly 1996). The implication of this assumption for sustainability is far-reaching, as illustrated by the experience of the small Pacific island nation of Nauru:

> In 1900 one of the world's richest phosphate deposits was discovered on Nauru and today, as result of just over ninety years of phosphate mining, about 80 percent of the island is totally devastated. At the same time, the people of Nauru have had, over the past several decades, a high per capita income. Income from phosphate mining enabled the Nauruans to establish a trust fund estimated to be as large as $1 billion. Interest from this trust fund should have insured a substantial and steady income and thus the economic sustainability of the island. Unfortunately, the Asian financial crisis, among other factors, has wiped out most of the trust fund. The people of Nauru now face a bleak future. Their island is biologically impoverished and the money Nauruans traded for their island home has vanished. The 'development' of Nauru followed the logic of weak sustainability, and shows clearly that weak sustainability may be consistent with a situation of near complete environmental devastation . . . [Thus] A substitution of natural for human-made capital may be one-way: once something is transformed into manufacturing capital there is no way to return to the original situation.
>
> (Ayres et al. 2001: 4)

13.4 THE ECOLOGICAL ECONOMICS APPROACH TO SUSTAINABILITY: STRONG SUBSTITUTABILITY

The ecological economics approach to sustainability begins with a worldview that the natural world is not only finite, but also non-growing and materially closed (see Chapters 2, 11 and Appendix B). Furthermore, it is postulated that the general capacity of this finite natural world is being put under strain by the size of the human economy, as measured by the aggregate use of throughput—low-entropic matter—energy (Boulding 1966; Common and Perrings 1992; Daly 1996). Proponents of this so-called 'full-worldview' insist that this new reality demands a shift in our vision of how the human economic system is related to the natural world. What has become increasingly evident is that 'economic growth' is unsustainable, especially if it is based on the increasing use of throughput from the natural ecosystem. Why is that so?

In the 'full-world' scenario, natural and human-made capitals can no longer be viewed as substitutes. In fact, a more realistic way to view the future relationship between these two components of capital is as *complements*. This suggests that a combination of both types of capital assets is needed in the production process. Thus, contrary to what has been suggested by the neoclassical approach to sustainability, an economy cannot continue to function without natural capital (i.e., natural resources are essential inputs in economic production).

Furthermore, it is expected that natural capital will be the limiting factor in the future. That is, fishing will be limited not by the number of fishing boats, but by the remaining fish population; petroleum use will be limited not by refining capacity, but by geologic deposits and by the atmospheric capacity to absorb CO_2 (Daly 2007; Dieren 1995). Most importantly, human-made capital (machines, buildings, etc.) cannot be substituted for scarce terrestrial energy without a limit. A certain minimum energy is required in any transformation of matter or performance of work (Ayres 1999; Georgescu-Roegen 1975). To that extent, then, natural capital is the key factor in any consideration of sustainability. *Strong*

sustainability is used to describe the ecological economics approach to sustainability because it insists on the presence of a certain minimum amount of natural capital at all times.

Accordingly, under the strong sustainability criteria, minimum amounts of both natural and human-made capital assets should be independently maintained in real physical/biological terms. This condition for sustainability clearly acknowledges that, as inputs of production, both natural and human-made capitals are complements.

Alternatively, the requirement for strong sustainability is stated in terms of the maintenance of a non-declining natural capital. This is done simply to stress the point that natural capital (i.e., deposits of minerals, soil, forest products, the ozone layer, coral reefs, and so on) are essential for the production of goods and services, the provision of environmental amenities, and for life-support.

In this respect, natural resources (i.e., natural capital) that are not market-priced are included in strong sustainability. This can be explained because, unlike weak sustainability, strong sustainability does not insist on valuation: the assessment of capital inputs in monetary terms so that tradeoffs can be considered. For strong sustainability, as mentioned above, it is sufficient to express the minimum and non-declining natural capital requirements in real physical/biological terms based on ecological principles and the laws of thermodynamics.

Thus, the *sustainability rules* of the ecological economics approach to sustainability (strong sustainability) are stated in the following manner:

1. The rate of exploitation of renewable resources should not exceed the regeneration rate.
2. Waste emission (pollution) should be kept at or below the waste-absorptive capacity of the environment. For the flow of degradable wastes, the rate of discharge should be less than the rate at which the ecosystem can absorb those wastes. For stock or persistent wastes (such as DDT, radioactive substances, etc.) the rates of discharges should be zero since the ecosystem has no capacity to absorb these wastes.

3. The extraction of nonrenewable resources (such as oil) should be consistent with the development of renewable substitutes. This is equivalent to the compensatory investment of the so-called Hartwick rule.

4. Certain ecosystems and environmental assets that are critical in providing unique and essential services (such as the ozone layer in the upper atmosphere or life-support in general), distinctive and irreplaceable non-use values (such as spotted owls, the Yellowstone National Park, and so on) should be preserved. More on this in the next section.

The rationale for maintaining a non-declining natural capital is based on ethical considerations, intergenerational equity in particular. In this respect, the 'ideal' amounts of the natural capital requirements may be kept at a level that would be adequate to ensure that, *at a minimum, future generations will be left no worse off than current generations.*

However, this is just one among several alternative ethical criteria that could be applied, to address the concern for intergenerational equity. Furthermore, unlike the neoclassical economics approach to sustainability, there is no pretention that the tradeoffs across generations will be efficient, that is, demonstrate intergenerational efficiency. This is because, as stated earlier, strong sustainability explicitly considers natural capital assets that have no directly observable or imputable market prices, hence there is no mechanism with which to formally assess tradeoffs (i.e., alternative choices).

Furthermore, the above ethical concern may be considered narrow to the extent that it tends to be human-centered or anthropocentric in its perspective. It is argued that *ecological sustainability needs to go beyond human interests.*

At least in principle, the ecological economics approach to sustainability includes concerns extending beyond the human species to the wellbeing of some other species and their life-support systems. In this respect, strong sustainability attempts to treat the economic subsystem and ecological systems in an integrated manner (see Case Study 13.1). Thus, the criteria for strong sustainability are: weak sustainability plus something else. The 'something else' refers to the additional natural capital requirements required to safeguard those aspects of environmental functions that are difficult, if not impossible, to assign values.

In other words, the 'something else' refers to the *critical natural capital* (CNC) needed, the maintenance of which is essential for environmental (as opposed to economic) sustainability (Ekins 2003). These additional requirements are generally listed (as shown above) in *physical/biological* terms. The decision about what to include on this list is done on a more-or-less

CASE STUDY 13.1 SUSTAINABLE FOREST MANAGEMENT PRACTICES: THE CASE OF THE MENOMINEE INDIAN RESERVATION

The Menominee Indian Reservation of Wisconsin is a federally recognized sovereign 'nation'. The reservation was established in 1854. It occupies 234,000 acres, about 95 percent of which is covered with mixed hardwood/coniferous forests. Today, the population of the Menominee community is about 8,000 and half of them live on the reservation. About 25 percent of the workforce makes their living on jobs directly related to the management, harvesting and processing of timber.

The Menominee Indians claim that they have been practicing sustainable forestry since the birth of their reservation more than 140 years ago. In fact, sustainable forest management practice is part of the present-day Menominee Constitution. In general, sustainable forestry is defined as harvesting trees at a rate within the forests' capacity to regrow (more on this in Chapter 16). Furthermore, the Menominee sustainable forestry practice refers 'not only to forest products and social benefits, but also to wildlife, site productivity, and other ecosystem functions' (Menominee Tribal Enterprises 1997: 9).

To assure this, the Menominee Indians follow forestry management principles that rely on both their strong traditional beliefs as the stewards of nature and state-of-the-art forestry technology. The 'annual allowable cut' from the reservation forest is determined on the basis of a 15-year cutting cycle with a 150-year planning horizon, employing various methods including selective cutting, shelterwood and small-scale clear-cutting only when it can improve stand quality and diversity. Up-to-date information on changes in timber volume and growth is provided through the use of the continuous forest inventory (CFI) method.

The production, marketing and product distribution aspects of the tribe are handled by the Menominee Tribal Enterprise (MTE). MTE claims that silviculture, not market forces, determines how much wood is cut. It is estimated that when the reservation was established, it contained 1.2 billion feet of timber. Since then, 2 billion feet have been cut, and 1.5 billion feet are standing today. The standing timber volume inventory now is greater than at the time when the reservation was created in 1854.

Although several efforts including a gaming (casino) operation are under way to diversify the economic basis of the Menominee community, the forest, with its multiple products, continues to be one of the major sources of employment and income. While the Menominee forest is one of the most intensively managed tracts of forest, it still remains the best example of biodiversity in the Great Lakes region. From the air, it has been described as 'a big green postage stamp', or 'an island of trees in a sea of farmland'. The contrast can be seen from space, and entering the reservation along Highway 55 has been described as entering a 'wall of trees'. In this respect, although on a small scale, the Menominee Reservation has provided a successful model of sustainable development for the twenty-first century. During the Earth Day celebration of 1995 the United Nations formally recognized the exemplary achievements of the MTE in its forest-based sustainable development practices. A year later, Vice President Al Gore presented the Menominee with the President's Award for Sustainable Development.

ad hoc basis, with priorities given to carrying capacity, ecological stability, resilience and biotic diversity (although not necessarily in this order).

Let me end this section by noting some of the criticisms of strong sustainability. As would be expected, most of the criticisms come from neo-classical economists. These criticisms seem to emerge because the strong sustainability criteria pay little, if any, attention to efficiency. A case in point is that the sustainability criterion which states 'the rate of exploitation of renewable resources should not exceed the rate at which these resources renew themselves' says nothing about the choices that have to be made when there are multiple situations that would satisfy this requirement.

For example, for a renewable resource such as fish there can be an *infinite* number of sustainable harvests (where annual harvest equals the annual growth in fish population or biomass), depending on the underlying fish population. In this case, society has to make a decision regarding the fish population that would be consistent with the 'optimal' sustainable harvest. That being so, it is not sufficient to just ascertain that the harvest is sustainable. The above general rule does not address this important issue.

Another criterion that we looked at earlier is that 'waste emission should be kept at or below the waste-absorptive capacity of the environment'. This criterion completely ignores economic considerations. As discussed in Chapter 3, the 'optimal' level of pollution can be in excess of the absorptive capacity of the environment.

Therefore, for the aforementioned reasons, neo-classical economists are generally skeptical about the relevance, as a guide to policy, of sustainability criteria that are stated in biophysical terms. Their objection arises from the fact that sustainability criteria of this nature lack economic context (i.e., consideration of all the relevant tradeoffs) and in so doing ignore considerations of *efficiency*.

Criticisms of a different nature arise from some ecologists because the strong sustainability criteria are not deemed sufficiently inclusive. For example, in an extreme case those who are proponents of the 'deep ecology' movement would argue that the equity considerations of the strong sustainability criteria should include concern for the wellbeing of every species (not just humans) as well as the integrity of the biosphere as a whole. In other words, strong sustainability should be *even stronger*. The discussion in the next section briefly attempts to respond to some of these concerns.

13.5 THE SAFE MINIMUM STANDARD APPROACH TO SUSTAINABILITY

The safe minimum standard approach traces its origin to the work of three pioneering and eminent natural resource economists, Ciriacy-Wantrup (1952), Krutilla (1967) and Bishop (1978). It began as a practical guide to natural resource management under conditions of extreme uncertainty, such as the preservation of individual species (e.g., the Pacific Northwest spotted owl or the African elephant). It was argued that *irreversibility* would be a key issue to consider for problems of this nature, meaning that beyond a certain threshold (or critical zone) the exploitation of natural resources may lead to irreversible damage. For example, the Pacific Northwest spotted owl would be declared extinct if its population dropped beyond a certain minimum, and this minimum is greater than zero. Therefore, in managing natural resources of this nature, it is extremely important not to extend resource use beyond a certain *safe* minimum standard (SMS). Otherwise, the social opportunity cost of reversing direction might become 'unacceptably large'. However, it is important to note that *considerable uncertainty exists regarding both the cost and the irreversibility of particular human impacts on the natural environment*. Thus, in this sense, uncertainty is central to the concept of the safe minimum standard.

What specific relevance does the SMS approach to resource management have to sustainability? Is SMS in any way related to either weak or strong sustainability, and if so, in what specific ways? The answers to these questions lie in understanding the implications of irreversibility and the potential social opportunity cost associated with it. In situations where human impact on the natural environment is regarded as potentially large and irreversible, the SMS suggests that human and natural capital cannot be safely deemed adequate substitutes. When viewed from a long-term resource management perspective, the substitution possibilities between natural and human-made capital become uncertain. In this respect, sustainability warrants the maintenance of *non-declining natural capital* as the safe minimum.

Understood this way, the SMS approach to sustainability does not completely invalidate the standard economics approach to resource assessment and management, or even the concept of sustainability. Instead, SMS narrows the scope and the applicability of the standard economics conception of sustainability by restricting its relevance to human impacts on the natural environment, where the potential consequences are regarded as small and reversible. In this situation, Hartwick's compensatory investments could be applied, and social opportunity costs could be assessed using standard cost–benefit analysis (see Chapter 9).

It is also obvious that, to some degree, the SMS and the ecological approaches to sustainability share common features. Both approaches adhere to the notion of limits in substitution possibilities between human and natural capital. However, these two approaches provide different explanations for limits in factor substitutions. The SMS uses *irreversibility* while the ecological economics approach relies on *all-encompassing physical laws* (of which ecological irreversibility is only a part).

In many respects, the SMS approach to sustainability can be perceived as a *hybrid* between the neoclassical and the ecological economic approaches to sustainability. It does not attempt to reject the basic tenets of the standard economics approach to sustainability, resource assessment, and management

301

philosophies. At the same time, in broad terms, it follows with the ecological economics' notion that nature imposes limits on factor substitutions in some ways.

Finally, it is important to note that the *operational rule* of SMS is quite straightforward. When the level of uncertainty and the social opportunity of current activities (such as global warming, ozone depletion, and the protection of rare, threatened or endangered ecosystems and habitats) are both high, the prudent course entails erring on the side of the unknown (see Case Study 13.2). This is, in fact, identical to the precautionary principle discussed in Section 9.6. In the end, the important message conveyed by this rule is the *social imperative for safeguarding against large-scale, irreversible degradation of natural capital*.

CASE STUDY 13.2 HABITAT PRESERVATION OF ENDANGERED FISH SPECIES IN THE VIRGIN RIVER SYSTEMS: AN APPLICATION OF THE SAFE MINIMUM STANDARD APPROACH

This case study is based on an article that appeared in the journal *Land Economics* (Berrens et al. 1998). This article dealt with two regional case studies from the southwestern United States, the Colorado and Virgin River systems. The primary objective of these studies was to analyze the regional and subregional economic impacts of the US Federal Court order for the preservation of endangered fish species in the designated areas. The rules for this court order were based on the provisions of the Endangered Species Act of 1973. These rules are consistent with the safe minimum standard (SMS) approach. Individual areas can be excluded from the designation of critical habitat, and therefore extinction of species is allowed if, and only if, the economic impacts of preservation are judged to be extremely severe or intolerable.

For brevity, only a summary of the economic impact analyses of the Virgin River study area is presented. This study area involved two counties: Clark County, Nevada, and Washington County, Utah. The problem stemmed from a precipitous decline in the fish populations observed in this area. The declines were caused by physical and biological alterations of the Virgin River systems primarily resulting from extended uses of water for agricultural, municipal and industrial purposes. The critical habitat designation was considered in order to restore the Virgin River systems to conditions that would allow the recovery of the endangered fish species.

The implementation of the above consideration will result in less diversion of the river water for commercial or human uses. The economic consequences of this were measured in terms of changes in output and employment. This in turn was done by comparing the economic activity with and without taking the needs of the endangered fish species into account. For the Virgin area study, the study covered a time horizon of over 45 years (1995–2040) and the economic impact analyses were performed using input–output (I–O) models.

The overall economic impact of critical habitat designation was found to be negative but insignificant. The present value of the lost output was estimated to range between 0.0001 and 0.0003 percent from the baseline — the regional economic development scenario over the study's time span in the absence of the federal court order for habitat preservation on behalf of the endangered fish species. In terms of employment, the reduction was estimated to range between nine and 60 jobs. Subregional variations were observed in both the output and employment impacts. To put this into proper historical perspective, between 1959 and 1994 the regional economy in the Virgin study area grew on average by 3.01 percent.

Overall, the economic impacts of critical habitat designation were found to be far below the recommended threshold for exclusion, which was a 1 percent deviation from the baseline projection of the aggregate economic activity. As a result, on the basis of regional economic impacts no sufficient grounds could be established on which to recommend exemption from fish species protection in the Virgin River area.

13.6 CHAPTER SUMMARY

In this chapter, three alternative conceptual approaches to SD were discussed: the Hartwick–Solow approach (i.e., neoclassical), ecological economics, and the safe minimum standard (SMS).

Careful examination of the above approaches to sustainability reveals that they share the following common features:

1. In principle, there appears to be a tacit recognition of biophysical limits to economic growth.
2. Sustainable economic development is envisioned as a viable and desirable course of action.
3. A non-declining capital stock (composed of natural and human-made capital) is regarded as a prerequisite for sustainability.
4. Sustainability requires consideration of both efficiency and equity.

However, the three approaches also differ in three very important ways:

1. They differ in the ways they perceive the relationships between human-made and natural capital. In the Hartwick–Solow approach, these two categories of capital are viewed as *substitutes*. This implies that the composition of the capital stock to be inherited by future generations is irrelevant. The ecological and the SMS approaches, in contrast, regard human-made and natural capital assets as *complements*. For this reason, keeping a certain minimum level of natural capital intact is deemed to be essential.
3. Differences exist in the degree of emphasis placed on equity relative to efficiency. In the Hartwick–Solow approach to sustainability, the emphasis is on intertemporal efficiency: the efficient allocation of societal resources over time. In the ecological approach, the emphasis is on intergenerational equity. The SMS approach emphasizes equity only to the extent that present actions are suspected to cause irreversible harmful effects on future generations.
4. Differences exist in the consideration given to species other than humans. The Hartwich–Solow approach relies on valuation methods that are unapologetically anthropocentric, whereas the ecological and SMS sustainability models attempt to incorporate some considerations of the wellbeing of nonhuman species. For this reason, these two approaches use biological and physical indicators as an integral part of their sustainability criteria.

All three approaches presented in this chapter are plagued by the difficulties associated with obtaining the necessary information to determine the 'appropriate' size of the non-declining capital stock. To this extent they are theoretical models.

The determination of the 'appropriate' capital stock size requires, at minimum, the following:

1. Information on resource prices extending over a long period of time (forward markets for resources);
2. Estimation of shadow prices for environmental services that are not traded in the market;
3. Determination of the social discount rate;
4. Adjustment of the conventional measure of a national accounting system to account for the depreciation of natural capital;
5. Detailed information on the physical, biological and ecological conditions of natural resources;
6. Identifying critical natural capital (aspects of natural capital with poor substitution possibilities); and
7. The establishment of social, legal and political institutions intended to effectively operationalize the concept of SD. The implication of all this is that progress toward SD may be slowed considerably because of unreasonably large administrative, information and legal costs.

Another practical consideration that tends to hamper the implementation of SD programs is concern for *intragenerational* equity (concern for the poor living today). In considering sustainability, the emphasis has been on intergenerational equity: the wellbeing of future generations. Given this, sustainability stresses investment in long-term projects at the expense of current consumption. However, concern about those who are poor today entails adopting a policy that leads to increased current consumption, rather than increased investment.

Despite the practical difficulties cited above, the interest among economists on the subject matter of SD continues to grow. This development has contributed to an increased academic focus on the following three important issues:

1. *Intergenerational equity*: the key issue here is the ethical legitimacy of discounting.
2. *Biophysical limits*: here the issue is no longer about the existence of ecological limits as such, but on how to deal with the perceived limits. This is, indeed, the essence of SD.
3. *Sustainable national income accounting*: in recent years, an increasing level of attention has been given to ways in which the conventional national accounting system might be overhauled in such a way that defensive environmental expenditures and the depreciation of natural capital are accurately reflected (a subject matter to be discussed in the next chapter).

REVIEW AND DISCUSSION QUESTIONS

1. Briefly identify the following concepts: intergenerational equity, intragenerational equity, intergenerational efficiency, weak sustainability, strong sustainability, critical natural capital, the Brundtland Report, and the Hartwick rule.
2. Read the following statements. In response, state 'True', 'False' or 'Uncertain' and explain why:
   (a) The necessary condition for *strong* sustainability is non-declining natural capital and nothing else.
   (b) In principle, the safe minimum rule to sustainability and the precautionary principle are one and the same.
   (c) The main difference between weak and strong sustainability is the size and not necessarily the nature of the non-declining capital stock requirements.
3. Are the statements in (a) and (b) below saying the same thing? (Hint: think about the tradeoffs between concerns of intra- and intergenerational equity.)
   (a) Sustainability is principally about intergenerational equity.
   (b) 'Sustainability is not exclusively or even primarily an environmental issue. It is fundamentally about how we choose to live our lives, with an awareness that everything we do has consequences for the 7 billion of us here today, as well as for the billions more who will follow, for centuries' (from the foreword section of the *Human Development Report 2011: Sustainability and Equity, a Better Future for All*).
4. The safe minimum standard (SMS) is just a minor variation of the strong sustainability rule. Is this true? Explain.
5. In a world so divided in so many ways, sustainable economic development on a global scale will amount to nothing but a figment of human imagination or, to put it mildly, just wishful thinking. Do you agree with this statement? What do you make of the many world summits on SD that have been held over the past two decades, the latest being the Rio+20 Earth Summit 2012 in Brazil? Would it be fair to say that the talks and the agendas for actions of the past world summits on SD have been, to put it bluntly, 'much ado about nothing'? Take a side and discuss your position.
6. Beckerman (1994: 191) in his article entitled 'Sustainable Development: Is it a Useful Concept?' wrote the following: 'It is argued that "sustainable development" has been defined in such a way as to be either morally

repugnant or logically redundant. "Strong" sustainability, overriding all other considerations, is morally unacceptable as well as totally impractical; and "weak" sustainability, in which compensation is made for resources consumed, offers nothing beyond traditional economic welfare maximization'. Do you share Beckerman's view of SD? Explain.

7. 'Debates over what environmental sustainability means often focus on whether human-made capital can substitute for natural resources — whether human ingenuity will relax natural resource constraints, as in the past. Whether this will be possible in the future is unknown and, coupled with the risk of catastrophe, favours the position of preserving basic natural assets and the associated flow of ecological services' (UNDP 2011: 2). Does this remark provide a good rationale for the relevance of any one the three types of sustainability concepts (i.e., weak sustainability, strong sustainability, and SMS) discussed in this chapter? Explain.

REFERENCES AND FURTHER READING

Arrow, K., Bolin, B. and Costanza, R. (1995) 'Economic Growth, Carrying Capacity, and the Environment', *Science* 268: 520–1.

Ayres, R. (1999) 'The Second Law, the Fourth Law, Recycling and Limits to Growth', *Ecological Economics* 29, 3: 473–83.

Ayres, R., van den Bergh, J. and Gowdy, J. (2001) 'Viewpoint: Weak Versus Strong Sustainability', *Environmental Ethics* 23: 155–68.

Beckerman, W. (1994) 'Sustainable Development: Is it a Useful Concept?' *Environmental Values* 3: 191–209.

Berrens, R. P., Brookshire, D. S., McKee, M. and Schmidt, C. (1998) 'Implementing the Safe Minimum Standard Approach: Two Case Studies from the U.S. Endangered Species Act', *Land Economics* 2, 74: 147–61.

Bishop, R. C. (1978) 'Endangered Species and Uncertainty: The Economics of a Safe Minimum Standard', *American Journal of Agricultural Economics* 60: 10–18.

Boulding, K. E. (1966) 'The Economics of the Coming Spaceship Earth', in H. Jarrett (ed.) *Environmental Quality in a Growing Economy*, Washington, DC: Johns Hopkins University Press.

Common, M. and Perrings, C. (1992) 'Towards an Ecological Economics of Sustainability', *Ecological Economics* 66: 7–34.

Costanza, R., Perrings, C. and Cleveland, C. J. (1997) 'Introduction', in R. Costanza, C. Perrings and C. J. Cleveland (eds.) *The Development of Ecological Economics*, London: Edward Elgar.

Daly, H. E. (1973) *Towards a Steady-state Economy*, San Francisco: W. H. Norton.

—— (1996) *Beyond Growth: The Economics of Sustainable Development*, Boston, MA: Beacon Press.

—— (2007) *Ecological Economics and Sustainable Development: Selected Essays of Herman Daly*, London: Edward Elgar.

Dasgupta, P., Lavin, S. and Lubchenco, J. (2000) 'Economic Pathways to Ecological Sustainability', *BioScience* 54, 4: 339–45.

Dieren, W. (ed.) (1995) *Taking Nature into Account: A Report to the Club of Rome*, New York: Springer-Verlag.

Ekins, P. (1993) 'Limits to Growth and Sustainable Development: Grappling with Ecological Realities', *Ecological Economics* 8, 3: 269–88.

—— (2003) 'Identifying Critical Natural Capital: Conclusions about Critical Natural Capital', *Ecological Economics* 44, 277–92.

Georgescu-Roegen, N. (1975) 'Energy and Economic Myths', *Southern Economic Journal* 41, 3: 347–81.

Gowdy, J. M. and McDaniel, C. N. (1999) 'The Physical Destruction of Nauru: An Example of Weak Substitutability', *Land Economics* 75, 2: 333–9.

Hamilton, K. and Hartwick, J. M. (2005) 'Investing Exhaustible Resource Rents and the Path of Consumption', *Canadian Journal of Economics* 38, 3: 615–21.

Hartwick, J. M. (1977) 'Intergenerational Equity and the Investing of Rents from Exhaustible Resources', *American Economic Review* 67, 5: 972–4.

—— (1978) 'Substitution among Exhaustible Resources and Intergenerational Equity', *Review of Economic Studies* 45: 347–54.

Hicks, J. R. (1946) *The Value of Capital*, 2nd edn., Oxford: Oxford University Press.

Howarth, R. B. (1997) 'Sustainability as Opportunity', *Land Economics* 73, 4: 569–79.

Krutilla, J. V. (1967) 'Conservation Reconsidered', *American Economic Review* 57, 4: 787–96.

Maler, K-G. (2008) 'Sustainable Development and Resilience in Ecosystems', *Environmental & Resource Economics,* 39: 17–24.

Menominee Tribal Enterprises (1997) *The Menominee Forest Management Tradition: History, Principles and Practices*, Keshena, WI: Menominee Tribal Enterprises.

Pearce, D. W. (2005), 'Environmental Policy as a Tool for Sustainability', in D. Simpson, M. A. Toman and R. U. Ayres (eds.) *Scarcity and Growth Revisited*, Washington, DC: Resources for the Future.

Pearce, D. W. and Atkinson, G. (1998) 'The Concept of Sustainable Development: An Evaluation of its Usefulness Ten Years after Brundtland', *Swiss Journal of Economics and Statistics* 134, 3: 251–69.

Perrings, C. A. (1991) 'Reserved Rationality and the Precautionary Principles: Technological Change, Time, and Uncertainty in Environmental Decision Making', in R. Costanza (ed.) *Ecological Economics: The Science and Management of Sustainability*, New York: Columbia University Press.

—— (1995) 'Ecological Resilience in the Sustainability of Economic Development', *Economic Applique* 48, 2: 121–42.

Pezzey J. and Toman, M. (2005) 'Sustainability and Its Economic Interpretations', in D. Simpson, M. A. Toman and R. U. Ayres (eds.) *Scarcity and Growth Revisited*, Washington, DC: Resources for the Future.

Siegfield von Ciriacy-Wantrup, S. (1952) *Resource Conservation: Economics and Policy*, Berkeley, CA: University of California Press.

Simpson, D., Toman, M. and Ayres, R. (2005) 'Introduction: The New Scarcity', in David Simpson, Michael A. Toman and Robert U. Ayres (eds.), *Scarcity and Growth Revisited*, Washington DC: Resources for the Future.

Solow, R. M. (1974) 'The Economics of Resources or the Resources of Economics', *American Economic Review* 64: 1–14.

—— (1986), 'On the Intertemporal Allocation of Natural Resources', *Scandinavian Journal of Economics* 88: 141–9.

—— (1993) 'Sustainability: An Economist's Perspective', in R. Dorfman and N. Dorfman (eds.) *Selected Readings in Environmental Economics*, 3rd edn., New York: W. W. Norton.

World Bank (1992) *World Development Report 1992: Development and the Environment*, New York: Oxford University Press.

WCED (World Commission on Environment and Development) (1987) *Our Common Future*, New York: Oxford University Press.

Chapter 14

Green accounting and alternative indicators of sustainability

---

LEARNING OBJECTIVES

After reading this chapter you will be familiar with the following:

- Why the standard national income account (SNA) may fail to consider the damages or contributions to wellbeing of many environmental services, and what can be done to incorporate these missing environmental values.
- A general conceptual framework for an environmentally adjusted net national income account.
- Environmentally adjusted 'sustainable' national income accounting that is rooted in a theoretical foundation of weak sustainability.
- Major shortcomings associated with the greening of the SNA.
- The creation of the system of integrated environmental and economic accounting (SEEA), with its satellite system that organizes environmental and economic statistics.
- Alternative indicators of environmentally adjusted sustainability and social wellbeing:
  - (a) The environmentally adjusted net domestic product (EDP);
  - (b) The environmentally adjusted net genuine savings (GS); and
  - (c) The index of sustainable economic welfare (ISEW).
- Physical indicators of sustainability: ecological footprint (EF).

It has been customary to measure the successes and failures of the economic performance of nations according to the annual growth-rate of gross domestic per capita income over time. However, over the past 30 years it has become increasingly clear that, for many 'resource dependent' countries, economic progress as measured by the standard indicators of economic performance consistently signaled unabated economic progress, while the physical and social evidences indicated the opposite. This chapter is about the recent development of alternative indicators of aggregate economic and social performances to avoid persistent

policy failures with regards to the environment and the development of many emerging nations.

14.1 INTRODUCTION

Modifying national income accounting systems to promote an understanding of the links between the economy and the environment has been taken as a first step towards the integration of *sustainability* into the performance indicators of national economies. With this in mind, this chapter will examine how the values of environmental assets and the costs of natural-resource depletion and environmental degradation can be explicitly incorporated into 'conventional' national income accounts.

This is done in the following order. In Section 14.2, the concept of environmentally adjusted national income accounting (EANIA) will be explored. A systematic development of this concept requires a good understanding of the conventional national income accounts and some basic macroeconomic identities and economic indicators, which are also discussed. In Section 14.3, using weak sustainability as a tool, attempts will be made to explicate the conditions necessary to transform the environmentally adjusted system of national income accounts (developed in the previous section) into 'sustainable' national income accounts (i.e., green accounting). This section also discusses some of the major shortcomings of green accounting as a concept. In Section 14.4, four commonly used indicators (three monetary and one physical) of sustainability are examined. Efforts are made to identify the important policy implications as well as the major shortcomings associated with each of the four sustainability indictors discussed. Section 14.5 offers a summary of the chapter.

14.2 ENVIRONMENTALLY ADJUSTED SYSTEMS OF NATIONAL INCOME ACCOUNTING

The system of national income accounts (SNA) and GDP

The basic premise of this section is that since the core accounts of the system of national accounts (SNA) do not explicitly include natural resources and the environment, adjustment is needed to incorporate these missing environmental variables. The SNA is a conceptual framework that establishes the statistical (i.e., the collection, compilation, classification and analysis of data) standards according to which national governments measure macroeconomic activities in a market-economy setting. As will be shown shortly, the SNA is the foundation of gross domestic product (GDP), the most widely used indicator of macroeconomic activities.

The SNA is a relatively recent invention. The first formal application of the SNA was carried out by the US government in 1937 under the guidance of Simon Kuznets, a Nobel Laureate in Economics. In response to the widespread application of the general framework of the SNA throughout the world, the United Nations System of National Accounting (SNA or UNSNA), was first published in 1953 (Haggart 2000). This was done to standardize the SNA so that international comparisons of all significant macroeconomic activities are possible. The SNA has been revised three times since its inception, in 1968, 1993 and 2008.

The data for GDP, the most widely used barometer for measuring the aggregate economic activities of a nation, is extracted from the 'flow' account of the SNA. Formally, GDP is defined as the market value of all goods and services produced by a nation during a specific calendar year. It is important to note that GDP, unlike the gross national product (GNP), measures the total value of goods and services produced within the territorial boundaries of a nation. In other words, while GNP represents the value of all goods and services produced by all nationals of a country, GDP is computed after considering the *net* income from assets abroad (i.e., total capital gains from investment abroad and income earned by foreign nationals domestically).

One thing that should immediately become evident from the above definition of GDP is that the aggregation of all the assortments of goods and services produced (cars, mouse traps, restaurant services, and so on) are calculated using market prices. This would allow all the production and investment activities of a nation to be expressed in a monetary unit, such as the dollar. GDP can be computed in three ways: (1) by adding up income (*wages* as compensation to labors, *rent* as payment for resources, and *profits* as rewards for entrepreneurial risk taking) received from the production of goods and services; (2) by adding up expenditures on goods and services; and (3) by adding up the 'value added' by labor and capital when inputs purchased from other producers are transformed into output.

For example, a gallon of milk at a grocery store may be sold for $2.10. Before it reached the shelf of the store, this same gallon of milk was sold for $0.85 by the dairy farmer, and $1.60 by the wholesaler and distributor of milk. In this example, the value added at each stage of milk production and delivery was 85 cents at the dairy farm level, 75 cents at the wholesale level, and 50 cents at the grocery store level. The sum of the value added (0.85 + 0.75 + 0.50) equals $2.10—exactly equal to the expenditure of consumers on a gallon of milk when purchased at the grocery store).

Understood in this way, GDP measures the 'flow' of the total *income* (GDI) or total *expenditure* of a nation. These measures are generated from economic activities during a specified period of time, usually a calendar year. Thus, GDP provides a 'snapshot' of the macroeconomic activity of a nation.

For example, a quarterly report of GDP may be used to gauge the business climate of a nation, that is, whether the nation is in the recessionary, recovery, or expansionary phase of the economy. This would be important for short-term macroeconomic policy and investment decisions in the business sector of the economy. On the other hand, when year-to-year reports of GDP are viewed over time, they can be used as an indicator of economic growth. An increasing trend of GDP is usually seen as a sign of increased economic prosperity. Lastly, GDP divided by the total population of a nation, the so-called GDP per capita, is used as a proxy for measuring the standard of living in a nation. A growing per capita income implies that the average citizen of a nation is doing well.

Thus, GDP can be used as an indicator of the business climate of an economy, economic growth, or standard of living in a country. Judgments about who is doing well, or not so well, are often rendered (both in absolute and relative terms) by looking at the historical performance of countries on the basis of either GDP or GDP per capita. Thus, GDP could provide information that is very important for business people, investors and policymakers. International agencies such as the United Nations and the World Bank can also use GDP in measuring the relative economic performance of emerging nations over time.

However, as discussed in Chapter 6, we know that economic indicators such as GDP or GDI per capita may not account for the 'side-effects' of economic activities on the natural environment. Furthermore, the costs of environmental damages, as well as the values of the services of important environmental assets, may have been omitted from GDP because these resources have no market prices. Given this, what we would like to examine next are the conceptual challenges involved in developing a comprehensive system of national income accounts that incorporates the environment in the computation of GDP.

Towards environmentally adjusted national income accounts

The conceptual challenges of developing a comprehensive framework of national income accounts that attempt to incorporate the side-effects of human economic activities on the environment cannot be fully captured without a closer examination of the basic components of GDP. GDP as a 'flow' of aggregate expenditures can be mathematically expressed as:

$$GDP = C + I_g \qquad (14.1)$$

where C represents *private* and *public* consumption expenditures and I_g represents gross investment. Note that net export (i.e., export minus import) is not included in the above national income identity. This assumption of a closed economy is done mainly to make the analysis in this section simple. Furthermore, no differentiation is made between private and public consumption.

Since it will be important for later discussion, it should be noted that from the outset GDP only measures the *flow* of expenditures (i.e., income), and not the *stock* (i.e., wealth) of a nation. For example, I_g in Identity 14.1, measures the value of the *new* capital formation (new machines, housing, etc.) that is added to the already existing capital stock (infrastructure) of a nation during the current fiscal year. *The GDP for a given year does not explicitly provide any information about changes in the value of the initial capital stock (infrastructure)*—which plays a major role in determining the productive capacity of a nation.

The initial capital stock essentially represents part of the wealth of a nation. Rich nations will have much larger initial capital stock (i.e., infrastructure) than poor countries. The value of capital that is explicitly included in the GDP's measure of a given year is the addition (hence, the flow) to the initial stock. In other words, this is what the variable I_g in Identity 14.1 represents.

It should be noted, however, that capital stocks, old or new (like machines, factories, roads, etc.), are *depreciable* assets. In other words, when a nation produces goods and services to be used for the current year, a certain amount of the 'old' capital stock is being used up or consumed. Thus, allowances for the depreciated capital assets have to be made if a country wants to safeguard its wealth (productive capacity) from future decline. In the conventional system of national income accounting, this is done by subtracting the estimated value of depreciation allowance for capital from GDP in order to arrive at what is known as the 'net national product' (NNP). That is,

$$NNP = GDP - d_m \qquad 14.2$$

where the variable d_m represents the value for the depreciation allowance for capital. It is important to note, however, that d_m represents the depreciation value of the initial capital stock or the stock of the manufactured (produced) capital of a nation at the beginning of a given calendar year. In general, there is no insurmountable 'valuation' problem associated with these kinds of capital assets because their values are assessed on the basis of actual market prices.

However, an economy also uses resources extracted or harvested from 'capital stocks' provided by nature, such as farmland, mineral reserves, forestland, wetland preserves, coral reefs, and so on. These resources are either renewable (such as fish stock and forest) or nonrenewable/exhaustible (such

as mines of bauxite ores, aquifers and fossil-fuel reserves). To complicate matters, an economy is supported by life-support systems such as the waste assimilative capacity of the environment, the ozone layer of the stratosphere, and so on. From here on, as was done before, 'natural capital' is used as the generic phrase to describe capital assets provided by nature with detectable uses in the economic enterprises of humanity.

At this point, it is natural to ask the following two questions: (1) How is the 'flow' of resources extracted or harvested from natural capital valued and incorporated in GDP?; and (2) What can be done to account for the depreciation of natural capital? As we shall see shortly, the extent to which these two questions can be answered in a satisfactory manner determines what can and cannot be done to conceptualize an EANIA.

Based on our discussion in Chapter 8, we know that 'valuation' of environmental assets is more of an art form than a science. This remains so, despite the advances made by economists to impute monetary values on many aspects of ecosystem services. For a moment, let us set this problem (as posed in question 1 above) aside and merely look at the rationale for considering the depreciation of natural capital and why it should be subtracted from GDP.

A simple example may help illustrate the need for such an adjustment. Suppose we have a nation known for its rich diamond reserves and the proceeds from the sale of diamond ores account for a significant portion of this country's GDP. According to the standard SNA, the net proceeds (income) generated from the sales of diamond ore (i.e., the market value of total sales minus the extraction cost) will be included in the GDP (El Serafy, 1997; Repetto, 1992). Issues with valuation are not present here because diamond is a market-priced commodity. Therefore, this nation can always increase its GDP or NNP by simply allowing for more diamond extraction.

However, natural capital (such as diamond mines) is subject to depletion. Each time ores are extracted and sold there will be that much less left in the ground. Thus, a decision to extract more diamond in order to increase the GDP in any given year will have an effect on the 'flow' of income of this country in the future. In other words, if future economic viability is an important consideration to the government of this nation, allowances have to be made for its ever diminishing natural capital stock (i.e., diamond reserve). Unfortunately, the standard SNA does not do this. Once this is realized, at least conceptually, a problem of this nature can be resolved by making sure that NNP is attained after accounting for the depreciation of both human-made capital and the depletion of exhaustible resources, such as diamond. The next section will discuss how this adjustment process is carried out.

However, the above adjustment only addresses nonrenewable natural capital. What about natural capital assets that are renewable, but can be 'potentially exhausted' if overexploited? This occurs when renewable resources are harvested at rates exceeding their regenerative capacity over an extended period of time. Examples include the degradation of pastureland due to overgrazing, the depletion of fish stocks due to overfishing, and deforestation due to the excessive harvesting of forestland for timber, among others.

Again, the standard SNA treats proceeds from the sale of resources harvested from renewable natural-resource stocks as part of the income of a nation. However, this is done without any mechanism to account for the effects that the current harvest rate of renewable resources may have on the flow of future income. Clearly, an environmentally adjusted NNP has to confront this reality if the unfortunate and very costly incidences of overfishing, deforestation, overgrazing, excessive soil erosion, and so on, are to be avoided. How this is actually done will be addressed in the next section.

In summary, an environmentally adjusted NNP would be conceptually expressed as follows:

$$NNP_e = GDP - d_m - d_n \qquad 14.3$$

where NNP_e represents the environmentally adjusted net national income, and d_n is the allowance for the depreciation of natural capital assets. Identity 14.3

captures the essential elements that are needed to modify the SNA in such a way that an environmentally adjusted net national income can be derived.

However, even setting aside the 'valuation' problems (see Chapter 8) associated with arriving at reasonable estimates of an environmentally adjusted net national income, the discussion in this section so far has only addressed part of the issue we are examining in this chapter. To complete the task, sustainability has to be incorporated within the framework of environmentally adjusted national income. The next section deals with the conceptual challenge of accomplishing this task.

14.3 ENVIRONMENTALLY ADJUSTED 'SUSTAINABLE' NATIONAL INCOME ACCOUNTING

In the last section, we developed a macroeconomic identity, Identity 14.3, which conceptually represents environmentally adjusted net national income. Like any other macroeconomic identity this is a static concept, as it represents the income flow of a nation resulting from economic activities that occurred during a given year. How can we make an identity of this nature represent income flows that are sustainable over an indefinite period of time? This is a dynamic concept because the income in any given year cannot be determined without considering the effect that it will have on future income flows. In other words, incomes are expected to be intertemporally related.

This requires a much clearer definition of income. To do this, we return to the Hicksian concept of income as discussed in Chapter 13. Hicks (1946) defined a person's income as 'what he can consume during the week and still expect to be as well off at the end of the week as he was at the beginning'. At the macroeconomic level this can be interpreted as the *maximum amount* that can be spent by a nation during a given year, while making sure that *capital assets remain intact so that productivity in the future is not compromised by lack of sufficient capital*. This concept of income is clearly consistent with the *weak* sustainability discussed in Chapter 13. Thus, using weak sustainability as a tool, we reinterpret Identity 14.3 as follows:

$$NNP_e = GDP - d_m - d_n, \qquad 14.3$$

Or,

$$NNP_e = (C + I_g) - d_m - d_n \qquad 14.3a$$

Identity 14.3 and 14.3a are the same, since GDP = C + I_g.

A closer look at Identity 14.3a reveals what a nation needs to do if it wants to maintain a sustained level of consumption, C, while keeping its 'human-made' and 'natural' capital stocks, or, more aptly, its productive capacity, undiminished. This would require the allowance for depreciation of human-made capital (d_m) and resource depletion (d_n) to be reinvested so that the productive capacity of the nation remains intact (El Sarefy 1997; Hartwick 1978). Note also that d_m and d_n together represent the *savings* (since they are required to be subtracted out from C) a nation would need to make in order to ensure that the productive capacity in subsequent years is not compromised. Intergenerational caring, like that advocated by the Brundtland Commission's definition of sustainability, is subtly implied here (see Chapter 13).

One final point needs to be made before completing this part of the discussion. Simply because the allowance for natural capital depletion, d_n, has been reinvested into some other capital assets, does not necessarily suggest that depletion will cease to occur. Thus, if resource depletion is not expected to impair the future productive capacity of a nation, human-made and natural capital are assumed to be close *substitutes* (Solow, 1986). Clearly, this assumption is consistent with weak sustainability and the broader neoclassical economics worldview.

It is important to note that, to make the explanation simple, so far d_n has been assumed to represent depletion allowance that may imply exhaustible resources. However, in general, d_n would include depletion of both renewable and nonrenewable resources. For renewable resources, depletion refers to a level of resource exploitation beyond certain critical thresholds (Sadoff 1992). It is also important to note that renewable resources can serve as substitutes for exhaustible resources. A nation can maintain its productive capacity by reinvesting the proceeds from the sales of an exhaustible resource, such as fossil fuels, into renewable energy resources, such as wind or solar energy (Hartwick 1978; Solow 1986). Thus, factor substitution is not limited to human-made and natural capital. In other words, within the domain of natural capital assets, factor substitution occurs between renewable and non-renewable resources.

By way of summary, the two conditions for an environmentally adjusted sustainable flow of national income can be stated as:

1. NNP_e (net national product or income) as shown in Identity 14.3a above, which indicates the amount a given nation can produce or consume without undermining its capacity to produce the same amount in the future.

2. Furthermore, for the above condition to hold, nations are expected to reinvest their savings in such a way that their productive capacity will remain intact. How this is done (the mix of the capital portfolio) is not very important because natural and human-made capital assets are assumed to be close substitutes.

This represents the theoretical underpinning of environmentally adjusted sustainable net national income accounting (i.e. green accounting). Since this theory has been structured within the conceptual framework of the SNA, at first glance it appears to be relatively easy to put it into practical use (more on this in the next section). However, there are still several conceptual problems with this particular theoretical formulation of green accounting, unless, of course, one is from the neoclassical school of economics. Therefore, this section ends with a brief outline of some of the major criticisms of greening the SNA based on weak sustainability:

1. *Thresholds in critical natural capital (i.e., strong sustainability) are not considered*: this objection

clearly comes from the proponents of the ecological approach to sustainability. As discussed in Chapter 13, strong sustainability requires both economic and environmental sustainability to be fully satisfied. In principle, both weak and strong sustainability consider this to be the case. The two approaches to sustainability differ on the specific nature of the requirements for satisfying environmental sustainability. Weak sustainability considers only those environmental assets that have market value or can be imputed using shadow prices.

This is a major limitation and, as discussed in Chapter 13, leaves out ecologically important ecosystem functions (such as the carbon absorptive capacity of forests, the diversity of plant and animal species supported by wetland ecosystems, and so on) that are not only critical for sustaining the future economic performance of a nation, but also the health of the biosphere as a whole. In short, the environmentally adjusted national income account, if it is structured within the existing framework of the SNA, will not be able to account for ecosystem functions that cannot be remedied through factor substitutions. Some (Ekins 2003; El Serafy 1997; Hecht 1999) have suggested that *one way to address* this legitimate and critically important concern is to use *physical* indicators of sustainability along with the indicators derived from an environmentally adjusted national income account (more on this in the next section).

2. *Defensive environmental expenditures should be netted out*: defensive expenditures are real costs incurred by society to prevent or avoid damage(s) to the environment caused by the side-effects of everyday production and consumption activities (Daly 1996). Examples include the extra expenditure on: health care for problems caused by air pollution; cars to equip them with catalytic converters; and the cleanup of offshore oil spills.

In the conventional system of national accounting, defensive expenditures of this nature are treated as part of the national income. But this is erroneous, given that defensive expenditures actually represent a *loss* of income that cannot be spent again for consumption or investment, but can be spent only to repair or prevent environmental damage caused by the side-effects of economic activities.

In fact, an environmentally defensive expenditure actually represents a real-income transfer from the human production system to the environment (Daly 1996). Thus, *if the goal is to estimate a measure of 'true' net income, environmentally defensive expenditures should be deducted (not added, as is normally done) from NNP* (Ibid). In other words, in regards to defensive expenditures, correction is warranted because the SNA counts what is supposed to be a 'cost' as income. As will be evident in the next section, Daly and others have suggested an alternative sustainability indicator that incorporates a feature to address the problem associated with defensive expenditures.

3. *Green accounting should be cognizant of social factors relevant to human development*: the key issue here is a comprehensive system of national income accounting that is designed to reflect economic and environmental sustainability, which, as much as possible, should also be consistent with sustainable 'economic welfare' (Daly 1996; Max-Neef 1995; Stockhammer et al. 1997). In other words, in addition to the physical environment, social aspects of the human condition with an appreciable impact on peoples' quality of life (such as literacy, income inequalities, access to primary health care, and so on) should be considered (more on this in the last section of this chapter).

4. *In the presence of external trade, sustainability indicators at the national level may be flawed*: this criticism arises from the observation that countries normally conduct their economic activity without taking the resource flow with their trading partners into consideration. Under this circumstance, it is quite conceivable that a nation appearing to have done well under the standard measures of economic performance (i.e., GDP or GDP per capita) may actually be

pursing an *unsustainable* path of economic activity once the balance sheet for resource flows from the trading that took place with the rest of the world is carefully scrutinized. Japan is a good example of this. In the limit, unless one believes that 'trade can substitute for nature', some measures of sustainability are likely to indicate that a country like Japan is unsustainable (Ayres 2000).

Trade could also distort sustainability in some other ways. Some have argued that there is an ecological imbalance in the flow of materials of international trade (Muradian and Martinez-Alier 2001). The economies of most of the world's poor countries depend on exports of either nonrenewable resources that are subject to depletion and environmental degradation and/or renewable resources that are susceptible to irreversible environmental degradation. If the international conditions that determine the prices for primary products fail to account for environmental costs, then there is an apparent transfer of wealth from poor countries to rich countries (Muradian and Martinez-Alier 2001).

The causes for price distortions could be market failure as well as other social and political factors. When there exists unequal 'ecological' exchange, the environmental problems associated with the trade of natural resources may include the rapid depletion of resources, habitat destruction (especially deforestation), species loss, land degradation, and water and air pollution.

The main message here is that trade may have the effect of complicating matters when environmental sustainability is considered at both national and global levels, and this should be taken into consideration.

5. *No explicit consideration is made to account for technological change and the discovery of new resources*: the framework for environmentally adjusted sustainable national income accounting has been developed with the requirement that capital stock remain intact. However, nothing is said about technology, although the implicit assumption has been that no appreciable change

in technology has taken place over time. The main point here is that, viewed from a very long-term perspective, if the rates of growth in technology are greater than the rates of growth in population on a consistent basis, indicators based on green accounting that assume no change in technology are likely to be conservative (Hamilton, et al. 1997). In other words, they will have a positive bias towards future generations. This assumes, of course, that there are no negative intergenerational externalities associated with technological advancement—which is not an unlikely issue.

It is also true that the discussion of green accounting thus far has not stated explicitly the effects of discovering new reserves. The SNA-based environmentally adjusted sustainable income of a nation, NNP_e, assumes 'known reserves' of mineral and other exhaustible resources. The question then is, what would happen to NNP_e when new reserves are discovered? It turns out that this will not pose any major problems. The SNA simply re-evaluates the depletion allowance, d_n, based on the new estimate of total reserves. Note, however, that the income flow (i.e., NNP_e) would be expected to increase under this circumstance, indicating that discoveries of new reserves (i.e., increases in wealth) will have the effect of increasing the sustainable flow of income across generations. This observation also suggests that the flow of sustainable income of any nation is subject to change for a variety of exogenous factors, such as the discovery of new reserves or changes in technology (Hamilton et al. 1997).

14.4 INDICATORS OF ECONOMIC AND ENVIRONMENTAL SUSTAINABILITY

Based on the discussion in Section 14.3, it is evident that a comprehensive framework of sustainable national income accounting can be developed conceptually. That is, within the framework of the SNA from which the GDP is derived, it is possible to create 'satellite' accounts with the ultimate effect of integrating the data needed from both the economy and the environment for nations to construct macro-economic models that track indefinitely sustainable income flows. This 'greening' of the SNA would yield income flows that are weakly sustainable. That is, the environmentally adjusted sustainable net national product (NNP$_e$) would represent the maximum amount of income that can be expended for current consumption without impairing the future productive capacity of a nation (i.e., keeping capital stock intact).

However, while conceptually straightforward, greening the national income accounting is formidably challenging to put into practice. In fact, due to problems associated with environmental 'valuation,' the general consensus maintains that *fully corrected green accounting is impossible* (El Serafy 1997a). With this in mind, in this section we will examine three widely used indicators of sustainable income: the *environmentally adjusted net domestic product* (EDP) of the United Nations; the *genuine net savings* (GS) of the World Bank, and the *index of sustainable economic welfare* (ISEW) of Daly and Cobb (1989). One thing that these three indicators have in common is that they operate within the general framework of the SNA-based EANIA discussed thus far. To this extent, they are 'monetary' indicators of sustainability. The fourth sustainability indicator discussed at the end of this section differs from the other three. It is a 'physical' indictor of sustainability, namely, the *ecological footprint* (EFP).

The environmentally adjusted net domestic product (EDP)

As discussed in Chapter 13, in 1987 the United Nations launched the Brundtland Commission to examine and report on the principle causes of persistent policy failures with regards to the environment and the development of many emerging nations. It became increasingly evident that during the 1970s and 1980s that the economic performance of many 'resource dependent' countries showed no problems as measured by standard indicators (such as GDP and GDP per capita), but that physical and social evidences indicated the opposite. That is,

these countries were using their resources in ways that appeared to be environmentally unsustainable (Bartelmus 2008).

This was later substantiated by the publication of a major study conducted by Robert Reppetto and his colleagues (1989) at the World Resources Institute. The publication was entitled *Wasting Assets: Natural Resources in the National Accounts* and it offered, among others, novel and systematic approaches for evaluating the depreciation of natural resource assets using Indonesia as a case study. It was shown that, once adjusted to account for the depreciation of its forests, petroleum reserves and soil assets, Indonesia's GDP and growth rates sank significantly below conventional figures.

Acting on the report of the Brundtland Commission report, the 1992 Earth Summit in Rio de Janeiro declared sustainable development to be the key to integrating social, economic and environmental dimensions of development into planning and policy making. Its Action Plan, *Agenda 21*, considered combined environmental and economic accounting as 'a first step towards the integration of sustainability into economic management'.

The following year, in 1993, the SNA, an international standard of national accounts, was revised so that for the first time it incorporated a 'satellite system' for organizing hard data and other information pertaining to natural resources and the environment. This development led to the creation of the System of integrated Environmental and Economic Accounting (SEEA). Its primary purpose is to provide a systematically organized set of aggregate environmental and economic information for which indicators of performance can be derived (Alfieri and Olsen 2007; Haggart 2000).

The SEEA was revised in 2003, although without much structural change. Structurally, the SEEA comprises four major categories of accounts: flow accounts for pollution, energy and materials; environmental protection and resource expenditure accounts; natural resource asset accounts; and valuation of non-market flow and environmentally adjusted aggregates. The United Nations Statistical Division (UNDS) is the lead agency responsible for carrying out several projects in SEEA around the world. Other international agencies working closely in cooperation with UNSD are the United Nations Development Programme (UNDP), the United Nations Environmental Programme (UNEP), the International Monetary Fund (IMF), the World Band, and the Organization for Economic Co-operation and Development (OECD).

As would be expected, the quality of the data among the various satellite accounts differs widely. The monetary satellite account is still a 'work in progress' surrounded by many controversies. This remains so despite, as discussed in Chapter 7, the major advances that have been made in environmental valuation techniques over the past two decades. It is important to note that there is also a measurable difference in the quality of data between countries. Despite these difficulties, using the SEEA database it is now common practice to measure an environmentally adjusted net domestic product (EDP) on a country-by-country basis.

The EDP per capita is computed by deducting *environmental costs* from *net* domestic product and dividing it by the total population of the nation under consideration (see Idenity 14.4 below). Understood this way, EDP per capita is equivalent to the standard notion of GDP per capita except that it is calculated after accounting for both the deprecation of human-made capital and the costs to the environment associated with the normal performance of an economy on the basis of production and investment activities at an aggregate level:

$$EDP/P = (NDP - E_c)/P \qquad 14.4$$

where E_c and P represent environmental cost and population, respectively. The *environmental costs* include: expenditures on environmental damage controls, the depletion of exhaustible resources, and the degradation of environmental assets. It is important to note, however, that environmentally adjusted national income accounts do not automatically guarantee sustainability. Sustainability has the additional requirement that capital stocks (natural and manufactured) are kept intact. In other words,

the reinvestment of depreciated and depleted capital stocks must occur.

The policy relevance of an indicator like EDP per capita cannot be underestimated. An increase in EDP per capita over time would suggest a rising standard of living that is associated with economic growth after accounting for environmental costs and the normal wear-and-tear of human-made capital. For policy-makers, this should be helpful because it assures them that the economy is growing, even after full consideration of both the economic and environmental assets of the nations. In this regard, EDP per capita demonstrates a marked improvement in providing an indication of sustainable economic growth when compared to GDP per capita.

Since the Earth Summit (1992), many countries (including several developing nations) have made noticeable progress in establishing an appropriate institutional framework for the implementation of sustainable development. For example, the Philippines began work on resource accounts in 1990, as did Namibia in 1994 (Hecht 1999). These countries and many others have been primarily motivated towards sustainable development because they are increasingly convinced that taking a long-term view on the management and utilization of environmental resources (i.e., the sustainable use of environmental resources) is in the best interest of their citizens.

However, there is considerable diversity in the type of strategy and degree of effort that has been put forth, reflecting considerable differences among national priorities and circumstances. As Salah El Serafy (1997b, 217) puts it, 'fully integrated resource accounting is a priority concern for those developing countries that are running down natural resources, and for which conventional accounting distorts macroeconomic measurement, analysis and policy'. To this end, the works that have already been accomplished due to the establishment of the SNA satellite system (i.e., SEEA) should be celebrated, and the continued efforts to improve the quality of the environmental data (in particular the monetary accounts) should be supported. This can be said despite the many shortcomings of SEEA (and therefore, EDP) that will be briefly addressed next.

Environmentally adjusted indicators, such as EDP, that depend on SEEA for their data are not without their critics. One of the criticisms of SEEA-based indicators raised most often has been that they are strongly associated with the SNA methodology. Thus, there is a built-in bias towards the monetization of environmental damages and the valuation of environmental assets. This bias often led to the assessment of the cost of environmental damages and the 'value' of environmental assets based on *arbitrary* assumptions. Therefore some argued that, while the idea of environmentally adjusted national accounting is a worthwhile effort, the stress on 'valuation' makes the entire process unnecessarily complex (El Serafy 1997). According to this view, not all environmental assets have to be 'priced' in order to design environmentally adjusted indicators that are of considerable value to decision makers.

The other criticisms of SEEA revolve around the methods used to evaluate depletion allowance and the degradation of environmental assets. For example, it is argued that the estimation for depletion allowances should be based on 'user cost' instead of replacement cost, as is often done (El Serafy, 1997b). User cost refers to the imputed cost of environmental resource use, and it is estimated on the basis of present value. This is relevant (El Serafy 1997) because valuation based on replacement cost tends to overestimate the cost of depletion allowance. Since this cost is relatively large, it is likely to have a significant effect on the final outcome of the adjusted net domestic product.

Furthermore, the replacement cost approach imputes the cost of environmental degradation based on the total expenditures on pollution-damage control. Some argue that this is misleading because expenditures on damage control measure a reaction to environmental damages, not the damage itself (Stockhammer et al. 1997). Finally, it should be pointed out that SEEA-based environmentally adjusted indicators, such as EDP, only indicate weak sustainability. To such an extent, some have suggested that they should be supplemented with physical indictors of sustainability that address the broader concern of ecological sustainability.

Genuine savings (GS)

This environmentally adjusted indicator of sustainability was developed under the sponsorship of the World Bank (WB) and has been utilized by many countries as a policy guide for their sustainability initiatives. This indicator operates within the general framework of the SNA and uses environmental statistics from the satellite accounts of SEEA. The main idea behind the genuine savings as an indicator of sustainability is straightforward and it is imputed using the following formula:

$$GS = (GDP - C) - d_m - d_n + h_e - e_d \qquad 14.5$$

where,

$GDP = C + I_g$, as defined in Identity 14.1

$GDP - C$ = gross domestic investment, I_g

d_m = the depreciation of human-made (produced) capital

d_n = the value of resource depletion (energy, minerals and forests are included)

h_e = the value of investment in human capital. This represents one of the unique features of GS because the standard national accounting treats expenditures on human capital as *consumption*. On the other hand, estimates of genuine savings treat human capital as investment (a factor that would increase the productive capacity of a nation), therefore it should be added as shown in Identity 14.5 above. The World Bank uses current education expenditure as a proxy for the value of the investment in human capital.

e_d = Imputed value of environmental degradation. This variable is subtracted out from gross saving $(GDP - C)$ to adjust for the welfare loss of people and producers who have been negatively affected by environmental pollution. The World Bank estimates health effects (reduced mortality due to particular emissions) and damages caused by CO_2 emissions to impute the value of environmental degradation on a global basis.

Thus, the GS indicates the 'true' level of savings in a country after depreciation of human-made capital, depletion of resources (minerals, energy, forests), investments in human capital (as measured by current education expenditures), and damages from local and global air pollutants are taken into account. Note that Identity 14.5 assumes a closed economy where aggregate savings must equal aggregate investment.

The World Bank popularized this indicator not so much because it is a superior indicator of sustainability as such, but for two other reasons. First, there exists easily accessible data of relatively high quality with which to estimate GS. Second, it has a real practical value to the extent that it shows that a negative GS is unsustainable. In this sense, GS is useful to the extent that it can serve as an indicator of non-sustainability. Since 1999, the World Bank publishes GS for over 150 countries on a regular basis. The name used at the World Bank for GS is 'adjusted net savings' and this is done to conform with the original name for this indicator given by Pearce and Atkinson (1993).

For many developing countries, genuine savings are found to be *negative*. What is even more revealing is that for many 'resource dependent countries', the adjusted net genuine savings comes out as *negative* while their gross domestic savings (GDP − C) is *positive*. This should not be totally surprising given the considerable impact that adjustment for resource depletion would have on GS. For example, according to the 2005 World Bank report, the net adjusted genuine savings rate (GS as a percentage of GDP) for Saudi Arabia was −26.5 while the gross saving rate for the same year was +29.4. The main reason for this was the adjustment factor for energy depletion which was estimated to be −51. In general, for resource-dependent countries such as Saudi Arabia, persistent negative net genuine savings rates should suggest that their use of natural capital is unsustainable.

On the other hand, since GS is positively influenced by expenditures on human capital (education) it tends to boost the estimated value of this indicator for many developed countries, such as Japan and many Western European countries. However, for these countries the adjustment for human capital alone does not appear to change the direction of the sign of the final estimates of GS. That is, even without the adjustment for human capital, the estimated value of GS would have remained positive.

In the past, the World Bank routinely used GDP per capita as an indicator of economic performance for countries around the world. The outcomes from decisions made on the basis of such an indicator have been repeatedly disappointing because of failures to detect resource uses that later turned out to be unsustainable. A classic example of this is Nauru, a very small Pacific island nation, where the unsustainable use of its phosphate mining in pursuit of economic growth as measured by GDP has actually caused irreparable damage to the economy (see Chapter 13).

It was primarily to resolve failures of this nature that the World Bank made the decision to develop a new indicator and eventually decided to adopt the genuine savings rate. This indicator has been in use for over a decade now. Despite the shortcomings listed below, the use of genuine savings rates should mark a significant improvement over GDP per capita by the mere fact that it tries to explicitly incorporate human and environmental factors that have been overlooked by conventional indicators, such as GDP per capita. This should be considered a step in the right direction, especially when it is applied to many developing countries where the link between economics and the environment is extremely critical.

The shortcomings of GS as a sustainability indicator are numerous and very similar to those discussed earlier pertaining to the adjusted net domestic product, EDP. Among them, the major ones include:

1. GS indicators are only concerned with weak sustainability. No account is made for factors relevant to test for strong sustainability;

2. The estimate of GS is based on unreliable data and methodologies (Everett and Wilks 1999);

3. Assigning monetary values to reduced mortality, education and many features of the environment, is an art rather than a science and, as such, is difficult to validate (Ibid);

4. Some have objected to the way that resource rents are calculated and to the use of discounted

rates (Weitzman 1998). The choice of these two factors will have a significant effect on the imputed value of resource depletion;

5. Since GS is GDP dependent, nations with higher GDPs are far less likely to obtain a weak or negative genuine savings result (Everett and Wilks 1999);

6. Some argue that it is overly simplistic to try to measure combined economic and environmental impacts using a single indicator that is based on a simple criterion of sustainability. Such a criterion does not inform decision-makers about the causes and or solutions for environmental problems (Ibid).

7. Both EDP and GS are constructed without any consideration of the fact that GDP, as conventionally measured, is not a good indicator of wellbeing (more on this later). To some, this is seen as a major weakness, especially if these two indicators are going to be used as measures of sustainable economic welfare (Daly and Cobb 1989). The next sustainability indicator to be discussed, the index of sustainable economic welfare (ISEW), was developed to address this omission.

The index of sustainable economic welfare (ISEW)

The concept of social 'welfare' has been briefly mentioned before, but deserves further exploration due to its significance as an indicator of wellbeing. Interest in this subject is not new to economics. In fact, welfare economics has been a branch of economic studies going as far back in history as the early twentieth century. The British economist, Arthur Cecil Pigou (1877–1959), was credited with much of the early work on the theory of welfare economics and its application to public policies.

As a subject, welfare economics not only deals with the efficient allocation of resources, but, most notably, on how the total goods and services of an economy are distributed. A central focus of welfare economics involves how resources (income) are distributed and how redistributions of income could affect the 'common good'. We have already observed the application of welfare economics in Chapter 8 in the development of the theoretical underpinnings of cost–benefit analysis. In general, welfare economics deals with the evaluation of economic policies in terms of their effects on the wellbeing of the community using well established and theoretically sound criteria (such as 'actual' and 'potential' Pareto improvements discussed in Chapter 8).

GDP is not a measure of economic welfare (i.e., general wellbeing). Although at times it seems to be used in that way (e.g., an increase in GDP per capita causes an improved standard of living), no respectable economist will argue that GDP has been designed with the intention of measuring social welfare (Nordhaus and Tobin 1972). What GDP is expected to measure is the performance of an economy on the basis of production and investment activities at an aggregate level—the total pie, so to speak. Similarly, the environmentally adjusted indictors discussed thus far (i.e., EDP and GS) cannot qualify as measures of economic welfare because, like GDP, they are functionally dependent on the SNA.

It was to fill this missing gap that Herman Daly (an economist) and John Cobb (a theologian) conceived the basic idea of what is now known as the *index of sustainable economic welfare* (ISEW) in their book, *For the Common Good* (1989). The aim of this index has been to combine the economic, ecological and social aspects of human endeavors, which are often separated. Furthermore, the ISEW is used as an indicator of economic performance in the same way as GDP, EDP and GS, but has the added benefit of being used as a yardstick for measuring economic wellbeing.

Since ISEW aims to measure sustainable economic welfare, its mode of analysis is based entirely on *consumption*. This is because the theoretical foundation of ISEW is based, not on the concept of Hicksian income, but on Irvin Fisher's concept of income and capital (Lawn 2003). For Fisher, *income* (which is equated with services) is the ultimate psychic satisfaction enjoyed by the final users of produced goods. On the other hand, *capital* refers to all stocks of material objects that yield services that people would like to have. Thus, according to Tobin (2005: 211), Fisher's concept of capital would include:

> land and other natural resources as well as reproducible goods; objects owned by households and governments as well as by businesses; houses and other consumer durable goods as well as producers' durables; objects whose yields are always in kind, like houses occupied by their owners, as well as those whose yields are marketed for cash; the bodies of human beings—perhaps their minds too—as well as nonhuman objects.

Note that, in both the definition of income and capital, *service* is the operative word. This is why the ISEW insists on converting all economic activities into their equivalent consumption.

The first step in the computation of the ISEW starts with *personal consumption expenditures*. Consistent with the Fisher conception of income, personal consumption represents the services or 'psychic' income enjoyed by the final users of produced goods (Lawn 2003). This part very much corresponds to the aggregate consumption part of the standard GDP. However, the process does not end here.

The second step is to *weight* the personal consumption expenditures with an index of income inequality. Normally, the *Gini coefficient*—a standard measure of income inequality with value ranging between 0 and 1— is used. A Gini coefficient of unity will indicate perfect equality. The rationale for doing this is based on the notion that the distribution of income can have a significant impact on a nation's economic *welfare* (Ibid). Holding personal expenditures constant, a decrease in the Gini coefficient (i.e., increasing gap in income distribution) over time is likely to have a *negative* effect on the economic welfare of a nation. This is because, according to the law of diminishing marginal utility (utility refers here to psychic benefits from incremental personal consumption), as the income gap of a nation increases, the marginal benefit (utility) gained by the rich from additional consumption will be less than the marginal benefit (utility) gained by the poor.

In plain English, this suggests that a poor person would derive more satisfaction from an increase in income (consumption) than would a rich person. Hence, any move towards an equitable distribution of income would likely lead to increased social welfare. Since the aggregate personal consumption expenditure obtained from data based on conventional national income accounting doesn't explicitly account for this potential, it should be normalized using an index of income inequality, that is, the Gini coefficient. It is important to note that, in taking this step, the ISEW considers income distribution *per se* to be an integral part of economic welfare.

The third step in the calculation of ISEW involves the estimation of the rate of consumption (depreciation) of *consumer durables*. This is done by finding the difference between the *cost* of consumer durables (such as cars, household furniture, personal computers, and so on) and the *service* annually yielded by previously purchased consumer durables. The value for the services from previously owned consumer durables is computed as a percentage of the total value of the aggregate stock of consumer durables in a given year (Ibid). This is expected to represent the rate of depreciation (more appropriately, consumption) of consumer durables. This value is *subtracted* is from the *weighted* personal consumption expenditure that was done in step one.

The fourth step in calculating the ISEW involves determining the annual rate of consumption (depreciation) of publicly provided capital, such as highways, schools, national parks, and so on. The value for the services for publicly provided capital is computed in the same manner as the consumer durables (i.e., as the percentage of the total value of all the existing stock of publicly provided human-made capital). The final value is supposed to represent the annual depreciation rate (or the rate of consumption) of publicly provided capital. Since this depreciation in the services rendered from the existing aggregate stock of publicly provided human-made capital is consistent with the Fisherian concept of income and capital it should be *added* in the ISEW.

The fifth step is to impute the value of the *services* of unpaid household labor. This is done to recognize that services such as childcare, even when performed by unpaid household members, have consumptive values. Thus, in the calculation of the ISEW the imputed value of household labor is *added* as part of the income flow because household labor, even when it is unpaid, contributes to the psychic income of a nation. This is an item that is completely ignored in conventional national income accounting.

The steps undertaken thus far would complete the *consumption base* of the ISEW. Once this is done, the sixth step taken in the process of computing the ISEW involves the estimation of the various *social* and *environmental* costs normally excluded or not properly accounted for in the calculation of the conventional gross domestic product. These social costs are identified in the following two ways: (1) the *disservices* (i.e., negative psychic incomes) generated by economic activities, such as urban congestion, auto accidents, crime, traffic jams, long hours spent commuting, among others; and (2) the *defensive expenditures* that society has incurred to either *repair* (such as reduce crime or reduce traffic jams) or to internalize external costs (such as money spent by households to install pollution-control devices). Defensive expenditures represent a *loss* of income that cannot be spent again for consumption or investment, but can be spent only to repair or prevent environmental damages or social ills caused by normal economic activities (Daly 1996). Thus, the calculation of the ISEW requires that these two types of social costs should be *deducted* from the total. This is not done in the conventional method of national income accounting.

The last step in the computation of the ISEW involves the estimation of the environmental costs borne by future generations (i.e., intergenerational external costs). These costs include: the depletion of nonrenewable resources (normally assessed using the replacement cost method); the use of renewable resources beyond their regenerations (assessed by the user-cost method); and long-term environmental damages arising from factors such as global warming, ozone depletion, and threats to species extinctions (using the various methods of environmental valuation discussed in Chapter 7).

In summary, ISEW per capita is computed the following way:

$$ISEW/P = [\alpha(PCE) + D]/P$$

where the variables PCE, α, and P represent personal consumption expenditures, the parameter used for weighing income inequality, and population, respectively. D represents an amalgamation of a number of benefits and costs that include the following: the *difference* between the expenditure on consumer durables and the service flows from consumer durables + the services obtained from the provision of publicly provided capital goods + the services provided by unpaid domestic labor – the defensive social and environmental costs – the *sum* of the *allowances* for the depletion of exhaustible resources, the overuse of renewable resources, and the external costs to future generations arising from long term environmental damages. It is important to note that *for the ISEW to meet the condition of sustainability, capital stock needs to be kept intact.* Note also that in the calculation of the ISEW all values are measured in monetary terms and using data generated using the general framework taken from the SNA. In this sense, ISEW can only be an indicator of weak sustainability.

Over the past two decades, the ISEW has been applied in several studies of both developed and developing countries. The results of these studies are somewhat varied, depending on the specific economic, social and environmental circumstances of the countries under consideration. However, one interesting observation that has emerged from these studies is *the widening gap between trend lines for the index of GDP per capita and the ISEW for advanced countries.* More specifically, after certain time-periods, these countries tend to show a decline in their economic performance as measured by the ISEW, despite continued growth of per capita GDP. Based on this empirical observation, Manfred Max-Neef (1995: 117) noted that 'for every society there seems to be a period in which economic growth (as conventionally measured) brings about an improvement in the quality of life, but only up to a point—the threshold

321

point—by which, if there is more economic growth, quality of life may begin to deteriorate'. This so-called 'threshold hypothesis' continues to be substantiated by a growing number of empirical studies.

The implication of this hypothesis is that, due to negative factors associated with social ailments (such as crimes, divorces, etc.), income inequalities, and environmental deterioration, after a certain threshold point economic growth (as conventionally perceived) would lead to a decline in quality of life. This is another inverted-U hypothesis, but this time relating to economic growth and quality of life as measured by an indicator such as the ISEW. According to Max-Neef (1995), the threshold point occurred in the early 1970s for the United States and in the mid-1970s for the United Kingdom.

The ISEW has been criticized for several reasons. Among them the major ones are as follows:

1. It cannot 'truly' claim to measure economic welfare to the extent that it relies on the SNA for imputing values on the basis of market prices.
2. Leisure is not considered.
3. The computation of the ISEW is marred by a number of arbitrary assumptions, and different valuation methods are used for different components of the ISEW so that consistency is not always guaranteed.
4. It is argued that the valuation of exhaustible resources is based on 'cost escalating factors' that are difficult to defend. Similarly, the valuation for long-term environmental damage is based on the assumption that it has a cumulative effect over time. The upshot of these two assumptions is that they inflate costs (Neumayer 2000). Using this as his basis, Neumayer questions the validity of the threshold hypothesis.

14.5 PHYSICAL INDICATORS OF SUSTAINABILITY: ECOLOGICAL FOOTPRINT

The three sustainability indicators discussed thus far have one thing in common. All three attempt to measure sustainability based on criteria that are expressed in monetary units. This often requires relying on market or shadow (imputed) prices, and when these are not available, resorting to environmental 'valuation' methodologies that, as shown in Chapter 7, use arbitrary assumptions and, as such, tend to be questionable. Furthermore, it is almost impossible to monetarily measure the impacts of economic growth on the structure and function of ecosystems without having a clear idea about the associated ecological thresholds and the risks involved in transgressing such limits (such as loss of biodiversity and the ability of ecosystems to withstand external shocks—ecological resilience).

Thus, a proxy of 'weak' sustainability indicators, such as EDP, GS and ISEW, leave out many important factors that are crucial in any consideration of ecological sustainability (such as ecosystems function and structure). In this respect, these monetary-based indicators may have failed in meeting the criteria of *strong* sustainability. As will be evident below, the main reason for considering physical indicators of sustainability is in response to this apparent shortcoming of the indicators of sustainability discussed thus far. The view taken here is that, given the seemingly intractable practical problems associated with designing indicators that satisfy the criteria of 'strong' sustainability, the second-best solution would be to supplement indicators of weak sustainability (such as EDP, GS and ISEW) with physical indicators of sustainability relevant to the specific problem on hand.

There are several physical indicators of sustainability (such as the sustainability gap indicator, carrying capacity and ecological footprint, among others) that can be considered for use at any given point in time. However, this section covers only one indicator, namely, the ecological footprint (EFP). This indicator is chosen not so much for the popularity it currently enjoys but rather, as will be evident shortly, for its implicit assumption that long-run economic wellbeing depends upon meeting the criteria of strong sustainability (Bicknell 1998).

The EFP concept and calculation method was first developed in 1990 by Mathis Wackernagel and William Rees at the University of British Columbia.

In 1996, Wackernagel and Rees published the book *Our Ecological Footprint: Reducing Human Impact on the Earth*. Conceptually, what does the EFP entail, and how is it measured? In what specific ways does it indicate sustainability or unsustainability? What are the major strengths and weaknesses of this indicator? These are the questions addressed in the rest of this of this section.

Ecological footprint as a concept

According to the *Living Planet Report* (WWF 2010: 11), from a global perspective 'the EFP tracks humanity demand on the ecosystems by measuring the area of biologically productive land and water required to provide the renewable resources people use and to absorb the CO2 waste that human activities generate'. There are three key issues in this definition that need to be clarified.

The first issue deals with the *demand* (i.e., resource consumption) placed on the biosphere from the global population. This demand is expressed in terms of the *productive land* needed for food, housing, transportation, consumer goods and services, and land to assimilate waste, such as CO_2 released from the burning of fossil fuels. Thus, at a given point in time estimates of the EFP convey the productive *land* needed to satisfy current levels of resource consumption. The unit used to express resource consumption is the global hectare (2.47 acres) and the calculation of EFP is based on the average person's annual consumption. Thus, EFP per capita would be expressed as:

$$EFP/P = L_{w/h}/P$$

where $L_{w/h}$ represents total area in global hectares (gha) of biologically productive land used to satisfy current consumption annually, and P represents population. It is also important to note that, as defined here, EFP is a static concept since it refers to current consumption assuming no changes in technologies, resource use patterns or lifestyles.

The second issue pertains to the total supply of resources available from the biosphere in the form of biologically productive land and sea areas for specific human uses—the *biophysical constraints*. In the current literature of the EFP, six major land-use categories are identified: energy land, built-up or degraded land, gardens, cropland, pasture and managed forest. The productivity of each land-use category depends on their respective *bio-capacity*, which is entirely determined by nature (i.e., according to the ecological principles discussed in Chapter 2). *Productivity* for any land-use category is measured according to the *average ability of the world to produce resources and absorb wastes*, using gha as the unit of measurement. Thus, the physical weights applied to each land-use category (such as pastureland) for a specific consumption category (such as cattle grazing) are fixed by nature. What this implies is the use of a fixed rate of substitution between different categories of land-use (van den Bergh 1999).

The third issue that should be noted is the focus EFP places on *renewable resources* for the following two reasons: (1) the fact that 'biological productivity' is a central concept in EFP clearly suggests that the resources under consideration have the capacity to regenerate themselves within the bounds established by nature; and (2) *nonrenewable resources are unsustainable by definition*, and as such they are irrelevant in the consideration of long-term ecological sustainability. Hence, given the EFP's focus on renewable resources, ecological sustainability can imply comparisons of the actual throughput of renewable resources relative to what is annually renewed. More specifically, *consumption should not exceed the regenerative capacity of the renewable resources*. This way, the natural capital (renewable resources) remains intact. Unlike the Hartwick rule (which is basically for optimal depletion of nonrenewable resources), the EFP rule is expressed entirely in *physical terms*.

Thus, it is fairly easy to observe that the EFP is an indicator of ecological sustainably entirely based on a 'bio-physical' context. It does not represent economic or social welfare, it simply conveys ecological wellbeing (Ayres 2000). It is in this sense that the EFP may be considered a good proxy in meeting the criteria for *strong* sustainability.

Finally, it is important to point out that the methodology for computing EFP is quite involved and difficult to present here in any meaningful detail. Interested readers are strongly encouraged to read a very useful publication prepared by Ewing et al. (2008) entitled 'Calculation Methodology for the National Footprint Accounts, 2008 Edition'. The calculations of EFP therein are primarily based on international data sets published by international agencies, such as the Food and Agriculture Organization of the United Nations and the International Energy Agency. For a complete list of source data please refer to a publication by Ewing et al. (2010) entitled 'The Ecological Footprint Atlas 2010'.

Ecological footprint as indicator of sustainability: global context

Keeping the above three points in mind, and setting aside the complex processes involved in the calculation of the EFP, ecological sustainability is attained when the aggregate *demand*, or the amount of productive land required to support the consumption of the global population annually (i.e., the total EFP), is met without exceeding the *total supply* of the biologically productive land available to satisfy demand on an annual basis (i.e., the earth's bio-capacity).

In this context, if demand exceeds supply, an ecological *deficit* will occur. More specifically, because we are dealing with renewable capital assets, an ecological deficit implies that the amount of biologically productive land needed for human consumption and waste generation exceeds what is annually renewed or added through the natural regeneration process. In other words, the world is dipping into its natural capital and this is clearly unsustainable. In recent years, there have been several studies which indicate that the world is in this unfavorable ecological predicament.

For example, according to the 2010 Edition of the *Living Planet Report* (WWF 2010), in 2007 the total global ecological footprint was estimated to be 18.09 billion gha or 2.7 gha per person (see Table 14.1). For the same year, the bio-capacity was estimated to be 12.06 billion gha or 1.8 gha per person. This suggests an ecological deficit of 0.9 billion gha per person. Furthermore, this situation has been the norm since the early 1980s. That is, the world has been in ecological *deficit* for about three decades (WWF 2010).

Another interesting figure to look at is the ratio of EFP to bio-capacity. For 2007 this figure was 1.5 (i.e., 2.7/1.8). This means that, at the current rate of global

Table 14.1 *Global Footprint from 1961 to 2006*

	1961	1965	1970	1975	1980	1985	1990	1995	2000	2005	2007
Global Population (billion)	3.1	3.3	3.7	4.1	4.4	4.8	5.3	5.7	6.1	6.5	6.7
Total Ecological Footprint	2.4	2.5	2.8	2.8	2.8	2.6	2.7	2.6	2.5	2.7	2.7
Cropland Footprint	1.1	1.1	1.0	0.9	0.8	0.8	0.7	0.7	0.6	0.6	0.6
Grazing Land Footprint	0.4	0.4	0.3	0.3	0.3	0.2	0.2	0.2	0.2	0.2	0.2
Forest Footprint	0.4	0.4	0.4	0.4	0.4	0.3	0.3	0.3	0.3	0.3	0.3
Fishing Ground Footprint	0.1	0.1	0.1	0.1	0.1	0.1	0.1	0.1	0.1	0.1	0.1
Carbon Footprint	0.3	0.5	0.9	1.0	1.1	1.1	1.2	1.2	1.2	1.4	1.4
Built-up Land	0.1	0.1	0.1	0.1	0.1	0.1	0.1	0.1	0.1	0.1	0.1
Total Biocapacity	3.7	3.5	3.1	2.9	2.6	2.4	2.3	2.1	2.0	1.8	1.8
Ecological Footprint to Biocapacity ratio	0.63	0.73	0.88	0.97	1.06	1.07	1.18	1.24	1.29	1.45	1.51

Source: www.footprintnetwork/images/uploads/2010_NFA_data_tables.xls

resource consumption, the earth needs 1.5 years to produce and replenish the natural resources that humanity is consuming in a single year. The implications of these findings are far reaching, because excess consumption and waste emissions beyond the earth's bio-capacity can only occur at the cost of other living species and the further weakening of the life-support functions of the biosphere. In fact, it is confirmed by the *Living Planet Report* (WWF 2010) that, worldwide, biodiversity decreased by nearly 30 percent between 1970 and 2007.

Findings of the above nature will have significant policy implications, especially when they are substantiated by additional physical evidence, such as a gradual but persistent trend of deforestation in areas of the world regarded as ecologically sensitive, or the accumulation of CO_2 in the atmosphere dating back to the industrial revolution. The 2010 Edition of LPR showed that the footprints (i.e., gha of productive land per capita available) for cropland, grazing land, and forestland have shown steady decline over the past five decades. On the other hand, over the same period the carbon footprint has been increasing at a faster rate. In 1961 the carbon footprint was 0.3 gha per capita. This means the equivalent of 0.3 gha per person was needed for CO_2 uptake in that year. After a steady increase over the past five decades, the carbon footprint reached 1.4 gha per capita by 2007—an increase of 433 percent (see Table 14.1).

As dire as the situation may seem however (as discussed in Chapter in 9 in some detail), the policy measures needed to remedy ecological problems whose impacts are understood only in a global context are very difficult (if not impossible) to implement because they depend on the unified actions of the world community. For this reason, from a policy perspective, it will make much more sense if sustainability criteria are framed within the geopolitical boundaries of nations or regions. Can this be done effectively using the EFP analyses? The answer to this question will be the subject of the next subsection.

Ecological footprint as indicator of sustainability: national/regional context

Conceptually, the EFP can be assessed for activities, regions, nations, or even individual people. However, as we shall see shortly, many criticisms of the EFP as an indicator of sustainability arise when it is used within the context of clearly demarcated geopolitical boundaries. Among others, one of the reason for this is because nations with well demarcated political boundaries may share ecosystems (wetland preserves, fishery grounds and forestland) and this complicates the computation of bio-capacity at national or regional levels (Ayres 2000; van den Bergh and Verbruggen 1999).

Setting aside the added difficulties associated with computing the bio-capacity on a country-by-country basis, in all other respects the EFP for a country is estimated using methodologies identical with those used for the world as a whole (Ewing et al. 2008). Reports of global EFP are often accompanied with corresponding estimates on a country-by-country basis. Disaggregated data of this nature are reported semiannually in the *Living Planet Report* (WWF 2010).

For example, in 2003 the EFP per capita for the US, China, Brazil, Canada and Germany were 9.6, 1.6, 2.1, 7.6 and 4.5, respectively (WWF 2006). All of the EFP per capita figures are expressed in terms of gha per person. On the other hand, for these same countries the estimates of the corresponding bio-capacity per capita were 4.7, 0.8, 9.9, 14.5 and 1.7, respectively.

Thus, the US, China and Germany were experiencing ecological *deficits* of –4.8, –0.9 and –2.8, respectively. On the other hand, Brazil and Canada were showing ecological reserves of 7.8 and 6.9, respectively. All figures are based on per capita gha.

In general, studies based on EFP analysis have consistently shown that many countries are running an ecological deficit, especially those with advanced economies. These findings have important implications, as William Rees (1996: 1) explains:

> most so-called advanced countries are running massive unaccounted ecological deficits with the

rest of the planet. Since not all countries can be net importers of carrying capacity, the material standards of the wealthy cannot be extended sustainably to even the present world population using prevailing technology.

Here is another observation based on recent data from the 2010 Edition of LPR that pretty much echoes Rees' concern (WWF 2010: 19):

> The Ecological Footprint according to four political groupings which broadly represent different economic levels, illustrates that higher income, more developed countries generally make higher demands on the Earth's ecosystems than poorer, less developed countries. In 2007, the 31 OECD countries—which include the world's richest economies—accounted for 37 percent of humanity's Ecological Footprint. In contrast, the 10 ASEAN countries and 53 African Union countries—which include some of the world's poorest and least developed countries— together accounted for only 12 percent of the global Footprint.

The above observations not only indicate global unsustainability, but also the ethical (normative) implications of the differentiated impacts of such ecological externalities. Findings of this nature could be used to justify the implementation of public-policy instruments, such as the Clean Development Mechanism (CDM), as defined by Article 12 of the Kyoto Protocol (see Chapter 10). The idea is for advanced countries with 'ecological deficits' to compensate developing countries through investing in projects that stand to benefit these countries.

Let us conclude the discussion in this subsection by providing brief mentions of the pros and cons of the EFP as an indicator of ecological sustainability. Supporters consider the following to be the strengths of the EFP as an indicator of sustainability:

1. It has an immediate intuitive appeal;
2. It is the only indicator that attempts to meet the criteria for strong sustainability;
3. It can be effectively used to complement the monetary based indicators of sustainability.
4. It is flexible since an EFP can be assessed for persons, activities, regions, or the world as a whole.
5. It could provide important policy clues in making decisions regarding an ecologically optimal sustainable *scale*.

On the other hand, some scholars downplay the value of EFP as an indicator of sustainability for the following reasons:

1. Its calculation is based on a number of arbitrary assumptions and the quality and sources of the data are questionable (van den Bergh and Verbruggen 1999);
2. It gives too much emphasis on energy. The land appropriated for fossil-fuel energy use makes up 50 percent of the EFP estimate for most developed countries (Ibid; Ayres 2000);
3. The total productive land available for use is hypothetical. It comprises only 25 percent of the earth's surface and the ocean is not included (van den Bergh and Verbruggen 1999);
4. It is anti-trade by its insistence that no country should have an ecological deficit (Ayres 2000);
5. It is a static indicator of sustainability since its calculation is based on current technological and resource use patterns. Most importantly, the EFP analyses tend to downplay intensive land use, especially in agriculture (Fiala 2008);
6. It does not allow substitutions between different forms or land-uses;
7. Its policy implications at national and regional levels are unreliable. This is because, as discussed above, it is extremely difficult to estimate biocapacity on the basis of arbitrarily drawn (from an ecological perspective) geopolitical boundaries.

14.6 CHAPTER SUMMARY

Modifying national income accounting systems to promote an understanding of the links between the economy and the environment is a first step towards the integration of sustainability into performance indicators of national economies. With this in mind, the primary motivations of this chapter have been to explore the recent advances in the development of environmentally adjusted indicators of sustainability within the general framework of the system of national income accounts (SNA). Why is the adjustment needed, and what are the adjustments that need to be incorporated?

The idea that the 'conventional' SNA does not explicitly consider the *costs* of natural resource depletion and environmental degradation has been firmly established for some time. Hence, to the extent that the SNA has this well-recognized shortcoming, it renders GDP (or GDP per capita) to be ineffective indicators of environmental sustainability. This is, of course, unless adequate adjustments are made in the way the SNA is structured to incorporate the missing key environmental variables.

Thus, the two major challenges facing international efforts to develop a 'green national income accounting' that is anchored within the general framework of the SNA have been:

1. The restructuring of the SNA at a fundamental level so that it will include the needed environmental data; and
2. The development of valuation techniques such that the environmental data are monetized as much as possible.

It was to this end that, in 1993 (a year after the *Earth Summit* in Rio de Janeiro) the SNA was revised so that, for the first time, it incorporated a 'satellite system' for organizing hard data and other information pertaining to natural resources and the environment.

This development led to the creation of the 'system of integrated environmental and economic accounting' (SEEA). Its primary purpose is to provide a systematically organized set of aggregate environmental and economic information from which indicators of sustainable performance can be derived. The SEEA was revised in 2003 and comprises four major categories of accounts: flow accounts for pollution, energy and materials; environmental protection and resource expenditure accounts; natural resource asset accounts; and valuation of non-market flow and environmentally adjusted aggregates.

Using the SEEA database it is now common practice to measure an environmentally adjusted net domestic product (EDP) on a country-by-country basis. More formally, EDP = NDP − total environmental cost, where NDP is net domestic product. In this formulation, the total environmental cost attempts to include *estimates* of the monetary values of the harms caused by pollution and allowances for the depreciation of natural capital (i.e., depletion of nonrenewable resources and harvest of renewable resources that are considered to be above the regenerative capacity of the resources under consideration). Several studies showed that, for several resource dependent countries, economic performances measured on the basis of EDP were a great deal lower than their GDP would have indicated.

Environmentally adjusted national income accounts, such as EDP, can provide helpful policy guidance. First, they have the potential to reveal important information about the sector(s) of an economy where resource misallocations due to environmental externalities are evident. Second, closer examination of the data used to compute an indicator like EDP may identify the major sources of sustainability or unsustainability.

Another sustainability indictor that was discussed in this chapter is 'genuine savings' (GS). This measure-of-sustainability index starts with the recognition of the importance of savings to the future growth of a country. More specifically, it stipulates that in using the framework of the environmentally adjusted SNA, the savings should be computed in such a way that the depreciation of human-made capital, the imputed value of resource depletion and environmental degradation, and new additions to human capital are explicitly and appropriately considered. Thus, the adjusted net genuine savings measures the 'true' level of savings in a country after the depreciation of human-made capital, depletion of resources (minerals, energy, forests), investment in human capital (as measured by current education expenditures), and damages from local and global air pollution are taken into account.

For many developing countries, genuine savings are found to be *negative*. What is even more revealing is that, for many resource-dependent countries, the adjusted net genuine savings comes out as negative while their gross domestic savings is positive. This should not be totally surprising given the considerable impact that adjustment for resource depletion would have on GS.

The third sustainability indicator discussed in this chapter is the 'index of sustainable economic welfare' (ISEW). This indicator differs from EDP and GS in that it attempts to measure sustainable economic welfare (wellbeing). For this reason, the index is constructed through the explicit incorporation of social and environmental factors that have not been addressed by EDP and GS. Such social factors include unpaid household labor and income distribution, and socially defensive expenditures (such as traffic jams). ISEW also includes additional environmental factors, namely environmentally defensive expenditures. All of these environmental and social factors are not included in the system of national accounting (SNA). Finally, since ISEW is a measure of welfare, all of the variables are converted into consumptive equivalents. This is done to confirm that utility is derived only from the act of consumption. To do this, however, investment expenditures have to be converted to consumptive equivalences. This is done by treating investment expenditures as future consumption derived from net investment.

Over the past two decades, the ISEW has been applied in several studies throughout both developed and developing countries. The results of these studies are somewhat varied, depending on the specific economic, social and environmental circumstances of the countries under consideration. However, one interesting observation that has emerged from these studies is the widening gap between trends lines for the index of GDP per capita and the ISEW for advanced countries. More specifically, after certain time-periods, these countries tend to show a decline in their economic performance as measured by the ISEW, despite continued growth of per capita GDP

It is important to note that all of the environmentally adjusted sustainability indicators discussed in this chapter do not automatically guarantee sustainability. Sustainability, as discussed in Section 14.3, has the additional requirement that capital stocks (natural and manufactured) are kept intact at some predetermined level. In other words, the reinvestment of depreciated and depleted capital stocks must occur.

This chapter outlined the major weaknesses associated with the three sustainability indicators that are formulated within the general framework of SNA, namely EDP, GS and ISEW. Since they are dependent on SNA, these indicators measure sustainability in monetary units. However, in so doing they can only serve as indicators of *weak* sustainability. This is because ecological factors that cannot be expressed in monetary units are ignored. Advocates for *strong* sustainability measures consider this to be a major flaw.

The fourth sustainability indicator considered in this chapter is the ecological footprint (EFP), and it is done with the expectation that it can be used as a proxy for strong sustainability. EFP is expressed in physical units. Setting aside the methodological complexities involved in the calculation of EFP, sustainability is measured by looking at the amount of productive land required to support the consumption of the global population annually. The world is said to be in an ecological deficit (on an unsustainable course) if the amount of biologically productive land needed for human consumption and waste generation exceeds what is annually renewed or added through the natural regeneration process. In other words, the world is dipping into its natural capital and this is clearly unsustainable. In recent years there have been several studies to indicate that the world is actually in this unfavorable ecological predicament.

The approach used to calculate EFP is flexible enough to apply it to an individual country or even for an individual person. However, problems will arise when it is used in this way because there is no perfect alignment between geopolitical and ecological boundaries.

One important issue, with significant policy and ethical implications, with studies based on EFP is that advanced countries are running massive unaccounted ecological deficits with the rest of the world. This is significant because it validates the massive resource transfers that are occurring from the poor nations to the rich nations. Furthermore, it implies that the cause for observed global unsustainability is the overconsumption of resources in the rich countries.

The EFP has several major weaknesses that have been already outlined in this chapter. However, one major shortcoming of EFP that is worth mentioning again is the fact that its calculation relies on methodologies that require making a number of arbitrary assumptions, and the quality and sources of the data are questionable. In addition to this, from an economic perspective EFP is calculated upon a methodological framework that does not allow for substitutions between different forms of land-uses (or resources, in general).

Finally, it is important to point out that these measures are *static* indicators of sustainability since their calculations are based on current technological and resource use patterns. This is an important issue to keep in mind if these sustainability indicators are to be used for policy considerations that intend to address equitable intergenerational transfer (distribution) of resources.

REVIEW AND DISCUSSION QUESTIONS

1. Briefly describe the following concepts: the system of national income accounts (SNA), depreciation of human-made capital, allowance for resource depletion, socially defensive expenditures, environmentally defensive expenditures, ecological footprint, the Gini coefficient, ecological deficit, welfare economics, threshold hypothesis.

2. Clearly explain the differences among the following alternative national accounting identities: (a) gross domestic product (GDP); (b) net national product (NNP); and (c) environmentally-adjusted net national product (NNP_e).

3. National income accounts of the type discussed in question 2 above are said to measure the 'flow' of income or expenditures of a nation in given year. Why is the term 'flow' significant? Explain.

4. National income estimates derived from the use of accounting methods based on the SNA (such as GDP, NNP and NNP_e) are said to be *static*. That is, they measure the flow of aggregate income or expenditure at a point in time. If this is the case, what specific condition has to be stipulated to make an environmentally adjusted net national product (NNP_e) an indicator of sustainability? Explain why a sustainability indicator that is based on NNP_e can only meet the condition for weak sustainability (i.e., why it cannot be an used as an indicator of strong sustainability).

5. Read the following statements. In response, state 'True', 'False' or 'Uncertain' and explain why:

    (a) In the presence of external trade, sustainability indicators at the national level may be flawed.

    (b) If the genuine savings rate (GS) of a resource-dependent country (such as Congo, Venezuela, Indonesia) has been consistently *negative* over the past 15 years, it is a clear indication that this country is a net exporter of resources. In an era of globalization this should not suggest any impending economic problem.

    (c) Many developed nations (such as Japan, Germany and US) are in ecological *deficit*. That is, for each country the ecological footprint or the amount of biologically productive land needed for consumption and waste generation exceeds the natural regeneration process. This is clearly unsustainable.

    (d) Money spent on repairing environmental damages, as such expenditure on devices put on smokestacks to control pollution, normally increases GDP. This is a flawed accounting approach because expenditures of this nature are not economically productive.

6. Why do some critics suggest that the so-called sustainability indictors, such as the GS and the ISEW, are better utilized as indicators of non-sustainability than sustainability? Explain.

7. A distinguishing feature of environmentally adjusted domestic product (EDP) as an indicator of sustainability is that it treats human capital as an investment, as measured by the total expenditures on education. This is a departure from the norm since human capital is conventionally treated as a consumption expenditure. Try to identify the pros and cons to this approach.

8. Empirical studies over the past two decades have shown a widening gap between trend lines for the index of GDP per capita and the ISEW for many advanced countries. This seems to validate the claim made by the so-called threshold hypothesis. That is, economic growth as conventionally measured would lead to a decline in quality of life. (a) Provide a measured comment. (b) How do you reconcile the threshold hypothesis with the environmental Kuznets curve (ECK) hypothesis discussed in Chapter 12?

9. Beckerman (1994) argued that 'Apart from a few small developing countries heavily dependent on minerals or other finite primary products, the measurement of some wider concept of "sustainable' GNP is a waste of time and such estimates as have been made are virtually worthless'. Explain why you may agree or disagree with Beckerman's criticism of green national accounting? Be specific by providing examples to support your position.

10. In Chapter 2, the concept of carrying capacity (CC) was introduced. It was defined as the population of a given species that can be supported indefinitely in a given well demarcated habitat (land) without irreversibly damaging the ecosystem on which it is dependent. Thus, CC can be represented by the ratio of land over population (L/P). In this chapter we define the ecological footprint (EFP) basically as the ratio of P/L, that is, the amount of productive land needed to support a given population. Thus, viewed this way, these two concepts appear to be inversely related. To perhaps indicate the close ties between these two concepts the founders of EFP, Wackernagel and Rees, initially use the phrase 'appropriated carrying capacity' to describe EFP. Given this, speculate as to why no one seems to talk about using carrying capacity as an indicator of sustainability with the same fervor as they do for ecological footprint.

11. For a hypothetical country, XYZ, what information does each of the following sustainability indicators convey (be specific):
    (a) Net genuine savings per capita (GS/P) > 0.
    (b) Ecological footprint per capita (EFP/P) < 0.
    (c) Index of sustainable economic welfare per capita (ISEW/P) < 0.

12. Can you provide a real-world situation (i.e., a specific country in the world) that could possibly satisfy the above three sustainability indexes at the same time? Explain.

REFERENCES AND FURTHER READING

Alfieri, A., and Olsen, T. (2007) 'Integrated Environmental and Economic Accounting', Paper prepared for the 2nd meeting of the Oslo Group on Energy Statistics, Delhi, India, 5–7 February: 1–11.

Ayres, R. (2000) 'Commentary on the Utility of the Ecological Footprint Concept', *Ecological Economics* 32: 347–9.

Bartelmus, P. (2008) 'Measuring Sustainable Economic Growth and Development', *Encyclopedia of Earth*: www.eoearth.org

Beckerman, W. (1994) 'Sustainable Development: Is it a Useful Concept?' *Environmental Values* 3, 3: 191–209.

Bicknell, K.B., Ball, R.J., Cullen, R. and Bigsby, H.R (1998) 'New Methodology for the Ecological Footprint with an Application to the New Zealand Economy', *Ecological Economics* 27: 149–60.

Castaneda, B. (1999) 'An Index of Sustainable Economic Welfare (ISEW) for Chile', *Ecological Economics* 28: 231–44.

Daly, H. E. (1996) *Beyond Growth: The Economics of Sustainable Development*, Boston, MA: Beacon Press.

Daly, H. and Cobb, J. (1989), *For the Common Good: Redirecting the Economy toward Community, the Environment, and a Sustainable Future*, Boston, MA: Beacon Press.

Ekins, P. (2003) 'Identifying Critical Natural Capital: Conclusions about Critical Natural Capital', *Ecological Economics* 44: 277–92.

El Serafy, S. (1997a) 'Green Accounting and Economic Policy', *Ecological Economics* 21: 217–29.

El Serafy, S. (1997b) 'The Environment as Capital', in R, Costanza, C. Perrings and C. J. Cleveland (eds.) *The Development of Ecological Economics*, London: Edward Elgar.

Everett, G. and Wilks, A. (1999) 'The World Bank's Genuine Savings Indicator: A Useful Measure of Sustainability?' Unpublished report, London: Bretton Woods Project.

Ewing, B., Reed, A., Rizk, S. M., Galli, A., Wackernagel, M. and Kitzes, J. (2008) 'Calculation Methodology for the National Footprint Accounts, 2008 Edition', Oakland, CA: Global Footprint Network. www.footprintnetwork.org/atlas

Ewing, B., Moore, D., Goldfinger, S., Oursler, A., Reed, A. and Wackernagel, M. (2010) 'The Ecological Footprint Atlas 2010', Oakland, CA: Global Footprint Network. www.footprintnetwork.org/atlas

Fiala, N. (2008) 'Measuring Sustainability: Why the Ecological Footprint is Bad Economics and Bad Environmental Science', *Ecological Economics* 67, 4: 519–25.

Gallet, C.A., List, J.A.', Shogren, J. F. (1999) 'Reconsidering the Savings due to the 1970 Clean Air Act Amendment', University of Central Florida, Mimeo.

Goklany, Indur M. (1999) 'Clearing the Air: The Real Story of the War on Air Pollution, Washington, DC: Cato Institute.

Haggart, B. (2000) *The Gross Domestic Product and Alternative Economic and Social Indicators*, Montreal: Government of Canada Depository Service Program, http://dsp-psd.pwgsc.gc.ca/Collection-R/LoPBdP/BP/prb 0022-e.htm

Hamilton, K. (2005) 'Testing Genuine Saving', *World Bank Policy Research Working Paper 3577*, Washington, DC: Environmental Department, World Bank.

Hamilton, K. and Bolt, K. (1997) 'Genuine Savings as an Indicator of Sustainability', *Working Paper GEC 97-03*, Norwich: University of East Anglia, Centre for Social and Economic Research on the Global Environment (CSERGE).

Hartwick, J. M. (1978) 'Substitution among Exhaustible Resources and Intergenerational Equity', *Review of Economic Studies* 45: 347–54.

Hecht, J. (1999) 'Environmental Accounting: Where We Are Now, Where We Are Heading', *Issue 135 Resources*, Washington, DC: Resources for the Future.

Hicks, J. R. (1946) *The Value of Capital*, 2nd edn., Oxford: Oxford University Press.

Lawn, P. A. (2003) 'A Theoretical Foundation to Support the Index of Sustainable Economic Welfare (ISEW), Genuine Progress Indicator (GPI), and Other Related Indexes', *Ecological Economics* 44: 105–18.

Lutz, E. (ed.) (1993) , Washington, DC: World Bank.

Max-Neef, M. (1995) 'Economic Growth and Quality of Life: A Threshold Hypothesis', *Ecological Economics* 15: 115–18.

Muradian, R. and Martinez-Alier, J. (2001) 'Trade and the Environment from a "Southern' Perspective"', *Ecological Economics* 36: 281–97.

Neumayer, E. (2000) 'On the methodology of ISEW, GPI and Related Measures: Some Constructive Suggestions and Some Doubt on the "Threshold" Hypothesis', *Ecological Economics* 34: 347–61.

Nordhaus, J. and Tobin, W. (1972) 'Is Growth Obsolete?', in *Economic Growth*, National Bureau of Economic Research General Series, No. 96E, New York: Columbia University Press.

Norton, Seth. (2002) 'Population Growth, Economic Freedom, and Rule of Law', PERC Policy Series, PS-24, Bozman, MT: PERC, Feb.

Pearce, D. and Atkinson, G. (1993) 'Capital Theory and the Measurement of Sustainable Development: An Indicator of "Weak" Sustainability', *Ecological Economics* 8, 2: 103–8.

Pigou, A. C. (1920) *The Economics of Welfare*, London: Macmillan.

Rees, W. (1996) 'Revisiting Carrying Capacity: Area-based Indicators of Sustainability', *Population & Environment* 17, 3: 195–215.

Repetto, R. (1992) 'Accounting for Environmental Assets', *Scientific American* 266: 94–100.

Repetto, R., McGrath, W., Wells, M., Beer, C. and Rossini, F. (1989) *Wasting Assets: Natural Resources in the National Accounts*, Washington, DC: World Resources Institute.

Sadoff, C. W. (1992) 'The Importance of Accounting for Natural Resources and the Environment', *TDRI Quarterly Review* 7, 2: 17–23.

Solow, R. M. (1986) 'On the Intertemporal Allocation of Natural Resources', *Scandinavian Journal of Economics* 88: 141–9.

Stockhammer, E. et al. (1997) 'The Index of Sustainable Economic Welfare (ISEW) as an Alternative to GDP in Measuring Economic Welfare. The Results of the Austrian (revised) ISEW Calculation 1955–1992', *Ecological Economics* 21, 1: 19–34.

Tobin, J. (2005) 'Fisher's the Nature of Capital and Income', *American Journal of Economics and Sociology* 64, 1: 207–14.

United Nations Statistics Division (1993) 'Satellite System for Integrated Environmental and Economic Accounting', *Integrated Environmental and Economic Accounting. Handbook of National Accounting. Studies in Methods,* Series F, No. 61, New York: United Nations Press.

United Nations Statistics Division (2012) 'National Accounts Main Aggregate Database', http://unstats.un.org/unsd/snaama/selQuick.asp, accessed 06/05/2012.

Van den Bergh, J. and Verbruggen, H. (1999) 'Spatial Sustainability, Trade and Indicators: An Evaluation of the Ecological Footprint', *Ecological Economics* 29, 61–72.

Wackernagel, M. and Rees, W. (1996) *Our Ecological Footprint: Reducing Human Impact on the Earth*, Gabriola Island, BC: New Society Publishers.

Weitzman, M. (1998) 'Why the Far Future Should Be Discounted at the Lowest Possible Rate', *Journal of Environmental Economics and Management* 36: 301–8.

World Commission on Environment and Development (WCED) (1987) *Our Common Future*, New York: Oxford University Press.

WWF (2006) *Living Planet Report 2006*, Oakland, CA: Global Footprint Network.

—— (2010) *Living Planet Report 2010: Biodiversity, Biocapacity and Development*, London: The World Wide Fund for Nature, www.footprintnetwork.org/press/LPR2010.pdf, accessed 08/06/2011.

Chapter 15

The business case for environmental sustainability

Commerce can be one of the most creative endeavors available to us, but it is not worthy of business to be the convenient and complicit bedfellow to a culture divorced from nature. While commerce at its worst sometimes appears to be a shambles of defilement compared to the beauty and complexity of the natural world, the ideas and much of the technology required for the redesign of our businesses and the restoration of the world are already in hand. What is wanting is collective will.

(Hawken 1993: 17)

LEARNING OBJECTIVES

After reading this chapter you will be familiar with the following:

■ A brief historical sketch of the events over the past three decades that led to some fundamental changes in the dominant business paradigm towards the environment.

■ The World Business Council for Sustainable Development (WBCSD) and its role as an agent for change and an advocate for the business perspective on sustainability.

■ Eco-efficiency as business response to sustainability: how the profitability of companies can increase while their impacts on the environment are decreasing

■ Real-world examples of eco-efficient and not so-eco-efficient companies.

■ Eco-effectiveness as business response to sustainability: the revolutionary idea that industrial systems can be organized in a cyclical system where the byproducts and wastes are reused and/or recycled as raw materials for another product or process, with an ultimate goal of eliminating waste.

■ Eco-effectiveness in practice: two case studies.

■ New concepts introduced in this chapter include: the triple-bottom line; corporate social responsibility; corporate sustainable reports; green washing; industrial ecology; closed-loop system; upcycling; remanufacturing; lifecycle design; design for the environment; industrial symbiosis; eco-industrial park; biomimicry; and industrial metabolism.

When it comes to the issue of protecting the environment, business is often viewed as the problem. This chapter is written with two things in mind: (1) to show that if environmental sustainability is to become a reality, business must be a part of the solution; and (2) to show the real potentials that exist for businesses to have constructive and leading roles in the global movement towards a sustainable economy.

15.1 INTRODUCTION

Until about 20 years ago, the dominant business paradigm has been rather indifferent towards nature. Little attention was given to what business took from nature as raw materials, to what it produced using these resources, and to what it put back into nature as waste (Hawken 1993; McDonough and Braungart 2002). At the fundamental level, the business of business was literally taken to be the production of goods and services demanded by the market at the lowest price.

However, as discussed in Chapter 3, in a free-market oriented economy, prices failed to account for harmful side-effects (i.e., externalities) arising from business activities. The outcomes of this, as Paul Hawken (1993: 12) succinctly puts it, have been that:

> First, business takes too much from the environment and does so in a harmful way; second, the products it makes require excessive amounts of energy, toxins, and pollutants; and finally, the method of manufacturing and the very products themselves produce extraordinary waste and cause harm to present and future generations of all species including humans.

The standard response to this apparent dilemma has been, as discussed in Chapters 5 and 6, environmental regulation through governmental legislative action. These regulations were intended, at least in theory, to correct environmental externalities in such a way that the cost of doing business would properly account for the use of nature both as a source for raw materials and as a repository of waste. In the recent past, as briefly outlined below, the way businesses responded to environmental regulations, or lack thereof, depended on a variety of circumstances, including the economic, political and social conditions of the time, and the public awareness about emerging environmental concerns. The scope of those concerns may have been local, regional, national, or even global.

The 1970s: environmental regulation and its aftermath

During the 1970s (i.e., 'the decade of the environment') businesses were subjected to an increasing level of environmental regulation. This was also a decade when the pressure from the public for businesses to do more to protect the environment was perhaps at its zenith. The regulatory regime at this time was based on the command-and-control method. In general, the response of the business sector to this growing public pressure and environmental regulatory burden was to find ways of reducing the environmental impacts of their production activities in ways that are considered to be *cost-effective*. That is, as discussed in Chapter 5, to invest in pollution-control technologies as long as the incremental benefit from doing so is greater than the monetary penalty imposed by law.

This approach to coping with environmental problems invariably tends to stress *cleanup* over the *prevention* of waste at its *source*. This is because under the command-and-control environmental regulation regime, firms are not given any other option(s) but to control the flow of waste before it enters into the environment (i.e., the air, water and land) as specified by law.

This approach to pollution control encouraged the development of *end-of-pipe* treatment technologies since the emphasis was on treatment or filtration of wastes prior to discharge into the environment, as opposed to making changes in the process that caused the waste in the first place. In situations where environmental pollution was considered hazardous, *cradle-to-grave* waste disposal and management technologies were adopted. In this case, the emphasis was on proper handling, transportation and disposal of waste to ensure safe management over its life cycle (McDonough and Braungart 2002).

The 1980s: environmental deregulation and its aftermath

As discussed in Section 6.4, in the United States the sentiment of the public towards the protection of the environment started to fade by the late 1970s. This was a period of double-digit inflation and stagnant economic growth. In this depressed economic climate, environmental regulation was suspected of causing a decline in productivity and an increase in business uncertainty. Pollution-intensive corporations, particularly in the mining and manufacturing sectors (such as coal, steel, petrochemicals, autos, pharmaceuticals, paper, textiles, etc.) of the economy, were particularly sensitive to the impacts of environmental regulations on their operations and profitability. This sentiment against environmental regulations was not limited to the US, since the economic downturn of the 1980s was truly global.

The upshot of this was a growing sentiment against any kind of government regulation, and most notably those concerning the environment. In the United States and Western Europe, this kind of public attitude towards government regulation favored conservative politicians and resulted in the elections of Ronald Reagan as the President of the United States (1980–88) and Margaret Thatcher as the Prime Minster of the UK (1979–90).

The administrations of both of these leaders made government deregulation (including the environment) a priority with a goal of relieving corporations from the 'excessive' burden (cost) of regulations. With respect to environmental regulation, this entailed a marked shift towards a market-oriented approach of pollution-control instruments; more specifically, the *transferable pollution permit*. It was also in the 1980s that *pollution prevention* started to make strong headway because firms started to see that reducing waste at the *source* actually saves money (more on this later).

The late 1980s: the dawning of the sustainability movement

However, the strong sentiment against environmental regulation did not last long. By the late 1980s, concern over the health of the global environment started to make headline news throughout the world. This time the environmental problems, such as ozone depletion, desertification, deforestation, global warming and loss of biodiversity, were more global in nature and quite serious in their reach and implications.

The publication of *Our Common Future* by the World Commission on Environment and Development in 1987 provided further evidence of emerging environmental problems on a global scale unless serious steps were taken to redefine the relationship between the human economy and the natural world. More specifically, the report in this book (popularly known as the Brundtland Report) was able to forcefully and effectively articulate the urgent need by the world community to embrace the concept of *sustainable development* as a guiding principle of 'economic growth' (for more on this see Chapter 13).

As discussed in Chapter 13, The Brundtland Report was instrumental in setting the stage for the United Nations Conference on the Environment and Development (UNCED) that took place in Rio de Janeiro, Brazil, in 1992. The organizers of this landmark international conference, popularly known as the Rio Earth Summit, invited many prominent business leaders from around the globe and challenged them to come up with the business case for sustainability.

The response to this challenge was the publication of *Changing Course: A Global Business Perspective on Development and the Environment* (Schmidheiny 1992). This book was published by the World Business Council for Sustainable Development (WBCSD)—a business association literally formed at the eve of the Earth Summit. Currently, the WBCSD has about 200 members from over 30 countries and 20 major industrial sectors. It is a CEO-led organization involving about 1,000 business leaders. The WBCSD considers the promotion of *eco-efficiency* as its primary mission. A detailed examination of eco-efficiency as a concept and its practical application in the business world is the subject of the next section.

15.2 ECO-EFFICIENCY: BUSINESS RESPONSES TO SUSTAINABILITY

Eco-efficiency is a basic component of sustainability that applies to running your business. It means reducing the amount of resources used to produce goods and services, which increases a company's profitability while decreasing its environmental impact. The underlying theme is simple: pollution is waste, and waste is anathema because it means that your company is paying for something it did not use. Given the clarity of this logic, it's amazing how few companies have diligently pursued eco-efficiency.

(Savitz and Weber 2006: 34–5)

As discussed in the previous section, the traditional way of controlling the wastes generated from industrial activities has been through the use of end-of-pipe technologies. This strategy of waste treatment has been considered inadequate for the simple reason that waste is not entirely precluded from re-entering the natural environment in some other way (Ayres and Ayres 1996; McDonough and Bruangart 2002). For example, the environmental impact of sulfur dioxide (SO_2) emissions on communities living in close proximity to a coal-fired electric power plant can be mitigated by requiring the company to install a tall smokestack. However, the effect of this kind of solution, the so-called pollution through dilution, will be to transfer the environmental impact of pollution from the local community to the region. The same thing can be said about using landfills to store hazardous wastes, which ultimately leads to groundwater contamination. This can be a serious problem, especially when the pollutants under consideration are highly toxic or persistent (McDonough and Bruangart 2002).

Eco-efficiency departs from the above approach in that the focus is entirely on pollution *prevention*. In other words, eco-efficiency works on the fundamental principle that it is environmentally more effective to prevent pollution at the *source* rather than removing it after it has been created. At the operational level, this can be achieved through the following four steps:

1.   As far as possible, avoid or eliminate the discharge of highly toxic pollutants into the biosphere, such as DDT, dioxin and so on. This step may require an externally imposed Regulation;

2.   Reduce waste through product design and reformulation;
3.   Reuse waste materials; and
4.   Recycle waste materials.

Thus, the above four Rs (regulate, reduce, reuse and recycle) are the guiding principle of eco-efficiency: the ultimate goal is *to produce more using less* (Hawken 1993). Note that the first R, regulation, is regarded as important for two reasons. First, toxins are highly dangerous since the natural environment lacks built-in mechanisms to deal with them effectively. Second, businesses are unlikely to undertake tasks that tend to be too costly simply out of concern for protecting the natural environment, especially when the ownership of the environmental resources under consideration are not clearly defined, such as large bodies of water or the ambient air. On the other hand, the other three Rs (reduce, reuse and recycle) are actions that can be undertaken willingly by businesses once they come to realize that there is money to be made by reducing waste.

Since the Rio Earth Summit, the focus of the WBCSD has been to create awareness in business communities throughout the world about the benefits of implementing the basic principles of pollution prevention outlined above. The main idea is this: being eco-friendly is not inconsistent with profitability. Greening business simply entails creative ways of avoiding waste in the first place and/or using waste as a resource. The rewards that emerge from such efforts come from the realization of the following benefits and/or avoided costs:

■   Avoidance or deferment of pollution-control equipment costs;
■   Reduction in material and energy costs arising from improved product design and manufacturing processes;
■   Increase in sales of existing products arising from improved customer loyalty and increase in sales of new products, such as recycled materials or products made out of recycled materials;
■   Improved management and labor relations— since, to implement waste prevention programs

on a company-wide basis requires good coordination of information and cooperation among all stakeholders; and

■ Constant focus on innovation and long-term profitability.

There are several companies that can be used to illustrate the potential benefits of eco-efficiency when employed as part of an ongoing business strategy. Below three companies—3M (Minnesota Mining & Manufacturing), Coca Cola and Nike—are used to provide examples of the various ways in which eco-efficiency can be used to enhance profits while at the same time pursuing goals that are explicitly designed to lower the overall environmental impacts of the company.

The pollution prevention pays (3P) program at 3M

3M was one of the earliest companies to implement a pollution reduction program, popularly known as 'pollution prevention pays' (3P). This program was first introduced in 1975, which is rather remarkable given that it took the rest of the corporate world more than a decade to fully realize the potential gain of incorporating eco-efficiency as an integral part of their overall business strategies.

The 3P initiative at 3M works with the philosophy that it is better to prevent pollution than to clean it up later. This philosophy was initiated internally and represents one of the most prominent and enduring cultures of the company. One of the major contributions of the 3P initiative has been to make the company constantly strive for innovation. In this regard, the focus of the innovations have been to reduce the use of resources by *preventing* waste at the source—through product reformulation, process modification, equipment redesign, and recycling and reuse of waste materials. The 3M corporation sustains the momentum for innovative ideas through an award system that is designed to recognize exceptional achievements—the 3P Awards. Furthermore, people working for 3M are recognized as the 'fourth P' and participation in any activities that contribute to the advancement of 3P initiative is voluntary.

The company's records show that, as of 2010, 'the program has resulted in the elimination of more than 3 billion pounds of pollution and saved them nearly $1.4 billion'. In 2010 alone, during the 35-year anniversary of the 3P program, the company reported savings of $40 million. This excludes the intangible benefits that 3M receives for being known as an environmentally friendly company.

The success of 3M has important management implications. The adoption of eco-efficiency as a business strategy on a company-wide basis requires effective, visionary and committed leaders from higher up the management ladder. This is necessary to instill the cultural, organizational and procedural changes needed to make strategies that are based on a vision of eco-efficiency work to their full potential (Dillon 1994). The successful implementation of eco-efficiency also requires the development of companywide strategies and guidelines for: (1) integrating environmental considerations into product design processes; (2) ensuring that all stakeholders are fully informed and working cooperatively for a clearly defined mission of the company; and (3) developing fair and well-conceived systems of reward for achievements that are considered to be exceptional.

These are important management prerequisites, and their full realization poses major challenges to many companies. Quite often companies adopt eco-efficiency mainly in the segment of their operations where both the economic and environmental advantages are very obvious. This piecemeal approach to eco-efficiency, and its inherent limitations, will be evident in the next company discussed: Coca Cola.

Coca Cola's water conservation initiative

Water is unquestionably the most basic and important ingredient for a company that produces beverages. Water is also used for beverage manufacturing processes such as rinsing, cleaning, heating and cooling. Coca Cola has nearly 900 bottling plants scattered around the globe involving different communities endowed with varying qualities and quantities of water.

337

Coca Cola is aware of the fact that steady availability of high quality water is crucial for its long-term survival. For this reason, 'water stewardship' has been one of the most important sustainability goals of the company. More specifically, the company's ultimate goal has been to 'work to safely return to nature and communities an amount of water equivalent to what we use in the beverages and their production'. This goal is accomplished by taking specific steps to reduce, recycle and replenish water as allowed by the conditions of the specific bottling plant.

Reduction of water usage is accomplished by implementing proven water-efficient practices in each bottling plant. According to a report by Coca Cola, 'In 2008, on average we used 2.43 liters of water to produce one liter beverages. One liter goes into the beverage itself, and 1.43 liters are used for manufacturing process such as rinsing, cleaning, and cooling. We are nearly half way to our 2012 goal of 2.17 liters per liter which will be a 20 percent improvement'.

The Coca Cola Company also has a specific, ambitious goal for as well. The goal is to 'return to the environment, at a level that supports aquatic life, the water we use in our manufacturing operations by the end of 2010 through comprehensive wastewater treatment'.

The third step Coca Cola is undertaking to conserve water involves replenishment. This is done through efforts such as: watershed protection; expansion of community drinking water and sanitation access; increasing the efficiency of water for agriculture and other similar uses; and education and awareness program. Many of these types of initiatives have been done in collaboration with the Worldwide Fund for Nature (WWF) and representatives of the local communities where beverage bottling plants are located. The ultimate goal of Coca Cola is to: 'Replenish (balance) the water used in our finished beverages by participating in locally relevant projects that support communities and nature. We will meet and maintain the goal of being fully balanced by 2020'.

Despite this, however, the march towards environmental sustainability at Coca Cola is not pursued on a company-wide basis to the extent that it does not require every aspect of its operation to be guided by the principle of eco-efficiency. In other words, eco-efficiency has yet to be regarded as one of the major business cultures of Coca Cola enterprise. Clearly, unlike 3M, environmental sustainability is pursued in a piecemeal fashion at Coca Cola. There are many risks associated with this kind of strategy. The most obvious risk is that Coca Cola's initiative of water conservation might be perceived as 'green washing'—an effort used to disguise the company's environmental abuses in other aspects of its operations.

Nike's drive towards sustainability

Nike is the world's leading supplier of athletic shoes and apparel and a major producer of sports equipment. The company prides itself on making innovation and product performance its first priority. Its first step towards a comprehensive assessment of the environmental impact of its products started in the late 1990s. The assessment was done by developing a 'material analysis tool', which is used to evaluate materials in *four* categories—chemistry, energy impact, physical waste and water impact—and ranks materials in such a way as to help product designers to make material choices that reduce environmental impact without sacrificing performance. In general, the entire shoe production process is guided by the following four principles:

1. *Use materials with benign environmental impact*: that is, the rubber, leather, nylon, polyester and foams used to make Nike's line of athletic shoes are chosen after careful assessment of their impacts on the environment and with full consideration of the alternative materials available for use. Key issues considered in the choice of each material are toxicity, recyclability and the potential for reuse or remanufacturing. Nike does this systematically and in a rigorous manner using its 'material analysis tool' mentioned earlier.

2. *Waste reduction*: at Nike, waste reduction is pursued in various ways. Among others, Nike's efforts to reduce waste include: constant

improvements in the design of products to prevent the initial creation of waste; improvements in the efficiency of the manufacturing process and product design so that scraps are minimized; reduction in weight and packaging materials; and finding ways to reuse and recycle waste materials.

Nike encourages the recycling of materials through its Reuse-A-Shoe Program. This program is instituted to encourage consumers to bring their used shoes to a Nike store so the materials (rubber, foam and fabric) can be recycled and/or reused. Nike uses recycled athletic shoes to make sports surfaces, playgrounds, rubber gym flooring basketball courts, and so on. This can be easily done because the three parts of the athletic shoes (i.e., the outsole which is composed of rubber, the middle sole which is composed of foam, and the shoe's upper which composed of several kinds of fabrics) can be easily separated in the recycling process.

3. *Reduction in solvent use*: Nike uses solvents to glue the various components of its athletic shoes together. Some of the solvents used by Nike contain toxic substances, and reducing or eliminating the use of these substances is a very high priority to any company that strives towards environmental sustainability. Nike claims that 'from 1995 through 2008, the average solvent used to produce a pair of shoes is reduced from 1.75 cups to 1 tablespoon—a reduction of 43 percent'. Clearly this remains one of the most challenging aspects of Nike's move towards sustainability.

4. Innovation: ongoing commitment to design innovation with two things in mind: (1) less toxicity (with an ultimate goal of eliminating toxic substances, such as PVC, and reducing the use of solvents, wherever possible); and (ii) less waste.

Nike appears to have a long-term commitment to environmental sustainability. The top managers of the company appear to embrace the view that working towards environmental sustainability is essential in order that Nike remain competitive in the long-run. However, whether Nike's commitment to environmental sustainability will be extended to include the company's other line of products, such as sports apparel, equipment and accessories, is not entirely clear.

The above three companies (3M, Coca Cola and Nike) clearly illustrate the various ways in which corporations choose to engage themselves in environmentally sustainable business practices. Clearly, as these three cases indicate, the degree to which companies commit themselves to the design and production of products that are healthy, both to humans and the natural environment, varies considerably. For example, in the case of 3M waste prevention has become one of the enduring cultural norms of the company. For 3M, reducing waste is a company-wide commitment and includes all the aspects of the company's operation.

On the other hand, Coca Cola's commitment to environmentally sustainable resource use is pursued with a focus on the conservation of a single, though very important, resource: water. However, there is no clear evidence that Coca Cola's commitment to environmental sustainability goes beyond water conservation in any meaningful way. Even in making this effort, Coca Cola is regularly accused by environmental groups of ethical violations of its water use in some parts of the world. Claims have been made accusing the company of appropriating water in ways that would adversely affect the inhabitants of some countries with a very low water supplies. For poor countries this may cause lower production of food and other basic necessities.

The situation at Nike appears to fall on the spectrum somewhere in-between 3M and Coca Cola. Nike, although a latecomer when compared to 3M, appears to be making steady and tangible progress in making its athletic-shoe production environmentally friendly. At the same time, though, it is important to note that Nike has a long way to go to make environmental sustainability a part of its well-recognized corporate culture, so that it can change its famous and enduring product brand label to a 'green' Nike 'Swoosh'.

Marketing eco-efficiency: the triple-bottom-line

As discussed earlier, the idea of eco-efficiency started to be taken seriously on the eve of the Rio Earth Summit under the auspices of a group of enlightened business leaders who later founded the World Business Council for Sustainable Development (WBCSD). From the outset, the WBCSD has had some marketing work to do. This is because of the natural inclination of corporate CEOs to be blinded by the drive for short-term profitability. However, for corporations to embrace eco-efficiency, they have to think long-term, since eco-efficiency requires investment in material choices and product designs that are front loaded with short-term costs. Thus, if environmental sustainability is to be taken seriously by the corporate world, business leaders have to start to think in terms of the long-term survival and growth of their companies. What has evolved out of this pressing need to change the corporate culture is the idea of the 'triple-bottom-line'. This idea has been promoted quite aggressively by the WBCDS since its inception as an organization in 1992.

The triple-bottom-line as an ongoing business ethos started with the grand idea that survival and growth in the business world depends on long-term profitability. The key idea is to demonstrate to business leaders the connection between growth and profitability. It is argued that long-term profitability is likely to be enhanced when companies operate in ways that are perceived to be both socially and environmentally responsible (Savitz 2006). In the business world, perception (i.e., branding and promoting a company's image) is everything. The challenge is selling the idea to business leaders that caring about the wellbeing of their workers, their customers and the communities they live in, and the being a 'good steward' of the environment actually pays in the long-run. The question is how?

The long-term payoff of pursing corporate social responsibility (CSR) as an ongoing business strategy is realized through increases in workers' productivity, customers' loyalty, and communities' reciprocity of goodwill and cooperation. In other words, CSR can

be a good business model, but requires a long-term commitment. On the other hand, the rewards from developing and implementing long-term environmental stewardship strategies largely emanate from the potential cost savings that companies could realize through the adoption of production methods that are eco-efficient. A focus on a vision inspired by eco-efficiency makes companies strive for continuous innovation, galvanized by systemic integrations of technologies and human resources.

Thus, the possibilities are real for businesses to grow and prosper when their long-term strategies are guided by the achievement of these three complementary goals: social responsibility, environmental stewardship and profitability. Savitz and Weber (2006: 26) describe the outcomes of well-executed business strategies of this nature as 'the sustainability sweet spot', and go on to further elaborate on this:

> The sweet spot embodies the literal meaning of 'sustainability,' making your company *viable for the long term* by managing according to principles that will strengthen rather than undermine the company's roots in the environment, the social fabric, and the economy (the triple-bottom-line). A business that occupies the sustainability sweet spot (or that strives to fit as much of its activities into that favored zone as possible) should have real long-term advantage over its rivals.

Clearly, the sustainability sweet spot cannot be automatically attained, as it requires the well-coordinated execution of many facets of a company's operations on a sustained basis. For example, Nike has made measurable success in reducing toxic waste by finding substitutes for some of the solvents that are currently in use. However, it may still fail to pass the sustainability test outlined above if Nike tolerates the exploitation of workers in its production facilities that are located in several developing countries.

Eco-efficiency, triple-bottom-line, CSR and environmentally friendly products have been buzz words in the corporate world since the early 2000s. In recent years, there has been growing skepticism about how these buzz words are used in the corporate world. Moreover, some are starting to question the adequacy of eco-efficiency given the nature and magnitude of current environmental concerns. These two concerns are discussed briefly below.

The skeptics as critics of eco-efficiency

Skeptics, mostly environmentalists, question whether the lofty goal of achieving the triple-bottom-line may actually end up not benefiting the environment. The source of this skepticism comes from the realization that when social and environmental issues are lumped together without a clear delineation of the factors that separate or unite these two issues, the outcomes may not always work out in favor of the environment.

For example, as a general rule the focus of environmental sustainability has been intergenerational equity. On the other hand, the focus of corporate social responsibility has been primarily on social justice and intragenerational equity. It is not difficult to envision situations in which these two equity concerns could come into conflict. If and when this occurs, for many environmentalists, the odds are against future generations. This is because advocating for the wellbeing of future generations often entails working against the interests of labor unions and short-term-profit oriented CEOs and management teams. It is important to note that the voices of future generations are heard only through third parties that may not have the power and legitimacy needed to adequately represent them. Future generations have no vote.

Skepticism also arises from the mistrust people often have towards business, particularly big corporations. It is argued that the real motivation of many corporations in claiming that they are committed to producing eco-friendly products is to enhance their public image. This kind of corporate behavior is known as 'green washing'—a misleading use of green marketing and other related activities mainly designed to deceive the public into believing that a company's product positively contributes to the health of the environment. Worse yet, the possibility exist that companies could use green marketing to cover up

environmentally damaging practices. For example, as discussed earlier Coca Cola has been accused of using its water conservation projects to hide environmental damages arising from other aspects of its resource use and production activities.

Public skepticism such as those detailed above still persist despite the gallant efforts of many corporations to fight back by issuing what are known as corporate sustainability reports. Corporate sustainability reports are now featured on many companies' websites at regular intervals and they contain, among other items, mission statements, performance records, records of environmental sustainability achievements and future goals and commitments to various stakeholders (such as employees, customers, shareholders, society at large and the environment). It still remains the case, however, that these reports are internal documents prepared by corporations, though they do receive directives from the WBCSD.

Finally, the most stinging criticism of eco-efficiency comes from those critics who argue that, at the fundamental level, eco-efficiency does not explicitly confront the issue of biophysical limits (Hawken 1993; McDonough and Braungart 2002). In this respect, eco-efficiency does not represent a paradigm shift. Below are two variations of this line of criticism:

1. Corporations have yet to accept the worldview that the biosphere is a closed system with a finite amount of material resources available both for extraction and waste emissions. Furthermore, they still believe in the possibility of perpetual economic growth. Here is how Hawken (1993: 5) expressed his criticism of business in accepting the existence of absolute ecological limits:

> Business is the practice of the possible: Highly developed and intelligent in many respects, it is, however, not a science. In many ways business economics . . . lack any guiding principles to relate it to such fundamental and critical concepts as evolution, biological diversity, carrying capacity, and

the health of the commons. Business is designed to break through limits, not to respect them, especially when the limits posed by ecological constraints are not always as glaring as dead rivers or human birth defects, but are often expressed in small, refined relationships and details.

2. Eco-efficiency is pursued to reduce and *not* eliminate waste. Reduction does not halt depletion and destruction, it only slows them down. In other words, 'being less bad is no good'. Here is how McDonough and Braungart (2002: 62) express the essence of this particular view:

> Eco-efficiency is an outwardly admirable, even noble, concept, but it is not a strategy for success over the long term, because it does not reach deep enough. It works within the same system that caused the problem in the first place, merely slowing it down with moral proscriptions and punitive measures. It presents little more than an illusion of change. Relying on eco-efficiency to save the environment will in fact achieve the opposite; it will let industry finish off everything quietly, persistently, and completely.

So, what should the alternative to eco-efficiency be? To the ardent critics of eco-efficiency, the clear alternative is *eco-effectiveness*—the subject of the next section.

15.3 ECO-EFFECTIVENESS: A SHIFT FROM LINEAR TO CYCLICAL THINKING

> If humans are truly going to prosper, we will have to learn to imitate nature's highly effective cradle-to-cradle system of nutrient flow and metabolism, in which the very concept of waste does not exist. To eliminate the concept of waste means to design things—products, packaging, and systems—from the very beginning on the understanding that waste does not exist.
> (McDonough and Braungart 2002: 104)

Eco-effectiveness is a radically different strategy that companies may employ to guide their business activities in a direction that is consistent with practices that contribute to the quality of the environment on a long-term basis. Eco-effectiveness operates on a core principle that an industrial system is considered to be most *effective* when production activities are organized in a *cyclical system* where the byproducts and wastes are reused and/or recycled as raw materials for another product or process, with an ultimate goal of eliminating waste.

The practical applications of this core principle require knowledge of many factors that are found at the intersections between *industrial* and *ecological* systems. A relatively new field of study that attempts to provide the conceptual framework, methodological tools, and the visions for dealing with resource management problems that involve both industry and the natural environment, is called *industrial ecology*. One of the early proponents of this field of study, Hardin Tibbs (1992: 5), defined industrial ecology this way:

> Industrial ecology involves designing industrial infrastructures as if they were a series of interlocking manmade ecosystems interfacing with the natural global ecosystem. Industrial ecology takes the pattern of the natural environment as a model for solving environmental problems, creating a new paradigm for the industrial system in the process . . . The aim of industrial ecology is to interpret and adapt an understanding of the natural system and apply it to the design of the manmade system, in order to achieve a pattern of industrialization that is not only more efficient, but that is intrinsically adjusted to the tolerance and characteristics of the natural system. The emphasis is on forms of technology that work with natural systems, not against them.

Consistent with the above definition, industrial ecologists often use the word *metabolism* to describe the interactions of all the activities (i.e., flow of matter and energy) within an industrial infrastructure in the same context as this word is used to connote the internal processes of a living organism (see Chapter 2). The specific phrase used to describe this vision of the internal workings of an industrial process is *industrial metabolism*, and Ayres (1994: 23) explains it as 'the whole integrated collection of physical processes that convert raw materials and energy, plus labor, into finished products and wastes in a (more or less) steady-state condition'. One of the most important implications of the industrial metabolism perspective is the fact that 'it is essentially "holistic" in that the whole range of interactions between energy, materials, and the environment is considered together— at least in principle' (Ibid: 35).

Another fundamental perspective of industrial ecology that is conveyed by the definition given above is 'nature knows best'. Thus, the natural ecosystem should be the *modus operandi* for our industrial systems (Benyus 1997; Frosch and Galopoulos 1989). In other words, imitating nature's economics is not only a good thing but also the right thing to do for industry (Benyus 1997). Clearly, this represents a fresh perspective amounting to a paradigm shift, given that the tendency of mainstream industrial society has been to view nature as an obstacle that needs to be conquered rather than appreciatively imitated

The question then becomes, in what specific ways should the industrial system imitate nature? Before answering this, one must bear in mind that the principal concern of industrial ecology is, as much as possible, to eliminate waste. This is also done with a full recognition of the limits imposed on any transformation of matter and energy by the laws of nature —principally the first and second laws of thermodynamics (see Chapter 2). Under this scenario, for the industrial world to imitate nature implies the following (Ibid):

1. Use waste as a resource;
2. Avoid toxic substances from entering into the biosphere;
3. Evaluate products and process performances using methodologies and operational tools that rely on the systems approach;

4. In as much as possible, rely on sunlight and/or non-polluting renewable energy resources to run industries;
5. Value diversity and acknowledge the existence of biophysical limits; and
6. Use innovations that are inspired by nature.

Proponents of industrial ecology strongly believe that these are guiding principles that can be implemented without too much difficulty, provided that modern industrial society is willing to *design* products and industrial processes with a clear focus on reducing negative environmental impacts at the *source* (Hawken 1993). In industrial ecology, therefore, product and process designs are given prominence.

In such an undertaking, the role of nature is a very important one. It is used to provide *prototypes* for the designs of industrial processes (Benyus 1997). It is in this specific way, therefore, that eco-effectiveness is guided by 'innovations that are inspired by nature'. The rest of this section elaborates on the *six* fundamental ideas outlined above to explain how industrial systems can be designed so that they adhere to the principles that are so fundamental to eco-effectiveness.

Use waste as a resource

As discussed in Chapter 2, in a natural ecosystem, energy and materials flow in a *closed-loop cyclical* system wherein the waste of one organism is used as nutrients (food) by other organisms. In the *linear* industrial system, resources from the earth and the biosphere are extracted, manufactured, and put to use (through consumption). Throughout this chain of *independently* organized processes or activities, damaging wastes are disposed of (discharged) into the environment. The challenge, then, is to design, in as much as possible, industrial structures and processes where the flow of *materials* and *energy* circulate in ways that are analogous to a closed-loop cyclical system (Ayres and Ayres 1996). This is done by adhering to the following basic principles:

1. Products must be *designed* in such a way that byproducts and wastes are minimized. This is an

important starting point because it adheres to the principle of waste *prevention*—reduction of waste at the *source*. This focus on design at the very moment when a product is conceptualized makes the role of industrial ecology that much more significant.

2. As discussed in Chapter 2, the second law of thermodynamics informs us that it is impossible to design a perfect matter–energy transformation system. Given this, at any step in industrial activities, from extraction to manufacturing and consumption (use), byproducts and wastes are inevitable outcomes. If the byproducts and wastes of industrial activities are *biodegradable*, their dispersion into the natural environment will pose no lasting harm to the environment. However, this is the case only if the biodegradable wastes are not contaminated with toxic and/or hazardous materials—a common feature of existing landfill and waste disposal practices (McDonough and Braungart 2002). It is also assumed that the amount of waste is not overwhelmingly large. That is, for any type of waste that is disposed into the environment, as discussed in Chapter 3, the *scale* and *rate* of the waste discharge should always be important considerations.

3. For byproducts and wastes that are not biodegradable, it is important to ensure that, in as much as possible, they can be *reused*, *remanufactured*, or *up-cycled*. Remanufacturing (i.e., the direct use of a byproduct in making a new product) and up-cycling (i.e., converting waste materials and discarded products into new

materials or products of equal or better quality) requires that products are designed for easy *disassembly*, so that at the end of their lifecycle the component parts can be put to multiple uses without diminution in *quality* (Garner and Keoleian 1995; McDonough and Braungart 2002). It is important to note that up-cycling is different from conventional recycling. Up-cycling requires that the *quality* of the recycled material is not materially downgraded. The opposite of up-cycle is down-cycle, for example, a recycled paper.

As illustrated in Figure 15.1, the above three requirements taken together would allow the flow of high-quality materials in a closed-loop industrial cycle. This represents a cyclical *cradle-to-cradle* mode of thinking wherein, as Hawken (1993: 71) states, 'every product or byproduct is imagined in its subsequent forms even before it is made. Designs must factor the future utility of a product and the avoidance of waste, from its inception'.

Avoid toxic wastes entering into the biosphere

Since the publication of *Silent Spring* (Carson 1962), humanity has been awakening to the harsh reality of the devastating and lasting effects of human-made toxic substances on the health and vitality of natural ecosystems. Given this reality, an industrial system that is designed to imitate nature should make the *prevention* of toxic wastes from entering into its waste stream a high priority. This has to be the case

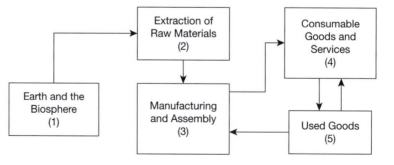

Figure 15.1 *Closed-loop materials flow. The key idea here is that 'used goods' are either re-manufactured or re-used as consumer goods and services.*

because natural ecosystems have no mechanisms to deal with synthetic toxic substances (Benyus 1997). The question then becomes, what practical steps can be taken to eliminate the use of synthetic substances that are either suspected or known to be toxic to the environment and human health? This is a very difficult question to answer given the increasing dependence of the human economy on synthetic materials and chemicals. While there are no completely satisfactory ways of dealing with this problem, the following list represents a small sampling of ideas that have been suggested as a way of responding to this question (Allenby and Fullerton 1991; Benyus 1997; Hawken 1993):

- Design and redesign products and manufacturing processes so that they don't create hazardous and biologically useless waste in the first place;
- Find substitutes for toxins;
- Industries who use chemicals should work with end users so that wastes are properly and safely disposed of;
- Legislate and enforce environmental laws to make the penalty for releasing toxic wastes into the environment (and the fees for their storage) expensive;
- Identify substances that are persistent toxins using the six criteria laid out by Dr. Karl-Henrik Robert, founder of the Natural Step (a highly respected and influential environmental organization that has been in existence since 1989):

> Is the substance natural? No. Is it stable? Yes. Does it degrade into harmless substances? No. Does it accumulate in bodily tissues? Yes. Is it possible to predict the acceptable tolerances? No. Can we continue to place the substance into the environment? No, not if we want to survive
>
> (Hawken 1993: 53)

Evaluate product and process performance

It is argued that the performance of a manufacturing system that is designed to allow the flow of materials and energy in a closed-loop cycle should be evaluated using methodologies and operational standards that are *holistic*. That is, the whole range of interactions between energy, materials and the environment is considered together (Ayres 1994). Several methods exist for doing performance evaluation of this nature. The following three widely-used performance evaluation tools—lifecycle assessment, design for the environment, and lifecycle design—are briefly discussed below as a way of illustrating the issues involved in the evaluation process of industrial activities that are designed to function within the framework of a closed-loop cycle system (Allenby and Fullerton 1991; Keoleian and Menerey 2004).

- *Life cycle assessment (LCA)*: the US EPA defines LCA as 'a tool to evaluate the environmental consequences of a product or activity holistically, across its entire life'. LCA is system-oriented because it attempts to integrate environmental requirements into each stage of the product development and manufacturing process so that total impacts caused by the entire industrial system can be reduced.

  Evaluation using LCA normally follows three distinct steps. The first step is *inventory analysis*. This entails the identification of materials and energy resources and their flow patterns within the industrial system, including waste releases into the environment. This is followed with *impact analysis*, which deals with qualitative and quantitative assessments of the consequences to the environment. The environmental assessment attempts to address not only ecological and human-health effects, but also concerns of resource depletion. The third and final step involves *improvement analysis*. In this stage, the aim is to contemplate actions that can be taken to improve upon the current conditions, with a focus on reducing environmental impacts. Since it requires a large amount of data and human resources, LCA is often costly to undertake.

- *Design for the environment (DfE)*: is a scheme used to evaluate the environmental impacts of products by identifying and using a series of matrices in an attempt to develop and then incorporate environmental requirements into product design. Examples of the matrices used in DfE assessment formulations may include: non-toxic process and production materials; minimum energy utilization; minimum emissions and byproducts; recyclability; material selection to enable and facilitate reuse; disassembly; use of adhesives; minimum packing materials; and so on.

- *Life cycle design (LCD)*: LCD is closely related to DfE, is product specific, and tries to incorporate general principles for lifetime requirements, such as testability, reliability, maintainability, upgradeability, instability, safety and product liability, and human factors. That is to say, LCD attempts to address environmental concerns (www.npd-solutions.com/lifecycle.html).

The most important lesson to be drawn from the above discussion is the significance of using performance evaluation tools in order to reduce environmental risks over the lifecycle of products rather than merely reducing pollution at the manufacturing site (Dillon 1994; Keoleian and Menerey 2004).

Rely on sunlight and other renewable energy resources to run industry

In a totally closed natural ecosystem, only solar energy would come from outside, while all materials would be constantly reused and recycled within. However, modern industrial systems continue to excessively rely on fossil fuels to run production activities (i.e., extract resources, produce goods and services, build infrastructures, and recycle byproducts, treat or dispose of wastes, and transport materials and people).

The three obvious pitfalls of industries' overreliance on fossil fuels to run their machines are: first, fossil fuels are nonrenewable and non-recyclable finite resources. Second, the use of fossil fuels is the major source of CO_2 emissions into the atmosphere —the largest component of GHGs and the main contributing factor to global warming. Third, not only are industries using the wrong sources of energy (i.e.,

fossil fuels), but they are also found to operate on average at an energy efficiency level far less than the theoretical thermodynamic potential (Ausubel 1996).

The question is, what can be done to effectively transition from an industrial system that is designed to be highly inefficient in its energy use and that relies heavily on energy resources that are scarce and exhaustible and whose byproducts are major contributors to global warming? For those who believe in the vision inspired by eco-effectiveness, the answer to this is that it demands a fundamental change in the way energy is currently used. Below are a few representative steps that can be taken by businesses to address the energy related concerns discussed thus far (Ayres and Ayres 1996; Benyus 1997):

- Design products for energy efficiency from the outset;
- Design manufacturing processes and industrial facilities (including buildings) with energy efficiency in mind; and
- Take a long-term view and steadfastly evaluate the options for alternative energy resources that are environmentally benign.

This kind of mindset is what is needed to facilitate creative ways of thinking about how to organize and manage businesses that are profitable in the long-run. However, it is very important to understand what the difficulties associated with making these adjustments are. For example, a decision to use renewable energy (such as wind, solar, hydro, etc.) to power industry would require different ways of thinking, not only about location but, most importantly, about the basic structure of modern industrial systems. In general, renewable energy resources are most effectively utilized in systems that are composed of relatively small and decentralized units. In such a setting, value is placed on diversity over uniformity. This distinction will be addressed next.

Value diversity and acknowledge the existence of biophysical limits

As discussed in Chapters 2 and 10, diversity optimizes the potential gains from *symbiosis cooperation*—

a mutually beneficial relationship among different groups and species of organisms within a given ecosystem. This is how McDonough and Braungart (2002: 122) describe this situation: 'Each inhabitant of an ecosystem is therefore interdependent to some extent with the others. Every creature is involved in maintaining the entire system; all of them work in creative and ultimately effective ways for the success of the whole'.

If nature is taken as a model, what should the lessons be for human industrial systems from the brief discussion above regarding diversity? A complete answer to this question can be quite involved. Thus, the following represents only a partial list of possible responses (Engbert 1995; Hawken 1993):

■ *Recognize symbiotic interdependence*: a well-known *eco-industrial park* in Kalundborg, Denmark, is

often used to illustrate the significance of this point (for more on this see Exhibit 15.1). This case study clearly illustrates the following pertinent issues: First, significant saving of valuable resources (such as water and energy) can be realized by organizing companies and communities into a network of mutually beneficial association. Second, the benefits (economic and environmental) is greater the more interdependent and diverse the participants within the network are functionally. Third, symbiotic cooperation is most advantageous when diverse firms are interconnected at community and local levels (i.e., within close geographic proximity).

■ *Recognize biophysical limits*: this requirement has evolved from the difficulty of envisioning sustainable industrial systems that fail to consider the 'absolute' biophysical limits imposed by

---

EXHIBIT 15.1   THE KALUNDBORG INDUSTRIAL PARK

This park is located in a small industrial zone about 75 miles west of Copenhagen and has a history that goes as far back as the early 1970s. The big players in this network of industrial cooperation consist of five companies and the town of Kalundborg, which has a population of about 20,000. The five companies (by what they produce) include: Denmark's largest electric power station (coal fired); Denmark's largest oil refinery; a pharmaceutical company; a plasterboard factory; and a fish farm. These five companies and the Kalundborg municipality are linked through a network of pipes to exchange their byproducts and wastes in ways that clearly represent a symbiotic cooperation. In other words, what brought together this diverse group together is the recognition that there are economic benefits to be gained if they work in a mutually interdependent and cooperative manner. Most importantly, this cooperative relationship has positive environmental impacts since their mutual desire is to use waste (more specifically, steam, steam gas, heat, water, sludge, and fish wastes) as raw materials.

In this case, what happens is that one company's byproduct becomes an important resource to one or several of the other companies in the industrial symbiosis network. For example, the power station is coal-fired and operates at about 40 percent thermal efficiency. This suggests that a significant portion of the energy generated goes up the stack as steam. However, through the mutually agreed-upon association created by the power company, pipes were constructed to redirect the waste steam to heat factory operations in the pharmaceutical and oil refining companies, as well as the Kalundborg heating station.

The power station is in fact the biggest player in this network of industries and, as a community, it clearly benefits from exchanging its byproduct (waste steam) to other parties in the network. However, the power station also benefits from its relationship with the oil refinery in another way. It receives fuel gas (a byproduct of the oil refinery) to be used as a substitute for coal. Thus, the interaction between two parties in the network is not necessarily one way. (For a complete discussion of this case please see http://indigodev.com/Kal.html.)

nature. This is a very important issue to consider given the evidence for the growing dominance of humans over nature in ways that have serious implications on the *resilience* of the biosphere as a whole (see Chapter 11). Business has a major role in this development because, as Benyus (1997: 7) observes, it 'regard[s] limits as a universal dare, something to be overcome so we can continue our expansion'. This behavior persists because of business' natural affinity to the possibility of perpetual material growth (i.e., growth in profit, sales, and so on).

However, the new reality of 'general' resource scarcity (see Chapters 9, 10 and 11) dictates that businesses have to make profound changes in the way they organize, manage and run their enterprises. This is because 'at this point in history, the problem is not a shortage of raw materials (although that will come), it's that we have run smack against the limits of the Earth's resilience' (Ibid: 207).

McDonough and Braungart (2002: 150) challenged the conscience of business enterprises by pointing out that 'if commerce shuns environmental, social, and cultural concerns, it will produce a large-scale tragedy of the common, destroying valuable natural and human resources for generations to come'. Even though it may appear very difficult to imagine a corporation basing its performance on a mission that is based in protecting the environment for the sake of distant generations and the health of global ecosystems, there are already a few daring business enterprises that have started this difficult journey with measurable success. In almost all of these cases, the catalysts appear to be leaders with incalculable imaginations, practical wisdom, courage and a strong faith that humans can be awakened to a cause that is meant to protect nature and, in so doing, protect themselves.

Use innovations that are inspired by nature

In recent years there has been growing academic interest in studying how materials are designed and manufactured in nature so that they can be put to some practical use in the human economy. This, as Benyus (1997: 2) puts it, 'conscious emulation of life's genus' is now called *biomimicry*. As it specifically applies to business, the biomimics (i.e., those practicing biomimicry) are discovering how nature uses the sun and simple compounds in order to produce totally degradable fibers, ceramics, plastics and chemicals.

One commonly observed trait of nature has been that 'it manufactures its materials under life-friendly conditions—in water, at room temperature, without harsh chemicals or high pressure' (Ibid: 97). Despite this, 'nature manages to craft materials of a complexity and a functionality that we can only envy'. This is the bright promise that nature provides to today's industrial society, of a future that could be free of toxins and hazardous wastes. This problem of waste is one of the most vexing and growing threats that industrial society has to find solutions to, since what is at stake is the health and vitality of humans, and of natural ecosystems, on an unprecedented scale. No doubt, industries could play a central role in finding solutions to this problem.

The possibility that we might be able to stop our production of toxic waste is also creating an increasing level of excitement and engagement among the practitioners of industrial ecology and biomimicry in order to work on the discovery of materials and manufacturing processes that are designed with cradle-to-cradle qualities in mind. To those who are committed to the view that 'technologies that produce byproducts society cannot absorb are essentially failed technologies' (Ibid: 256), epitomise what the notion 'innovations that are aspired by nature' literally conveys.

In this section, the concept of eco-effectiveness and its implications for the prevailing industrial paradigm have been explored. However, much of the discussion has been rather conceptual. In the next section, the extent to which eco-efficiency can be applied in the real world is demonstrated using two case studies: a small-scale farm operation and a medium-sized corporation.

15.4 ECO-EFFECTIVENESS: AS A VISION OF SUSTAINABLE BUSINESS PRACTICE

As discussed in the previous section, eco-effectiveness operates with a grand vision that an industrial system is *effective* if what it produces does not pose undue harm to any form of life in the biosphere. In other words, the products as well as the methods used to produce goods and services are designed in such a way that the material-flows within the entire production system(s) maintain their high quality in a closed-loop industrial cycle. In an industrial system of this nature there is effectively *zero* waste. As discussed earlier, this vision of zero waste is inspired by one of the most enduring qualities of well-functioning natural systems, which is that 'waste equals food'.

In this respect, eco-effectiveness is different from eco-efficiency in two very important ways. First, eco-effectiveness relies entirely on nature as its *modus operandi*. In other words, 'nature knows best' is taken as an article of faith. Second, eco-effectiveness operates on the principle that a total elimination of waste should be the abiding goal of an industrial production system. A system that operates with only the partial fulfillment of this grand vision as its goal (such as eco-efficiency) is rendered unsustainable in the long term. The question then becomes, to what extent can a production system be designed to satisfy the lofty vision of eco-effectiveness: zero waste? In other words, can the vision of eco-effectiveness be fully operationalized?

In this section, an attempt will be made to answer the above questions using two case studies. These cases are: *Polyface Farm* (a small family farm in Virginia's Shenandoah Valley); and *Interface, Inc.* (the world's largest manufacturer of modular carpet, with headquarters in Atlanta, Georgia). These cases attempt to illustrate both the challenges and opportunities of serious efforts directed toward eco-effectiveness.

Polyface Farm: imitating nature for profit

Polyface Farm, a grass-based livestock and poultry farm, serves as an excellent case study to illustrate how nature's way of growing food could be put to work on a commercial scale—a size of about 100 acres. This farm is envisioned and choreographed by its founder William Salatin and it has been in existence since 1961. It has been an economically viable enterprise since its inception. The fundamental reason for the successful and sustained economic performance of Polyface stems from the fact that it produces niche products (pastured beef, eggs, poultry, pork, mutton, turkey and rabbit meat) primarily intended for the *local* market. As a policy, Polyface do not ship their products.

As is evident from the nature of their products, on this small family farm a half-dozen animal species are raised together to form an ecological community with *synergetic* and *symbiotic* relationships. The narrative of this case study is based on an article by a well-known freelance writer on ecology and other related environmental issues, Michael Pollan (2002). As you read this article, pay special attention to how this farm is designed with cradle-to-cradle thinking—the core principle of eco-effectiveness. On this farm waste equals food, and in this important respect Polyface Farm is *beyond organic* (i.e., the conventional idea of organic farming—a farming practice that closely approximates eco-efficiency). Enjoy reading this innovative and noble endeavor of an enterprising family inspired by a vision of creating a model farm as a *restorative* enterprise, which, perhaps surprisingly, ends up being profitable as well.

In the second day of spring, Joel Salatin is down on his belly getting the ant's-eye view of his farm. He invites me to join him, to have a look at the auspicious piles of worm castings, the clover leaves just breaking, and the two inches of fresh growth that one particular blade of grass has put on in the five days since this paddock was last grazed. Down here among the fescues is where Salatin makes some of his most important decisions, working out the intricate, multispecies grazing rotations that have made Polyface one of the most productive, sustainable, and influential family farms in America.

This morning's inspection tells Salatin that he'll be able to move cattle into this pasture in a few days' time. They'll then get a single day to feast on its lush salad bar of grasses before being replaced by the 'eggmobile,' a Salatin-designed-and-built portable chicken coop housing several hundred laying hens. They will fan out to nibble at the short grass they prefer and pick the grubs and fly larvae out of the cowpats—in the process spreading the manure and eliminating parasites. (Salatin calls them his sanitation crew.) While they're at it, the chickens will apply a few thousand pounds of nitrogen to the pasture and produce several hundred uncommonly rich and tasty eggs. A few weeks later, the sheep will take their turn here, further improving the pasture by weeding it of the nettles and nightshade the cows won't eat.

To its 400 or so customers—an intensely loyal clientele that includes dozens of chefs from nearby Charlottesville, Virginia, and Washington, DC—Polyface Farm sells beef, chicken, pork, lamb, rabbits, turkeys, and eggs, but if you ask Salatin what he does for a living, he'll tell you he's a 'grass farmer.' That's because healthy grass is the key to everything that happens at Polyface, where a half-dozen animal species are raised together in a kind of concentrated ecological dance on the theme of symbiosis. Salatin is the choreographer, and these 100 acres of springy Shenandoah Valley pasture comprise his verdant stage. By the end of the year, his corps de ballet will have transformed that grass into 30,000 pounds of beef, 60,000 pounds of pork, 12,000 broilers, 50,000 dozen eggs, 1,000 rabbits, and 600 turkeys—a truly astonishing cornucopia of food from such a modest plot of land. What's more, that land itself will be improved by the process. Who says there's no free lunch?

Sustainable is a word you hear a lot from farmers these days, but it's an ideal that's honored mostly in the breach. Even organic farmers find themselves buying pricey inputs—cow manure, Chilean nitrate, fish emulsion, biological insect controls—to replace declining fertility of the soil or to manage pest outbreaks. Polyface Farm isn't even technically organic, yet it is more nearly sustainable than any I've visited. Thanks to Salatin's deft, interspecies management of manure, his land is wholly self-sufficient in nitrogen. Apart from the chicken feed

and some mineral supplements he applies to the meadows to replace calcium, Polyface supplies its own needs, year after year.

Salatin takes the goal of sustainability so seriously, in fact, that he won't ship his food—customers have to come to the farm and pick it up, a gorgeous adventure over a sequence of roads too obscure for my road atlas to recognize. Salatin's no shipping policy is what brought me here to Swoope, Virginia, a 45-minute drive over the Blue Ridge from Charlottesville. I'd heard rumors of Polyface's succulent grass-fed beef, 'chickenier' chicken, and the superrich eggs to which pastry chefs attribute quasimagical properties—but Salatin refused on principle to FedEx me a single steak. For him, 'organic' is much more than a matter of avoiding chemicals: It extends to everything the farmer does, and Salatin doesn't believe food shipped cross-country deserves to be called organic. Not that he has any use for that label now that the USDA controls its meaning. Salatin prefers to call what he grows 'clean food,' and the way he farms 'beyond organic'.

That it certainly is. The fact that Salatin doesn't spray any pesticides or medicate his animals unless they are ill is, for him, not so much the goal of his farming as proof that he's doing right. And 'doing it right' for Salatin means simulating an ecosystem in all its diversity and interdependence, and allowing the species in it 'to fully express their physiological distinctiveness'. Which means that the cows, being herbivores, eat nothing but grass and move to fresh ground every day; and that chickens live in flocks of about 800, as they would in nature, and turkeys in groups of 100. And, as in nature, birds follow and clean up after the herbivores—for in nature there is no 'waste problem,' since one species' waste becomes another's lunch. When a farmer observes these rules, he has no sanitation problems and none of the diseases that result from raising a single species in tight quarters and feeding it things evolution hasn't designed it to eat. All of which means he can skip the entire menu of heavy-duty chemicals.

You might think every organic farm does this sort of thing as a matter of course, but in recent years the movement has grown into a full-fledged industry, and along the way the bigger players have adopted industrial methods—raising chickens in factory farms, feeding grain to cattle on feedlots, and falling back on monocultures of all kinds. 'Industrial organic' might sound like an oxymoron, but it is a reality, and to Joel Salatin industrial anything is the enemy. He contends that the problems of modern agriculture—from pollution to chemical dependence to foodborne illness—flow from an inherent conflict between, on one hand, an industrial mind-set based on specialization and simplification, and, on the other, the intrinsic nature of biological systems, whose health depends on diversity and complexity.

On a farm, complexity sounds an awful lot like work, and some of Salatin's neighbors think he's out of his mind, moving his cows every day and towing chicken coops hither and yon. 'When they hear "moving the cattle," they picture a miserable day of hollering, pickup trucks, and cans of Skoal,' Salatin told me as we prepared to do just that. 'But when I open the gate, the cows come running because they know there's ice cream waiting for them on the other side.' Looking more like a maitre d' than a rancher, Salatin holds open a section of electric fencing, and 80 exceptionally amiable cows—they nuzzle him like big cats—saunter into the next pasture, looking for their favorite grasses: bovine ice cream.

For labor, in addition to his six-foot, square-jawed, and red suspendered self, the farm has Salatin's wife, Teresa (who helps run their retail shop and does the bookkeeping), children Rachel and Daniel, and a pair of paid interns. (Polyface has become such a mecca for aspiring farmers that the waiting list for an internship is two years long.) Salatin, whose ever-present straw hat says 'I'm having fun' in a way that the standard monogrammed feed cap never could, insists, however, that 'the animals do all the real work around here.' So the chickens fertilize the cow pasture, the sheep weed it, the turkeys mow the grass in the orchard and eat the bugs that would otherwise molest the grapes, and the pigs well, the pigs have the sweetest job of all.

After we moved the cows, Salatin showed me the barn, a ramshackle, open-sided structure where 100 head of cattle spend the winter, every day consuming 25 pounds of hay and producing 50 pounds of waste. Every few days, Salatin adds another layer of wood chips or straw or leaves to the bedding, building a manure layer cake that's three feet thick by winter's end. Each layer he lards with a little corn. All winter the cake composts, producing heat to warm the barn and fermenting the corn. Why corn? There's nothing a pig likes more than 40-proof corn, and nothing he's better equipped to do than root it out with his powerful snout. So as soon as the cows go out to pasture in March, the 'pigerators,' as Salatin calls them, are let loose in the barn, where they proceed systematically to turn and aerate the compost in their quest for an alcoholic morsel.

'That's the sort of farm machinery I like—never needs its oil changed, appreciates over time, and when you're done with it, you eat it.' Buried clear to their butts in compost, a bobbing sea of hams and corkscrew tails, these are the happiest pigs you'll ever meet. Salatin reached down and brought a handful of the compost to my nose; it smelled as sweet and warm as the forest floor in summertime, a miracle of trans-substantiation. After the pigs have completed their alchemy, Salatin spreads the compost on the pastures. There, it will feed the grasses so that the grasses might again feed the cows, the cows the chickens, and so on until the snow falls, in one long, beautiful, and utterly convincing proof that, in a world where grass can eat sunlight and food animals can eat grass, there is indeed a free lunch. Did I mention that this lunch also happens to be delicious?

Interface Inc.: a company with a mission for zero waste

Interface is the world's largest producer of modular carpet for commercial, institutional and residential markets. The company was found in 1973 by a visionary industrialist, Ray C. Anderson, who recently passed away (August 8, 2011). Anderson started his company with only 15 employees. Since its founding, through more than 50 acquisitions, Interface has grown into a billion-dollar corporation with manufacturing on four continents and sales in more than 110 countries.

Anderson, an environmental crusader and renowned sustainability visionary, was committed to show his fellow business leaders and other skeptics that reaching for sustainability provides a company with a competitive edge in more ways than one. He is widely known as 'America's Greenest CEO'. Anderson credited Paul Hawken, the author of *The Ecology of Commerce* (1993), for the inspiration he needed to initiate Interface's journey to sustainability, *Mission Zero*, in 1994. Mission Zero is Interface's grand vision of a total commitment to completely eliminating the negative environmental impact the company may have on the natural environment by 2020. As the current Chairman of the Board of Directors for the company, Dan Hendrix, put it 'Mission Zero gives voice to the grand promise that Interface Inc. will be sustainable, leaving zero footprint, by the year 2020. Mission Zero also unites the Interface companies in our commitment to consider the environmental impact of every creative, manufacturing and building decision we make'.

As will be evident from the discussion below, the progress toward Mission Zero has been quite impressive. Several reasons account for this. First, at Interface, the cultural transformation that needs to take place within the company to make Mission Zero a success has been total. Mission Zero is driven by a shared commitment for success. Second, continued success towards achieving the ultimate goal of Mission Zero has been effectively sustained by a steady stream of new innovations. Interface has created a team of experts, the Eco Dream Team, whose main charge has been to think creatively and in a timely manner about the future challenges of Mission Zero. Third, Interface operates with a principle of unparalleled transparency and accountability in transmitting information on the progress and challenges of its journey to sustainability. Every element of their progress is carefully cataloged, measured and reported (using programs, sources and methods that are credible and easily verifiable).

Below is a chronicle of some of the major goals and associated achievements of Interface as it marches to reach the summit of its sustainability journey by 2020: unless otherwise stated, the information below is extracted from the company's website, www.interfaceglobal.com

A. Energy use

- Commitment 1: Reduction in total energy efficiency through various technological means.
- Commitment 2: 100 percent of energy needs from renewable sources by 2020.
- Achievements as of 2010: total energy use per product unit on average is down by 43 percent since 1996. Renewable energy use at carpet factories has reached a level of 30 percent of total energy use. This is a major milestone given that renewable energy use accounted for no more than 10 percent of the total energy use only about a decade ago.

B. Climate: Reduction in GHGs emissions

- Commitment: A carbon neutral company by 2020.
- Achievements as of 2010: reduced company-wide GHG emissions by 35 percent from the baseline year of 1996. Most of this gain in emissions reduction is associated with Interface's progress in achieving measurable success in energy efficiencies, fuel switching, and the use of renewable energy resources.
- From 1996 through 2008, Interface has cut its net GHG emissions by 71 percent (in absolute tons), while sales increased by two-thirds (Anderson and White 2009).

C. Waste reduction

- Commitment: zero waste. 'Waste is broadly defined as any cost that does not produce value to customers. This includes everything from scrap materials and defective product to misdirected shipments or incorrect invoices'. The waste reduction goal includes the entire supply chain and involves constant searching for improvement in product design, packaging and transportation (more on this later).

- Achievements as of 2010: a reduction of 76 percent in total waste to landfills from the company's carpet factories since 1996.

D. Product design and manufacturing process

- Commitment: to produce products designed for sustainability through constant focus on innovative methods in the design of products and manufacturing processes. The ultimate goal is to enable the company to manufacture sustainable, closed-loop products.
- Achievements:
  - As of 2010, 40 percent of raw materials were recycled and bio-based. This is a considerable achievement when one notes that a decade ago only 3 percent of raw materials were recycled. Using current technologies products can be manufactured with 64–75 percent total recycled content, including more than 30 percent post-consumer recycled content.
  - Bio-based materials are renewable materials that Interface is discovering and using in order to reduce its heavy dependence on virgin petroleum-based raw materials. This remains one of the major challenges of Mission Zero.
- New product designs:
  - Entropy: a new residential carpet collection. Its development is inspired by biomimicry, more specifically by imitating how nature designs a floor. The advantages associated with this product are less manufacturing waste and the capability for non-directional installation.
  - TacTiles: carpet tile installation system without the need for glue. This process is inspired by examples from nature.
  - Cool Carpet: the world's first carbon neutral carpet. This product was introduced in

the marketplace in 2003. As of 2010, more than 142 million square yards of Cool Carpet have been sold, retiring more than 2 million metric tons of verified emission reduction credits.

E. Transportation

- Commitment: Identifying and reducing the company's global transportation footprint by creating partnerships with other companies and government programs and through the promotion and implementation of innovative internal transportation programs and transportation efficiency initiatives.
- Achievements:
  - Since 2003, Interface has been a charter member of the US EPA's SmartWay Partnership program—a federal program specifically designed to reduce transportation emissions.
  - Trees for Travel: program designed to track and neutralize the carbon emissions from employees' air travel. 'Interface has planted more than 118,000 trees to neutralize the carbon emissions from business related air travel since this program started in 1997'.
  - Interface uses several innovative programs specifically designed for providing incentives to employees to choose more fuel-efficient modes of transportation and detailed internal policy guidance on shipping with a focus on minimizing their transportation footprint.

F. Other commitments and achievements

- Interface is committed to reducing the environmental impact of its facilities (such as factories, showrooms, office spaces, etc.). Many of the company's facilities are LEED certified.
- Interface operates on a management principle that permeates a culture of cooperation among its employees and management. A culture of cooperation is viewed as crucial to keep employ-

ees 'connected to Mission Zero and empowered to effect change'.

- Interface has been named by Fortune as one of the 'Most Admired Companies in America' and the '100 Best Companies to Work For'—twice.
- From 1996 through 2008, Interface earnings doubled.

In *Business Lessons from a Radical Industrialist*, Anderson (Anderson and White 2009: 6) had this to say about the success of a company he created from scratch:

> Based on our experience since 1994, I can promise this: Done right, sustainability doesn't cost. It pays. And the view from the summit—looking out on a clean, healthy world for which our children and grandchildren will thank us—will make every step you and I take today for ourselves, and for them, worthwhile.

Interface is living proof that managing business with environmental stewardship in mind is not inconsistent with making profit. This is the lasting legacy of a visionary entrepreneur like Anderson.

Criticisms of eco-effectiveness as a viable sustainable business practice

Eco-effectiveness is based on the core principle that it is possible to design an industrial infrastructure in such a way that a closed cycle of the 'flow-of-energy-and-matter' is possible. It is also possible to imagine that manufacturing plants, and even economies, can be designed in a similar fashion. In such a system material wastes could be eliminated, although its sustainability requires a continuous flow of free energy from an external source—the second law of thermodynamics. Thus, the focus of eco-effectiveness is *eliminating* material waste and minimizing energy waste within the theoretical boundaries of thermodynamic efficiency. Several criticisms have been raised about eco-effectiveness, stemming from both the robustness of its theoretical foundations and the limits

associated with its practical applications. The major criticisms are:

1. For its theoretical foundation, eco-effectiveness relies on industrial ecology, and, as such, natural science and engineering are heavily emphasized. Some critics argue that this biophysical perspective should be linked with management and policy studies (Korhonen et al. 2004).

2. Industrial ecology, with its focus on the flow of matter and energy, appears to downplay the importance of the flow of information, which is critical for system efficiency. In other words, consideration of the flow of information may not be done explicitly in the design of manufacturing or industrial systems.

3. The sustainability criterion of zero waste is made without *formal* consideration of economic efficiency—alternative resource use and opportunity costs.

4. Considerable debates exist as to the notion of an industrial ecosystem and several of its implications, such as the potential of industrial symbiosis, the role of eco-industrial parks in environmental management (Korhonen 2005).

5. Problems relating to the validation of tools, methods and weighing metrics: the methods used to evaluate the performance of industrial activities that are designed to operate within a framework of a closed-loop system are incomplete and perhaps misleading. This refers to the measure used to gauge the mass of emissions and waste, the assessment of overall environmental impacts using mass as a proxy, and the measure of toxicity of chemical compounds and their effects on human health.

6. Its basic assumption of innovations inspired by nature may be overly simplistic because it does not account for the human elements in industry that would not allow it to perform in the same way as nature does. Place-specific, local, evolution-based relationships, changes and arrangements, etc.

15.5 CHAPTER SUMMARY

This chapter has explored the various conceptual ideas and practical tools businesses can utilize to embark on a journey towards sustainability. It was shown that such a journey requires, among others, visionary and daring leaders who are capable of getting the support needed from all of the stakeholders in their business enterprises. This is needed so that inevitable changes are accepted without too much delay and the working environment is conducive for the continuous breeding of new and innovative ideas.

Working towards environmental sustainability is invariably challenging because, as the late Chairman of the Board of Interface put it, 'conventional wisdom and the status quo are powerful sedatives. Like opiate they dim our vision and blur our minds'. The conventional wisdom in this case is to associate environment with cost. In the business world cost is something not to pursue but to avoid.

As discussed in this chapter, since the late 1980s there has been some rethinking in the business world about the association of environment with cost. The change in this mindset has not originated by accident—it occurred with what may appear to be the sudden realization by the world community that the global environment is at risk. It was at the eve of the Rio Earth Summit in the summer of 1992 that a group of visionary business leaders created an organization that eventually came to be known as the World Business Council for Sustainable Development (WBCSD).

Currently, the WBCSD has about 200 members from over 30 countries and 20 major industrial sectors. It is a CEO-led organization involving about 1,000 business leaders. One of the major initiatives of WBCSD has been its engagement in the promotion of *eco-efficiency* to business enterprises of all sizes throughout the globe. The primary aim of this endeavor has been to convincingly convey the idea that waste minimization pays.

However, this is not an entirely novel idea. A prime example of this being 3M, which initiated its eco-efficiency program in early 1970s, almost 15 years before it got the attention it deserved. The version of the eco-efficiency initiative by 3M is known as the 3P program and it stands for Pollution Prevention Pays. The 3P program has had a long and successful history of accomplishment, both in terms of working for the environment (i.e., reducing waste) and saving considerable amounts of money for 3M. Its success is largely attributed to the fact that the commitment to reducing waste touches almost every aspect of the company's operations. It is also a program initiated internally by visionary leaders who, from the start, attempted to make the 3Ps an integral part of the company's culture. The people working at 3M are regarded as the 4th P.

The three operational principles of eco-efficiency are: reuse, reduce, and recycle—the 3Rs; and the order is important.

Since the 1990s, partly due to the efforts of the WBCSD, many companies around the world have been making demonstrable efforts to move towards business practices that embrace the ideals of sustainability by promoting the use of eco-efficiency criteria in product standards and waste management. This has been met with varying degrees of success. Success largely depends on the extent to which waste minimization strategies are applied within the domain of a given company. Piecemeal approaches to any sustainability effort yield suboptimal results and even unintended negative consequences. For example, effort may be looked upon as 'green-washing' deployed by a company to hide a more serious environmental abuse.

In recent years, eco-efficiency has been perceived as an inadequate response to the growing environmental destruction by humanity. Given the magnitude of the problem, it is argued that it is not enough to merely focus on waste reduction. What is needed is a fresh approach to industrial design that is conceived with the complete *elimination* of waste as its ultimate objective.

This means that, like in nature, the industrial system should operate in a closed-loop cyclical system. That is, as Hawken (1993) succinctly describes it, 'every product or byproduct is imagined in its subsequent forms even before it is made. Designs must factor the future utility of a product and the avoidance of waste, from its inception'. This *holistic* approach, as discussed in this chapter, requires a *holistic* approach to problem solving.

Eco-effectiveness is the term used to describe the approach where nature is taken as the *modus operandi* for industrial systems. Nature is to be imitated not conquered—a change in the mindset of humanity that very much represents a paradigm shift.

Eco-effectiveness does not totally invalidate eco-efficiency. However, it added some important elements in the design of industrial systems in such a way that waste is not permitted to leave the system. This is done by requiring that byproducts and wastes should be not only reused, but also up-cycled and remanufactured. In addition, eco-effectiveness insists on, at a minimum, the isolation of toxic wastes and hazardous materials entering into other waste streams. In principle, toxins are to be avoided.

The practical applications of eco-effectiveness require knowledge of many factors that are found at the intersections between *industrial* and *ecological* systems. A relatively new field of study that attempts to provide the conceptual framework and methodological tools for dealing with resource management problems that involve both industry and the natural environment is called *industrial ecology*.

As discussed in this chapter in some detail, several ideas are developed from the emergence of this new sub-discipline. Among them are: the notion of an industrial ecosystem—fashioned with interdependency, symbiotic and synergetic relationship; mutual dependencies and cooperation are just as important as competition; the value of system functionality with built-in redundancy; diversity; and the role of eco-industrial parks in environmental management.

This chapter offered two case studies where eco-effectiveness has been effectively applied. The first case study, the Polyface Farm (a small family farm in Virginia) showed how a grass-based livestock and poultry farm can be profitability run using a farming practice that literally allows the imitation of the nutrient cycles of a natural ecosystem. On this farm, waste is always converted to food. Polyface Farm is 'beyond organic' because not only is the use of chemicals and toxins outlawed, but the farm also operates with a zero tolerance of waste. The second case study is Interface, Inc.—the world's largest manufacturer of modular carpet. This company, lead by its visionary founder, embarked on an initiative that is known as 'Mission Zero'. The goal of this initiative is to reduce the footprint of Interface to zero by 2020. The case-study outlined the many remarkable successes that Interface has made on the way to achieving of this grand journey towards sustainability: perhaps the most ambitious undertaken by any company.

What became apparent in examining these two case studies is the importance of leadership from senior management to achieve the necessary cultural and organizational changes.

The chapter ended with an outline of some of the major weaknesses of eco-effectiveness, and how some of the observed shortcomings could be ameliorated through specific public-policy initiatives.

REVIEW AND DISCUSSION QUESTIONS

1. Briefly identify the following concepts: eco-efficiency, the 4Ps, the triple-bottom-line, corporate social responsibility (CSR), the sustainability sweet spot, corporate sustainability report, eco-effectiveness, industrial ecology, closed-loop system, up-cycling, remanufacturing, lifecycle assessment, green-washing, design for the environment, lifecycle design, industrial symbiosis, eco-industrial park, biomimicry, and industrial metabolism.
2. Compare and contrast the following pairs of concepts:
    (a) *Cradle-to-cradle* versus *cradle-to-grave*; as competing waste-treatment philosophies.
    (b) *Life cycle assessment* versus *design for the environment*; as alternative methods (strategies) for assessing the potential environmental impact of inputs (materials) and waste releases associated with ordinary industrial production processes.

    (c) *Industrial metabolism* versus *eco-industrial parks*; as metaphors to relate industrial processes with natural ecological processes.

3. Read the following statements. In response, state 'True', 'False' or 'Uncertain' and explain why:

    (a) The difference between recycling and up-cycling is purely semantic.

    (b) Biomimicry is a failed science from the outset because there is nothing to learn from nature since all of the elements in a natural ecosystem are products of evolution, which are impossible to imitate.

4. Why do some critics argue that, while the eco-industrial park is a good concept, it remains inapplicable to practice in the real world? Are you convinced with this view point? Why or why not?

5. Eco-efficiency is just a piece-meal approach to eco-effectiveness. Thus, pursuing eco-efficiency as business strategy is not only good in itself, but it also allows companies to see the advantages of working, if not for, then with nature. Do you agree? Explain.

6. Given the myopic nature of industry leaders and industrial society as a whole, do you think that the premise of 'the triple-bottom-line' is viable? In other words, can private firms operate in such a way that the interests of stock owners, workers, society at large, future generations and nature are thoughtfully, realistically and strategically considered? Discuss.

7. Dillon (1994: 203) suggested the following to be the most important implications of industrial ecology to the functioning, organization and management of a firm that is guided by a vision of eco-effectiveness. Write an essay explaining why these four specific cases can be viewed as being instrumental to the enduring success of firms' who are inspired by a vision of eco-effectiveness. Be specific.:

    (a) Commitment of senior management—to achieve the needed cultural, organizational and procedural changes;

    (b) Development of companywide strategies and guidelines—to ensure that product responsibility is carried out appropriately;

    (c) Creation of multidisciplinary networks;

    (d) Harmonization of product-responsibility programs and goals with other company practices and goals—to ensure that environmental issues are considered along with traditional criteria such as cost, quality and performance.

8. 'Commerce can be one of the most creative endeavors available to us, but it is not worthy of business to be the convenient and complicit bedfellow to a culture divorced from nature. While commerce at its worst sometimes appears to be a shambles of defilement compared to the beauty and complexity of the natural world, the ideas and much of the technology required for the redesign of our businesses and the restoration of the world are already in hand. What is wanting is collective will'. After reading the materials covered in this chapter, do you agree with this assessment by Paul Hawken? How many Andersons are out there in the real world that can take Hawken's challenge to heart and act upon it diligently and for the long haul?

REFERENCES AND FURTHER READING

Allenby, B. and Fullerton, A. (1991) 'Design for Environment—A New Strategy for Environmental Management', *Pollution Prevention Review*, Winter issue: 51–61.

Anderson, R. and White, R. (2009) *Business Lessons from a Radical Industrialist*, New York: St. Martin's Press: 1–6.

Ausubel, J. H. (1996) 'Can Technology Spare the Earth', *American Scientist* 84: 166–77.

Ayres, R. U. and Ayres, L. (1996) *Industrial Ecology: Towards Closing the Materials Cycle*, London: Edward Elgar Publishers.

Ayres, R. U. (1994) 'Industrial Metabolism: Theory and Policy', in B. R. Allenby and D. Richards (eds.) *Greening Industrial Ecosystems*, Washington, DC: National Academy Press: 23–49.

Benyus, M. J. (1997) *Biomimicry: Innovation Inspired by Nature*, New York: Harper Perennial.

Carson, R. (1962) *Silent Spring*, New York: HarperCollins.

Dillon, P. S. (1994) 'Implications of Industrial Ecology and Firms', in B. R. Allenby and D. Richards (eds.) *Greening Industrial Ecosystems*, Washington, DC: National Academy Press: 201–7.

Engbert, H. (1995) 'The Industrial Symbiosis at Kalundborg', in T. Gladwin and T. Freeman (eds.) *Business, Nature and Society: Towards Sustainable Enterprise*, Burr Ridge, IL: Richard D. Irwin.

Frosch, R. A. (1992) 'Industrial Ecology: A Philosophical Introduction', *Proceedings of the National Academy of Science* 89, 3: 800–3.

Frosch, R. A. and Gallopoulos, N. E. (1989) 'Strategies for Manufacturing' *Scientific American* 189, 3: 144–52.

Garner, A. and Keoleian, G. (1995) *Industrial Ecology: An Introduction*, National Pollution Prevention Center for Higher Education, University of Michigan: 1–32.

Hawken, P. (1993) *The Ecology of Commerce: A Declaration of Sustainability*, New York: Harper Collins Press.

Indigo Development (2003) 'The Industrial Symbiosis at Kalundborg, Denmark', http://indigodev.com/Kal.html, 7/23/2011.

Interface, Inc. www.interfaceglobal.com/Company/History.aspx

Keoleian, A. G. and Menerey, D. (2004) 'Sustainable Development by Design: Review of Life Cycle Design and Related Approaches', *Journal of the Air and Waste Management Association* 44, May 1994: 646.

Korhonen, J. (2005) 'Industrial Ecology for Sustainable Development: Six Controversies in Theory Building', *Environmental Values* 14: 83–112.

Korhonen, J., von Malmborg, F., Strachan, P. A. and Ehrenfeld, J. R. (2004) 'Management and Policy Aspects of Industrial Ecology: An Emerging Research Agenda (Editorial)', *Business Strategy and the Environment* 13: 289–305.

McDonough, W. and Braungart, M. (2002) *Cradle to Cradle: Rethinking the Way We Make Things*, New York: North Point Press.

Pollan, M. (2002) 'Sustaining Vision', *Gourmet Magazine*, August Issue.

Savitz, W. A. with Karl Weber (2006) *The Triple Bottom Line*, San Francisco, CA: Jossey-Bass.

Schmidheiny, S. (1992) *Changing Course: A Global Business Perspective on Development and the Environment*, Boston, MA: MIT Press.

Thomas, V., Thomas, T., Lifset, R., et al. (2003) 'Industrial Ecology: Policy Potential and Research Needs', *Environmental Engineering Science* 20, 1: 1–9.

Tibbs, H. (1992) 'Industrial Ecology: An Environmental Agenda for Industry', *Whole Earth Review*, Winter 1992: 4–19.

World Commission on Environment and Development (1987) *Our Common Future*, Oxford: Oxford University Press.

Part V

Environmental sustainability in developing countries

Part six consists of one chapter, Chapter 16, which investigates the complex and seemingly paradoxical interrelationship among population, poverty and environmental degradation in the developing countries of the world. The chapter starts with a detailed analysis of the population problem, both globally and with a focus on developing countries. This is followed by an exploration on a long-held thesis that a link exists among poverty, population and environmental degradation. The analysis of this theory, to its fullest extent, takes up a large part of the materials presented in Section 16.5.

Some of the major issues addressed in this chapter include the following: (1) A close look at the intricate nature of poverty that is so prevalent in developing countries, and at how this economic condition contributes to population growth and environmental degradation; (2) the significance of gender equality, and more specifically improvements in the economic status of women, as an important social variable for the amelioration of environmental degradation and population control; (3) strategies to empower the poor in such a way that they become motivated to take actions that are consistent with their economic security, while inflicting the least amount of damage to their environmental assets; (4) the changes in governance structures that are considered crucial in fostering the development and implementation of

institutional programs and/or policies to protect the environment, while meeting the basic needs of the poor; and (5) the extent to which international development aid programs and trades have either been benefiting or hurting economic development aspirations and the ecological integrity of developing countries.

This chapter deals with *real* problems facing about three-quarters of the world's population. These problems are real in the sense that they contribute to the visible incidences of malnutrition suffered by a significant percentage of the world population: poor sanitation facilities, exposing people to high level of health risk; large-scale land degradation and critical water shortages that continue to contribute significantly to loss in agricultural productivity; mass species extinction resulting from deforestation and the devastation of fragile coastal ecosystems; a noticeable decline in some fish species that are vital sources of protein for many people around the world; pollution of all sorts; and so on.

These are indeed serious problems and they demand the immediate attention of the global community (the poor and the rich) to work together for causes that are singularly intended to achieve sustainable development on a global scale. They are indisputably among the major challenges confronting humanity in the twenty-first century.

Chapter 16

Population, poverty, and environmental degradation in the developing world

There are many reasons to be optimistic about the future. More people are better fed and housed than ever before, global literacy rates are increasing and more people have access to better health care. Despite these significant gains, however, the need to arrest the increase in poverty while at the same time reversing the current trends of environmental degradation remains one of the world's greatest challenges. It is essential to tackle these two challenges simultaneously, since it is abundantly clear that the poor suffer disproportionately from the effects of environmental decline.

(UNDP Report on Poverty and Environmental Initiatives 1999: iii)

LEARNING OBJECTIVES

After reading this chapter you will be familiar with the following:

- The disparities in conditions relating to populations, economies, and the environment within the so-called 'developing' nations.
- Why the world population problem may be viewed predominantly as a concern of the developing nations, but why its long-term implications leaves no country untouched.
- Understanding the causes for the failure of past development experiments designed to alleviate poverty and reduce environmental degradation.
- The social, economic and institutional challenges associated with efforts to decouple the poverty, population and environmental links in developing countries.
- Fresh initiatives for decoupling the poverty, population and environmental links, including:
  (a) Gender equity and the alleviation of poverty and environmental degradation;
  (b) Improved governance for the alleviation of poverty and environmental degradation;
  (c) Empowering the poor to work towards environmental sustainability;
  (d) Social and economic equity and environmental sustainability; and
  (e) Fair and equitable international trade regimes.

This chapter deals with the economic struggles and the serious environmental degradation that are afflicting four-fifths of the world's population. What is clearly evident for most of these countries, especially the bottom quarter (the very poor) is the unsustain-ability of the business-as-usual practices of economic development. Sustainability in this context suggests that the poverty, population and environmental linkages cannot be decoupled without a comprehensive and fresh look at the social and political dynamics of these countries. This may be a messy process, but it is a necessary one.

16.1 INTRODUCTION

In Section 11.3 the interrelationships among population growth, economic growth and environmental degradation were analyzed within the context of the Malthusian tradition. It was observed that although population growth has not yet threatened us with the immediate Malthusian catastrophe envisioned by many, it remains a serious problem. This is because rapid population growth is considered to be one of the major contributing factors to the vicious cycle of poverty and environmental degradation in many parts of the developing countries (Hughes et al. 2009).

The primary aim of the present chapter is to systematically examine the exact nature of the interrelationships between population, poverty and environmental degradation in the developing world. As will be evident, those interrelationships are not only multifaceted and as such complex but also, in many respects, *paradoxical*. This is not to suggest that environmental and social problems of such complexity and magnitude defy 'practical' solutions, although as Martin Lewis (1992: 191) put it, 'the patterns of destruction experienced here are markedly distinct from those of the industrialized zone, calling for the development of a separate body of both social–environmental theories and economic–ecological programs'.

In analyzing this issue, it is important to note that the 'developing world' is composed of a heterogeneous group of countries and not all of them are at the same stage of economic development or encounter the same levels of population and environmental problems. As will be shown shortly, some countries in this group have been quite successful, both in controlling their population growth and in maintaining steady growth in their economy, as conventionally measured by an increase in GDP per capita.

However, while these countries are making demonstrable progress (transitioning) in their struggle to increase their standard of living on the *average*, they are plagued by an increasing level of air

and water pollution, and by an accelerated rate of resource depletion. These problems exhibit themselves through deforestation, soil erosion, overfishing and damage to marine and coastal ecosystems such as coastal wetlands and coral reefs (Trainer 1990).

For these countries, it appears that economic growth was attained at significant costs to their *natural capital assets*—the very resources critical for sustainable development. Furthermore, the economic success (in terms of increased per capita income) of this group of countries has been clouded for two reasons. First, because of the lopsided nature of the income distribution in the countries of this group, it has been difficult to make significant headway on the war on *poverty*. In general, it appears that the very poor have not benefited from economic growth during the past four decades (UNDP 2011). Second, the economies of these countries still remain vulnerable to international macroeconomic conditions and the policy measures taken by the major international loan-granting institutions, such as the IMF and the World Bank.

Leading examples of these 'transitioning' countries are Argentina, Brazil, Mexico, India, South Korea, China, Taiwan, and so on. For these countries poverty remains a serious problem, not because of a lack of measurable progress in economic performance as measured by GDP per capita, but because of other social, political and institutional problems (more on this later).

On the other hand, many of the so-called least developed countries located mainly in sub-Saharan Africa, Central America and Southeast Asia, plus small island states from Oceania and the Caribbean, are confronted with problems of poverty and environmental degradation *simultaneously* (Hughes et al. 2009). One of the major reasons for this is the failure of these countries to control their rapid rates of population growth.

According to the United Nations Report on World Population Prospect (2004: 11):

> Since the 1970s, the least developed countries have experienced, on average, the highest population growth rate in the world. Even though they

represent a relatively small share of the world population, just under 12 percent in 2005, it is expected that the overall population increment in those countries will account for 37 percent of all world population growth during the period 2005–2050.

In many of the poorest developing countries population has been growing faster than GDP, indicating a *negative* annual growth in per capita income. In these countries poverty and population growth are exerting dangerous pressure on the carrying capacity of the ecosystem, and producing widespread desertification and deforestation (Bhattarai and Hammig 2001; Hughes et al. 2009; Lewis 1992; Trainer 1990).

Although these differences exist, the developing world has certain common characteristics. To a varying extent, population is still a major problem to most of these countries. Urbanization is another problem that these countries seem to share. In most of the developing nations, women are treated as second-class citizens and the poor are often marginalized. Globalization and international trade offer both major threats and opportunities to safeguarding the natural resource base of the developing nations. Most of these countries have unstable governments and an unequal distribution of income and wealth, and they seem to lack the tradition and institutional infrastructure that are necessary for establishing clearly defined ownership over renewable resources, such as forests, fisheries and arable land (Turner, et al. 1993).

As will become evident, these *governance* issues are major contributing factors to both the short- and the long-term economic, population and environmental problems of these nations. Until comprehensive solutions to these problems are found, both those countries that seem to be doing well economically, and those that are failing to develop, will continue to share what appears to be a common experience: a severe form of environmental degradation (Lewis 1992).

This chapter has limited objectives. Consistent with the theme of the book, the main focus is the *environment*. Thus, poverty (or development) and population are discussed to the extent that they have

significant adverse impacts on the physical environment of the developing world. It also endeavors to recommend a number of practical policy measures that should be instituted in order to decouple the links between poverty, population and the environment. The following list highlights the key issues addressed in this chapter.

- It is not only the number of people, but also their lifestyles, political systems, and social structures that define the relationship between humans and environment.
- Poverty is associated with environmental degradation, but there is not necessarily a direct causal relationship.
- It is not economic growth as such but the way in which 'development' takes place (is conceived and implemented) that is important in the alleviation of poverty and environmental degradation.
- The status of women is a particularly important variable in the interactions between population, poverty and the environment.
- Reform of the governance structures of many developing countries is a prerequisite to encouraging the sustainable use of environmental resources.
- Events such as structural adjustment programs, macroeconomic reform and globalization can be important in stimulating overall economic growth and greater economic efficiency. On the other hand, these same events may put many developing countries in a situation to overexploit natural resources in order to handle balance-of-payment problems or to deal with changing global market conditions.

16.2 GLOBAL POPULATION TRENDS: CAUSES AND CONSEQUENCES

One of the most vivid experiences of the developing world in the past 60 years has been the rapid increase in population growth. This has been a concern for a number of reasons, and one of these concerns has been the notion that rapid population growth may in fact be the main culprit for continued environmental degradation in the developing world. There are a number of empirical studies that support the existence of causal relationships between rapid population growth and environmental degradation (Allen and Barnes 1995; Cropper and Griffith 1994; Ehrlich and Holdren 1971; Repetto and Holmes 1983; Rudel 1989; Stern et al. 1996). However, most of these findings are valid only within certain *contexts*, and as such cannot be used to establish a general causal relationship between population growth and environmental degradation. The idea that seems to emerge is that *while population growth is important, it is not the sole or even primary cause for environmental degradation.*

Thus, even in countries where rapid population growth is occurring, environmental degradation is best understood when the population factor is combined with other variables, such as poverty, the status of women, governance structures (e.g., land tenure systems or traditions, income distribution, political systems, social structures, and so on), and markets and other institutional failures (Hughes et al. 2009). In addition, when the concern for the environment is placed in a global context, it is not only the number of people but also that 'the geographic distribution of people throughout the globe, the concentration of people in urban areas, and the demographic characteristics of regional populations have an important influence on the effects of human activity on the environment' (Population Reference Bureau 1998: 1).

In this section, using published data, an attempt is made to examine the exact nature of the population problem in developing nations. This is done by looking at the growth trends and spatial distribution of *world* population so that the problem (i.e., population growth in developing nations) is understood both historically and relative to developed nations.

An unprecedented level of steady population growth has been one of the dominant characteristics of the twentieth century. This is a significant change, considering that for several millennia human population was growing at an insignificant rate, with deaths largely offsetting births. As shown in Figure 16.1, the world population was initially growing at a steady but

very low rate, reaching the first billion mark in about 1800. In other words, it took millions of years for the world population to reach its first billion. However, as is evident from Figure 16.1, since about the turn of the seventeenth century the world population has been growing at a much faster pace. A look at Table 16.1 makes this point quite clear. While it took millions of years for the human population to reach the first billion, it took merely 130 years to add the next billion. Although the rate of growth seems to have been declining since the mid-1970s, it now takes only 12 years for the world population to grow by a billion. According to the medium-variation projection of the 2010 Revision of World Population Prospects, the world population is expected to reach 9.1 billion in 2050.

In addition, the situation becomes even more striking when we focus our attention on the most recent world population trends. At the beginning of the twentieth century there were between one and 1.5 billion people in the world. For the first half of the century (1900–50), world population grew at a relatively low rate, averaging about 0.8 percent per year (World Resources Institute 1987). By the 1960s there were 3 billion people on earth, and the annual growth rate was reaching the 2 percent mark (Ibid.). In the next decade (1960–70) the world population grew at an accelerated rate until it reached a new plateau—an annual rate of increase of 2.06 percent (Ibid.). Rapidly declining death rates, together with continued high birthrates—especially in the developing regions of the world—contributed to this rapid rate of growth.

Yet since the early 1970s, the growth rate of the world population has been showing a slow but steady decline. Specifically, the annual rate of growth has declined from 1.96 percent in 1970 to approximately 1.16 percent today (World Population Prospects: The 2010 Revision). This drop is attributable mainly to a decrease in birthrates worldwide, as a result of intense educational campaigns to promote birth control, along with specific preventive actions (such as improvements in reproductive health and access to contraception) undertaken by various government and private agencies.

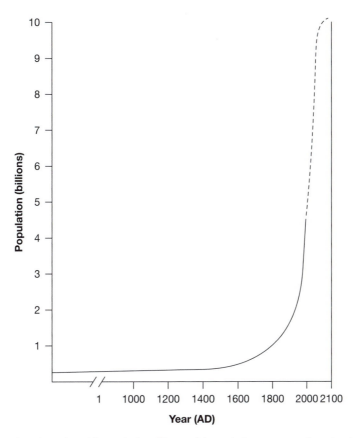

Figure 16.1 *Past and projected world population. The world population was growing at a steady but a very low rate, reaching the first billion in about 1800. On the other hand, exponential growth of world population has been the dominant feature of the twentieth century.*

Table 16.1 *An approximate time it took for the world population to grow by a billion*

Approximate Time	Population in Billions	Time it Took to Grow in Years
— to 1800	1	(Millions of Years)
1800 to 1930	2	130
1930 to 1960	3	30
1960 to 1974	4	14
1975 to 1987	5	13
1987 to 1999	6	12
2000 to 2011	7	12

Source: Population Reference Bureau estimates (1800 to 2011), 2011 World Population Data Sheet.

365

Despite the progress that has been made to slow down the annual rate of population growth, more people are being added to the earth's total each year (see Table 16.2). Several factors explain this, among which the most significant are: (1) the continuing decline in mortality rates; (2) the absolute size of the world population (7 billion as of 2011); and (3) the immense momentum built up from the current age composition of the population (i.e., the fact that roughly half of the world's population is under the age of 25, with all or most of their reproductive years ahead of them).

As shown in Table 16.2, while the world is adding more people every year, the number of people added during the current decade (2010–20) will be less than the previous decade (2000–10). This should not be surprising given the steady decline in the rate of population growth over the past four decades. Despite this, even in the most recent decade, on average, the planet adds about 76 million people each year, the equivalent of 9 New Yorks.

So far the focus has been on the population trends of the world as a whole. However, these trends, based on aggregate data, do not reveal the wide differences in population growth rates (see Table 16.3) and the distribution of population (see Table 16.4) that persist between the different regions of the world, especially between developed and developing nations.

For two centuries (1750–1950) the population of these two groups of nations grew at low rates— between 0.4 and 0.9 percent, respectively (McNamara 1984). Furthermore, during this period the rate of growth of developed nations was slightly higher than that of developing nations. However, as shown in Table 16.3, since 1950 the average annual rates of population growth of developing nations have started to outpace those in developed nations by considerable margins.

For example, between 1960 and 1965, the average growth rate for developing nations was roughly *twice* that of developed nations (2.32 versus 1.21 percent). Forty years later, between 2000 and 2005, the population of developing nations was growing at a rate 3.5 times faster than that of developed nations (1.46 versus 0.42 percent). Stated differently, if these rates persist over a long period, it will take less than

Table 16.2 World population growth by decade, 1950 to 2010

Year	Population by Decade (Billions)	Increase Average Annual (Millions)	Increase (Millions)
1950	2.556	—	—
1960	3.042	486	49
1970	3.721	679	68
1980	4.452	731	73
1990	5.288	836	84
2000	6.088	800	80
2010	6.853	756	76

Source: US Census Bureau, International Data Base.

50 years for the population of developing nations to double, and over 160 years for that of developed nations. (It is important to note that, as shown in Table 16.3, the rates of population growth vary among the various groups of the developing nations. What is particularly noticeable is that sub-Saharan African countries are lagging considerably behind countries in South America and Asia in their effort to reduce population growth.)

Clearly then, as seen in Table 16.4, such differences have resulted in a significant shift in the distribution of global population towards developing nations. At the beginning of the twentieth century, a third of the world population lived in developed nations, and this proportion remained constant until about 1950. Since the 1950s, though, the share of the world population living in developed nations has been declining steadily. By the year 2005, less than one-fifth (18.7 percent) of the world population lived in developed nations. That is, approximately four out of every five people in the world currently live in a developing nation.

Moreover, this trend is expected to continue in the foreseeable future. As shown in Table 16.4, a recent United Nations medium-variant projection of world population for the year 2050 is estimated to be 9.1 billion. Although the predicted estimate of world population in 40 years is subject to a wide range of variation, one trend of future global population

Table 16.3 Annual rates of population growth (as percentages) by regions, 1950 to 2005

Region	1950–55	1960–65	1970–75	1980–85	1990–95	2000–05
Sub. S. Africa	2.23	2.53	2.78	2.98	2.80	2.50
South America	2.80	2.77	2.35	2.19	1.69	1.38
Asia (excluding Middle East)	1.87	2.15	2.24	1.83	1.56	1.17
Developing Nations	2.04	2.32	2.40	2.12	1.86	1.46
Developed Nations	1.28	1.21	0.89	0.70	0.54	0.42
Total World	1.78	1.95	1.94	1.74	1.54	1.24

Source: World Resource Institute (Population: Growth rate and total pollution).

Table 16.4 Population trends, 1900 to 2050 (millions)

Region	1950	1985	2000	2005	2050
Developing Regions	1,681 (67)	3,657 (76)	4,837 (79)	5,253 (81.3)	7,840 (86.4)
Africa	224	555	872	906	1,937
Asia	1,292	2,697	3,419	3,905	5,217
Latin A.	165	405	546	561	783
Developed Regions	835(33)	1,181 (24)	1,284 (21)	1,211	1,236 (13.6)
Total	2,516	4,837	6,122	6,465 (18.7)	9,076

Source: World Resources 1988–89, p. 16. © 1988 by the World Resources Institute. Reprinted by permission. (The numbers inside the brackets indicate percentage of the world population.)

Source: United Nations Department of Economic and Social Affairs/Population Division, World Population Prospects: The 2004 Revision, Volume III: Analytical Report. (Data for 2005 and 2050.)

growth remains indisputable. That is, the world population will definitely increase in the future, and most of this increase will occur in developing countries. According to the United Nations estimate (see Table 16.4), it is expected that in 2050, 86.4 percent of the people in the world will be living in developing countries (Ibid.). That is, 17 out of every 20 people in the world will live in the poorer nations.

What the above observations clearly indicate is that the world population problem is predominantly a concern for developing nations. The question is, then, to the extent that a link exists between rapid population growth and environmental degradation, what can be done to ameliorate the population problem in these poor nations? As discussed above, the fact the wealthy nations have done far better in controlling their population growth than the poor ones may suggest that *poverty* is a factor to be considered in finding a long-term resolution to both the population and environmental problems of developing countries (Cropper and Griffith 1994). However, to link poverty with population and the environment should not necessarily imply that economic growth is the *panacea* to the problems of population and the environment in the developing nations. To make economic development work for the poor (and in turn for the environment), it is important to have a general understanding of the nature and circumstances of poverty in developing nations. The next section will address this issue.

16.3 UNDERSTANDING POVERTY AND ITS INTERACTIONS WITH POPULATION AND THE ENVIRONMENT

> We recognize that poverty, environmental degradation, and population growth are inextricably related and that none of these fundamental problems can be successfully addressed in isolation. We will succeed or fail together.
>
> (WCED 1987: 45)

Poverty may mean different thing to different people. It is generally conceptualized in terms of income, and formally defined as people living below a certain predetermined income level. For example, several recent publications from the United Nations identify *absolute* poverty as people existing on less than one dollar per day (Bhalla 2002). It was estimated that almost half of the world, over three billion people, live on less than $2.50 a day (Hughes et al. 2009; World Bank 2008). Most of these people live in sub-Saharan Africa and South Asia. However, it would be rather misleading to think that abject poverty is limited to the so-called poor developing countries. Brazil, an economically emerging country, has over 10 million people (about 5 percent of the total population) living on an income below $2 per day (World Bank 2011).

Alternatively, poverty may be defined in terms of *assets* instead of income (Hughes et al. 2009). In this case, poverty may refer to a lack of income-generating assets that would enable the provision of an adequate level of basic necessities. Assets may include natural capital (the ownership of land), human capital (work skills), social capital (human relations), physical capital (tools of the trade), and financial capital (e.g., cash savings). For the absolute poor, individual ownership of these assets may be beyond their reach. On the other hand, collectively the poor may own a substantial amount of the various forms of the asset categories mentioned above, and pro-poor public policies may put stress on how to better *allocate* and *manage* these assets so that the economic circumstances of the poor will be improved. In addition, as will be observed soon, this asset-based definition of poverty is particularly helpful in examining the poverty–environmental interactions.

Another key issue that needs to be recognized in relating poverty with the environment is the fact that poor people are not a *homogenous group*. Most importantly, significant differences exist between the *rural* and *urban* poor in terms of their relationship to the environment.

In rural areas, 'the destitute are those who have very few assets, are marginalized, and who are continually forced to live from hand to mouth. They have no recourse but to exploit the environment around them, even if it means degrading its long-term value for their needs' (UNDP 1999: 27). In this respect, the rural poor are heavily dependent upon natural resources for their livelihoods. A good many of them reside in communities where land is collectively (communally) owned and the productivity of the land is very low or sub-marginal. Often, the rural poor live in regions where the ecosystem, as a whole, is fragile, and the carrying capacity of the land is visibly overstressed (Hughes et al. 2009).

Under these circumstances, the pressure from population growth is relieved by territorial expansions that entail deforestation and other similar ecological encroachments, or by migrating to an already crowded urban area. The essential message here is that 'attacking poverty in rural areas is then necessarily a matter of improving poor people's ability to derive sustenance and income from more productively sustainably-managed natural resources' (UNDP 1999: 28). In other words, in rural areas it is more effective to attack poverty by means of *improving the management and utilization of natural resources* rather than the other way around.

On the other hand, the very poor or destitute *urban* dwellers in developing countries have different impacts on the environment. The urban poor live in densely populated regions often characterized by substandard housing, inadequate or polluted water, lack of sanitation and solid waste systems, outdoor air pollution, and indoor air pollution from low-quality cooking fuels. Under these living conditions, health risks are heightened because of the concentration of people and production. Thus, viewed in this way, it seems that many of the linkages between the urban poor and the environment occur in the form of the effects of the environment on them, rather than the other way around.

The policy implication of this is that improving the environment in urban areas can reduce poverty because it improves poor people's health (Ibid.). In this regard, poverty alleviation measures through economic growth (increased per capita income) could benefit the environment. This, as discussed in Chapter 12, seems to be confirmed by empirical studies based on the environmental Kuznets curve (EKC) hypothesis. These studies consistently found a strong association between growth in GDP per capita and reduction in air pollutants that are known for causing local health risks, and that can be treated without great expense, such as sulfur dioxide, dark matters and sanitation (Panayotou 1993; Selden and Song 1994).

Of course, although relatively small on a per capita basis, the urban poor also consume products and produce wastes that have significant negative impacts on the environment. This situation is worsening as the population of the urban poor in the developing regions of the world increases rapidly. Among the key findings of the 'World Urbanization Prospects: The 2003 Revision', prepared by the United Nations Department of Economic and Social Affairs' Population Division, were:

1. Population growth will be particularly rapid in the urban areas of less developed regions, averaging 2.3 percent per year during 2000–2030. Migration from rural to urban areas and the transformation of rural settlements into urban places are important determinants of the high urban population growth anticipated in less developed regions.
2. Almost all the growth of the world's total population between 2000 and 2030 is expected to be absorbed by the urban areas of the less developed regions. By 2017, the number of urban dwellers will equal the number of rural dwellers in the less developed regions.

This rapid population increase in urban areas in less developed countries has created a host of social and environmental problems. Many cities are unable to expand their infrastructure and services fast enough to keep pace with population growth. Furthermore:

> urban growth often encroaches on farmland, destroys wildlife habitats, and threatens sensitive ecosystems and inshore fisheries. In Jordan, for example, the rapid growth of Aman and Zarqa has led to the gradual depletion of a major underground water reserve, which has reduced water availability for farmers and desiccated an internationally important wetland.
>
> (Population Reference Bureau 1998: 3)

From what have been discussed so far, it is important to note that the rural and urban poor are *interdependent* groups. A worsening condition of the natural environment in the regions where the rural poor reside could initiate mass migration from the rural to urban poor areas. The obvious effect of this would be to further deteriorate the living and environmental conditions of cities.

On the other hand, the rapid and unplanned growth of urban areas affects the natural environment of the urban poor by adversely affecting the waterways, wildlife habitats and other sensitive ecosystems. Recognition of this kind of *interdependence* between the rural and urban poor clearly implies that policy initiatives intended to improve the environment of the rural poor would not only benefit this group but also the urban poor, and vice versa. This statement would remain valid to the extent that migration of the rural poor to urban areas remains a major concern and the growth of the urban poor is viewed as having a significant effect on the natural environment upon which the rural poor depends for their survival.

The discussion in this section clearly reveals that the interactions of poverty, population and the environment are *complex* and depend on the contexts under which they are examined. It was observed that defining poverty in terms of *assets* would make the interactions between the environment and poverty more evident, at least from a policy perspective. Furthermore, it was shown that the interactions of population, poverty and the environment are sensitive to *location*—urban versus rural poor. Most importantly, it was shown that recognition of these points has important policy implications. In the next section, an effort will be made to show why, over the past three decades, major public policy measures intended to eradicate poverty in developing countries have failed. As will become evident, there have been difficulties in understanding the full extent of the population, poverty and environment interactions, difficulties that are the root cause of this failure.

16.4 THE FAILURE OF PAST POLICY MEASURES TO REDUCE POVERTY AND ENVIRONMENTAL DEGRADATION

In the 1960s, when many developing countries were engaged in a desperate struggle to make the difficult transition from colonialism to political independence, a serious push was made to raise the standard of living in these nations (Bandyopadhyay and Shiva 1989). The motivation for this was the depressing level of poverty in many developing nations, especially in the newly independent nations of Africa and Southeast Asia. As a world organization, the United Nations responded to this concern by inaugurating several development programs specifically intended to alleviate poverty in developing nations. Furthermore, the 1972 United Nations Conference on the Human Environment identified poverty as both a cause and a consequence of environmental degradation. This was a landmark event in the sense that it raised the awareness of the pervasive nature of poverty to the world as a whole and called for unified actions to deal with it.

In this first era of 'development push', in almost all the UN-sponsored efforts, economic 'development' was conceived of as the cure for poverty. Economic development was understood as an increase in per capita GDP, and countries tried to increase their GDP without any attempt to differentiate between economic development and economic growth (Goodland and Daly 1992). Furthermore, it was hypothesized that growth in GDP not only alleviates poverty by creating jobs for the poor, but could also create a surplus with which to clean up the environment and control crime and violence (Homer-Dixon, et al. 1993). By the same token, in accordance with the theory of demographic transition, achieving a high

standard of living was expected to lead to a decline in fertility rates, and hence a decline in the rate of population growth. Thus, as discussed in Chapter 12, economic development was conceived as a remedy, not only for poverty, but also for *population growth* and *environmental degradation*.

To further strengthen these claims, the need for *economic development* was argued for in terms of the 'vicious cycle of poverty and environmental degradation'. The main implication of this is that low-income countries are destined to remain poor indefinitely unless something is done to raise their standard of living on a sustainable basis (Todaro 1989). It was argued that countries with a low standard of living spend a high proportion of their income on *current consumption needs*. This means low savings and low investments, which leads to low productivity. With no hope of improving productivity, it was argued that these countries would remain poor. Furthermore, the persistence of poverty coupled with population pressure would lead to the migration of the poor to ever more fragile lands or more hazardous living sites, forcing them to overuse environmental resources. In turn, the degradation of these resources would further impoverish them. The question of interest therefore, was what could be done to resolve this seemingly persistent problem of poverty?

Using the traditional model of development, *capital accumulation* was sanctioned as the way of alleviating poverty, or as a catalyst for economic development (Solow 1994; Todaro 1989). This was based on the notion that capital accumulation, by enhancing the productivity of labor and other factors of production, would ultimately lead to *increase in the per capita income* of a nation. It was with this in mind that the development projects of the 1960s and 1970s were primarily focused on capital formation to promote growth. These included large capital-intensive projects involving dams, assembly lines and large-scale energy and agricultural projects. These projects were financed largely by international loans agencies, such as the World Bank and the International Monetary Fund (IMF).

In addition, it was argued that the economic condition of developing nations could be further enhanced by engaging in *free trade* with the industrial countries of the West (Bhagwati 1993; Bhalla 2002). The trade relations between these two groups of nations are largely characterized by exports of primary resources (such as wood, minerals, fruits, spices, etc.) from the developing nations, and imports of industrial products from developed countries (such as machines, tractors, transportation vehicles, etc.). The justification for such trade relations is based on the fundamental premise that free trade leads to the attainment of a mutually beneficial outcome for all the parties involved. That is, international trade is not a zero-sum game even when the total benefits are not shared evenly among the trading parties.

By the early 1980s it became increasingly evident that the traditional approaches to economic development, which basically depended on *capital formation* and *free trade*, did not live up to expectations. In fact, the evidence seemed to suggest that in many respects these development experiments had failed to improve productivity in many developing countries. Today, there are some who claim that some countries are worse off now than five decades ago, when the official United Nations development programs were initiated (Daly 1993). More specifically, there are now more people in the developing world who are in desperate poverty than ever before; environmental degradation in this part of the world has reached crisis proportions, and many developing countries are politically unstable and burdened with debilitating international debts. How did this come about? What explanations can be given for such unintended and unfortunate outcomes? Simply put, what went wrong?

These are indeed difficult questions to address. Any attempt to offer comprehensive answers requires careful scrutiny of the political, social, institutional, economic and environmental dimensions of the programs that are specifically intended to alleviate poverty in developing nations. What follows is an attempt to do this under the following three broadly defined themes: economic growth and the environment; international trade and the environment; and governance, economic growth, poverty and the environment.

Economic growth and the environment

As stated earlier, the campaign to alleviate poverty in the developing world had as its primary focus the increase of per capita GDP. Furthermore, this aim was expected to be achieved through increased capital formation and exposure to international markets. This traditional approach to economic development has two major flaws when consideration is given to the environment.

First, as discussed in Chapter 14, the conventional measure of GDP does not account for the depreciation of natural or environmental capital. Thus, a focus on increasing GDP is likely to have a detrimental effect on the natural environment in the long run (Goodland and Daly 1992; Stockhammer 1997). More specifically, some empirical evidence exists indicating that a decline in natural capital alongside the accumulation of various other forms of capital (man-made, human, and social) has contributed to economic growth (OECD 2002: 15). The natural capital that is being degraded in quality includes groundwater resources, fish stocks, the global atmosphere, and the capacity of ecosystems to assimilate toxic chemicals. This is the natural resource base critical for sustainable development.

Second, traditionally capital formation was conceived of in terms of large-scale capital-intensive projects such as dams, highways, factories and agriculture, etc., and these projects were implemented without adequate assessment of their impacts on the natural ecosystem (Goodland and Daly 1992). Furthermore, these projects were *not necessarily pro-poor*. That is, they didn't necessarily encourage the development and implementation of infrastructure and/or technologies that benefited the poor or protected the integrity of the environment. To the contrary, large-scale economic development projects seemed to offer a disproportionately large benefit to the already advantaged groups, such as large-scale farm operators, established firms with strong ties to international corporations, middle-class urban dwellers, etc. This pattern of economic development contributed to a further increase in income inequality between the rich and the very poor, which is regarded by many as one of the major drivers of poverty (Hughes et al. 2009)

The upshot of this has been continued environmental degradation, which manifests itself in a variety of forms, such as deforestation, soil erosion, increasing levels of urban air and water pollution, and increasing damage to coastal and marine ecosystems leading to diminishing fishery stocks and the destruction of coral reefs.

In the developing world, where the economy is primarily agrarian, the environment is an important input for many production activities (Hughes et al. 2009). Thus, environmental degradation has an adverse effect on productivity, and the outcome of this is a reduction in income. The important implication of this result is that poverty-alleviation programs are likely to fail in the long-run if they are pursued with a primary focus on increasing GDP or per capita GDP. Growth ideology of this nature undermines the economic significance of the natural environment (Goodland and Daly 1992). In the developing world the poor depend on the environment, and *protecting the environment should be an important element of poverty alleviation* (Bandyopadhyay and Shiva 1989; Hughes et al. 2009).

International trade, development and the environment

As discussed earlier, the conventional wisdom has been to view international trade as a vehicle for accelerated economic growth in the developing nations (Antweiler et al. 2001; Bhagwati 1993; Bhalla 2002). However, although somewhat inconclusive, the empirical evidence seems to suggest that commercialization or international trade is an important factor contributing to rapid rates of tropical deforestation and the extinction of some valuable animal and plant species worldwide (Bhattarai and Hammig 2001; Koop and Tole 1999; Repetto and Holmes 1983; Rudel 1989).

More specifically, trade with developed nations appears to accelerate deforestation in Latin America and Southeast Asia, and intensify the rate of desertification and the extinction of some animal and plant species in sub-Saharan Africa (Bhattarai and Hammig 2001; Rudel 1989). The implication of this is that, contrary to conventional wisdom, free trade has *not* been consistent with environmentally sustainable trade (Daly 1993). Does this suggest that, from the perspective of natural resource conservation, there is something inherently wrong with the trade between developed and developing nations? How could this be possible when, at least conceptually, international trade among sovereign nations is based on the premise of attaining 'mutually beneficial outcomes'?

From the perspective of natural resource and environmental management, the problem with international trade arises when one examines the way benefits and costs are imputed. Under a free trade regime the value of all international exchanges is assessed on the basis of *market prices*. As discussed in Chapter 3, a number of factors can lead to distortions in market prices, and the chance for this to happen is even greater when we are dealing with international trade involving environmental and natural-resource commodities. For our purposes we should note two factors in particular that may lead to price distortions in the natural-resources markets of developing countries.

First, generally the economies of developing countries tend to be weak and quite unstable. They are often confronted with an urgent need to finance both domestic and international *debt*. In their desperate attempt to finance such debt, the governments of these countries are likely to offer their natural resources for sale at a discount (Korten 1991). Case Study 16.1 illustrates this point, showing how, because of the pressure to pay its external debts, Brazil in the 1970s and 1980s was aggressively pursuing economic policies that encouraged cattle ranching, and in so doing accelerated the rate of deforestation. Furthermore, the case of Nauru, as discussed in Chapter 13, is another good example of the unsustainable use of natural resources (in this case phosphate deposits) by a poor country.

The second and probably most important factor contributing to natural resource price distortion is market failure. That is, market prices for natural resources in these regions do not take account of

CASE STUDY 16.1 RANCHING FOR SUBSIDIES IN BRAZIL

Theodore Panayotou

In the 1960s, the Brazilian government introduced extensive legislation aimed at developing the Amazon region. Over the next two decades, a combination of new fiscal and financial incentives encouraged the conversion of forest to pasture land. During the 1970s, some 8,000–10,000 square kilometers of forest were cleared for pasture each year. The proportion of land used for pasture in the Amazonian state of Rondonia increased from 2.5 percent in 1970 to 25.6 percent in 1985 (Mahar 1989).

It is now clear that transforming the Amazon into ranchland is both economically unsound and environmentally harmful. Without tree cover, the fragile Amazonian soil often loses its fertility, and at least 20 percent of the pastures may be at some stage of deterioration (Repetto 1988b). Indeed, cattle ranching is considered one of the foremost proximate causes of deforestation. Furthermore, ranching provides few long-term employment opportunities. Livestock projects offer work only during the initial slash-and-burn phase. Negative employment effects have been observed when income-generating tree crops such as Brazil nuts are eradicated for pasture (Mahar 1989).

Nonetheless, the incentives designed to attract ranching, which were administered by the government's Superintendency for the Development of the Amazon (SUDAM), were powerful. Fiscal incentives included ten- to fifteen-year tax holidays, investment tax credits (ITCs) and export tax or import duty exemptions . . . SUDAM evaluated projects and financed up to 75 percent of the investment costs of those that received favorable ratings using tax credit funds.

Starting in 1974, subsidized credit also played a crucial role in encouraging numerous ranching projects. The Program of Agricultural, Livestock and Mineral Poles in Amazonia (POLAMAZONIA) offered ranchers loans at 12 percent interest, while market interest rates were at 45 percent. Subsidized loans of 49–76 percent of face value were typical through the early 1980s (Repetto 1988a) . . .

The subsidies and tax breaks encouraged ranchers to undertake projects that would not otherwise have been profitable. A World Resources Institute study showed that the typical subsidized investment yielded an economic loss equal to 55 percent of the initial investment. If subsidies received by the private investor are taken into account, however, the typical investment yielded a positive financial return equal to 250 percent of the initial outlay. The fiscal and financial incentives masked what were intrinsically poor investments and served to subsidize the conversion of a superior asset (tropical forest) into an inferior use (cattle ranching). Moreover, a survey of SUDAM projects reveals that five projects received tax credit funds without even being implemented (Mahar 1989).

Source: Green Markets: The Economics of Sustainable Development, San Francisco, CA: International Center for Economic Growth (1993). Reproduced by permission of the author.

---

externalities (Daly 1993; Ekins 1993). For example, when lumber is exported from a country in Southeast Asia to Japan or France, the importing country will pay the prevailing market price, which is highly *unlikely* to include the environmental effects of the logging operations and the forgone benefits (these include both the *use* and the *non-use* values) from preserving the resource under consideration for future use. Thus, if no mechanism is used to internalize these exter-

nalities, free-trade based on market prices will lead to the undue exploitation of natural resources upon which a vast number of the poor nations' people depend for their livelihood. Perceived in this way, free-trade leads to the environmentally unsustainable and economically inefficient appropriation of resources on a global scale (Daly 1993; Ekins 1993).

In addition to the above factors, international trade may work against the poor for the following reasons:

1. The integration of poor areas into national or international economies, or the popularization of products that were formerly consumed only locally, can create demand that outstrips sustainable supply. Resources that had been used only for local consumption can suddenly be over-exploited as markets increase, as happened in the case of the shrimp industry in Southeast Asia (UNDP 1999).

2. Trade for industrial or niche export markets often exposes rural households to high levels of risk. This is particularly true where the trade has encouraged people to move away from a more diversified and less risky agriculture-based livelihood (Ibid.).

3. Structural adjustment programs (generally imposed by IMF) may limit countries in their ability to provide subsidies to the poor. Furthermore, externally imposed macroeconomic adjustments often tend to encourage the reallocation of resources (in the form of new investment opportunities) towards the fastest-growing sectors of the economy, and this task often entails the withdrawal of resources away from long-term investment in the resources of the poor (Ibid.).

4. In recent years, a new and disturbing phenomenon of trade is emerging. Transnational companies are buying agricultural land from countries with major food insecurity (such as Ethiopia) with the clear intention of exporting most of the produce from the land. For this reason and others, land acquisitions have caused displacement, dispossession and disenfranchisement. This kind of failed trade policy could have been prevented were it not for the existence of major institutional (governance) failures (Cochrane 2011). This is the subject of the next subsection.

Governance, economic growth, poverty and the environment

The issue of governance refers to the political, social and economic institutions that are necessary to manage and protect environmental resources and the interests of the often-marginalized poor. For the subject of interest here, an effective governance system is judged according to what it attempts to do to promote social equity and environmental sustainability without unduly disrupting the normal functions of an economy. 'Achieving these goals requires, above all, approaches of governance that foster citizen participation in policy-making and that promote integrity, transparency, and accountability in the management of public resources' (OECD 2002: 40).

As the discussions below indicate, these are key institutional elements that are lacking in many developing countries even today, let alone during the 1960s, 1970s and 1980s when economic growth was pushed with little or no scrutiny. In the absence of a good governance structure ambitious programs of economic development often meant *economic growth at the expense of the environment and sometimes the poor*. To a large extent, the main culprits for the persistent lack of good governance practices in less developing countries have been political instability, biased land tenure systems, the widespread corruption of government officials, and insufficient experience in conducting democratically structured governance systems (Dicklitch 2004). In some countries, there appears to be strong and persistent resistance to a freely elected and representative government system.

Establishing institutions that ensure the stable functioning of society and economies, including the enforcement of civil and property rights, requires political leaders that have a broad mandate from their constituents and the ability to stay in power until the official term of their administration has expired. For most developing countries, political instability and insecure tenure over many valuable renewable resources, such as forests, fisheries and arable lands, continually negate public-policy efforts to stabilize population, control pollution and conserve resources (Bulte and van Soest 2001; Panayotou 1993; Turner et al. 1993).

One of the most unfortunate, but recurring, realities in many developing countries is political instability. It is especially true of countries in Africa, Southeast Asia and Central and South America, which frequently face internal strife that sometimes erupts into prolonged tribal conflict and even civil war. Thus, in this kind of political climate it would be, if not impossible, extremely difficult to implement effective population and resource conservation policies based on long-term visions. Instead, public policies are conducted on a piecemeal basis, and generally as a reaction to crisis situations. What this entails is an apparent lack of responsible stewardship in resources that are critically important to the long-term survival of the nation (Homer-Dixon et al. 1993).

To make matters worse, in many of these countries properties are publicly or communally owned, and often ownership is not clearly defined. Consequently, as discussed in Chapter 3, market prices need to be corrected. But this requires that developing countries have the appropriate regulatory and institutional framework to internalize environmental externalities. In many developing countries this kind of market failure tends to persist because of their governments' inability to administer and enforce the laws that are intended to correct externalities.

One reason for this is that these are countries that can least afford to pay for protecting the environment. As a result, even when the effort to protect the environment or conserve resources is there, regulations are inconsistently applied and regulatory agencies are too poorly staffed and informed to be able to monitor and implement regulations effectively. The fact that corruption is rampant further complicates this problem.

The ultimate effect of this has been a rapid degradation of valuable environmental assets resulting from extensive and random land-clearing, imprudent farming practices, and excessive water and air pollution (Cole 2007). This situation is likely to continue unless some means are found to strengthen the institutional weaknesses that are at the core of the problems—that is, to *define* and *enforce* clear rights of access and use of resources to producers, consumers and governments, so that societal resources are prudently used. As Case Study 16.2 clearly demonstrates, this does not mean that countries need

CASE STUDY 16.2   COMMUNAL TENURE IN PAPUA NEW GUINEA

Theodore Panayotou

Unlike most of the developing world, Papua New Guinea has maintained its communal tenure customs while adapting to the requirements of an increasingly market-oriented economy. While the latter requires clear land ownership, Papua New Guinea's experience has shown that converting land from communal to freehold ownership may confuse rather than clarify the rights of ownership. The widespread land degradation encouraged by the insecure tenure, loss of entitlements and open access characteristic of state-owned land elsewhere has been absent from Papua New Guinea.

Most countries have responded to market pressures for clear ownership by imposing a new system of private or state ownership. In contrast, Papua New Guinea's land law builds upon the customs governing its communally held land. The country's Land Ordinance Act calls for local mediators and land courts to base settlements on existing principles of communal owner-

ship. Consequently, 97 percent of the land remains communal, has been neither surveyed nor registered, and is governed by local custom (Cooter 1990).

This communal tenure seems to provide clearer ownership rights, with all their environmental and market implications, than private ownership. Settlements that convert communal land to freehold are often later disputed, and reversion back to customary ownership is a frequent outcome. Yet unlike state-owned land in other developing countries, communal land in Papua New Guinea is neither in effect unowned nor public. Rather, the bundle of rights deemed 'ownership' in the West does not reside in one party. For example, individual families hold the right to farm plots of land indefinitely, but the right to trade them resides in the clan (Cooter 1990).

The island's communal systems have long resulted in the sustainable use of its more densely populated highlands. Even with a nine-thousand-year agricultural history, a wet climate and population growth of at least 2.3 percent, the highlands remain fertile. The population, which is primarily agricultural, enjoys a per capita income more than twice that of El Salvador, Western Samoa and Nigeria (Cooter 1990). In marked contrast to much of the developing world, only 6 million of its 46 million hectares of forestland have been converted to other uses (Australian UNESCO Committee 1976).

The lack of deforestation comes as no surprise since those who control the land have an interest in the sustainable, productive use of the forest. Rather than dealing with a distant government in need of quick revenues and foreign exchange, companies seeking logging rights must negotiate directly with those who have secure tenure and who use the land not only to farm, but also to gather fruit, hunt and collect materials for clothing, buildings and weapons (Panayotou and Ashton 1992). Because the communal tenure patterns provide an entitlement to all clan members, individuals have little incentive to sacrifice future value for current use.

Source: *Green Markets: The Economics of Sustainable Development*, San Francisco, CA: Institute for Contemporary History, (1993). Reproduced by permission of the author.

to adopt private ownership of resources. Effective property rights systems could take several forms; what matters is that governments match property tenure laws with the social context.

In addition to the problems with land tenure systems, in most developing nations the distribution of farmlands is grossly uneven. For example:

> In 1960, the smallest 50% of holdings controlled less than 3% of agricultural land, in 1970, the median of the reported figure is 4% . On the other hand, the largest 10% of holdings controlled 65% of the land in 1960; for 1970, the median for all developing countries figure was 70%.
>
> (Repetto and Holmes 1983: 610)

The effect of this has been the more intensive use of small farmlands, primarily for the purpose of growing crops for domestic needs. This practice is greatly intensified when internal population pressures increase. Yet owners of large lands allocate most of their holdings for commercial or cash crops, such as coconuts, sugar, fruits, vegetables, cotton and tobacco, primarily for export. Moreover, these crops are grown with the extensive application of pesticides. Thus, the unequal distribution of landholdings that exists in most developing countries not only shifts land use from domestic to export needs, but also places these countries at greater environmental risk. This situation can be ameliorated only through *land*

reform (wealth redistribution) designed to more or less equalize landholdings and/or through *export restrictions*.

To sum up, clearly the discussions in this section suggest that the failure of the poverty alleviation programs in developing countries during the 1960s, 1970s and a good part of the 1980s, was primarily due to the improper implementation of many well-intentioned economic development programs. The focus of these programs was very much on pursuing economic growth at all costs.

This was justified with the rather naïve notion that it is only through economic growth (an increase in average per capita income) that the eradication of poverty will be possible, and that this should be pursued even if it is done at the cost of the environment. Furthermore, the belief was also that, in the long run, as suggested by the EKC hypothesis, economic growth will be good for the environment. Furthermore, it was argued that increases in the living standards of the poor would slow population growth (see Chapter 12).

However, as the discussions in this section have showed, the economic development programs during these three decades miserably failed to achieve their intended goal: the eradication of poverty. This was because the programs were not properly focused on either the problem of the poor and/or the elements of the natural environment (assets) that specifically affects the poor. Furthermore, the problem was further compounded by the fact that economic growth was pursued without much consideration of the *institutional factors* relevant to the promotion and enforcement of social equity and the sustainable use of the natural environment. The question is now, what can be done to remedy these past mistakes? The next section attempts to answer this question.

16.5 NEW INITIATIVES TOWARDS POVERTY AND THE ENVIRONMENT

In terms of international development programs, the 1980s was a decade of transition. This was a decade during which searches for new and comprehensive initiatives related to poverty, population, overconsumption and the environment started to be considered seriously. More specifically, it was during this decade that a conceptual shift from 'traditional economic growth' towards 'sustainable development' started to take place. This new movement was formally articulated in 1987 by the publication of a book entitled *Our Common Future*, popularly known as the Brundtland Report (WCED 1987). As discussed in Chapter 13, it was from this report that sustainable development obtained its most commonly accepted definition as 'development that meets the needs of the present without putting the future at risk'. With reference to the main theme of this chapter, in the Introduction section of the report, Dr. Gro Harlem Brundtland wrote,

> There has been a growing realization in national governments and multinational institutions that it is impossible to separate economic development issues from environmental issues; many forms of development erode the environmental resources upon which they must be based, and environmental degradation can undermine economic development. Poverty is a major cause and effect of global environmental problems. It is therefore futile to attempt to deal with environmental problems without a broader perspective that encompasses the factors underlying world poverty and international inequality.
>
> (Ibid: 3)

What this report brought into focus was that environmental problems are not only linked to poverty as it exists in the developing countries but also to *inequalities in global patterns of consumption and production*. This globalization of the environmental problem was in fact the driving force for holding the United Nations Conference on Environment and Development (the Earth Summit) in Rio de Janeiro in 1992. Agenda 21, the action program adopted at this conference, devoted a chapter to the relationship between poverty and environmental programs.

This Rio Summit was followed by a number of other global conferences throughout the 1990s, all dealing with specific aspects of the interactions between population, poverty and the environment from a global perspective. Among these conferences, the most notable ones were: the Cairo Conference on Population and Development (1994); the Copenhagen World Summit on Social Development (1995); the Beijing Fourth World Conference on Women (1995); the Istanbul Habitat II conference (1996); the 2000 Millennium Summit; the World Summit on Sustainable Development (WSSD) in Johannesburg in 2002; and the 2005 World Summit. The unifying theme of these conferences has been sustainable development and the specific topic (namely, population, environment, social and economic equity, gender, human settlements, etc.) of each conference reflected the perspective under which sustainable development has been pursued.

In June of 2012 the United Nations will be holding a conference during the twentieth anniversary of the Earth Summit, the Rio+20 Earth Summit. At this event, the main topics are again sustainable development and poverty eradication. Another related issue the conference will be addressing is the institutional framework of sustainable development.

It could be argued that there has been a big gulf between the goals of the global conventions of the above nature and their actual achievements. However, in spite of this, the cumulative effects of the above conferences have been to change the perception of global communities regarding how to deal with problems of poverty, population and the environment in the following concrete manner:

■ First and foremost, these problems are viewed as being global, and as such their solutions require cooperative international actions. A case in point is the establishment of the Millennium Development Goals (MDGs). Adopted by world leaders in the year 2000 and set to be achieved by 2015, the MDGs provide concrete, numerical benchmarks for tackling extreme poverty in its many dimensions. There are eight MDGs, which are broken down into 21 quantifiable targets that are measured by 60 indicators. The MDGs also provide a framework for the entire international community to work together towards a common end.

Another related development has been the Poverty and Environmental Initiative (PEI) of the UN Development Programme (UNDP) and the UN Environmental Programme (UNEP). This partnership was established in 2005 to help countries increase their capacity to turn mainstreaming poverty–environment linkages into country-led MDG progress (Hughes et al. 2009).

■ Second, there is a growing realization in the international community that economic growth cannot be considered a solution of underdevelopment by itself, and that the way in which development takes place matters a great deal.

■ Third, enduring solutions to poverty, population and the environment require a careful examination of some specific issues that have been somewhat neglected until recently. These issues include, *gender*, *governance*, *the empowerment of the poor*, and *social and economic equities*. The rest of the chapter deals with discussions of these *four* general issues and how they contribute to a better understanding of poverty, population interactions and their possible remedies.

Gender equality and the alleviation of poverty and environmental degradation

It has been only in the past quarter of a century that gender equity started to receive serious attention as an important variable in the population–poverty–

environment relationship. Given that we live in a male-dominated world, gender equity necessarily refers to the much-needed improvement in women's social and economics status. Why is this important? In many societies the status of women is closely associated with rates of fertility and infant and child mortality, health and nutrition, children's education, and natural resource management (Population Reference Bureau 1998). Invariably, a decline in the population growth rate is evident wherever the status of women has been elevated. This how Nierenberg (2002: 9) described the significance of this issue:

when girls go to school free of fear of violence and sexual coercion and when women reach economic, social, and political parity with men, they have fewer children and give birth later on average than their mothers did. Assuming good access to health and family planning services, fertility almost invariably declines to or below replacement level. That slows the growth of population. It is increasingly clear that the long-term future of environmental and human health— and, critically, the global population peak—is bound up in the rights and capacities of youth, especially young women, to control their own lives and destinies.

There is always a danger in advocating an improvement in the status of women purely based on the premise that their reproductive decisions and actions are valued or have implications for population growth and/or poverty. The argument is that gender equality and the reproductive and sexual health of women are basic human rights and, as such are of *intrinsic* value. These were the positions taken in the International Conference on Population and Development (ICPD) in Cairo in 1994, and, to a much greater degree, at the Fourth World Conference on Women in Beijing in 1996.

This issue as to whether one argues for the equality of women on the basis of either a purely instrumental or a purely human rights perspective should not be an important issue in itself. What is important is the recognition that no meaningful policies on population, poverty and the environment can be formulated without an explicit account of the important roles women play in these areas of human endeavor. This warning or declaration is especially pertinent to the developing countries in which women's participation in much of the important social, political and economic decision-making is severely limited.

Equal access to education is the most effective way to empower women. By 'empower' what is meant here is a woman's ability to maintain control over the resources and decisions that affect her life:

> Educating girls and women gives them higher self-esteem, greater decision-making power within the family, more confidence to participate fully in community affairs, and the ability to one day become educated mothers who pass on their knowledge to their own daughters and sons.
>
> (Nierenberg 2002: 16)

Not surprisingly, a major contributor to later pregnancies and lower fertility is at least six or seven years of schooling (Ibid.). Investment in women's education, at least at the primary school level is, therefore, crucial for two reasons: (1) to provide girls and women with invaluable knowledge and information on reproductive health (i.e., the capacity to plan, prevent and postpone pregnancy); and (2) to provide women with the necessary confidence to voice any social, political and economic issues that have the potential to affect their life and livelihoods. Most importantly, it can give them the confidence to demand equal access to land ownership.

In the final analysis, women play critical and unique roles in societal endeavors that are specifically targeted towards population stabilization, poverty eradication and environmental sustainability. However, the contributions of women to the problems of population, poverty and the environment (or sustainable development in general) can never be fully materialized until women are given the unfettered rights to control their own lives and destinies. According to the UNDP (2011: 10):

> Recent studies reveal that not only is women's participation important but also how they participate—and how much. And because women often show more concern for the environment, support pro-environmental policies and vote for pro-environmental leaders, their greater involvement in politics and in nongovernmental organizations could result in environmental gains, with multiplier effects across all the Millennium Development Goals.

Yes, some elements of women's 'rights' are subject to different interpretations and often require a good understanding of their social context. However, the social context of women's rights should never be used to either make excuses or find justifications to deny the rights of women to their own bodies, equal access to education and land ownership, and equality in the workplaces.

Improving governance for poverty alleviation and environmental sustainability

It is not difficult at all to find examples of resource management projects and development programs that failed miserably in the implementation process mainly due to lack of 'good' governance systems. As discussed earlier, governance refers to the social institutions that are necessary to facilitate the management of public resources. With reference to resource management, good governance practices require not only the consideration of efficiency (lower transaction costs) but also equity and political realities. Above all, the efficacy of good governance greatly depends on the commitment of bureaucrats to creating a working environment that promotes integrity, transparency and accountability (UNDP 1999). That is, those with leadership roles have to demonstrate that they are the servants of the public and work with the objective of promoting the 'greatest good for the greatest numbers'.

The issue here is not a choice of political ideology (i.e., dictatorship, democracy or socialism), but rather the identification of general institutional 'principles' for effective resource governance. With regard to resource management, the general principles that are often sought as hallmarks for good governance include the following human and organizational conditions: (1) the protection of individual civil liberty; (2) decentralized decision-making processes; (3) easy access to relevant information; and (4) minimal or no impediment to resource mobilization (Ibid.). These principles, taken together, may be closely associated with commonly held views of *democratic principles* but not entirely with *democratic political ideologies*.

The main economic rationale for using the above general principles of governance is that they are expected to reduce *transaction costs* in the management of resources. Furthermore, these are also principles that are most likely to offer groups that are often marginalized (such as the poor, the residents of remotely located rural areas, etc.) a much better chance to decide what to do about their *own resources*. It is for this reason, therefore, that resource governance, guided by the *four* principles above, is essential in any serious effort to alleviate poverty or prevent the degradation of natural resources that are so vital to the livelihood and self-esteem of the poor.

In practice, what do the above principles of governance entail in terms of the structures of government organizations specifically designed to protect the interests of the poor and the environment, especially in the developing world?

1. Governments must find ways to hold themselves, private corporations and international institutions *accountable* for their environmental performance. No one should be allowed to exercise authority over natural resources without being accountable for its actions.

2. Governments should strive to place authority over environmental resources to those individuals or groups whose claims as stakeholders are verifiably legitimate. This often entails *decentralizing* responsibility for natural resource management to local governments and communities. Decentralized decision-making facilitates participation among stakeholders and the reallocation of resources (resource mobilization). Furthermore, decentralized decision-making, to the extent that it provides greater authority to

local institutions, may be made sensitive to the needs and aspirations of marginalized groups such as the poor. Of course, the decentralization of the decision-making process of government institutions cannot occur without political will at the highest level.

3. Government leaders should not only have adequate means to defend their territories from outside invaders, but should also be able to make trade, environmental and other international treaties to the benefit of their people. It is not any more adequate to identify globalization with trade. More than ever before, poverty, population and environmental problems are becoming increasingly global concerns, and their resolution demands global governance. Understanding the dynamics of global governance is critical to any government that tries to maximize the benefits to its people arising from an alliance with global treaties.

How could this kind of governance be actualized? Or, what would it take to actualize such governance in practice?

1. Legitimacy of the government. Those who are in leadership roles have a legitimate claim to the authority they exercise over their constituencies. Authority is obtained by legitimate means and without violations of human rights.

2. Political stability. Stable government is critical for making policies that are oriented towards the long-term.

3. Institutions that enable the smooth transition of political power.

4. An intolerance for corruption.

These suggestions need *not* necessary result in a government that strictly adheres to the principles of political democracy. A case in point is Cuba—a socialist country that is governed by an absolute dictator. However, Cuba has done quite well in eradicating extreme poverty, although this does not suggest that a dictatorship (even a benevolent one) is what is needed to eradicate poverty in developing countries.

The issue of governance remains a critical issue, mainly because it is one area in which a great deal of improvement is needed. It is perhaps for this reason that it is one of the top agenda items for discussion at the 20+Rio Summit in June 2012.

Empowerment of the poor and environmental sustainability

As stated earlier, it is important to recognize that *collectively* the poor in any country have both tangible and intangible assets (properties) of their own. For example, the rural poor in developing countries live in a certain geographic area with certain a climate, vegetation and land quality. They have skills and indigenous knowledge that help them cultivate their land for survival. They have histories, cultures and traditions that glue communities together and provide their identity and pride. In many African and Asian and Latin American countries the rural poor, despite their impoverishment, are often proud of who they are, and they revere their natural surroundings that are so crucial for their survival (UNDP 1999).

The same thing can be said about the urban poor. That is, they possess assets (tangible and intangible) that are peculiar to their surroundings. In general, although most of them are descendants of the rural poor, the urban poor do not have too strong a tie with land. Ownership of land is possible for only a very small minority group. What the urban poor have as resources are: plenty of unskilled and semi-skilled *labor* resources, and under-utilized *entrepreneurial* skills.

Empowerment of the poor starts with the recognition that the poor have resources that can be used and improved upon to provide them with decent living standards on a sustainable basis (Hughes et al. 2009). It also recognizes that the poor (as a community) understand their situation better than outsiders, and as such are capable of planning and implementing projects that are intended to improve their wellbeing. This is not to say that the poor do not need outside (financial or otherwise) assistance. The assertion here is that outside aid that is meaningful to poor communities is that which allows these communities to have a *complete say* regarding what the aid will be used for.

As discussed earlier, many development aid programs failed (or, indeed, fail) mainly because they never consider empowering the poor. The poor are often viewed as being helpless since they are destitute, disorganized in their community affairs or simply rootless, and ignorant about their natural surroundings (UNDP 1999). The decisions regarding what should be beneficial for the poor were often left to decision-makers at the central government level, in NGO's and in other international organizations such as the World Bank, IMF, EC, OECD, and so on.

Under these kinds of decision-making environments, should it be surprising to hear that development projects intended to alleviate poverty in rural areas often end up benefiting, not the rural poor (the targeted population), but the big landlords, government bureaucrats and other mediators of the aid packages (Wedemann and Thielke 2005)? These misallocations of resources (and, in some instances, outright blunders) can be stopped only if the poor (collectively) are recognized as a social entity capable of determining their own economic fates.

Furthermore, when the poor are recognized as equal partners in the decision-making process that involves their economic fates, among others, the wisdom of using *endogenous knowledge* will not be overlooked. This is clearly a way of avoiding the implementation of inappropriate technologies.

Further, poor people are not homogenous groups. There are different categories of urban poor and each sub-group could have conflicting needs and objectives. The same can also be said about the rural poor. Given this reality it would be wrong to view the poor as a homogenous entity. What this implies is that development programs have a better chance of succeeding if they are targeted at a certain clearly identifiable social group (or groups) living within a certain geographic region. This way, the money earmarked to reduce poverty in certain region is not used for other purposes .

Finally, it is important to note that investing in programs intended to eradicate poverty does not come without a cost (the opportunity cost). Money spent on the poor could come only by taking away resources that would have been spent on some other social projects. Thus, decision-makers need to make sure that investment to alleviate poverty is done within a framework of a cost–benefit analysis. However, such cost–benefit analyses should take into consideration the issues of *equity* discussed in the next subsection. If this is done, it will get rid of the possibility of looking at investment in the poor regions as being nothing more than *handouts*. In the long run, such an attitude will be detrimental to the poor. What the poor need is not charity but development assistance of various sorts that have a proven record in improving wellbeing on a sustainable basis (UNPD 1999).

Social and economic equities and environmental sustainability

As discussed earlier, the existence of a highly unequal distribution of assets (i.e., the total tangible and intangible capital holdings of individual households—land ownership being the most obvious) is still a serious problem in many developing countries. Obviously, the direct result of this has been the notably skewed income and wealth distributions that are so prevalent in most of these nations. This reality has been challenged, not only on the basis of *equity* (which is easy to do), but also on *efficiency* grounds. The claim has been that the highly unequal distribution of income or assets often has the tendency to suppress rates of economic growth (UNDP 1999).

What the argument above suggests is that in many developing countries reforming the distribution of assets can be justified on *both* equity and efficiency grounds. As Deininger (2003) showed, in the long term there is a clear correlation between economic growth and land inequalities. By providing land access for large numbers of people, and a sufficient economic basis to live and invest, more equal land distribution encourages consumption and investment among millions of households, with clear impacts on growth. Furthermore, a good case could be made that pro-poor asset reforms would lead to the improved management and conservation of environmental

resources (Ibid). Clearly, in many situations asset reforms could be imperative, and the issue of paramount significance is how to conduct the intended reforms successfully. This suggests that the redistribution of assets can take different forms, and that successful reforms often require careful scrutiny among alternative modes of asset reforms.

The method of asset redistribution used most often appears to be *land* reform. Land reform has been an emotional issue in developing countries. It generally means the confiscation of land from those with large holdings and its subsequent redistribution to those who have little or no land. Historically, in most instances, this kind of land reform has been shown to be socially divisive and very damaging to an economy in the long-run. This is because agricultural productivity and investments in agriculture are quite sensitive, not just to the size of landholdings, but to the way in which the land reform has been instituted—how ownership rights are defined and secured. Thus, while land reform can be justifiably used in cases were land distribution is highly skewed, its social divisiveness and adverse impact on the economy warrants caution.

Alternative asset reforms exist. Below is a list of asset reforms that are particularly relevant to the concerns of the poor and the environment. These reforms are, generally, aimed at protecting, improving, and/or expanding the asset base of the poor. They are also intended to give the poor entitlement to assets that are clearly delineated so that self-interest would lead to the use of improved resource management strategies. For expanded discussions on each of the issues listed below, refer to the United Nations Development Program (UNDP) publication, *Attacking Poverty While Improving the Environment: Toward Win–Win Policy Options*, September, 1999.

1. *Turning communal property resources over to the poor as individuals or to organizations composed of the poor*: the important issue here is that the poor have property that they claim as their own and as such have self-interest in managing it wisely.
2. *Providing the poor with long-term rental contracts for the use of public lands.*

3. *Granting of formal tenure rights*: to individuals or groups currently squatting on public lands or in urban areas.

4. *Co-managing resources with the poor*: this entails forming partnerships between local people and the state (government) to develop strategies for asset improvement and protection of resources. A good example of a successful co-management program is the Campfire program in Zimbabwe (see Case Study 16.3 below).

5. *Co-investing with the poor*: government working with local communities (such as farmer organizations) to make socially beneficial long-term

investments possible. Investments of this nature may include: soil conservation; irrigation and drainage infrastructure; grazing land rehabilitation; land-leveling; or micro-watershed re-vegetation. If the poor are to succeed, they also need to be trained. In urban areas co-investing with the poor may involve improving access to better water supplies, sanitation and energy services to reduce the health effects associated with indoor cooking, smoking and poor hygiene.

6. *Developing technologies that are targeted to directly benefit the poor*: this may entail a deliberate 'reallocation of research funds away from the most

CASE STUDY 16.3   THE CAMPFIRE: A WILDLIFE CONSERVATION PROGRAM IN ZIMBABWE

Zimbabwe's Campfire (Communal Areas Management Programme for Indigenous Resources) was officially established in 1989. Conceptually, the focus of Campfire has been wildlife management in communal areas, particularly those adjacent to National Parks. Zimbabwe has set aside, in perpetuity, more than 12 percent of its land as protected wildlife areas and most of these protected areas are surrounded by communal lands (Child et al. 1997). Historically, the communal lands were inhabited through forced settlement during the colonial period. Many of the communal lands have too little or unreliable rainfall for agriculture, but provide excellent wildlife habitat. It is estimated that 42 percent of the Zimbabwean population live on rural communal lands (Ibid.).

Before the Campfire, the relationships between the wildlife that inhabited the protected area and the rural poor living in the communal lands were antagonistic. Given the precarious conditions of the rural poor, damages caused by wildlife to crops or livestock were major threats to people's very livelihoods. In particular, elephant damage was a significant factor in crop loss in many parts of the district. Evidently, before Campfire some 200 to 300 crop-raiding elephants were shot annually by the local people (Ibid.). Furthermore, the local people often found themselves acting as allies to

poachers. Given this situation, one of the major goals of Campfire has been to change the psychology of the rural people that considered wildlife as a menace rather than an asset. How was this accomplished?

Conceptually, the primary aim of the Campfire program has been to devolve the control and benefits of wildlife and other natural resources to the lowest accountable units at sub-district level. It attempts to do this through well-designed and carefully coordinated *co-management systems* among interested parties, in particular, the rural community representatives (Campfire Association), the different branches of government bodies dealing with wildlife management (Department of National Parks and Wildlife Management, Ministry of Local Government, Rural and Urban Development), and some private and non-private organizations (Action, African Resources Trust, Centre for Applied Social Sciences, University of Zimbabwe, and World Wide Fund for Nature—Zimbabwe). In this respect, Campfire has become a forum for a wide range of issues, including representation, economic participation, and the governance of communal areas. Campfire is concerned with the nature of rural communities and collective decision-making as well as with the technical challenges of the sustainable use of wildlife.

383

At the operational level, Campfire begins when a rural community, through its elected representative body, the Rural District Council, asks the government's Wildlife Department to grant them the legal authority to manage its wildlife resources, and demonstrate its capacity to do so. The Wildlife Department, upon granting the 'appropriate authority', informs the Rural District Council regarding hunting quotas and revenue-sharing procedures that are specifically applicable to their own district at that point in time. In this regard, the aims of the Wildlife Department are two-fold: (1) to ensure transparency in revenue sharing; and (2) to foster the application of sound conservation practice in wildlife management. Under the current legal set-up in Zimbabwe, all funds generated by Campfire projects go first to Rural District Councils, and this body must disburse at least 50 percent of wildlife revenues to the producers (areas or regions from which the wildlife resources have been harvested or extracted). Over 90 percent of all Campfire revenues are currently generated by safari hunting in which foreigners visit Zimbabwe to shoot game animals (Africa Resources Trust 1996).

Thus, by granting people control over their resources, Campfire makes wildlife valuable to local communities. It is in the self-interest of the rural community to carefully manage protected lands and their wildlife. In this respect, Campfire is an attempt to use economic incentive to encourage the most appropriate wildlife management system in communal areas, particularly those adjacent to National Parks, where people and animals compete for scarce resources.

Overall, Campfire has been a very successful experiment in sustainable resource management. According to a report by the World Wide Fund for Nature (WWF), Campfire has increased household income in communal areas by 15 to 20 percent. Furthermore, over 50 percent of the revenues from Campfire have been used for much-needed community development projects, such as: drilling wells to provide clean water for residents; building schools and health clinics; fencing arable and residential land; road development; and installing grinding mills (Africa Resources Trust 1996).

favored environments and toward the resources upon which the poor depend most—fragile and rainfed lands, livestock development, agro-forestry systems, and subsistence crops' (Ibid.: 17). The aim is for capacity building sufficient to secure a better future for the poor and a sustainable use of the environment.

In the final analysis, the problems of population, poverty and the environment that are facing most developing nations are extremely serious, requiring immediate action. Furthermore, even if action is taken immediately, the fruits of these policy measures will not be seen for quite a while, which implies that the solutions necessitate long-term vision and much short-term sacrifice. This is the dilemma that most developing nations are presently facing. It would be unrealistic to expect these countries to confront their problems effectively without the presence of a stable domestic government and land-tenure systems that preserve the prudent use of natural resources.

Furthermore, what seems to be increasingly obvious is that if developing countries are to succeed in their continued struggle for economic and environmental security, they need significant financial and technical assistance from developed nations. This assistance, however, needs to be specifically targeted towards slowing the pace at which natural resources are inefficiently exploited. Whether or not international assistance contributes to self-sufficiency and resource conservation will depend, in large part, on the discipline with which aid is used by the recipient. When it is not applied appropriately, time and again international aid has proven to be counterproductive (Korten 1991; Wedemann and Thielke 2005).

There are three main ways in which developed countries could help ameliorate ecological crises in developing countries:

1. They could eliminate natural-resource price distortions in international markets. This would require the realignment of trade and international relations between the poor and the rich nations.

2. They could reduce their resource consumption in such a way that an imminent threat of resource depletion and a threat to the health of the global environment are averted. This is important because currently developing countries supply a *disproportionate share* of the minerals and ecological resources needed to satisfy the lavish lifestyle of affluent industrial nations.

3. They should compensate poor nations for their disproportionate use of the global commons. An example of an existing method for achieving this is the Clean Development Mechanism (CDM) as defined by Article 12 of the Kyoto Protocol, which involves rich nations undertaking environmental improvements (such as afforestation or rural electrification projects using solar panels) in developing countries as offsets for increased carbon emissions (see Chapter 9 for more on this).

Finally, the main lessons of this chapter are that the population, poverty and environmental problems of developing countries have no simple solutions, and that a comprehensive approach to resolving these problems demands the careful assessment of all the political, social, economic, technical, ecological and ethical aspects of these problems. While the poor nations of the world should be held *accountable* for solving their own economic and environmental problems, reality dictates that meaningful resolutions to these problems require *international cooperation* in the effort to make global resource consumption and international trade environmentally sustainable.

Furthermore, it is important to note that the rich nations have a moral obligation to find solutions to the poverty and environmental crisis in developing countries since they are *directly* responsible for many of the regional and global environmental problems resulting from their overconsumption of resources on a per capita basis. A significant percentage of the total global petroleum, paper, metals, wood and fishery products are consumed by the population of the developed (rich) nations (see Table 16.5 below). These products originate from territories that are under the jurisdictions of the developing countries and are extracted at significant environmental costs that are not adequately reflected in their market prices. Moreover, with the increasing globalization of the natural resources market, the developed nations' contribution to environmental stresses and resource depletion in developing regions of the world is likely to grow in the future.

Table 16.5 *Share of population, resource consumption, and waste production in percentages*

Country	Population	Fossil Fuel Consumption	Metal	Paper	Hazardous Waste
US	5	25	20	33	72
Other Developed Countries	17	35	60	42	18
Developing Countries	78	40	20	25	10

Source: World Population and the Environment: A Data Sheet for the Population Reference Bureau, Copyright 1997. Reprinted by permission of the Population Reference Bureau.

16.6 CHAPTER SUMMARY

This chapter has dealt with the interface of population, development and environment, with specific reference to developing nations.

A comprehensive analysis of global demographic trends indicates that the world population problem, as it relates to poverty and environmental degradation, is predominantly the concern of developing nations. Some of the disturbing facts about these countries in relation to population, poverty and the environment can be depicted in the following ways:

1. In many developing countries, population has been growing at or above 2 percent annually. For some sub-Saharan countries, population is expected to double in about 20 years—implying a rate of growth of 3.5 percent. This is in contrast to a rate of population growth in developed countries that is currently averaging about 0.6 percent annually. Some developing countries are actually experiencing a decline in population.
2. It was estimated that a total of 1.3 billion people (about one fifth of the world population) live in absolute poverty—people existing on less than $1 per day (Population Reference Bureau 1998). Most of these people live in sub-Saharan Africa and South Asia.
3. Most developing countries are plagued by an increasing level of air and water pollution and by an accelerating rate of resource depletion, which exhibit themselves through deforestation, soil erosion, overfishing and damage to marine and coastal ecosystems such as coastal wetlands and coral reefs (Trainer 1990). For example, it was estimated that currently, 14×10^{16} of tropical forests are lost annually worldwide—a landscape predominately occupied by developing nations (Bonnie et al. 2000)

In the past the majority of these countries have been forced to pursue aggressive economic development policies just to maintain their existing standard of living, often with the reckless abandonment of environmental considerations. The result of this has been deepening poverty and mounting environmental degradation.

The failures of past development aid programs as led primarily by the World Bank and other closely affiliated international organizations (such as the IMF) were attributable to several interrelated factors. Among them were:

1. *The indiscriminate and therefore inappropriate use of capital-intensive technologies*: mostly financed by the World Bank, these investment projects were implemented *without adequate consideration* of their impacts on income distribution (equity) and the environment.
2. *Forced exposure to unbalanced and unfair international trade*: primarily for the purpose of financing mounting international debts, these trades typically had significant negative impacts on the poor and the environment. Debts are often financed through the sale of natural resources at bargain prices, and through the diversion of resources that would have otherwise been used to support development programs for the poor and the protection of the environment.
3. *Institutional failures*: not enough attention was given to the political, legal (especially the legal rights of resource ownership), social and cultural circumstances at the time these countries were granted international loans to finance development projects. For example, offering loans to governments lacking clear mandates from their own constituents, and with a past history of lack of accountability, were major contributing factors to the failure of large internationally financed projects.
4. *Market failure and market distortion*: as discussed in Chapter 7 and elsewhere at some length, the free market often fails to value 'ecosystem services'. For example, forests provide watershed protection, biodiversity conservation and carbon sequestration and the consequent reduction in GHG emissions. As valuable as these

services are to society, forests are exploited solely on the basis of the market values of the wood products and non-forest uses such as agriculture. The consequence of this has been the degradation and loss of forestland at alarming rates. A related issue is the excessive exploitation of extractive natural resources (such as forests, minerals, etc.) due to market distortion resulting from subsidies (for a specific example of this see Case Study 16.1).

In recent years, there appears to have been a new realization that population, poverty and environmental degradation in developing countries are highly interrelated and do not exhibit a *linear* pattern. Thus, the economic problems of the developing world cannot be resolved by looking at population, poverty or environmental concerns separately. In order to evaluate the options that are available to raise the standard of living of the average person in developing countries, without inflicting major damage to the environment, it is necessary to have a comprehensive understanding of the interrelationships among them, however complex they are perceived to be.

The following represent some of the key features of the new development strategies, mainly aimed at achieving a level of economic progress that is considered to be environmentally sustainable:

1. *Investments that are pro poor and pro environment*: this should be done knowing that it entails sacrifices. As discussed in some detail in this chapter, such a strategy has a number of implications for the way the poor and their assets are viewed, and a new understanding of the link between poverty and the environment.
2. *Recognizing and supporting the role of women*: a recognition and an unconditional endorsement of the special role that women play in population control, poverty alleviation and the management of the environment. How this could be achieved is detailed in Section 16.5.
3. *A change in governance structure*: the adoption of decision-making schemes that demand transparency and accountability, and that encourage the full participation of the stakeholders relevant to the decision under consideration. In addition, it is acknowledged that decisions that affect the poor and the environment are most effective when they are dealt with at the community level that are most impacted—this is to suggest a preference for decentralized community based decision-making. Of course, a decision-making process of this nature cannot occur without political will at the highest level.
4. *The issue of equity*: in countries where income distributions are highly skewed, which would be the case for the majority of developing nations, serious consideration should be given to finding mechanisms to redistribute income (resources). Highly uneven income distribution is not only unwarranted on ethical or moral grounds, but it is also considered as a drag on rates of economic growth in the long run.

Specific policy targets for the decoupling the population, poverty and environmental problems of developing nations include the following:

1. Improving the economic and social status of women.
2. Working through institutional reforms that encourage decentralization and the transparency of decision-making processes, allow full participation of all the stakeholders, and demand accountability for the decision outcomes.
2. Correcting the most obvious forms of market and government failures. For example, ending subsidies of any sort that have the effects of either favoring the rich or causing the unwarranted exploitation of natural resources.
3. Encouraging the adoption of technological devices that increase productivity and minimize damage to the environment. Furthermore, the adoption of new technologies should always be subjected to comprehensive and carefully designed cost–benefit analyses that search for economically sound, environmentally benign and resource-saving technologies. If ecological sustainability is an important consideration, as it should be, the choice of technology is an important factor that needs to be carefully considered (Goodwin 1991; Norgaard and Howarth 1992).

4. Reducing national debt could help most developing countries to focus more on the long-term benefits of their natural resource endowments, rather than putting them up for sale at a discount for the purpose of financing their debt. This could be achieved, either by granting outright debt relief, or by debt refinancing mechanisms that are gradual and more cognizant of the economic circumstances of debtor nations.

5. Realigning international trade to eliminate, as far as possible, natural resource price distortions in international markets. This, of course, requires the full cooperation of rich nations as they are the parties who would be affected negatively by such an arrangement.

6. Providing international aid (grants) specifically aimed at conserving resources because of their far-reaching global implications. A prime example of this would be Madagascar's (one of the world's poorest countries) decision to designate the Masoala Peninsula (a 33,000 hectare area) as a national park. This came at great cost (in terms of opportunities forgone) to Madagascar and, according to a study by Kremen et al., this country 'is paying 57 to 96 percent of the total cost' (2000: 1831). On the other hand, the *net* benefit to the global community from Masoala National Park for carbon conservation (carbon sequestration and the consequent reduction in GHG emissions) alone was estimated to be in the range of $67.5 and $645.5 million (Ibid.). This project also has the added benefit of conserving biodiversity, which is not considered in this study.

REVIEW AND DISCUSSION QUESTIONS

1. Briefly identify the following concepts: relative versus absolute poverty, urbanization, capital formation, vicious cycle of poverty, gender equity, governance, institutional failure, endogenous knowledge, appropriate technology, structural adjustment, desertification, communal land, the World Bank, the IMF, the UNDP, and NGO.

2. Read the following statements. In response, state 'True', 'False' or 'Uncertain' and explain why:
    (a) It is not only the number of people, but also their lifestyles, political systems, and social structures that define the relationship between humans and the environment.
    (b) *Laissez-faire* policies towards reproduction will inevitably burden society with the problem of ruinous overpopulation.
    (c) Poverty and the environment are inextricably linked in a downward spiral.
    (d) Markets are not always environmentally friendly, and not always supportive of poor people.
    (e) Poverty reduction and concern for the environment are incompatible.
    (f) The status of women is an extremely important variable in the population–environment relationship.

3. Poor people degrade the environment more than the non-poor because the poor implicitly use a high discount rate in valuing current over future production. Do you agree or disagree with this logic? Explain your position.

4. At the United Nations Conference on the Human Environment in 1972 (also known as the Stockholm Conference), the then Indian Prime Minister Ms. Indira Gandhi proclaimed that 'poverty is the greatest polluter'. Discuss.

5. Free trade could lead to the overexploitation of natural resources upon which a vast number of the people in poor nations depend for their livelihood. Discuss.

6. The root cause of underdevelopment and environmental degradation is the 'overdevelopment' of a handful of rich nations. Discuss.

7. In a report by the UNDP in its Poverty and Environment Initiative (1999: 2–3), the following remark was made regarding the UN conferences on development and the environment. What do you think can be done to get out of this unfortunate quandary? Explain your answer using specific examples:

Though serious and successful efforts to address both poverty and environment are underway in many places, they remain exceptions. While there is broad agreement on the 'why' and the 'what,' there has been far less agreement about the 'how.' Too often, politicians and technical experts have found themselves at odds. Policymakers complain that the experts have not given them substantive practical solutions. Experts accuse policymakers of lacking political will. This fruitless debate has contributed to the disappointing gulf between the goals of the global conventions and their actual achievements.

8. The same UNDP report as above, makes the following statement (Ibid.). Is this an economic or an ethical argument for more public investment that protects the environment and benefits the poor? Explain.

    The political process of reallocating funding toward projects that benefit the poor and the environment can be made easier if 'pro-environment/pro-poor' guidelines are used for public investments. This includes properly valuing long-term environmental benefits (greening the internal rate of return) and weighting investment criteria to recognize the fact that a particular monetary return on investment for the poor is more valuable for increasing net well-being than the same return on investment is for the non-poor.

REFERENCES AND FURTHER READING

Africa Resources Trust and the CAMPFIRE Association (1996) *Zimbabwe's Campfire: Empowering Rural Communities for Conservation and Development*, Harare, Zimbabwe: IUCN-ROSA.

Allen, J. C. and Barnes, D. F. (1995) 'The Causes of Deforestation in Developed Countries', *Annals of the Association of American Geographers* 75, 2: 163–84.

Antweiler, W., Copeland, B. R. and Taylor, M. S. (2001) 'Is Free Trade Good for the Environment?' *American Economic Review* 91, 4: 877–908.

Australian UNESCO Committee for Man and the Biosphere (1976) *Ecological Effects of Increasing Human Activities on Tropical and Subtropical Forest Ecosystems*, Canberra: Australian Government Publishing Service.

Bandyopadhyay, J. and Shiva, V. (1989) 'Development, Poverty and the Growth of the Green Movement in India', *The Ecologist* 19: 111–17.

Bhagwati, J. (1993) 'The Case of Free Trade', *Scientific American* 269: 42–9.

Bhalla, S. (2002) *Imagine There's No Country: Poverty, Inequality, and Growth in the Era of Globalization*, Washington, DC: Institute for International Economics.

Bhattarai, M. and Hammig, M. (2001) 'Institutions and the Environmental Kuznets Curve for Deforestation: A Cross-country Analysis for Latin America, Africa, and Asia', *World Development* 29, 6: 995–1010.

Bonnie, R., Schwartzman, S., Oppenheimer, M. and Bloomfield, J. (2000) 'Counting the Cost of Deforestation', *Science* 288: 1828–32.

Bulte, E. H. and van Soest, D. P. (2001) 'Environmental Degradation in Developing Countries: Households and the (Reverse) Environmental Kuznets Curve', *Journal of Development Economics* 65: 225–35.

Child, B., Ward, S. and Tavengwa, T, (1997) 'Zimbabwe's CAMPFIRE Programme: Natural Resource Management by the People', *IUCA-ROSA Environmental Issues Series No. 2*, Harare, Zimbabwe.

Cochrane, L. (2011) 'Food Security or Food Sovereignty: The Case of Land Grabs', Feinstein International Center, *The Journal of Humanitarian Assistance* 2: 30–1.

Cole, M. A. (2007) 'Corruption, Income and the Environment: An Empirical Analysis', *Ecological Economics* 62: 637–47.

Cooter, R. D. (1990) 'Inventing Property: Economic Theories of the Origin of Market Property Applied to Papua New Guinea', *Memo*, Berkeley, CA: University of California.

Cropper, M. and Griffith, C. (1994) 'The Interaction of Population Growth and Environmental Quality', *American Economic Association Papers and Proceedings* 84, 12: 250–4.

Daly, H. E. (1993) 'The Perils of Free Trade', *Scientific American* 269: 50–7.

Deininger, K. (2003) *Land Policies for Growth and Poverty Reduction: A World Bank Research Report*, Oxford: Oxford University Press.

Dicklitch, S. (2004) 'African Corruption is a Crime Against Humanity', *The Christian Science Monitor*, August 9.

Ehrlich, P. R. and Holdren, J. P. (1971) 'Impact of Population Growth', *Science* 171: 1212–17.

Ekins, P. (1993) *Trading Off the Future?: Making World Trade Environmentally Sustainable*, London: The New Economics Foundation.

Goodland, R. and Daly, H. E. (1992) 'Ten Reasons why Northern Income Growth is Not the Solution to Southern Poverty', in R. Goodland, H. E. Daly and S. El Serafy (eds.) *Population, Technology and Lifestyle: The Transition to Sustainability*, Washington, DC: Island Press.

Goodwin, N. R. (1991) 'Introduction — Global Commons: Site of Peril, Source of Hope', *World Development* 19: 1–15.

Homer-Dixon, T. F., Boutwell, J. H. and Rathjens, G. W. (1993) 'Environmental Change and Violent Conflict', *Scientific American* 268: 38–45.

Hughes, B., Irafai, M. T., Khan, H., Kuman, K. B., Rothman, D. S., Soloizano, J. R. (2009) *Reducing Global Poverty: Patterns of Potential Human Progress, Volume 1*, New Delhi: Oxford University Press.

Koop, G. and Tole, L. (1999) 'Is There an Environmental Kuznets Curve for Deforestation?' *Journal of Development Economics* 58: 231–44.

Korten, D. C. (1991) 'International Assistance: A Problem Posing as a Solution', *Development* 3/4: 87–94.

Kremen, C., Niles, J. O., Dalton, M. G., Daily, G. C., Ehrlich, P. R., Fay, J. P., Grewal, D. and Guillery, R. P. (2000) 'Economic Incentives for Rain Forest Conservation Across Scale', *Science* 288: 1828–32.

Lewis, M. W. (1992) *Green Delusions: An Environmentalist Critique of Radical Environmentalism*, Durham, NC: Duke University Press.

McNamara, R. S. (1984) 'Time Bomb or Myth: The Population Problem', *Foreign Affairs* 62: 1107–31.

Nierenberg, D. (2002) *Worldwatch Paper #161: Correcting Gender Myopia: Gender Equity, Women's Welfare, and the Environment*, Washington, DC: The Worldwatch Institute.

Norgaard, R. B. and Howarth, R. B. (1992) 'Economics, Ethics, and the Environment', in J. M. Hollander (ed.) *The Energy–Environment Connection*, Washington, DC: Island Press.

OECD (2002) *Working Together Towards Sustainable Development: The OECD Experience*, Paris: OECD Publishing.

Panayotou, T. (1993) 'Empirical Tests and Policy Analysis of Environmental Degradation at Different Stages of Economic Development', *World Employment Programme Research Working Paper WEP 2-22/WP 238*, January, Geneva: International Labour Office.

Panayotou, T. and Ashton, P. S. (1992) *Not by Timber Alone: Economics and Ecology for Sustainable Tropical Forests*, Washington, DC: Island Press.

Population Reference Bureau (1996) *Population Today 24*, Washington, DC: Population Reference Bureau.

—— (1997) *Population Today 25*, Washington, DC: Population Reference Bureau.

—— (1998) *Population Bulletin 53*, Washington, DC: Population Reference Bureau.

Repetto, R. and Holmes, T. (1983) 'The Role of Population in Resource Depletion in Developing Countries', *Population and Development Review* 9, 4: 609–32.

Rudel, T. K. (1989) 'Population, Development, and Tropical Deforestation', *Rural Sociology* 54, 3: 327–38.

Selden, T. and Song, D. (1994) 'Environmental Quality and Development: Is there a Kuznets Curve for Air Pollution Emission?' *Journal of Environmental Economics and Management* 27: 147–62.

Solow, R. M. (1994) 'Perspectives on Growth Theory', *Journal of Economic Perspectives* 8, 1: 45–54.

Stern, D. I., Common, M. S. and Barbier, E. B. (1996) 'Economic Growth and Environmental Degradation: The Environmental Kuznets Curve and Sustainable Development', *World Development* 24: 1151–60.

Stockhammer, E., Hochreiter, H., Obermayr, B. and Steiner, K. (1997) 'The Index of Sustainable Economic Welfare (ISEW) as an Alternative to GDP in Measuring Economic Welfare: The Results of the Austrian (revised) ISEW Calculation 1955–1992', *Ecological Economics* 21, 1: 19–34.

Todaro, M. P. (1989) *Economic , Development in the Third World*, 4th edn., New York: Longman.

Trainer, F. E. (1990) 'Environmental Significance of Development Theory', *Ecological Economics* 2: 277–86.

Turner, K., Pearce, D. and Bateman, I. (1993) *Environmental Economics: An Elementary Introduction*, Baltimore, MD: Johns Hopkins University Press.

United Nations Department of Economic and Social Affairs (UNDESA)/Population Division (2003) *World Urbanization Prospects: The 2003 Revision*, New York: United Nations Publications.

United Nations Report on World Population Prospects (2004), *World Population Prospects: The 2004 Revision Analytical Report*, New York: United Nations Publications.

UNDP Report on Poverty and Environmental Initiative (1999) *Attacking Poverty While Improving the Environment: Towards Win–Win Policy Options*, New York: UNDP.

UNDP (2011) *Human Development Report 2011: Sustainability and Equity, a Better Future for All*, New York: UNDP, http://hdr.undp.org/en/media/HDR_2011_EN_Summary.pdf, accessed 06/04/2011.

WCED (World Commission on Environment and Development) (1987) *Our Common Future*, New York: Oxford University Press.

Wedemann, E. and Thielke, T. (2005) 'Is Aid the Problem, Not the Solution?' *New York Times*, July 6.

World Bank (2008) *World Development Indicators*, Washington, DC: World Bank Publishing.

—— (2011) *World Development Indicators*, Washington, DC: World Bank Publishing.

World Population Prospects: The 2010 Revision (2011) http://esa.un.org/wpp/Other-Information/faq.htm.

World Resources Institute (1987) *World Resources 1988–89*, New York: Basic Books.

—— (1992) *World Resources 1992–93*, New York: Oxford University Press.

—— (1995) *World Resources 1995–96*, New York: Oxford University Press.

Resource scarcity, economic efficiency and markets: How the invisible hand works

Markets respond to price signals. If a resource, whether it is a barrel of oil, a patch of Louisiana swamp or old-growth forest, or a breath of fresh air, is priced to reflect its true and complete cost to society, goes the argument, markets will ensure that those resources are used in an optimally efficient way.

(Alper 1993: 1884)

A.1 INTRODUCTION

This Appendix systematically develops the analytical (theoretical) foundation of the neoclassical approach to resource scarcity, allocation and measurement. The broader aims of Appendix A are the following: (1) to specify the conditions under which Adam Smith's notion that individuals working in their self-interest will promote the welfare of the whole of society holds good; and (2) to show formally the conditions under which market price can be used as a measure of resource scarcity. To address these two issues fully and systematically, the chapter starts by outlining the basic conditions for a model of a perfectly competitive market.

Before doing this, however, it may be instructive to explain in a few words why the contents of Appendix A are relevant to the study of environmental economics. One of the discoveries in environmental economics is the 'failure' of the private market (transactions among private individuals based on the free expression of self-interest) to allocate environmental resources optimally. Despite this, neoclassical economists continue to insist on the use of market-friendly policy instruments for the allocation of environmental resources. If one wants to understand the root causes for the unshakable faith

that neoclassical economists have in the market, the materials covered in this Appendix will be very valuable.

A.2 BASIC ASSUMPTIONS

In an idealized capitalist market economy, the well-being of consumers (the final users of goods and services) is of paramount importance. What this means is that the effectiveness of an economy is judged by how well it satisfies the material needs of its citizens—the consumers. Therefore, given that resources are scarce, an effective economy is one that is capable of producing the *maximum* output from a given set of basic resources (labor, capital and natural resources). Of course, the implication of this is that scarce resources must be utilized (produced and consumed) efficiently.

The question then, is: What conditions must a market system satisfy in order to be considered an efficient institution for allocating scarce resources? In other words, what are the conditions consistent with the ideal or perfect form of market structure? According to prevailing economic thought, a market has to satisfy the following broad conditions in order to be regarded as an efficient institutional mechanism for allocating resources:

1. *Freedom of choice based on self-interest and rational behavior*: buyers and sellers are well informed and exhibit 'rational' behavior. 'Rational' here refers to the notion that the behavior of a buyer or a seller is consistent with her or his pursuit of self-interest. It is further stipulated that these actors in the market are provided with an environment conducive to the free expression of their choices. Note that choice is an inevitable byproduct of resource scarcity.

2. *Perfect information*: economic agents are assumed to be provided with full information regarding any market transactions. They are also assumed to have perfect foresight about future economic events.

3. *Competition*: for each item subjected to market transactions, the number of buyers and sellers is large. Thus, no one buyer or seller can single-handedly influence the terms of trade. In modern economic jargon, this means that both buyers and sellers are price-takers. This is assumed to be the case in both the product and the factor markets.

4. *Mobility of resources*: in a dynamic economy, change is the norm. Significant shifts in economic conditions could result from a combination of several factors: changes in consumer preference, income, resource availability and technology. To accommodate changes of this nature in a timely fashion, resources must be readily transferable from one sector of the economy to another. This is possible only when barriers to entry and exit in an industry are absent (or minimal).

5. *Ownership rights*: all goods and services, as well as factors of production, have clearly defined ownership rights. This condition prevails when the following specific conditions are met:

   (a) The nature and characteristics of the resources under consideration are completely specified;

   (b) Owners have a title with exclusive rights to the resources they legally own;

   (c) Ownership rights are transferable—that is, ownership rights are subject to market transactions at terms agreeable with the resource owner(s); and

   (d) Ownership rights are enforceable (Randall 1987)—that is, property rights are protected by binding social rules and regulations.

When the above *five* conditions are met, an economy is said to be operating in a world of perfectly competitive markets. In such a setting, Adam Smith (the father of modern economics) declared over two centuries ago that the market system, through its invisible hand, will guide each individual to do not only what is in her or his own self-interest, but also that which is for the 'good' of society as a whole. A profound statement indeed, which clearly depicts the most appealing features of the market economy in its ideal form. In the next section, this will be demonstrated systematically using demand and supply analysis.

A.3 EVALUATING THE PERFORMANCE OF A PERFECTLY COMPETITIVE MARKET ECONOMY

A market may be identified as a *social institution*—where buyers and sellers of a certain product are able to consummate business transactions on the basis of their self-interest and on terms that are considered to be mutually beneficial for all participating parties.

The performance of an institution cannot be based solely on its daily operations. A valid judgment on the performance of an institution should be based on the enduring qualities of long-term outcomes. In this regard, the claim often made by mainstream economists is this: provided that all the assumptions of the model of perfect competition discussed in Section A.2 are satisfied (freedom of choice and enterprise, consumers and producers as fully informed price-takers, mobility of resources and clearly defined ownership rights), in the long run the market system will tend to *allocate resources efficiently*. Furthermore, market prices will *measure the true scarcity value of resources*.

To demonstrate these claims in a systematic manner, let us suppose that Figure A.1 represents the long-run equilibrium condition of a product

Figure A.1 *Market equilibrium price is attained when* $Q_d = Q_s$.

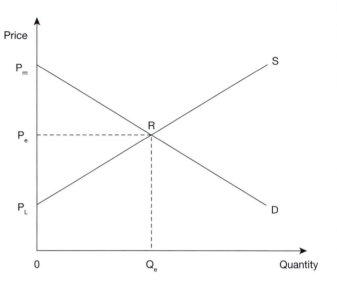

produced and sold in a perfectly competitive industry. In this case, P_e and Q_e represent the market equilibrium price and quantity, respectively. It is important to note that the long-run equilibrium price is that which prevails after the existence of above-normal profits have attracted new firms to enter the industry (or below-normal profits have forced some firms to exit). It is, in other words, a situation in which all firms in that particular industry are just making *normal profits*.

Normal profit means that, in the long run, firms in a given industry cannot make a return from their investment above what they would have been able to earn if they had invested in some other industry with similar operating conditions and a similar risk environment. To see the 'social' significance of this long-run equilibrium situation, let us separately analyze the economic conditions of the consumers and producers.

Consumers' surplus

Figure A.2 shows the same demand function as the one in Figure A.1. Thus, P_e and Q_e represent the long-run market equilibrium price and output. P_m is the price where the quantity demanded is zero. Thus, it can be interpreted as the maximum price consumers are willing to pay for this product rather than go

without it. By focusing on the demand alone, we will now be able to demonstrate the implication of long-run market equilibrium for consumers' welfare.

The demand curve depicts the *maximum* price consumers are willing to pay for a given quantity of the product provided in the market. For example, P_m is the *maximum price consumers are willing to pay rather than go without the product*. On the other hand, at the market equilibrium quantity, Q_e, the consumers are willing to pay the price P_e. For quantities between zero and Q_e, consumers will be willing to pay prices higher than P_e and lower than P_m. Note that the prices consumers are willing to pay successively decline as the quantity of a product available in the market increases. This diminishing willingness to pay is, of course, consistent with the law of demand.

To illustrate the above concept let us assume that, in a given market, there are some eager consumers who would be willing to pay as much as $20 for a gallon of gasoline. If the gasoline price in this market were more than $20, no one would buy any. If the price of gasoline were less than $20, then we can be sure that some amount of gasoline would be purchased. Suppose the actual market price is $1.50; those consumers who were willing to pay as much as $20 now essentially save $18.50 for every gallon of gasoline that they purchase. It is this kind of saving that is being conveyed by the concept of *consumers' surplus*.

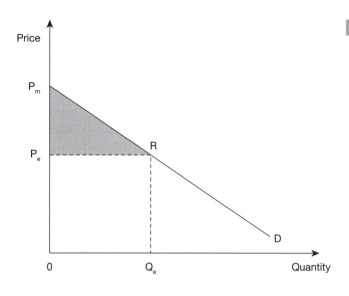

Figure A.2 *Consumers' surplus represented here by the shaded triangle.*

Looking at demand as a measure of willingness to pay also lends itself to the interpretation of price as the *marginal private benefit to consumers*. That is, a consumer whose sole interest is to maximize utility will not purchase an additional unit of a product unless the benefit derived from the incremental unit is at least equal to the market price. The fact that the price or marginal private benefit declines as the quantity of the product increases is also consistent with the law of diminishing marginal utility.

If prices can be looked at as a measure of marginal private benefit then, conceptually, we can compute the total private benefit by summing all the marginal benefits for a given range of the output demanded. For example, in Figure A.2, for the market equilibrium of output, Q_e, the *total* consumers' benefit would be measured by the sum of all the prices starting from P_m all the way up to and including P_e. The area of trapezoid $0P_m RQ_e$ represents this. *In an ideal (competitive) market, in the long run this area would tend to be maximized.*

The reasons for this are not difficult to see. Given that both consumers and producers are *price-takers* and resources are freely mobile, the long-run equilibrium condition ensures that firms are operating efficiently (minimizing their costs of production). In addition, due to the free mobility of resources, firms are not able to make an above-normal profit. If this

situation prevails, then the market equilibrium price, P_e, represents the lowest price firms can charge in the long run. If P_e represents the lowest price, it follows that Q_e is the largest output that could be forthcoming to the market. Thus, the trapezoid area $0P_m RQ_e$ represents the largest total consumers' benefit.

This *total* consumers' benefit is composed of two parts. The first part is rectangle area $0P_e RQ_e$, which represents what the consumers actually paid to acquire the market clearing output, Q_e. The second segment is the area of the triangle $P_e P_m R$, which represents the sum of all the prices above the equilibrium price that consumers would have been willing to pay. Since consumers did not actually pay higher prices for some units, but paid P_e for every unit up to Q_e, the sum of these prices, which is shown by the area of triangle $P_e P_m R$, represents consumers' surplus. In other words, *consumers' surplus is the difference between the total willingness to pay* (area $0P_m RQ_e$) *and what consumers actually paid*, which is represented by the area $0P_e RQ_e$. What is significant here is that, in the long run, consumers' surplus is *maximized*. This is easy to demonstrate given that the long-run equilibrium price, P_e, represents the lowest feasible price for producers. This is an important conclusion since it confirms economists' assertions that, in the long run, a market economy left alone would do what is best for consumers: maximize their surpluses.

To offer a simple numerical illustration of consumers' surplus and total willingness to pay, let us suppose that the market equilibrium price and quantity in Figure A.2 are $5 and 2,000 units, respectively. In addition, let P_m, the maximum price consumers are willing to pay for this product, be $9. First, given this information, consumers' surplus (the shaded area in Figure A.2) can be obtained using the formula 1/2 (the product of the base and the height of the relevant triangle); in this case it would be 1/2 (2,000 × 4), which is equal to $4,000. Second, in acquiring the 2,000 units, consumers paid a total sum of $10,000 (the product of the market equilibrium price and quantity). In Figure A.2 this $10,000 represents the area of the rectangle $0P_eRQ_e$. On the basis of these two findings, it can be inferred that the *total* willingness to pay is $14,000 (area $0P_mRQ_e$ in Figure A.2), since consumers have gained $4,000 in surplus while paying $10,000 for the purchase of the equilibrium quantity, 2,000 units.

Producers' surplus

Figure A.3 is a replica of the supply curve in Figure A.1. The supply curve could be interpreted as showing the *minimum* prices producers are willing to accept to provide various levels of output in a market. For example, P_L represents the lowest price producers require before participating in any production activity. Similarly, P_e is the minimum price the producers would accept to provide the last unit of the equilibrium output, Q_e. Alternatively, as discussed earlier, the supply curve is intimately related to production costs. More specifically, the supply curve represents nothing more than the mapping of the incremental (marginal) costs of production. Thus, if we employ these two interpretations of the supply curve, P_e can be understood in the following two ways. In one sense it shows the minimum price producers are willing to accept in order to bring forth the last unit of Q_e in the market. Alternatively, it represents the *marginal cost* of producing a given level of output. Note that these dual interpretations apply equally to all prices along the supply curve.

If the supply curve in fact represents the mapping of the incremental costs of production, in Figure A.3 the trapezoid area $0P_LRQ_e$ represents the total cost of production at the output level where the long-run equilibrium, Q_e, is attained. This area is obtained by summing the marginal costs (or the minimum acceptable prices to producers) along the relevant output range. In a competitive market setting (where producers are price-takers and resources are freely mobile), this long-run production cost is minimized and accurately reflects the opportunity costs of the scarce resources being used in the production process.

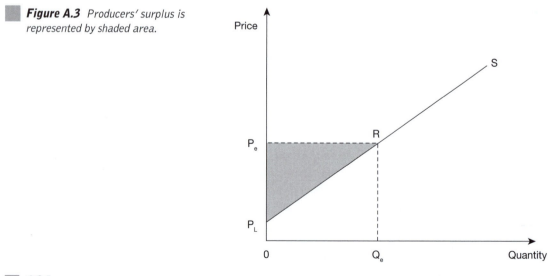

Figure A.3 *Producers' surplus is represented by shaded area.*

In Figure A.3 we have already established that area $0P_LRQ_e$ represents the *total* cost of producing the equilibrium level of output, Q_e. However, at the equilibrium level of output and price, the total producers' receipt (revenue) is represented by area $0P_eRQ_e$. The difference between the total revenue and total production cost, triangle area P_LP_eR in Figure A.3, is *producers' surplus*. What can this surplus be attributed to? There is no clear-cut answer to this question in the existing economic literature. For our purpose, we consider producers' surplus to be the cumulative payments to those producers exhibiting entrepreneurial capacity which is above that of the marginal producer (the last producer to enter the market).

To provide numerical illustrations of the concepts of producers' surplus and production cost, again let the market equilibrium price and quantity be $5 and 2,000 units, respectively. Furthermore, let P_L, the minimum price acceptable to the producers, be $2. Given this information, producers' surplus (the area of the shaded triangle in Figure A.3) would be $3,000 ($1/2 \times 3 \times 2,000$). Furthermore, the total receipts (revenue) of the producers from the sale of 2,000 units would be $10,000 ($5 \times 2,000$) or area $0P_eRQ_e$. Thus, the total production cost would be $7,000 ($10,000 − $3,000), or the area of the trapezoid $0P_LRQ_e$. This total value represents either *the sum of all the minimum prices that producers are willing to accept or the sum of all the marginal costs in producing the output ranging from 0 to 2,000 units*.

Net social surplus and how it is maximized

Finally, let us go back to Figure A.1 to tie together what we have been discussing so far concerning the long-run equilibrium condition under a competitive market setting. In Figure A.1 we noted that area $0P_mRQ_e$ represents the consumers' total willingness to pay (private benefit) associated with the consumption of the equilibrium level of output, Q_e.

As discussed earlier, under a perfectly competitive market setting this benefit is maximized. On the other hand, area $0P_LRQ_e$ shows the cost of producing the equilibrium level of output, Q_e. As previously dis-

cussed, this cost is *minimized*. Thus, area P_LP_mR represents the *net* surplus, which is composed of the consumers' and the producers' surpluses. From the above arguments, it should be noted that this social (consumers' and producers') surplus is *maximized*— one of the hallmarks of an ideal market system.

Pareto optimality and the invisible hand theorem

One alternative approach that is frequently used to arrive at the above conclusion is the notion of Pareto optimality. An equilibrium condition is said to be Pareto optimal if the move in any direction cannot be made without making at least one member of a society worse off. To see this, suppose in Figure A.4 that P_e and Q_e represent the long-run equilibrium price and output, respectively. Suppose the output is increased to Q_1. What would be the effect of this increase in output from Q_e to Q_1? The answer is rather straightforward. To begin with, the increase in output from Q_e to Q_1 will require an additional production cost, as shown by the area Q_eRTQ_1 (the area under the supply curve over the relevant output range). Similarly, the area Q_eRUQ_1 (the area under the demand curve along the relevant output range) measures the benefit associated from this incremental output. Thus, in this situation the cost outweighs the benefit by the triangle area RTU.

The curious should try to perform the following numerical exercise. Consistent with earlier examples, assume the equilibrium price and quantity in Figure A.4 to be $5 and 2,000 units. Assume that output is now increased from Q_e to Q_1 or from 2,000 to 2,100. Furthermore, the supply price at Q_1 (point T along the supply curve) is given as $7 and the demand price at this same level of output (point U along the demand curve) is $3.

This information demonstrates the following: (1) the increase in the production cost as a result of the increase in output by 100 (from 2,000 to 2,100, represented in Figure A.4 by area Q_eRTQ_1) is $600; (2) the increase in consumers' benefit resulting from a 100-unit increase in output (area Q_eRUQ_1 in Figure A.4) is $400. Findings (1) and (2) clearly

Figure A.4 *Pareto optimality and its implications.*

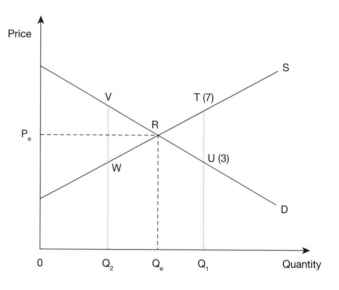

indicate that to increase output from Q_e to Q_1 would result in a net loss of $200 ($400 − $600 = −$200).

On the other hand, if output were restricted, falling from Q_e to Q_2, the area $Q_e RVQ_2$ would measure the forgone benefit associated with this action. However, as a result of this reduction in output there would be a cost saving measured by the area $Q_e RWQ_2$. In this case the forgone benefit would outweigh the cost saving by the area of the triangle RVW. Thus, from the argument presented so far, a movement away from the equilibrium in either direction would lead to a net loss. This clearly confirms that long-run equilibrium outcome in a setting of perfectly competitive markets is Pareto optimal. Note that *Pareto optimality implies economic efficiency—* a condition in which the *net* benefit of producers and consumers taken together is maximized. After all, as we have seen above, any deviations from the equilibrium are associated with a reduction, not a gain, in net benefits. Indeed, this amounts to a backhanded proof of Adam Smith's invisible hand theorem.

A.4 PRICE AS A MEASURE OF RESOURCE SCARCITY

Whenever the prevailing (equilibrium) market price for a product is positive, it follows that the product under consideration is scarce. But scarce in what

sense? To respond to this question adequately, let us refer to Figure A.5 below. In this figure, the market equilibrium price is P_e given that S_0 is the relevant supply curve. From the consumers' viewpoint, this price measures their willingness to pay for the last unit of the equilibrium output, Q_e. In other words, it measures consumers' marginal private benefit (MPB) at the equilibrium level of output. On the other hand, from the producers' perspective, the prevailing market price, P_e, measures the minimum price they are willing to accept in offering the last unit of the equilibrium output in the market. In an ideal market, where the marginal producers are just making a normal profit, this would be equivalent to the marginal private cost (MPC) of producing the last unit of output.

Given the above argument, in an ideal market setting the long-run equilibrium price has an implication that goes far beyond a market clearing condition. This price equates marginal private (consumers') benefit with that of marginal private (producers') costs. That is,

$$P_e = MPB = MPC$$

Furthermore, in cases where ownership rights are clearly defined, there will be no difference between *private* and *social* benefits and costs (see Chapter 3).

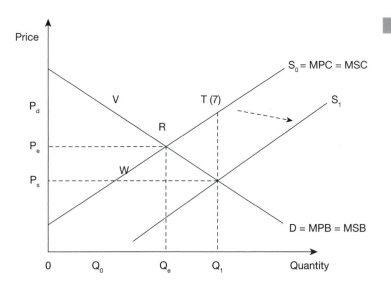

Figure A.5 *Market price as a measure of resource scarcity and as an indicator of resource misallocation.*

Thus, in ideal market conditions the long-run equilibrium price of a product is a measure of both the marginal social benefit and the marginal social cost. That is,

$$P_e = MPB = MSB = MPC = MSC$$

It is in this context that mainstream economists base their long-standing claim that *in a free competitive market, a market price tends to reflect the true scarcity value of a resource under consideration.* True in exactly what sense? In the sense that, in the long run, *market price reflects the social cost of using resources* (land, labor, capital, etc.) to produce *output at the margin.*

Note that market price would fail to reflect social cost if the price were artificially set either below or above the market equilibrium price, P_e. If either one of these situations occur the result will be what economists commonly refer to as a 'misallocation of resources'.

To see the significance of this, let us suppose that a decision is made to lower the market price from P_e to P_s in Figure A.5. To make this possible the supply curve needs to be shifted from S_0 to S_1, otherwise, P_s will not be a market-clearing price. Suppose this is accomplished through a market intervention mechanism, such as a government subsidy (either as a tax break or cash grant) to the firms producing the product under consideration. The question is then, 'How will this result in a misallocation of societal resources?'

At the new and artificially established equilibrium price, P_s, the market clearing output will increase from Q_e (the socially optimal output) to Q_1. For it to do so, more resources (labor, capital and natural resources) are now allocated for the production of the output under consideration. However, for any output level beyond Q_e, the MSC (the supply prices along S_0) of using these resources exceeds the prevailing market price, P_s. Clearly, then, these resources are not being used where they benefit society the most—they are *misallocated*.

A.5 RENT AS MEASURE OF RESOURCE SCARCITY: THE RICARDIAN RENT

David Ricardo (1772–1823), another distinguished English economist, was one of the earlier critics of Malthus's doctrine on population and resource scarcity. His objection was not Malthus's gloomy prophecy of the future condition of human material progress, but rather on the emphasis Malthus had given to population. For Ricardo, human material progress would not be hampered in the long run by the explosive growth of human population as Malthus had envisioned, but by the *progressive decline in the quality and quantity of extractive resources*, most importantly, agricultural land. What follows is an explanation for this alternative view on resource scarcity and its implication to long-run economic growth.

Agricultural land varies in its natural productive capacity—fertility. For agricultural land (and for that matter for most extractive resources such as coal, gold, fisheries, and so on), the normal pattern tends to be to extract these resources sequentially in accordance with quality and accessibility. Plots of land with high natural fertility (or mines containing high-grade ores) are put to use first because their *real cost* is low. Real cost is defined here as the amount of labor, capital and other resources needed to make farmland available for cultivation.

To illustrate this point and its broader implications, in Figure A.6 the horizontal line P_0 to A represents the *long-run* supply curve of available farmland that is of high and uniform quality (in terms of fertility). A maximum amount, C_0, (measured either in acres or hectares) of this quality of land is assumed to exist. A second segment of the supply curve is represented by another horizontal line, B to C. This parallel upward shift of the supply curve from P_0–A to B–C reflects the increase in real cost arising from the change in the quality of the land—from fertile to marginal farmland. A total amount of marginal land ($C_1 - C_0$) is presumed to be available for use. The land available

beyond C_1 is considered to be submarginal in terms of its fertility (quality) and line E to F represents the supply curve for this type of land. It is assumed that there is no constraint to the amount of submarginal land available for use.

If the demand for farmland remains at D_0 or below, consideration of cost will favor the use of land from the first category only—fertile land. P_0 represents the equilibrium market price for a unit of farmland of this quality. This price also represents the real cost to owners for making a unit of their farmland available for cultivation. If this is the case, there will be no difference between what the owners of the land receive as income and the cost of making the land available for cultivation. That is, the owners receive zero rent. Rent is defined at the *total payment to owners for a factor of production in excess of the minimum price necessary to bring the resource available for use.*

With the above analysis in mind, from Figure A.6 it can easily be observed that both *real cost* and *rent* increase as demand for farmland grows and progressively inferior land is brought into cultivation. It is easy to observe the increase in real cost from P_0 to P_1 as demand increases from D_0 to D_1, likewise from P_1 to P_2 as demand further increases from D_1 to D_2. This increase in real cost simply reflects the fact that progressively more resources (in terms of labor, capital, and so on) are needed to cultivate a unit of

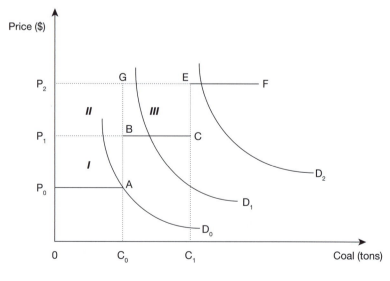

Figure A.6 Ricardian scarcity. This model indicates that successive increases in demand (D_0, D_2, D_3, etc.) are met with corresponding increases in resource prices (P_0, P_1, P_2, etc.) due to successive declines in the quality of extractive resources, such as coal mines.

land as the quality (fertility) of the available land continues to decline.

How did the increase in rent come about? The reasons for this are more subtle than for the increase in real cost discussed above. To see this, let us observe what happens to rent when the demand for farmland increases from D_0 to D_1. This would necessitate the cultivation of marginal land and the increase in real cost (or price of land) from P_0 to P_1. Now, as a result of this development, owners of farmland of the superior grade will start to earn rent since their cost is still P_0, while the market price for farmland is now P_1. This suggests that owners of the fertile land collectively will earn a total rent as represented by the area P_0P_1BA (or the area of the rectangle I). It is important to recognize that this rent is attributable solely to differences in the quality of land.

Similarly, when demand is further increased to D_2, the total rent to owners of the fertile land increases from area P_0P_1BA to P_0P_2GA or the combined areas of rectangles I and II). In addition, the owners of the marginal land are now able to realize rent that is measured by area BCEG (or the area of rectangle III). Thus, as a result of the shift in demand from D_1 to D_2, the total rent has increased from area P_0P_1BA (the area of rectangle I) to area P_0P_2ECBA (or the area of rectangles I + II + III).

The above observation is the essence of what is known in modern economics literature as *Ricardian scarcity*. It suggests a steady increase in rent (and real cost) as quality of land (or any other extractive resources) decline. According to Ricardo, it is the *steady increase in rent as land-use expands that would ultimately stifle long-term human economic progress*. In this particular context, to Ricardo *population is relevant only to the extent it has an effect on what happens to demand*.

Essentially, then, to Ricardo the major impediment to human material progress would emerge not so much from demand but rather from supply side constraints. This was a hotly debated issue by Malthus and Ricardo, and was responsible for producing several written exchanges that are still of significant interest to economic historians.

An important caveat should be made here. Ricardo did not develop his theory of rent and scarcity to suggest a biophysical limitation to economic growth. His motivation was actually aimed at demonstrating that the primary beneficiaries of the Corn Laws, by artificially restricting the import of agricultural products into England at a time when both population and demand for farm products were growing, were the landlords—who were the rent seekers. By implication, Ricardo was also suggesting that landlords stifle growth through their rent-seeking behavior.

A.6 IMPORTANT CAVEATS

It is important to note that, while the analysis presented in Appendix A has covered the basic elements necessary for understanding the mainstream economic notion of resource scarcity and its measurement, it did so with several obvious limitations. The most significant of these are as follows:

1. The economic analysis thus far has been strictly *static*; no time element has been considered. This is a major drawback given that environmental economics, by its very nature, deals with the intertemporal allocation of resources—that is, how environmental resources are managed over time.

2. The economic analyses were calculated assuming the existence of *perfectly competitive markets*. Given this institutional setting, we observed that private decision-making would actually lead to a socially optimal allocation of resources. Furthermore, there would be no discrepancy between the individual (private) and social assessment of benefits and costs. But what happens if the conditions for perfectly competitive markets fail to materialize? This is, indeed, an important issue in environmental economics and a subject matter fully addressed in Chapter 3.

3. In the economic analysis so far, nothing has been said about resources that have values but may *not* be captured through the normal operation of the market system. An example would be the value of preserving an animal species such

as the Northwest spotted owl. A species of this nature has very little use-value—benefits or satisfactions received by humans from a direct utilization of services (or amenities)—and therefore is likely to be unaccounted for under the normal operation of market processes. This particular issue becomes even more serious when it is realized that market prices are formed on the basis of human preferences alone. This issue will be dealt with in Chapter 7.

4. In Appendix A efforts have been made to show how, at a point in time, prices for final products are determined through the free-market mechanism. To what extent information on current market prices could be used to predict a future scarcity event has not been adequately addressed.

More specifically, the *uncertainty* associated with predicting a future scarcity condition on the basis of past price-trends has not been addressed. The position taken so far is that current resource prices are a good predictor of future scarcity events. This would be the case in a world of perfectly competitive markets where economic agents were operating with perfect foresight and costless information. Under those circumstances, if there is reason to judge that the cost of obtaining a certain resource in the future will be much greater than it is now, speculators will hoard that material to obtain future price, thereby raising the present price. So, current price is our best measure of both current and future scarcity.

A.7 SUMMARY

The objectives of Appendix A have been twofold. The first aim was to clearly specify the theoretical conditions under which individuals working in their self-interest will promote the welfare of the whole of society — the so-called 'invisible hand theorem'. The second was to show the extent to which *product* can be used as measures of resource scarcity.

To address these issues fully and systematically, the following three key assumptions were made:

1. Markets are perfectly competitive;
2. The economy is evaluated on the basis of its long-term performance; and
3. The criteria for evaluating market performance are based on the market's ability: (a) to attain efficient allocation of resources so that, in the long run, the aggregate social surplus is maximized; and (b) to transmit accurate signals of resource scarcity.

It was shown that, given the above assumptions, a market system uses *price* information to facilitate the production and exchange of goods and services. These prices are formed by the interaction of market demand and market supply.

Furthermore, when one assumes the existence of clearly defined ownership rights in the product market, demand and supply reflect marginal social benefit (MSB) and marginal social cost (MSC), respectively. Thus, the long-run equilibrium is attained when the following condition is satisfied: $P_e = MSB = MSC$, where P_e is the long-run equilibrium price. This condition has the following important implications:

1. The fact that $MSB = MSC$ suggests that, in the long run, competitive markets allocate resources in such a way that the *net* social benefit (the sum of consumers' and producers' surplus) is maximized. This is because no reallocation can be made without adversely affecting the net social benefit. Thus, in the long run, competitive markets are Pareto efficient.
2. Market price is a measure of the value 'society' attaches to a product. That is, $P_e = MSB$.
3. The market equilibrium price of a product, P_e, is a measure of the 'social' cost of using basic resources (labor, capital, land, etc.) to produce the desired product. That is, $P_e = MSC$.
4. Market price, P_e, is a 'true' measure of resource scarcity because there is no discrepancy between the social value of the product (what people are willing to pay) and the social opportunity cost of the resources used to produce this product. One important implication of this observation is that market intervention, through subsidies or support prices, would cause a distortion of important social opportunity costs and in so doing lead to a misallocation of resources.

REFERENCES AND FURTHER READING

Alper, J. (1993) 'Protecting the Environment with the Power of the Market', *Science* 260: 1884–5.

Nicholson, W. (1998) *Microeconomic Theory*, 7th edn., Fort Worth, TX: Dryden Press.

Pindyck, R. and Rubinfeld, D. (1998) *Microeconomics*, 4th edn., New York: Macmillan.

Randall, A. (1987) *Resource Economics: An Economic Approach to Natural Resource and Environmental Policy*, 2nd edn., New York: John Wiley.

The development of ecological economics: A brief historical sketch

Ecological economics treats a subject that goes as far back as the pre-classical Physiocrats—the economists of the French school of the mid-seventeenth century (Christensen 1987; Cleveland 1987). One of the fundamental premises of the Physiocratic school of economic thought was that all economic surpluses are derived from the productive power of 'land'. Thus, land was regarded as the ultimate source of material wealth. To underscore this point, one of the most celebrated economists of the Physiocratic School, Sir William Petty (1623–83), wrote that 'land is the mother and labor is the father of wealth'. In other words, the human economy is anchored by a biophysical reality—land and its productive capacity.

A major turning point in the historical development of 'biophysical' economics occurred with the advance in the understanding of the laws of *thermodynamics* in the early nineteenth century (Ayres 1984; Cleveland 1987; Georgescu-Roegen 1971). What emerged from this was an increasing use of these laws (especially the first and second laws) to explain physical and biological systems in terms of energy and material flows. This analytical approach led to the recognition of the indispensable role that energy plays both as a catalyst and a limiting factor in all systems that require a continuous transformation of matter–energy for their own continuous functionality. The natural ecosystem and the human economy are two such systems.

By the late nineteenth century, several physical scientists and economists started to advocate the use of energy as a basis for a unified value theory. It was argued that all transformations require energy, that its flow is unidirectional, and that there is no substitute for it. It therefore makes sense to use energy as a numeraire—a denominator by which the value of all resources is weighed (Odum and Odum 1976). As Costanza (1980) correctly observed, this is equivalent to attempting to express the value of economic activities in terms of their embodied energy.

The most recent breakthrough in the development of ecological economics has occurred since the early 1960s and the emergence of the space age. The unique attribute of this new development was the joint use of the laws of thermodynamics and ecology to understand the functioning of the human economy and its relationship with the biosphere in terms of the exchanges in the flow of matter and energy between these two systems (Daly 1968). This required the study of economics from an interdisciplinary and a systems perspective.

Kenneth Boulding set the stage for this new perspective on economic analysis with his classic essay *The Economics of the Coming Spaceship Earth* (1966). The main focus of his essay was to explain the transition that is taking place in the relationship between the natural and human economy. He described this transition as being from a 'cowboy economy' without limits to a 'spaceman economy' in which 'the earth has become a single spaceship, without unlimited reservoirs of anything, neither for extraction nor for pollution'. For all practical purposes the earth is a closed ecological sphere.

Another major early contributor to the development of the modern phase of ecological economics was Nicholas Georgescu-Roegen. His insightful and substantive contributions to ecological economics were meticulously articulated in his book *The Entropy Law and the Economic Process* (1971). In this book he explained at some length the implications of the laws of thermodynamics for the economic process (i.e., the transformation of matter–energy into products, services and waste). The central message of this book was that 'the economic process is solidly anchored to a material base, which is subject to definite constraints. It is because of this constraint that the economic process has a unidirectional irrevocable evolution'.

For Georgescu-Roegen, therefore, it is impossible to understand the full extent of the opportunity cost of any economic activity without a good understanding of the implications of the law of entropy. He (1993: 80) argued that 'environmental low entropy is scarce in a different sense than Ricardian land. Both Ricardian land and the coal deposits are available in limited amounts. The difference is that a piece of coal can be used only once'. He then suggested that the neoclassical economic school of thought, by not giving sufficient attention to this law, has failed to recognize the 'unidirectional' nature of the economic process.

The third major contributor to the modern version of ecological economics is Herman Daly, a student of Georgescu-Roegen. Daly's contributions to ecological economics are numerous. He is particularly recognized for his effort to conceptualize an alternative to the neoclassical growth paradigm. His first attempt to do this was done in his edited book *Towards a Steady-state Economy* (1973).

Daly's vision of growth is unlike the neoclassical growth model in that he attempts to explicitly incorporate the ecological and physical realities articulated by Boulding and Georgescu-Roegen. In fact, one could safely claim that the steady-state economy represents a theoretical economic growth model that explicitly attempts to incorporate the biophysical limits and ethical considerations proclaimed or implied by Georgescu-Roegen and Boulding. The main message of Daly's work on this front has been to show that the *scale* of the human economy relative to the global natural ecosystem has become large enough to cause significant stress on the limited capacity of the natural global ecosystem to support the economic subsystem. Thus, boundless economic growth cannot mesh with such biophysical reality (Daly 1992, 1996).

Daly is also credited for his effort to vividly articulate the interdependence of economic (social) and environmental systems by using metabolism as a metaphor (1996). Here is how Ropke (2004: 300–1) described this particular effort of Daly's:

> Daly . . . intended to recast economics as a life science focusing on the metabolistic character of economic activities, the 'passage of low-entropy matter–energy through its life-supporting input–output transformations into high-entropy waste' and emphasizing the large size the human economy had achieved in relation to the natural environment.

Clearly, this can be viewed as restating what has been already articulated by Boulding, but Daly presented the influence society has on nature much more vividly and made it easier to grasp by using the concept of metabolism—a biological term that concerns our own digestive system. He made the concept more accessible by drawing a parallel between our metabolic system and the earth's capacity to assimilate, cleanse and replenish what we put into nature as byproducts of our economic system. However, it is important to note that the relevance of this metaphor is predicated with the assumption that the size of the human economy relative to the natural ecosystems is large (Daly 1968; Ropke 2004). If Daly's argument is to be taken seriously, sustainability requires understanding the 'similarities between patterns of interaction in natural and social systems and on self-regulation inside systems through communication and feedback mechanism' (Ropke 2004: 299). From a modeling perspective, this requires systems-thinking with interdisciplinary and intradisciplinary focus.

405

Where is ecological economics today? Consistent with Daly's view above, as the world has gradually but surely shifted from a relatively 'empty world' to a relatively 'full world', the relevance of ecological economics for addressing global environmental and resource concerns has been widely recognized. The resurgence of interest in ecological economics has been particularly dramatic over the past three decades. Ecological economics was institutionalized in 1988 with the establishment of the International Society for Ecological Economics (ISEE) and it was accompanied by the Journal of Ecological Economics, dedicated to the publication and dissemination of scholarly works in the field. Presently, it enjoys a sizeable number of paying members, and it is truly international in both its mission and membership composition.

It is beyond the scope of this textbook to present all the major contributors to the recent advances in ecological economics. For those who are interested, I refer you to the following three articles: (1) 'Foundations of Ecological Economics' (Pearce 1987); (2) 'Biophysical Economics: Historical Perspective and Current Research Trends' (Cleveland 1987); and (3) 'The Early History of Modern Ecological Economics' (Ropke 2004).

I will end the discussion in Appendix B by listing the general topics of some of the significant recent scholarly contributions of ecological economics.

- The *complementarity* of natural and human-made capital;
- The limits as well as the opportunities of conserving energy through technological means;
- The pervasive nature of environmental externalities;
- The development of systems-based, interdisciplinary and transdisciplinary-based economic analysis;
- The valuation of ecosystem services;
- The development of alternative indices for social wellbeing, such as the index of sustainable economic welfare (ISEW);
- Boundary issues on biophysical limits: 'safe' biophysical boundaries and the risk of overshooting;
- Systems resilience and its implications to continued economic growth; and
- Sustainability and sustainable economic development.

REFERENCES

Ayres, R. U. and Nair, I. (1984) 'Thermodynamic and Economics', *Physics Today* 37: 63–8.

Boulding, K. E. (1966) 'The Economics of the Coming Spaceship Earth', in H. Jarrett (ed.) *Environmental Quality in a Growing Economy*, Washington, DC: Johns Hopkins University Press.

Christensen, P. (1987) 'Classical Roots for a Modern Material–Energy Analysis', *Ecological Modelling* 38: 75–89.

Cleveland, C. J. (1987) 'Biophysical Economics: Historical Perspective and Current Research Trends', *Ecological Modelling* 38: 47–73.

Costanza, R. (1980) 'Embodied Energy and Economic Valuation', *Science* 210: 1219–24.

Daly, H. E. (1968) 'On Economics as a Life Science', *Journal of Political Economics* 76: 392–406.

—— (1973) *Towards a Steady-state Economy*, San Francisco, CA: W. H. Freeman.

—— (1992) 'Allocation, Distribution, and Scale: Towards an Economics that is Efficient, Just, and Sustainable', *Ecological Economics* 6: 185–93.

—— (1996) *Beyond Growth*, Boston, MA: Beacon Press.

Georgescu-Roegen, N. (1971) *The Entropy Law and the Economic Process*, Cambridge, MA: Harvard University Press.

—— (1993) 'The Entropy Law and the Economic Problem', in H. E. Daly and K. Townsend (eds.) *Valuing the Earth: Economics, Ecology, Ethics*, Cambridge, MA: MIT Press.

—— (1996) *Energy and Economic Myths*, New York: Pergamon Press.

Odum, H. and Odum, E. (1976) *Energy Basis for Man and Nature*, New York: McGraw Hill.

Pearce, D. W. (1987) 'Foundations of Ecological Economics', *Ecological Modelling* 38: 9–18.

Ropke, I. (2004) 'The Early History of Modern Ecological Economics', *Ecological Economics* 50: 293–314.

Index